Natural Resources and Aboriginal People in Canada
Readings, Cases, and Commentary

Edited by

ROBERT B. ANDERSON
AND
ROBERT M. BONE

Captus Press

Natural Resources and Aboriginal People in Canada
Readings, Cases, and Commentary

This Selection Copyright © 2003 by Robert B. Anderson and Robert M. Bone
and Captus Press Inc.

All rights reserved. No part of this book may be reproduced, stored in a retrieval system, or transmitted, in any form or by any means, electronic, mechanical, photocopying, recording, or otherwise, without prior written permission of the copyright holders.

The publisher and the editors gratefully acknowledge the authors, publishers and organizations for their permission to reproduce their work in this book. Care has been taken to trace ownership of copyright material contained in this book. The publisher will gladly take any information that will enable the rectification of any reference or credit in subsequent editions and apologizes for any errors or omissions.

National Library of Canada Cataloguing in Publication

    Natural resources and Aboriginal people in Canada : readings, cases and commentaries / editors, Robert B. Anderson, Robert M. Bone

Includes bibliographical references and index.
ISBN 1–55322–039–0

    1. Native peoples — Canada.   2. Natural resources — Canada.   3. Natural resources — Government policy — Canada.   I. Anderson, Robert Brent, 1951–   II. Bone, Robert M.   III. Title.

E78.C2N39 2003   333.7'089'97071   C2003-903158-6

Captus Press Inc.
Mail: Units 14 & 15, 1600 Steeles Avenue West
      Concord, Ontario
      Canada   L4K 4M2
Telephone: (416) 736–5537
Fax: (416) 736–5793
Email: info@captus.com
Internet: http://www.captus.com

Canada *We acknowledge the financial support of the Government of Canada through the Book Publishing Industry Development Program (BPIDP) for our publishing activities.*

0 9 8 7 6 5 4 3 2 1
Printed in Canada

Table of Contents

PREFACE vii

Section 1
Two World Views: Conflict, Accommodation and Synthesis

CHAPTER 1   Conflicting World Views   7
  (a) The Lockean Basis of Iroquoian Land Ownership
    John Douglas Bishop   7
  (b) Capitalism and the Dis-empowerment of Canadian
    Aboriginal Peoples
    Michelle Mann 18

CHAPTER 2   Accommodation and Synthesis. 30
  (a) Traditional Ecological Knowledge in Environmental
    Assessment and Management
    Peter J. Usher 30
  (b) Co-management of Aboriginal Resources
    Tracy Campbell 47
  (c) And Now for Something Completely Northern:
    Institutions of Governance in the Territorial North
    Graham White 53
  (d) Modern Aboriginal Economies: Capitalism with a
    Red Face
    David Newhouse 70
  (e) The Politics of TEK: Power and the "Integration" of
    Knowledge
    Paul Nadasdy 79
  (f) Knowing Home: Nisga'a Traditional Knowledge and
    Wisdom Improve Environmental Decision Making
    John Corsiglia and Gloria Snively 103

Section 2
Land Use and Renewable Resources

CHAPTER 3   Introduction.................................. 117

   (a) The Nunavut Tunngavik Inc.: An Examination of Its Mode of Operation and Its Activities
André Légaré 117

   (b) Neither Boom Nor Bust: The Renewable Resource Economy May Be the Best Long-term Hope for Northern Communities
Heather Myers 139

   (c) Options for Appropriate Development in Nunavut Communities
Heather Myers 146

   (d) Institutionalized Adaptation: Aboriginal Involvement in Land and Resource Management
David C. Natcher 159

   (e) Inuit Perceptions of Contaminants and Environmental Knowledge in Salluit, Nunavik
Sylvie Poirier and Lorraine Brooke 173

CHAPTER 4   Forestry................................... 192

   (a) First Nations Economic Development: The Meadow Lake Tribal Council
Robert B. Anderson and Robert M. Bone 192

   (b) First Nations in Forestry
First Nations Forestry Program 222

   (c) Aboriginal Forestry in Canada
Michael J. McDonald 230

CHAPTER 5   Hunting/Trapping/Country Food................ 257

   (a) First Nations Claim Equal Rights to Manage National Parks
Dennis White Bird 257

   (b) The Harvest of Beluga Whales in Canada's Western Arctic: Hunter-based Monitoring of the Size and Composition of the Catch
Lois A. Harwood, Pamela Norton, Billy Day, and Patricia A. Hall 262

   (c) "A Clear Intention to Effect Such a Modification": The *NRTA* and Treaty Hunting and Fishing Rights
Robert Irwin 279

   (d) Community Perceptions of the Beverly-Qamanirjuaq Caribou Management Board
Anne Kendrick 303

(e) Towards a Model of Co-management of Provincial Parks in Ontario
Roger Spielmann and Marina Unger 326

CHAPTER 6   Water 350
(a) Water Issues and Treaty Negotiations: Lessons from the Yukon Experience
Andrew R. Thompson and Nancy A. Morgan 350
(b) The Blood Tribe Agricultural Project, Standoff, Alberta
Anna Classen 359

CHAPTER 7   Fishery 365
(a) Lobster Wars
Parker Barss Donham 365
(b) Lobster Wars and the Media
Parker Barss Donham 369
(c) Lobster Wars: 2001 Edition
Parker Barss Donham 371

Section 3
Non-Renewable Resources

CHAPTER 8   Oil and Gas 379
(a) The Mackenzie Valley Pipeline Inquiry
Robert B. Anderson 379
(b) Power Shifts in the Canadian North: A Case Study of the Inuvialuit Final Agreement
Robert M. Bone 382
(c) New Pipe Dreams: In the 1970s, Native Protests Helped Stop the Mackenzie Valley Pipeline. Now, Native Leaders Want to See It Built
Brian Bergman 393
(d) Shell Game: Transnationals Everywhere Are Attempting to Recast Themselves as Eco-friendly
Stephanie Boyd 397
(e) Metis Concerned about Expansion of Suncor's Oil Sands Operations, Called Project Millennium
Marie Burke 400
(f) Sour Gas, Bitter Relations
Ginger Gibson, Eric Higgs and Steve E. Hrudey 401

CHAPTER 9   Mining. 412
   (a) The Nasty Game: How Environmental Assessment
      Is Failing Aboriginal Communities in Canada's North
      Susan Wismer *412*
   (b) Northern Gems: Natives Battle a Proposed $12-billion
      Diamond Mine
      Tom Fennell *422*
   (c) Nunavut Open for Business: It's a Delicate Balance
      between Creating a Sustainable Mining Industry
      Yet Maximizing Our Resources Potential
      Paul Okalik *426*

Preface

Natural resource use has always been a fundamental element of Aboriginal culture. The nature of that use has changed over time. Three periods can be identified. The first is the period prior to first contact with Europeans. During this period, the traditional Aboriginal world view held sway uncontested. The phrases "natural resources" and "natural resource" management fail to capture the relationship between people and the land during this period. The land and the things of the land were not viewed as separate from people or to be managed and exploited. Instead, people and the earth in all its parts were considered as one. The world was a web of interrelationships and obligations, not a supply of resources to be used and managed to the benefit of people. This does not mean that Aboriginal people did not use the resources of the land. Of course they did, but when they did, it was as a part of a complex and reciprocal relationship inseparable from culture, values and spirituality.

The second period is one of European colonization and then state-building, extending from first colonization until the very recent past. During this period, the traditional Aboriginal world view, while not eliminated, was marginalized, and the European view dominated. The land and its resources were seen as separate from people — factors of production along with human and financial capital to be combined together to meet market needs. The phrase "resource management" and its connotations are associated with this period. So too is the notion that something can be good for people and bad for the environment, which makes that benefit an entirely relative one.

The final period is the current one. Two forces are at play. The first is the emergence of the environmental movement and the sustainable development paradigm. Globally, there is an increasing realization that humans and the environment are inseparable, and that the notion that something can be good for people and bad for the environment is ludicrous — something akin to the traditional Aboriginal world view. The other force is the considerable control Aboriginal people are regaining over their traditional lands and resources in Canada and elsewhere. With the emergence of the sustainable development paradigm and increasing Aboriginal control over vast tracts of lands and resources, there has also been a growing acknowledgement of the traditional Aboriginal world view, and attempts to incorporate "traditional environmental knowledge" (TEK) in the "sustainable" management of natural resources. This theme forms the central thrust of this text on natural resources and Aboriginal people in Canada.

There is an important sub-theme. Since contact with Europeans, Aboriginal use of natural resources has evolved. There has been a cultural adjustment involving a blending of traditional and commercial utilization of natural resources. Today, traditional harvesting of wildlife from the land and water continues to play an important role in Aboriginal communities by supplying country food and by reinforcing traditional customs and values. At the same time, commercial use of natural resources by Aboriginal firms and individuals has increased as Aboriginal people participate more actively in the market economy, sometimes sustainably and sometimes not.

In the early 1990s, two books, *Aboriginal Resource Use In Canada* by Kerry Able and Jean Friesen, and *Aboriginal People and Natural Resources in Canada* by Claudia Notzke, recognized a growing interest among Aboriginal people in developing their natural resources for commercial purposes, and in the critical links between Aboriginal rights, land title, and increased access to natural resources by Aboriginal people. The 1990s have seen (i) increased Aboriginal interest in participating in the market economy; (ii) modern land claim agreements providing greater control over traditional lands and encouraging Aboriginal development of the natural resources of these lands; and (iii) court rulings, such as the Marshall Decision, that have confirmed and expanded Aboriginal rights to natural resources. The passage of time has rendered both books outdated; hence this new book.

To bring some structure to the task of addressing our theme and sub-theme, we have divided the material in this book into three sections. Each section begins with a commentary that discusses the cases and articles within the section identifying key issues, problems and opportunities.

Section 1 of this book contains articles that set out the nature of the two world views (traditional and modern); the conflict between them over the period from first contact between Europeans and the Aboriginal people living in what is now Canada to the present; the recent trend to incorporate TEK, culture and values in such things as land claims agreements, advisory boards, joint business ventures, co-management regimes, and environmental assessment; and the more fundamental search for a sustainable development paradigm in which traditional values and practices occupy a central place. From this foundation, the book explores emerging issues in the various resource "sectors", including forestry, fisheries, traditional land use, oil and gas, diamond and other mining and the like, in Sections 2 and 3 — Renewable Resources and Non-renewable Resources, respectively.

Natural Resources and Aboriginal People in Canada serves two audiences. First and foremost, it is designed for college and university students who are exploring the complex interrelationships among Aboriginal people, non-Aboriginal people and natural resources. Such courses are commonly part of Native Studies programs. In addition, they are becoming increasingly common in "mainstream" disciplines such as commerce, geography, economics, law, political science and sociology, and in interdisciplinary programs dealing with land use, environmental studies, sustainable development, and planning.

The second audience is a broader one. It serves those concerned about the interrelationships among Aboriginal people, non-Aboriginal people, the land, and natural resources. Aboriginal and non-Aboriginal business executives, political leaders, and policy makers will find *Natural Resources and Aboriginal People in Canada* a useful reference.

SOURCES
Abel, Kerry and Jean Friesen (eds.). 1991. *Aboriginal Resource Use in Canada: Historical and Legal Aspects*. Winnipeg: University of Manitoba Press.
Notzke, Claudia. 1994. *Aboriginal Peoples and Natural Resources in Canada*. North York: Captus University Publications.

Section 1

Two World Views:
Conflict, Accommodation and Synthesis

This section contains articles on three themes. The first is the nature of the two world views (traditional Aboriginal and Euro-Canadian) and the conflict between them over the period from first contact to the present. The second theme is the recent trend to accommodate traditional values and practices in such things as land claims agreements, advisory boards, joint business ventures, co-management regimes, and environmental assessment. The final and more fundamental theme centres on the search for a sustainable development paradigm based on the synthesis of TEK, and modern scientific knowledge. In the remainder of this introduction, we provide an overview of the selected articles and their relationship to these themes.

The first theme, conflicting world views, is a complex and challenging one. It is not our purpose to explore either the traditional Aboriginal or Euro-Canadian world views in great depth. We leave that to others, like Gregory Cajete (2000), who has done a thorough job of exploring the traditional Aboriginal perspective in *Native Science: Natural Laws of Interdependence*. Our task is limited to providing basic insight into these contrasting world view(s) and the conflict between them from first contact between Europeans and Aboriginal North Americans to the present. To do this, we have chosen two articles. They are "Capitalism and the Dis-empowerment of Canadian Aboriginal People" by Michelle Mann and "The Lockean Basis of Iroquoian Land Ownership" by John Douglas Bishop. As the titles suggest, our focus is on conflicting economic systems and related conflicting views of land ownership and natural resource use.

In "Capitalism and the Dis-empowerment of Canadian Aboriginal People", Mann begins with a description of the period between first contact and the mid 1700s. She says, "This period was generally marked by a spirit of cooperation ... and respect for each other's sovereignty". According to Mann, one of the reasons for this cooperation was the Europeans' reliance on Aboriginal people's "knowledge of the land and how to survive in it". European respect for Aboriginal sovereignty and traditional knowledge, and the related spirit of cooperation, did not last beyond the middle of the 18th century. In its place, a trend toward assimilation, disempowerment and marginalization began to emerge. Mann asks and then answers the questions, "How did this change in colonial attitude come about", and, "What purpose did it serve?" She finds the answers to these questions in the evolving European economic system — the emergence of capitalism — and the thirst of capitalism for land and resources.

Aboriginal and European views about the land and resources differed prior to the emergence of the capitalist economy. However, these differences were not a source of conflict during the fur trade era; the views could and did coexist. With the simultaneous decline of the fur trade and the rise of capitalism, this peaceful coexistence came to an end. Under capitalism, land and its resources became inputs of production: inputs that had to be owned by individuals before they could be used. This view was (and still is) in stark contrast to the traditional view of land as a place to live and the source of life. John Douglas Bishop, in "The Lockean Basis of Iroquoian Land Ownership", explores these contrasting views on land and land ownership in more depth. He explains how Europeans came to "own" the land and resources, at least according to their own rules.

The remaining articles in Section 1 explore the grudging respect for traditional knowledge and practices that has begun to emerge, and the place that these views have been accorded in "modern" land use and resource management. The articles do this under the two remaining themes: (I) accommodation in the existing system and (ii) a synthesis of "traditional" and "modern" into a new, sustainable paradigm.

Three articles address accommodation. They are "Traditional Ecological Knowledge in Environmental Assessment and Management" by Peter Usher, "Co-management of Aboriginal Resources" by Tracy Campbell, and "And Now for Something Completely Northern" by Graham White. There are also three pieces that explore the synthesis of Aboriginal and non-Aboriginal views into something new that respects both and draws on the strengths of each. They are David Newhouse's "Modern Aboriginal Economies: Capitalism with a Red Face", "The Politics of TEK: Power and the 'Integration' of Knowledge" by Paul Nadasdy, and "Knowing Home: Nisga'a Traditional Knowledge and Wisdom Improve Environmental Decision Making" by John Corsiglia and Gloria Snively.

Peter Usher begins "Traditional Ecological Knowledge in Environmental Assessment and Management" with the statement:

> It has become a policy requirement in Canada, and especially in northern Canada, that "traditional knowledge" (TK) or "traditional ecological knowledge" (TEK) be considered and incorporated into environmental assessment and resource management.

Then, in the subsection entitled "The Problem", he goes on to say that

> Although the general policy requirement is in place, its wording is neither clear nor consistent, and there is virtually no guidance on how to implement it ... All parties need to know in practical terms (I) what TEK is, (ii) what information it provides, (iii) how this information can be documented and (iv) brought into the environmental assessment process, and (v) how it should be expected to affect both the process and the outcome [numbering added].

In the remainder of his paper, Usher addresses these five points. In doing so, he strives to find a way to include or accommodate TEK in a "modern scientific approach" to environmental assessment and resource management. Contrast this approach to the transformational role of TEK in the approach to land and resource management discussed by Nadasdy in "The Politics of TEK: Power and the 'Integration' of Knowledge".

In "Co-management of Aboriginal Resources" Tracy Campbell offers further insight into recent attempts to accommodate TEK in resource management activities. She begins her paper by exploring the reasons for the move to the inclusion of Aboriginal people in resource management after centuries of exclusion. At the core is a growing realization by governments and corporations of the nature and extent of Aboriginal rights to land and resources. Governments and corporations did not come to this realization willingly but, rather, did so reluctantly when forced to do so by the Constitution, the courts, quasi-judicial bodies like the Berger Inquiry, and the continuing demands and protests of Aboriginal people. Nonetheless, it is now accepted that Aboriginal people must be involved in decisions on land use and resource management. Campbell goes on to describe co-management as a method of achieving this inclusion. As in Usher's description of

TEK in environmental assessment, Campbell describes a system that allows Aboriginal participation and accommodates, to some extent, Aboriginal views on what should be done on the land and with its resources.

While certainly an improvement over centuries of exclusion, Nadasdy and Corsiglia and Snively argue that the co-management process (like the environmental impact assessment process) remains a "western scientific and economic one" that accommodates TEK, but only to a limited extent and on non-traditional terms. As you will see, in their papers Nadasdy and Corsiglia and Snively argue instead for a complete transformation of the entire land use and resource management paradigm into one that has TEK and the world view from which it emerges at its core. In this new approach, "western science" will be a useful tool, but it will not determine the nature of the process or its outcomes. Nor will the economy and the environment be seen as separate when what is good for one is often bad for the other.

This is not a new idea, nor is it restricted to the Aboriginal context in Canada. The sustainable development paradigm began its rise to popular prominence in 1987 with the publication of "Our Common Future", the report of the World Commission on Environment and Development (usually called the Brundltland Commission). Among other things, the Commission attached great importance to TEK, arguing that the world views that gave rise to this knowledge were "sustainable" in the past, and could form the foundation for sustainable development in the future. Nadasdy and Corsiglia and Snively illustrate this view in their papers.

Paul Nadasdy begins his paper "The Politics of TEK: Power and the 'Integration' of Knowledge" with the statement:

> The widespread recognition that something called "traditional ecological knowledge" even exists represents, in itself, an important first step toward the full participation of aboriginal communities in the management of land and resources.

However, he goes on to say:

> In spite of 15 years of effort ... to develop a method for integrating scientific and traditional knowledge ... scientists remain essentially at a loss regarding traditional ecological knowledge; many are still not quite sure what it is, much less how to use it or integrate it.

Nadasdy explores the reasons for this failure, and finds them in power relations as much as in the very real, fundamental differences between the two types of knowledge.

Essentially, he argues that efforts at integration to date have attempted to force TEK to fit the existing the Western scientific view of what knowledge is and how knowledge should be used. This is so because those that hold the Western scientific view also hold the power to determine how TEK is gathered and used. This has resulted in efforts to "integrate" TEK that have attempted to "compartmentalize" it when it is holistic; "distill" it when its strength is its richness and breadth of content; and render it universal when it is "local" and based on generations of people and their relationship to their "place" or "territory". As a result, what is called TEK and is "integrated" is no longer TEK, only an abstract of it. Nadasdy concludes that any meaningful attempt to improve resource management practices and empower local aboriginal communities must acknowledge this aspect of the current attempt to "integrate TEK" and science and develop a new approach.

Describing this new approach, Nadasdy says:

> local beliefs, values and practices themselves — not merely abstract forms affixed to them — must be accepted as a valid basis for action. This will require changes in current practices of resource management and environmental assessment.

Nadasdy argues that the necessary change is one from an advisory to a decision-making role for those who know and live TEK. The role of Western science will continue to be important, informing the process but no longer controlling it.

The final paper in Section 1, "Knowing Home: Nisga'a Traditional Knowledge and Wisdom Improve Environmental Decision Making" by Corsiglia and Snively, provides a "face" and a "place" for the discussion of TEK. It also shows that we have moved some distance toward the approach argued for by Nadasdy, and that this process will continue as comprehensive land claims agreements evolve over time, and courts will continue to clarify the nature and extent of Aboriginal rights to lands and resources, and Aboriginal people exercise these rights.

The Supreme Court of Canada has made a number of key rulings that have had great impact on Aboriginal people and their access to natural resources. Until recently, the federal and provincial governments did not recognize that Aboriginal people had claims to land beyond those defined by treaties. In 1973, this legal position was shaken by the Calder case. Calder argued that the Nisga'a had Aboriginal title to their traditionally occupied land because they had never surrendered it to the Crown. While the Supreme Court narrowly ruled against Calder, the court did recognize that the Nisga'a had Aboriginal property rights, and therefore, Aboriginal title existed until the claim was extinguished (in the Calder case, three of the seven judges believed that the Nisga'a claim had been extinguished, but all seven recognized that Aboriginal people had a claim on lands traditionally occupied by them prior to contact). After this ruling, the federal government accepted the principle of Aboriginal title, and Ottawa set in motion a process of negotiations. The Inuvialuit Final Agreement (1984) marked the first modern land claims agreement between Ottawa and an Aboriginal group (the Inuvialuit) who claim much of the Western Arctic. Table 1 provides a summary of key Supreme Court of Canada decisions that have affected Aboriginal title and, therefore, improved their access to natural resources.

Finally, some brief comments on the papers by White and Newhouse. Both address efforts to accommodate Aboriginal culture, values and practices in modern activities other than co-management and environmental impact assessment/resource management. White does so in the context of building new governments and government agencies in the Yukon and what was once the Northwest Territories. It is an interesting article. Though general, it is relevant to resource management because it is governments (old and new) that write the "rules of the game".

Newhouse talks about capitalism, but not just any capitalism. He talks about a capitalism transformed to some extent by the incorporation of Aboriginal values and practices. Aboriginal companies are increasingly involved in "resource development". If such companies reflect traditional values, and respect and use both

TABLE 1. Recent Supreme Court of Canada Decisions

Case	Date	Outcome
Nowegijick	1983	Treaties must be liberally interpreted.
Guerin	1984	Ottawa must recognize the existence of inherent Aboriginal title and a fiduciary (trust) relationship based on title.
Sioui	1990	Provincial laws cannot overrule rights contained in treaties.
Sparrow	1990	The term "existing rights" was defined as anything in Section 35(1) of The Constitution Act 1982 was defined as anything unextinguished.
Delgamuukw	1997	The oral history of Indian people must receive equal weight to historical evidence in land claim legal cases.
Marshall	1999	Mi'kmaq have the right to catch and sell fish (lobster) to earn a "moderate living".

TEK and modern scientific knowledge appropriately, they can be part of the process that transforms land use and resource management in "Indian country". An example of this dynamic process unfolding can be found in Section 2 in "First Nations Economic Development: The Meadow Lake Tribal Council".

CHAPTER 1

Conflicting World Views

(a) The Lockean Basis of Iroquoian Land Ownership[†]

John Douglas Bishop

I. INTRODUCTION[1]

John Locke's theory of property was carefully designed to render claims to land ownership by North American Native people illegitimate; as a result of this agenda, his theory is Eurocentric, gender biased, and blind to many aspects of Native culture. Locke's involvement in the colony of Virginia gave him a vested interest in showing that land in North America was unowned at the time of contact, and he provided the basis for a discourse on property that many European settlers for generations were eager to believe.[2] The case for this view has most forcibly been made in recent articles by James Tully,[3] who intends to cast doubt on the applicability of Lockean property theories to Native land ownership. If Tully's views become generally accepted, and it seems likely some version of them will be,[4] defenders of Native ownership claims will have a basis for rejecting Lockean style property theories altogether, or at least for rejecting their applicability to Native land. Tully, for example, argues for recognition of dual Native and English common law property discourse, neither of which is Lockean. Not that the rejection of Lockean discourse is new; there has been a long history of rejecting its application to North America. Even in Locke's day, alternative views of property were proposed for Europeans settling in North America. In the nineteenth century, Chief Justice Marshall explic-

---

[†] First appeared in *Journal of Aboriginal Economic Development* 1(1): 35–43. Reproduced with permission of the author and CANDO.

itly rejected Lockean foundations for property claims in *Johnson and Graham's Lessee v. M'Intosh* (1823).[5]

This paper will examine an alternative to rejecting the application of Lockean property theory to Native lands at the time of contact. It will be argued here that if the Lockean approach to property is corrected for Eurocentric and gender bias, and for blindness to Native cultures, then Native ownership of both agricultural and hunting lands at the time of contact has a firm Lockean basis.

As a test case for showing that Lockean property theory supports Native ownership, this paper will discuss Iroquoian land usage.[6] The mixture of hunting and farming that formed the basis of the Iroquoian economy at the time European settlers began questioning Iroquoian land ownership makes this a useful example. However, this paper is not intended as a contribution to the study of the Iroquoian system of land ownership; it is an attempt to identify biases and theoretical problems in Lockean property theory by trying to apply that theory to a non-European culture and economy. Showing that Iroquoian land ownership has a Lockean basis in not to say that Iroquoian property rights are best analyzed in Lockean terms; it only shows that Lockean theory has failed in denying Iroquoian ownership of the land they farmed and hunted on.

The removal of biases from Lockean property theory and the application of the theory to Iroquoian land usages are part of a larger discussion concerning both the interpretation of Locke's writings and the coherence of Lockean style property theories. Some of the key issues in that larger debate that are crucial to our current concerns can be correlated with discussion of specific aspects of Iroquoian culture and economy; the following lists these and the section in which they will be discussed:

Issue of Lockean Interpretation or Coherence	*Iroquoian Culture or Economy*
III group ownership	• farming methods
IV enclosure	• governing structures
V nature of improvement	• temporary clearing of farm land
VI nature of labour	• care of hunting grounds
VII Lockean proviso	• cultural significance of hunting

However, before dealing with these specific issues, this paper will first outline very briefly Locke's theory of property and his view of North American Native people.

II. LOCKE'S THEORY OF PROPERTY

In the beginning, God gave all of nature to humankind in common (II, 25);[7] all people had an equal right to gather natural resources for their own use. Once gathered (or "appropriated"; II, 26), an item belonged to the person who made the effort to gather it, but nature itself remained common property. One owned the apples one picked (II, 28), but not the apple tree; the deer one hunted (II, 30), but not the forest. Ownership was conferred by the effort expended to make an item available for personal use; an object became personal property when someone "hath mixed his labour with" it (II, 27). Once acquired, owners of objects were entitled to dispose of them in any fashion they chose except letting them spoil unused.

When applied to land, the theory holds that all land was originally owned in common, but that anyone who chose could acquire a rightful property claim to a specific piece of land by labouring to make it more productive. One could, and this example is appropriate for the woodlands of North America, clear the forest, plough the soil, and cultivate crops.[8] This would entitle a person to own not only the crops but also the land that had been cleared.

The portion of the Lockean theory outlined so far refers to the original appropriation of property — that is, how a piece of land goes from being part of the common property of all people to being the private property of a particular individual. Once a piece of land is private property, the owner, while alive, can choose to transfer ownership to any other person and, upon dying, can designate anyone as heir (subject to the owner's moral responsibility to dependants).

This theory of appropriation has an implied limit in that a person is not entitled to acquire more land than they can productively cultivate. Locke also places two constraints on appropriation of land.[9] First, a person cannot claim so much land that it produces more than the owner can consume before the produce goes bad. The other constraint is the famous Lockean proviso: a person is only entitled to transfer property from common to private ownership if "enough and as good is left for others." The interpretation of this proviso is much discussed,[10] and later in this paper it will be discussed with reference to the settlers on Iroquoian territory. Locke argues that the development of money removes these constraints on the amount of property a person can own; once money provides a means of stored value, ownership of property can be unlimited.[11]

Interpreters of Locke have argued variously for labour, merit, efficiency, and desert as the basis of Locke's theory of original appropriation.[12] However, underlying any or all of these is Locke's theory of natural rights and natural law. In a state of nature, people can be aware of and are morally bound by the Law of Nature. Ashcraft usefully distinguishes natural law as the moral foundation of Locke's theory from empirical claims which Locke uses to apply natural law to specific historical situations, like seventeenth century North America.[13] In these terms, what the present paper will do is return to the natural law foundations of original appropriation and reassess the application of this to North America using recent empirical information unavailable to Locke.[14]

The Law of Nature, among other things, imposes on all people a duty to undertake actions that tend to preserve the human species.[15] Because certain forms of labour increase the likelihood of preservation, we have a duty to perform those kinds of labour. Since original appropriation of property encourages and makes possible those kinds of labour, original appropriation of private property becomes a right.[16] This is related to efficiency in that more efficient use of land also tends towards human preservation. However, Locke nowhere argues that efficiency overrides private property once ownership is established; his theory is obviously not a utilitarian theory in which land must always be reassigned to the most efficient use. Thus efficiency is only relevant at the time of original appropriation and only in so far as it helps Locke derive property rights from natural law. The duty to preserve humanity is the primary aspect of natural law used in the current paper.

In the chapter on property it is clear that Locke thought most of America was still owned in common by mankind (II, 26) — meaning all of mankind, not just Native Americans. He also seemed to think that most of America was vacant (II, 36). Native Americans wandered wherever they wanted in a vast, empty continent; Locke seemed quite concerned that they might get lost (II, 36). He did not seem to think that they had identifiable territories, cultivated farm land, or assigned hunting grounds. Economically, they hunted and gathered; nowhere does Locke acknowledge agriculture outside the civilizations of Meso and South America.

Trade, according to Locke, was in the form of barter and was limited because Native Americans had no money (II, 49). For the most part, they had not entered civil society because they had no regular government (II, 108).[17] He repeatedly refers to the natives of North America as an example of people living either in a state of nature or under the "youngest" forms of civil society (II, 49; II, 108).[18] When necessary, decisions would be made by "the people" or their representatives in a council. Locke's image is of free and independent individuals living in the state of nature coming together to make decisions with no individual claiming power or authority over any other.[19] Only when fighting a war would they elect as temporary commander the bravest or strongest man present.

How accurate is this picture as applied to the Iroquoian of the seventeenth and eighteenth centuries? Not very.[20] The issue of mostly vacant land held in common will be discussed later in this paper. The Iroquoian economy was based on agriculture, with hunting and gathering important supplements to the three cultivated staples — corn (i.e., maize), squash, and beans. Money of various sorts played some role in the economy, more as a medium of exchange than as stored value; Locke was right in thinking that the Iroquoian did not have an insatiable desire to acquire endless amounts of gold or to accumulate unlimited possessions of any sort.[21] The Iroquoian did have extensive trade connections throughout North America before the European arrival. And long before attempts were made to settle the lands, the fur trade with the French, Dutch, and British had become a significant part of the Iroquoian economy.

On government, Locke was completely wrong. The Iroquois had formed the Five (later Six) Nation Confederacy as a sophisticated, complex, and well-defined system of governance, and the Huron were a confederacy of four peoples.[22] The Iroquois confederacy had been formed in the fifteenth century (prior to Columbus); it was functioning throughout Locke's lifetime and throughout the eighteenth century when settlers were moving onto Iroquoian lands. However, Iroquoian government had neither the sort of authority to enact laws nor the executive power and control that European governments were used to.[23]

III. GROUP OWNERSHIP

Locke always assumed that land would be appropriated and owned by individuals. Prior to the formation of government by social contract, a piece of land was either commons available for individual appropriation, or it was the property of an individual who had invested labour in improving it. After the formation of government, there could be agreement to leave some land unappropriated; such "commons" would belong to the community in the English fashion, but such community ownership was only possible subsequent to the formation of government, and would be exceptional even then because the purpose of forming government was the protection of private property. Individuals would own most of the land.

For the Iroquoian, land was not the property of individuals; both agricultural land and hunting grounds were assigned to clan segments, villages, or bands. This group ownership could not be by community agreement after the fashion of English commons since Locke viewed Native people as being in a stage prior to the formation of government. Furthermore, government could not be formed in a community in which all productive land was group owned since governments are formed by agreement of individuals for the protection of their individual property; if there was no individual property, government would not be formed to protect ownership. A Lockean justification of Iroquoian group ownership cannot, therefore, be based on social contract and the formation of government.

If a Lockean basis of group ownership is possible, it must be derived directly from natural law. Interpretations of Locke's views on natural law vary, but Tully[24] agrees with Simmons and others in thinking that natural law for Locke included a natural liberty of the individual bounded by a natural duty to preserve mankind and by certain natural obligations. Group ownership of land puts limits on natural liberty because it makes use of the land contingent on the agreement of the other members of the group, and on social obligations to share labour and produce. This appears to conflict with the whole point to Locke's argument on property, namely, that owning property does not depend on getting anyone's agreement, and does not involve obligations to society. To justify the limits on natural liberty that group ownership involves, what one needs to show is that the survival of the group imposed natural obligations to share work and produce among the community.

Locke acknowledged that wives and children have a claim in natural law on a man's property, which takes precedence over, for example, the claims of a victim of aggression against an aggressor's property, or the claims of a conqueror in war.[25] The claims of the wife and children are based on the belief that recognition of such claims advances the survival prospects of humanity. The extension of such claims from immediate family to the extended family or community would depend on showing that given a particular culture, technology, and situation, the survival prospects of the group were enhanced by group ownership.

Given the immense labour involved in clearing forests with fire and stone axes, and given the need for cooperation in hunting, it is not unreasonable to claim that shared labour and group ownership of land enhanced Iroquoian survival. If so, then group ownership has a clear Lockean basis in natural law.

IV. ENCLOSURE

Locke explicitly claims that land in North America was not enclosed, and connects this with his claim that such land was still common property. For example, he talks of "... the wild Indian, who knows no enclosure, and is still a tenant in common ..." (II, 26). It is certainly true that Iroquoian hunting grounds were not physically enclosed, and Iroquoian agricultural land was not enclosed in the cow and sheep proof fences and hedges common in England. This physical difference may have contributed to Locke's and other Europeans' failure to perceive Native land ownership systems.[26] However, Locke's own argument shows that such physical enclosure is not necessary to justify ownership; legal "enclosure" is sufficient once government has been established. Locke claims that laws are the "fences to properties of all members of the society" (II, 222), and elsewhere says that "the people hav[e] reserved to themselves the choice of their representatives as the fence to their properties ..." (II, 108).

However, laws can only be fences once government is established, and Locke quite clearly saw North America as being still in a state of nature (II, 49). In a state of nature land can be private property, but it is not fenced by laws and government since these do not exist.[27] Without government, the Iroquoian could not claim enclosure by laws, and so without physical enclosure there could be no ownership.

But Locke's Eurocentric biases has led him to an error here; legal enclosure does not require a government capable of legislating and enforcing property rights; all that is required is a method of recognising property claims and resolving disputes. This the Iroquoian had for both hunting and agricultural land. Hunting grounds and agricultural land were assigned to particular clan segments or families. These assignments lasted over many generations and, hence, became part of tradition.[28] Boundary and trespass disputes, if minor, were handled by local chiefs. Disputes between different nations of the Iroquois Confederacy would be settled through council meetings called and supervised by the Onondaga chiefs. Locke was probably right in suggesting Native leaders had only limited power to make laws concerning land ownership and limited powers of enforcement. But these are not needed to prove Lockean ownership; only a system of recognising land ownership is necessary for enclosure in a state of nature. Locke's image of North American Native people running "wild" (II, 26) in a huge forest without boundaries reflects only his failure to perceive non-physical enclosure.

It can be concluded that Iroquoian land, whether used for agriculture or hunting, was "enclosed" in the required sense that ownership was recognised by defined social structures.

V. NATURE OF LAND IMPROVEMENT

One of the most powerful Lockean arguments against Native ownership of land is the claim that land appropriation depends on the labour of clearing and cultivating, and that since Native peoples had not laboured on the land, the land could be appropriated by settlers willing to do so. This argument is powerful, but not correct. Its application to Iroquoian agricultural lands and hunting grounds needs to be discussed separately.

The failure of Locke and other Europeans to perceive the extent of Native agriculture was probably partly due to the Lockean argument that agriculture usually implied ownership; the easiest way to deny ownership was to deny the facts. In the case of the Iroquoian, the application of Lockean property theory to agricultural land is complicated by the fact that improvement was not permanent. Because of the lack of manure, land was cleared, farmed for ten to thirty years, and then not used for agriculture.[29] It needs to be shown that labour leading to non-permanent improvement confers ownership.

On Locke's theory it does. For Locke, labour is relevant only to the initial appropriation of land from the commons, not to its continued ownership. Locke assumed that improvements would be permanent or maintained, but there is nothing in his theory of appropriation that requires this. To require continual labour or improvement would radically change the theory to a utilitarian one in which continued ownership would depend on continued assessment of its productivity. This would undermine Locke's entire attempt to establish property rights, and replace it with an argument for the utility of property.[30] Once the Iroquoian cleared land, Locke would have to recognise that it had been appropriated. Ceasing to farm it subsequently is irrelevant to continued ownership.[31]

VI. HUNTING GROUNDS

The Lockean argument against Iroquoian ownership of hunting grounds was that the Iroquoians had not invested labour in clearing the land and subduing nature; since their labour had only been directed towards hunting animals, not improving the land, they owned the animals they killed, but not the land they hunted on. Their hunting grounds were therefore still the common property of all mankind, and could be appropriated by anyone willing to labour at clearing a portion of them. It has been pointed out that this argument will always justify farmers appropriating the land of hunters,[32] but I will argue that this Eurocentric bias in favour of farming is not inherent in Locke's argument and that hunters can claim a Lockean basis for owning their hunting grounds.

A Lockean based claim for ownership of hunting grounds rests on three factors: socially recognised assignment of hunting territories, care of hunting territories by restraint, and hunting's contribution to the survival of the community.

For the Iroquoian at the time of contact, hunting territories were associated with particular clans and assigned to families within the clan by tradition. Within the Five (later Six) Nation Confederacy and their client bands, there were recognised procedures for resolving disputes. This social recognition of the assignment of specific hunting grounds to identifiable people or groups is sufficient to establish "enclosure" for purposes of a Lockean argument; physical enclosure is irrelevant, and in this case incompatible with usage since the animals needed to wander. As argued above, group ownership of such "enclosed" hunting grounds by families, clans or bands is as relevant to Lockean arguments as individual ownership.

Within assigned territories, families would hunt certain species in certain areas some years and times of years. Other years and times of years, they would refrain from hunting. The purpose of these hunting patterns was conservation.[33] The patterns were set by a combination of tradition and close observation of the fluctuations of animal numbers and their migration patterns. Decisions were based on the principles of respect for tradition and respect for nature and living things. Religion instilled a belief in the sanctity of people living in spiritual harmony with the rest of nature,[34] but the economics of family survival lay behind caring for hunted species by sometimes refraining from hunting at certain times and places. Later, when the English and French fur traders started to provide the Iroquoian with access to insatiable European markets and to European made goods, the ethic of care was sorely stressed, but there clearly had been some care by restraint at the time of contact.

Such restraint satisfies Locke's argument in the same way labouring to improve the land does. For Locke, investing labour in improving common land conveys private ownership of the land because of a combination of two factors: first, such labour improves productivity and, hence, people's chances of survival; and second, it would not be undertaken unless private ownership of the resulting benefits, which requires private ownership of the land, is assured. Care by restraint fulfils both these requirements every bit as well as land improvement; restraint would not be undertaken unless those who restrained their hunting reaped the benefit, and given the technical level of Iroquoian society, restraint that prevented over-hunting of particular species in particular areas at certain times would increase the chances of human survival.

Thus, if one returns to the natural law obligation to provide for the survival of the community, restraint can justify ownership of hunting grounds in precisely the same way that labour justifies ownership of farm land. The extent to which this changes the labour theory of appropriation needs to be noted. If this conclusion is correct, labour allows appropriation not because the activity somehow "mixes" something of the labourer with the land, but because labour in some situations is required by natural law. Natural law, in other situations, may require other types of behaviour, such as restraint. Any behaviour required by natural law confers property rights in a fashion similar to labour if the property rights permit or encourage the behaviour required.

This conclusion is actually more restricted than some current interpretations of the requirements of Lockean arguments. Simmons argues at length that ownership does not require labour, but that "property can be acquired by incorporation into our purposive activities."[35] The conclusion of the present paper is restricted to activities required by natural law. When discussing Simmons' view of purposive activity, Tully points out the implication, which is argued for in the present paper, that North American Native people owned North America at the time of contact.[36] Tully thinks this shows that purposive activity is not a correct interpretation of Locke's intention, but we are here trying to show that Locke's intention of dismissing Native ownership of hunting grounds was inconsistent.

VII. THE PROVISO

The previous section argues that there are Lockean grounds for recognising Native ownership of hunting grounds; this section, on the contrary, assumes that the hunting grounds were the common property of humanity, and argues that, even on that assumption, appropriation of hunting grounds by European settlers does not have a Lockean justification.

As mentioned above, Locke placed two constraints on the right to the appropriation of common land; a person could not justifiably appropriate land that would produce more than they and their family could consume before it spoiled, and the appropriation had to leave "enough and as good" for others. The second of these is the famous Lockean proviso. There have been many interpretations of the

Lockean proviso;[37] the two that need to be examined in the current context are: (a) that the Iroquoian were left as well off as they were before the settlement; or (b) that there was suitable land left for the Iroquoian to settle on and farm in the same way as European settlers.

If the first of these interpretations is assigned to the proviso, then the proviso was clearly violated by the settlement of Iroquoian hunting grounds. That the Iroquoian hunters were less well off after settlement is clear from their bitter complaints throughout the eighteenth and nineteenth centuries that settlers were interfering with hunting.[38] The effect of settlement on hunting is clearer when it is realized that any particular settlement would be in the hunting territory of a particular clan or community, and thus the burden would fall not imperceptibly on the Iroquoian people as a whole, but very perceptibly on specific groups of individuals.

The other interpretation of the phrase "enough and as good" would imply that there was as much land left for each Iroquoian as each settler had acquired, and that the Iroquoian portion could be made as productive as the settlers' lands. In other words, there was enough land left to allow the Iroquoian to give up hunting and become European-style farmers. Accepting this argument implies that farmers everywhere have a natural right to force hunters to become farmers since the farmers are entitled to settle on hunting grounds until the hunters have only enough land left to live if they adopt farming.[39] A couple of things need to be said about this version of the proviso. First, if the settlers are within their rights to enforce their right of settlement, this version of the theory of original appropriation collapses into a right of conquest whenever the hunters object to giving up their hunting grounds. And the Iroquoian plainly did object.

Locke was keen to establish that original appropriation does not require the permission of the rest of humanity; and, in the event of interference in "justified" appropriation, he thought a state of war would be justified.[40] However, he did not view his theory of original appropriation as a justification of war, and did not give serious thought to the possibility that as a matter of fact that might be the normal result.[41] Locke repeatedly uses phrases such as, "there could be little room for quarrels or contentions ..." (II, 31); there was not "any prejudice to any other man ..." (II, 33); or the "rest of mankind" would have no "reason to complain or think themselves injured" (II, 36). The problem with this second interpretation of the proviso is that hunters clearly did see themselves as injured, and saw themselves as thinking they had good grounds for thinking so. It was empirically not true that there was "no room for quarrel" (II, 38).

Second, this interpretation of the proviso does not deal with the historic fact that North American Native people (such as the Cherokee[42]) who cleared land for European style farming simply made the land more attractive to Europeans and lost it anyway. And it must be remembered that the argument applies only to Iroquoian hunting grounds, not to the land they used for agriculture.[43] The impact of this second interpretation of the proviso is that no value at all is placed on lifestyles that use the commons as commons, even if those lifestyles (having avoided the tragedy of the commons somehow) have existed for centuries.[44] But it seems that this is the only interpretation of original appropriation and the proviso that can justify the right of settlement on Iroquoian hunting grounds. The justice of this interpretation in the context of aboriginal rights has been explored elsewhere.[45]

VIII. CONCLUSION

John Locke's theory of original appropriation of land was intended to show that North America in the seventeenth century was unowned, and that Europeans had a right to appropriate land in America by clearing and farming it. This theory of appropriation was based on natural law and certain beliefs about Native American cultures. But Locke was led into inconsistencies by his biases; consistent Lockean arguments from natural law in fact show that North American Native people had already appropriated both farm land and hunting grounds, and hence that most (or all) of North America was private property at the time of contact. Given the culture, technology and situation of North American Native peoples, Lockean arguments based on natural law show that group ownership of property is as legitimate as individual ownership, that physical enclosure of private property is not required even prior to the formation of governments, that temporary land improvement is sufficient to legitimise appropriation, and that care by restraint is as adequate for appropriation as labour for improvement. It can be further shown that even if Native hunting grounds were still common property, the Lockean proviso would make appropriation by settlers illegitimate anyway. Locke failed in his attempt to deny Native ownership of land at the time of contact.

NOTES

1. For a much longer version of this article, which expands on the philosophical issues of Lockean property theory, see: "Locke's Theory of Original Appropriation and the Right of Settlement on Iroquois Territory," *Canadian Journal of Philosophy*, Sept. 1997.
2. Lockean discourse was not the only discourse about property; much of the debate between European and Native property claims depends on other theories of rights and property, such as treaty rights, aboriginal rights, or the right of conquest; this paper deals only with the Lockean theory of property.
3. James Tully, "Rediscovering America: The Two Treatises and Aboriginal Rights," in G.A.J. Rogers, ed., *Locke's Philosophy: Content and Context* (Oxford: Clarendon Press 1994); James Tully, "Aboriginal Property and Western Theory: Rediscovery of a Middle Ground," in Ellen Frankel Paul, Fred D. Miller, and Jeffrey Paul, *Property Rights* (Cambridge: Cambridge University Press 1994); James Tully, "Property, Self-Government and Consent," *Canadian Journal of Political Science*, 28 (1995).
4. Richard Tuck, "Three Great Empires — and Their Defenders: the Diverse Conquerors of the Americas," *Times Literary Supplement*, No. 4860 (1996) 15.
5. Tully, "Aboriginal Property and Western Thought," 158.
6. I will follow Trigger's usage in which "Iroquoian" refers to the Hurons, the peoples of the Five (later Six) Nation Confederacy, and other peoples speaking languages of the same group. "Iroquois" will refer only to the peoples of the Five (or Six) Nation Confederacy. Trigger points out that the Iroquois and Hurons, despite their on-going warfare with each other, had similar economies in the immediate pre-contact period (12). I am not aware of any differences in their economies that affect the arguments of this paper. See Bruce Trigger, *The Huron: Farmers of the North* (Fort Worth: Holt, Rinehart and Winston 1990).
7. The second of Locke's Two Treatises of Government will be referred to as II followed by the paragraph number from J.W. Gough's edition (Oxford: Basil Blackwell, 1942).
8. That Locke had precisely this in mind is argued by Arneil, 602–603; and by James Tully, "Aboriginal Property and Western Theory," 160. Locke's phrase is "tills, plants, improves, cultivates ..." (II, 32).
9. Tully refers to these as the internal or spoilage limit, and the external or sufficiency limit; James Tully, "Property, Self-Government and Consent," 120.
10. See for example: Robert Nozick, *Anarchy, State and Utopia* (New York: Basic Books 1974); and Jan Narveson, "Property Rights: Original Acquisition and Lockean Provisos" (Unpublished manuscript, University of Waterloo 1995).

11. For a discussion of how Locke applies the constraints only to original acquisition, see Macpherson 203–20. Shrader-Frechette argues against Macpherson and others on this point (206–19); I will take the view that natural law continues to apply after original acquisition, but that the specific constraints do not apply unless they are entailed by natural law in particular situations, which they are generally not for Locke in commercial society. This position may be consistent with Shrader-Frechette's discussion. See C.B. Macpherson, *The Political Theory of Possessive Individualism* (Oxford: Oxford University Press 1962); and Kristin Shrader-Frechette, "Locke and the Limits on Land Ownership," *Journal of the History of Ideas* (1993).
12. cf. Shrader-Frechette, 201–19.
13. Richard Ashcraft, *Locke's Two Treatises of Government* (London: Unwin Hyman 1987), ch. 2, esp. 50–56.
14. Locke had, in fact, read extensively the writings about North American Native People that were available in his day; cf. Tully, "Rediscovering America," 168. He obviously considered empirical information relevant.
15. Tully, "Property, Self-Government and Consent," 107; also Knud Haakonssen, *Natural Law and Moral Philosophy: From Grotius to the Scottish Enlightenment* (Cambridge: Cambridge University Press, 1996) 55.
16. For a discussion of the debate surrounding this interpretation of Locke, see Tully, "Property, Self-Government and Consent," 113–18.
17. Also Tully, "Rediscovering America," 169. In "Aboriginal Property and Western Theory" 164, Tully argues that Locke gave three reasons for not recognising that Native Americans had government. These are: the war chief could not "declare war or peace," "the councils often appointed *ad hoc* arbitrators of justice," and there was a "lack of crime, property disputes, and litigation."
18. See also Tully, "Rediscovering America," 169.
19. ibid.
20. Tully discusses the inaccuracy of Locke's views of the property and government systems of Native Americans, including the Iroquois, in "Aboriginal Property and Western Theory," 163.
21. Trigger, 48, 95.
22. Trigger, ch. 6.
23. Jennifer Roback, "Exchange, Sovereignty, and Indian-Anglo Relations," in Terry Anderson, ed., *Property Rights and Indian Economics* (Lanham, MD: Rowan and Littlefield 1992) 13–16; Bruce Benson, "Customary Indian Law: Two Case Studies" in Anderson, ed., *Property Rights and Indian Economics* 28; Trigger, 80–96.
24. Tully, "Property, Self-Government and Consent," 108.
25. The gender bias in this paragraph is Locke's.
26. cf. for example, Flanagan's discussion (591–92) of John Winthrop's "General Considerations for the Plantation in New-England" (1629). It is clear from the quotation Flanagan gives that for Winthrop, it was the lack of physical enclosure (and the lack of "manurance") that meant Indian lands were unowned and available for settlement. Thomas Flanagan, "The Agricultural Argument and Original Appropriation: Indian Lands and Political Philosophy." *Canadian Journal of Political Science*. Vol. 22, 3 (1989), 589–602.
27. Tully, "Rediscovering America," 169.
28. Tully, 181; also William Cronon, *Changes in the Land: Indians, Colonists, and the Ecology of New England* (New York: Hill and Wang, 1983) 58–67, for a discussion of how land assignment varied with use. Tully's and Cronon's discussions are in terms of North-eastern Native peoples in general, as are most discussions of hunting grounds. There appear to be only limited studies of the Iroquoian assignment of hunting grounds, but see Trigger, 34–39.
29. Trigger, 30–32.
30. For a discussion of the differences between rights and utility theories of property, and arguments showing Locke's is a rights theory, see Jeremy Waldron, *The Right to Private Property* (Oxford: Clarendon Press 1988), especially 5–19.
31. On actual abandonment of property, see Simmons, "Historical Rights and Fair Shares," 171.
32. Tuck, 15.
33. The extent to which the Iroquoian and other Native peoples practised care of hunting grounds by restraint is greatly debated; see Claudia Notzke, *Aboriginal Peoples and Natural Resources in Canada* (Toronto: Captus, 1994) 145–149 for recent comments on and references to this debate. For purposes of my argument, the extent of care is irrelevant; any level of care would satisfy Locke's argument. Also, the collapse of the care ethic under pressure of the fur trade with Europeans (as

is discussed by Notzke, 147) is also irrelevant, since this would have been subsequent to the original appropriation of the hunting grounds.
34. Tully, "Rediscovering America," 190.
35. Simmons, "Historical Rights and Fair Shares," 183; also 162.
36. Tully, "Aboriginal Property and Western Thought," 116–17.
37. For a survey of interpretations of the proviso, see Narveson, "Property Rights."
38. Williams, 235.
39. Besides scholarship on Locke such as Tully's, this question has provoked philosophical debate: cf. Michael McDonald, "Aboriginal Rights," in William Shea and J. King-Farlow, eds., *Contemporary Issues in Political Philosophy* (New York: Science History Publications, 1976); David Gauthier, untitled review of William Shea and J. King-Farlow, eds., *Contemporary Issues in Political Philosophy*, *Dialogue*, Vol. 18 (1979), 432–40; Nichola Griffin, "Aboriginal Rights: Gauthier's Arguments for Despoliation,' *Dialogue*, Vol. 20 (1981), 690–96; Thomas Flanagan, "The Agricultural Argument and Original Appropriation: Indian Lands and Political Philosophy," *Canadian Journal of Political Science*, Vol. 22, 3 (1989), 589–602; Nichola Griffin, "Reply to Professor Flanagan," *Canadian Journal of Political Science*, Vol. 22, 3 (1989), 603–606; and Thomas Flanagan, "Reply to Professor Griffin," *Canadian Journal of Political Science*, Vol. 22, 3 (1989), 607. The discussion in the current paper is more restricted, dealing only with the issue in the context of Locke's theory. If these papers are debating about a Lockean type proviso (and it is not clear that this is the context of all of the debates) then they presuppose that Indian hunting grounds are common property and can be appropriated subject to the proviso. It might be more appropriate, as Griffin points out ("Reply to Professor Flanagan," 604), to view this debate as about expropriation.
40. Tully, "Rediscovering America," 170–71.
41. See Ashcraft, ch. 8, for Locke's views on a state of war (which was not the same as the state of nature, as it was for Hobbes); see Williams, ch. 5, 6, and 7, for the history of the idea that Europeans had a right to wage war against Natives if the Natives in the slightest way interfered with settlement.
42. Ronald Wright, *Stolen Continents: The "New World" through Indian Eyes* (Toronto: Penguin 1993) ch. 9; also Flanagan, 601.
43. It is now recognised that the extent of Native agriculture was far greater at the time of European contact than was realized at the time. The discourse of the right of settlement may explain why Europeans, including Locke who nowhere acknowledges Native agriculture in North America, did not see this.
44. As Tully expresses a somewhat similar conclusion: "This is the flaw in almost all the purported solutions to appropriation without consent: they presuppose agreement on the values and goods of the commercial system" ("Property, Self-Government and Consent," 127).
45. See footnote 38 above.

(b) Capitalism and the Dis-empowerment of Canadian Aboriginal Peoples[†]

Michelle Mann

INTRODUCTION

It is generally acknowledged that European colonialists sought to establish new colonies in North America, from approximately 1500 onwards, for the purposes of trade, expansion and settlement. However, the role of capitalism as a driving force

---

[†] The views expressed are solely those of the author. First appeared in *Journal of Aboriginal Economic Development* 1(2): 46–54. Reproduced with permission of the author and CANDO.

behind the dis-empowerment of Aboriginal peoples, both past and present, is not generally acknowledged. In Canada, both on a general level and in particular cases, we can see how the needs of capital direct the interaction between Aboriginal peoples and the state.

HISTORICAL BACKGROUND

The initial period of European contact in Canada ranges from approximately 1500 AD to the early 1800s, and is the period of the first treaties between the British Crown and Aboriginal nations. When British colonialists first made contact in Canada, they encountered "organized" Aboriginal communities, with their own forms of governance and economic systems. Contact during this period was generally marked by a spirit of co-operation between the two nations and respect for each other's sovereignty.[1] The reasons for the colonialists' initial co-operation and respect for the sovereignty of Aboriginal peoples were practical rather than theoretical. As noted in the Report of the Royal Commission on Aboriginal Peoples (RCAP): "Relations were established in a context in which Aboriginal peoples initially had the upper hand in population and in terms of their knowledge of the land and how to survive in it".[2]

Initially, Aboriginal peoples were also partners in the colonialists' economic endeavours, trading fish, furs and material goods, and reaping trade benefits from pursuing their traditional way of life: hunting, fishing, trapping, trading, canoeing, and transportation.[3] Yet another reason behind this early spirit of co-operation was the colonialists' need for Aboriginal nations as military allies both against each other and against the United States. At this stage of the colonial/Aboriginal nations relationship, the support or neutrality of an Aboriginal nation could only be gained by diplomacy, not force.[4] Thus, despite the imperial ambitions of the Europeans, the early stages of this political relationship between European and Aboriginal nations were significant in as much as European powers recognized Aboriginal peoples as autonomous political nations, capable of governing themselves and of entering into relationships with others.

However, towards the end of this period, there was the beginning of a shift in how the colonial powers viewed the Aboriginal nations with whom they were dealing. Government policy reflected an increasing trend towards assimilation, dis-empowerment and enfranchisement of Aboriginal peoples from approximately the mid 1700s through to 1970. By 1876, the first *Indian Act*[5] had been enacted[,] as had various other legislative instruments of enfranchisement and assimilation. This is also the time period in which Aboriginal peoples were increasingly confined to life on reserves, in order to free up their traditional lands for colonial development.

How did this change in colonial attitude come about, and what purpose did it serve? It is not surprising to find that legislation pertaining to Aboriginal peoples throughout the period of 1500 to 1970 indicates that an overwhelming concern of the colonialists was land, and much less so the autonomy or well being of Aboriginal peoples. By the end of the eighteenth century, several factors had evolved that cleared the way for the colonialists to act on their ambitions. By the late 1700s, Aboriginal populations had drastically declined as a result of imported diseases, while the colonial population was continually increasing due to immigration from the colonial countries as well as a rapid influx of loyalists after the American Revolution.[6] These new immigrants pursued agriculture and the export of timber, particularly in the Maritimes, leading to incursions on the Aboriginal land base.[7]

In other areas of Canada, such as Upper Canada, the immigrants' need for land led to the Crown negotiating treaties for the purchase of Aboriginal lands, which the state then made available for purchase by the immigrants.[8] Further, the end of the War of 1812 and the normalization of relations between the United States and Great Britain meant that the colonialists no longer needed the Aboriginal nations as military allies.[9] Finally, the colonial economic base had shifted, as the fur trade declined, and immigrants increasingly desired both land with which to undertake agricultural pursuits, and access to natural resources in order to meet their own needs and that of markets elsewhere.[10]

In fact, not only had the colonial economic base shifted; but during the period from the late 1700s to approximately the mid 1800s, the economic system of England had undergone revolutionary change. The concurrent development of industrialization and *laissez faire* economics in England had parented a new form of capitalism.[11] Prior to the late 1700s, England's capitalism had been held somewhat in check by mercantilism, an economic philosophy that allowed the state extensive powers in regulating and controlling the economic life of the nation.[12]

Towards the end of the 18th century, mercantilism came increasingly under attack, as critics decried the role of government in regulating economic life.[13] Adam Smith, the pre-eminent critic of the time, argued that the government's primary function was to maintain competitive conditions, for only under such a government would the unrestricted self-interest of the individual operate for the public good.[14] The industrial revolution in Britain, combined with *laissez faire* economic theory, gradually forged a new model of capitalism in which free enterprise reigned and capitalists experienced relative freedom from government control. By the mid 1800s, the incentive for private enterprise was no longer encumbered by the state.

It was against this historical background that the way of life of the Aboriginal and non-Aboriginal cultures increasingly became incompatible, as the colonialists resolved that the Aboriginal way and claims to the land would not interfere with their progress. As stated in the RCAP report, "... Aboriginal people came to be regarded as impediments to productive development".[15] The question then, of how the Aboriginal-colonial relationship went from an initial spirit of "contact and co-operation" to one of dis-empowerment and assimilation, involves a closer examination of the goals of capitalism and their centrality to the colonial effort.

GOALS OF CAPITALISM

Capitalism must, by its very nature, expand, seeking new markets and labour forces, in order to keep generating profit and new capital. This need for new markets and the expansion of trade fueled colonialism, as European powers sought to continue their economic growth abroad. As noted by Michael Parenti, "What is unique about capitalism is its perpetual dynamic of capital accumulation and expansion — and the dominant role this process plays in the economic order."[16] In order to generate revenue out of the new territory, colonialists required land on which to base their expansion. As noted by Adam Smith, the success and affluence of a new colony is dependent upon one economic factor: the availability of "plenty of good land".[17] Land in Canada in the 1840s was described as "no lottery, with a few exorbitant prizes and a large number of blanks, but a secure and certain investment."[18] However, not only was it necessary that land be available for use, but also that it be owned and controlled in order to satisfy the needs of capitalists.

Economic power under capitalism can be defined as the "control, authority or influence over others which arises from the ownership of property".[19] Indeed, the right of ownership in productive assets is one of the three basic institutions of capitalism.[20] "Private property is a person's socially enforceable claim to use, or to exclude others from the use of, or to receive the benefits of, certain rights".[21] Thus, not only did capitalism necessitate that land be available for the colonialists, but also that it be subject to private ownership. Under capitalism, inequality in economic power is equivalent to inequality in political power. Even more simply put, domination over things equals domination over people.

The state in capitalist society has as its principal task the legitimation and enforcement of property rights.[22] Those with capital created the capitalist state to guard the rights capital has appropriated, and to protect those rights from the antagonisms of society at large.[23] Historically, one can see how capital controlled the state via the institution of property qualifications for the right to vote, and the right to hold office.[24] Focusing on the concept of property ownership as the power to exclude others reduces the concept of property to one referring to relationships rather than things. Property rights then, like human rights, become rights of an individual *vis a vis* other individuals.[25]

These ideological dimensions of capitalism were in direct conflict with the belief systems of the Aboriginal peoples the colonialists encountered. Private property concepts and their accompanying power imbalance have fostered an individualist interpretation of collective interests in capitalist society. Shared rights and obligations are of marginal importance, and exploiters of the community are supported by the state.[26] In contrast, Aboriginal peoples traditionally functioned as a collective, governed by the interests and survival of the group. Private property and the exclusive ownership of land or resources were not part of the Aboriginal way of life. This interconnectedness of all things has been well documented:

> Aboriginal cultures are non-Anglo-European. We do not embrace a rigid separation of the religious or spiritual and the political. We have extended kinship networks. Our relations are premised on sets of responsibilities (instead of rights) among individuals, the people collectively and toward land.[27]

Thus, in addition to capitalism requiring that the land itself be subjected to private ownership, there was a corresponding theoretical imperative of overriding the communal way of life of Aboriginal peoples. In furtherance of private property, capitalism requires the subsumption of all earlier property forms. The capitalist state is constantly engaged in the process of creating private property for capitalists out of communal property. This is achieved by creating conditions whereby capital can realize itself by overcoming barriers imposed by alternative systems of production.[28] This involves the transformation of "the social means of subsistence and of production into capital".[29] In addition to its role as supplier of land, the new colony also had a role to play in increasing trade for its home country. "Foreign countries in North and South America, which accounted for one-thirteenth of the total British export trade in 1821, took more than one-seventh in 1831; the exports trebled in value during these years.[30]

FIRST NATIONS' CASE STUDIES

It is within the context of the land and resource rights of First Nation peoples, including hunting, fishing, and harvesting, that we can see more clearly the state role as legitimator and enforcer of private property rights, both past and present. In this context, there emerges a continuing pattern of state interference in transferring common property into state property and, finally, into private property. Since the early stages of colonialism in Canada, the state has engaged in the process of alienating land from Aboriginal peoples as a collective group, transferring land to state control. The state then created private property out of this land, transferring much of it to corporations such as the Hudson's Bay Company, and the Canadian Pacific Railway.[31] This exemplifies the pattern of property transfer: from common to state to private.

Perhaps nothing so blatantly emphasizes this state role as section 25 of *The Indian Act, 1876* (and its precursor, the *Royal Proclamation, 1763*), which required, by law, that any Aboriginal surrender of reserve land must be in the name of the Crown.[32] Subsequent to the surrender, the Crown could then act to transform the surrendered land into private property. While the government purpose behind this section was said to be the protection of Aboriginal peoples from unscrupulous colonialists, the state role in the transfer of property from communal to state to private is clearly evident. Further, this provision remains in the current *Indian Act*.[33]

Not long after this legislation was enacted, a case came before the Privy Council of Britain that highlighted the state role as protector of the interests of capital. At issue in the case of *St. Catherine's Milling and Lumber Co. v. R.* (1888) was whether certain Aboriginal lands that had been surrendered belonged to the province or the Dominion of Canada. The St. Catherine's Milling Company had received a cutting permit from the federal government for the land in which the province claimed to hold beneficial interest. In 1873, the federal government had entered into a treaty with the Saulteaux Ojibway providing that the First Nation surrendered their right and title to certain land in exchange for specific considerations. One very important treaty provision was that:

> ... subject to such regulations as may be made by the Dominion Government, the Indians are to have the right to pursue their avocations of hunting and fishing throughout the surrendered territory, with the exception of those portions of it which may, from time to time, be required or taken up for settlement, mining, lumbering or other purposes.[34]

Thus, while the First Nation surrendered their title to the land, they were to retain the right to hunt and fish in their traditional territory. However, the limitation placed on this right that excepted areas taken up for mining and lumbering proved problematic for the First Nation. While the First Nation may have meant to preserve some semblance of their traditional way of life in the form of maintaining hunting and fishing rights, it is evident that the government retained control over this right, rendering it a "qualified privilege", dependent on the "goodwill" of the Crown.[35] Given the discretion of the Crown, the First Nation had little protection when the lumbering company sought and received a permit from the government to cut away one million feet of lumber from the land.[36]

This early case, essentially a battle between the federal and provincial Crown as to who had the jurisdiction to award the lumber licence, does not consider the damaging effect that the cutting away of one million feet of lumber would have on the area wildlife and on the treaty right to hunt. While the federal licence at issue was held to be invalid, and had to be reissued by the province, the rights to the lumber ended up in the control of a private company, without consideration of the First Nation's hunting and fishing rights.

This case illustrates the pattern of the transfer of property rights, from communal to state to private. While the title to the land remained with the Crown, the permit given to the private company effectively overrode the First Nation's communal interests in the property. Further, the provision in the treaty that excepted areas of land required or taken up for settlement, mining, lumbering or other purposes from the First Nation's hunting and fishing rights meant that the licence given to the lumbering company was to the exclusion of the rights of the First Nation. Thus, the lumbering company had a right both to use, and to exclude others from the use of, certain rights relating to the land.

Further, capitalism as a system was served by further reducing or eliminating the extent of the First Nation's rights to hunt and fish and thereby engage in alternative systems of production. Through the transfer of this land from the First Nation to the state, and the issuance of a licence to private business, the Aboriginal means of subsistence and of production was effectively transformed into capital.

Similarly, in British Columbia, where much of the land and resources are subject to comprehensive claims based on Aboriginal title, the First Nations have found themselves battling state supported private corporations for the preservation of their rights. Many of the Aboriginal claims to land and resources are subject to a lengthy treaty making process engaged in with both the federal government and the province since 1993. With this process underway, B.C. Indian Chiefs issued a demand to the government that development be halted on lands subject to a claim for Aboriginal title.

This request was denied by the Aboriginal Affairs Minister for British Columbia as "irresponsible" because it would send the wrong signals to investors and "could harm investment or job creation in B.C."[37] Further, the Minister stated that "We intend to carry on with our responsibility, which is to keep the economy vibrant and healthy".[38] As a result, the First Nations lost their bid to have the province stop issuing Crown logging and other resource permits until the implications of the Supreme Court of Canada decision in *Delgamuukw* could be ascertained.[39]

More specifically, the Haida of British Columbia went to court in an attempt to protect their lands and resources from a private logging company, MacMillan Bloedel, given exclusive rights to cut on Crown lands. The Haida claim Aboriginal title to a large area of British Columbia, much of which was subject to a provincial tree farm licence issued to MacMillan Bloedel. The government renewed the 25-year licence in both 1981 and 1995. The Haida went to court by way of judicial review, seeking to set aside both renewal decisions of the Minister of Forests.[40]

The case centred around the question of whether or not Aboriginal title and rights constituted an encumbrance within the meaning of the B.C. *Forest Act*, thereby precluding the Minister from issuing the licence. The Court concluded that the Aboriginal title and rights did indeed constitute an encumbrance, and allowed the Haida's appeal, thereby preventing the province from giving logging companies exclusive rights to Crown land where Aboriginal rights and title had been established.

However, the Haida's desire was to end MacMillan Bloedel's licence to log on about 190,000 hectares of their claimed homeland altogether. As stated by the lawyer for the Haida: "What's at stake ultimately is the Haida culture, ... the continuing right of Haida people to access our forests to keep our culture alive".[41] She further noted that the exclusive nature of the provincial licensing system is at odds with Aboriginal title, creating the prospect for "fundamental change".[42] It is important to note that while this case was a victory for the Haida, it was determined on the hypothesis that the Aboriginal title and rights claim of the Haida had been established. The question was determined by the court on the assumption that the Haida had title and other Aboriginal rights over the area in question, including the land, water, flora, fauna and resources.[43] This reaffirms that the government and the courts are not willing to protect areas subject to a claim for Aboriginal title or rights pending their determination.

In Vancouver, the Saulteau First Nation commenced an action for judicial review against decisions of the Ministry of Energy and Mines and the Ministry of Forests concerning permits that had been issued to the gas conglomerate Amoco Canada. The Saulteau, a small Treaty 8 Band from Northeast British Columbia, opposed the issuance of permits to Amoco for the development of an exploratory gas well by Energy and Mines, and for cutting timber by the Ministry of Forests, on land subject to Aboriginal treaty rights and title.[44] Against the protests of this First Nation, Amoco had begun exploratory drilling in a watershed area for which the First Nation had been seeking legislated protection for several years.[45] The corporation expects to find a "world class" deposit of deadly but very valuable sour gas.[46] If successful in this endeavor, the corporation plans to establish more exploratory and development wells, along with pipelines and processing plants.

The goal of the Saulteau in this court action was to have the two Ministerial decisions set aside, and for orders requiring the respondent Ministries to consult further with them before any new decision was made regarding Amoco's application to develop an exploratory well and for the necessary cutting permits to provide access to that wellsite. While there had been extensive consultations between this and other concerned First Nations, and the Ministries and Amoco, the Saulteau felt these consultations were inadequate and continued to oppose the development of an area accepted by the court to be a spiritual site for the First Nations.[47] The court found that while the Saulteau First Nation "are adamant in their opposition to this project, they have been afforded the fulfilment of the duty upon the Crown to be consulted."[48] The First Nation's petition was consequently dismissed.

Accordingly, the Chief of the Saulteau First Nation questioned:

> ... how can Glen Clark [Premier of British Columbia] say he's respecting and looking after our Treaty and Aboriginal rights and interests when he stands to gain hundreds of millions

in royalty revenues if Amoco is successful[?] I'd say he's in a clear conflict of interest![49] (emphasis added)

Further, he added:

> They've completely missed the point ... we're trying to protect the water, wildlife and pristine ecosystem which still exists there — it's where our Elders prophesied a hundred years ago, we must depend upon the future for our basic sustenance — that's something money just can't buy.[50]

The comments of this Chief accurately reflect the conflicted role of the state as the guardian of Aboriginal and treaty rights, and the promoter and protector of capitalism.

And while the state has "missed the point" on the values and way of life of this First Nation, it only too well recognizes the point of capitalism: to maximize profit, while simultaneously overriding alternative systems. In fact, the B.C. government has openly acknowledged that a motivating factor behind their negotiation of treaties in British Columbia is the creation of a stable climate for economic development.[51]

Across the country, in Quebec, the Grand Council of the Crees of Eeyou Istchee undertook an action in the Quebec Superior Court in July 1998 to prevent the destructive forest management practices in that area, and challenge the state support of this exploitation.[52] The Grand Council is also seeking a court order requiring the Quebec government to abide by the terms of the James Bay and Northern Quebec Agreement and to respect its own *Forestry Act*. Their position is that from the signing of this agreement onwards, the Quebec government has not respected its commitment to the Cree people to ensure that forestry development is conducted in such a way as to protect Cree rights.[53] The 1975 agreement promises:

- A procedure whereby environmental and social laws and regulations and land use regulations may from time to time be adopted if necessary to minimize the negative impact of development in or affecting the Territory upon the Native people and the wildlife resources of the Territory;
- The protection of Native people, societies, communities, economics, with respect to developmental activity affecting the Territory;
- The protection of wildlife resources, physical and biotic environment, and ecological systems in the Territory with respect to developmental activity affecting the Territory.[54]

The Crees contend that the terms of this modern day treaty are not being fulfilled and are, in fact, being ignored by Quebec in the implementation of policies, laws and regulations determining how forestry operations may be undertaken.[55]

As a result of this neglect, the Crees contend, the Quebec forestry industry is mining out Eeyou Istchee, clear cutting forest habitat, and rapidly depleting Cree hunting territory. While under the treaty, development must incorporate the commitment of government to protect the Cree traditional way of life and the environment, this has not occurred. Cutting is taking place in the absence of land-use planning, and without consultation with the affected Cree communities. The result is that "An age old system of land management and social organization is being destroyed".[56] As the Grand Chief of the Grand Council of Crees, Matthew CoonCome, stated:

> *It is intolerable that the solemn promises of Quebec to the Crees be left up to industry to determine.* The Agreement of 1975 calls for laws and regulations in this situation and Quebec has failed to put into place the required protections. This attack on our rights has been systematic, and long-term and has survived successive governments in the Province.[57] (emphasis added)

The Crees are asking that the court prohibit the defendant corporations from carrying out forestry practices that violate Cree international, Aboriginal, and treaty rights throughout the Eeyou Istchee. They are also seeking an order requiring all forestry operations in the area to undergo federal and provincial impact assessment. Finally, they seek damages for breaches by Canada and Quebec of their constitutional, treaty and other duties.[58]

Again, this case illustrates the state role in furthering the goals of private capital. Despite having entered into a modern day treaty in 1975 with the Crees, the state continues to support private capital even where that necessitates breaching treaty and Aboriginal rights. The Grand Chief highlights the fact that the government's obligations towards Aboriginal peoples are often effectively, if not formally, left to the determinations of private industry. As well, this case evidences the role of the state in supporting the success and profitability of capital, particularly where the sacrifice is "an age old system of land management and social organization". The Cree way of life and its alternative systems face absorption, driven by the needs of capital to continue growing and expanding whatever the human or environmental cost.

Further east, there is increasing conflict in New Brunswick as First Nations communities declare their rights to harvest trees on Crown land. The Maliseet and Mi'ikmaq First Nations contend that their 18th century treaties with the Crown prove that the Crown lands of New Brunswick were never ceded or surrendered and are still Aboriginal lands.[59] In the words of one First Nations logger, "the land belongs to the native people and we have the right to harvest the natural resources".[60] This issue came to the forefront when a Mi'ikmaq was charged with unlawfully cutting bird's eye maple, under section 67 of the *Crown Lands and Forests Act*.[61] The accused was originally acquitted at trial and on appeal by the Crown, with the appeal judge finding that the First Nations had land and treaty rights that included the right to harvest trees on Crown lands.[62]

Briefly, the facts of the case are that the accused had cut three logs of very valuable Bird's eye maple on Crown land with no authority from the Minister. The land where the logs were cut was licensed to Stone Consolidated Inc.[63] The Crown appealed the judge's decision to the New Brunswick Court of Appeal, which reversed the previous courts, concluding that on the evidence provided, the defence had established neither a treaty right nor an Aboriginal right to commercial harvesting.[64] Leave to appeal this decision to the Supreme Court of Canada was subsequently denied.[65]

While the legal issues in this case concern the relevant treaty provisions and the question of the existence of an Aboriginal right to commercial harvesting, it is interesting to consider the parties involved and the interests at stake. In this case, Mr. Paul cut three logs on Crown land that was licensed to a major timber company. It is clear that it is in the interest of this company and other logging companies to have a monopoly on tree harvesting in the area, as this maximizes their profit. The restriction of an Aboriginal right to harvest commercially is clearly not in the interests of the impoverished Aboriginal communities. Nor does it appear to be in the interests of the community in general, as there is no mention of any environmental or conservation concerns in the various judgments.

However, as discussed above, it is the role of the state to protect the interests of capital in order to perpetuate the system. The charging and trial of this First Nations person for cutting three logs on an area licensed to a major corporation brings to mind a quote from Adam Smith:

> When some have great wealth and others nothing, it is necessary that the arm of authority should be continually stretched forth.... Laws and governments may be considered in this and in every case as a combination of the rich to oppress the poor and preserve to themselves the inequality of the goods.[66]

It is also noteworthy that at the Court of Appeal level, several lumber companies were granted intervener status in the case.[67] What possible interest could these corporations have in Aboriginal and treaty rights, other than that of protecting their profit margin?

In response to a recent report generated by the New Brunswick government on this issue, one Aboriginal owner of a logging company commented:

> What I wanted to see in this report was more willingness to share the resource.... They should have recommended that some of the big companies drop a portion of their annual allowable cut, maybe 10 per cent apiece. There should have been some compromise.[68]

It comes as no surprise that most of New Brunswick's six million hectares of forest land is owned by or reserved for big forestry companies.[69] The Aboriginal peoples who lived in New Brunswick long before European settlers made contact have not only been deprived of their rights to the land itself, but also to its produce. These peoples, who now live in a state of high unemployment and poverty, are being denied even the most basic Aboriginal rights to natural resources of which they once had free rein. Even absent a detailed discussion of Aboriginal and treaty rights, it is clear whose interests are being protected in this case. It is not the interests of the environment, and it is most definitely not the interests of the Aboriginal people in the area. Rather, it is the interests of private capital these lumber corporations seek to preserve through the protection of the state. For the large lumbering companies to "share" the resource, or "compromise", would translate into loss of profit, rather than the growth of capital.

CONCLUSION

Given the historical and constitutional importance of treaty and Aboriginal rights, it is appropriate that these issues take centre stage in the debate. However, an examination of the interests that oppose the rights for which Aboriginal peoples seek recognition can be instructive. The question of whose interests are being served is one that should be asked in order to understand what exactly Aboriginal peoples face in their struggles for recognition.

Not only are corporations granted property rights by the state, but they also have the capital, and thus the political power, to enforce those rights. In contrast, many First Nations find that their Aboriginal rights are largely unrecognized and unprotected because the people as a whole are economically, and thus politically, dis-empowered. Given that the state is in the contradictory role of protector of capital and guardian of Aboriginal and treaty rights, it is worth considering the role of capitalism as a basis for the dis-empowerment of Aboriginal peoples historically and in the present day. It may be that the origin and continuance of Aboriginal dis-empowerment is largely economic, having less to do with the race or culture of the occupiers of the land, but more to do with the land and resources themselves.

NOTES

1. Royal Commission on Aboriginal Peoples, *Looking Forward, Looking Back*, vol. 1, ch. 2 (Ottawa: Supply and Services Canada, 1996), at 38.
2. Ibid., ch. 5 at 100.
3. Ibid., at 101.
4. Ibid., at 102.
5. *The Indian Act, 1876*, S.C. 1876, c. 18. (39 Vict.)
6. Royal Commission on Aboriginal Peoples, *Looking Forward, Looking Back*, vol. 1, ch. 6 (Ottawa: Supply and Services Canada, 1996), at 137.
7. Ibid.
8. Ibid.
9. Ibid., at 138.
10. Ibid.
11. C. Breunig, *The Age of Revolution and Reaction, 1789–1850* (New York: W.W. Norton & Company, 1977) at 174.
12. Ibid.
13. Ibid.
14. Ibid.
15. Royal Commission on Aboriginal Peoples, *Looking Forward, Looking Back*, vol. 1, ch. 6 (Ottawa: Supply and Services Canada, 1996), at 138.
16. M. Parenti, *Democracy for the Few*, 5th ed. (New York: St. Martin's Press, 1988) at 15.
17. E. Williams, *Capitalism and Slavery* (London, England: Andre Deutsch Limited, 1987) at 4.
18. Ibid.
19. L. Osberg, *Economic Inequality in Canada* (Toronto: Butterworths, 1981) at 32.
20. S. Pejovich, *The Economics of Property Rights* (Netherlands, Kluwer Academic, 1990) at 27.
21. L. Osberg, *Economic Inequality in Canada* (Toronto: Butterworths, 1981) at 165.
22. W. Clement, *Class, Power and Property* (Ontario: Methuen, 1983) at 211.
23. Ibid., at 214.
24. M. Parenti, *Democracy for the Few*, 5th ed. (New York: St. Martin's Press, 1988) at 55.
25. S. Pejovich, *The Economics of Property Rights* (Netherlands, Kluwer Academic, 1990) at 27.
26. D. Hay, "The Criminal Prosecution in England and its Historians" (1984) 47 Mod. L.R. 6 at 21.
27. Monture-Okanee and Turpel, "Aboriginal Peoples and Canadian Criminal Law: Rethinking Justice", [1992] *U.B.C. Law Review*, 239, at 256.
28. W. Clement, *Class Power and Property* (Ontario: Methuen, 1983) at 215.
29. Ibid., at 213.
30. E. Williams, *Capitalism and Slavery* (London, England: Andre Deutsch Limited, 1987) at 132.
31. W. Clement, *Class Power and Property* (Ontario: Methuen, 1983) at 215.
32. *The Indian Act, 1876*, S.C. 1876, c. 18 (39 Vict.).
33. *Indian Act*, R.S. 1985, c. I-6 , s. 37.
34. *St. Catherine's Milling and Lumber Co. v. R.* (1888), 14 App. Cas. 46 (P.C.).
35. Ibid.
36. Ibid.
37. "Minister refuses to halt development on native lands", *Vancouver Sun*, February 5, 1998, A6.
38. Ibid.

39. Ibid.
40. *Haida Nation v. British Columbia (Minister of Forests)* (1997), 45 B.C.L.R. (3d) 80 (B.C.C.A).
41. "Haida challenge logging rights", *Vancouver Sun*, May 8, 1998, B8.
42. Ibid.
43. *Haida Nation v. British Columbia (Minister of Forests)* (1997), 45 B.C.L.R. (3d) 80 (B.C.C.A).
44. *Chief Stewart Cameron and the Saulteau First Nation v. Ministry of Energy and Mines, Ministry of Forests and Amoco Petroleum Company Ltd.*, October 23, 1998, Vancouver, Docket A982279, (B.C.S.C.) (Unreported).
45. "BC Band blames NDP premier for BP-Amoco Lawsuit", *Khatou News*, October 1998.
46. Ibid.
47. *Stewart Cameron, and the Saulteau First Nation v. Ministry of Energy and Mines, Ministry of Forests and Amoco Petroleum Company Ltd.*, October 23, 1998, Vancouver, Docket A982279, (B.C.S.C.) (Unreported).
48. Ibid.
49. "BC Band blames NDP premier for BP-Amoco Lawsuit", *Khatou News*, October 1998.
50. Ibid.
51. "The Effect of Treaty Settlements on Crown Leases and Licences", Ministry of Aboriginal Affairs, British Columbia, Communications Branch, Internet site.
52. *Mario Lord et al. v. The Attorney General of Quebec et al.*, Checklist of positions taken in the Proceedings by Plaintiffs, 1998, Internet site of the Grand Council of Crees.
53. Forestry Practices Violate Cree Rights", July 15, 1998, Internet site of the Grand Council of Crees.
54. Ibid.
55. Ibid.
56. Ibid.
57. Ibid.
58. Ibid.
59. "N.B. natives dismiss report as inadequate", *Globe and Mail*, March 26, 1999, A5.
60. Ibid.
61. *Crown Lands and Forests Act*, S.N.B. 1980, c. C-38.1.
62. *R. v. Paul*, [1998] 1 C.N.L.R. 209.
63. Ibid., at 210.
64. *R. v. Paul*, (1998) 158 D.L.R. (4th) 231 (N.B.C.A.).
65. [1998] 4 C.N.L.R. iv (note) (S.C.C.).
66. D. Hay, "The Criminal Prosecution in England and its Historians" (1984) 47 Mod. L.R. 6 at 25.
67. *R. v. Paul* (1998), 158 D.L.R. (4th) 231 (N.B.C.A.) at 234.
68. "N.B. natives dismiss report as inadequate", *Globe and Mail*, March 26, 1999, A5.
69. Ibid.

CHAPTER 2

Accommodation and Synthesis

(a) Traditional Ecological Knowledge in Environmental Assessment and Management[†]

Peter J. Usher

THE POLICY ENVIRONMENT

The Policy Requirements

It has become a policy requirement in Canada, and especially in northern Canada, that "traditional knowledge" (TK) or "traditional ecological knowledge" (TEK) be considered and incorporated into environmental assessment and resource management. All comprehensive claim agreements in Canada's territorial North call for aboriginal beneficiaries to be involved directly in wildlife management. For example, the Inuvialuit Final Agreement (IFA) of 1984 states as a principle that "the relevant knowledge and experience of both the Inuvialuit and the scientific communities should be employed in order to achieve conservation" (Canada, 1984: article 14:5). In 1993, the Government of the Northwest Territories adopted a Traditional Knowledge Policy, which recognized that "aboriginal traditional knowledge is a valid and essential source of information about the natural environment and its resources, the use of natural resources, and the relationship of people to the land" and undertook to "incorporate traditional knowledge into Government decisions and actions where appropriate" (GNWT, 1993: 11). Two recent federal environmen-

---

[†] From *Arrtic*, 53(2) (2000): 183–93. Permission to reproduce has been granted from Arctic Institute of North America and the author.

tal assessment panels (for the BHP diamond mining project in the Northwest Territories and the Voisey's Bay nickel mining project in Labrador) were instructed to give, respectively, "full and equal consideration to traditional knowledge" (MacLachlan et al., 1996: 74), and "full consideration to traditional ecological knowledge whether presented orally or in writing" (Griffiths et al., 1999: 203).

Forthcoming federal legislation on species at risk is expected to include explicit requirements to take account of TEK, and the draft terms of reference for the Committee on the Status of Endangered Wildlife in Canada (COSEWIC) already require the status of species to be assessed according to criteria "based on science and to include traditional and local knowledge" (Anon., 1999: 1). At the international level, the Convention on Biological Diversity refers to the knowledge of indigenous and local communities (article 8[j]), and the recently amended Canada-United States Migratory Birds Convention requires the "use of aboriginal and indigenous knowledge" for migratory bird management (article II).

The requirement that the environmental knowledge of aboriginal people be given admissibility and weight in quasi-judicial proceedings and by co-management and other stakeholder bodies, is the outcome of several developments over the last two decades. These include a growing recognition that aboriginal people have knowledge that can usefully contribute to these processes; advocacy from many quarters, including the Royal Commission on Aboriginal Peoples (RCAP, 1996: 678–680), that aboriginal knowledge be so utilized; the negotiation of comprehensive claims across the North; and evolution of formal environmental assessment and review processes. There are also related legal developments. The Supreme Court of Canada has decided that the rules of evidence must allow for the consideration of oral history in the proof of aboriginal rights and titles R. v. Van der Peet, 1996; Delgamuukw v. British Columbia, 1997), and that consultation is a key requirement to justify the infringement by governments of those rights R. v. Sparrow, 1991; Delgamuukw v. British Columbia, 1997). A number of lower court rulings have set standards for consultation and for the consideration of advice given by a body constituted in the context of aboriginal rights (e.g., Nunavut Tunngavik Inc. v. The Minister of Fisheries and Oceans, 1997).

The Problem

Although the general policy requirement is in place, its wording is neither clear nor consistent, and there is virtually no guidance on how to implement it in the public arenas where knowledge claims must be tested. This suggests an insufficient understanding on the part of policymakers of what TEK actually is, and hence of the implications and practicalities of incorporating it into formal decision-making processes.

Neither the Canadian Environmental Assessment Agency, nor the co-management bodies established by the comprehensive claims, nor COSEWIC, nor the Supreme Court has given specific instructions in guidance documents, operating procedures, or judgements on how to implement this requirement. For example, in both of the environmental assessments cited above, it was left to the panels themselves to decide how to implement this requirement and how to instruct proponents to respond to it in their Environmental Impact Statements (EIS). This lack of guidance and clarity has been problematic for regulators, adjudicators, proponents, and intervenors alike (see, for example, MacLachlan et al., 1996: 14–16; Stevenson, 1997). All parties need to know in practical terms what TEK is, what information it provides, how this information can be documented and brought into the environmental assessment process, and how it should be expected to affect both the process and the outcome.

Inconsistent definition is a key problem with the policy requirements cited. Some refer to "traditional ecological knowledge" or TEK, and some to "traditional knowledge" or TK. Some refer specifically to aboriginal knowledge, others only to local knowledge. It appears that TEK is conceived of as something specific to place, if not also to particular people, and it is differentiated presumably in both form and content from other types of knowledge generally and from science specifically. The BHP Panel was instructed to consider TK, which according to GNWT policy (1993) includes "knowledge and values ... acquired ... from spiritual teachings." This instruction led Howard and Widdowson (1996) to assert that requiring the use of TEK in environmental assessment is inappropriate, and even unconstitutional, in a secular context. The subsequent controversy (viz. Berkes and Henley, 1997; Howard and Widdowson, 1997; Stevenson, 1997) demonstrates the problem of applying a well-intended but ill-defined policy. There has also been insufficient attention to appropriate methods of organizing and presenting TEK for the required purposes.

This discussion considers how to remedy these deficiencies, and it shows how TEK and science can be presented and judged in comparable terms in the public arenas of environmental assessment and management. My observations are informed by my experience as a member of an environmental assessment panel and as chair of a wildlife co-management body, as well as by my own research and practice. My purpose is not simply to advocate the use of TEK. That case has already been made, and the appropriate institutional framework has already undergone significant change. My objective is rather to address the problem of implementation. If the unconvinced are to become convinced, then TEK must be seen to make a clear and positive contribution where it is already mandated to do so.

The Context of Implementation

Environmental assessment and co-management are public policy-making tools that are open and responsive to both public opinion and stakeholder rights and interests. The present system is the outcome of years of advocacy and negotiation, and it is within that framework that the key participants have agreed to work. This is not necessarily to say that these are the only or the best possible arrangements, and no doubt they will continue to evolve. For the existing system to work, however, there is an overriding requirement for common rules and protocols, transparency of procedure, and clarity of outcome for all parties.

Of the various policy arenas noted at the outset, the environmental assessment process is the most structured and visible, in which participants can contribute both information and opinion on a wide range of matters. Environmental assessment also has been implemented across Canada for over two decades. To a greater degree than the other policy arenas, it has formal procedures, including public hearings, for obtaining and adjudicating information and opinion. (However, in the case of federal environmental assessment, at least, these procedures are not strictly judicial, as evidence is neither led nor cross-examined by legal counsel, and panels have some discretion in setting and applying their procedures.) Environmental assessment panels are accountable for how they gather and use information, and their recommendations must be based transparently on that information. Panel reviews are always subject to public scrutiny and may also be subject to legal challenge if they violate the principles of administrative fairness. I therefore focus this discussion on environmental assessment, although it applies more generally to a variety of resource management issues.

Environmental assessment and management involve human intervention: deliberate actions whose consequences, intended or unintended, must be understood and predicted, so far as is possible, to ensure the most desirable (or avoid the most undesirable) outcomes. To integrate science and TEK for this purpose, information from both sources must be collected, organized, and communicated. This must be done systematically, using established protocols, so as to minimize the dangers of overgeneralizing from limited information and untested assumptions (Wenzel, 1999: 120). Neither opinions alone, however firmly or sincerely held, nor facts alone, however accurately recalled or precisely recorded, are sufficient. The policy arenas in which these matters are resolved are ones in which knowledge claims must be tested and validated, not merely asserted. Thus, no information, no form of knowledge, and no knowledge claim can be undisclosed or kept privileged from examination.

DEFINING TEK FOR ENVIRONMENTAL ASSESSMENT AND MANAGEMENT

Definitions

Many commentators have attempted to dichotomize TEK (or sometimes TK) and Western science in terms of their respective ideological underpinnings, substantive content, methods, epistemology, and context (e.g., Bielawski, 1992; Freeman, 1992; Johnson, 1992; Berkes, 1993; Mailhot, 1993; Stevenson, 1996). While constructing archetypes of the two can be instructive, Agrawal (1995) rightly notes the practical and philosophical limits of posing them as pure categories. Contemporary TEK explanations can hardly be unaffected by aboriginal people's knowledge (scientific or otherwise) of the wider world. For example, field science programs have been employing aboriginal Northerners since at least the 1960s, including some who are elders today. They are aware of what scientists actually do and find out, and even if they do not agree, they have considered scientific knowledge critically against their own. While there are indeed differences between TEK and science, their essential similarity may be more important for the purposes of this discussion.

I use the term "TEK" here because it has passed into common usage, and also, in the same way as Wenzel (1999: 114), in preference to "TK" because it is more specific. Stevenson (1996: 280–283) likewise distinguishes among traditional ecological knowledge, other traditional knowledge, and nontraditional knowledge, as various forms of indigenous knowledge that can contribute to environmental assessment. For this discussion, then, TEK refers specifically to all types of knowledge about the environment derived from the experience and traditions of a particular group of people. TEK is, nonetheless, a problematic descriptor of that knowledge. By using the term "traditional," one risks implying a static or archaic form of knowledge that is inherently nonadaptive, whereas the acute observations and sophisticated knowledge that some aboriginal people have of their environment are both evolving and current.

Although it is appropriate in this context to use "traditional" as though it were interchangeable with "aboriginal," TEK as defined below is not restricted by genetics or heritage to aboriginal persons (for a discussion of the use of local harvesters' knowledge in fisheries management, for example, see Neis et al., 1999). TEK could be characterized as the knowledge claims of those who have a lifetime of observation and experience of a particular environment and as a result function very effectively in that environment, but who are untutored in the conventional scientific paradigm.

I also refer to "science" (or "Western science," as used by some commentators, even though it is not exclusively Western), as the chief knowledge claim conventionally contrasted with TEK, even though it is also an ambiguous term. There are, of course, competing knowledge claims within the realm of "science," based not only on differing interpretations of the same evidence but also on differing paradigms and premises. What is loosely called science in the public policy arena (including technology, engineering, and management) combines a particular set of values with systems of knowing based on empirical observation, rationality, and logic, as opposed to received or felt truths or, exclusively, sensory perception or "lived experience" (viz. Fernandez-Armesto, 1999).

A Classification of TEK

The concept of TEK has been applied to at least the following categories of information, which are distinguishable on substantive and epistemological grounds.

Category 1: Factual/rational knowledge about the environment. This includes statements of fact about such matters as weather, ice, coastal waters, currents, animal behaviour, traveling conditions and the like, which are typically based on (a) empirical observations by individuals of specific events or phenomena; (b) generalized observations based on numerous experiences over a long time; or (c) generalized observations based on personal experience reinforced by the accounts of others both living (shared experience, stories, and instruction) and dead (oral history and customary teachings).

In practical terms, this broad category of TEK is largely about what works, and sometimes about how and why it works. It also includes, for example, indicators of ecosystem health, such as the appearance or behaviour of animals, the taste and texture of country food, or unusual occurrences or conditions. Category 1 TEK thus ranges from specific observations to explanatory inferences, constituting explanations of what people observe and the relations and connections among them, or more broadly, an understanding of why things are as they are. As observations accumulate, both in frequency and over time, raw data become information about patterns and associations of phenomena. The boundary between observation and inference is not always evident, however, because people may state as fact or consequence what scientists would characterize as inference or deduction. But, in principle, what is not a statement of fact is a potentially testable hypothesis.

Category 2: Factual knowledge about past and current use of the environment (e.g., patterns of land use and occupancy, or harvest levels), or other statements about social or historical matters that bear on the traditional use of the environment and hence the rights and interests of the local aboriginal population in the regional environment. Statements of fact are based on a range of knowledge from personal experience and observation to oral history. I refer to information about past and current use of the environment as a separate category here because it is so often relied on in environmental assessment and management (Usher, 1993; Duerden and Kuhn, 1998), but this information constitutes a different body of knowledge rather than being a different form of knowledge. While oral history information is included in this category, it is important to note that oral history in its largest sense — which includes such matters as the history, traditions, and origins of the people, their identity, and their assertions of their rights and titles — goes well beyond any conventional definition of TEK.

Category 3: Culturally based value statements about how things should be, and what is fitting and proper to do, including moral or ethical statements about how to behave with respect to animals and the environment, and about human health and well-being in a holistic sense.

Category 4: Underlying the first three categories is a culturally based cosmology — the foundation of the knowledge system — by which information derived from observation, experience, and instruction is organized to provide explanations and guidance. It is the framework with which people construct knowledge from facts. This foundation may include systems of classification of natural phenomena that differ from Western scientific approaches such as the Linnaean ordering of species. While this category is the least articulated and hence the least accessible to outsiders, some understanding of it may be needed to interpret or understand the other three categories of knowledge.

From a Western scientific perspective, TEK includes empirical facts or associations based on observation and experience, explanations of fact, a culturally specific way of organizing and understanding information, a set of values, and — in a very broad sense — cultural norms about how to do things. From an aboriginal perspective, TEK is what people learn from experience, from family and community, and from stories handed down about how to live fully and effectively in their environment. It is thus both knowledge of how things work and a guide to action.

To sum up, I have distinguished four categories of TEK: (1) Knowledge about the environment; (2) Knowledge about the use of the environment; (3) Values about the environment; and (4) The knowledge system. Each of these categories has a place in environmental assessment, although where and how they do so will vary. However, I will focus on factual knowledge about the environment (Category 1) because it is in principle testable in the same way that scientific knowledge is, and because it can be used for prediction and monitoring of environmental effects.

Some Characteristics of TEK

Any reasonably aware and competent person who regularly engages in small-scale artisanal activity in a natural environment year after year — whether it be farming, husbandry, or fishing — is likely to accumulate a wealth of observations that will enable him or her to make certain generalizations, comparisons, and conclusions about natural phenomena. (I specify "artisanal" in this context to distinguish from industrial activities in which individuals engage in only a particular component of the work and have neither opportunity for comprehensive observation, nor a requirement for comprehensive environmental knowledge. It is perhaps this artisanal characteristic that has given rise to the suggestion that TEK is "holistic," in contrast to "reductionist" Western science.)

Several factors enhance this knowledge among aboriginal people, however. Their harvesting activities often occur over a very large area, and over long periods of the year. Thus the geographical and temporal scope of their environmental knowledge is generally much greater than that of a farmer or coastal fisherman, whose scope of operation is bounded by legal or customary property rights or by highly restricted harvesting periods. The diversity of activities, of animals and plants harvested, and of types of landscapes or coastal areas used is generally greater, and consequently the breadth of aboriginal environmental knowledge and the scope for drawing connections among phenomena is greater. The fact that human activity on the land typically occurs within a framework of communal rather than private property relations, as well as mutual aid, facilitates continuity and sharing of experience. Long continuity of practice and of the geographic extent of land use greatly increase the likelihood that information will be transmitted and accumulated over generations.

In contrast, where the levels of socioeconomic diversification and personal mobility, and the rate of social change, are high (as typically occurs with industrialization and urbanization), knowledge of useful particularities about the local environment is less likely to be widely shared. And where property and access rights are commonly bought and sold, intergenerational knowledge of the same place is the exception rather than the rule. While TEK is thus not unique to aboriginal culture or ethnicity, it is far more likely to be prevalent among aboriginal people who continue to participate in a mixed, subsistence-based economy because of the property relations and continuity of practice that typify their communities. Such circumstances may nonetheless also exist among nonaboriginals, such as the settler families of long residence in Labrador and in Newfoundland outport communities.

The circumstances that foster TEK are neither uniformly distributed nor permanent among aboriginal communities. In places where, for whatever reason, few if any members of the community have recent or current experience of a particular area or phenomenon, there may not be much TEK that will be useful to environmental assessment. However, TEK does not always need to be of great antiquity to be valid or useful. New and evolving environmental knowledge may also contribute to environmental assessment.

In TEK, factual observations may be very precise and recalled in extraordinary detail. Typically, people are careful to distinguish between what they actually saw and what they were told by someone else, and hesitate to generalize beyond their personal experience. This type of knowledge tends to be localized and restricted to personal, uninstrumented observations, with little concern for precision in measurement, and it is normally unrecorded. The emphasis is on observing conditions, trends, and variations (especially extreme or abnormal ones), rather than on establishing norms and averages or testing the strength of associations. Conclusions based on this information tend to be verified or reinforced through trial and error, rather than by experimental design and formal hypothesis testing.

TEK confirms inferences and associations when repeated experience shows that they work, but the situation is less clear when such confirmation does not occur. Even unassailable observations may lead to an incorrect inference or association, and such erroneous conclusions may persist when TEK cannot actually verify them. On the other hand, even widely used scientific methods of verifying and interpreting data, including statistical tests, do not preclude erroneous conclusions, and are not without controversy and uncertainty (Johnson, 1999).

Category 1 TEK has a substantial time-depth, ranging from "living memory" (personal experience), to the memory of several generations, preserved as oral history. It thus provides a diachronic or "natural history" perspective, rather than synchronic perspective. Hence a "baseline" is not conceived as a static, snapshot phenomenon but as a more fluid and evolving one that offers a clearer perspective on deviations from "normal" conditions. TEK can thus contribute to environmental assessment by providing a broader and deeper understanding of baseline conditions and a fuller understanding of local environmental processes, at a finer and more detailed geographical scale, than conventional scientific knowledge can offer. Category 1 TEK is also important because it deals with outcomes and prediction: what people think will happen and why.

It makes good sense to involve people who spend a lot of the time on the land in environmental assessment and management, for the obvious reason that they get to see things more often, for longer, and at more different times and places than is normally the case for scientists. These observations, and the resulting hypotheses, can complement observations that contemporary scientists are in a position to make (but aboriginal people are not) through such techniques as magnification, remote sensing, or chemical or genetic analysis. Scientists' observations are instrumented, quantified, and recorded, and are more likely to be guided by a specific hypothesis, but are otherwise in principle similar to those of aboriginal observers.

Category 1 TEK, particularly that based on direct observation, can be unique to the individual, especially if the particular areas of use or types of activity are highly specialized, for example in a family harvesting area such as a trapline or fishing site. Such TEK is likely to be specialized by gender (for example, where men harvest and women process food, they observe different things) and by age and experience. TEK for a large region may in these circumstances emerge as a mosaic of individual or family knowledge, whose totality may not be known by any single individual. Where no members of the group are in a position to observe something (for example, what happens in places that are seasonally inaccessible or at depth in the ocean), there is no Category 1 TEK, except perhaps some inferences or speculations.

Although TEK is based on careful and repeated personal observation, it does not consist merely of personal observation or opinion. Some persons are more knowledgeable and experienced and wiser than others, and they are widely acknowledged as such in their communities. TEK becomes authoritative in aboriginal communities through continuity and sharing of experience, through telling and retelling: hence the importance of the oral tradition. The fact that human activity on the land typically occurs within a communal framework facilitates this continuity and sharing of experience. TEK is more than just isolated or unconnected personal observations: it is cumulative and shared experience validated by testing in practical circumstances for its effectiveness. TEK is part of a pool of knowledge particular to a group of people, and the more durable and widely agreed-upon elements are part of their cultural heritage. Finally, TEK is not privileged or secret knowledge in the way that certain other cultural phenomena, such as ritual, healing, or spirituality, may sometimes be.

INTEGRATING TEK IN ENVIRONMENTAL ASSESSMENT AND MANAGEMENT

Types of TEK Required for Environmental Review

In considering how TEK contributes to each of these phases of an environmental assessment, it is essential to distinguish among facts based on observation, which can be verified; inferences or hypotheses, which can be tested; and values and norms, which are matters of personal preference, community consensus, or cultural standards. Any or all of these can legitimately be brought forward and considered in a public review, but [who] brings each type forward, and the way each will be treated, is different. The first two types must be subject to verification and testing, but the third cannot be subject to such tests, although it can and should be authenticated as representative. Environmental assessment often presents a new challenge to TEK, as it does to science, precisely because it tries to predict the outcome of what is at least partly a novel and untested situation. Under the federal environmental assessment regime, there are four phases of a typical public review of a development proposal that would involve TEK.

Phase 1: Scoping, or identification of issues, which leads to the guidelines for the review. This phase may involve scoping hearings at which participants identify the key concerns regarding the proposed development. The guidelines identify what are sometimes termed the "Valued Ecosystem Components" (VECs), which focus the review around the values at risk (Beanlands and Duinker, 1983). This phase requires TEK from Categories 2 and 3. Category 2 TEK helps to establish "the current use of lands and resources for traditional purposes by aboriginal persons" that may be adversely affected (this is mandated by the definition of "environmental effect" under the Canadian Environmental Assessment Act, Article 2[1]). Category 3 TEK identifies, from the aboriginal perspective, the key phenomena, places, and processes that may be adversely affected, and why they are important. While Category 4 TEK is more difficult to present in the assessment process, it may provide different perspectives on the ecosystem and human-environment interrelations and hence on what might constitute a VEC. It is the responsibility of affected parties, acting as intervenors, to bring TEK from Categories 2, 3, and 4 to the public review process.

Phase 2: Preparation of an Environmental Impact Statement (EIS) by the proponent, in response to the guidelines. The EIS includes a description of the proposed project, a description of the existing environment (certainly consisting of a baseline description and ideally identifying key environmental processes), predictions of the effect of the project on the environment, and proposals for mitigating adverse effects. While all categories of TEK may be useful for the EIS, for practical reasons elaborated below it may sometimes be either impossible or inappropriate for the proponent to fully incorporate TEK into the EIS.

Phase 3: Public review of the EIS, which may include public hearings. The factual and explanatory aspects of TEK (Category 1) can be applied both to baseline description (or profiling) and, in certain respects, to impact prediction. Category 1 TEK can also include prior experience with development impacts, and hence can contribute to understanding cumulative effects. Public hearings generally involve separate technical and community sessions. Category 3 TEK is appropriate to community sessions, while Category 1 and Category 2 TEK can be introduced in both types. How this information is introduced, and by whom, is discussed further below.

Phase 4: Monitoring and follow-up, if the project is approved and proceeds. A follow-up program, as defined in Article 2(1) of the Canadian Environmental Assessment Act of 1992, has two purposes: to verify the accuracy of the environmental assessment and to determine the effectiveness of mitigation measures. Such programs have been established by multi-party agreement to monitor the effects of both the BHP diamond mine in the Northwest Territories and low-altitude military flights in Labrador and Quebec. The Voisey's Bay Panel recommended that the parties negotiate an environmental co-management mechanism for the ongoing requirements of permitting and regulatory review of the project as it evolves, and the administration of the follow-up program (Griffiths et al., 1999: 155–160). Category 1 TEK can and should be used for monitoring impacts on VECs and for testing impact hypotheses and predictions in a follow-up program (see LGL et al., 1986 for an outstanding example of integrated TEK and science construction of indicators and hypotheses for monitoring).

Stevenson (1996: 283) proposes a similar phased use of TEK in the environmental assessment process.

The Need for Equivalency

Mobilizing science for specific environmental assessments is a highly organized and structured process. The proponent engages scientists to gather baseline data, test hypotheses, or answer certain questions according to recognized methods; to communicate the results in consulting reports and peer-reviewed journals; and to appear as expert witnesses. Regulators and intervenors engage scientists for similar purposes, or at least to review the work of the proponent's scientists. Specific questions are asked and answered by research programs directed to the problem at hand.

This is in contrast to TEK, in which a lifetime's experience is drawn upon to consider whatever problem arises (Gunn et al., 1988: 25). TEK exists in people's heads; even if some aspects of it have been written down, that information may not apply directly to the specific project or question. Mobilizing TEK for environmental assessment is, to date, not a well-organized or structured process, and it is certainly not a straightforward or unambiguous exercise.

For Category 1 TEK to be given full and equal consideration as a knowledge claim in a public forum, it must be documented in a way that is equivalent or comparable to (although not necessarily the same as) scientific claims about environmental assessment and management. Such documentation has at least two requirements. The first is to compile and assemble TEK in an organized and systematic way. Not everything every aboriginal person utters is TEK, and it is both inappropriate and unhelpful to present TEK as a random collection of utterances. Random or opportunistic recording of whatever individual aboriginal persons might say about environmental conditions in the course of casual conversation, or even at public meetings, does not provide useful information for assessment, any more than miscellaneous and unorganized scientific observations do. The second requirement is to distinguish clearly between observations and inferences, in the same way that in scientific reports, results are separated from conclusions. If scientists (and, more importantly, adjudicators) who are not familiar with TEK do not accept its inferences or conclusions, they are liable to discount the observations on which they are based as anecdotal — or worse, as unreliable.

Without these precautions, the use of Category 1 TEK in environmental assessment can be seriously compromised. The risk is that TEK will be seen as a haphazard collection of sometimes conflicting and apparently unreproducible observations that are not clearly grounded in space and time, resulting in untestable statements about the environment and about the environmental effects of a particular activity. If individual assertions of TEK conflict, then whose are authoritative? And how does one go behind what is said in order to establish the basis of a knowledge claim? It follows that TEK is most likely to assist an environmental assessment if it is presented as a study report, i.e., a written document that organizes and synthesizes TEK for the purpose of the assessment and specifies the basis of the knowledge presented. (Technical sessions of public hearings normally require written presentations submitted in advance.)

Documenting and Presenting TEK in Environmental Assessment

When TEK has been used for environmental assessment, it has almost always been recorded, organized, and presented by trained persons who use accepted social scientific methods, and who are employed by aboriginal organizations for that purpose. (The exception is of course Category 3 TEK, which is generally presented directly by aboriginal persons or organizations in nontechnical hearings.) The use of technical reports by trained intermediaries does not and should not preclude, or take precedence over, direct statements of TEK by those who have it, at public hearings. However, such reports provide an essential communications bridge by converting what appear (to those unfamiliar with TEK) to be anecdotes or opinions to usable and testable data and hypotheses within a widely recognizable framework.

Methods for obtaining and organizing Category 2 TEK are already well established (e.g., Freeman, 1976; Ellanna et al., 1985; Usher and Wenzel, 1987). There are also emerging norms for TEK research specifically directed to assessment and management issues (Neis et al., 1999). A key method of data collection is the semidirected interview (Nakashima, 1990; Ferguson and Messier, 1997; Huntington, 1998; Fienup-Riordan, 1999), although focus group methods can also be used.

Interviews are generally conducted using maps as a recall and recording aid, because Category 1 TEK is geographically specific. The use of chronologies as recall aids to ground TEK data in time is also recommended. A competent interviewer must have a good working knowledge of the geography and chronology of the region, and of local environmental processes and harvesting practices, to be able to ask questions that follow up and probe further the information offered by informants, without the aid of an interview guide. This is especially important for establishing sources of knowledge and the basis of individual knowledge claims (Wenzel, 1999: 117). The normal methods of controlling (or at least accounting) for response bias and recall failure must be adhered to.

Interviews should be conducted in the preferred language of the participant, and if the interviewer does not have this capacity, an interpreter is required. The interviewer or interpreter must be proficient enough to know specific environmental terminology and taxonomy, place names, and the like, and this is not necessarily the case with younger members of the community. Such interviews can take several hours to complete and may require more than one session.

Taken together, these methods help to ensure the authenticity and validity of TEK obtained through interviews. For the purposes of impact assessment, the question of validation applies only to TEK Categories 1 and 2, because it is these specific knowledge claims that are being compared (or contrasted) to scientific knowledge claims. A cooperative or synthetic approach to integrating scientific and traditional environmental knowledge requires validation through independent corroboration, internal consistency of evidence, and similar approaches.

Validation, or corroboration, is required of any fact or conclusion brought before a public review, and in this respect TEK is not privileged. However, any panel, and any proponent, is well advised to approach this question in a careful and respectful manner. Challenges to specific facts or conclusions can appear to bring TEK of Categories 3 and 4 into question as well, not to mention the personal integrity and competence of those who have TEK.

TEK documentation requires time and money. However, research programs along the lines described above can usually be completed within a year, which is less time than many scientific baseline programs for environmental assessment require. Early examples of scholarly documentation of TEK (viz. Nelson, 1969; Usher, 1971; Freeman, 1985; Feit, 1988) used the method of participant observation. However, TEK documentation does not necessarily require extended periods of participant observation (and the apparently nonsystematic approach sometimes associated with that method). TEK research can be faster, and certainly cheaper, than a typical biophysical science program (Freeman, 1979: 358), and with shrinking science budgets in the public sector, these are important considerations. True, it is rare to find much existing literature or relevant databases for TEK when it comes time to prepare or review a EIS. But it is often the case that scientific baseline information and understanding of environmental processes at the local scale are similarly deficient. If introduced early in the process, TEK can be used to guide scientific research on impacts by identifying key locations and processes that can inform hypothesis testing and focus sampling programs.

Documentation and communication of TEK, regardless of who does it, require the support, cooperation, and involvement of the community involved. Individuals from outside the community who seek TEK need to negotiate the basis for doing so. This is a standard requirement of ethical research guidelines, and is sometimes also a permitting requirement. Researchers must gain the trust of and be accountable to the persons providing TEK. They do this by, among other things, fully disclosing the objectives and uses of the research, obtaining informed consent of individual participants, involving the community in the design and conduct of the research, and entering into an agreement about data ownership and access.

The most effective way of obtaining verifiable and generalizable knowledge begins by interviewing the most knowledgeable persons in the community, who are the proper sources of TEK. The community consultation process must therefore include the identification of those persons, although it is ultimately the individuals' prerogative as to how and with whom they will share TEK, and thus whether they wish to participate in the project. TEK research is not an opinion poll, and mass sampling methods are neither required nor appropriate.

The fact that TEK research must be under community control raises a key question for proponents and regulators in project review. Not only may the proposed development itself be controversial: its review may occur in the context of larger political concerns, for example, unresolved land claims or the negotiation of impact and benefit agreements. Under such circumstances, an affected aboriginal community is unlikely to choose proponent-designated researchers to act as intermediaries in encoding, analyzing, and presenting local TEK, and indeed, if the community were opposed to the project, it could hold up the review by simply failing to provide TEK. Even if the project itself is viewed favourably by the local population, there is often a reluctance to share TEK with outside researchers or agencies because of a concern that it will be misinterpreted or decontextualized (Stevenson, 1996, 1997). It is therefore neither reasonable nor appropriate to require a proponent to incorporate TEK directly into its EIS.

An Example: The Voisey's Bay Environmental Assessment

In 1996, the Voisey's Bay Nickel Company Ltd. (VBNC) filed an application to proceed with a mine and mill project in northern Labrador. This application triggered an environmental review under federal and provincial legislation. A joint environmental assessment panel was constituted in January 1997 to review the proposal. Scoping hearings were conducted in 1997, and the proponent submitted an EIS in December. Public hearings were conducted in 1998, and the panel submitted a report in March 1999 (Griffiths et al., 1999).

Recognizing the problems that would arise in obtaining TEK under the controversial circumstances of the project (relating chiefly to unresolved land claims and benefits agreements), the panel's guidelines provided the proponent (Voisey's Bay Nickel Company) with two options for ensuring that TEK (and TK in general) would be given full consideration in the review. The company could either (1) "make best efforts, with the cooperation of other parties, to incorporate into its EIS aboriginal knowledge to which it has access or which it may reasonably be expected to acquire through appropriate diligence, in keeping with appropriate ethical standards and without breaching obligations of confidentiality," or (2) "facilitate the presentation of such knowledge by aboriginal persons and parties themselves to the Panel during the course of the review" (Anon., 1997: 6–7).

Neither the Labrador Inuit Association nor the Innu Nation (the two primary affected aboriginal parties) was willing to provide TEK directly to the proponent. The Voisey's Bay Nickel Company had already provided financial support to both to undertake issue identification (INTFMA, 1996; Williamson, 1996). Their reports, which provided primarily Category 3 TEK, assisted the panel during the scoping phase, and VBNC used these reports, as well as the Labrador Inuit Association's documentation of land use and ecological knowledge (Williamson, 1997), in its EIS. However, as neither party chose to provide Category 1 TEK directly to VBNC, the company chose the panel's second option, to ensure that TEK that it could not otherwise obtain would in fact be made available for the review. Proponents anticipating a public review may be well advised to engage in similar processes at the same time they begin their own scientific research program.

Both aboriginal parties opted to minimize the use of trained professionals as intermediaries at the public hearings, but in different ways. The Labrador Inuit Association provided TEK chiefly through the innovative procedure of assembling panels of Inuit experts (established as such through their long experience) at technical hearings. These individuals provided information on the local estuarine, marine, and sea-ice environments, and predicted certain effects of the proposed marine and air transport systems on those environments, in conformity with the Panel's Public Hearings Procedures (Anon., 1998). These experts, selected by the Labrador Inuit Association, provided Category 1 TEK with specific reference to the project description. Their evidence was presented, questioned, and considered in the same way as other expert evidence at the public hearings.

The Innu Nation used trained intermediaries to assist in the preparation of a report on Innu TEK (Clement, 1998), and video documentation of Innu circumstances and concerns. The former included Category 1 and Category 4 TEK, although its impact predictions appeared to be based on general knowledge (or opinions) of previous industrial development, with no reference to VBNC's description of its proposed project. The video addressed the concerns and views of Innu regarding the project, thus restating issues identification and concerns noted at the scoping hearings, rather than addressing Category 1 TEK regarding specific project effects. The chief difference between the LIA and Innu presentations of TEK was that the LIA's addressed the effects of the project actually described by the proponent (to the best of the LIA's understanding of that description), while the Innu presentations referred to the effects of other developments that Innu had experienced, without reference to the specifics of VBNC's proposed project.

Category 1 TEK was particularly relevant to the Panel's findings and recommendations regarding the proposed marine and air transport systems. This information went well beyond both the proponent's EIS, and the evidence of nonaboriginal technical experts. The Voisey's Bay case shows that the use of professional intermediaries to organize and present TEK can be minimized. However, I believe that the need for professionals is best assessed in each case, on the basis of the technical requirements of the particular arena, how adversarial the proceedings are likely to be, what other requirements for that information may exist, and what resources are available to those who would put it forward. Certainly, the primary role of the professional for this purpose is not to verify or improve on TEK, but to organize it and make it accessible. Interpretation, while to some extent unavoidable (and not necessarily undesirable if it is clearly stated as such), should be kept to a minimum in an environmental review, so that adjudicators receive the benefit of local TEK with a minimum of filtering by the researcher.

CONCLUDING OBSERVATIONS

Many aboriginal people regard TEK as unique and particular to their culture and locality, and as a positive and empowering attribute of their aboriginal identity. For them, the use of TEK in environmental assessment and management affirms the validity and relevance of their knowledge, experience, and competence, and reverses a long history in which those attributes were ignored or discounted. Yet many people, both aboriginals and researchers, have expressed concerns about the use of TEK in this context. One such concern is that TEK, and those who present it, be treated with respect. Another is the risk of appropriation and dispossession of TEK (Stevenson, 1997; Wenzel, 1999). Aboriginal people are often resistant to the idea that TEK can be codified in writing and thus taken away, removed, or separated from the cultural context in which it operates.

There has been considerable discussion in some legal and human rights arenas on issues of "intellectual property rights" with regard to TEK, but no firm principles have been established. Questions have been raised about whether Western legal principles of intellectual property rights properly or adequately apply, whether other legal concepts are required, and whether more restrictive regimes would be effective, or have desirable outcomes in a broader sense (viz. Brown, 1998; Wenzel, 1999). In the international development field, some proponents of the use of indigenous knowledge advocate collecting and archiving TEK as though it were a data set, although as Agrawal (1995) notes, this entails processes of codification and reification that contradict the very qualities that some TEK advocates maintain are the crucial differences between TEK and science. The data set approach appears to have few advocates in Canada, at least in the context of environmental assessment and management.

Wenzel (1999: 118) poses the question: "Who has the right to access and interpret traditional ecological knowledge?" and cites a range of views from different commentators. However, once such knowledge is placed in the public arena in support of a public policy choice, the answer must be that everyone has the right to interpret it, just as all have that right with respect to any other knowledge claim. Some have observed that courts of law, or even panel reviews, are not the best places to judge the merits of scientific claims, and that scientists are best qualified to do that. There is a risk that any knowledge, taken out of the context in which it was generated, can be misinterpreted or even deliberately misused. Achieving transparency and accountability in public policy-making processes is a better way to minimize that risk than withholding knowledge and information from them. Ethical treatment of TEK does not and should not include sole control over interpretation.

The public (including the aboriginal public) is increasingly aware that there are competing knowledge claims within the realm of science, and that each may be accompanied by inherent limitations and risks of error. TEK, as a form of science, is not infallible in this regard, and its use and acceptance in public policy making will not be enhanced by assertions that TEK is above critical examination of its premises, data, methods, and conclusions. Some might observe that I have sought to fit TEK to existing environmental assessment and management processes, rather than the other way around. I would respond that it is in the interests of all to demonstrate the power of TEK in the arenas and by the processes that have already been negotiated, as so many have advocated, before moving on.

REFERENCES
AGRAWAL, A. 1995. Dismantling the divide between indigenous and scientific knowledge. Development and Change 26(3): 413–439.
ANONYMOUS. 1997. Environmental impact statement (EIS) guidelines for the review of the Voisey's Bay Mine and Mill Undertaking. 20 June 1997. Available from Canadian Environmental Assessment Agency, Fontaine Building, 200 Sacre-Coeur Blvd., Hull, Quebec K1A 0H3.
———. 1998. Procedures for public hearings. Environmental Assessment Panel Reviewing the Voisey's Bay Mine and Mill Proposal. 6 August 1998. Available from Canadian Environmental Assessment Agency, Fontaine Building, 200 Sacre-Coeur Blvd., Hull, Quebec K1A 0H3.
———. 1999. Terms of reference, Committee on the Status of Endangered Wildlife in Canada (COSEWIC). Draft March 23 1999. Available at Canadian Wildlife Service, Environment Canada, Hull, Quebec K1A 0H3.
BEANLANDS, G., and DUINKER, P.N. 1983. An ecological framework for impact assessment in Canada. Hull, Quebec: Federal Environmental Assessment Review Office.
BERKES, F. 1993. Traditional ecological knowledge in perspective. In: Inglis, J.T., ed. Traditional ecological knowledge: Concepts and cases. Ottawa: Canadian Museum of Nature. 1–9.
BERKES, F., and HENLEY, T. 1997. Co-management and traditional knowledge: Threat or opportunity? Policy Options 18(2): 29–31.
BIELAWSKI, E. 1992. Inuit indigenous knowledge and science in the Arctic. Northern Perspectives 20(1): 5–8.
BROWN, M. 1998. Can culture be copyrighted? Current Anthropology 39(2): 193–222.
CANADA. 1984. The Western Arctic Claim: The Inuvialuit Final Agreement. Ottawa: Minister of Indian Affairs and Northern Development.
CLEMENT, D. 1998. Aeneid utashinimuau: The Innu people's rock. Available from Canadian Environmental Assessment Agency, Fontaine Building, 200 Sacre-Coeur Blvd., Hull, Quebec K1A 0H3.
DUERDEN, F., and KUHN, R. 1998. Scale, context, and application of traditional knowledge of the Canadian North. Polar Record 34(188): 31–38.
ELLANNA, L.J., SHERROD, G.K., and LANGDON, S.J. 1985. Subsistence mapping: An evaluation and methodological guidelines. Technical Paper No. 125. Juneau: Division of Subsistence, Alaska Department of Fish and Game.
FEIT, H. 1988. Self-management and state-management: Forms of knowing and managing northern wildlife. In: Freeman, M., and Carbyn, L., eds. Traditional knowledge and renewable resource management in northern regions. Occasional Publication No. 23. Edmonton: Boreal Institute for Northern Studies. 72–91.
FERGUSON, M., and MESSIER, F. 1997. Collection and analysis of traditional ecological knowledge about a population of arctic tundra caribou. Arctic 50(1): 17–28.
FERNANDEZ-ARMESTO, F. 1999. Truth: A history and guide for the perplexed. New York: St Martin's Press.
FIENUP-RIORDAN, A. 1999. Yaqulget qaillun pilartat (what the birds do): Yup'ik Eskimo understanding of geese and those who study them. Arctic 52(1): 1–22.
FREEMAN, M.M.R., ed. 1976. Report, Inuit land use and occupancy project. 3 Vols. Ottawa: Department of Indian Affairs and Northern Development.
———. 1979. Traditional land users as a legitimate source of environmental [expertise]. In: Nelson, J.G., Needham, R.D., Nelson, S.H., and Scace, R.C., eds. The Canadian National Parks: Today and tomorrow, Conference II: ten years later. Waterloo University Studies in Land Use History and Landscape Change No. 7. Waterloo, Ontario: University of Waterloo Press. 345–361.

———. 1985. Appeal to tradition: Different perspectives on wildlife management. In: Brosted, J., Dahl, J., Gray, A., Gullov, H., Henriksen, G., Jorgensen, J., and Kleivan, I., eds. Native power: The quest for autonomy and nationhood of aboriginal peoples. Oslo: Universitetsforlaget. 265–281.

———. 1992. The nature and utility of traditional ecological knowledge. Northern Perspectives 20(1): 9–12.

GNWT (GOVERNMENT OF THE NORTHWEST TERRITORIES). 1993. Traditional knowledge policy. Yellowknife: Government of the Northwest Territories.

GRIFFITHS, L., METCALFE, S., MICHAEL, L., PELLEY, C., and USHER, P. 1999. Environmental Assessment Panel-Report on the proposed Voisey's Bay Mine and Mill Project. Ottawa: Minister of Public Works and Government Services.

GUNN, A., ARLOOKTOO, G., and KAOMAYOK, D. 1988. The contribution of ecological knowledge of Inuit to wildlife management in the Northwest Territories. In: Freeman, M., and Carbyn, L., eds. Traditional knowledge and renewable resource management in northern regions. Occasional Publication No. 23. Edmonton: Boreal Institute for Northern Studies. 22–30.

HOWARD, A., and WIDDOWSON, F. 1996. Traditional knowledge threatens environmental assessment. Policy Options 17(9): 34–36.

———. 1997. Traditional knowledge advocates weave a tangled web. Policy Options 18(3): 46–48.

HUNTINGTON, H.P. 1998. Observations on the utility of the semi-directive interview for documenting traditional ecological knowledge. Arctic 51(3): 237–242.

INTFMA (INNU NATION TASK FORCE ON MINING ACTIVITIES). 1996. Ntesinan nteshiniminan nteniunan—Between a rock and a hard place. Sheshatshiu, Labrador: Innu Nation Office.

JOHNSON, D.H. 1999. The insignificance of statistical testing. Journal of Wildlife Management 63(3): 763–772.

JOHNSON, M., ed. 1992. Lore: Capturing traditional environmental knowledge. Ottawa: Dene Cultural Institute and International Development Research Centre.

LGL LTD., ESL ENVIRONMENTAL SCIENCES LTD., ESSA ENVIRONMENTAL AND SOCIAL SYSTEMS ANALYSTS LTD., and P.J. USHER CONSULTING SERVICES. 1986. Mackenzie Environmental Monitoring Project 1985–1986. Final report to Indian and Northern Affairs Canada, Environment Canada, Fisheries and Oceans Canada, Government of the Northwest Territories, and Government of the Yukon. Available at the Library of the Department of Indian and Northern Affairs Canada, 10 Wellington Street, Hull, Quebec K1A 0H4.

MacLACHLAN, L., KENNY-GILDAY, C., KUPSCH, W., and SLOAN, J. 1996. NWT Diamonds Project. Report of the Environmental Assessment Panel. Ottawa: Minister of Supply and Services.

MAILHOT, J. 1993. Traditional ecological knowledge: The diversity of knowledge systems and their study. Background Paper No. 4, Great Whale Environmental Assessment. Montreal: Great Whale Public Review Support Office.

NAKASHIMA, D.J. 1990. Application of Native knowledge in EIA: Inuit, Eiders, and Hudson Bay Oil. Canadian Environmental Assessment Research Council. Ottawa: Minister of Supply and Services.

NEIS, B., FELT, L.F., HAEDRICH, R.L., and SCHNEIDER, D.C. 1999. An interdisciplinary method for collecting and integrating fishers' ecological knowledge into resource management. In: Newell, D., and Ommer, R.E., eds. Fishing places, fishing people. Toronto: University of Toronto Press. 217–238.

NELSON, R. 1969. Hunters of the northern ice. Chicago: University of Chicago Press.

RCAP (ROYAL COMMISSION ON ABORIGINAL PEOPLES). 1996. Report of the Royal Commission on Aboriginal Peoples. Vol. 2, Restructuring the relationship. Ottawa: Minister of Supply and Services.

STEVENSON, M. 1996. Indigenous knowledge in environmental assessment. Arctic 49(3): 278–291.

———. 1997. Ignorance and prejudice threaten environmental assessment. Policy Options 18(2): 25–28.

USHER, P.J. 1971. The Bankslanders: Economy and ecology of a frontier trapping community. Vol. 2, Economy and ecology. NSRG-71-2, Northern Science Research Group. Ottawa: Department of Indian Affairs and Northern Development.

———. 1993. Northern development, impact assessment, and social change. In: Dyck, N., and Waldram, J.B., eds. Anthropology, public policy, and Native peoples in Canada. Montreal and Kingston: McGill-Queen's University Press. 98–130.

USHER, P.J., and WENZEL, G.W. 1987. Native harvest surveys and statistics: A critique of their construction and use. Arctic 40(2): 145–160.

WENZEL, G.W. 1999. Traditional ecological knowledge and Inuit: Reflections on TEK research and ethics. Arctic 52(2): 113–124.

WILLIAMSON, T. 1996. Seeing the land is seeing ourselves. Final report, Issues Scoping Project. Available from Canadian Environmental Assessment Agency, Fontaine Building, 200 Sacre-Coeur Blvd., Hull, Quebec K1A 0H3.
———. 1997. From sina to sikujaluk: Our footprint. Available from Canadian Environmental Assessment Agency, Fontaine Building, 200 Sacre-Coeur Blvd., Hull, Quebec K1A 0H3.

(b) Co-management of Aboriginal Resources[†]

Tracy Campbell

Conflict related to natural resource management in development situations seems to be a common occurrence. This of course is not a new phenomenon; on the contrary, conflict has always been present in varying degrees since the beginning of resource exploitation in Canada. However, in today's context of finite natural resources, the intensity of that conflict appears to be rising exponentially, as more interests than ever before are competing for use of and access to both renewable and nonrenewable resources. One area of natural resource management and development seems to have an unusually high incidence of conflict — where natural resource management affects aboriginal communities.

There are several reasons for the presence of conflict when natural resource development, particularly forestry and oil and gas development, collide with First Nation peoples. First, relatively large-scale, hinterland resource projects take place in areas, usually northern, where there are small, isolated aboriginal communities. Second, resource development is occurring in territories where traditional hunting, trapping, fishing, and gathering activities still play a vital role in subsistence lifestyles practised by First Nations, especially in the North. Third, and perhaps most important, the rights of First Nations to traditional territories and the natural resources therein are ill-defined by both the Canadian governments and the judiciary. The special rights of aboriginal people as guaranteed by treaty are not generally considered when resource development projects are proposed or resource management plans are prepared. Consequently, resources located on aboriginal traditional territory often become the focus for conflict between government, natural resource industries, and First Nation peoples.

In Canada, lands and related resources claimed by First Nations as aboriginal traditional or treaty territory are extensive. Ongoing disputes, whether they involve adequate reserve size, sacred areas, or the exercise of treaty rights, touch every Canadian province and territory. However, for First Nations to gain a measure of control over land outside reserve boundaries is extremely difficult. Though Section 35(1) of the Constitution Act, 1982 "recognized and affirmed" existing aboriginal rights, the manner in which and degree to which those rights extend has yet to be fully clarified by the courts or recognized by any level of government. Thus, the

[†] From *Information North*, 22(1) (1996): 1–6. References omitted. Permission to reproduce has been granted from the Arctic Institute of North America.

amount of land and related natural resources that should fall under aboriginal control is disputed by federal and provincial governments, resource industry representatives, and public interest groups alike. Further, the amount of land and resources which currently does fall under direct aboriginal control is insignificant. First Nation people claim the land and resources on treaty or traditional territory is theirs; government and industry maintain that aboriginal rights to land off-reserve translates into something significantly less.

Historically, First Nation peoples have been excluded from any meaningful input into how, where, when, or why resource development occurs on traditional territory. It has largely been left up to both the federal and provincial governments and resource industries to decide on specific parameters for development. This policy of exclusion has had significant negative economic and social impacts on aboriginal communities. Their lack of input into and control over what happens in the traditional territory around them is the most critical issue facing First Nation communities today.

The dispute over rights of access to and use of natural resources off-reserve (treaty or traditional territory) raises fundamental questions regarding the special relationship between First Nation people and the rest of Canada. It is no wonder that disputes arise; opinions concerning what First Nations are 'entitled' to are strongly held and expressed, on both sides of the issue. These disputes often result in comprehensive or specific land claims within the federal government framework or legal battles within the judiciary as means to resolve conflict. However, more and more frequently, disputes result in roadblocks, blockades, or other confrontational protests by First Nations against development on claimed aboriginal territory, as some aboriginal people see the conflict resolution mechanisms as either too slow or essentially ineffective.

The reasons for supporting aboriginal participation in the management and development of surrounding land and resources are compelling. Its justification can be strongly linked to the fundamental importance of maintaining the social validity of aboriginal communities so inextricably and historically tied to the land. For many aboriginal communities, subsistence practices such as hunting, fishing, and trapping on traditional territories relate more to issues of culture, lifestyle, and identity than to questions of economy, although economic considerations cannot be minimized. Reserve economies are fragile and inadequate, unable to support aboriginal populations. In fact, reserves as they were originally designed were never meant to support reserve communities independently; they were an interim measure taken by the federal government for the purpose of assimilation of the aboriginal population into the nonaboriginal mainstream (Price, 1991). That anticipated assimilation did not occur. In today's context, benefit from inclusion into the natural resource economies surrounding reserves would go a long way toward restoring the economic sustainability of aboriginal communities.

First Nations have never had a strong voice in influencing what goes on around their communities. Fortunately, however, the process by which natural resource activity is carried out on both treaty and traditional territory is changing, albeit slowly. In the last decade, both the relationship between government and industry and the manner of carrying out resource extraction have become somewhat less exclusive. The public participation movement, arising from increased public concerns about environmental integrity and the sustainability of resource development, has affected this process by demanding that others with different opinions regarding resource development have input into the decision-making. First Nations are similarly insisting on a more inclusive approach to natural resource use and development on traditional and treaty lands. This is especially apparent in British Columbia, where aboriginal land claims and natural resource development have increasingly become inseparable issues. However, the reasons aboriginal people have taken this stance have more to do with control than with environmental protection, although these two factors go hand in hand. That is to say, aboriginal people are demanding more control in decision-making when development affects traditional territory. The extent to which First Nations are in fact included in the development dialogue is a matter which has yet to be determined.

Several institutionalized mechanisms are available to First Nations for resolving disputes involving land and resources, which include both formalized land claims and litigation. However, land claims are extremely slow to reach negotiation, settlement, or implementation phases, and litigation is both lengthy and costly. Meanwhile, development continues unabated on aboriginal territory. This situation makes for explosive conditions on many reserves in Canada, as impatient and often militant leaders demand change. Consequently, a new arrangement which attempts to mitigate resource development conflict involving disputed territory has been gaining popularity among many of those involved in resource management, including First Nation people. This new approach is known under several names, such as co-management, joint management, or joint stewardship. Co-management has been described by some as an inclusionary, consensus-based approach to resource use and development. Co-management has also been described as the sharing of decision-making power with nontraditional actors in the process of resource management. Nontraditional actors would include those other than either state managers or industry, such as local resource users, environmental groups, or aboriginal people. One important element of co-management is that it stresses negotiation rather than litigation as a means to resolve conflict. Co-management has also been used to describe the process of combining western scientific knowledge and traditional environmental knowledge for the purpose of improving resource management.

Unfortunately, there is not, as yet, a clear and precise definition of co-management. Co-management has been used to describe agreements involving both renewable and nonrenewable resources; for both aboriginal and nonaboriginal conflict situations; for both single resource and multi-resource scenarios; for both single jurisdiction and multi-jurisdiction situations; on both provincial and territorial lands. Similarly co-management has been used to describe arrangements ranging from public participation initiatives, to land claim settlements and self-government initiatives. What co-management has evoked from many parties affected by resource management is an extremely positive response: co-management has become the buzzword in the field of natural resource management.

Although gaining in popularity among several different fields, co-management has not had a long history. In fact, there is no co-management effort which goes substantially beyond a decade. What has resulted thus far is a proliferation of co-management agreements without corresponding research into the field, as the number of authors who have published on co-management is indeed small. Although research on co-management is still quite new, the principles of co-management as nonconfrontational, inclusionary, and consensus-based have been hailed by the academic community, industry leaders, government representatives, and First Nations alike as a viable means by which resource conflicts on aboriginal territory may be resolved. What has yet to emerge is a comprehensive examination of what co-management changes within the realm of natural resource management and development. Conversely, what has also yet to emerge is a comprehensive examination of what co-management does not change.

Co-management's increased popularity is not surprising: the theory behind it is indeed attractive. Also, co-management arrangements established within land claim settlements in the northern territories appear to be working extremely well. However, the co-management agreements that are being offered within a provincial context do not offer the same set of circumstances as co-management in the territories. The history and context of co-management within the northern settlement agreements is a far cry from the realities of provincial jurisdictions over natural resources experienced in the provinces. A danger arises when the blanket term "co-management" is used to describe any and all alternative dispute resolution models used for natural resource management.

It is important to note where co-management theory and practice got their impressive start. Co-management first appeared in the literature in the early 1980s, as a means to describe several initiatives involving migratory wildlife and fisheries management. These initiatives tended to be somewhat informal and advisory in nature, most often involving aboriginal people. Institutionalized co-management agreements have, up until this time, been used in the context of settled land claim agreements involving aboriginal people in Quebec and in the northern territories. However, the experience of co-management in Quebec was extremely limited and highly criticized. It is the political and legal circumstances in the northern territories that allowed co-management to get its successful start.

One such claim is the Inuvialuit Final Agreement (IFA) signed in 1984, the first "comprehensive" settlement in the territories. The terms of the IFA included a lump-sum compensation payment, the equivalent of full title to lands in and around the six Western Arctic communities of Inuvik, Aklavik, Tuktoyaktuk, Paulatuk, Sachs Harbour and Holman (Category I lands: 11 000 sq. km), and shared or joint management of resources on additional territory (Category II lands: 78 000 sq. km) (Dickerson, 1992: 103). Boards and committees established under the IFA to administer Category I and II lands and resources are unique in Canada. They include the Fisheries Joint Management Committee, the Wildlife Management Advisory Council (NWT), the Wildlife Management Council (North Slope), the Environmental Impact Screening Committee, and the Environmental Impact Review Board. Joint management on these boards and committees is accomplished through a 50% Inuvialuit representation. Consensus-based, they employ nonadversarial methods of negotiation, and enjoy a reputation of being successful from both state and industry perspectives. In addition, each community developed its own conservation and management plans that are consistent with the regional plan developed in 1988.

Co-management within the terms of IFA works extremely well. It is likely that other comprehensive land claim settlements in the North, such as the Council of Yukon Indians Agreement (1990), the Gwich'in Agreement (1992), the Sahtu/Dene/

Metis Agreement (1993), or the Nunavut Agreement (1993), will also feature successful co-management committees that bring First Nations as equal partners in decision-making into the process of natural resource management and development.

In the co-management of the northern settlement agreements, territorial governments, industry representatives, and First Nations in the territories know exactly who has rights to what. Co-management works in these circumstances precisely because settled land claims clarify who has rights and access to land and resources surrounding aboriginal communities. First Nations in the territories have a legally defined place at the negotiating table to develop, implement, and institutionalize co-management structures, which in turn, gives them a clear voice in the process of resource management and development. In the provinces, these circumstances simply do not exist. Rights to off-reserve land and resources are not clearly defined. Many First Nation peoples believe that treaty rights guarantee a continued right of access to traditional territory for hunting, trapping, fishing and gathering. Others do not agree.

The guarantee of hunting, trapping, fishing, and gathering rights protected by treaty can be seen as trapped within a vicious circle of government policy. Provincial governments view treaty matters as a federal responsibility, while the federal government sees jurisdiction over natural resources, either as a result of the Natural Resources Transfer Agreement, 1930 or through the Terms of the Union, as a provincial responsibility. First Nation people have concerns about exercising their treaty rights on provincially regulated Crown land when treaty rights are a federal matter. Further, it is extremely difficult to exercise federal treaty rights on provincial Crown land when neither government level has any desire to step over the carefully delineated lines of constitutional jurisdiction. Thus, when the provincially managed boreal forest is being cut down, drilled on, and dug up, treaty rights are seen as a federal matter. And development continues.

With the successful reputation that co-management enjoys in the North, it is no wonder that its principles and theories have recently been used in the attempt to include First Nations in resource management within the provinces. In fact, co-management terminology is currently being used by both provincial governments and resource industries to describe arrangements that include First Nations in the decision-making process in any capacity. However, the co-management being offered First Nations in the provinces is not the same as the co-management agreements which have been operating successfully in the northern territories for the past ten years.

Perhaps because of the broad interpretation of co-management initiatives appearing within the literature, Berkes et al. (1991) and Berkes (1994) developed a "continuum of co-management" to describe the range of ways in which co-management was being used (Table 1). These degrees of co-management show just how broad a range the terminology can be used for. Level 1 describes how decisions by state managers have been made in the past; Level 7 describes a situation much like a settled land claim, where power over a jurisdiction is shared equally with the state. Unfortunately, most of the co-management agreements in the provinces operate at the lowest levels of authority transfer described by Berkes.

Among other fundamentals, co-management implies that each participant at the negotiating table has equal rights of participation. That is, each participant brings to the process an enforceable position, ideally established in law and policy, which

TABLE 1. Levels of aboriginal participation in co-management agreements. Adapted from Berkes (1994: 19).

Co-management operating within Northern Land Claim Agreements	7	Partnership, Community Control
	6	Management Boards
	5	Advisory Committees
	4	Communication
	3	Co-operation
Co-management operating within provincial setting	2	Consultation
	1	Informing

Co-management operating within Northern Land Claim Agreements	Partnership of equals; joint decision-making institutionalized; delegated to community where feasible.
	Community is given the opportunity to participate in developing and implementing management plans.
	Partnership in decision-making starts; joint action on common objectives.
	Start of two-way information exchange; local concerns begin to enter management plans.
	Community starts to have input into management (i.e., use of local knowledge, research assistants).
Co-management operating within provincial setting	Start of face-to-face contact; community input heard but not necessarily heeded.
	Community is informed about decisions already made.

can then be formally institutionalized in the co-management process. This situation, which has developed in the northern territories because of settled land claims, is not possible under the present circumstances within the provinces. In fact, unless a drastic change occurs within the relationship aboriginal people currently have with the provincial and federal governments, co-management is simply an empty promise.

An examination of various agreements described as co-management in the provinces proves fascinating. Negotiated between either a First Nation and a provincial government or a First Nation and a resource company, these agreements show that aboriginal input is indeed being courted. They feature terms such as inclusionary, consensus decision-making, partnership, and joint stewardship, terms that are utilized in co-management agreements operating under settled comprehensive land claim agreements in the territories. At first glance, these agreements appear to be a major breakthrough, insofar as they imply 'equal' partnerships between industry, government, and First Nations. These initiatives are indeed a step forward from the position resource management used to operate from, but closer examination shows that they differ substantially from the co-management practised in the context of settled land claims. Indeed, even among the agreements that Berkes would consider to be at the lowest level of power transfer, there are wide variations. Many factors affect the type of agreement which may result. For example, the strength of the relationship a First Nation community establishes with the provincial ministry involved affects the negotiations, which in turn affect the terms of the agreement. The political strength of the First Nation community, the willingness of the resource company to open a dialogue and the impetus for negotiations to develop in the first place (i.e., the presence of an immediate conflict situation) also have an influence on the type of agreement considered.

The co-management agreements now appearing on the provincial natural resource scene should be looked at for what they don't include, such as a substantial transfer of decision-making power, or even a share of royalties for resources harvested from traditional territories. There may be a danger for First Nations in pursuing this type of co-management in preference to formalized land claims or even litigation, because it takes the focus away from some fundamental questions regarding the relationship between First Nations and the rest of Canada. Such agreements may offer limited economic development strategies or job creation in 'partnership' with resource companies, but fail to raise the larger issues of treaty rights and self-government.

Unfortunately for First Nation people in the provinces, neither land claim settlements, nor recognition of aboriginal title through the courts, nor implementation of the spirit and intent of the treaties will happen anytime in the near future. In fact, intolerance on the part of the Canadian public towards aboriginal claims for land and resources within the provinces seems to be growing. Co-management as it stands now may be the only practical road left open to First Nations to begin dialogues with government and industry.

There is a danger [in] using co-management terminology and theory without a significant transfer of decision-making power. Without a significant power transfer, such as that described in Berkes et al. (1991), the problem of land disputes will remain and First Nations will remain frustrated over their lack of input. Further, if promises of change through co-management are not delivered to First Nation communities, this frustration will most likely increase.

(c) And Now for Something Completely Northern: Institutions of Governance in the Territorial North[†]

Graham White

This essay examines some of the distinctive or unique institutions of governance in the territorial North. The purpose of so doing is two-fold: first, to draw to wider attention [to] the unusual and innovative structures and processes of government operating in the North and second, to demonstrate that alternatives beyond the sta-

---

[†] From *Journal of Canadian Studies*, 35(4) (2001): 80–99. Reproduced with permission of the publisher.

tus quo exist for national and provincial political institutions, provided that they reflect the values and experiences of the societies in which they are embedded.

The influence of Aboriginal peoples on political institutions and processes is a prominent theme. In addition, variations between and among the three territories (due in substantial measure to the different positions and approaches of their Aboriginal peoples) are high-lighted. Northern institutions are treated not as exotic curiosities, but as responses to particular political needs and social contexts.

The North has long stirred the Canadian imagination and shaped the Canadian identity. They may know little of it or harbour highly idealized notions of it, but for Canadians the North looms large in ways tangible and intangible: artistic inspiration, definition of nationhood, wealth from its bountiful resources and romantic (if usually unfulfilled) ideas of personal adventure. In the realm of politics and political institutions, however, the North scarcely registers for most Canadians. Beyond a vague awareness of the creation of Nunavut in 1999, they know almost nothing of northern governance and would likely be dismissive of any suggestion that they have anything to learn from how northern government and politics are organized.

This essay argues that much of interest and value is to be learned from the political and governmental institutions of northern Canada — defined here as the Territorial North — which are in important ways qualitatively different from those in Ottawa and the provinces. Not, of course, that Canada "south of 60" is likely to adopt the institutional arrangements found in the territories or that they would perform in the South as they do in the North, save perhaps in the realm of Aboriginal self-government. Rather, the northern experience is important because it demonstrates, first, that options beyond the status quo exist for the structuring and operation of the central institutions of governance, and second, that the effectiveness of these institutions depends in substantial measure on the extent to which they are meaningfully rooted in their societies.

None of this is to suggest that territorial institutions are ideal. Indeed, as the analysis shows, they can be problematic in conception, deeply flawed in operation and highly uncertain in durability. In addition, the essay cites innovative ideas for structuring governance that came to naught, as well as unimaginative adoption of institutional arrangements from elsewhere. All told, however, an examination of northern political institutions offers important insights into such fundamental issues as the linkage between society and governance and the organization of government so as to render it at once effective and legitimate.

Questions about the underlying nature of northern institutions are raised, if not definitively answered. These include whether the institutional differences between North and South are essentially cosmetic or are indeed substantial; the extent to which northern institutions are rooted in the distinctive elements of northern society and, in particular, whether they reflect Aboriginal influences; and whether the distinctive features of northern institutions are simply a function of the small scale or the political immaturity of territorial politics.

The prime emphasis of the essay is on governmental rather than political institutions, so that enormously important Aboriginal organizations receive little attention. Most of the analysis is devoted to the so-called "consensus government" system in Nunavut and the Northwest Territories, the co-management boards established under the settled comprehensive land claims, the attempts at melding "public" and Aboriginal self-government regimes and the Nunavut government's commitment to decentralize its structure radically and to imbue its operations with Inuit Qaujimajatuqangit (roughly, "Inuit traditional knowledge").

THE TERRITORIAL NORTH: A SOCIAL AND POLITICAL OVERVIEW

Only the briefest outline of territorial society and politics can be offered here.[1] For many Canadians, the North is a largely undifferentiated mass: cold, remote and beautiful, inhabited principally by Aboriginal peoples living in desolate conditions. To be sure, the territories share important commonalities of climate, geography, demography, economy and identity. They are sparsely populated — in the three territories barely 100,000 people are spread across nearly four million square kilometres; their economies all depend heavily on natural resources and on government and are hampered by difficult communications, distance from markets and lack of diversity; winters are indeed long and harsh; the proportion of Aboriginal peoples is far higher than in any province; and a strong sense of being northern — and distinctive — pervades the three territories.

At the same time, the three territories differ substantially on important dimensions. Geographic and climatic variations are significant. Most notably, Nunavut lies entirely north of the tree line whereas most of Yukon and the NWT are moderately to heavily forested, and winters are perceptibly harsher in Nunavut. Though air travel is essential throughout, the three territories' transportation systems differ a good deal: all but one Yukon community is on the all-weather road system; several NWT communities are not accessible by road at all or only by winter ice-roads or exceedingly roundabout routes; Nunavut has no roads linking communities. As well, important differences exist in the economic bases of the three territories. Transportation, economic and cultural links to other places also distinguish the territories. Yukon's primary links are with British Columbia and Alaska; the NWT's main connections are with Nunavut and Alberta; Nunavut has links with NWT, Manitoba, Quebec (especially Nunavik, the Inuit region of northern Quebec), Newfoundland and Greenland. Most significantly, the territories are vastly different in social composition. The Aboriginal population of Yukon is about 20 per cent, in the NWT it is 50 per cent and in Nunavut it is 85 per cent. Even these figures understate the differences: the Aboriginal population of Nunavut is virtually all Inuit; in Yukon, the Aboriginal population is primarily Dene, in some 14 separate First Nations; in the NWT, the Aboriginal population is quite diverse, comprised of Inuvialuit (Inuit of the Beaufort area), Metis and Dene, with significant linguistic and other divisions fragmenting the Dene. Even the degree of urbanization — and thus the domination of the territorial capital — ranges widely: seven of ten of Yukoners live in Whitehorse, Yellowknife contains about 40 per cent of the NWT population and less than 20 per cent of Nunavummiut live in Iqaluit.

Politically, the pattern is similar: common basic features overlaid with significant cross-territory variations. The territories are something of "proto-provinces"; in all substantive ways they are autonomous self-governing entities exercising a wide range of jurisdictional powers, but they lack formal constitutional status. Their "constitutions" are federal statutes and Ottawa retains nominal authority to set aside territorial legislation, though this power is likely as much a dead letter as the federal government's disallowance power over provincial legislation. Very high proportions — up to 90 per cent in the case of Nunavut — of territorial government revenues come as transfers from Ottawa, but virtually all such funding takes the form of unconditional grants, so that federal influence over territorial expenditure decisions is minimal. The territories exercise almost all important province-like powers: education, health, welfare, municipal government, local transportation and so on; the principal — and in the North, critical — exception is lands and resources. As was the case with Alberta, Saskatchewan and Manitoba prior to 1930, Ottawa retains ownership (and primary though not complete control) of Crown lands and the nonrenewable resources on and under them. Federal policy aims at complete devolution of land and resources to the territories (jurisdiction over oil and gas was transferred to Yukon in 1998), though progress has been slow.

Territorial autonomy is of recent provenance. Until the 1970s, the territories were little more than internal colonies of the federal government. For example, until 1967 Ottawa was the capital of the Northwest Territories while its "government" consisted of a committee of federal bureaucrats under the direction of an all-powerful commissioner. Through the 1970s and early 1980s, however, Ottawa devolved — sometimes willingly, sometimes grudgingly — most of its powers, plus funding for them, to the territories. In classic colonial fashion, the federal bureaucrats who oversaw the transfer of effective power to the territories unquestioningly assumed that territorial governance should follow the British cabinet-parliamentary model of executive-legislative relations, and acted accordingly. As good neutral public servants, they did nothing to promote the emergence of political parties, though they doubtless expected this to follow in the wake of responsible government, as it had elsewhere in Canada. In Yukon, parties did indeed come to the fore in the 1970s and have dominated politics since; no independent MLA has been elected in Yukon since the mid-1980s. Not so in the NWT or Nunavut.

CONSENSUS GOVERNMENT

The best-known northern departure from southern political models is the consensus government system in the NWT and Nunavut. (Nunavut carried the consensus system over from the pre-division NWT, though not automatically or unreflectively.) In essence the system is a non-partisan Westminster cabinet-parliamentary regime. All the key constitutional principles underlying British-style responsible government exist. The authority of cabinet derives from its capacity to maintain the confidence of the House by winning key votes. Ministers are responsible to the assembly for policy and administration (thus permitting a politically neutral public service). Cabinet solidarity prevails. Only cabinet can place before the assembly measures for raising taxes and directing expenditures.[2] Political parties, however, play no role in the assembly; members (MLAs) seek election and serve as independents.

From this curious juxtaposition comes a set of parliamentary structures and processes at once strange and beguiling to southern Canadians. The premier and the cabinet are selected by secret ballot of all MLAs; the premier assigns ministers to portfolios and may subsequently shuffle them. Exceptionally, the premier may dismiss a minister (the constraints are political rather than constitutional) but ministers are more likely to be deposed by those who originally put them in office, the "ordinary" or "regular" (i.e., private) members of the assembly. Thus, power relations between the premier, ministers and private members differ substantially from those characterizing the premier-dominated cabinets and cabinet-dominated legislatures of southern Canada.

The premier is truly, as in parliamentary ages past, the "first among equals" since ministers are beholden to the MLAs rather than to the premier for their posts. Cabinet effectively finds itself in a permanent minority, though its numerical weight — six or seven in 19-member houses — requires it to win over only a very few MLAs to carry a vote. Nothing so adversarial or organized as a formal opposition exists but strong committees offer non-ministers opportunities to co-ordinate strategy and seek support for their political concerns.

Ministers are certainly far more powerful than ordinary MLAs, not least because of their control over the bureaucracy, but the private members have opportunities for influence far beyond that enjoyed by their counterparts in other Westminster systems. MLAs exert influence both as individuals and through the legislative committee systems, which engage deeply in issues of policy and administration and have unusually good access to government information and officials.

The tone of debate is civil and respectful — astonishingly civil compared to the "sandbox" mentality of party bickering in southern parliaments — and MLA's views and proposals are taken seriously by ministers. Moreover, though power is clearly concentrated in cabinet, a unique parliamentary institution plays a key role in government decisions. South of 60 (and in Yukon), each party caucus meets regularly to devise strategy and to discuss party positions; in Nunavut and the NWT, caucus includes all MLAs, including the Speaker. Caucus meets at least weekly when the assembly is in session and periodically holds two- or three-day strategic planning sessions outside the capital. It does not usurp cabinet's power but does review key political and policy issues, and its views are often decisive.

The Nunavut legislature is overwhelmingly Inuit and the NWT has had an Aboriginal majority since the mid-1970s. Accordingly, for some participants and observers, the consensus system derives from northern Aboriginal political culture, which avoids division and confrontation — and voting — through decision-making premised on thorough, respectful discussion of the issues from which a genuine consensus emerges. Others, including Aboriginal MLAs, contend that decision-making in the assembly is nothing like the true consensual style found at the community level. For them, Aboriginal influences on the Westminster system do not go much beyond the cosmetic — members' preference for moosehide jackets and sealskin vests over three-piece suits — with the explanation for the unusual parliamentary structures and processes lying principally in the absence of parties.

Undoubtedly, the absence of parties is critical. But why are there not parties? One answer might be that the NWT and Nunavut remain politically immature: as in the western provinces, which initially did not have party systems, parties will appear once the territories develop sufficiently. This explanation overlooks several key points: the consensus system has endured for the better part of two decades, during which several attempts at instituting a party system (including most recently in the 1999 NWT election) failed; federal politics in the North are entirely organized on a party basis; and Yukon, which is no more sophisticated politically than the other territories, has been dominated by parties since the 1970s. Ultimately, it is not that parties have yet to emerge or coalesce; rather, parties have been consciously rejected by a great many northerners (primarily but not exclusively Aboriginal) as unsuitable to northern needs and conditions.

Some believe party politics are quietly emerging in the NWT. Following the 1999 election, veteran MLA Steve Kakfwi not only secured election as premier, he effectively managed, through adroit backroom politicking, to get his "slate" of ministerial candidates elected as the cabinet. The tight cabinet coherence, strident and well-organized opposition from ordinary members (led by ministers deposed by the Kakfwi slate) and the premier's well-known Liberal ties presage for some the demise of consensus government. Others maintain that nothing fundamental has changed: well-organized factions of MLAs have existed in the past, ministers still hold office at the pleasure of the ordinary members and the tenuous bonds of political association Kakfwi has forged among his team are far removed from those characterizing a genuine party. Reports of the death of consensus government in the NWT seem, at the least, premature.

In Nunavut the threat to consensus government comes not from political manoeuvring but from the possibility of fundamental structural change. The designers of the Nunavut government contemplated grafting a popularly elected premier onto the consensus system. Creating strong, accountable leadership in this way was mooted as a means of overcoming the failings of the consensus system. Uncertainty on key practical issues — should the premier be elected simultaneously with other MLAs; could the assembly remove a premier elected by the public — together with the need to focus on more pressing issues meant that the idea was put into abeyance. Little has been heard of it since the Nunavut Assembly came into being, doubtless in part because MLAs recognize that it would entail substantial loss of power on their part, but it remains an idea with considerable public appeal. If adopted, of course, it would fundamentally alter the Nunavut political system since a popularly elected first minister is essentially incompatible with the basic tenets of Westminster-style responsible government.

It is easy for southern Canadians, repelled by the mindless partisanship, suffocating party discipline and general ineffectiveness of Parliament, to see only the positive side of consensus government. Inevitably, of course, consensus government has its failings: it can be highly parochial and inclined to behind-the-scenes log-rolling on capital projects, government jobs and the like; factionalism and individualism in the legislature and the premier's limited control over cabinet can undercut policy coherence and make it difficult to address important but potentially divisive issues; it depends heavily on moderation and accommodation on MLAs' part, so that it is vulnerable to instability and disruption if only a few members refuse to play by the unspoken rules; while cabinet accountability to MLAs is very strong, government accountability to the public is weak since voters can only pass judgement on their MLAs, not on past or prospective governments.[3]

Northerners, well aware of these shortcomings, often sound as cynical about their elected representatives as any other Canadians. And parties may well supplant the consensus system. Yet northerners have clearly crafted practical adaptations to the British cabinet-parliamentary model that have endured because the adaptations meet peculiarly northern needs and are congruent with, if not necessarily derived from, central elements of northern society and culture.

Curiously, one area in which northerners have shown a singular lack of imagination in modifying southern models is electoral representation and voting regimes. All MLAs in the three territories are, as in southern Canada, elected through single-member plurality electoral systems. The vigorously contested concepts of representation that suffuse northern politics might have been expected to lead to departures from southern electoral orthodoxy but this has not occurred; indeed, the overwhelming acceptance of single-member plurality is remarkable. A noteworthy, though ultimately unsuccessful, exception was the imaginative proposal of the Nunavut Implementation Commission, the body charged with designing Nunavut's political-governmental system, to establish a "gender-equal" legislature. The idea, which generated great interest not only in Canada but abroad, was to create dual-member ridings in which all voters would cast two votes: one for a candidate on the male list and one for a candidate on the female list. Though most of Nunavut's political elite came to support the proposal, it was decisively rejected in a referendum.

LINKING ABORIGINAL SELF-GOVERNMENT TO PUBLIC GOVERNMENT

Southern Canadians often presume that the numerical preponderance of Aboriginal MLAs and ministers, together with Aboriginal influences on consensus government, means that the NWT government constitutes "Aboriginal government." Many Aboriginal organizations in the NWT, however, take a very different view. They reject the territorial government as fundamentally illegitimate — having been imposed by Ottawa on Aboriginal peoples without their consent or involvement — and in no way embodying their inherent right to self-government. Along with Yukon First Nations, they have been vigorously pursuing far-reaching self-government regimes. (The Inuit, by virtue of their overwhelming numbers in Nunavut, are satisfied with "public government."[4])

Each of the settled comprehensive claims in Yukon and the NWT includes government commitments to negotiate self-government across a wide range of areas.[5] Seven of Yukon's 14 First Nations have finalized self-government agreements. In the NWT, no agreements have been finalized, but regional negotiations have been under way for several years; some are close to completion.

The emerging self-government regimes constitute a third order of government in Canada — the Yukon self-government agreements, for example, explicitly employ such terms as "citizen" and "constitution." Moreover, these self-government agreements entail extensive jurisdictional sweep, with First Nations laws replacing territorial laws in areas where the First Nations decide to exercise their powers. In terms of power and authority, Yukon First Nation governments more closely resemble provinces than municipalities. Some of the most interesting and critical questions arising from the establishment of self-government relate to the linkages between public and self-government regimes.

Differing demographic patterns and political contexts have resulted in different linkage issues coming to the fore in Yukon and the NWT. With the typical Yukon

First Nation numbering only a few hundred, the capacity of their governments to provide services in all areas in which they possess jurisdiction is a concern. In the realm of land and resource management, Yukon First Nation governments are moving towards extensive and sophisticated structures. In other areas, such as health, which depend on expensive technical expertise, practical realities require arrangements with the Yukon Territorial Government (YTG) for delivery of certain services and programmes. This could entail either contracting the YTG to deliver services or joint YTG-First Nation government processes.

The finalized self-government agreements establish principles and frameworks and also set out the wide range of jurisdictions that the First Nations governments can exercise as they see fit, with specific arrangements in particular policy fields to follow. Some detailed Programme and Service Transfer Agreements (PSTAs) have been completed for the transfer of federal responsibilities to First Nations, though on-the-ground changes have been limited since band governments had already been delivering, on Ottawa's behalf, many of the transferred programmes and services. More substantial change will emerge from the negotiation of PSTAs covering activities performed by the Yukon government. Each First Nation will ultimately sign a series of agreements with the territorial government for transfer of programmes and services. The possibility thus exists for substantial variation in the provisions of different First Nation governments' PSTAs, as well as in the specific policy areas over which individual First Nations choose to exercise their jurisdiction. Negotiations to date, however, reflect a common approach from the First Nations involved (and, indeed, a single negotiating table), so that the initial sets of PSTAs may not vary significantly from one First Nation to the next.

A central feature of the Yukon self-government agreements is the authority of each First Nation government to legislate in a wide range of areas, including language, culture, health, education and social services, for all its citizens regardless of where they live in the territory. The arrangements between individual First Nations and the YTG will take the form of highly detailed protocols and contracts guaranteed to make the eyes of all but the most dedicated bureaucrats and accountants glaze over. Mundane and picayune as these agreements may be, however, they are crucially important (and thus more difficult to negotiate than might be thought) because they embody the practical realization of fundamental and often contentious principles: Who really sets policy? What are the political and bureaucratic accountability relationships? How are Aboriginal values and interests accommodated in policy implementation and programme delivery?

Similar issues arise in self-government negotiations in the NWT. Capacity problems are generally less acute since the First Nations are large (most claims groups number between 2,000 and 3,000). Some claims do provide the possibility of self-government regimes for individual communities, so that the community of Deline (population 600), for example, commenced formal self-government negotiations several years ago. In the NWT, unlike in Yukon, tremendous effort has been expended on the "macro-politics" of linking public and self-government institutions. With the non-Aboriginal population and the territorial government so dominant in Yukon, the primary links between the YTG and the First Nations governments take the form of a multilateral intergovernmental process; they are not played out within the YTG. By contrast, the role of Aboriginal organizations and governments within the central institutions of the territorial government is a primary issue in the NWT.

Since the mid-1980s enormous time and effort have been expended in attempts at developing a constitution for the NWT to satisfy the aspirations and interests of both Aboriginal and non-Aboriginal residents. Institutional mechanisms were clearly needed, within the territorial government, to co-ordinate, reconcile and possibly meld Aboriginal interests (as embodied in self-government regimes) with territory-wide interests (primarily, but not exclusively, non-Aboriginal). Establishing a widely acceptable design for the composition, powers and decision rules of the legislature and the executive has proven especially difficult.

As well, the question of how to structure the relationship between the NWT government and community governments generates highly divergent views. Aboriginal views of governance give pride of place to community institutions, but while the territorial government has for many years proclaimed a strong commitment to empowering communities and regions, its failures outweigh its successes. In many communities, band councils, public municipal governments and Metis locals are all involved in governance, so that local government in the NWT raises both practical questions of co-ordination and conceptual issues of public versus self-government. In an imaginative innovation, the NWT government created the possibility for local people to meld the three governing elements in a "charter community" structure, but few communities have chosen to go that route. If the record of successes at the community level is mixed, attempts to build regional governments in the NWT have uniformly failed. In important ways, of course, the emerging self-government regimes will transform concepts and structures of regional government.

Over the years, several groups have been formed to work out a constitutional accommodation. Typically they have brought together leaders of Aboriginal organizations, NWT politicians and representatives of groups such as the NWT Association of Municipalities and the Native Women's Association of the NWT. The federal government has generally not played a direct role in developing specific constitutional schemas. It certainly takes, however, a strong interest in these processes and powerfully affects them, for example, through its insistence on maintaining the integrity and capacity of the territorial government and its clear preference for implementing the inherent right to self-government in the NWT through public government. Ottawa also funds most of the constitutional processes.

These groups have consulted widely, met endlessly and issued hosts of reports and papers. Though agreement remains elusive and key participants strongly hold to apparently irreconcilable views, discussion has for the most part been amicable and civil. Certainly, fundamental issues of governance have been extensively and publicly debated in ways rarely if ever seen elsewhere in Canada. In 1995, by way of illustration, the closest Canada has come to a constituent assembly took place in Yellowknife to consider constitutional possibilities. Progress, however, has been slow, not least because, with leaders of important Aboriginal organizations disputing the legitimacy and effectiveness of the territorial government for their needs and aspirations, the very existence of what might be termed the "territorial, quasi-provincial public government model" remains deeply problematic for some.

With resolution of mega-constitutional exercises still some distance away, no clear picture of the new institutional framework has emerged. To be sure, as self-government agreements come into play the structure and nature of the NWT government will be significantly affected. At a minimum, in a few years the institutions of governance in the NWT will look quite unlike those anywhere else, reflecting the territory's singular social composition and political imperatives. Not only will there be strong, wide-ranging Aboriginal self-government regimes, but territorial government will be, in effect, an exercise in decidedly asymmetrical federalism. The central institutions of government are likely to contain significant consociational elements (NWT politicians wisely avoid such jargon, preferring the term "partnership"). One model illustrates just how unusual the eventual arrangements may seem to southern Canadians.

In a 1996 draft constitutional package entitled Partners in a New Beginning, a broadly based Constitutional Working Group proposed that the territorial legislature consist of two chambers, a 14-member General Assembly (elected by all residents) and an eight-member Aboriginal Peoples Assembly (elected by those belonging to the eight organized Aboriginal groups). Passage of legislation would require majority votes in both chambers or a two-thirds majority of the entire Assembly. Cabinet would be composed of four members from the General Assembly and two from the Aboriginal Peoples Assembly. Responsible government principles would prevail initially, but no clear commitment to them was voiced — indeed, the possibility of moving away from them was evident (Constitutional Working Group). The Partners model was quickly scuppered by non-Aboriginal opposition to the departure from conventional liberal principles, most notably the idea of Aboriginal persons having two votes versus one for non-Aboriginals. The point is not that a revamped form of this proposal is likely to find general favour, but to emphasize the distinctiveness of the possible solutions under active discussion.

CLAIMS-MANDATED CO-MANAGEMENT AND REGULATORY BOARDS

The territorial North is home to a set of unusual institutions of governance in the realm of land, environmental protection and wildlife management. The co-management and regulatory boards deriving from the settled comprehensive claims are neither federal nor territorial, nor are they a form of Aboriginal self-government (indeed, they are explicitly established as "institutions of public government"). Instead, they exist almost as a distinct order of government: independent of territorial and federal governments and of Aboriginal organizations, exercising on occasion substantial governmental authority.

These boards represent political compromises. Aboriginal organizations pushed for control over land and wildlife, which are central to Aboriginal peoples. Government insisted on maintaining its authority over use and management of public lands. The boards are thus designed to involve Aboriginal peoples in a very direct way in land, environment and wildlife issues without turning full control over to them. The boards have jurisdiction over the entire territory included in the claims; that is, they are not restricted to the (very extensive) lands owned outright by the Aboriginal organizations. Examples of these boards include the Nunavut Wildlife Management Board, the Mackenzie Valley Environmental Impact Review Board, the Inuvialuit Fisheries Joint Management Committee and the Yukon Land Use

Planning Council. In terms of scope, legal authority and Aboriginal participation, no similar bodies exist in the provinces.

Structure, formal mandate, membership, procedures and extent of de jure and de facto decision-making authority vary a good deal across these boards, as does their effectiveness, but they do share important common features. Since, as "modern-day treaties," land-claim agreements are constitutionally protected under section 35 of the Constitution Act 1982, the boards enjoy a similar, constitutionally protected status. This differentiates them — not least by imbuing them with substantial legal authority — from various co-management schemes in the provinces that bring together Aboriginal peoples and their organizations with federal and/or provincial governments. Provincial co-management regimes are typically narrow in scope as well as limited in formal powers.

Boards are tripartite in that members are appointed (or nominated) by the federal government, the territorial government and the Aboriginal organization responsible for overseeing claim implementation. In some, each nominates the same number of members; in others, the Aboriginal organization's appointees equal those of both governments. The formal assumption is that board members act on their own independent judgement rather than as delegates of the entity that appointed them, though the reality is sometimes different. Certainly it would be rare, indeed improper, for governments or Aboriginal organizations to attempt to instruct nominees on specific policy issues or decisions. At the same time, some board members do see themselves as representing the Aboriginal or government perspective. Since the Aboriginal organizations almost invariably appoint Aboriginal persons while territorial governments often and the federal government occasionally do likewise, Aboriginal members form the majority on most boards.

The claims typically require the federal government to fund the boards. For the most part, funding levels and mechanisms have been satisfactory, so that boards have been able to carry out their administrative, regulatory and research functions with adequate financial resources, although some boards have encountered funding problems.

One regulatory board threatened to shut down with several months left in the fiscal year unless it received adequate funding. Some boards, especially in Nunavut, strongly objected to Ottawa's policy of applying to them funding mechanisms designed for Indian bands and special projects (which, for example, required the return of unspent monies at the end of the fiscal year). A recent change towards more flexible funding arrangements specifically designed for claims boards has resolved most such complaints. The boards enjoy complete independence in hiring and other internal administrative matters.

Basic policy directions are set by the elected governments, territorial and federal, and are implemented by the bureaucracies directly accountable to them. The boards lack the authority and legitimacy of governments, but they can play a pivotal role in certain decisions and in policy development; they have minimal involvement in policy implementation. The tasks they perform range from the mundane and routine, such as assigning polar bear quotas to communities, to exceptional and crucial, for example, reviewing the environmental impact of proposed diamond mines or pipelines (the Mackenzie Valley Environmental Impact Review Board carries out the functions the Canadian Environmental Assessment Agency performs elsewhere in Canada). Some boards have the capacity to issue binding decisions, but board decisions for the most part only have the status of advice to government, and the responsible minister can overrule board decisions. In reality, however, the boards are much more than simply advisory bodies whose recommendations government may or may not accept. In most instances, ministers are faced with negative options: unless they formally overturn a board decision within a specified time period, the decision stands. This effectively reverses the political onus: rather than the boards expending political capital to convince government to accept their decisions, government faces political difficulty should it wish to veto a board recommendation. And indeed, fewer than a handful of important board decisions have been overturned.

A noteworthy illustration of the boards' influence occurred in 1996 when, on the basis of studies confirming the sustainability of a limited harvest, the Nunavut Wildlife Management Board issued the first permit in decades for the legal harvest of a bowhead whale. The federal minister came under substantial domestic and international pressure to cancel the hunt, but in the end did not do so. Subsequent licences for additional bowhead harvests were issued in 1999 and 2000.

As this example confirms, elected government, rather than the boards, makes the final decisions on major policy issues, yet the boards are powerful players in matters relating to wildlife, environment and land use in the North. Were their influence put to a stark test, it is unlikely that they would have the legal authority to prevent a major development project such as a mine or road, yet politically it would be very difficult for a government to allow such a project to proceed over strong board objections.

The boards have been generally successful at incorporating Aboriginal peoples and their perspectives into government decisions affecting critically important land, wildlife and environment issues. Not all boards have risen effectively to the challenges before them; some are essentially reactive, largely limiting themselves to processing requests for permits and approvals, and thus failing to take advantage of substantial opportunities to develop and influence policy. Moreover, while the boards certainly involve Aboriginal peoples in important governance questions, they typically do so by way of structures and processes that are little influenced by Aboriginal culture and sensibilities and that are overwhelmingly Euro-Canadian in orientation and outlook. Formal processes, sometimes highly legalistic, adversarial and heavily scientific, dominate. Also problematic is the extent to which land and wildlife issues, in subtle but important ways, come to be defined in Western rather than in Aboriginal terms. One close observer has remarked that "co-management arrangements oppress traditional Inuit forms of management. 'Wildlife' provisions within most land claims agreements are infused with the biases, concepts and procedures of western science and the conservation bureaucracy, many of which are alien to Inuit hunters and their traditional management practices" (Stevenson 4).

INUIT QAUJIMAJATUQANGIT

As this last point suggests, methods of operating and the values they embody are defining issues for Aboriginal governments and for governments of jurisdictions with large Aboriginal populations. How governments do things can be as important as what they do. Truly Aboriginal governance thus entails not simply control of governmental institutions but Aboriginal modes of thought and action. In Nunavut, the objective of establishing an Inuit government meant not just creating a government numerically dominated by Inuit, but also a government operating according to Inuit norms and culture.

Central to the realization of an Inuit government is the success of establishing Inuktitut as the working language of the government of Nunavut. Not only would this ensure that unilingual Inuktitut residents were adequately served by their government, it would also represent a key step towards the goal of a government rooted in Inuit culture. Yet ensuring that all or most Nunavut officials worked in Inuktitut — at best, an uncertain prospect — would be no guarantee that the government functioned in a genuinely Inuit fashion. A bureaucracy suffused with Euro-Canadian precepts and processes is not an Inuit institution, whatever the language of memos and meetings.

Hence the creators of Nunavut were concerned to imbue their government with Inuit values. This abstract goal has found somewhat more explicit form in the government's commitment to Inuit Qaujimajatuqangit. Inuit Qaujimajatuqangit (IQ) is roughly translated as "the Inuit way of thinking and living." The Nunavut Social Development Council described it as "the very foundation of governance in our new Territory... [which] encompasses all aspects of traditional Inuit culture including values, world-view, language, social organization, knowledge, life-skills, perceptions and expectations" (Nunavut Social Development 1).

The Nunavut government has sponsored conferences, established working groups and continually reaffirmed its support for IQ. Not surprisingly, however, concrete manifestations of precisely how IQ is to inform governance have been slow to emerge. Specific proposals include suggestions that the experience and insights of elders be explicitly sought and incorporated into policy development (all policy, not just that relating to wildlife, the environment and related topics for which traditional Inuit knowledge has obvious relevance); that government working hours and conditions be made more conducive to Inuit lifestyles, for example, through a flexible leave policy to accommodate the unpredictable opportunities for hunting; that IQ orientation programmes be developed for new and non-Inuit employees; and, of course, that language training be provided with the goal of making Inuktitut the working language of government. Given the huge task of building governmental capacity, together with the financial and logistical barriers to extensive language training and cultural orientation, only limited progress has been registered on these proposals.

At the same time, the government commitment to IQ is more than noble rhetoric. An essential step in promoting value-change in a large organization is recognition of the deep-seated nature of values and the importance of constant reflection on how the desired values might be put into practice. In other words, awareness of IQ is part and parcel of implementing it. Beyond that, however, serious attempts are being made at embedding policy development in IQ. A noteworthy example is Maligarnit Qimirrujiit, the Nunavut Law Reform Commission. Established as one of the first acts of the new government, Maligarnit Qimirrujiit is charged with reviewing the laws Nunavut inherited from the NWT, to, in the words of Premier Paul Okalik, "identify laws that are inconsistent with the vision and goals of

Nunavummiut: laws that are not in keeping with Inuit Qaujimajatuqangit" (Legislative Assembly 77). Commissioners have no legal training, and may not speak English; their task is not to submit existing laws to close textual analysis but to consider them from a cultural point of view. Their first report made recommendations pertaining to vital statistics and official name policy, official languages and "custom adoption" practices. Not all of their proposals reflected a distinctive IQ perspective — suggestions to provide important government forms in Inuktitut and to review the pay and training of Custom Adoption Commissioners hardly required an Inuit sensibility — but some certainly did. For example, the Commission pointed out that the non-Inuit practice of naming buildings for deceased persons is contrary to traditional Inuit culture and offensive to Inuit elders (Maligarnit Qimirrujiit).

The work of Maligarnit Qimirrujiit demonstrates in a concrete way how IQ can be incorporated into public policy. Quite different and decidedly more problematic is the question of how IQ might influence the structure, processes and operating principles of the Nunavut government. Even if the Nunavut bureaucracy were to give pride of place to Inuktitut, provide cultural training to non-Inuit, offer flexible leaves and regularly consult with elders, it would still be a large, bureaucratic organization profoundly shaped by the powerful values implicit in the Euro-Canadian bureaucratic model. The central features of this model are largely incompatible with the principles of IQ: rigid hierarchy, formal processes, concentrated power, professional specialization, political neutrality, inflexible rules, [separation] of private and public domains and the like.

Other efforts at instituting IQ range from the highly abstract to the decidedly practical. At the one extreme, for example, an official involved in the IQ initiative argues that the traditional Inuit family-kinship model can provide a workable basis for government management (Arnkak 11). At the other, the Languages Commissioner of Nunavut observes that "the process of launching formal complaints against a large institution like the government is completely foreign to the Inuit way of life" and thus has developed plans for community-based exercises in soliciting and responding to Inuit concerns about language rights (Languages Commissioner 3).

Embedding the policies and operations of the government of Nunavut in IQ is a long-term undertaking; few organizational changes are as slow or as difficult as fundamental value shifts. Typically, though, the objectives of the IQ commitment are at once sweeping and distinctively northern. Value change has been a prominent, if imperfectly realized, goal in southern bureaucracies for some time, but the objective has largely been to imbue government with such private-sector values and approaches as "customer service," entrepreneurship and business planning, which may have been uncommon in traditional public administration but were hardly alien to it. The cultural transformation sought for government in Nunavut is rooted in a fundamentally different world view.

DECENTRALIZING THE NUNAVUT GOVERNMENT

Though IQ is primarily about values, the notion of rendering the Nunavut government an Inuit organization also has structural implications. On the surface, the design of the government seems quite conventional, and in many ways it is: the basic administrative structure consists of a largely unexceptional set of central agencies and line departments. The number of [departments] is relatively small (11), but the overall array of departments — Education, Justice, Health and Social Services, Finance and the like — as well as the typical departmental organization — a politically neutral deputy minister, supported by one or more assistant deputy ministers with staff organized into a fixed hierarchy — would seem decidedly orthodox to anyone familiar with provincial governments.

To be sure, pragmatism — often cited as an Inuit trait — inclined the designers of the Nunavut government towards the conventional in establishing bureaucratic structures. And yet, in one elemental respect the organization of government in Nunavut is to be boldly innovative. Once fully realized, it will be perhaps the most decentralized government in the world, certainly far more decentralized than any other Canadian jurisdiction.

Every modern government is decentralized in the sense of having networks of regional offices to deliver services and co-ordinate activities. In this regard Nunavut is already highly decentralized, with field offices in virtually all communities. Decentralization in Nunavut, however, entails much beyond this: a very high proportion of the departmental "headquarters" functions, which in other governments are almost invariably situated in the capital city, are being located in communities throughout the territory. Thus, while the deputy minister and some departmental staff will remain in Iqaluit, whole units — policy development, finance and other specialized operational and departmental offices, as well as government boards — are being relocated to the communities, the largest of which has barely 2,000 residents. When decentralization is complete, by way of illustration, the Department of Sustainable Development will have divisions and corporate functions, as well as associated boards, in six communities beyond Iqaluit.

All this — indeed, the entire operation of the Nunavut government — is made possible by state-of-the-art electronic communications networks. Inevitably, in a project as large and technology-dependent as this, initial operations have been uneven: bandwidth limitations and reliability of service in some communities have been recurrent problems. Glitches have caused inconvenience but have not occasioned fundamental impediments to government operations.

Decentralization has several objectives. Spreading government functions throughout the territory was seen by some as in keeping with Inuit political culture, which prizes government close to the people. On a more tangible level, decentralization entails sharing the economic benefits of government — stable, well-paid jobs and valuable infrastructure — widely. With employment and economic development opportunities so limited in Nunavut, the direct and spinoff jobs and the facilities associated with the government presence are critically important. Finally, locating middle-rank and senior bureaucratic posts in small communities is an integral component of a key strategic aim of the Nunavut project: ensuring the Inuit character of the Nunavut government through strong Inuit participation throughout the bureaucracy. Potential Inuit recruits would not face the barriers and disincentives of leaving their home communities either in initially taking up government jobs or in seeking advancement to more senior levels.

The decentralization initiative has its critics and sceptics. Some argue that the costs — both start-up and operating — are far out of proportion to the potential benefits. Others worry that decentralization will produce an administrative nightmare, rendering routine processes hopelessly cumbersome and inefficient. Still others doubt that distributing jobs to the communities will contribute much to Inuit hiring and retention in the bureaucracy, on the premise that few Inuit in small communities will be qualified for the available jobs. Moreover, critics warn, decentralization will render recruitment of non-Inuit (primarily from southern Canada) difficult and costly.

Decentralization will not be complete for several years and even then a good deal of time will have to elapse before a thorough reckoning of its success will be possible. At that, it will not be easy to weigh identifiable costs and shortcomings against the intangible benefits deriving from the fundamentally different government that decentralization will create. None the less, one conclusion about the consequences of this bold initiative seems inescapable: decentralization will fundamentally shape the nature of governance in Nunavut.

CONCLUSION

This essay has highlighted unique and unfamiliar aspects of northern governance institutions. And while other examples could be cited of distinctive northern governmental and political institutions — Nunavut's unique unified court system and the remarkable relationships emerging between the public governments of the territories and the Aboriginal land-claim organizations, to mention just two — many institutional features of northern governance are commonplace and unexceptional.

Still, it should be clear that central elements of government in the territorial North differ substantially from those of the provinces and the federal government. It would be easy to dismiss such differences as simply exotic curiosities, as irrelevant to southern governance as the life experiences of northern Aboriginal hunters are to the everyday concerns of suburban commuters. Yet this would be a mistake. Not that southern legislators are about to renounce their party ties and adopt a system of consensus government or that provincial governments should contemplate imbuing IQ principles into their operations. Rather, the relevance of northern institutions lies in their implicit message that governmental structures and processes can, within the confines of Westminster principles and the exigencies of the modern bureaucratic state, be organized in ways quite different from those dominant — indeed all but invariable — in Ottawa and the provinces. The key lies not in adopting specific organizational and cultural forms of governance but rather in developing institutions that reflect and advance the jurisdiction's social organization and values.

The pathologies impairing Canadian governmental institutions are often traced to the rigidities and anachronisms of the Westminster cabinet-parliamentary system. And to be sure, institutions that emerged in the context of mid-nineteenth-century British and Canadian social and political conditions can seem highly unsuitable to current needs. The northern experience, however, suggests that the Westminster system is far more flexible and adaptable than is usually thought. Indeed, its strength lies in its compatibility with a wide range of political-institutional arrangements. The problem may not be that the basic precepts of the Westminster system are hidebound and restrictive, but that the one variation that has become entrenched in

Ottawa and the provinces is seen so widely as definitive and immutable and thus impervious to challenge or reform.

Finally, if the extent to which northern governmental institutions are truly rooted in Aboriginal political culture is a matter of debate, the influence of the North's Aboriginal peoples — their interests, aspirations and political ideas — is indisputable. Gilles Paquet has written that "our evolving arrangements with the First Nations are likely... to act as an important catalyst in the transformation of our weltanschauung and of our philosophy of governance" (Paquet 103). The unique constellation of northern governmental institutions offers powerful support for this view.

NOTES

1. For a recent overview of society and politics in the territorial North, see the chapters by Floyd McCormick (Yukon), Peter Clancy (NWT) and Jack Hicks and Graham White (Nunavut) in The Provincial State in Canada: Politics in the Provinces and Territories, eds. Keith Brownsey and Michael Howlett (Peterborough: Broadview Press, 2001).
2. One minor exception: elsewhere it is the first minister who advises the sovereign or her representative to dissolve the elected House (i.e., call an election); in the NWT and Nunavut this prerogative is effectively in the hands of the Assembly.
3. For a discussion of the strengths and weaknesses of the consensus system vis-a-vis the party system, see the exchanges between Frances Widdowson and Albert Howard and me in Policy Options (January-February, May, September and November 1999).
4. "Public government" extends to all residents of a jurisdiction (including the right to vote and hold elected office); Aboriginal self-government represents and serves Aboriginal peoples, who are the only ones entitled to vote or hold office.
5. All of Nunavut and all of Yukon are covered by single claims; although the Yukon claim is an umbrella agreement, under which the various First Nations negotiate specific arrangements. Three claims — those of the Inuvialuit, the Gwich'in and the Sahtu Dene and Metis — cover the northern half of the NWT; the Dogrib claim in the central NWT is close to finalization, but in the Deh Cho and Akaitcho regions (essentially south and west of Great Slave Lake) quite different processes are unfolding.

WORKS CITED

ARNKAK, JAYPETEE. "What is Inuit Qaujimajatuqangit?" *Nunatsiaq News.* 25 August 2000.
CONSTITUTIONAL WORKING GROUP OF THE WESTERN CAUCUS of the Legislative Assembly and the Aboriginal Summit. Partners in a New Beginning. Yellowknife, 1996.
LANGUAGES COMMISSIONER OF NUNAVUT. *First Annual Report.* Iqaluit 2000.
LEGISLATIVE ASSEMBLY OF NUNAVUT. *Hansard.* 25 October 1999.
MALIGARNIT QIMIRRUJIIT/NUNAVUT LAW REFORM COMMISSION, *First Report to the Premier.* Iqaluit, October 2000.
NUNAVUT SOCIAL DEVELOPMENT COUNCIL. "Towards An Inuit Qaujimajatuqangit (IQ) Policy for Nunavut." Iqaluit 1999.
PAQUET, GILLES. "Tectonic Changes in Canadian Governance." How Ottawa Spends 1999–2000. *Shape Shifting: Canadian Governance Toward the 21st Century.* Ed. Leslie Pal. Toronto: Oxford University Press, 1999. 75–112.
STEVENSON, MARC G. "Inuit and Co-management: Principles, Practices and Challenges for the New Millennium." Paper presented at the North Atlantic Marine Mammal Commission conference, "Sealing the Future," St John's, Newfoundland, 1997.

(d) Modern Aboriginal Economies: Capitalism with a Red Face[†]

David Newhouse

INTRODUCTION

In March 1993, Victor Buffalo, Chairman, Peace Hills Trust Company, spent a few days as our Distinguished Visitor. He spoke to several classes and gave a public lecture about the Samson Cree Nation, the problems that it faces, and the role that Peace Hills Trust plays in helping to resolve these problems. After one of the lectures, a few students approached me and my colleagues to express their indignation that Mr. Buffalo had been invited to speak. They explained that Mr. Buffalo was not an Indian because he had not once used the word "sharing" in his presentation, he was wearing a suit and he was exploiting his own people. The exploitation was the making of a profit through the loaning of money. Mr. Buffalo's company loans money to Indian bands on the basis of cash flow, using the contribution agreements of the government as a form of collateral rather than the usual collateral of plant, equipment and land. His company has been able to do things that non-aboriginal bankers have been reluctant or unwilling to do.

A decade and a half ago, I chaired, for a short time, the Department of Indian Affairs and Northern Development's Ontario Region Indian Economic Development Loan Board. I saw many of the early attempts at business development on Indian reserves in southern Ontario. I remember being struck by the projects that I saw and their differences from mainstream businesses. On the surface the proposals looked the same: they contained cash flow and profit projections, investments in plant and equipment, the usual things that one expects to find in business plans. The heart of many of the proposals was not profit in the normal accounting sense but the creation of jobs. Profits were the way in which more jobs could be created and, hence, more people employed.

There have been enormous and significant changes within aboriginal society within the last generation. We need to reflect upon them in order to discern their meaning and impact. I present these stories as examples of the type of change of the last two decades and as a prelude to my topic. I have been asked to write on the unique perspectives that aboriginal belief systems have for development, how these can be preserved, and what lessons these might have for future development efforts both within aboriginal communities and the mainstream. These are difficult questions, and I'm not sure that they can be answered satisfactorily in the short time available to prepare this paper. I want, however, to provide some clues to the answers, and suggest not that further research be undertaken in this area, but that the processes that are underway within aboriginal communities be supported through the development of aboriginal institutions.

[†] First appeared in *Journal of Aboriginal Economic Development* 1(2): 55–61. Reproduced with permission of the author and CANDO.

THE MODERNIZATION OF ABORIGINAL SOCIETIES

My premise is that aboriginal societies are undergoing a process of modernization. I have written about this process in a previous paper (The Development Of Modern Aboriginal Societies, October 1992). This process is resulting in the development of new identities and new social, political, cultural and economic institutions within aboriginal societies. These institutions, in my opinion, will be primarily Western in nature and will be adapted to operate in accordance with aboriginal traditions, customs and values. One only has to look at the rapid development of organizations over the last decade to see evidence of this process. The 1990 Arrowfax Directory of Aboriginal Organizations lists 3,000 for-profit business and 3,000 not-for-profit businesses. The 1992 edition of the same directory showed a significant increase in the number of listings. A 1997 report by Aboriginal Business Canada shows 14,000 Aboriginal Businesses. Many of these organizations were not in existence a decade ago. At the same time, there is a growing desire to attempt to base the organizational cultures upon the contemporary interpretations of traditional ideas.

In addition to the growing set of organizations, which is akin to Drucker's idea of a society of organizations, there are other indicators of the modernization of aboriginal society: a steady growth in the off reserve population, continuing convergence of Indian birth rates and family size with the Canadian norms, adoption of English as a lingua franca, adoption of Western-style elected governments, (most evident in the band councils on Indian reserves), an increasing number of aboriginal students attending secondary and post secondary education institutions, and a move towards textual transmission of knowledge rather than oral transmission. There are now two generations of aboriginal people who have not lived on reserve and for whom reserve life is unknown. There is also a small but emerging aboriginal urban middle class. In some ways, aboriginal life is qualitatively different than it was two decades ago.

I don't know if this process of modernization is good or bad. The rapid rate of change, however, is causing a certain amount of social dislocation and problems, which we read, see or hear about in the various media of Canada. While the pace of change may be rapid, it would be unfair to say that it proceeds evenly across all aboriginal communities.

The million or so aboriginal people in Canada live in the midst of 30 million others. It is impossible for aboriginal people not to be affected by this contact and not to be changed by it. Aboriginal people are also surrounded by a capitalist economy and, because of its strength and appeal, will be affected by it. The question I have been asked to address needs to be placed in that context. The result is a slightly different set of questions: Given this context, and given that capitalism is an extremely adaptable system, what unique perspectives do aboriginal people bring to the ongoing debate about the practice of capitalism? How will aboriginal people adapt themselves to capitalism? Can aboriginal people find a way to adapt capitalism to their own particular world views?

I think that this is already occurring around us. I call this resultant aboriginal adaptation *capitalism with a red face*, for nowhere have I seen an outright rejection of capitalism by aboriginal people. In fact, I see a desire to adapt this particular political-economic system and to make it work in accordance with aboriginal belief systems. In addition, I see the adoption of policies and programs, by all governments, both aboriginal and not-aboriginal, all designed to further the development of this system within aboriginal society.

WHAT IS CAPITALISM?

Capitalism is a way of life, first of all and foremost. Then it's a world view, and finally, it's a political-economic system. Many people focus only on the economic aspects of capitalism. They believe once they have described how this feature works, that they understand it.

At the heart of capitalism is a particular view of man and a notion of social progress. Man is viewed as a being who is continually striving to improve his material and social well-being. Progress is measured through a continual improvement in individual material position. Most important, this progress occurs as the result of the actions of individuals, each of whom engages in this constant striving. It is the collection of individual effort that results in improved collective well-being. Individuals possess capital or labour that can be used to produce profits or surpluses. The goal of every individual is to produce an economic surplus, which can be saved for use at a future date, spent on consumables, or invested in order to produce additional surpluses. Individuals may pool their surpluses and use them for that group's good, or governments may appropriate them in the form of taxes in order to produce public goods that are available for all.

This notion of individual effort and social competition is important, for it is what drives capitalism. Without it, many of the gains would not be possible. One could argue that the work of this Royal Commission is paid for through the collective surpluses of individual workers.

Capitalism has proven to be a remarkably adaptable and versatile system and appears to be the preferred economic system throughout the world today. Nations as varied as Japan, the United States, India, and members of the former USSR are adapting it to their various cultures. Many are also involved in the search for a solution to one of capitalism's most difficult problems: achieving an equitable distribution of wealth in a society.

Aboriginal people in Canada appear to have accepted the fundamental premises of capitalism: the notion of progress as defined through social competition and the notion that one possesses either capital or labour, which can be used to produce surpluses.

There is no fear that capitalism cannot be adapted to aboriginal realities. In fact, it is being done throughout Canada, where economic programs, community infrastructures and education programs are encouraging its adoption. Individuals are being encouraged to use their own capital to establish enterprises to make profits, the rules of access to capital are being examined and revised, capital investment institutions (trust companies, caisse populaires, cooperatives, aboriginal capital corporations) are being established, governments are setting up small enterprise assistance programs for aboriginal individuals and communities, and some First Nations governments are tentatively thinking about some form of taxation and user fees on individual and corporate incomes.

It has been a popular belief in recent years that aboriginal people did not engage in economic activity; that, somehow, this type of activity was inconsistent with aboriginal culture and values. The historical record shows a much different picture: aboriginal people were active in the fur trade, assuming a major role in it (the Hurons were said to have been responsible for 50% of the fur trade in the 1600s), and were good traders. One of the names of the Micmac was "Taranteens", which meant "trader", and which reflected their role as excellent middlemen between the hunters of the north and the agriculturalists of the south.

Cree businessmen in the late 1800s in northern Saskatchewan were excellent business people: so good, in fact, that many of the surrounding business people wanted to restrain their ability to trade. In fact, throughout the whole of contact, aboriginal people have engaged in trade with those who arrived here; and prior to that, they traded with each other. For example, Oolichan grease was traded far into the interior of the country along trails that became known as "grease trails." In the present day, one only has to examine the huge powwow circuit that has grown up over the last few years or the rapid growth in the sale of cigarettes on Indian reserves to see the great increase in the number of people who are engaging in trade and making a profit: that most fundamental of capitalist activities.

With this background, the questions to be asked become clearer: what can aboriginal belief systems contribute to the practice of capitalism in aboriginal communities, what adaptions will be made to it, and what can governments do to assist in this adaption process to mitigate the inequities of the capitalist system?

ABORIGINAL BELIEF SYSTEMS

In 1991, the Manitoba Public Inquiry into the Administration of Justice and Aboriginal People reported: "Aboriginal peoples do not adhere to a single life philosophy, religious belief or moral code. Indeed, there are and have been considerable differences among tribes. That the aboriginal peoples of North America, for the most part, hold fundamental life philosophies different from those of the dominant European-Canadian society is now taken for granted." (p. 20).

At the core of aboriginal belief systems is a difference in the perception of one's relationship with the universe and the Creator. In the Judeo-Christian tradition, which is arguably the philosophical basis for much of European-Canadian society, there is the notion that humankind (mankind, in some interpretations) was to fill the earth and to have dominion over it and all that was contained within it. In Ojibway thought, which is taken to be representative of traditional aboriginal thought in general, mankind does not have dominion over the earth and all its creatures. Instead, mankind is dependent upon all parts of the creation for survival. In this view, man is the least important entity of the creation.

Despite the differences in traditional lifeways, James Dumont in a 1992 presentation to the Royal Commission on Aboriginal Peoples argued for a set of generalized Native primary values that he defined as arising from vision, ie. a special way of seeing the world as a native person and a capacity for holistic or total vision. With this ability to see the whole comes respect: respect for creation, respect for knowledge and wisdom, respect for the dignity and freedom of others, respect for the quality of life and spirit in all things, and respect for the mysterious.

From this core of vision and respect, he argues that there arise seven primary traditional values:

1. **kindness:** a capacity for caring and desire for harmony and well-being in interpersonal relationships;
2. **honesty:** a necessity to act with the utmost honesty and integrity in all relationships, recognizing the inviolable and inherent autonomy, dignity and freedom of oneself and others;
3. **sharing:** a willingness to relate to one another with an ethic of sharing, generosity and collective/communal consciousness and cooperation, while recognizing the interdependence and interrelatedness of all life;
4. **strength:** conscious of the need for kindness and respecting the integrity of oneself and others, to exercise strength of character, fortitude and self-mastery in order to generate and maintain peace, harmony and well-being within oneself and in the total collective community;
5. **bravery:** the exercise of courage and bravery on the part of the individual so that the quality of life and inherent autonomy of oneself and others can be exercised in an atmosphere of security, peace, dignity and freedom;
6. **wisdom:** the respect for that quality of knowing and gift of vision in others (striving for the same within oneself) that encompasses the holistic view, possesses spiritual quality, and is expressed in the experiential breadth and depth of life;
7. **humility:** the recognition of oneself as a sacred and equal part of the creation, and the honouring of all life, which is endowed with the same inherent autonomy, dignity, freedom and equality.

These values should be interpreted and translated into community processes, institutions and codes of behaviour. Another important factor to consider is the collectivist orientation of aboriginal society. While the interpretation of this value orientation varies quite widely, its usual interpretation is that the needs of the group, whether it be the family, clan or nation, take precedence over the needs of the individual. It is also important to realize that traditional aboriginal people viewed life as a journey. The practice of capitalism within aboriginal society will be affected by these factors as well as by modernizing trends as described earlier. It is this world view and value set that aboriginal people bring to the debate about the practice of capitalism.

There is, and will continue to be, considerable debate about whether traditional values are, indeed, compatible with capitalism. Within the aboriginal community, there is a considerable effort underway to ensure that traditional values are understood and made the centre of aboriginal life again: a process sociologists call revitalization, which I call retraditionalization. It is this process of relearning and reinterpreting traditional values within a contemporary context that offers some hope for the development of aboriginal economies that operate in accordance with aboriginal ideas and values.

However, the achievement of this ideal, an aboriginal economy operating with traditional values, is made difficult. Many aboriginal people have bought into the fundamental premises of capitalism and of its promises of a better material life. Yet I think that there is sufficient desire to try to create something that is uniquely aboriginal out this blend of traditionalism and capitalism, what I call: red capitalism.

WHAT WILL RED CAPITALISM LOOK LIKE?

Aboriginal values and world views will affect the practice of capitalism and, hence, the process of economic development in the following ways:

1. The concept of personal and social development itself will be much broader. Using a holistic view, development will be viewed as encompassing four dimensions: physical, mental, emotional and spiritual, the same dimensions as contained within the Cree Medicine Wheel. The development process itself will have to include all four elements at the same time, and not just along the economic (physical) dimension.
2. Development itself will be seen as a process, and not as a product. Based upon the aboriginal view that life itself is a journey, the development process will also be seen as a journey, not as an end state to be achieved. This is not to say that movement along the journey cannot be measured, but that the emphasis will be upon the quality of the journey rather than the specific place to be reached. This view of development may mean that there will be a willingness to pursue long term results over short term improvements.
3. Development will be seen as a joint effort by the individual and the collective and its institutions: in this case, the community and government. The process itself will tend to be collaborative rather than competitive. One can see this happening in the manner in which individuals who attempt to start businesses without the legitimizing support of either community or governments are treated or dealt with.
4. In addition to the notion of joint effort and somewhat along the same lines, development will be seen as a partnership between the individual and the world. In a world in which the fundamental value is respect, one needs to have permission of the world in order to change it, to transform it into something else. If one sees oneself as an integral part of the world, indeed as its least important creation, then one would hesitate to act in a way that shows a lack of respect. This will affect the choice of development projects engaged in and the type of technology employed.
5. The development effort will emphasize human capital investment rather than individual capital accumulation. This focus on the human aspects of development will cause developers to explicitly consider the effects of their activities upon the quality of life, which includes the environment, and will affect development choices. Decisions may be reviewed by Councils of Elders. Decision criteria may be established to explicitly require an analysis of these aspects.
6. Traditional wisdom as interpreted by the elders will be used to guide planning and decision making. Elders may be accorded a formal place in planning and development efforts through a variety of mechanisms: Councils of Elders who must approve plans and advisory councils that sit at the same table as Councillors or as advisors to individuals.

7. The issues surrounding wealth distribution will be tackled using aboriginal values of kindness and sharing. There will be expectations that individuals who have or who are accumulating wealth will somehow share it with community members.

    Indeed, the current notion of success as defined by capitalism in material terms will be challenged and broadened. The adaption of capitalism will also alter traditional systems for determining social status. At present, elders who possess knowledge and experience of traditional lifeways are highly revered. The continued use of a material definition of success in aboriginal society may change this hierarchy as those who have material wealth move to the top of the social scale.

8. The economic institutions that are established will be primarily Western in nature, with adaptions to ensure that they operate in a manner appropriate to the local aboriginal community. This means the development of a wide range of Western looking organizations: cooperatives, individual proprietorships, partnerships, corporations owned by individuals and governments, joint ventures — in fact, the myriad of ways in which economic activity can be undertaken.

    In addition to this infrastructure of primarily economic institutions, there will develop a whole range of secondary economic support institutions, such as development agencies, management advisory groups, loan funds, etc., whose primary function is not economic activity itself, but increasing the efficiency of the economy.

9. The desire to arrive at decisions by consensus will guide the development of community and organizational structures and processes that are consistent with this value. This has implications for the development planning process itself. Planners and decision makers will not be able to proceed with plans unless a consensus, using an acceptable process, has been reached that this is what should be done. In addition, decision makers will not be able to make decisions without ensuring that broad community consensus exists for a particular direction and course of action. The current business approach to decision making, which is based on "number crunching", ie. quantitative information, will be broadened.

10. The notions of honesty and respect will result in a heightened sense of accountability for economic institutions and decision makers. This accountability will be focused on two issues: (1) adherence to the direction as consensually agreed upon; and (2) adherence to aboriginal notions of holism and development.

Much of this is now happening. A quick glance at recent developments within aboriginal society shows they include:

1. an increasing number of primary and secondary economic institutions: small and medium sized businesses; financial institutions, such as trust companies, caisse populaires, credit unions, aboriginal capital corporations; economic support organizations, such as sectoral support programs, community development corporations, training and development organizations, consultants and advisors, etc.;

2. elder stewardship in decision making through advisory councils, inclusion as board members or advisors in organizations;
3. adoption of community economic development models with their broad notions of development and the subsequent development of indicators to permit communities to gauge their movement;
4. continued and expanded use of programs designed to provide aboriginal people with the skills, knowledge and capital to participate in the broader Canadian economy.

The desire for a much improved material quality of life, the recentness of the above developments, the general lack of understanding of the workings of aboriginal economies, the acceptance of the fundamental premises of capitalism by many aboriginal people and the tentative acceptance by Canadians of the notion of aboriginal self government all indicate that great care needs to be taken in the choice of interventions by governments and outside agents in order to support the development of a capitalism that is consistent with aboriginal ideas and values.

What Can Be Done to Assist in This Development?

The process of modernization and the adoption of capitalism as the dominant political-economic system within aboriginal society is well underway. It would be sheer folly to attempt to reverse the process or to attempt dramatic shifts in direction. I would argue that the forces of modernization are much too great to resist, especially in this area. The questions, however, remain: what should our strategy be, and what can we reasonably do to influence the future course of events?

There are, in my opinion, three possible courses of action:

1. One could do very little at this time. One could take the view that the process is underway, aboriginal people are gaining access to the Canadian economy and are participating in it in increasing numbers, in contrast to the recent past when economic participation was legally ruled out.

    The adoption of this approach, given the fragile nature of aboriginal economies, would, I think, prolong the current situation for an indefinite period. Development would continue, but at a very slow pace, not keeping up with the demand for an improved quality of life. In addition, aboriginal values would probably have a difficult time surviving, given the highly competitive nature of the Canadian and global economies.
2. One could increase the level of effort within existing programs. The reasoning would be that an increased level of effort will directly result in a quicker improvement in the quality of life for aboriginal individuals. The adoption of this approach would permit an increased level of economic activity but does not do much to support aboriginal values and world views.
3. One could adopt a strategy of institution building within aboriginal society: i.e., one could make its focus the building of institutional capacities within aboriginal communities, which could then begin to deal with the various problems and issues of aboriginal life.

This is the course of action that I suggest for the economic development area.

A society's values are reflected in its institutions just as much as in its day to day practices. In fact, institutions assume a large role in the preservation and transmission of culture and values. Much of the thinking that needs to be done with respect to aboriginal economic development and values needs to be undertaken by aboriginal people. On an individual and collective basis, aboriginal people are making daily decisions based on their understanding of their values. Much needs to be done to support that decision making.

It would be useful to establish an economic research and policy development institute whose main function is to identify issues such as those I've raised in this paper and to research them on behalf of aboriginal individuals, communities, organizations and governments. It would develop the culturally appropriate tools and make them available for use by individuals and communities. It would also be able to provide policy analysis and advice to aboriginal governments using aboriginal perspectives and values.

At the present time, an institution of this sort does not exist. This is not to suggest that there is little being accomplished in this area. In fact, there is a considerable amount of research and experiential learning taking place. Much of this needs to be captured and fed back into the community in a form that is usable and viewed as legitimate. An institute of this sort could do that.

The question, then, as I see it, is not one of preserving aboriginal world views and values, but of finding ways to assist in the creative interpretation of these world views and values in the contemporary reality: a process that is already underway.

BIBLIOGRAPHY

BYRNES, J., *Aboriginal Enterprise Development: Themes and Issues* (publisher unknown, 1989).
DICKASON, O., *Canada's First Nations, A History of Founding Peoples from Earliest Times* (McClelland and Stewart, 1992).
DUMONT, J., "Aboriginal People and Justice", Presentation to Royal Commission on Aboriginal Peoples, Canada, 1992.
HAMILTON, A.C. and SINCLAIR, C.M. *The Report of the Aboriginal Justice Inquiry of Manitoba, Volume 1* (Queen's Printer, Manitoba, 1991).
LANGDON, S., *Contemporary Alaskan Native Economies* (University Press of America, Inc., 1986).
LOCKHART, R.A., *Issues Perceived as Critical to the Construction of Native Management and Economic Development Models* (The Working Group on Native Management, 1992).
MERREL, J.H., *The Indians' New World: Catawbas and their Neighbours from European Contact Through the Era of Removal* (W.W. Norton and Company, 1989).
NEWHOUSE, D.R., "From the Tribal to the Modern: The Development of Modern Aboriginal Societies", Presentation to Royal Commission on Aboriginal Peoples, Canada, 1992.
RUFFING, L., *Navajo Economic Development Subject to Cultural Constraints* (American Indian Policy Review Commission, date unknown).
STANLEY, S., *American Indian Economic Development* (Mouton Publishers, Paris, 1978).
VECSAY, C. and R. VENABLES, *American Indian Environments: Ecological Issues in Native American History* (Syracuse University Press, 1980).
WIEN, F. *Rebuilding the Economic Base of Indian Communities: The Micmac in Nova Scotia* (The Institute for Research on Public Policy, 1986).

(e) The Politics of TEK: Power and the "Integration" of Knowledge[†]

Paul Nadasdy

INTRODUCTION

Use of the term "traditional ecological knowledge" (TEK) is now commonplace in discourse concerning the management of land and resources across the North American Arctic and Subarctic. The past decade and a half has seen an explosion in the number of conferences, symposia, and workshops devoted to traditional ecological knowledge across the North, not to mention the growth of a substantial academic literature on traditional knowledge and the establishment of numerous regional, national, and international working groups, information networks, and other organizations concerned with promoting and disseminating research on the topic. The principal objective of this activity has been to "collect and document" traditional ecological knowledge and to "integrate" it with scientific knowledge of the environment. The hope is that by integrating the knowledge of aboriginal people who have spent their lives out on the land with that of scientific experts, we will increase our overall understanding of the environment and that this new integrated knowledge will allow improvements in existing processes of environmental impact assessment and resource management. There is also some hope that the integration of traditional knowledge with science will help to empower the aboriginal people and communities who are the holders of this knowledge.

The widespread recognition that something called "traditional ecological knowledge" even exists represents, in itself, an important first step toward the full participation of aboriginal communities in the management of land and resources. In spite of nearly 15 years of effort by countless scientists, resource managers, aboriginal people, and social scientists to develop a method for integrating scientific and traditional knowledge, however, there has been little actual progress toward achieving it. Despite the establishment of numerous co-management regimes across the North, scientists and resource managers remain essentially at a loss regarding traditional ecological knowledge; many are still not quite sure what it is, much less how to use or integrate it with scientific research. A recent review of the literature on TEK, for example, noted that a large proportion of this literature still focuses on the potential use of TEK rather than on actual applications (Kuhn and Duerden 1996: 79). Many works continue to advocate the use of TEK and its integration with science without describing a method for achieving this goal. In the meantime, aboriginal people continue to express dissatisfaction and impatience with current efforts to use TEK in the real world of land claims and resource management. Why, given the duration, intensity, and interdisciplinary nature of the effort to integrate traditional and scientific knowledge, has there been so little success? This paper seeks to answer this question by taking a new approach to the integration of TEK and

---

[†] From *Arctic Anthropology*, Vol. 36, Nos. 1 & 2, pp. 1–18. © 1999. Reproduced by permission of the University of Wisconsin Press.

science. Rather than focusing on obstacles to integration that arise from differences in form between the two "types" of knowledge, as most of the literature has done, I will consider instead the power relations underlying the project of integration itself.

This paper is based on 32 months of fieldwork in Burwash Landing, a village in the Southwest Yukon Territory, Canada. The community is located on the Alaska Highway 280 km north of Whitehorse, the territorial capital. It has a year-round population of approximately 70 people, most of whom are members of the Kluane First Nation.[1] In addition to participant observation of daily life in the community throughout this period, I attended land claims negotiations, resource management meetings, TEK-related conferences, workshops, and symposia in Burwash Landing and Whitehorse as well as elsewhere in the region.

CONVENTIONAL PERSPECTIVES ON THE INTEGRATION OF SCIENCE AND TEK

There are two conventional ways of explaining why it has been so difficult in practice to integrate traditional knowledge and science. One type of explanation is encountered primarily in official and formal settings; the other can be heard only in more informal and unofficial contexts. At conferences, workshops, and other formal arenas for the discussion of traditional knowledge and co-management, as well as in the vast majority of the academic and policy-oriented literature on the topic, participants and authors are likely to identify and focus on certain obstacles to the integration of traditional knowledge and science. These, they argue, arise from the fact the two types of knowledge are incommensurable. In contrast to traditional knowledge, which is assumed to be qualitative, intuitive, holistic, and oral, science is seen as quantitative, analytical, reductionist, and literate. Indeed, one cannot examine the question of traditional knowledge for long without being confronted by a barrage of such dualistic comparisons (often arranged neatly in a table) purporting to sum up the differences between traditional and scientific knowledge. The assumption is that since traditional knowledge is expressed in a form that is vastly different from, and largely incompatible with, that of science, there are a whole host of essentially technical problems that accompany the effort to integrate them. Most of these problems relate to difficulties in accessing and collecting TEK or with translating it into a form that can be utilized by resource managers. This approach views the present lack of progress towards integration as resulting from the complexity of these problems and the difficulty in developing strategies and methodologies capable of effectively dealing with them.

This official type of explanation, by focusing on the "integration of knowledge systems" as a technical problem, is inadequate because it ignores the political dimensions of the issue of knowledge integration. Rather than merely assuming, as many do, that integrating traditional knowledge with science will automatically lead to improved resource management and aboriginal empowerment, we must closely examine the assumptions underpinning this project. By doing so, it will become apparent that the practice of traditional knowledge research and its integration may well be reinforcing, rather than breaking down, a number of Western cultural biases that in the end work against full community involvement in managing local

(e) The politics of TEK: Power and the "integration" of knowledge / 81

land and wildlife. Before developing this argument further, I will turn to a brief discussion of a more hidden discourse surrounding traditional knowledge and its integration with science.

There is a fairly common form of explanation regarding the current failure to integrate traditional knowledge and science which is almost completely absent from both the literature and formal arenas of discussion on traditional knowledge. It is encountered almost exclusively in informal or even "private" conversations. It is more likely to be heard in the home or in the bar than in the meeting room. Though they very rarely do so in one another's presence, both aboriginal people and non-native scientists and resource managers are equally likely to engage in this hidden discourse about traditional knowledge. In these relaxed informal settings people are more likely to give voice to their suspicions regarding the hidden agendas of others and on the "real" motives behind their involving the term "traditional knowledge." Expressions of this sort are extremely varied, running the gamut from vague uneasiness, through racist explosions of distrust and contempt, to thoughtful and cogent argument. It is not my intention here to deal exhaustively with the dynamics and meanings of this hidden discourse on traditional knowledge, but only to point out some of its major currents.

A number of First Nations people, for example, in expressing to me their frustration with traditional knowledge and co-management processes, have come to the conclusion that many scientists and managers have no real intention of trying to integrate traditional knowledge with science, but are merely paying lip-service to the idea because it has become politically expedient to do so. As a result, they often interpret the failure of scientists and resource managers to deal seriously with traditional knowledge as a calculated strategy for retaining control over the management of land and resources. In this context, First Nations people are increasingly likely to (and some of them already do) view most "official" talk about traditional ecological knowledge as insincere or even as willful obfuscation. For their part, a number of scientists and resource managers have expressed to me, in private conversation, their own doubts about the existence and efficacy of traditional knowledge. Most who have expressed these reservations to me feel that, though traditional knowledge may very well have existed at one time, drastic changes in the lifestyle of aboriginal people have so eroded this type of knowledge that it effectively no longer exists. As a result, they tend to view aboriginal people's insistence on the use of traditional knowledge with suspicion. I have heard it expressed more than once by scientists and resource managers that "traditional knowledge" is simply a political ploy invented by aboriginal people to wrest control of wildlife from "qualified" scientific managers. On one occasion a biologist told me outright that the only value she sees in consulting with native elders is that she must do so in order to secure community support for her projects, which in the current political climate is now required.

It is perhaps not surprising that by now many people on all sides of the traditional knowledge debate have become suspicious of the whole idea. Though confusion and uncertainty about the role of traditional ecological knowledge in the co-management process are as widespread as ever, the term traditional knowledge itself (the acronyms "TK" and/or "TEK" have by now almost completely replaced it)[2] is thrown around with ever greater (and more indiscriminate) abandon. Indeed, it often seems as though the term "TEK" is now used precisely to *avoid* rather than to engage in the difficult task of specific cross-cultural negotiation and understanding that is inherent in the idea of co-management. Even if "traditional knowledge" is not the deliberately mystifying political jargon that some from every perspective in the debate are beginning to suspect it to be, it is nevertheless in danger of becoming — if it has not already done so — a meaningless buzzword, its use masking more than it reveals.

Unofficial explanations for the failure to integrate traditional knowledge and science are, if anything, more riddled with bias and unexamined assumptions than are the official explanations. Even so, we ignore this hidden discourse at our peril, not only because many of those involved with the issue profess to "really think" these things, but also because this hidden discourse focuses on a dimension that is almost completely lacking from the official explanations: power. In these informal discussions, people do not concern themselves with abstract questions of epistemology nor with the nuances of different information gathering techniques; instead, they concentrate on the political dimensions of the issue: How are the different actors in the management process using the term traditional knowledge? What meanings and agendas are promoted or masked through their use of the term? How are thoughts and actions constrained and directed by these meanings? Who benefits from all this? This paper takes these questions and concerns seriously. Accordingly, I will not approach the issue of integrating traditional knowledge and science from a technical perspective, but from a political one. I will begin by questioning — rather than proceeding from — some of the basic assumptions underlying the concept of traditional knowledge.

"TRADITION," "ENVIRONMENT," AND "KNOWLEDGE:" UNEXAMINED ASSUMPTIONS OF TEK

As Morrow and Hensel (1992) argued of the Alaskan context, many terms used in relation to the management of land and wildlife, such as "subsistence," "conservation," and "traditional use," have no counterparts in the languages or cultural practices of aboriginal people. As a result, these terms, while seemingly straightforward in meaning, are actually contested on a fundamental level. Since all parties assume that the contested terms refer to agreed-upon realities, when in fact they serve only to mask deep cultural differences, the use of these terms can lead to serious misunderstandings and perceptions of bad faith between the parties. Their use also has the effect of biasing the discourse in favor of scientific managers by restricting the ways in which it is possible to talk (and think) about these issues. Morrow and Hensel's language-based argument is directly applicable to an examination of the political dimensions of traditional knowledge and TEK research.

Though the way of life to which the term "traditional ecological knowledge" refers is far from new, the term itself has only recently been adopted by resource managers and First Nations people alike. The term and its components, "tradition," "environment/ecology," and "knowledge," are contested on a fundamental level and constrain people's thought and action in significant ways. This paper will focus on these terms, especially "knowledge," and their role in structuring the way that people can act upon and think about TEK and its relation to science.

Morrow and Hensel speak directly to the term "traditional," which, as used and understood by most non-natives, has the effect of assuming that cultural practice is frozen at a particular point in time (usually the distant past). This allows the dismissal of more recent practice, however consistent it may actually be with local beliefs and values, as "inauthentic," giving non-native resource managers and others the power to define, in important ways, what constitutes "authentic" native culture and to judge and act upon the behavior of aboriginal people accordingly. To illustrate this they recount a case in which two Yup'ik boys were charged with shooting a muskox out of season (Morrow and Hensel 1992: 40–41). Muskoxen are rarely found around the village in question, so the boys had consulted the village elders for guidance before shooting it. The elders had advised the boys to shoot the animal, because it had offered itself to them and might be offended if they did not. The boys shot the animal and the meat was distributed within the village in a culturally accepted manner. Thus, they interpreted and acted upon the unusual appearance of the muskox in a manner that was consistent with local Yup'ik ideology. Yet, the judge in the case rejected a defense based on "customary and traditional" practice and ruled against the boys on the grounds that muskoxen are not traditional game animals in the area.

This illustrates how the idea of "tradition" can be used by non-natives to deny the adaptability and dynamism of aboriginal culture. Many non-natives view changing practices and lifestyles in aboriginal communities as "evidence" that traditional knowledge is disappearing. This allows them to discount the opinions and knowledge of aboriginal people who do not live according to their preconceived notions of a traditional aboriginal lifestyle. More than once I have heard a non-native dismiss an aboriginal person's claim to possess traditional knowledge with a statement like, "He doesn't have any traditional knowledge. He went to school and drives a truck and a skidoo just like me." Use of the modifier "traditional" enables people to hold such views by implying that aboriginal culture is static. This allows them, like the judge in the above example, to deny that First Nation people have the ability to adapt to new circumstances without abandoning their culture altogether. Use of "traditional" also makes it easy for scientists and resource managers to disregard the possibility that aboriginal people might possess distinct cultural perspectives on modern industrial activities such as logging or mining.

As with "tradition," use of the English terms "environment" and "ecological" in discussions of TEK tends to bias the discourse toward a Euro-Canadian perspective. These terms are products of a Western conception of the world. Implicit in their use is the notion that human beings are separate and distinct from the rest of the world, and it is specifically the non-human part of the world which constitutes the "environment." Though some ecologists and others have begun to point out that humans are indeed part of the environment (e.g., in the debate over global warming), this has done little in practice to break down the conceptual separation between humans and the environment in Western thought. There are very few Euro-Canadians who would consider kinship, for example, to be an ecological topic. Yet, there are those who do not subscribe to this rigid Western distinction between humans and the environment, among them many of the aboriginal people of the Yukon, who have referred to themselves explicitly as "part of the land, part of the water" (McClellan 1987: 1). In the absence of a strict separation between humans and the environment, the very idea of separating "ecological" from "non-ecological" knowledge becomes nonsensical. This is powerfully illustrated by native elders who, when asked to share their knowledge about the "environment," are just as likely to talk about "non-environmental" topics like kinship or respect as they are to talk about animals and landscapes. Every time researchers or bureaucrats dismiss or ignore these parts of an elder's testimony as irrelevant, they are actually imposing their own culturally derived standards of relevance.

The most fundamental and least examined (in the discourse on TEK, at any rate) concept underlying the idea of TEK is that of "knowledge." The goal of most Tek research is to collect, preserve and/or utilize traditional knowledge. Yet, traditional knowledge is not really "knowledge" at all in the Western sense of the term. Aboriginal people themselves constantly point this out when they say that traditional knowledge is not so much knowledge, as it is a "way of life." This should come as no surprise to anthropologists who have long regarded knowledge as culturally constructed (e.g., Bulmer 1967; Evans-Pritchard 1937; Gladwin 1970). As a result, they have tended to approach it not simply as an abstract "product" of the human intellect, but as one aspect of broader cultural processes that are embedded in complex networks of social relations, values, and practices which give them meaning. Indeed, all of the finest ethnographic treatments of local knowledge in the North (Cruikshank 1990; Nelson 1983; Tanner 1979, to name but a few) have made this point explicitly, and with scarcely a single incidence of the expression "TEK" between them. Despite the warnings from anthropologists and aboriginal people themselves, however, the discourse on TEK continues to treat traditional knowledge as a set of discrete intellectual products which are completely separable from the cultural milieu that gives them meaning.

To understand why this is the case, we need to look at the context in which TEK research has been carried out and in which its results are being used. Most TEK research in Canada has grown out of the land claims process, in which First Nations entered into negotiations with federal and provincial and/or territorial governments to settle the question of aboriginal rights to land and self-government. Early traditional knowledge studies were carried out to document patterns of native land use for specific land claim negotiations (Freeman 1976). Increasingly, however, the purpose for collecting TEK has been to incorporate it into co-management and environmental impact assessment processes established under or in conjunction with these land claim agreements (e.g., Allen 1994; Berger 1977; Brody 1982; Freeman and Carbyn 1988; Inglis 1993; Johannes 1989; Johnson 1992; Nakashima 1990; *Northern Perspectives* 1992; Roberts 1996).

Though the idea of incorporating TEK into processes of state resource management and impact assessment is a fairly new one, systems of state-sponsored wildlife management and impact assessment are themselves far from new. Indeed, not only do both fields have relatively long histories as established disciplines in applied science (especially wildlife management), both have been formally institutionalized through the establishment of complex state bureaucracies. Moreover, these bureaucratic structures have long been the exclusive domain of scientists and resource managers who necessarily have a great deal personally invested in scientific management *as a profession*. Because of this, they tend to view TEK (at best) as a supplementary body of information which does not threaten the fundamental assumptions of wildlife management itself. This is evident from the rhetoric about *incorporating* TEK *into* the management process, which assumes that the value of TEK lies in its use by wildlife managers. That traditional knowledge might be used to re-think unexamined assumptions about how people should relate to the world around them (including other humans), which unconsciously form the basis of scientific wildlife management itself, is a possibility that scientists and resource managers never entertain. It is this perspective on the relation between TEK and the management process that has led directly to the goal of "integrating" TEK and science in the first place.

This approach allows the project of integrating the two knowledge systems to be reduced to the technical exercise of combining two alternative sets of "data," while the management system into which this new "integrated knowledge" is inserted remain essentially unchanged (see also Cruikshank 1998: 53). The imperative integration means that TEK must be expressed in forms that are compatible with the already existing institutions and processes of scientific resource management. The problem with this approach to TEK is that it ignores the cultural processes in which different "ways of knowing" are embedded and treats traditional knowledge (to say nothing of scientific knowledge) as simply another type of information or source of data. In practice this has had two important and interrelated effects on the way TEK researchers have approached the rich constellation of social relations, practices, values, and beliefs to which the term TEK supposedly refers: they have had to both compartmentalize and distill it.

THE COMPARTMENTALIZATION OF TEK

Scientific knowledge and practice are compartmentalized. Indeed, the same can be said of all that Western scientists and scholars classify as "knowledge." There are "social science," "natural science," "pure science," "applied science," and so on, each subdivided into a whole array of disciplines and subdisciplines which are quite distinct from one another both intellectually and socially. Historians of science and sociologists have argued that this compartmentalization has more to do with the politics of institutionalized knowledge production in the West than it does with any corresponding divisions in the "real" world (e.g., Foucault 1980; Rabinbach 1990; Said 1978; Worster 1977). The production and compartmentalization of knowledge do not occur in a world of pure intellect, but are aspects of broader trends in the development of capitalism and state structures (e.g., Foucault 1978; Lukács 1971; Marcuse [1964]; Merchant 1980). This compartmentalization has profound effects on how people can think about knowledge and the ways in which it can be used. This is especially obvious to those who do *not* accept the basic assumptions underlying compartmentalization.

An experienced hunter in Burwash Landing, who has dealt extensively with both government officials and biologists, explained to me once why he felt the government could not effectively manage wildlife. He complained that government officials would not act without first gathering knowledge from all its experts. But this is easier said than done, he explained, because the government has forestry experts, water experts, and mining experts; it has sheep biologists, moose biologists, wolf biologists, and bear biologists; and none of these people knows anything outside of their own specialty. Since any management efforts necessarily must include a number of different resources, the government is powerless to act without endless meetings in which these specialists attempt to "educate" one another; and even then no one really understands the environment as a whole. He specially contrasted this situation to his own knowledge of the land and that of others in the community who have spent considerable parts of their lives out on the land. He said that survival in the bush depends on one's knowledge of the environment as a whole. It is not enough to know only about bears or moose; one must know about *all* of the animals out there — how they behave, what they eat, how they interact with one another, and how they think. To illustrate his point, he listed off about ten different species of animals and the relative sizes of their populations in the area over the past 15 years. He said that biologists do not know as much about the environment as they think they do, because if you put them out in the bush alone they would not be able to survive.

While it may not be entirely fair to criticize the knowledge of biologists on this count (since it is not their goal or intention to be able to "live on the land" in this way), this statement does highlight the radically different social contexts in which scientific resource managers and aboriginal people are embedded. Compartmentalization, which is an essentially unquestioned necessity associated with living and functioning in the world of bureaucratized state management, is seen as quite strange and counterproductive by one who does not accept that social context as given. Indeed, most aboriginal people are quite explicit about the uncompartmentalized nature of the lifestyle that is referred to as "traditional knowledge." To survive on the land one must "know about" not only certain animals, but how they fit into a complex web of practices, values, and social relations that encompass not only all animals, plants, and land forms, but humans as well.

All general *descriptions* of traditional knowledge encountered at TEK workshops and found in the introductions to management-oriented TEK studies echo this sentiment; indeed, much is made of the holistic nature of TEK in all the rhetoric surrounding TEK. Yet, despite all this, one continuously comes across TEK reports with titles like "Traditional Ecological Knowledge of Beluga Whales" (Huntington 1995) or "Collection and Analysis of Traditional Ecological Knowledge about a Population of Arctic Tundra Caribou" (Ferguson and Messier 1997), and community level workshops are being held regularly across the North for the explicit purpose of gathering "Moose TEK," or "TEK about Dall sheep." As these titles imply, many TEK studies focus on single species or at most a handful of related or "important" species — almost always large game animals or medicinal plants. This focus on individual species conforms not to the views of native elders and hunters, but to the needs and specifications of the scientists and government officials who are managing these populations in an established institutionalized setting.

Scientists and resource managers concerned with managing a population of Dall sheep, for example, are primarily interested in data on sheep. They may have some interest in a few other species (e.g., major prey or predator species such as, in the case of Dall sheep, coyotes, wolves, or eagles), but in general they are not at all interested in "unrelated" animals such as ground squirrels, salmon, moose, or otters. The integrated holistic view of the world that hunters value and, indeed, depend upon for their very survival cannot be accommodated by the institutional structure of the state management system into which they are being "incorporated." For the experience of local hunters to be useful at all to scientists and resource managers, it must be compartmentalized in a way that corresponds to the divisions which already exist in the practice of scientific resource management. So, sheep biologists deal with sheep TEK; bear biologists deal with bear TEK; moose biologists deal with moose TEK, and so on. Since scientific knowledge of the environment is divided and compartmentalized, scientists treat TEK, in so far as it is "knowledge," as compartmentalizable along similar lines.

The experiences and lives of First Nations people, however, cannot be compartmentalized in a way that corresponds to the categories of scientific management. The lack of correspondence that inevitably results from the attempt to do so leads to two types of problem. The first is that there are categories in the field of scientific resource management which appear to have no analogues in TEK. This creates the illusion that First Nations people have nothing to say regarding these topics. Examples of this type are categories such as "mining" and "forestry." Though aboriginal people certainly used both minerals and trees in precontact times, their practices had little resemblance to contemporary industrial mining or forestry. The knowledge that they did possess concerning the location of these resources and how to obtain them [is] seen as rudimentary and outdated, unable to provide even supplementary data for foresters or geo-physicists (though there are some significant exceptions to this[3]). Nor do these activities seem to be surrounded by the same richly elaborated set of beliefs and practices as is, for example, hunting. Most scientists and resource managers conclude therefore that no TEK exists regarding these "modern" topics; though there may be such a thing as "moose TEK," there is no "forestry TEK" or "TEK on mining." This assumption is given additional weight by the use of the modifier "traditional," as noted above.

On numerous occasions at meetings and workshops on mining or forestry in Whitehorse, I have heard questions and concerns regarding traditional knowledge dismissed with the assertion that, in essence, there is no such thing (though it is usually phrased somewhat more delicately than this). This assertion is an illusion caused by the false compartmentalization of TEK. Though aboriginal people did not engage in industrial forestry or mining in precontact times, they do nevertheless have distinct beliefs, practices, and values regarding trees and the earth (not to mention any number of more general beliefs and values) which are relevant to the practice of activities such as mining and forestry (Kari 1995; McClellan 1975; Nelson 1983). By channeling all discussion into the institutionally accepted language of science-based resource management, the assertion that "there is no TEK on mining/forestry" effectively limits the ways in which First Nations people can participate in the debates surrounding these industries. Though they are welcome to participate, the "truth" of their input is evaluated strictly according to the standards of forestry, ecology, geology, or geo-physics. Because there is supposedly no TEK about forestry or mining to compete with these accepted disciplines, scientists and resource managers can confidently assume that they hold a monopoly on knowledge in these fields. This is especially significant in the Yukon, where mining has long been one of the most important resource-based activities, and governments are at this moment struggling to develop a management plan for a newly emerging timber industry.

The second problem arising from the compartmentalization of TEK is that whole aspects of aboriginal people's reality fall outside the established categories of scientific resource management. A whole array of stories, values, social relations and practices, all of which contribute substance and meaning to aboriginal people's relationship to the environment, must be "distilled out" of TEK before it can be incorporated into the institutional framework of scientific resource management.

THE DISTILLATION OF TEK

As discussed above, scientists and resource managers interested in gathering the TEK of Dall sheep, for instance, are not particularly interested in hunters' opinions or observations regarding ground squirrels or otters, since these seemingly have nothing to do with sheep. Their interests, however, are even more circumscribed than this. It is not simply that they are interested only in sheep; rather, they are only interested in *certain kinds of information* regarding (only) sheep. Resource managers are typically interested in information on the numbers of sheep sighted by First Nation members and the years and locations of these sightings. They are not interested in (nor are they able to make use of) a wide variety of the elements of an aboriginal hunter's world view (which to her or him are directly related to sheep), such as the stories, values, and social relations that transmute those sheep from a set of population figures into sentient members of the social, moral, meaning-filled universe of the hunter and his or her family. These vital aspects of the hunters' rich and complex relationship with sheep are distilled out in any attempt to collect or use TEK in the management process. A specific example should illustrate the nature of this distillation process.

In an attempt to manage a population of Dall sheep in the southwest Yukon, the Kluane First Nation and the Yukon Territorial Government established the multi-stakeholder Ruby Range Sheep Steering Committee to make recommendations to the Yukon Fish and Wildlife Management Board. The committee was explicitly mandated to consider both scientific and traditional knowledge in the formulation of their recommendations. First Nations people, including elders and hunters, spoke to the committee, and some sat on it and participated regularly in its meetings. They were asked to recall the numbers of sheep they had seen over the years as well as when and where these sightings and occurred. A series of maps was prepared from their accounts. As far as the scientists and government officials involved in the process were concerned, this meant that they had fully and fairly considered the traditional knowledge of the community; they proved either unwilling or unable to make use of other types of information offered by the community. In discussions about regulating sheep hunting, for example, a number of Kluane First Nation members expressed concern over the current practice of restricting hunters to shooting only full curl rams (these are fully mature rams eight years old or older). They argued that these animals are especially important to the overall sheep population because of their role as teachers; it is from these mature rams that younger rams learn proper mating and rutting behavior as well as more general survival strategies. Thus, killing too many full curl rams has an impact on the population far in excess of the number of animals actually killed by hunters. One person specifically likened it to killing off all the elders in the community; though the actual number of people killed might not be great, the damage to the community in terms of knowledge and social reproduction would be incalculable.

The scientists and resource managers present at the meetings neither dismissed nor refuted this argument. They simply ignored it. Community members had raised these concerns hoping to switch from a full curl rule to a quota system as a means for limiting the sheep kill in the area. Both methods effectively limit the number of animals that can be killed, but a quota system would spread the kill more evenly over the entire population, rather than focusing it on a particular age group. Yet, even after community members made this argument, biologists continued to assert that there was no need for a quota, because the full curl rule was sufficient to limit the number of sheep taken. There are three possible reasons for the biologists at these meetings to have ignored the community's argument against the full curl rule. First, restricting the hunt to full curl rams (the big "trophy" sheep) is clearly preferable to big game outfitters, several of whom were also present at these meetings. Second, some of them may simply not have taken this "social" information about sheep very seriously. Third, those who did take it seriously (and I believe there were at least a few who did) were unable to make use of it, because it cannot be expressed quantitatively. In addition, it would be difficult to "prove" this information scientifically.

Contrast this to justifications for a ban on hunting ewes (along with the females of nearly all big same species), which is supported without question by biologists and resource managers (and was mentioned by them several times over the course of these meetings). The argument for this ban is that since ewes bear young, they represent not only themselves but all of their unborn potential offspring as well. Thus, killing an ewe has a much greater impact on the future population than the death of a single animal. This argument strongly resembles that made against shooting full curl rams by Kluane First Nation members, except that it is mathematical and biological as opposed to social in nature. In contrast to the case of full curl rams, it is a simple matter to calculate the number of potential offspring that will be affected by the shooting of an ewe. Everything that one needs to know about sheep to make this calculation can be expressed numerically (e.g., average numbers of offspring, number of reproductive years per ewe, and so on).

Community members attending these meetings expressed frustration at the tendency of scientists to treat animals as numbers. As one hunter put it:

> The sheep don't fall out of the sky. They don't create on a piece of paper in somebody's office. They are born, raised out there in the wild. That's where they are born; that's where they die. They don't happen in somebody's office. It doesn't matter how many numbers you put on that piece of paper; out there is still the same.

To this hunter, sheep are not numbers. They are sentient beings with their own social structure, whose lives are quite independent from the mathematical manipulations of biologists. As far as he and many other members of the Kluane First Nation are concerned, disruption of the sheep's social structure can do at least as much damage to their population as the death of hordes of "potential offspring," who exist only as numbers on paper. Understanding how animals think and behave is every bit as important to them as the numbers sought by biologists; yet, scientific resource managers are unable to accommodate this kind of information. Many aboriginal people see the biologists' approach as ultimately disrespectful to the animals themselves. As the same hunter once told me after one of these meetings, "Biologists think animals are stupid. They're not."

In the relatively exceptional cases when TEK studies do elicit non-numerical information, such as descriptions of the behavior of sheep and their predators, they tend to treat these accounts as isolated incidents of pure observation, exhibiting little interest in (or dismissing as useless) the *meaning* of such behavior (i.e., how does the hunter interpret this behavior in the context of certain stories, beliefs, and social relations to which it directly relates?); instead, they confidently assign their own meanings and interpretations to these observations. Even those management-oriented TEK studies which have explicitly tried to gather more than just animal population figures (e.g., the collection of personal histories described in Ferguson and Messier 1997) have usually only done so to "tighten up" these population figures (to get more precise data for time and place). Scientists and resource managers usually do not even acknowledge, much less attempt to make use of, the stories, beliefs, and values which inform the hunters' view of the world and specify the proper relationship between themselves and the animals in question. Since these non-quantitative understandings can not really be "translated into the language of TEK," they tend to "drop out of the database" (Cruikshank 1998: 57–58).

The distillation process, however, is not yet complete even when the lived experiences of elders and hunters have been reduced to a set of numbers and lines on maps. These distilled "artifacts" of TEK research often have a number of different and sometimes incompatible possible *meanings*, some of which can be utilized by resource managers and others which cannot. To illustrate this point, I will return to the case of the Ruby Range Sheep Steering Committee.

As part of its effort to increase cooperation in the management of sheep, the steering committee organized a joint ground-based sheep survey involving biologists and Kluane First Nation members. The group drove together down an arm of Kluane Lake and counted the number of sheep on the surrounding mountains. Using a spotting scope, they also determined the number of yearling lambs among them. The day was pleasant; the group shared a picnic lunch, and the survey was conducted in a spirit of goodwill and cooperation. On the face of it, there seemed to be little room for disagreement about the data. Everyone agreed on the two numbers generated by the study: the overall sheep count and the yearling count. Yet, later it became apparent that biologists and community members had interpreted these numbers very differently. The biologists were interested in generating a figure for lamb survival (expressed as the ratio of yearlings to total population). The total sheep count, however, had been very low (approximately 45). According to the biologists, this represented too small a sample from which to derive a reliable figure for lamb survival; thus, all of the day's data were useless. The community members understood the desire to get a yearling count, but they were more interested in the overall number of sheep. Several of them said that in the past they had counted hundreds or even thousands of sheep in that place at that time of year. For them, the low count was clear proof of the drastic decline in the population, dramatically bearing out the position they had taken in the committee meetings. The biologists dismissed this interpretation, saying that a ground-based survey is useless for determining the total number of sheep in the area, since for all anybody knew, most of the sheep could have been on the other side of the mountains. The community members in turn disagreed with the biologists, saying that in the past there had *always* been many sheep visible from the lake in the early spring and that the mountains had had two sides then too.

Thus, a seemingly straightforward number generated by a joint survey was assigned radically different meanings by scientists and community members. The biologists saw the number in the context of their understandings of statistical theory and population dynamics, while community members saw the same number in relation to their past experiences of that place. Everyone counted the same 45 sheep, but the biologists saw in them a sample size that was too small to be statistically valid, while community members saw them as too few sheep. In the end, the committee made no use of the numbers generated by the joint survey. The scientists' interpretation prevailed because there was no "proof" that the sheep population had ever been as high as the community members maintained; therefore, their interpretation of the number generated by the survey was not seen as reliable enough to be incorporated into the management process.

The imperative of incorporating TEK into the state management system has caused researchers to focus on extracting from communities only that kind of information which can be expressed in a few very specific ways — that is, in forms that can be utilized within the institutional framework of scientific resource management, such as numbers and lines on maps contained in reports, books, and other written documents — and then to interpret it in a manner consistent with the assumptions of scientific wildlife management. The practice of distilling these TEK artifacts out of the interrelated complexity of social relations has some very serious consequences. To begin with, the simple attempt to set down on paper that which all holders of traditional knowledge agree is a "way of life" necessarily distills out the social relations and practices that make it meaningful. In addition, the need to render this information into a form compatible with scientific data tends to remove those qualitative aspects of local experience which might otherwise have survived translation into written form.

Several First Nation people, who have themselves worked on traditional knowledge projects in the Yukon, have expressed to me their frustration that once this knowledge has been gathered, "it just sits there" in a filing cabinet or book. It is not passed on to young people and incorporated back into the daily life of the community, but filed away to be consulted occasionally in the course of land claim negotiations or resource management debates. Indeed, the artifacts produced by these traditional knowledge studies, useful though they may be in certain contexts (specifically, those for which they were produced), actually possess none of the characteristics that such studies themselves use in their definitions of TEK in the first place. That is, rather than being holistic, oral, qualitative, and intuitive, TEK artifacts tend to be categorized, written, quantitative, and analytical. They are closer in form to scientific documents than they are to the accepted (and idealized) descriptions of the type of "knowledge" they are supposed to represent. It should hardly be surprising, then, to find that these artifacts are largely useless to people's everyday lives — even the communities where they were produced.

TEK researchers are to some extent aware of the dangers of distillation and translation inherent in their work, but they usually treat these problems as technical difficulties to be overcome and ignore their political dimensions. The crucial question concerning the distillation of TEK should be: 'who is doing the distilling?' The answer to this question is not always obvious, because distillation is not usually the result of a conscious process. Instead, the very conceptualization of TEK as something to be gathered and incorporated into the management process virtually assures this distillation. All those who use the term TEK, for example, are (probably without even realizing it) participating in the process of distilling out "non-traditional" in favor of "traditional" knowledge; "non-ecological" in favor of "ecological" knowledge; and, most significantly of all, "non-knowledge" in favor of "knowledge." But who decides what qualifies as "traditional," or "ecological," or "knowledge"?

TEK artifacts are produced for the explicit purpose of being incorporated into existing institutions of scientific resource management. As a result, TEK researchers — native and non-native alike — have no choice but to conform to the meanings assigned to terms like "knowledge" and "traditional" by scientists and resource managers when designing and conducting TEK research as well as analyzing and expressing their results. If they do not, the TEK artifacts they produce will be useless to resource managers and therefore will not be incorporated into the management process. Thus, the meanings and categories used by scientists and resource managers end up shaping the process of distillation, which is essence sorts the life experiences of elders and hunters into the "relevant" and the "irrelevant," into useful "knowledge" and useless "non-knowledge." In effect, TEK researchers are — by the questions they ask, the "data" they record, and the TEK artifacts they produce — deciding *for* elders and hunters which of their experiences are relevant to the management of wildlife (though TEK researchers are themselves constrained by the needs and assumptions of the state management system). Thus, regardless of who exactly is conducting a specific TEK research project, they must — by the every nature of the project they are engaged in — distill out meaning and content so that it is acceptable and useful to scientists and managers. They irony is that the very people who know the *least* about "traditional knowledge" are the ones who set the standards of relevance by which it is distilled.

Distillation is also a product of the social context of TEK research and co-management processes. TEK research is often conducted through formal interviews or TEK workshops. Co-management decisions (or, as is usually the case, recommendations) are made at conferences and resource board meetings. Though these meetings and workshops are often held in local communities, they are nevertheless conducted in offices and conference rooms identical to those used by federal and territorial government officials. Thus, bureaucratic resource managers never find themselves in truly unfamiliar social contexts. This is true of scientists as well, since their participation in conferences and government meetings has long been an integral part of the process of doing science (see, e.g., Traweek 1988). This is certainly true for scientists involved in resource management in the Canadian North, a majority of whom either work directly for federal territorial governments or derive a large part of their income from government contracts. They attend conferences and other bureaucratic forums of resource management as a regular part of the work they do *as scientists*; and their work is specifically tailored to these kinds of use. Thus, though co-management may mean that scientists and resource managers have to travel out to the communities more often and must make use of TEK artifacts alongside those of science, they never have to leave the comfortable setting of the conference room to engage in the practice of resource management.

The situation is very different for many First Nation people called on to participate in TEK studies or co-management meetings. Elders and hunters must take time out from their lives to attend the necessary interviews, workshops, or meetings. They sit, often ill at ease, in the artificial and unfamiliar surroundings of conference rooms. Often they must endure one or more lectures by biologists on the "state of the resource" which are so full of jargon and "big words" that they understand very little of it. They are then expected to speak about the "resource" in question, but only about that particular resource and only about certain aspects of it (numbers, places, dates). When they feel the need to disregard these seemingly arbitrary limitations on the subject matter and choose to talk more broadly about matters they feel are important and relevant, they are allowed to speak (though they are sometimes subjected to gestures of impatience and disrespect, such as eye-rolling, audible sighs, and/or under-the-breath comments), but the conversation is invariably brought back "on topic," often after a brief but awkward silence, by a scientist or resource manager. After putting up with all of that, elders and hunters I have spoken with say over and over again that they see very little that they consider to be of practical value to them emerge from these processes. Small wonder that several elders and hunters have told me quite plainly that they find these affairs extremely frustrating, because it seems that government officials do not take them very seriously. I know several who view all such meetings as a waste of time and simply do not attend them anymore, despite their extensive experience on the land.

In the conference rooms, with their flip charts and overhead projectors, scientists and managers are in their element. They set the agenda, frame the discussion, ask the questions. First Nations elders and hunters, feeling out of place and a bit bewildered, follow along and answer the scientists' questions, filling the TEK "blanks" in their management scheme. Any attempt that an elder may make to reframe the discussion is usually viewed by scientists as irrelevant side-tracking. Elders and hunters are quite aware of the contextual bias inherent in these events. One hunter, who does not attend co-management meetings anymore, told me that this was because government people treat him and his knowledge as "old-fashioned" and useless. He said that they should hold one of these meetings out on his trapline during the winter. He would tell them they could discuss management after they got a fire going, built a brush camp, and got dinner ready. Then they might realize that he and other elders know a little something.

POWER AND THE "INTEGRATION" OF KNOWLEDGE SYSTEMS

This paper has argued that the project of incorporating TEK into the process of resource management leads inevitably to its compartmentalization and distillation. TEK researchers are not unaware that they are constrained in their efforts to record and express TEK, but they tend to see this as a necessary part of the effort to integrate TEK and science. An examination of the political dimensions of incorporating TEK artifacts into the state management system, however, demands a closer look at the notion of "knowledge integration."

As already argued, the very idea of such integration implicitly assumes that knowledge is an intellectual product which can be isolated from its social context. While anthropologists and others have long sought to demonstrate the sociocultural dimensions of so-called traditional knowledge systems throughout the world, only more recently have they begun to focus on the social dimensions of scientific knowledge production (e.g., Callon 1986; Longino 1990; Martin 1991; Todes 1989; Traweek 1988; Woolgar 1988). These studies indicate that all knowledge — *including* science — is embedded in larger social processes which give it meaning. Indeed, some (Feyerabend 1970 [sic]; Latour 1987, 1988) have contested even the assumption that science is an epistemologically distinct system of knowledge, preferring instead to see the legitimization of scientific artifacts (theories, data, and instruments) as a result of active social manipulation, rather than some elite epistemological status they happen to possess. If this is the case, what does it really mean to talk of "integrating" traditional knowledge and scientific knowledge?

Bruno Latour (1987) has described how the production of scientific knowledge is part of an overall social process that simultaneously produces not only the artifacts of science but *their utility as well*. He argues that the artifacts of science do not possess the seemingly magical universal and cross-cultural utility that people ascribe to them. Instead, they only "work" under certain very specific conditions that exist in the laboratories where they were produced. These artifacts do not gain acceptance and utility in the outside world because they "happen to work," but only through an intense process of negotiation and struggle to create those specific conditions outside the laboratory. This includes the creation of the necessary physical, social, and conceptual infrastructure without which the artifacts are useless. He argues, for example, that airplanes may work in principle, but without the enormous physical infrastructure that makes them work in practice (from runway systems and flight schools to the industries that produce the planes themselves and the fuel to fly them — not to mention the industries that make the machines for the petroleum and aerospace industries, and so on), they cannot really be said to "work" at all. Similarly, Newtonian mechanics might work everywhere in principle, but without the establishment and maintenance of an elaborate (and expensive) system of standardized measurements of length, weight, time, temperature, etc. (all of which are cultural constructions) and their prior application to the outside world, mechanics does not work in practice. For Latour not only the meaning but the very utility of a scientific theory or instrument is entirely dependent on the extension of the social, physical, and conceptual networks that gave rise to them.

Latour sees the extension of these networks as intimately connected to power. Scientists extend them primarily by representing local realities *in forms compatible with* science. In practice, this means expressing them in a written form which is amenable to mathematical manipulation. Thus, in another of his examples, the rich social and physical complexities of place are expressed as a set of numbers (latitude and longitude). The point of doing this is to render that place into a mathematical form that can be brought back to a "center of calculation" for collection and manipulation. As these centers accumulate more and more such sets of numbers from countless other places, scientists there can make new kinds of comparisons between realms that earlier may have seemed entirely unrelated (e.g., Hong Kong and Whitehorse, by virtue of their latitude and longitude, can now be directly and mathematically compared). This gives those in the center a new kind of power over all of the places to which these networks have been extended (i.e., all the places that have been assigned a latitude and longitude). Power accrues in these centers of calculation, however, not merely through the collection of information; even more important is their manipulation and interpretation of these abstractions. As scientists at the center extend their networks ever farther, they can begin to manipulate the abstractions brought back to them to form higher and higher order abstractions, such as maps, graphs, and theories. In the process they make choices about what kinds of information and meaning to preserve and produce (e.g., in generating a map from collected coordinates, cartographers must decide what kinds of information to preserve: angles or surface shapes). As a result, cartographers in the center gain enormous power when, for example, navigators all over the world begin to use their maps. This power is derived not from any inherent "truth" in the maps they produce, but from the fact that navigators have been trained to use and rely on these maps — not to mention the particular conceptions of space and time upon which the cartographers have based them.

Powerful as the abstractions produced by scientists can be, their purpose is not — nor has it ever been — to *represent* local knowledge. Indeed, local knowledge of place, for example, is far too rich and varied to be expressed by a set of numbers. Instead, the sole purpose of distilling these abstract forms from the complexities of local reality is to extend social/conceptual networks from the centers of calculation to the outside world. Until this has been accomplished, the artifacts of science are useless there. Four hundred years ago, for example, Athapaskan hunters in the Yukon, though they possessed profoundly detailed knowledge of the place in which they lived, would have regarded their latitude and longitude as both useless and meaningless. Not surprisingly, cartographers in London had no power over their lives. Once people far from the centers of calculation accept the concepts of latitude and longitude and begin using maps generated by cartographers thousands of miles away, however, they — like navigators — must implicitly accept and base their actions upon the cartographers' priorities and assumptions about the world. The illusion of universality that accompanies this extension of scientific networks makes local knowledge, which is rooted in its own social networks, seem extremely limited and unreliable by comparison. Though these seemingly universal abstractions do not negate local knowledge, they do greatly increase the power of scientists vis-à-vis local people.

Latour's argument puts TEK research and the production, compartmentalization, and distillation of TEK artifacts in a new light. It indicates that we might more usefully view the integration of TEK and science as a process that is extending the social and conceptual networks of scientific resource management into local communities rather than as part of an attempt to meld two distinct epistemological systems (which, from his point of view, do not even exist as such). TEK research is, in Latour's terms, extending the networks of scientific resource management into the "outside world" of First Nation communities by rendering the life experiences of native elders and hunters (through the processes of compartmentalization and distillation) into forms which can be used and interpreted far from these communities, in laboratories and centers of calculation (in this case, for example, the offices of the Department of Renewable Resources in Whitehorse). Rather than empowering local communities, as many people hope, this process actually concentrates power in hope, this process actually concentrates power in the centers of calculation at the expense of local people.

Indeed, viewed in these terms, there can be little doubt that TEK research and co-management have effectively extended the networks of scientific resource management into local communities. As long as TEK researchers continue to "collect" or "document" TEK as an intellectual product to be integrated with science, they will be helping to extend the networks of scientific resource management into local communities. This cannot help but concentrate power in the hands of scientists and resource managers in administrative centers like Whitehorse. After all, who uses these categorized and distilled TEK studies? As discussed above, community members who spend time out on the land have no use for the kinds of artifacts produced by standard TEK studies. They do not take those maps and reports out into the bush with them, and sometimes they even express their annoyance at continually being asked to contribute to such studies, which, as often as not, they view as pointless. Yet, more than once at conference and workshops on co-management or TEK, I have heard well-meaning bureaucrats and scientists plead with First Nations people to "tell us what traditional knowledge is, so we can use it." The fact that such pleas can be made again and again without anyone so mush as raising an eyebrow indicates the degree to which people have come to accept the extension of scientific resource management networks into the communities. By contrast, if a First Nation elder were to stand up at one of these meetings and ask a biologist to teach him/her then and there the principles of conservation biology "so we can use it," these same well-meaning officials would probably chuckle at the absurdity of the request and patiently explain to the elder how many years of training are required before one can be expected to master and use that kind of knowledge.

What makes people accept the notion that scientists and bureaucrats are in any way qualified to "use" traditional knowledge after one or even a dozen workshops on the subject? It is because they are expected to (and do in fact) use the numbers, lines on maps, and other artifacts generated by standard TEK research. These they *are* undoubtedly qualified to use, since they have been trained to read and manipulate exactly this kind of information. These numbers and maps are none other than the abstract forms affixed to local realities for the precise purpose of being manipulated by scientists and managers in the center. Just as is the case with latitude and longitude, however, TEK artifacts are emphatically *not* substitutes for local place-dependent knowledge and practice.

It is not only resource managers in the center, however, who use the artifacts of TEK. A growing segment of First Nation populations in the communities are making use of these artifacts. This segment is composed primarily, though not exclusively, of members of the younger generation who are engaged in negotiating land claims, setting up systems of self-government, and participating in bureaucratic co-management processes. Due to the nature of these activities, these community members have necessarily spent large periods of their lives in local First Nation government offices. They have earned degrees in law or resource management, and/or have taken courses in mediation and negotiation skills. Unlike most elders in their communities, they feel comfortable talking with biologists and government officials in the context of negotiations and co-management meetings. Because of the huge time commitments they have made, however, first to receive their formal education and then to work on land claims and co-management, they have spent a great deal less time out on the land then many of their elders (and even some of their peers). As a result, many of them, too, have to consult with their elders for the "traditional knowledge" perspective. While people in the communities are aware of the increasing bureaucratization of a segment of their own communities, see it as a problem, and are actively seeking ways to deal with it, the need to participate in land claims and co-management continue to tie many people to their desks at least eight hours a day. Thus, while many elders in the communities quite clearly reject the networks and assumptions of scientific resource management, the bureaucratization of the younger generation is testimony to the extension of these networks into the communities and into the bodies and minds of local people themselves.

As argued above, the extension of scientific resource management networks in this way does *not* nullify or replace local knowledge of place; it does, however, increase the power of scientists and resource managers vis-à-vis local hunters and elders. If we are serious about utilizing the life experiences of native elders and hunters (and not just the abstract representations of them embodied in TEK reports) to improve resource management practices and empower local aboriginal communities, we must acknowledge this aspect of the current attempt to "integrate" TEK and science and develop a new approach to the issue. Improved management and local empowerment cannot be achieved through any attempt to "include" local elders and hunters into the existing state-management system simply through the production and use of TEK artifacts. Instead, it will require that local beliefs, values, and practices themselves — not merely the abstract forms affixed to them — be accepted as a valid basis for action. This will require changes to current practices of resource management and environmental assessment to allow these people to play a meaningful role in these processes as *decision-makers*. In short, "traditional knowledge" cannot truly be "incorporated" into the management process until native elders and hunters have achieved full decision-making authority in that realm.

CO-MANAGEMENT IN THE YUKON AND PROSPECTS FOR THE FUTURE

This paper has argued that the project of "integrating" TEK with science and incorporating it into existing bureaucratic management structures will result neither in substantially improved management practices, nor in local aboriginal empowerment. Instead, what is needed is a radical rethinking of the basic assumptions, values, and practices underlying contemporary processes of resource management and environmental impact assessment. Before turning to a discussion of prospects for this kind of change in the case of the Yukon Territory, a cautionary comment on use of the term "management" (and, by extension, "co-management").

Much has been written about systems of indigenous, aboriginal, or self-management as opposed to state-management systems (Feit 1988; Usher 1986; Williams and Hunn 1982). While the point of this distinction is well taken, it is as dangerous a distinction to make as the one between "traditional" and "scientific" knowledge. The term "management" is every bit as riddled with assumptions and contested meaning as is "knowledge." Indeed, the two terms are inextricably linked in Western thought. The term "management" in relation to resources refers to the attempt by "managers" to use a particular resource rationally, based on their knowledge of that resource. Use of the term "management," therefore, implies not only the existence of "knowledge" as separate from practices, values, and social relations, but also of a formal institutionalized system of management complete with specialized managers. This is why many, scientists and resource managers especially, have been so reluctant to admit the existence of such a thing as indigenous management systems in the first place (preferring to argue that human impact was low in precontact times because of low population densities, or citing Pleistocene extinctions as evidence for the absence of such system[4]). The focus on systems of management (whether state, indigenous, or cooperative in nature) facilitates the extension of scientific resource management institutions into the communities. Why else label a set of practices, values, and social relations "indigenous resource management" if not to categorize and distill them so as to give scientific resource management something with which to interface?

In many jurisdictions throughout the North, governments and First Nations are setting up co-management regimes as the primary means for including traditional knowledge in resource management and environmental assessment processes. In some cases, co-management bodies are ad hoc responses to specific management problems, but many of them are being established through the land claims process. In the Yukon, both of these types of co-management presently exist, though in theory the co-management boards established by Yukon First Nation Final Agreements will replace all the ad hoc boards and committees currently in place as soon as all 14 of these agreements are signed and ratified. The Yukon Umbrella Final Agreement (UFA) provides for the creation of a whole array of co-management boards and councils which are to come into effect with the signing of the Final Agreements.

In the Yukon case, "co-management" essentially means that First Nation people will hold half of the seats on these boards. In addition, there are several general statements in the UFA and existing Final Agreements which call for the use of traditional knowledge and the empowerment of aboriginal people. Among the stated objectives of chapter 16 — Fish and Wildlife of the UFA, for example, are the following:

> To integrate the relevant knowledge and experience both of Yukon Indian People and of the scientific communities in order to achieve conservation,

and

> To enhance and promote the full participation of Yukon Indian People in Renewable Resource Management
> (Council for Yukon Indians 1993: 153).

This chapter then establishes 14 Renewable Resource Councils and the Yukon Fish and Wildlife Management Board. It goes on to describe their roles, powers, and responsibilities in the management of wildlife on a First Nation Traditional Territory- and a Yukon-wide basis, respectively. Despite the stated objectives at the beginning of the chapter, however, nowhere does it specifically require the boards to take traditional knowledge into account in formulating their recommendations; presumably the 50% First Nation representation was thought to be sufficient to ensure this. Significantly, all of the co-management bodies established under the UFA have purely advisory roles. Though the Fish and Wildlife Management Board, for example, is "established as the primary instrument of Fish and Wildlife Management in the Yukon" (Council for Yukon Indians 1993: 166), it in fact only has the power to make recommendations to the Yukon Minister of Renewable Resources. The minister is not obligated to follow these recommendations, but only to respond to them in writing within a specified period of time.

It remains to be seen how these and other co-management boards established under the UFA work in practice, but because of the many bureaucratic layers separating native elders and hunters from decision-making authority, it seems unlikely that the creation of these boards will lead to a transformation of the management process or to empowerment of local First Nations people as many hope it will. Reliance on distilled TEK research and the bureaucratization of First Nation people extend the networks of scientific resource management into the communities and work against the direct participation of hunters and elders in the management process.

In addition, members of co-management boards know that they must justify their recommendations to the minister and his or her scientific/bureaucratic advisors in the Department of Renewable Resources or else their recommendations will not be acted upon. In practice, this means that they must base their decisions on data which can be expressed in terms compatible with scientific resource management (which now includes the artifacts of TEK). This creates an automatic bias which works against these co-management boards submitting recommendations that are not primarily based on scientific data. It is not likely, for instance, that the Fish and Wildlife Board would recommend a management action based solely or even primarily on the advice of First Nation elders and hunters, even if they happened to have seats on the board. Finally, any such recommendation which did manage to survive the "self-censorship" of the board would be subject to review by the minister and the bureaucrats in the Department of Renewable Resources, who are unlikely to be convinced that any action is justified without scientific data to back it up. As long as First Nation people are compelled to subject their own way of life to external standards of validity established and imposed by scientists and resource managers, the state management system will remain essentially unaltered.

What is the solution then? Is it possible to develop a management process that makes full unbiased use of the way of life that is traditional knowledge? Such a process can only be achieved if elders and hunters are relieved of the burden of having to express themselves in ways that are foreign to them to justify their views to scientists and bureaucrats. This means essentially the devolution of control over local land and resources to aboriginal communities themselves, and it would have to include not only control over wildlife, but over all forms of development as well. As long as ultimate decision-making power over the land is held in distant administrative centers, local ways of life will continue to be undervalued or ignored in favor of the illusion of scientific universality.

This is not to say that there is no value at all in the practises of scientific resource management. Community-based aboriginal people themselves are among the first to admit the usefulness of some of the techniques and perspectives of relevant scientific disciplines, especially in light of the North's increasing population, heterogeneity, and its integration into global systems. Returning decision-making power over the land to local communities, however, would provide a counter-weight to the power-centralizing tendencies of scientific resource management. This would not preclude scientists from engaging in their own set of socially useful practices, but they would be doing so at the request and direction of local communities. Thus, scientists would no longer define and drive the process of resource management, but would act as a resource, providing communities — upon request — with a perspective on the environment that, by virtue of its greater scope for large-scale comparison, would help local people to deal with larger regional or global issues that cannot be well understood from a purely local perspective.

It seems unlikely that territorial and federal governments will be devolving this kind of control to local communities any time in the near future (though, ironically, the present climate of budget cutting and fiscal restraint, if it continues indefinitely, may provide just the incentive necessary to do so). In the meantime, however, the present role of "traditional knowledge" in the management process needs to be carefully re-thought. As Julie Cruikshank (1981: 86) put it, "the focus should not be on 'getting information before it is too late' but on developing mechanisms for its continued transmission...." The important work is to ensure that there continue to be those in communities who engage in the way of life to which the term traditional knowledge refers. This project may include some documentation of that lifestyle, but this must be done with great care to avoid undermining that way of life and further concentrating power in distant administrative centers. A rule of thumb for this kind of local research might be to ask the question, "who is going to actually use, interpret and/or manipulate it?" If the answer is not "local community members," then the research will probably do more harm than good.

CONCLUSION

The past 15 years have witnessed an explosion in the amount of research devoted to "traditional ecological knowledge" throughout the Arctic and the Subarctic. The self-proclaimed goal of much of this research has been to collect and document TEK and to integrate it with scientific knowledge for use in resource management, environmental impact assessment, and land claim negotiations. I have argued that the simple act of framing the problem as one of "integration" automatically imposes a culturally specific set of ideas about "knowledge" on the life experiences of aboriginal people. The goal of knowledge-integration forces TEK researchers to compartmentalize and distill aboriginal people's beliefs, values, and experiences according to external criteria of relevance, seriously distorting them in the process. The project of knowledge-integration also takes for granted existing power relations between aboriginal people and the state by assuming that traditional knowledge is simply a new form of "data" to be incorporated into already existing management bureaucracies and acted upon by scientists and resource managers. "Knowledge," however, (whether scientific or traditional) does not exist in some pure form, independent of power relations; rather, it is constituted by those relations and draws its validity from them. TEK researchers, insofar as they focus exclusively on the methodological difficulties of integrating distinct knowledge systems, help to obscure the power relations that shape the production and use of the knowledge they study. And, since it is scientists and resource managers, rather than aboriginal hunters and trappers, who will be using the new "integrated" knowledge, the project of integration actually serves to concentrate power in administrative centers, rather than in aboriginal communities.

NOTES

1. For those unfamiliar with the Canadian context, "First Nation" is the accepted term for referring to aboriginal people and their governments. It was adopted in acknowledgement of aboriginal people's founding status in the Canadian State, along with the "immigrant" English and French nations. The term has now largely replaced "band," an administrative term long used by the Department of Indian Affairs.
2. In other parts of the world, "Indigenous Knowledge" (IK), rather than TEK, has become the buzzword for engaging in these types of debates. The term "indigenous," however, is every bit as problematic as that of "tradition" (Cruikshank 1998: 48–49). In any case, the arguments in this paper apply equally well to a discussion of IK as to TEK.
3. Notable exceptions in the Yukon include the work of Lionel Jackson and Ruth Gotthardt (Jackson and Gotthardt 1990) on volcanic and earthquake activity. See also Julie Cruikshank (1981) for some more examples of how glaciologists and geologists have used (or might use) local knowledge of place to inform their work. In addition, because of the widespread historical use of fire as a management tool by aboriginal people all over the world, TEK on forest fires in one field of traditional knowledge related to forestry that is generally accepted as valid.
4. This latter argument is quite unconvincing given the role of scientific managers and the state in such management disasters as, e.g., the collapse of the eastern cod fishery, which illustrate clearly that the failure of animal stocks does not in itself indicate the absence of a management system.

REFERENCES

ALLEN, JAMES. 1994. *Traditional Knowledge Report: The Aishihik Recovery Area*. Report produced for Champagne and Aishihik First Nation and the Yukon Territorial Government.
BERGER, THOMAS. 1997. *Northern Frontier, Northern Homeland*. Ministry of Supply and Services Canada, Ottawa.
BRODY, HUGH. 1982. *Maps and Dreams*. Pantheon, New York.
BULMER, RALPH. 1967. Why Is the Cassowary Not a Bird? A Problem of Zoological Taxonomy among the Karam of the New Guinea Highlands. *Man* 2(1): 5–25.
CALLON, MICHEL. 1986. Some Elements of a Sociology of Translation: Domestication of the Scallops and the Fishermen of St. Brieuc Bay. In: *Power, Action and Belief*, edited by J. Law, pp. 196–233. Routledge and Kegan Paul, London.
COUNCIL FOR YUKON INDIANS. 1993. *Umbrella Final Agreement*. Ministry of Supply and Services Canada, Ottawa.
CRUIKSHANK, JULIE. 1981. Legend and Landscape: Convergence of Oral and Scientific Traditions in the Yukon Territory. *Arctic Anthropology* 18(2): 67–93.
———. 1990. *Life Lived Like a Story: Life Stories of Three Yukon Native Elders*. University of Nebraska Press, Lincoln.
———. 1998. *The Social Life of Stories: Narrative and Knowledge in the Yukon Territory*. University of Nebraska Press, Lincoln.
EVANS-PRITCHARD, E.E. 1937. *Witchcraft, Oracles and Magic among the Azande*. Clarendon Press, Oxford.
FEIT, HARVEY. 1988. Self-Management and State-Management: Forms of Knowing and Managing Northern Wildlife. In: *Traditional Knowledge and Renewable Resource Management in Northern Regions*, edited by Milton Freeman and Ludwig Carbyn, pp. 72–91. Boreal Institute for Northern Studies, Edmonton.
FERGUSON, M., and FRANCOIS MESSIER. 1997. Collection and Analysis of Traditional Ecological Knowledge about a Population of Arctic Tundra Caribou. *Arctic* 50(1): 17–28.
FOUCAULT, MICHEL. 1980. *Power/Knowledge: Selected Interviews and Other Writings 1972–1977*. Harvester Press, Brighton.
———. 1978. *The History of Sexuality. Volume I: An Introduction*. Vintage, New York.

FREEMAN, MILTON (editor). 1976. *Inuit Land Use and Occupancy Project* (three volumes). Ministry of Supply and Services Canada, Ottawa.
FREEMAN, MILTON, and LUDWIG CARBYN (editors). 1988. *Traditional Knowledge and Renewable Resource Management in Northern Regions.* Boreal Institute for Northern Studies, Edmonton.
GLADWIN, THOMAS. 1970. *East is a Big Bird: Navigation and Logic on Puluwat Atoll.* Harvard University Press, Cambridge.
HUNTINGTON, HENRY. 1995. Traditional Ecological Knowledge of Beluga Whales. *World Wildlife Fund Bulletin* 4: 20.
INGLIS, J.T. (editor). 1993. *Traditional Ecological Knowledge: Concepts and Cases.* International Program on Traditional Ecological Knowledge and International Development Research Center, Ottawa.
JACKSON, LIONEL, and RUTH GOTTHARDT. 1990. Recent Eruptions of Volcano Mountain and Native Oral Traditions. Paper presented at the 23rd Annual Meeting of the Canadian Archaeological Association, Whitehorse.
JOHANNES, ROBERT. 1989. *Traditional Ecological Knowledge: A Collection of Essays.* IUCN, World Conservation Union, Glund, Switzerland.
JOHNSON, MARTHA (editor). 1992. *Lore: Capturing Traditional Environmental Knowledge.* Dene Cultural Institute, Yellowknife.
KARI, PRISCILLA RUSSELL. 1995. *Tanaina Plant Lore: Denaíina Kíetíuna.* Alaska Native Language Center, Fairbanks.
KUHN, RICHARD, and FRANK DUERDEN. 1996. A Review of Traditional Environmental Knowledge: An Interdisciplinary Canadian Perspective. *Culture* 16(1): 71–84.
LATOUR, BRUNO. 1987. *Science in Action.* Harvard University Press, Cambridge.
———. 1988. *The Pasteurization of France.* Harvard University Press, Cambridge.
LONGINO, HELEN. 1990. *Science as Social Knowledge: Values and Objectivity in Scientific Inquiry.* Princeton University Press, Princeton.
LUKÁCS, GYÖRGY. 1971. *History and Class Consciousness.* Translated by Rodney Livingstone. The MIT Press, Cambridge.
MARCUSE, HERBERT. 1964. *One-Dimensional Man.* Beacon Press, Boston.
MARTIN, EMILY. 1991. The Egg and the Sperm: How Science Has Constructed a Romance Based on Stereotypical Male-Female Roles. *Signs* 16(3): 485–501.
McCLELLAN, CATHERINE. 1975. *My Old People Say: An Ethnographic Survey of the Southern Yukon Territory.* National Museum, Ottawa.
McCLELLAN, CATHERINE, et al. 1987. *Part of the Land, Part of the Water: A History of the Yukon Indians.* Douglas and McIntyre, Toronto.
MERCHANT, CAROLYN. 1980. *The Death of Nature: Women, Ecology and the Scientific Revolution.* Harper and Row, San Francisco.
MORROW, PHYLLIS, and CHASE HENSEL. 1992. Hidden Dissensions: Minority-Majority Relationships and the Use of Contested Terminology. *Arctic Anthropology* 29(1): 38–53.
NAKASHIMA, DOUGLAS. 1990. *Application of Native Knowledge in EIA: Inuit, Eiders and Hudson Bay Oil.* Canadian Arctic Resources Committee, Hull.
NELSON, RICHARD. 1983. *Make Prayers to the Raven: A Koyukon View of the Northern Forest.* University of Chicago Press, Chicago.
Northern Perspectives. 1992. Special Issue: Indigenous Knowledge. 20(1).
RABINBACH, ANSON. 1990. *The Human Motor: Energy, Fatigue, and the Origins of Modernity.* Basic Books, New York.
ROBERTS, KAREN. 1996. *Circumpolar Aboriginal People and Co-Management Practice: Current Issues in Co-Management and Environmental Assessment.* Proceedings of the Workshop on Circumpolar People and Co-Management Practice, Nov. 20–24, 1995 in Inuvik, NWT. Arctic Institute of North America, University of Calgary, Calgary.
SAID, EDWARD. 1978. *Orientalism.* Pantheon, New York.
TANNER, ADRIAN. 1979. *Bringing Home Animals: Religious Ideology and Mode of Production of the Mistassini Cree Hunters.* C. Hurst, London.
TODES, DANIEL. 1989. *Darwin without Malthus: The Struggle for Existence in Russian Evolutionary Thought.* Oxford University Press, New York.
TRAWEEK, SHARON. 1988. *Beamtimes and Lifetimes: The World of High Energy Physics.* Harvard University Press, Cambridge.
USHER, PETER. 1986. *The Devolution of Wildlife Management and the Prospects for Wildlife Conversation in the Northwest Territories.* CARC Policy Paper 3. Canadian Arctic Resources Committee, Ottawa.

WILLIAMS, N.M., and E.S. HUNN (editors). 1982. *Resource Managers: North American and Australian Hunter-Gatherers.* Westview Press, Boulder.
WOOLGAR, STEVE. 1988. *Science the Very Idea.* Travistock Publications, New York.
WORSTER, DONALD. 1977. *Nature's Economy: The Roots of Ecology.* Cambridge University Press, Cambridge.

(f) Knowing Home: Nisga'a Traditional Knowledge and Wisdom Improve Environmental Decision Making[†]

John Corsiglia and Gloria Snively

The knowledge and wisdom of ancient and contemporary indigenous peoples, especially their traditional ecological knowledge of specific homeplaces, represents a treasure trove of important but historically neglected environmental knowledge and wisdom. As problems associated with resource depletion, burgeoning human populations and ecological disasters worsen, increasing numbers of scientists, academics and environmental managers are turning to traditional ecological knowledge for reliable, time-proven information regarding ecological processes and sustainability practices.[1] The new literature on traditional ecological knowledge can provide important information and innovative strategies for implementing successful conservation and resource management programmes.

Traditional ecological knowledge combines current observation with knowledge and experience that has been acquired over thousands of years of direct human contact with specific environments. Although the term traditional ecological knowledge came into widespread use in the 1980s, the practice is timeless and predates the written record. A leading Canadian researcher in this field, Fikret Berkes, defines traditional ecological knowledge as:

> a cumulative body of knowledge and beliefs, handed down through generations by cultural transmission, about the relationship of living beings (including humans) with one another and with their environment. Further, [traditional ecological knowledge] is an attribute of societies; by and large, these are non-industrial or less technologically advanced societies, many of them indigenous or tribal.[2]

Traditional ecological knowledge interprets how the world works from the cultural perspectives unique to particular indigenous peoples. As such, it differs in a number of important ways from conventional Western science. Unlike conventional science, which generally presents itself as a culturally neutral and value-free system of universal knowledge, traditional ecological knowledge invariably focuses on community priorities within the local context. It is both remembered sensory information built upon repeated observation, and formal understandings that are usually trans-

---

[†] Reproduced from *Alternatives Journal: Environmental thought, policy and action*, 23(3) (1997): 22–27. Annual subscriptions $25.00 (plus GST) from Alternatives Journal, Faculty of Environmental Studies, University of Waterloo, Waterloo, Ontario N2L 3G1.

mitted orally in story form with abstract principles and important information encapsulated in metaphor.[3] The conceptual roots of traditional ecological knowledge relate more to the timeless mainstream of human experience than to the recent traditions of Western science, which grew up in the service of empire building and placed great emphasis on permanent records, mathematics, navigational systems and broad portable understandings.

Traditional ecological knowledge is contextual. The stories and testimonies of indigenous peoples are usually related to the context of the home place. Nisga'a elders, for example, generally prefer to confine their inquiry to issues that affect their own lands and communities and leave it to other groups to interpret their own issues and traditions. Thus, intermingled with the identification and description of the structure of a particular plant and its fruit may be the uses of the plant within the context of a particular family or community. Traditional ecological knowledge may include information relating to the use of the plant as a food source, its ceremonial uses, its complex preparation process, its use in purification rituals, and so on.[4] This contextual approach is in marked contrast with that typically used by Western scientists, for whom "environmental" and "social" influences are generally considered extraneous.

Aboriginal experimentation and innovation may take place at a more measured pace than in Western science. In her observations of the Athapaskan and Tlingit languages in the Yukon and Northwest Territories, anthropologist Julie Cruikshank notes:

> Observations are made over a lifetime. Hunting peoples carefully study animal and plant life cycles, topography, seasonal changes and mineral resources. Elders speaking about landscape, climate and ecological changes are usually basing their observations on a lifetime of experience. In contrast, because much scientific research in the North is university-based, it is organized around short summer field seasons. The long-term observations included in oral accounts provide important perspectives on the questions scientists are studying.[5]

Hasty conclusions and speedy reactions to circumstances are not generally valued in traditional science. Among the Nisga'a of northern British Columbia, for example, one rarely responds to a request for information or opinion quickly — it is more respectful to consider such a request for some time before making a response. Mistakes cannot be tolerated where footsteps take one near swift water rushing beneath river ice. Where a community is resident and stable, solutions to problems can be carefully preserved in oral form; and refined and re-applied over time.

Unlike Western science, which can reduce nature to its value-free mechanical properties, traditional knowledge usually begins with respect for the spiritual essence that infuses creation — all life-forms must be respected as essentially conscious, intrinsically valuable and interdependent.[6] In practical terms, traditional wisdom extends the caring relationships associated with family life to communities and even to the environment. We are all relations: it is wrong to exploit or waste other life forms, or to take more than one's share. Our children's deep interest in animals, plants, water, and earth should be trusted and encouraged. All creatures can be our teachers and although humans may readily affect other life forms, we need not see ourselves as superior.[7] One Nisga'a elder, for example, considered that wolves and bears are superior life forms because they "do not need to talk to communicate."[8]

ACCEPTING TRADITIONAL KNOWLEDGE

On the one hand, the unique features of traditional ecological knowledge described above may suggest its potential to complement and enrich Western science. On the other hand, the differences between traditional and conventional approaches to knowledge may be taken as evidence that traditional ecological knowledge cannot be classified as "real science".

Critics may make the mistake of dismissing traditional knowledge as inferior because of its origins in oral culture. Even though written information appears to have been required for the operation of vast empires, oral information systems have always been associated with the organization and management of countless small and stable human communities. As Julie Cruikshank writes:

> Oral tradition does not provide us with a series of data which stand by themselves. It is more like a prism which becomes richer as our ability improves to view it from a variety of angles. The question is not whether a particular tradition reflects the way a particular individual views the world, but whether it broadens the worldview of the listener.[9]

Western scientists and resource managers seem to be particularly vexed by the spiritual content of traditional ecological knowledge, which they consider superstitious and fatalistic. But, as Johnson and Ruttan point out, such critics fail to recognize that:

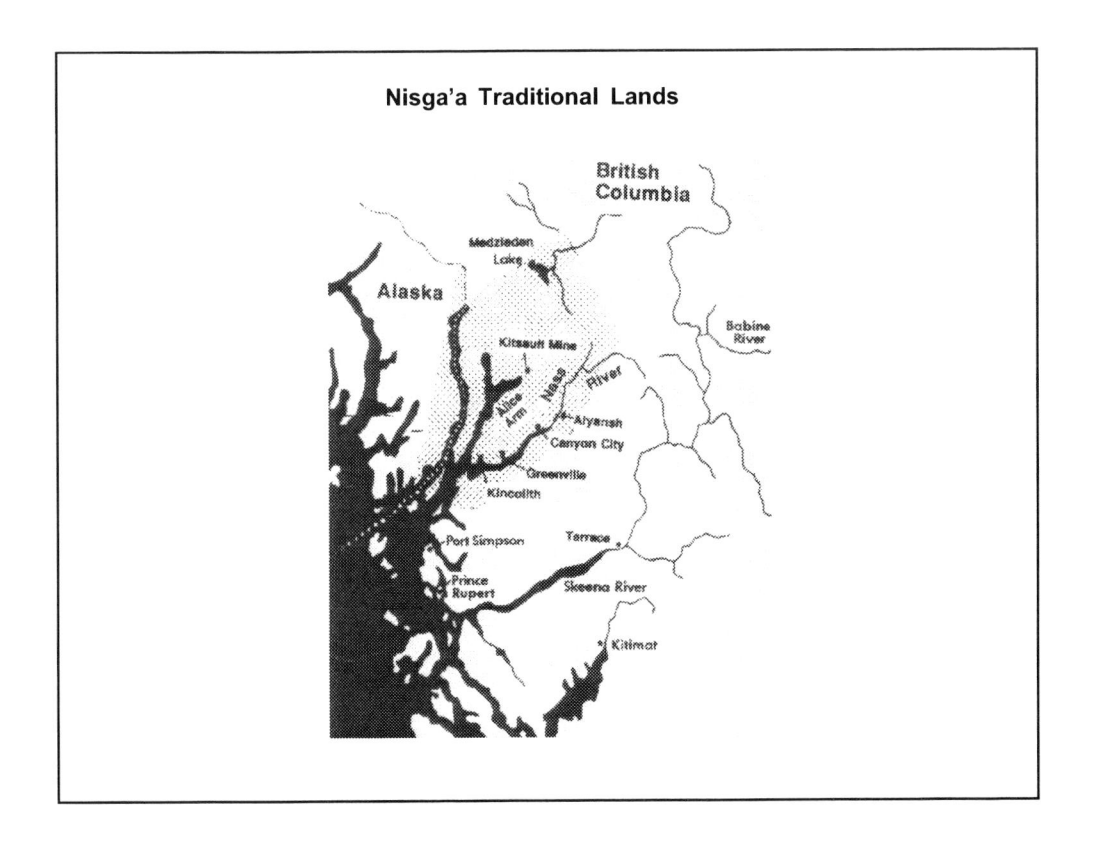

Nisga'a Traditional Lands

> Spiritual explanations often conceal functional ecological concerns and conservation strategies. Further, the spiritual aspect does not necessarily detract from the aboriginal harvester's ability to make appropriate decisions about the wise use of resources. It merely indicates that the system exists within an entirely different cultural experience and set of values, one that paints no more and no less valid a picture of reality than the one that provides its own (Western) frame of reference.[10]

The work of various researchers has shown that diverse indigenous groups — from the Arctic to the Amazon have developed systems of ecological knowledge that are sophisticated even by Western standards. For example, pioneering work by ecologists such as H.C. Conklin[11] and others documented that traditional peoples such as Philippine horticulturists often possessed exceptionally detailed knowledge of local plants and animals and their natural history, recognizing in one case 1600 plant species. Other kinds of indigenous environmental expertise have been acknowledged by Western scientists working in a variety of fields. For instance, ecologist W.O. Pruitt has been using Inuit terminology for types of snow for decades, "not in any attempt to be erudite, but to aid in the precision in our speech and thoughts." When dealing with ice phenomena and types of snow, "[t]here are no precise English words."[12]

The increased appreciation for traditional science, ancient and contemporary, has led to a wider acceptance of the validity of traditional knowledge as a basis for resource management.[13] Perceptive investigations of traditional environmental knowledge systems show that they may provide new biological and ecological insights, help locate and identify rare and endangered species, provide shortcuts for researchers investigating the local resource base, and help define protected areas. Thus, traditional knowledge can provide time-tested in-depth information about a local area that may improve the effectiveness of resource management strategies.[14]

LESSONS FROM THE NISGA'A

The Nisga'a people of British Columbia live in their Nass River Valley homeland near Alaska. They continue to use the Nisga'a language and to preserve the culture that connects them with their river and its valley.[15] Prior to contact with Europeans, the Nisga'a were at the hub of an extensive trading empire based on their monopoly control over vast runs of oolichan fish, which provided the oil required to make a winter diet of dried salmon digestible.[16] The Nisga'a became well known both for their wealth and the leadership and diplomatic systems that enabled them to manage, control and defend that wealth.

Nisga'a prosperity and management was disrupted by white incursion. For some 120 years — since Canada and the province of British Columbia began to "wage law" upon them — the Nisga'a have spearheaded legal campaigns to protect the ecological and economic integrity of their valley from white exploitation and degradation, especially from canning factories, and forest and mining operations. The Nisga'a also developed procedures for educating white newcomers so that they might learn how to "respect" flora, fauna, land forms and communities. Even now, when newcomers arrive at the Nass fishing grounds, they may be instructed to follow certain procedures.

One such caution instructs novice salmon fishers to consume all edible parts and return all unused wastes to the river Nass. Nisga'a people explain that the fish need the smell of the salmon remains in order to have a proper scent trail to find their way home from the open ocean. If we do not return the salmon remains to the river, the fish will feel insulted and will not come back. This principle was first recorded by Hudson Bay Traders in 1835, only three years after they had established themselves on the Nass River.[17] Later, when a cannery was allowed to operate on the Nass, the Nisga'a required that cannery operators return the wastage to the sandbars in order to create a natural "scent trail" for the fish to follow when they return home from the open ocean. This practice — along with the Nisga'a persistent petitioning of governments to address problems associated with White economic activities in the valley — is quite likely to have contributed to the survival, to date, of all the Nass River fishes that return from the sea to spawn.

The Nisga'a traditional science practitioner is trained to observe nature and behave with respect. Children are cautioned not to molest spawning salmon, or the spawning ground, when the fish are laying eggs. As a child, one is expected to watch adults performing specialized tasks with such attention that when one finally takes knife in hand to fillet a sockeye, every cut is made correctly and nothing is wasted. No one may drop a salmon. Trial and error is not an option — making a mistake is often serious near such a dangerous river and is almost always seen as a disgrace. In some Nisga'a families, children are still cautioned to focus their minds on the task at hand and never to think about other matters. When we allow our minds to wander, Watzq, the Otter, will emerge from the river in the form of our desires, trick us, and lure us into the river, where we will surely perish.[18]

In 1982, a Nisga'a fisher — a resident of Kincolith — observed mature "edible" crabs marching past the dock at the mouth of the Nass River, rather than staying in the deep water of Alice Arm. Suspecting that the unusual behaviour might have been caused by the new molybdenum mine at Alice Arm, the man conferred with others and the matter was reported to Nisga'a Tribal Council leaders.[19] The leaders engaged lawyers and biologists to provide "official scientific knowledge and official communication" about the matter. It was quickly established that the ocean floor was being affected by heavy metal tailings with a concentration of 400 grams of suspended solids per litre, 8000 times greater than that allowed by the Canadian government. Somehow, the company had obtained a permit that "entitled" them to emit an effluent that greatly exceeded the normal toxicity standard.[20]

We may rightly wonder at the Nisga'a fisher's ability to deduce the cause of the crabs' unusual behaviour. It is instructive to note that among the Nisga'a, and among other aboriginal peoples, formal observation, recollection, and consideration of extraordinary natural events is taken seriously. Every spring, members of some Nisga'a families still walk their salmon streams to ensure that spawning channels are clear of debris and that salmon are not obstructed in their ascent to spawning beds. In the course of such inspection trips, Nisga'a observers traditionally use all of their senses and pay attention to important variables: what plants are in bloom, what birds are active, when specific animals are migrating and where, and so forth. In this way, traditional communities have a highly developed capacity for building up a collective data base. Any deviations from past patterns are important and are noted.

While each member of the community is traditionally taught to function as a careful observer, the hereditary leaders are trained from childhood to specialize in co-ordinating resource management and information gathering. Ideally, communities were kept to a size (about 250) that enabled the chief to absorb and process the detailed information and understand the relevant variables. Leaders are considered highly developed emotionally and spiritually. They are thought to be "owned" by their communities and may not act from self-interest. Thus, the Nisga'a fishery management system assigns the hereditary chiefs powers to manage the allocation of fish and protect local habitat. According to fisheries biologist Mike Morrell:

> The great strength of the aboriginal systems of fisheries management is that the authority of the Chiefs is recognized throughout the Indian community and the rules are based on the shared philosophy and values of the entire society. As a result rules are self-enforcing and direct conflict is minimal.[22]

In an effort to improve the knowledge of salmon returns and protect Nass River fish stocks, the Nisga'a Fisheries Board is using both ancient and modern approaches. Observing that electronic fish sensors can be inaccurate, the Nisga'a have instituted an ingenious fish-counting system in the Nass River that combines ancient Nisga'a fish wheel technology with modern statistical methods of data analysis. The swift moving current powers a wheel comprised of an axle with three large flat dipnet-like vanes. As the river current turns the wheel by exerting force against the submerged vanes, the companion vanes rise in turn, gently catching and lifting fish as they swim up-river. As each vane rises from the horizontal, the fish slide toward wooden baffles that guide them out the side of the fishwheel [sic] and into submerged holding baskets. Returning fish are caught using the fish wheel at a lower river station, held in holding tanks until tagged, measured and released unharmed or kept for food. Fish are also caught at an upriver fish wheel station where the proportion of tagged fish is used to calculate returns. Reportedly, this procedure provides more accurate and reliable data than that collected by electronic tracking systems.[23]

Clearly, the Nisga'a are deeply concerned with the state of fish stocks; nothing in their ancient laws and stories authorizes them to give up their responsibility to the fish. Nisga'a stories and laws are all about living correctly in the Nass Valley.

TRADITIONAL NISGA'A WISDOM STORIES

There are a number of kinds of narratives among the Nisga'a and only the rightful heir and legitimate chief is permitted to know the full details of certain stories. Complete knowledge of a family story can function as proof of ownership of lands and resources. An origin story may also reveal something about the particular nature of a valley or mountain as well as notable human actions worthy of consideration and contemplation. Thus the remembering of legal, historical, ecological, spiritual and philosophical information associated with particular places is carefully distributed among holders of particular "names." But besides affirming a group's legitimate rights to control and enjoy lands and resources, traditional wisdom stories can teach respect-based principles that govern the interactions of people, nature and environment.[24]

A number of versions of the K'amlugides story are preserved in the ethnological record and some versions of the story have been published.[25] One story describes events that took place when a group of Nisga'a Wolf Clan members under K'amlugides was driven away from the Nass River by the Tseax volcano eruption. While they were enduring winter starvation conditions near present-day Prince Rupert (at the mouth of the Skeena River), they heard a wolf repeatedly call their leader's name. K'amlugides put on his ceremonial regalia and went out into the snow to meet the wolf and possibly his own death. He found a very large white wolf in distress and eventually determined that it was suffering with a deer bone lodged in its throat. K'amlugides spoke to the wolf and then reached into its throat and removed the bone. Within a few days, the wolves reciprocated by bringing K'amlugides and his extended family a supply of venison, and continued to do so for the remainder of that dark winter. The story teaches that a respectful attitude towards animals and their communications enables nature to respond to human needs. It teaches interdependence with nature. The descendants of the white wolf still guide the descendants of K'amlugides, and by extension K'amlugides' bravery and wisdom can instruct and guide us all.

It is instructive to compare the K'amlugides story with the story of St. Francis of Assisi and the wolf; where the injured wolf is healed, subdued, and then tamed. The St. Francis story legitimizes human domination and control over nature, and affirms human superiority — at best, Francis' wolf becomes a pet.

CONNECTING WITH TRADITIONAL SCIENCE

We live in a time when globalization is threatening to overwhelm and devastate regional and local interests. But the world is still inhabited by significant numbers of indigenous people who feel attached to their home places and attend upon those homelands with highly refined knowledge and wisdom. And where aboriginal peoples have been displaced or extirpated, much of their traditional knowledge and wisdom is still accessible through the records kept by those who displaced them. Traditional ecological knowledge can enrich environmental education by engendering respect for and feelings of attachment to home places.[26] It also dovetails with the many fields of study based on "knowing home" — ecofeminism,[27] bioregionalism,[28] and the emerging popularity of the study of "place" in geography and environmental psychology.[29]

Traditional knowledge also suggests that environmental managers need to think clearly about both knowledge and wisdom — it is irrational to dismiss traditional science as backward or irrelevant. Innovative, effective, and appropriate ecological understandings maybe embedded in the sands of time as well as in the silicone lattices of computer chips.

NOTES

1. For detailed discussions see the following excellent documents: *Traditional Knowledge and Renewable Resource Management in Northern Regions*, M. Freeman and L. Carbyn, eds. (Edmonton: University of Alberta, Boreal Institute for Northern Studies, Occasional Publication No. 23, 1988); Fikret Berkes, "Traditional Ecological Knowledge in Perspective," *Traditional Ecological Knowledge: Concepts and Cases*, J.T. Inglis, ed. (Ottawa: International Development Research Centre, 1993), pp. 1–9; and *Traditional Ecological Knowledge: Wisdom for Sustainable Development*, N.M. Williams and G. Baines, eds. (Canberra: Australian National University, 1993).
2. See F. Berkes, "Traditional" [note 1], p. 3.
3. See Julie Cruikshank, "Legend and Landscape: Convergence of Oral and Scientific Traditions in the Yukon Territory," *Arctic Anthology*, 18:2 (1981), pp. 67–93; and Julie Cruikshank, *Reading*

Voices: Oral and Written Interpretations of the Yukon's Past (Vancouver: Douglas & McIntyre, 1991).
4. M.J. Christie, "Aboriginal Science for the Ecologically Sustainable Future," *Australian Science Teachers Journal*, 37:1 (1991), pp. 26–31.
5. See Julie Cruikshank, "Legend" [note 3], p. 18.
6. See Hugh Brody's, *Maps and Dreams: Indians and the British Columbia Frontier* (Vancouver: Douglas & McIntyre, 1981). See also Brody's 1991 documentary NFB film on the Nisga'a "Time Immemorial".
7. Examples in J. Corsiglia and G. Snively, "Global Lessons From the Traditional Science of Long-Resident Peoples," *Thinking Globally About Mathematics and Science Education*, G. Snively and A. MacKinnon, eds. (Vancouver: University of British Columbia, Center for the Study of Curriculum and Instruction, 1995), pp. 25–52.
8. Harold Wright, Nisga'a elder, personal communication (1977).
9. See Cruikshank, "Legend" [note 3], p. 86.
10. For an interesting collection of essays, see Lore: *Capturing Traditional Environmental Knowledge*, M. Johnson, ed. (Ottawa: Dene Cultural Institute, 1992).
11. H.C. Conklin, *Hanunoo Agriculture: A Report on an Integral System of Shifting Cultivation in the Philippines* (Rome: Food and Agriculture Organization, Forestry Development Paper No. 5, 1957).
12. W.O. Pruitt, Jr, *Boreal Ecology* (London: Edward Arnold, 1978).
13. *First Nations' Perspectives Relating to Forest Practices Standards in Clayoquot Sound* (Victoria, British Columbia: Cortex Consultants, 1995).
14. See Berkes, "Traditional" [note 1]; Inglis *Traditional* [note 1]; and Williams and Baines *Traditional* [note 1].
15. Nisga'a Tribal Council, *Nisga'a: People of the Nass River* (Vancouver: Douglas & McIntyre, 1993). See also 1996 *Agreement in Principle* regarding Nisga'a management and decision making in the traditional Nisga'a Treaty lands. Information and perspective supplied here was kindly provided since 1977 by Nisga'a teachers, especially, Bertram McKay, Harry Nyce Sr., George Gosnell, Maurice Squires and the late Eli Gosnell.
16. The Nisga'a controlled, and at the same time shared, their important Nass River resources with Tlingit, Haida, Tsimshian, Tahltan, and Gitksan who rented oolichan fishing campsites, equipment and supplies.
17. W.F. Tolmie, Bancroft Notes on 1835 Port Simpson Hudson's Bay Company Journal, PC23 (Berkeley, California: Bancroft Library, 1887).
18. Harold Wright, Nisga'a elder, personal communication, 1980.
19. Roderick Robinson, Bertram McKay, Nisga'a elders, personal communications (1983).
20. D. Raunet, *Without Surrender, Without Consent* (Vancouver: Douglas & McIntyre, 1984).
21. Bertram McKay, Nisga'a elder, personal communication (1977) and (1993).
22. Mike Morrel, "The Struggle to Integrate Traditional Indian Systems and State Management in the Salmon Fisheries of the Skeena River, BC," *Co-operative Management of Local Fisheries: New Directions for Improved Management and Community Development*, E. Pinkerton, ed. (Vancouver: University of British Columbia Press, 1989), p. 235; also Martin Weinstein, "The Role of Tenure and the Potlatch in Fisheries Management by Northwest Pacific Coast Societies" (Vancouver: Paper presented to the American Fisheries Society Workshop, 1994).
23. Personal communication, Harry Nyce, Nisga'a elder (1996).
24. P. Knudtson and D. Suzuki, *Wisdom of the Elders* (Toronto: Stoddart Publishing Company, 1992).
25. M. Barbeau, *Totem Poles: Their General Character* (Ottawa: Department of Resources and Development, National Museum of Canada, Vol. 1, 1950–1952); and Tsimshian Narratives, J.J. Cove and G.F. MacDonald, eds. (Ottawa: Canadian Museum of Civilization, Mercury Series, No. 3, 1987).
26. Gloria Snively, "Bridging Traditional Science and Western Science in the Multicultural Classroom," *Thinking*, Snively and MacKinnon, eds. [note 7], pp. 53–76.
27. For an interesting overview see Heather Eaton, "Ecofeminist Spiritualities: Seeking the Wild or the Sacred?" *Alternatives*, 21:2 (1995), pp. 28–31.
28. See Michelle Summer Fike and Sarah Kerr, "Making the Links: Why Bioregionalism Needs Ecofeminism." *Alternatives*, 21:2 (1995), pp. 22–27.
29. Tony Hiss, *The Experience of Place* (New York: Alfred A. Knopf, Inc., 1990).

Section 2

Land Use and Renewable Resources

Aboriginal people have a special relationship with the land. This holistic relationship has a spiritual foundation that goes back to the beginning of the Aboriginal World in North America. The Sacred Circle of Life epitomizes Aboriginal beliefs, and its starting point is that all life is spiritual — animals, plants, and even the sun and stars. For Plains Indians the medicine wheel symbolized the circle of life. Seemingly forever, the land has nurtured Aboriginal people by providing food for their physical sustenance and cultural well-being. In return, Aboriginal people have a responsibility to care for the land and its many creatures. The land and its natural resources hold the key to Aboriginal cosmology and culture.

Contact with Europeans introduced Aboriginal people to a different culture — a culture based on the ownership of property. Contact brought about fundamental changes to the land and to the way of doing things. Some were mutually beneficial while others had negative consequences for Aboriginal people. The fur trade brought about a beneficial partnership between the white traders and the Indian trappers. The loss of the great buffalo herds crippled the hunting economy of the Plains Indians and Metis. In 1871, Chief Sweet Grass sadly but stoically informed Chief Factor W.J. Christie that "Our country is no longer able to support us." (Morris 1889: 171). The psychological blow to their traditional beliefs was overwhelming. But not all regions suffered so hard and so fast. The caribou and sea mammals in Canada's North did not endure the same fate as the buffalo, and so the land continues to provide food for the northern Indians and Inuit.

As Canada came under the control of Ottawa and the provinces, natural resources were subject to conservation, management, and licensing measures. Regulation of fish and wild animals falls under provincial jurisdiction, but responsibility for Treaty Indians lies with Ottawa. Conservation measures designed for the general public tended to adversely impact Aboriginal people, who depend on access to wild food for their physical well-being and survival. Moreover, such laws came into conflict with the traditional ways of managing wildlife.

While Aboriginal people living well beyond Canada's densely populated area could turn to the land for much of their sustenance, access to the land changed radically in the 1950s when Aboriginal people began to move into settlements. While these settlement dwellers continued to harvest resources from the land, the pattern of hunting had changed — time on the land was much less, and the hunting parties tended to consist of small groups of male hunters. Children remained in school where they were caught up in the settlement life. Within a generation, Aboriginal people's relationship with the land has had to adapt to new circumstances, which propelled them toward commercial use of natural resources. A combination of factors led to these new circumstances, including large-scale industrial projects, land claims agreements, court decisions that provide commercial access to resources, and the desire by Aboriginal individuals and organizations to engage in resource development as a means of helping themselves and their people. The Quebec Cree, for example, lost some of their prime hunting and fishing lands when these river valleys were flooded by the construction of the James Bay Project. In their negotiations with the province, the Quebec Cree obtained an income support program for their hunters and trappers. Known as *the Income Security Program for Cree Hunters and Trappers*, this popular program provides cash income for those who live on the land, thus relieving the province of providing social assistance payments for these hunters and trappers. A similar program exists for the Inuit of Nunavut, but in this case the funding comes from land claims funds through Nunavut Tunngavik Inc. (Légaré in Chapter 3).

By the 1980s, reassertion of Aboriginal control over their traditional lands was well underway. The next step was resource development by Aboriginal organizations. Writing in 1994, Claudia Notzke (303) expressed these new circumstances as:

> In a country that owes so much of its national character to resource frontiers created by immigrant society, it is now aboriginal people who advance into 'new territory' by reclaiming lands and resources as well as management power over them.

By the 21st century, First Nations had created a variety of business organizations that involved the commercial use of their natural resources. In an article by Tom Mason on the commercial development of reserve land known as the Truro Power Centre by Millbrook First Nation in Nova Scotia, the range of economic activities across Canada was impressive. Mason (2001: 45) reported that:

> Impressive as they may be, the strides that Millbrook residents are making are far from unique. In fact, they're part of a new wave of native-run businesses sweeping Canada, bringing once-poor First [Nations] a newfound prosperity. The Lac La Ronge Indian Band in northern Saskatchewan has developed Kitsaki Management Ltd to manage a portfolio of businesses that includes mining, insurance, trucking, and hospitality. BC's Osoyoos Indian Band Development Corp. is now operating eight businesses, including a vineyard and a saw mill. And Peace Hills Trust, an Alberta-based financial institution with about $800 million in assets, may soon be a Power Centre tenant.

While Mason's article is upbeat and focused on commercial successes, most First Nations are struggling to find their way in this commercial world that is so foreign to their traditional culture. One solution to this struggle of cultural adaptation is found in the comprehensive land claims agreements, which have created a dual structure, thus allowing a foot in the new world of commerce and the old world based on the land. In the case of the Inuvialuit Final Agreement, the Inuvialuit Game Council is concerned about the land and the harvesting of wildlife, while the Inuvialuit Regional Corporation represents the Inuvialuit's business arm.

In this section on land use and natural resource, we have selected works that are intended to stimulate thinking about the issue of commercial use of land and other natural resources. These articles will foster class discussion about the new approach to Aboriginal use of resources. Each author has looked at this special relationship from a particular perspective. We begin with four articles. Three examine the emergence of Aboriginal organizations that promote the development of natural resources. One deals with the troublesome issue of industrial wastes reaching the North and entering the food chain, thus affecting wildlife and the health of Aboriginal northerners whose diet contains large quantities of country food. The connection between the four articles is the recognition that external forces, whether market forces or global pollution, affect local decision-making and limit solutions.

Andre Légaré begins this process with a recent article that he translated especially for this book. Nunavut and Nunavut Tunngavik are new to the political landscape of the North. In his article, Legare discusses the role of Nunavut

Tunngavik Inc. and its activities, programs, and organization in terms of its relationship with the government of Nunavut. Nunavut Tunngavik Inc.'s specific role is the implementation of the Nunavut Land Claims Settlement.

Heather Myers argues in both of her papers that renewable resources offer better prospects for long-term economic development for Aboriginal northerners than large-scale industrial projects. Given the low level of involvement with large-scale industrial projects, Myers makes a persuasive argument. For local communities, small-scale local developments based on locally available natural resources are the order of the day. Such an approach to community development, Myers claims, would depend on the development and management of local renewable resources.

David Natcher focuses his attention on Aboriginal involvement in land and resource management, particularly of new organizations that lend themselves to dealing with the market economy. This process, according to Natcher, leads to a form of institutionalized adaptation.

Sylvie Poirier and Lorraine Brooke look at the issue of toxic wastes found in the food chain of wildlife in the Eastern Arctic. The wastes have two sources: internal — mining activities and garbage left on the land at cabins or by hunting groups; and external — global atmospheric and ocean circulation systems that bring industrial contaminants from other parts of the world to the North, which is a problem out of control. Poirier and Brooke report that Quebec Inuit are very concerned about contaminants in wildlife, but they are not modifying hunting and eating of country food.

Forestry

Robert Anderson and Robert Bone report on the remarkable economic advances made by the Meadow Lake Tribal Council in the forest industry. Access to a provincial timber lease was a critical element in this success story. Forming a joint venture with a new pulp mill operated by Miller-Western Inc. was another critical element. The Meadow Lake Tribal Council is now a serious player in logging and timber operations in northwest Saskatchewan. The spin-off effects for the First Nations belonging to the Meadow Lake Tribal Council have been profound, and have greatly increased the business confidence and self-esteem of many members of those First Nations.

First Nations in Forestry presents four short accounts of First Nations engaged in various forest activities — Babine Forest Products, Long Lake Forest Nursery, Logging at Lake St. Martin First Nation, and forestry partnership in La Ronge. The four reveal the range of First Nations involvement in the commercial forest business. The recent American restrictions on Canadian lumber and other wood products have hurt these firms. For instance, the proposed joint venture saw mill at La Ronge has been delayed until an alternative market for its lumber can be found.

Michael McDonald recounts how forest operations on traditional territories are complicated by the legal interpretation and application of Delgamuukw, Badger, and Sparrow in the forestry context of British Columbia, where few treaties have been signed. First Nations, McDonald argues, must seek business and political or even court solutions while treaty land entitlement and self-government negotiations continue. In the absence of settled claims, court rulings require that forestry firms conducting operations on lands claimed by First Nations consult with those First Nations, giving Aboriginal people the opportunities to participate in the company's forest operations.

Wildlife

Denis Bird discusses the important issue of joint management of national parks. This issue has far-reaching implications because most national parks are adjacent to traditional hunting areas. If such management includes hunting, trapping, and fishing rights for Aboriginal people within these parks, then the area available for these traditional pursuits would be greatly increased.

Lois Harwood, Pamela Norton and other federal government scientists looked at the question of sustainable harvesting of Beluga whales by the Inuvialuit. In their study of the Inuvialuit harvest of Beluga whales, Harwood and her fellow federal government authors have carefully documented the catch over time. One observation is the presence of large, older Beluga whales. They concluded that the current harvest, which is below traditional levels, takes place at a sustainable level.

Robert Irwin brings forward the issue of Indian hunting and fishing rights in the Canadian prairie provinces of Alberta, Saskatchewan and Manitoba. These rights are impacted by two separate regulatory structures: the Indian treaties and Section 12 of the Natural Resources Transfer Agreements. Irwin argues that Ottawa did not intend to extinguish treaty rights through the Natural Resources Transfer Agreements that gave the three prairie provinces control over natural resources.

Anne Kendrick focuses on the issue of co-management of wildlife resources. In this case, Kendrick has examined the Beverly-Qamanirjuaq Caribou Management Board. While only an advisory board, the members, representing a combination of community and government members, have over the years come to a better understanding of the critical issues. Community perceptions of the board, however, vary.

Roger Spielmann and Marina Unger have a different perspective on co-management of resources, focusing their attention on a co-management model based on co-management of provincial parks in Ontario.

Water

Andrew Thompson examines water legislation in Yukon as it affects Aboriginal rights. Water legislation consists of the Northern Inland Water Act and the Yukon Waters Act, which in 1993 replaced the Northern Inland Water Act in Yukon. While the Northern Inland Water Act covers all the territories, the Yukon Water Act was designed to provide stronger protection for Yukon waters and to protect Aboriginal water interests.

Anna Classen's account of the Blood Tribe Agricultural Project indicates the importance of controlling water flowing across Blood Tribe lands. With access to this water, the Blood Tribe is able to irrigate their lands and engage in commercial agriculture.

Fishery

Parker Barss Donham has prepared a series of newspaper accounts of how the Marshall Decision has had a profound impact on Aboriginal access to the lobster fishery on the East Coast. Donham provides insights into the behind-the-scenes implications. He claims that the national media has fuelled "white" hysteria about Aboriginal fishers depleting the lobster stocks. In fact, Donham claims that illegal fishing by white fishers at Yarmouth exceeds the total take by Aboriginal fishers.

REFERENCES

Mason, Tom. 2001. "Tribal Counsel", *Canadian Business*. 74(21): 41–45.

Morris, A. 1889. *The Treaties of Canada with the Indian of Manitoba and the North-West Territories*. Toronto: Belfords, Clarke.

Notzke, Claudia, 1994. *Aboriginal Peoples and Natural Resources in Canada*. North York: Captus University Publications.

CHAPTER 3

Introduction

(a) The Nunavut Tunngavik Inc.:
An Examination of Its Mode of Operation
and Its Activities[†]

André Légaré

INTRODUCTION

The Nunavut Tunngavik Inc.[1] (NTI) is a private Inuit Corporation created on April 1, 1993. NTI succeeded the Tunngavik Federation of Nunavut[2] (TFN) as the Inuit organization responsible for the implementation of the Nunavut Land Claims Agreement (NLCA). NTI represents and defends the interests of the 24,000 Inuit beneficiaries of the NLCA (DIAND 1993).

After 15 long years of negotiations, the comprehensive land claims settlement of the Nunavut Inuit was signed on December 16, 1991 by representatives from TFN and the Federal Government (cf. Légaré 2001). The NLCA was approved on November 6, 1992 by the Inuit of Nunavut and by the Canadian Parliament on June 10, 1993. The Agreement came into effect on July 9, 1993. The NLCA covers an immense geographical area of 1,931,511 sq. km. (Figure 1) sparsely populated by

---

[†] Research Associate, GETIC (Inuit and Circumpolar Studies Group), Faculté des sciences sociales, Pavillon Charles-De-Koninck, Local 0450, Université Laval, Québec, QC. G1K 7P4. e-mail: <Inukshuk@internorth.com>.

Originally published in André Légaré, "La Nunavut Tunngavik Inc.: Un examen de ses activités et de sa structure administrative," *Etude/Inuit/Studies*, 24(1) (2000). Author's translation. Reproduced with permission of publisher.

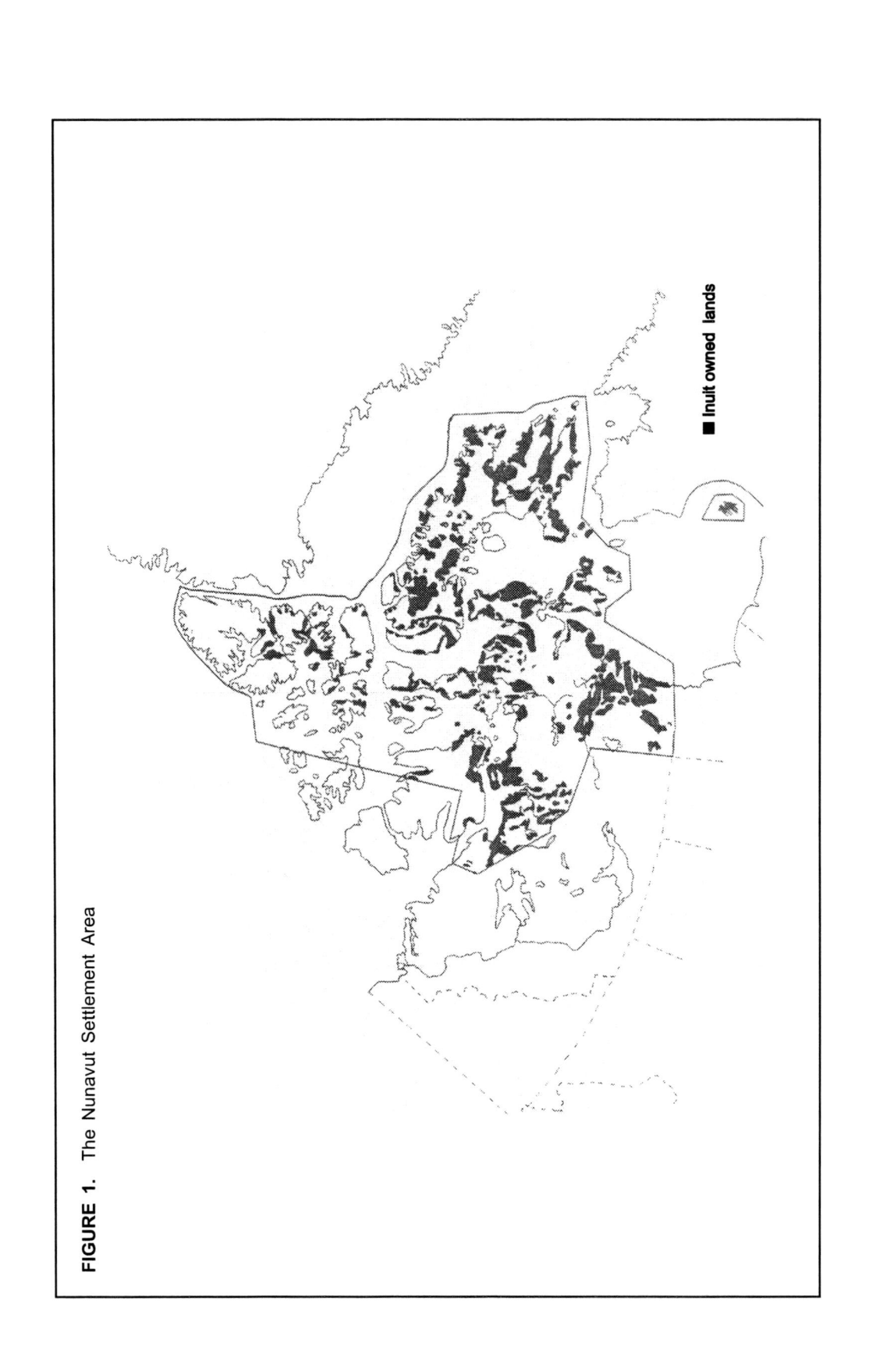

FIGURE 1. The Nunavut Settlement Area

■ Inuit owned lands

> **TABLE 1.** Synoptic Table of the Nunavut Land Claims Agreement
>
> Five Co-Management Boards are established for the management of lands and resources throughout the Nunavut Settlement Area (1,931,511 km^2).
>
> Inuit have the right to hunt, fish and trap throughout the Nunavut Settlement Area without needing to apply for permits.
>
> Inuit own 353,610 km^2 of land. This represents 18 per cent of all the lands of the Nunavut Settlement Area. In addition, Inuit have mineral rights (sub-surface ownership) over 36,257 km^2 of Inuit owned lands.
>
> Inuit receive 50 per cent of the first $2 million of royalties received by Canada each year from mining, oil and gas development on Crown Lands in the Nunavut Settlement Area. On Inuit owned lands Inuit may receive up to 100 per cent of all royalties.
>
> The Government of Canada will give to the Inuit $1.17 billion as financial compensation over a period of 14 years (1993–2007). This money is deposited in a Trust (Nunavut Trust).
>
> In exchange for the rights and benefits described in the Nunavut Land Claims Agreement, the Inuit have extinguished all of their land rights.
>
> Source: After DIAND, 1993

29,000 inhabitants; a majority are Inuit (83 percent). Table 1 summarizes the main points of the NLCA.

NTI's role is to make sure that the 212 sections contained in the 40 Articles of the NLCA are properly implemented. Its mandate is to ensure that all beneficiaries benefit from the rights established in the NLCA. Contrary to the Government of Nunavut, which is a public government representing the interests of all residents in Nunavut (cf. Légaré 1997), NTI is an Aboriginal organization representing solely the interests of the Inuit of Nunavut. In fact, Inuit beneficiaries are the shareholders of NTI.

The implementation of the NLCA has given birth to a multitude of public and Inuit institutions in Nunavut. NTI is the pivotal point of this kaleidoscope of institutions. In the following pages, I will examine the activities and organizational structure of NTI. The purpose of this essay is, in part, to portray the organizational chart of NTI in order to unveil its tasks. The essay also displays the functions of the various institutions that flow from the NLCA.

To fulfill these objectives, I will first examine the structure and the mode of operation of NTI. I will then highlight the working relations that exist between NTI and the new Government of Nunavut as well as the existing links between NTI and other public or Inuit organizations within Nunavut. Finally, I will analyze the programs and services administered through NTI for the benefit of the Nunavut Inuit. A particular emphasis will be put on the newly created Nunavut Hunter Support Program.

THE ORGANIZATIONAL STRUCTURE AND MODE OF OPERATION OF NTI

NTI is a private corporation whose members are the 24,000 Inuit beneficiaries of the NLCA (DIAND 1993: Art. 39). Its headquarters are located in the Nunavut capital of Iqaluit. NTI is composed of three levels of decision-making structures and eight departments (Figure 2): General Assembly, Board of Directors, Executive Committee, and departments.

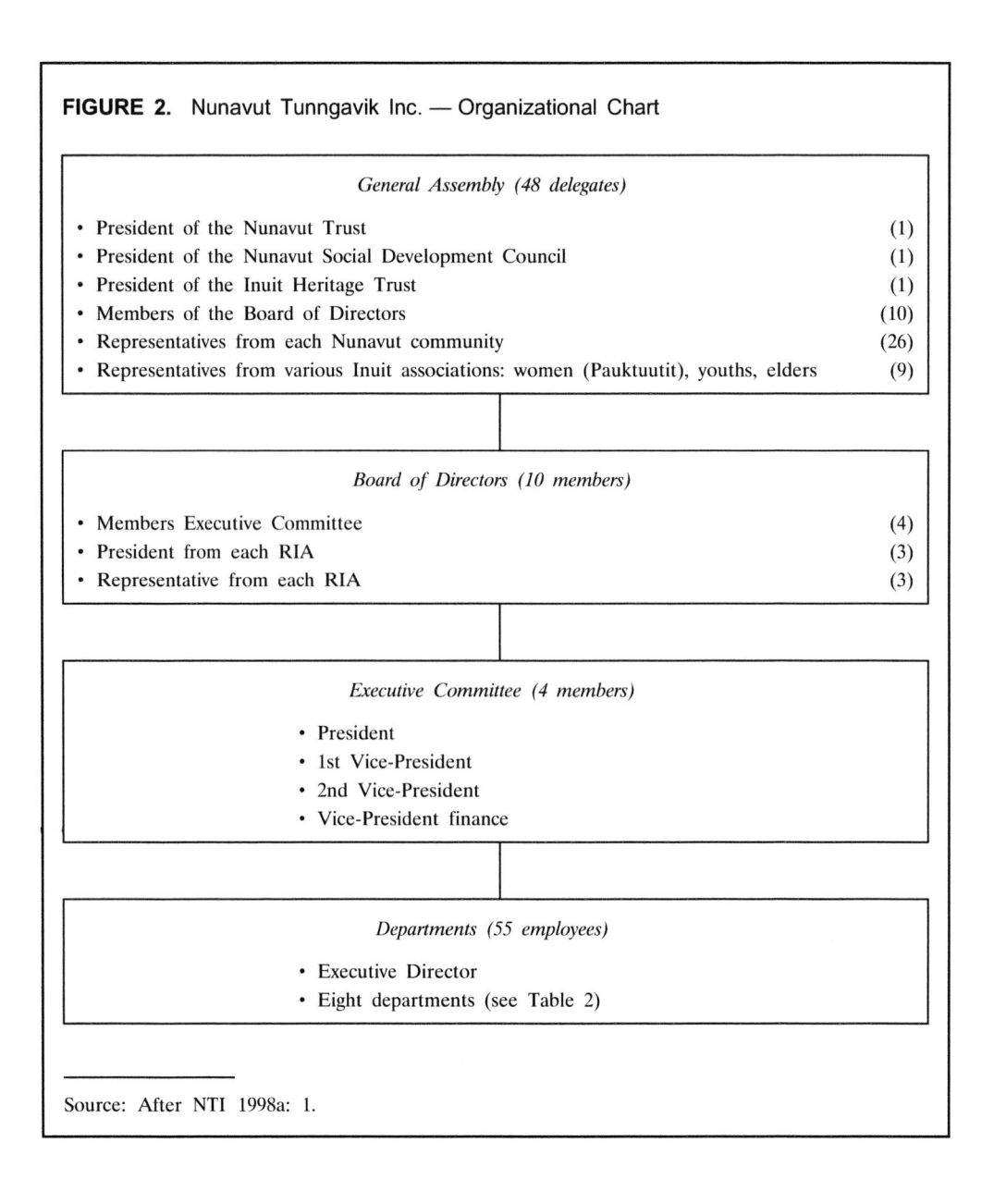

FIGURE 2. Nunavut Tunngavik Inc. — Organizational Chart

General Assembly (48 delegates)

- President of the Nunavut Trust (1)
- President of the Nunavut Social Development Council (1)
- President of the Inuit Heritage Trust (1)
- Members of the Board of Directors (10)
- Representatives from each Nunavut community (26)
- Representatives from various Inuit associations: women (Pauktuutit), youths, elders (9)

Board of Directors (10 members)

- Members Executive Committee (4)
- President from each RIA (3)
- Representative from each RIA (3)

Executive Committee (4 members)

- President
- 1st Vice-President
- 2nd Vice-President
- Vice-President finance

Departments (55 employees)

- Executive Director
- Eight departments (see Table 2)

Source: After NTI 1998a: 1.

The General Assembly

The General Assembly is the supreme decision-making body. A General Assembly is held once a year. It approves the annual budget of NTI. The General Assembly delegates can increase or restrict the spending level. The General Assembly can modify the programs and services delivered by NTI. It can also pass and amend the rules (bylaws) of NTI. Any changes to programs and bylaws must be approved by at least two-thirds of the delegates. A similar percentage of delegates is required for the passing of new bylaws or programs and services.

The Annual General Assembly consists of 48 delegates: President of the Nunavut Trust (1); President of Nunavut Social Development Council (1); President of the Inuit Heritage Trust (1); members of the Board of Directors of NTI (10); one representative from each Inuit community in Nunavut (26); three representatives from each of the following Inuit associations: women, elders, and youths (9).

Board of Directors

NTI has a ten-member Board of Directors. The members meet four times per year to review the decisions taken by the Executive Committee, and to prepare the yearly budget of NTI. The Board usually approves the decisions taken by the Executive.[3] In fact, to disapprove a decision taken by the Executive would be both complex and likely unsuccessful since it would require the convocation by the Board of a special General Assembly where two-thirds of the delegates would vote against a decision from the Executive.

All four members of the Executive Committee are also members of the Board of Directors. In addition, the President of each of the three Regional Inuit Associations (RIAs) is a member. Finally, each RIA sends a representative on the Board.[4] Thus, six of the ten members of the Board come from RIAs. This gives significant weight to regional interests within the Board. Some frictions have been known to arise between Executive members, who have a pan-Nunavut view of Inuit interests, and RIAs members who are more regionally oriented.

RIAs were creations of TFN in the mid-eighties. Originally, their purpose was to select Inuit-owned lands within each of their regions (cf. Fenge and Merritt 1989). With the implementation of the NLCA, they have now acquired a significant role in the administration of those lands.[5] Although RIAs do not have any public governmental responsibilities, they cover a geographical area similar to the administrative regions created by the Government of the Northwest Territories in 1983 (Légaré 1998: 18). Figure 3 shows the extent of those geographical regions: RIA Kitikmeot (Kitikmeot Region); RIA Kivalliq (Keewatin Region); RIA Qikiqtani (Baffin Region).

The Executive Committee

In theory, the most powerful structure within NTI is the General Assembly. In reality, the real power lies within the Executive Committee. Decisions taken by the Executive cannot be easily disapproved by the General Assembly unless there is a two-thirds support of delegates to do so.[6] The four members of the Executive are elected at large by Inuit beneficiaries, aged 16 and older, for a three-year mandate.

FIGURE 3. Regional Inuit Associations

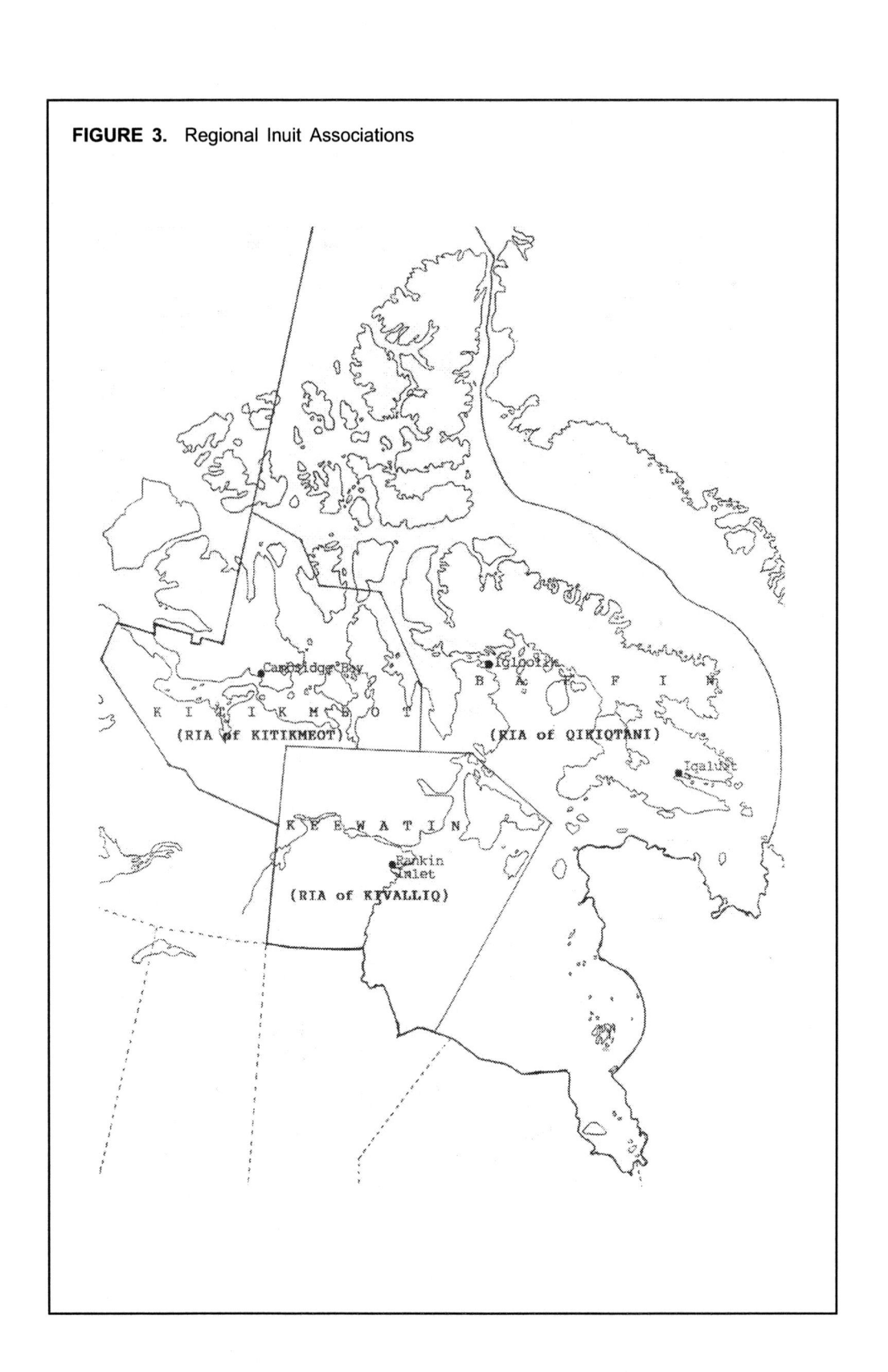

Usually, these elections result in low turnouts. At the first election, in March 1993, only 45 percent of the eligible voters went to the poll. In the last election, on December 10, 2002, in which Ms. Cathy Towtongie was elected President, there was a similar turnout of voters (45 percent). Many factors may explain this apathy. The small electorate is saturated by the number of elections in Nunavut: members for the Nunavut Legislative Assembly, members for the Municipal Councils, members for the local Hunters and Trappers Associations, RIA elections, NTI elections. On average, an Inuk voter would have to go to the poll three times per year! Many Inuit do not have any interest in politics and, simply, do not vote. Another reason possible for the low turnout is the fact that NTI elections are usually held in the spring when many Inuit hunters are on the land.

Members of the Executive meet once a month to implement the decisions approved by the General Assembly and to supervise the "day to day" operation of NTI. The Executive is composed of a President and three Vice-Presidents. Even though the President is ultimately responsible for all decisions taken by the Executive, he/she must be sure to always have the full support of the Executive on any initiatives. Indeed, Presidents (e.g., Paul Quassa) have been known, in the past, to be compelled to resign from their post because of lacking support from members of the Executive. This can be explained by the fact that Presidents are often exposed to criticisms and do not generally last for more than a three-year mandate, while the other members, who are not as much in the limelight, can last several years: Mr. James Eetoolook has held the post of First Vice-President for over seven years. In summary, NTI decision-making process can be best described as collegial, where power rests within the whole of the Executive.

The Departments

To properly implement its duties, NTI has a staff of 55 employees (secretaries, managers, accountants, researchers, etc.). Most of these employees are Inuit (90 percent). The work of the employees is supervised by the Executive Director whose task is to make sure that the decisions of the Executive are implemented. The employees work within one of the eight departments of NTI. Each of these departments falls under the authority of one of the members of the Executive Committee (Table 2).

NTI Budget

The money for the annual budget of NTI comes from the profits made by the Nunavut Trust. The Trust manages the compensation money received from Canada as part of the NLCA (DIAND 1993: Art. 31). For the annual fiscal year of 2000/2001, NTI required $21 million to administer its operations. This amount also included the budget dedicated to the administration of the three RIAs (Rodrigue 1999a: 16).

NTI Mode of Operation

Most regional and national Aboriginal organizations (Assembly of First Nations, Inuit Tapirisat of Canada, Makivik Corporation, Dene Nation, etc.) possess

TABLE 2. The Departments of the Nunavut Tunngavik Inc.

Departments	Description	Under Authority of
Business Development	Works with Inuit-owned businesses to provide jobs and income in the North.	President
Implementation	Ensures that the provisions of the NLCA are carried out properly.	President
Supervision Committee	Observes the activities of the Government of Nunavut and makes sure that government policies support the interests of the Inuit People.	President
Land Management	Ensures that everyone has fair access to Inuit-owned lands and gives Inuit a voice in deciding how Inuit-owned lands are to be used. Responsible for the cleanup of waste sites ("Dew Line").	1st Vice-President
Communications	Informs the Inuit population about NTI's policies, programs and services.	2nd Vice-President
Finance	Manages NTI finances.	Vice-President Finance
Human Resources	Implements capacity building programs and recruits NTI personnel.	Vice-President Finance
Enrolment and Eligibility	Works to enrol all Inuit with NTI in order to benefit from the NLCA.	Vice-President Finance

Source: NTI 1996: 1.

administrative structures inspired from a Euro-Canadian mode of organization. NTI does not differ to this rule. As with other Western corporations, Aboriginal organizations are largely bureaucratized (Nagata 1987: 62). This gives rise, as we have seen in the case of NTI, to a cumbersome structure of decision-making. How can one explain this Western mode of operation?

Two factors justify this mode of operation. First, in order to influence the political decision-makers at the federal and territorial levels of government, NTI must possess a structure that is legitimized in the eyes of Euro-Canadians, and comprehensible for the average government bureaucrat. To do so, NTI, like all other Aboriginal organizations, has a structure and a mode of operation similar to those found in Western corporations: "Since Native political organizations are run by principles recognizable to the dominant society..., the process has given them a legitimacy in the eyes of the dominant society that they might have otherwise lacked" (Sawchuk 1998: 167).

Second, NTI must adhere to Nunavut territorial laws dealing with corporations and private enterprises. These laws establish common denominators with regard to the management and structures of corporations and private enterprises: "Regulations such as the various societies acts, impose requirements on association board structure" (Sawchuk 1998: 162).

However, this Euro-Canadian mode of operation exercises an influence that goes well beyond the simple structure of Aboriginal organizations. It influences the political behaviour of some Aboriginal leaders. Recently, some Inuit beneficiaries have expressed three forms of criticisms towards NTI: (1) controversies among some members of the Executive; (2) a structure too cumbersome; (3) salaries too high.

Some past Executive members have had to give up their post because of questionable ethics. Several Inuit beneficiaries have expressed the desire to see greater accountability and stability among the Inuit leadership. To achieve this goal, some Inuit have proposed that NTI distance itself from the Euro-Canadian mode of operation, since this structure does not reflect Inuit traditions or customs. They want Inuit elders to have a key input in all NTI decisions. In so doing, these Inuit beneficiaries believe that, with the contribution of elders, NTI will inherit increased accountability, honesty, compassion and humility — qualities that Inuit elders believe are sometimes absent among the young Inuit leadership educated through the Euro-Canadian system: "This election and political process was never an Inuit custom. In Inuit based society, the young did not lead the elders. The Inuit elders have to be solicited as advisors and leaders" (Carpenter 1994: B25).

In addition, the cumbersome structure of NTI makes it hard for the average Inuit, not acquainted with the intricacies of administrative bureaucratic systems, to understand the role and activities of NTI. Some Inuit have said that NTI structure should be simplified and made more democratic. Currently, only a few Inuit participate in the decisions of NTI (i.e., the 48 delegates attending NTI Annual General Assemblies). Those decisions have often had significant impacts on the lives of the 24,000 Inuit beneficiaries. This highly centralized decision-making process is further reinforced by the dominant role of the Executive within NTI: "The leadership has yet to show openness and remain content to not distance themselves from totalitarian practices" (Peter 1995: 8).

Finally, several Inuit do not appreciate the fact that their leaders give themselves high wages. In a region where one finds the highest poverty rates in Canada, the President of NTI earns an annual salary of $135,000! "Tunngavik's high salaries will likely quicken the development of a class system within the Inuit society: a small, affluent, and politically powerful elite maintaining dominance over a cash poor badly educated and mostly unemployed underclass" (Nunatsiaq News 1993: 7).

In summary, the Euro-Canadian mode of operation shared by NTI has eased interactions between NTI and federal or territorial government officials. However, this highly centralized and bureaucratized mode of operation is foreign to Inuit traditional decision-making (cf. Mitchell 1996: 34–37).

THE RELATION BETWEEN NTI AND THE GOVERNMENT OF NUNAVUT

On April 1, 1999, the new Nunavut Territorial Government was officially inaugurated. The Government of Nunavut (GN) is a public government representing the interests of all Nunavut citizens (Inuit and non-Inuit). The new government has a similar political structure as the one found in the Northwest Territories (cf. Légaré 1998: 24–27).

Until recently, there was no common understanding as to the relationship between NTI and the GN. However, all of that changed on October 28, 1999, with the signature of the *Clyde River Protocol* (NTI, Nunavut, 1999) between the Premier of Nunavut Mr. Paul Okalik and the President of NTI Mr. Jose Kusugak. The *Clyde River Protocol* established the norms that will rule the relationship between NTI and the new Government of Nunavut: "... The Government of Nunavut and NTI agree to conduct their working relations in accordance with this protocol" (NTI, Nunavut 1999: 1). So as to better understand the relationship between these two political entities, I will now examine the content of the protocol.

The signatories recognized that the GN represents all the citizens of Nunavut. On the other hand, the protocol also recognizes that NTI is a private Inuit Corporation representing the large majority of Nunavut citizens (83 percent of the Nunavut population). The mandate of NTI is to defend and promote the Rights of Inuit as described in the NLCA: "The Government of Nunavut recognizes that NTI occupies a special place in the affairs of Nunavut as the primary Inuit organization with the mandate to speak for the Inuit of Nunavut..." (NTI, Nunavut 1999: Article A.1).

In order to avoid any political imbroglios between the GN and NTI, the Protocol establishes clearly that the two entities must collaborate to implement policies that have an impact on Inuit Rights: "... The Government of Nunavut and NTI recognize a particular need to maintain close, ongoing development within Nunavut; ... the status, protection and promotion of the Inuit language and culture within Nunavut" (NTI, Nunavut, 1999: Article B.2).

In addition, so as to harmonize the links between NTI and the GN, the Protocol suggests that the Executive Director of NTI and the Deputy-Minister of Intergovernmental Affairs of the GN discuss any policy proposal put forward by the Government of Nunavut that may have an impact on Inuit culture or Rights (NTI, Nunavut 1999: Article G).

It is still too early to grasp the impact of the *Clyde River Protocol* on the political scene of Nunavut. However, a quick analysis of the document allows us to establish a number of parameters. First, the protocol seems to define the dominant political role of NTI in relation to the GN. Second, the protocol emphasizes the fact that the new Government of Nunavut was created through the NLCA (DIAND 1993: Article 4). It further emphasizes that the GN must respect the Inuit Rights established in the NLCA. Finally, any policies put forward by the GN must not contradict the articles of the NLCA: "Kusugak said: the Protocol gives NTI a role when government policy is developed.... Before the Nunavut Government writes up reports they will have to talk to us" (Rodrigue 1999b: 16).

The *Clyde River Protocol* reinforces the position of NTI in relation to the GN. In fact, one may pretend that NTI is for now the real political force in Nunavut. Several factors may explain this conclusion: First, NTI is the most experienced and oldest political institution in Nunavut[7]; second, it represents a vast majority of Nunavut citizens; third, it is responsible for defending the Inuit Rights defined in the NLCA — those Rights are protected through section 35 of the 1982 Canadian Constitution; fourth, NTI insists on the fact that the GN was created through the NLCA, a document NTI is responsible for overseeing.

RELATIONS BETWEEN NTI AND OTHER PUBLIC AND INUIT INSTITUTIONS IN NUNAVUT

NTI has relations with numerous organizations in Nunavut. These relations are generally of two kinds: (1) designated; (2) delegated. In the former, NTI nominates members to the Boards of Directors of the organizations. However, these institutions (i.e., public co-management boards, Inuit Heritage Trust, Nunavut Social Development Council) are independent from the politics of NTI. Those institutions (Figure 4) result from the implementation of the NLCA. In the latter case, NTI holds no power of nomination; however, NTI delegates responsibility for the administration of Inuit-owned lands to these institutions: i.e., RIAs. Finally, the Nunavut Trust has its own unique relationship with NTI. I will now briefly examine the function of these institutions.

Public Co-Management Boards

The Nunavut Land Claims Agreement sets aside provisions for the creation of five Public Co-Management Boards (DIAND 1993: Article 10). These institutions (Table 3) are financed by Canada, and members to these organizations are nominated by NTI, the GN and Canada.[8] Once nominated, members do not defend the interests of the institutions that nominated them; rather, they defend the interests of all Nunavut citizens. As such, Co-Management Boards are considered public institutions even though one may suppose that Inuit Rights would be a high priority in the minds of members whenever decisions are to be taken on issues.

Co-Management Boards are responsible for the management of renewable and non-renewable resources throughout the Nunavut Settlement Area (Figure 1). Even though the Federal Cabinet has the power to veto decisions from Co-Management

FIGURE 4. NTI and Other Public and Inuit Institutions in Nunavut

[Diagram showing Nunavut Tunngavik Inc. at top, with designated relations to Public Co-Management Boards, Inuit Heritage Trust, and Nunavut Social Development Council; delegated relations to Regional Inuit Associations Qikiqtani, Kivalliq, Kitikmeot, which connects to Nunavut Trust; financial relations from Nunavut Trust back to Nunavut Tunngavik Inc.]

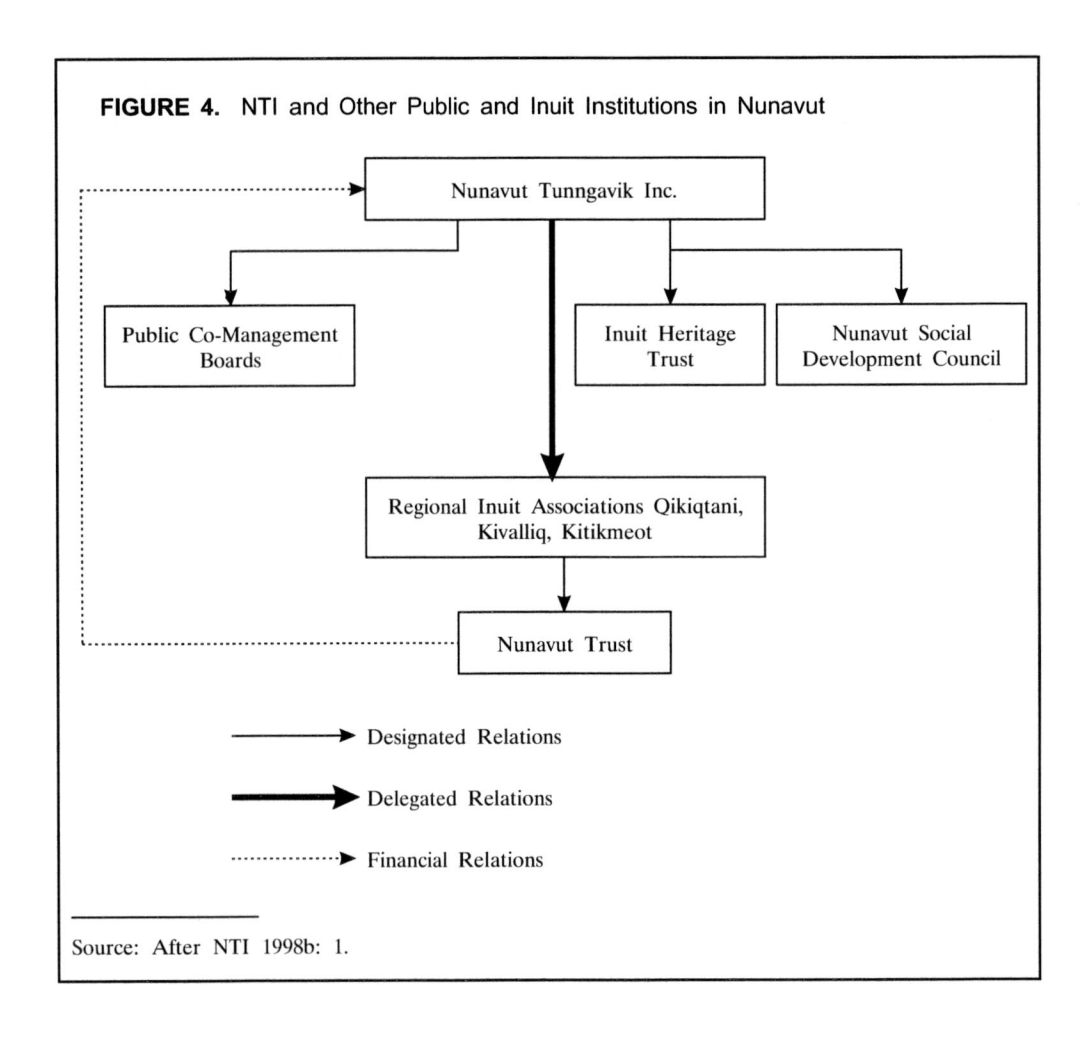

- Designated Relations
- Delegated Relations
- Financial Relations

Source: After NTI 1998b: 1.

Boards, this is rarely done. In fact, Cabinet can use this power only to protect the resources.[9]

A proponent who wishes to develop a mining or an oil and gas project in Nunavut would need the approval of some of these Co-Management Boards. Since at least half of the members of these Co-Management Boards are nominees from NTI and the remainders are also generally of Inuit descent, NTI is assured that the interests of Inuit are taken into account by these Boards. In fact, Co-Management Boards provide NTI with a significant role with regard to economic development in Nunavut. Even though these Boards are, in theory, public institutions, in reality their membership is largely Inuit, and NTI nominees compose the majority of members.

Inuit Heritage Trust

The Inuit Heritage Trust (IHT) was established in April 1994 through the implementation of Article 33 of the NLCA (DIAND 1993: 241). The four members

TABLE 3. Nunavut Public Co-Management Boards

Name: Nunavut Wildlife Management Board
Headquarters: Iqaluit
Members Designated (8): NTI (4); GN (1); Canada(3); Makivik[*]
Function: The Board supervises and regulates wildlife harvestings. Respecting conservation principles, it determines the quotas on fish and mammals harvested within the Nunavut Settlement Area.

Name: Nunavut Impact Review Board
Headquarters: Cambridge Bay
Members Designated (8): NTI (4); GN (2); Canada (2).
Function: The Board screens development project proposals. It gauges their impacts on the Arctic ecosystem. Ultimately the Board approves or disapproves project proposals.

Name: Nunavut Planning Board
Headquarters: Taloyoak
Members Designated (8): NTI (4); GN (2); Canada (2).
Function: The Commission is responsible for setting planning goals. It formulates and reviews land use plans. It ensures that development projects respect the Nunavut land use plans.

Name: Surface Rights Tribunal
Headquarters: Iqaluit
Member Designated (8): NTI (4); GN (2); Canada (2).
Function: The Tribunal determines the amount of indemnity given to NTI when a proponent damages the ecosystem of the Nunavut Settlement Area.

Name: Nunavut Water Board
Headquarters: Gjoa Haven
Members Designated (8): NTI (4); GN (2); Canada (2).
Function: The Board has responsibilities and powers over the regulation, use and management of water in Nunavut.

[*] The Makivik Corporation represents the Inuit of Nunavik (Northern Quebec). Because of the interest Makivik has on off shore islands located within Nunavut, it has one ex-officio member sitting on the Board.

Source: Légaré 1996b: 153.

of the Board of Directors are nominated by NTI for a period of three years. The IHT has the mandate to manage all archeological sites found in Nunavut. It is responsible for delivering archeological permits. The IHT is also responsible for establishing by-laws and policies regarding the protection of Nunavut archeological sites. Finally, it approves any proposed new name or name change for topographic sites in Nunavut.

Nunavut Social Development Council

The Nunavut Social Development Council (NSDC) was created in October 1996. From March 1993 to September 1996 NSDC was already one of the departments of NTI. Its Board of Directors has twelve members, all nominated by NTI for a duration of three years.

The role of the NSDC is clearly described in Article 32 of the NLCA (DIAND 1993: 239). It is mandated to do research on Inuit cultural and social issues. It is further mandated to advise the new Government of Nunavut on all Inuit cultural policies and on programs and services delivered by the GN that may have an impact on Inuit culture. The NSDC is also responsible for diffusion of Inuit Traditional Knowledge (*Inuit Qaujimajatuqangit*). Since the Government of Nunavut considers that *Inuit Qaujimajatuqangit* is an important component of its programs and policies, this consideration gives NSDC a significant say with regard to policy development by the GN. In the past, the NSDC has been highly critical of the way the GN manages Inuit culture in Nunavut: "Inuktitut is being replaced by English, children aren't learning Inuit traditions and government programs don't always include Inuit values" (Rideout 2001: 3). In sum, through the NSDC, NTI attempts to influence GN policy making.

Regional Inuit Associations

NTI has control and management over Inuit-owned lands throughout the Nunavut Settlement Area (DIAND 1993: Art. 39). NTI, however, has delegated some of its responsibilities over Inuit lands to RIAs (Kitikmeot, Kivalliq, Qikiqtani). At its inaugural Annual General Assembly, on July 10, 1993, NTI delegates voted in favour of giving management and control over surface Inuit-owned lands (317,353 sq. km.) to the RIAs. NTI kept its management authority over sub-surface Inuit-owned lands (36,257 sq. km.).

In summary, RIAs control Inuit surface lands located within their respective regions, while NTI has control over all Inuit sub-surface lands (i.e., mineral rights). Because sub-surface Inuit-owned lands are located under surface Inuit-owned properties, it is crucial for NTI to establish a good rapport with the RIAs with regard to Inuit land management so as to avoid any possible conflicts between NTI and the RIAs over non-renewable resource development.

However, past experiences have shown that the relationship between NTI and the RIAs in that regard has not always been smooth (Légaré 1996b: 153). In fact, the working relations between NTI and the RIAs over Inuit land management reminds us of the often strained relationship that exists between the provincial government and the federal government: "Quassa said, the haggling at the meeting reminds him of the way the federal government and the provincial battle it out for power" (Gregoire 1993: 10).

As we know, NTI represents the interests of all Inuit beneficiaries to the NLCA (DIAND 1993: Art. 19). However, the three RIAs believe that they are closer to the common interests of the Inuit since they are endowed with the responsibility of defending those interests from a regional perspective rather than pan-territorial. The RIAs wish to be granted all responsibilities with regard to control and management of Inuit-owned lands, whether those lands are surface or sub-surface owned. With exclusive control over Inuit lands, the RIAs believe that the regions will benefit more financially from land development: "... Regional Inuit Associations are the entities that should be in control of economic development in their regions" (Nunatsiaq News 1994: 7). "Some of what NTI is doing in land management and economic development should be left to the regions" (Gregoire 1994a: 5). Nevertheless, giving the RIAs increased power over land management could reveal itself as a double edged sword. Regions with greater mineral potential (i.e., Kitikmeot) could become much richer while less endowed regions would not benefit. At present, because NTI controls sub-surface riches owned by Inuit, any financial benefits are spread equally among all regions.

NTI Annual General Assemblies often reveal the rift between NTI and the RIAs on this issue: "NTI appeals to delegates at the year's annual general meeting to place Nunavut's interests ahead of their regional differences" (Wilkins 1997: 12). "Kono Tattuinee a delegate from Arviat said: ... We're working against each other, and that's not what Nunavut's about" (Van Rassel 1996: 13).

The Nunavut Trust

The Nunavut Trust was established by the TFN on April 1, 1990. Its mandate is described in Article 31 of the NLCA (DIAND 1993: 237). The Trust receives, manages and invests the 1.1 billion dollars that the Inuit of Nunavut received from Canada when they signed the NLCA (DIAND 1993: Art. 29). The Trust also receives and manages all resource royalties payable under the NLCA (DIAND 1993: Art. 25).

The six trustees who are responsible for the management of the Trust are appointed by the RIAs (two per region) for a period of three years. Even though the Trust is the sole funding provider of NTI and the RIAs, it is independent from both.

The money received by the Trust is invested into interest-bearing bank accounts, bonds, or share equities (e.g., Bell Canada). The funding of NTI's annual budget ($21 million for the fiscal year 2000/2001) comes from some of the interests and investment returns earned annually by the Trust. In 1999, the Trust made $31 million in profits from its investments (Ashbury 1999: B7). Surpluses not used by NTI are reinvested.

THE PROGRAMS AND SERVICES DELIVERED BY THE NUNAVUT TUNNGAVIK INC.

NTI is responsible for the delivery of two programs and services: (1) Nunavut Elders' Benefit Plan; (2) Nunavut Hunter Support Program (NTI 1998c). However, because of its major financial impact on almost all Inuit families, most of this section is dedicated to an analysis of the Nunavut Hunter Support Program.

The Nunavut Elders' Benefit Plan

The Nunavut Elders' Benefit Plan (NEBP) was established by NTI as a reward to Inuit elders. Their traditional knowledge and their use of the land helped in the drafting of the *Inuit Land Use and Occupancy Project* (Freeman 1976). This document legitimized Inuit claims in the Canadian Eastern Arctic (ITC 1976, 1977, 1979) and resulted in the finalization of the NLCA: "Kusugak said, the whole idea behind this is to thank the elders, after all, this whole claim — the land use part of the claim regarding hunting etc. — is all based on the knowledge of our old people and the support they gave us" (Gregoire 1994b: 20).

NTI administers and delivers the NEBP. All Inuit beneficiaries aged 46 and older as of December 31, 1994 are entitled to the program.[10] Those who on that date aged 50 and older will receive a monthly pension of $100, and those aged between 46 and 49 will receive a monthly pension of $75. The NEBP starts as the candidates reach their 55th birthday and will last for the rest of their lives. The NEBP cannot be transferred to other members of the family once the beneficiary has deceased. Finally, elders who were already aged 55 as of December 31, 1994, received an additional one-time amount of $1,000.

In 1997, 1,421 Inuit benefited from the NEBP. Eventually up to 2,125 Inuit elders could benefit. The costs for the delivery of this program amounted to $1.6 million in 1996 (NTI 1998c: 46). It is estimated that once all beneficiaries have deceased, the program will have cost NTI between $45 and $50 million.

The Nunavut Hunter Support Program

Traditional wildlife harvesting activities, such as hunting, fishing and trapping, are at the center of Inuit culture and lifestyle. They reinforce the social cohesiveness of Inuit society and play an important economic role (cf. Wenzel 1991). Sadly, those harvesting activities practised full time in the past by Inuit for their livelihood have now become threatened by new economic realities. The fur boycott launched by European countries in the 1970s and 1980s against the Canadian seal industry has dealt a serious economic blow to Inuit fur trapping.

Because of the European and American boycotts, fur prices have plummeted. In 1990, fur sales could only bring to an Inuk hunter a meagre annual income of $1,240 (RT & Assoc. 1993: 47). In 1980, the same hunter would have earned $11,258 for the sale of his furs. We can see now the economic disaster brought to Inuit hunters and to Inuit traditional way of life within a short span of a few years. The market prices for furs are so low now that it has become impossible for an Inuk hunter to make reasonable wages in the traditional economy.

In 1992, TFN asked the consulting firm RT & Associates to do a report analysis on the financial needs of Inuit families for whom wildlife harvesting was the primary economic activity. The report was submitted to NTI by RT & Associates in June 1993.

According to the report, in 1990, 90 percent of Nunavut households relied on harvesting for country food. In fact, 85 percent of all Inuit families were involved to various degrees in the traditional economy (RT & Assoc. 1993: 36, 40). It is estimated that the value-exchange coming from country food in Nunavut in 1990 amounted to $62.4 million. These numbers show the importance of hunting, fishing, and trapping in the economy of Nunavut. However, the high costs associated with the purchase of hunting equipment makes these activities prohibitive for the average Inuk hunter. In 1993, the costs of equipment items could be as high as

TABLE 4. Costs for Harvesting Equipment (1993)

Equipment	Purchase Cost	Annual Cost for Maintenance
Snowmobile	5,400	2,700
Canoe/Boat	4,500	750
Boat Motor	4,900	1,633
Rifles/Ammunitions	300	75
Tent/Cabin	500	250
Traps	1,800	120
Fishing Nets	400	200
ATV	3,500	875
Komatik	300	75
HF Radio	2,400	240
Tools	500	167
Gasoline	—	3,563
Camp Gear	2,000	1,000
Total	**$26,000**	**$11,648**

Source: RT & Assoc. 1993: 54.

$26,000 while annual maintenance of equipment, such as a snowmobile, could reach $11,648 (see Table 4).

Since they can absorb the high costs of equipment, the most successful hunters are those who have full-time employment in the wage economy (e.g., government employment) and practise wildlife harvesting as a part time activity. These are the weekend hunters. For the family households[11] who practise full time harvesting (there were 1,082 such households in 1993), it is necessary for the full time hunters[12] to have supplement incomes, beyond social assistance, to buy and maintain the yearly costs associated with hunting equipment.

After the mid-1980s, it was made clear to Inuit hunters that they could not rely on the sale of furs as a significant income source. Social assistance did not bring much help to the full time hunter. The TFN realized that the sole option for maintaining the traditional Inuit economy of wildlife harvesting was to provide a funding mechanism to the full time hunter. The TFN first tried to convince Canada to implement a Harvesting Support Program as part of the NLCA. However, Canada refused categorically, stating that these programs were funded by territorial or provincial governments. In fact, the James Bay and Northern Quebec Agreement, signed in 1975, is the only Comprehensive Claims Agreement in Canada where one finds such a program [in Section 30 of JBNQA 1976]. The program is wholly subsidized by the Government of Quebec. In 1992, the TFN decided to create and subsidize its own unique hunter support program. The Nunavut Hunter Support Program (NHSP) is now administered and financed by NTI.

TABLE 5. Annual Spending (1995–1988): Nunavut Hunter Support Program

Year	Amount
1995	$1,956,921
1996	1,928,195
1997	2,223,168
1998	2,707,000

Households where the main economic activities centre on hunting, fishing and trapping for at least six months of the year may apply for the NHSP.[13] The goal of the NHSP is to promote the Inuit traditional economy of wildlife harvesting. The program allows the full time hunter to acquire increased financial independence and greater self-esteem: "...a meaningful hunter income support program would allow many of our people to regain pride in their way of life" (Bell 1993: 7).

From 1993 to 1997, both NTI and the Government of the Northwest Territories invested a total of $30 million in this program. Most of that money has been put in short term saving accounts while the rest has already been spent (see Table 5). It is estimated that the investments earned from these savings will enable the program to be self-sufficient until the year 2010; after that date new money will be needed. The Nunavut Trust will likely be the new financial source (NTI 1998c: 43).

The NHSP is centred on households, not on individuals. Only one member per household can benefit from the program even if the household has more than one full time hunter. Each year about 250 households[14] are selected to benefit from the NHSP. The program runs on a five-year cycle (1995–2000, 2000–2005, etc.). Once selected, a household cannot be eligible for the program for the next four years. Households with the lowest annual income (lower than $26,000) were the first to be selected. By 2001, all households practising full time hunting fishing, and trapping were supposed to have benefited from the program.

The NHSP costs each year $2 million. Each household receives about $12,000. Most of this amount is delivered in forms of credit bonds, not cash.[15] The credit bonds are used by the hunter to purchase equipment (boat, snowmobile, rifle, etc.) through a dealership accredited by the program. The dealership will then get payment directly from NTI. This process guarantees that the funds are spent solely for hunting equipment.

The criteria for selection are established by local Hunter and Trappers Associations (HTAs).[16] It is expected that the HTAs are in the best position to know which households rely mostly on the Inuit traditional economy. On average, about 20 percent of households of each of the 26 Nunavut communities will, in the end, benefit from the NHSP.

Requests for selection to the program are submitted by households to HTAs in November of each year.[17] Names are selected in March of the following year.

Each submission is valued according to the following criteria: time dedicated to wildlife harvesting; the annual household income; the household need for new equipment; and the willingness to share country food with other residents of the community. The list of the selected candidates is then submitted for approval by NTI. The name lists submitted by the HTAs are generally approved by NTI. This gives significant power to the HTAs and has exposed the NHSP to some criticism.

Allegations of patronage and nepotism have plagued the NHSP: "...of the 14 Iqaluit hunters who got benefits only about one-third are legitimate full-time hunters. Iqaluit HTA used the program to reward their relatives. One man who got assistance is the brother of the HTA Chairman, and another has a full-time job" (Gregoire 1995: 19).

In addition, the HTAs do not check to see if the equipment provided to the candidates is used for the purposes requested: i.e., hunting, fishing and trapping. There were some cases where equipment newly acquired by the selected candidate was then sold by the candidate to other community residents in order to obtain cash. "...there are hunters that got snowmobiles through the program and two or three only are using these as transportation around the community" (Nunatsiaq News 1996: 7). "NTI is not actively involved in ensuring the goals of the program" (Nunatsiaq News 1998: 8). These complaints have convinced some local HTAs to withdraw from the program (e.g., Coral Harbour). In the spring of 1998, NTI decided to be more involved in the selection of candidates in order to alleviate some of the biases emerging from the selection process.

The NHSP is not the only hunter support program to have been under criticism. In Nunavik (i.e., northern Quebec) a hunter support program has been in existence since 1975, following the signature of the James Bay and Northern Quebec Agreement (Quebec 1976: Section 30). The Inuit Hunting, Fishing and Trapping Support Program (IHFTSP) was endorsed by the Quebec legislature in December 1982 (Quebec 1982).

The basic objectives of the IHFTSP are similar to those found in the NHSP. Both programs have been put forward so as to encourage the continuation of traditional Inuit harvesting activities and to ensure a supply of country food to Inuit households. However, the similarities stop there. There are four major factors that distinguish the IHFTSP from the NHSP: first, the IHFTSP is wholly financed by the government;[18] second, neither the Nunavik Inuit organization (Makivik Corporation) nor local HTAs exercise any control over the program; third, the program is geared toward individuals rather than households; fourth, the program encourages the commercialization of the hunt (cf. Duhaime 1990). Hunters are paid[19] according to the number and weight of animals they bring into the community. The country food is then put in a community freezer and distributed to all residents of the community.[20] No distinction is made here between low income or high income families; everybody is entitled to country food (Duhaime 1990: 50).

In 1997, 920 hunters participated in the IHFTSP; they earned, on average, $6,000. Some hunters made as much as $18,000. The program cost the Quebec Government $4 million (cf. Kativik 1998).[21] Generally, as one may expect, the most successful hunters were the weekend hunters who already benefit from full employment in the wage economy. They were able to afford the best equipment. In fact, the hunter support program in existence in Nunavik, contrary to the one found in

Nunavut, seems to be primarily beneficial to those who already enjoy high incomes. In summary, even though the NHSP has a number of deficiencies, it is more fair-minded in its distribution of funding support. The NHSP generally benefits low income, full time hunters.

CONCLUSION

The Nunavut Tunngavik Inc. is a private Inuit organization representing and defending the interests of all Nunavut Inuit. NTI is responsible for overseeing the implementation of the NLCA. Our analysis of NTI has revealed a number of important factors. First, NTI is a highly centralized institution whose organizational structure is based on Euro-Canadian corporate models. This structure is dominated by the four members of the Executive Committee, who are the real power brokers of NTI. In fact, NTI decision-making process is collegial, rather than presidential. Decisions are taken by the whole of the Executive, in which the President is just one of the members. Under these circumstances, the role of the President of NTI can best be described as one of a spokesperson presenting to the public the collegial decisions of the Executive.

Second, tensions between NTI and the RIAs will likely continue for as long as land management operations remain as they are: i.e., surface rights go to the RIAs, sub-surface rights to NTI. Third, with the exclusion of the Nunavut Trust, NTI has significant links (delegated, designated) with all institutions created through the NLCA. NTI therefore possesses a certain degree of influence over the decisions taken by these institutions. Fourth, programs and services put forward by NTI have generally been highly appreciated by Inuit beneficiaries. Even though our analysis has shown that the selection process of the NHSP should be improved and that a bigger annual budget should be requested to bring further financial comfort to full time hunters, the program has been, in general, quite successful and has helped increase wildlife harvesting activities in Nunavut.

Finally, the question remains: which is the main political power entity in Nunavut — the Government of Nunavut, or the Nunavut Tunngavik Inc.? The *Clyde River Protocol*, endorsed by the GN, seems to say that NTI is the real power broker in Nunavut. In fact, in its working relationship with the GN, one may portray NTI as a "watchdog" or as an "ex-officio opposition" to the Government of Nunavut. NTI does not hesitate to criticize the new government whenever it feels that its policies are not conscious of the provisions of the NLCA or of Inuit culture. The GN has taken the habit of consulting regularly with NTI, as proposed by the *Clyde River Protocol*, so as to avoid any imbroglios. Because of its central role in almost all institutions in Nunavut, and because of its power to influence the Government of Nunavut's political agenda, one must conclude that, at present, the Nunavut Tunngavik Inc. is the most powerful political force in Nunavut.[22]

NOTES

1. An English translation of the Inuktitut name "Nunavut Tunngavik Inc." would read as: "Foundation Our Land Inc."
2. The TFN represented the interests of the Nunavut Inuit during the negotiation period (1982–1993) that led to the conclusion of the NLCA.

3. The fact that four of the ten members of the Board are also members of the Executive may explain why, to this day, all past decisions taken by the Executive have been approved by the Board.
4. Each regional representative is elected for a three-year mandate to sit on the Board by the General Assembly of its RIA.
5. Each RIA has an organizational structure similar to NTI (i.e., General Assembly, Board of Directors, Executive Committee).
6. To this day, no decision taken by the Executive has been reversed by the General Assembly.
7. Of course one must take into account the previous existence of its predecessor: the Tungavik Federation of Nunavut (1981–1993).
8. All members of the Boards are nominated for a three-year mandate.
9. In 1996, the Federal Minister for the Department of Fisheries and Ocean Canada vetoed a decision from the Nunavut Wildlife Management Board regarding turbot quotas in the Davis Straight for Inuit fishermen in order to protect the species.
10. This program is in addition to the already existing federal and territorial pension plans to which all Nunavut citizens are entitled once they reach the age of 65.
11. Each household has an average six family members.
12. Full time hunters are generally heavily dependent on social assistance for their incomes. In Nunavut, 40 percent of adult Inuit are unemployed and rely on social assistance.
13. To qualify, a hunter must spend annually at least 960 hours on harvesting activities.
14. This number represents about 20 percent of all households whose main economic activity is wildlife harvesting.
15. Only $2,000 is given to the hunter for the purchase of gasoline.
16. There is a HTA in each of the 26 Nunavut communities.
17. In 1998, 1,986 households submitted requests, which is almost double the number who had given "Inuit traditional economy" as their full time economic activity in previous years. Are we witnessing a tremendous increase in full time hunting in Nunavut, or are we seeing unqualified people submitting requests? The latter is likely the answer.
18. The Government of Quebec is the sole funding source.
19. Payments are made by the Kativik Regional Public Government on behalf of the Quebec Government.
20. There are 14 communities in Nunavik.
21. The IHFTSP costs twice as much as the NHSP for a population of just 9,000 Inuit.
22. On a lighter note, it is interesting to note that the building housing the Legislative Assembly of the Government of Nunavut is actually owned by Nunavut Constuction Ltd., a subsidiary firm of NTI!

REFERENCES

ASHBURY, DOUG. 1999. "Nunavut Trust books 17 per cent gain", *News/North*, (May 17): B7.
BELL, JIM. 1993. "Patterson backs hunter income plan", *Nunatsiaq News*, (May 7): 7.
CARPENTER, MARY. 1994. "Inuit leaderships shattered kaleidoscope", *Nunatsiaq News*, (Dec. 2): B25.
DEAN, BERT. 1999. "Nunavut Harvester Support Program", *Ittuaqtuut*, 1(2): 12–13.
DIAND (Department of Indian Affairs and Northern Development). 1993. *Nunavut Land Claims Agreement*, Ottawa, Supply and Services.
———. 1994. *Inuit Lands: Nunavut* (poster), Ottawa.
DUHAIME, GÉRARD. 1990. "La chasse inuit subventionnée: tradition et modernité", *Recherches sociographiques*, 31(1): 45–62.
FENGE, TERRY and JOHN MERRITT. 1989. *Nunavut: Political choice and manifest destiny*, Ottawa, Canadian Arctic Resources Committee.
FREEMAN, MILTON M.R. 1976. *Inuit land use and occupancy project*, 3 vols., Ottawa, DIAND, Milton Freeman Research Ltd.
GREGOIRE, LISA. 1993. "Tunngavik Assembly to meet for first time", *Nunatsiaq News*, (July 2): 10.
———. 1994a. "Regional tensions surface at NTI assembly", *Nunatsiaq News*, (Dec. 9): 5.
———. 1994b. "Nunavut elders to get pension this year", *Nunatsiaq News*, (April 22): 20.
———. 1995. "Complaints cloud hunters' support plan", *Nunatsiaq News*, (June 16): 19.
ITC (Inuit Tapisisat du Canada). 1976. *Nunavut. A proposal for the settlement of Inuit lands in the Northwest Territories*, Ottawa: ITC.
———. 1977. *Speaking for the first citizens of the Canadian Arctic*, Ottawa.

———. 1979. *Political development in Nunavut*, Ottawa.
KATIVIK (Kativik Regional Government). 1998. *Inuit Hunting, Fishing, and Trapping Support Program*, Kuujjuak.
LÉGARÉ, ANDRÉ. 1996a. "Le gouvernement du Territoire du Nunavut (1999): un analyse prospective" *Études/Inuit/Studies*, 20(1): 7–43.
———. 1996b. "The process leading to a land claims agreement and its implementation: The case of the Nunavut Land Claims Settlement", *The Canadian Journal of Native Studies*,16(1): 139–63.
———. 1997. 'The Government of Nunavut (1999): A prospective analysis". In J.R. Ponting (Dir.), *First Nations in Canada*, Toronto: McGraw-Hill Ryerson Ltd.
———. 1998a. *The evolution of the Government of the Northwest Territories (1967–1995)*, Québec, Université Laval, Gétic, travaux de recherches.
———. 1998b. "Le Nunavut. Le compte à rebours est commencé", *Recherches amérindiennes au Québec*, 28(2): 101–106.
———. 2001. "The spatial and symbolic construction of Nunavut: Towards the emergence of a regional collective identity" *Etudes/Inuit/Studies*, 25(1/2): 141–68.
MITCHELL, MARYBELLE. 1996. *From talking chiefs to a Native corporate elite. The birth of class and nationalism among Canadian Inuit*, Montréal & Kingston, McGill-Queen's University Press.
NAGATA, SHUICHI. 1987. "From ethnic bourgeoisie to organic intellectuals: Speculations on North American Native leadership", *Anthropologica*, 29: 61–75.
NTI (Nunavut Tunngavik Inc.). 1996. *Nunavut Tunngavik: A guide to NTI Departments*, Iqaluit.
———. 1998a. *Nunavut Tunngavik Incorporated organization chart* (poster), Iqaluit.
———. 1998b. *NTI and Nunavut's network of organizations* (poster), Iqaluit.
———. 1998c *Nunavut Tunngavik Incorporated 1997 Annual Report*, Iqaluit.
NTI, Nunavut (Nunavut Tunngavik Inc. and Gouvernement of Nunavut). 1999. *The Clyde River Protocol*, Iqaluit.
NUNATSIAQ NEWS. 1993. "A good start for NTI", *Nunatsiaq News*, (Dec. 17): 7.
———. 1994. "What should NTI be doing", *Nunatsiaq News*, (Nov. 18): 7.
———. 1996. "NTI ignoring youth, says reader", *Nunatsiaq News*, (Jan. 19): 7.
———. 1998. "Aivilik's MLA critizes NTI's hunter support program", *Nunatsiaq News*, (March 13): 8
PETER, JACOPOOSIE. 1995. "The need for change", *Nunatsiaq News*, (Nov. 17): 8.
QUEBEC (Government of Quebec). 1976. *James and Northern Quebec Agreement*, Québec, Editeur officiel.
———. 1982. *Loi sur le programme d'aide aux Inuit bénéficiaires de la Convention de la Baie James et du Nord québécois pour leurs activités de chasse, de pêche et de piégeage (loi 83)*, Québec, Assemblée nationale.
RIDEOUT, DENISE. 2001. "NSDC chides Government on Inuit culture", *Nunatsiaq News*, (Oct. 12): 3.
RODRIGUE, MICHAELA. 1999a. "NTI delegates approve 2000–2001 budget", *Nunatsiaq News*, (Nov. 5): 16.
———. 1999b. "Nunavut government, NTI sign co-operation pact", *Nunatsiaq News*, (Nov. 5): 16.
RT & ASSOCIATES. 1993. *Nunavut Harvest Support Program. Background document*, Yellowknife.
SAWCHUK, JOE. 1998. *The dynamics of Native politics*, Saskatoon, Purich Publishing.
VAN RASSEL. 1996. "Office move opens regional tension", *Nunatsiaq News*, (Nov. 8): 13.
WENZEL, GEORGE. 1991. *Animal rights, human rights. Ecology, economy and ideology in the Canadian Arctic*, Toronto, University of Toronto Press.
WILKIN, DWANE. 1997. "Jose Kusugak: put Nunavut's interest first", *Nunatsiaq News*, (Oct. 31): 12.

(b) Neither Boom Nor Bust: The Renewable Resource Economy May Be the Best Long-term Hope for Northern Communities[†]

Heather Myers

Canada virtually ignored its Northwest Territories and northern peoples until after the Second World War. Then, as national security and other concerns prompted the federal government to devote some attention to the region, the poor conditions of some northern native peoples also came to light, prompting various housing, education and health initiatives.[1] In addition, resource development was pursued as a source of employment and income.

The prevailing assumption was that native peoples, particularly the younger generations, would be assimilated into the dominant industrial model of economic development. Other forms of small-scale development were viewed as a stop-gap measure.[2]

However, this assumption has proven erroneous. Non-renewable resource developments have not ensured adequate or stable employment, either for northern peoples or for imported workers. Furthermore, the younger generation has not shown a clear preference for moving from the land into industry.

For example, mining employed between 140 and 244 native persons in the Northwest Territories between 1990 and 1995 (9 to 12 percent of the total mining work force, and only about 1.5 percent of the native labour force).[3] Oil and gas exploration boomed in the 1970s and early 1980s, and many companies pursued native employment and business creation. But relatively few native people gained permanent or significant work and, in any case, job creation was fairly localized. Now that the oil boom is over, those jobs no longer exist.

However, northern peoples have needed to supplement their land-based income of food and materials with some kind of cash income. The current land-based lifestyle, and life in communities entail increasing cash expenses: paying for utilities, buying food or children's treats at the Bay, and buying ammunition, nets, snowmobiles and gasoline for hunting, fishing and trapping. This indicates a need for some form of development that would allow people to supplement their land-based income with cash. In the absence of this, social assistance and unemployment insurance must be used.[4]

Employment and economic patterns in the NWT are telling. Formal unemployment ranges from 17 to 50 percent in the smaller communities. In the average small northern community, there might be no more than 50 full-time jobs available, as school teachers, nurses, RCMP officers, hamlet administrators and workers, social workers or other territorial government officials, and store clerks. In a com-

---

[†] Reproduced from *Alternatives Journal: Environmental thought, policy and action* 22(4): 18–23. Annual subscriptions $25.00 (plus GST) from Alternatives Journal, Faculty of Environmental Studies, University of Waterloo, Waterloo, Ontario N2L 3G1 <ww.alternativesjournal.ca>.

munity of 500 to 1000, that represents much less than one job per household. Also, many of these jobs are filled by workers imported from outside the communities.

As a result, many people actively pursue a "mixed" household economy — combining some seasonal or part-time wage-paying work for cash income, with traditional pursuits such as hunting, fishing and trapping, crafts-making or carving.[5] These pursuits may provide domestic or subsistence income, that is, products and materials that are used within the household, and/or commercial income from sales of the products. So, although people may not be actively involved in the wage-paying "formal" sector,[6] they are not necessarily "unemployed". Official unemployment statistics, which only relate to one part of the economy, are therefore misleading.

The official 1994 NWT Labour Force Survey estimated that only 61 percent of natives were involved in the formal workforce in 1994, compared to 89 percent of non-natives.[7] To a degree, this reflects lower educational or skill levels among the native labour force (41 percent have never attended secondary school)[8] and a reluctance to leave one's home community to work elsewhere, but it also represents a preference to pursue other livelihoods. Analysis of regional harvest studies and individual community studies has suggested that in the mid- to late-1980s, 80 percent of native households in the NWT had at least one harvester.[9] Each brought home, on average, the equivalent of $10,000 to $11,000 in country food, fish, wood fuel, furs or hides — a substantial "subsistence income" of food and materials, which also reduces cash requirements. Other research has found that people actively pursue wage employment in order to fund their subsistence harvesting activities and may prefer part-time or seasonal jobs that allow them greater freedom to pursue traditional activities.[10]

So, despite predictions of the demise of the traditional economy of hunting, fishing and trapping, this sector of the northern economy has persisted, for economic as well as cultural reasons. But the conundrum remains. There are increasing needs for cash income to support harvesting activities as well as community life; but there are also few wage-paying job opportunities, and a continuing preference for participation in the traditional harvesting economy. Can these not be brought together to find a solution?

That question has been a quiet, persistent voice in northern development programmes, despite the prevailing government preference for large-scale resource exploitation and industrial development. Indeed, some economic development programmes funded in the North — notably the Government of Canada/GNWT Special Rural Development Agreement (1977) have included provisions for renewable resource-based development.

When oil was the driving force, the first federal-territorial Economic Development Agreement (1982) anticipated that the renewable resource sector would be a small-time supplement to major, non-renewable resource developments.[11] After the boom went bust, the importance of renewable resources was given greater emphasis in the second Economic Development Agreement (1987).[12] More recently, the territorial government has explicitly addressed the potential of the renewable resource sector for assisting in development of northern communities.[13]

Just how well renewable resource development projects have done in terms of employing northern peoples in their communities can be seen in the experience of seven main sectors of renewable resource development.[14]

RENEWABLE OPTIONS

Commercial fisheries have been conducted in Great Slave Lake and along the Arctic coast for several decades. The Freshwater Fish Marketing Corporation reports a value, from their sales alone, of $1.4 million in 1992/93.[15] These fisheries operate at various scales, from single fishers or families harvesting char during the short arctic season, to winter operations by snowmobiles on the ice, and larger boats, including some freezer-packer boats. These latter allow travel to more distant fishing areas, and better preservation of fish quality until it can be shipped south to market.

The industry is vulnerable to fluctuating fish prices dictated by southern producers and consumers, competition with salmon farms in Canada and Europe, and weather, which can interfere with fishing or transportation. There are some attempts to process fish more fully in the North, through filleting or smoking for instance, which will increase employment and income benefits within communities.

Forestry operations have also been conducted in the western NWT for many decades, first to supply road, mine, mission and pipeline construction needs, but now to supply lumber and building logs to the North and, to a degree, to the South. Aside from some larger existing mills, some communities are interested in developing small-scale logging and milling enterprises, both to serve the larger mills, and to supply local needs. The value of lumber produced in 1991/92 was estimated at $1.1 million, down from $2.2 million in 1980/81, while fuel wood production also decreased from about two million to one million dollars in the same period.[16]

A natural outgrowth of the traditional economy is the production of country food, and several successful community-based stores are processing meats and selling them locally or regionally. Initially, it seems surprising that these should do so well, given that many people still hunt for their own meat. Nonetheless, hunters will provide part of their harvest to the local country food outlet, and keep part for home consumption; they may even go back to the store and buy some of the meat they originally provided. The stores are able to produce jerky, corned meat, salamis and so on, adding to the value of the product, creating local employment as well as products that appeal to consumers.

Food production also generates harvest by-products: fur, leather, bone, antler, and associated crafts. These may support, for example, groups of women doing traditional tanning of moose hides, or organizing to produce and market handmade articles. This remains an important economic pursuit, particularly for older native women who may have few other opportunities. The 1989 Labour Force Survey found that 27 percent of NWT native persons participated in traditional crafts, generating perhaps eight million dollars per year.[17] Unfortunately, like many arts and crafts pursuits, the remuneration, while crucial, is very low considering the hours invested in production. Personal satisfaction and the need for cash counteract this to a degree, but northern women continue to seek ways to increase their return from craft production.

Further, this sector has suffered a number of setbacks because of southern, urban anti-harvest campaigns, as well as barriers such as the US *Marine Mammals Protection Act* and the European Community bans on sealskins and furs. From a northern perspective, however, people must still eat, and it is only common sense to use materials that would otherwise go to waste.

Tourism, sport fishing and sport hunting have existed for several decades in the NWT. Initially, sport fishing and hunting predominated, with lodges or camps often owned by non-native business people from southern Canada. Native people derived some employment from these ventures, usually as guides or cooks, but the local benefits were limited. More recently, they have sought greater control of this sector, by entering the guiding and outfitting business, and in some cases by owning lodges. The nature of this sector is changing. Other wilderness or cultural experiences are sought by visitors to the NWT, either to complement or substitute for fishing and hunting. To this end, a number of native-style camps have been set up for tourists, and some existing sport camps and lodges are including other activities. Together, these sectors now provide about $50 million in sales to the NWT economy, employing 1500 full-time and 2100 part-time workers, 57 percent of them northerners.[18]

DETERMINANTS OF SUCCESS

A survey of projects in these sectors reveals several characteristics that seem to bear on their success.[19]

Projects in northern communities span the gamut from cutting wood or collecting driftwood for sale in town as firewood; to collecting sea cucumbers (a previously unused resource) for sale to Japan; to operating large, mechanized sawmills. The record suggests that neither the very traditional, nor the very modern projects enjoy the same kind of success as those which combine elements of each. Country food stores, for instance, call on a variety of skills, from traditional hunting skills, to new butchering, packaging, sales and management skills. Several of these country food outlets have done very well at a community and regional level.

To a degree, this characteristic of tradition/innovation relates to project size — very modern projects tend also to be very capital-intensive — and the relationship of project size to project viability is very clear. According to my survey, projects costing less than $30,000 are more likely to continue to operate than those costing from $30,000 to over one million dollars, and are much less likely to need additional government funding. It may be that larger projects bring with them more complicated management demands, and greater pressures that can easily crush new businesspersons. Certainly, these results indicate that the viability of large-scale projects should be carefully weighed.

Management is also critical to the success of these ventures. The prevailing ideology of government programmes has been to support private entrepreneurship. In communities with more developed economies, and perhaps more role models or support networks, this may work. However, in the smaller, more remote communities, this contradicts the native philosophy of shared rather than owned resources, and it is an onerous demand to make of people who may have no business experience or exposure. In the smaller communities, renewable resource ventures that have a community-based organization at the helm, for example, a Hunters' and Trappers' Association, or a community or native development corporation, seem to have a better chance of success.

As mentioned above, the mixed economy is still important to many northern peoples, so employment opportunities that complement harvesting activities or family and community obligations may be most desirable. Many renewable resource-based ventures are necessarily seasonal. Char run for only a short season, as do tourists. This can cause some conflicts, for instance, if people wish to fish during the summer, or take their families camping, as well as run tours. Day-to-day flexibility therefore becomes more important. One community-based sawmill has deliberately followed this approach, allowing its employees to take time off for hunting or fishing. It requires greater flexibility on the part of management, as well as some responsibility from the workers, but can be workable and thus complement community needs.

Many of these renewable resource-based businesses will never make their owners or employees rich.[20] For example, the costs of fishing on Great Slave Lake seem to take up all but a couple of thousand dollars of revenues, regardless of the size of the operation.[21] A study of sport fishing lodges in the early 1980s revealed that 41 lodges made gross sales of $6.9 million, against expenses of $6.8 million.[22] Sawmills, particularly the larger ones, seem to be plagued by high costs of equipment purchase, operation and repair, and some have struggled to keep going, needing frequent government inputs.[23]

Average earnings of employees in sawmills and sport fishing lodges were about $2000 in the early 1980s, and these wages were used to supplement other forms of income.[24] More recent studies of char fishing in the central Arctic also showed that fishers used commercial fishing as a cash complement to domestic harvest of fish and wildlife. Some fished intensively, and earned up to $2400 after costs, but the average earnings were only $665. This provides short-term viability, covering the cost of fuel, food and maintenance, but not long-term costs of business operation or replacement of equipment.[25]

In one community studied, intensive fishing could generate sufficient income to achieve long-term viability for perhaps nine fishers; but people there preferred instead to share the fishery among many, although each participant would make significantly less income.[26] This highlights an interesting difference in attitude to income: the importance of sufficiency rather than accumulation.[27]

In all cases, those ventures that depend upon southern markets seem to be vulnerable to market forces outside northerners' knowledge or control. Fish prices are set in Winnipeg, Chicago or Montreal; meat prices must compete with southern beef and pork costs; lumber prices fluctuate, depending on the southern economy; northern tourism must compete with cheap charters to Mexico.

A number of enterprises have focused instead on local and regional markets, which can draw on and enhance local pride and regional linkages, while serving consumers whose preferences are more understandable. While the tourism, sport hunting and sport fishing cater primarily to southern clienteles, the commodities sectors — food, fish, by-products and forestry — can serve northern markets, replacing, to a degree, some expensive imported products. Indeed, in my survey, the commodity-based businesses aimed at northern markets did better than those oriented primarily to exports.

Overall, an impressive number of renewable resource development projects have continued to operate.[28] Successful enterprises include, for example, country food outlets, tour outfitters and native-style tourist camps, small and medium-scale fishing operations, and a native-process tannery for moose-hides. Notable, too, is the pride and determination with which people speak of their enterprises.[29]

MADE IN THE NORTH SOLUTIONS

Earlier government assumptions about economic development in northern native communities have proven to be faulty: northern native peoples do not necessarily want to mimic the southern, industrial, or "nine-to-five" model.

Traditionally based activities on the land provide important cultural and economic support for northern communities. In the pursuit of appropriate northern development, renewable resources can offer potential for income, while complementing community lifestyles and values. They will not provide a total answer to northern development, employment and income needs, but they will satisfy some key needs and values.

As the Northwest Territories comes to terms with its future prospects for diamond mining, it is important that renewable resources not be forgotten. They have supported people down through time and may still be what people need to fall back on when the mines eventually close. And although the wealth and employment provided by mining will be important to some, many will not feel these benefits. People in small, remote communities will still need to find their niche in the modern economy.

The northern situation provides a useful test of the concept of sustainable development. On one hand, these renewable resource-based ventures offer many desirable characteristics; they can be locally based and driven, small-scale, flexible, renewable, and true to indigenous tradition. On the other hand, the success of this form of development requires understanding and tolerance from the urban populations of Canada and other Western countries, who are usually the ones driving environment/development information and campaigns, and who have been the ones defining what is meant by sustainable development. Often the resulting definition has implied only non-consumptive uses of the environment or resources.

The ability of northern communities to achieve self-reliance will depend on developing options that are suitable to their resources, needs and values. Fundamentally, if sustainable, appropriate development is to be achieved by northern native communities, we must not repeat the mistake of imposing values and assumptions from southern Canada.

NOTES

1. R.Q. Duffy, *The Road to Nunavut: The Progress of the Eastern Arctic Inuit Since the Second World War* (Montreal: McGill-Queen's University Press, 1988); and M. Zaslow, *The Northward Expansion of Canada: 1914–1967* (Toronto: McClelland and Stewart, 1988).
2. See, for example, B.G. Sivertz, "The North as a Region," *Resources for Tomorrow Conference Vol. 2 Canada* (Ottawa: Queen's Printer, 1961).

3. R. Johnstone, Energy, Mines and Petroleum Resources, Government of the Northwest Territories (GNWT) (personal communication, March 1996); and *1994 NWT Labour Force Survey, Report No. 1: Overall Results and Community Detail* (Yellowknife: Bureau of Statistics, GNWT, 1994).
4. In 1992, social assistance payments, to a monthly average of 9889 beneficiaries, totalled $26.7 million (an average of $2696 each), while UIC payments to 2353 recipients were $38.3 million *Statistics Quarterly* (Yellowknife: Bureau of Statistics, GNWT, September 1995). The debate about how social assistance is used by northern peoples is a complex one. Does the use of social assistance undermine the validity of the renewable resource harvesting lifestyle, or is it just another source of available, useful cash? For a discussion and references on this topic, see P.D. Elias, *Northern Aboriginal Communities: Economies and Development* (North York, Ontario: Captus Press, 1995). The fact remains, however, that social assistance is not a proudly chosen source of income for most northern peoples, but a necessary evil, when domestic harvesting and the lack of local employment are unable to provide for households' cash needs.
5. See Elias, *ibid.*
6. Essentially, that part of the economy that can be measured in dollars. Peter Usher and David Ross provide an insightful discussion of the formal and informal sectors in *From the Roots Up: Economic Development as if Community Mattered* (Croton-on-Hudson, New York: The Bootstrap Press, 1986).
7. *1994 Labour Force Survey* [note 3]. The survey defines the workforce as persons above the age of 15, who are either employed, or are unemployed but available or looking for work.
8. *1991 Aboriginal Peoples Data; Northwest Territories: Schooling, Work and Related Activities* (Yellowknife: Bureau of Statistics, GNWT, 1993).
9. *Keeping on the Land: A Study of the Feasibility of a Comprehensive Wildlife Harvest Support Programme in the Northwest Territories*, R. Ames, et al. (Ottawa: Canadian Arctic Resources Committee, 1988).
10. C. Hobart, "Industrial Employment of Rural Indigenes: The Case of Canada," *Human Organization*, 41:1 (1982), pp. 54–63.
11. *An Economic Development Agreement Between the Government of Canada and the Government of the Northwest Territories* (Government of Canada/Government of the Northwest Territories, December 1982).
12. *Canada-Northwest Territories Economic Development Agreement* (Government of Canada/Government of the Northwest Territories, no date, but approximately 1987).
13. It must be noted that the territorial government, as well as the native communities and management boards are very cautious about all resource harvesting for commercial purposes; it is permitted only after intensive wildlife surveys confirm what additional harvest can be sustained by the population. Commercial quotas are obtainable only after subsistence harvesting requirements have been met. For some details of GNWT policy, see: *Building on Strengths: A Community-Based Approach* (Yellowknife: Economic Development and Tourism and Department of Renewable Resources, GNWT, 1990); *Tradition and Change: A Strategy for Renewable Resource Development in the Northwest Territories* (Yellowknife: Department of Renewable Resources, GNWT, 1993).
14. These results are taken from my doctoral research evaluating the patterns of renewable resource development in the NWT, and possible factors contributing to the success of such enterprises. See Myers, *An Evaluation of Renewable Resource Development Experience in the Northwest Territories, Canada* (Cambridge, England: unpublished doctoral thesis, University of Cambridge, 1994), or contact the author at the University of Northern British Columbia, Prince George, BC.
15. *Statistics Quarterly* [note 4].
16. *Tradition and Change* [note 13].
17. *1989 Labour Force Survey* (Yellowknife: Bureau of Statistics, GNWT, 1990).
18. *Canada-Northwest Territories Economic Development Agreement; Subsidiary Agreements*, (Government of Canada/Government of the Northwest Territories, no date, but approximately 1987)
19. The results reported here are based on an analysis of 70 projects — a sample representing 15 percent of projects funded in these sectors by six main funding programmes, between 1978 and 1992. See Myers, *Evaluation* [note 14].
20. In this survey, income information was considered private; I have relied instead on the limited published/report information where available. Five reports relevant to these sectors are cited below.
21. J. Mayo, *Report on Great Slave Lake Commercial Fishery Surveys* (Yellowknife: prepared for the Department of Economic Development and Tourism, GNWT, 1991).

22. D. Topolniski, *Regional Income Analysis of NWT Fishing Lodges* (Winnipeg: Department of Fisheries and Oceans, Government of Canada, 1982).
23. R. Lagimodiere, *An Evaluation of the Benefits and Costs of the Continued Expansion of Slave River Sawmill Ltd., Fort Resolution, NWT* (Ottawa: Department of Regional Economic Expansion, Government of Canada, no date).
24. Topolniski, *Regional Income* [note 22] and *ibid.*
25. L. Yonge, *An Economic Analysis of the 1987 Whale Cove Commercial Char Fishery* (Yellowknife: prepared for the Department of Economic Development and Tourism, GNWT by Faculty of Environmental Studies, York University, North York, 1988); and L. Yonge, *An Economic Analysis of the Eskimo Point and Maguse River Commercial Char Fishery, summer 1988* (Yellowknife: prepared for the Department of Economic Development and Tourism, GNWT by Faculty of Environmental Studies, York University, North York, 1989).
26. *Ibid.*
27. This has important implications regarding the question of overharvesting if sufficiency rather than surfeit motivate northern native peoples' decision making about resource use and development.
28. Given the history of development projects that have opened, run for a short time, then closed down, leaving a legacy of "failure" and pessimism, a primary measure of project success in this survey was simply "continuation".
29. For detailed case studies of other successful aboriginal enterprises, see Elias, *Northern Aboriginal Communities*, [note 4], and W. Wuttunee, *In Business for Ourselves: Northern Entrepreneurs*, (Calgary: Arctic Institute of North America, 1992).

(c) Options for Appropriate Development in Nunavut Communities[†]

Heather Myers

INTRODUCTION

The implementation of Nunavut is not only a chance to attempt self-government, but an opportunity to develop an economy more attuned to Inuit values and resources, and perhaps show the rest of the world what sustainable development really means. At the World Commission on Environment and Development (1987), and the United Nations Conference on Environment and Development (1992), and through documents such as the Inuit Regional Conservation Strategy, the Inuit have made arguments about the value and validity of their traditional land-based economy, and their need to be able to develop according to Inuit resources, traditions and values. More recently, at a conference on the Future of Work in Nunavut, in 1997, discussions covered the need and potential for new models of work and lifestyle, more appropriate to Nunavut. By creating a more "Inuit" economy, Nunavut can illustrate an alternative path to development, different from the traditional European economic model.

This paper will briefly describe the current economic situation in Nunavut, then examine a potential new field of development, and what needs to be done in order to support this alternative approach to sustainable economic development in

---

[†] From Études/Inuit/Studies, 24(1) (2000): 25–40. Reproduced with permission of the publisher.

Nunavut communities. The main concern of the research was to find economic development alternatives that were more appropriate to northern communities, in terms of resources available, skills required, and interests and values of the community residents. Information was drawn from government files on economic development programs, and interviews of a sample of 70 entrepreneurs across the Northwest Territories (NWT) whose enterprises are based on renewable resources, whether using traditional approaches or newer ones. The focus here will be on projects occurring in, or relevant to Nunavut.

THE SETTING FOR ECONOMIC DEVELOPMENT IN NUNAVUT COMMUNITIES

There is a relatively high birth rate in Nunavut, but relatively few jobs in the formal economy. Yet living in Arctic communities, or even supporting harvesting lifestyles requires cash. If Nunavut residents are not to be shackled to a welfare-dependent supply of cash, there is a pressing need to support the creation of new income-generating employment opportunities in Nunavut communities.

Where will the necessary jobs come from? Government? Governments everywhere are cutting back. While the Nunavut government is proportionately large given the population size, and plans to employ many new people (Nunavut Implementation Commission 1995), not everyone wishes to work for government, nor might they have the skills. Other employment alternatives will be required for Nunavut residents.

Will non-renewable resource development supply the work? Mining and hydrocarbon development, as an example, are typically localized, prone to boom-and-bust patterns, and in any case, relatively few Inuit have seemed to want to work full-time in mines or on rigs (Haagen 1982; Hobart 1982; Kleinfeld et al. 1983; Bone 1992). Mining employed only about 1.5 per cent of the native labour force in the NWT between 1990 and 1995 (Bureau of Statistics 1994a); oil development has also employed relatively few native people in permanent jobs, and is now virtually shut down because of world oil prices.

Many studies, particularly from the 1980s, when oil and gas development seemed likely to boom in the Arctic, have shown that northern peoples prefer to work part-time or periodically at wage-paying jobs, while continuing to pursue traditional economic activities of hunting, fishing, trapping and gathering (Kruse 1991; Kleinfeld et al. 1983). There is little current literature on this, but comments by John Amagoalik, Chief Commissioner of the Nunavut Implementation Commission, at a conference on the Future of Work in Nunavut, seemed to indicate an openness to a more Inuit style of work, rather than the "dog-eat-dog" model of the South (Nunatsiaq News 1997).

Could renewable resource-based development provide some of the necessary employment and income? Many studies have shown the continued importance of traditional Inuit economy (Brody 1987; Wenzel 1991; Condon et al. 1995). That traditional economy, especially in the eastern NWT, is a crucial part of community economies, providing an average of $11,000 in imputed value per native household in 1986 for domestic consumption alone; commercial production is on top of that (Ames et al. 1988). Current figures for country food and domestic production indicate that this value is little changed. More than 90% of aboriginal households consume country food, and more than 70% of those households hunt or fish (www.ssimicro.com 1998).

The community profiles from the 1994 NWT Labour Force Survey (Bureau of Statistics 1994b) show the continued participation in hunting and fishing, trapping, and crafts: in the Baffin communities, for example, anywhere between 34% and 76% of the labour force are involved in hunting and fishing, 3–39% in trapping, and 15–51% in crafts. Tellingly, these rates are not directly linked to employment rates. As might be expected, communities with lower employment rates, such as Igloolik and Sanikiluaq (57% employment), have high rates of participation in hunting and fishing (61% and 58% for the respective communities), and in crafts (35% and 27% respectively). However, communities with high employment rates, such as Resolute and Grise Fiord (90% and 84%) are also active in hunting (50% and 76%), trapping (13% in each), and crafts (27% and 34%).

Small business is contributing increasingly to the northern economy — 52% of NWT employment in 1986, and 41% of the total payroll (Robinson et al. 1991). Robinson et al. foresee a future for small enterprises in ecotourism, the "information economy" or trade in traditional knowledge, arbitration and meeting skills, in-the-North hide tanning, and services. I foresee a small business sector that draws on other traditional skills and resources, in country food, fisheries, tourism and sport hunting/fishing, and harvest by-products/crafts.

In contemplating what kind of development might serve northern communities' interests, some considerations are key. Obviously there is a need for households to acquire at least some cash income, because life in the communities is expensive. There is a need for local opportunities, in order to keep families together. Employment should ideally fit with the other economic pursuits of the family, whether they are hunting, looking after the elders or children, or sitting on boards and committees. As well, it would be ideal if jobs drew on the skills and interests that people already possess or else if they required skills that would be useful in other parts of community life. Finally, desirable work and development would complement Inuit values, knowledge, culture, lifestyles and resource use patterns.

The North is littered with the remains of failed economic development programs — whether they were driven by well-meaning motives or assimilationist ones — which have tended to introduce "southern" kinds of work or work expectations. But increasingly, as native voices have become louder, and to be fair, as more government personnel have become sensitive to northern realities, programs have allowed different kinds of economic development to be pursued. Thus, there is an increasing number of enterprises, designed and operated by northerners, that better reflect their interests, needs and abilities. A sample of these will be reviewed below, and their experiences will provide some useful lessons about what can work in the northern economy, and how enterprises can be designed to fit northern communities.

The descriptions below are drawn from the files of federal and territorial departments responsible for economic development programs in the North (the Special Agricultural and Rural Development Agreement, two federal/territorial Economic Development Agreements, and programs under the Government of the Northwest Territories' departments of Economic Development and Tourism, and

TABLE 1. Funding for renewable resource-based projects in the NWT, 1977–1992

Baffin	5,515,083
Ft. Smith	5,044,960
Ft. Simpson	313,430
Inuvik	2,465,212
Keewatin	2,781,817
Kitikmeot	595,329
Norman Wells	405,168
North Slave	551,807
Yellowknife	2,282,675
TOTAL	19,955,481

Renewable Resources). These data were complemented by interviews with entrepreneurs. In respect for proponents' privacy, no names or locations will be given, but their experiences provide valuable insights into the potential for small business development in the North, and into the interest of northerners in developing new economic options based on traditional resources, skills and values.

It should be noted that the amount spent by government programs on such traditionally-rooted renewable resource enterprises has been relatively small. Over the period included in this study (1977–1992), $19,955,481 was invested by the six programs, in enterprises that were traditionally-rooted, action-oriented and community-based in their labour or resource components[1]. This comprised 480 projects over the whole NWT. Table 1 lays out the total spending, by region in the NWT, on renewable resource-based community economic development projects. This is relatively small compared to the level of government investment in non-renewable resource development

ENTERPRISES ROOTED IN TRADITION

This survey focused on renewable resource enterprises, because of their link to the traditional native economy. The question of concern is: can such enterprises contribute to the community economies in the North? The renewable resource enterprises have been grouped into four sectors for discussion here: country food; commercial fishing; fur, leather, by-products and crafts; and tourism, sport hunting and sport fishing.

Country Food

There are several country food stores and producers operating in the Nunavut area, which were supported in an effort to balance the damage done by the European sealskin ban. These outlets have experimented with narwhal and caribou jerky-making, sausage-making, and char smoking among other things, and have learned some useful lessons. For instance, narwhal jerky is not very good but caribou jerky is so good that it is hard to keep up with demand. Furthermore, people can be conservative in their tastes, at least at first. As well, people expect local products to be cheaper than imported ones, making competition tough. It is apparent that local people will sell part of their harvest to the outlet, then sometimes buy it back in processed form. Work at the country food outlets is very popular in the communities, but the businesses benefit from a manager who demands high quality and performance. A very important lesson has been that a good manager is necessary, but that the enterprise must be able to pay a manager well. A country food outlet can serve the local community, region, and potentially other parts of the NWT, but cannot send products south without federal inspection, which is diffcult and expensive to arrange. Marketing is a key need of these enterprises, as it is for other northern enterprises.

Commercial Fishing

This sector has received a lot of attention from economic development programs over the decades. Nevertheless, it seems to have suffered frequently from failed attempts at new technology, expensive boats that consume any profits, inflated expectations of sales and incomes, high product transportation costs and uncontrollable market conditions or prices in the South. However, more moderately-sized fisheries seem to be able to succeed. One, for instance, involves 23 people in fishing and processing; the fishers work on 10 river systems, catches are picked up by float-plane, processed in a central fish-plant, then shipped south. When Department of Fisheries and Oceans regulations were relaxed, so that fish did not have to be inspected fresh, winter fishing and natural freezing became possible, and helped to reduce costs. This fishery has been self-sustaining, with a freight rate subsidy of 50%. Much of the fish is sold locally, but it also ends up in regional country food stores, local and regional restaurants, seafood outlets in Iqaluit and Yellowknife, and the local Hunters and Trappers Association (HTA). Though payment to fishermen is based on a share of the total catch rather than individual performance, there has only been a 15% turnover in the participants, indicating satisfaction with this approach to employment and development.

Fur, Leather, By-products and Crafts

This is an important sector, in that it seeks to continue or replace markets lost because of the sealskin bans and trapping bans, and also because it is a sector crucial to women's participation in traditional economic pursuits. The success of the Inuit carving and print-making enterprises suggests the potential for arts-based enterprises, and the interest they hold for people in the North.

Perhaps in compensation for anticipated consumer reactions against "consumptive use of wildlife," many projects in this sector seem to have been more oriented towards experimentation and capitalization: trials have been made with extracting seal-oil for use as fuel oil, a large-scale sealskin tannery, fur farming, and eiderdown collection. None of these "experiments" [has] been a great success; it is worth considering whether persistence and flexibility, and smaller project scales or expectations might have helped more projects in this sector to succeed. What have been successful are smaller-scale production ventures, where women can work at their own pace, and in the company of other women — materials distribution and craft production cooperatives, or traditional tanning of hides for instance. Again, marketing seems to be a major component of success for projects in this sector.

Tourism, Sport Hunting and Sport Fishing

For a long time, visitors to the North were attracted by the opportunity to hunt and fish there. This is changing somewhat, especially in the sport fishing sector, with the effect that more visitors seek cultural or "non-consumptive" wildlife experiences. Numerous outfitters exist in the Nunavut area, with infrastructures ranging from a Lake Winnipeg boat or kayaks, to tent camps, and permanent lodges — some operating quite successfully. HTAs offer sport-hunts for polar bear or caribou, often in partnership with southern, or southern-northern outfitting agents who can do the necessary marketing. Establishing fixed camps may require huge capital inputs; one project application estimated $650,000 to upgrade an existing fishing camp to serve thirty persons. Though feasibility studies may indicate that this camp could pay off its debt in ten years, it would still be a burdensome debt for one owner/operator with a six to twelve week season. The visitor season can be short, and sometimes operators combine outfitting with services to local people, such as bringing carving stone into town, or with other ventures such as snowmobile repair. Thus, this sector has the potential for bringing in revenues, and for complementing other on-the-land activities and economic pursuits.

FACTORS IN SUCCESS: COMPLEMENTING COMMUNITIES

Many enterprises like the ones described above are being tried in the North, and from an analysis of a sample of projects (Myers 1994), it is possible to draw some inferences about project characteristics that contribute to the success of these community-based developments. Table 2 defines three broad categories into which northern communities were divided for the 1990 Economic Development Strategy of the NWT. These are useful for suggesting the general characteristics of communities, as well as their needs and capabilities. Such categories also seem to have some bearing on the success of renewable resource enterprises.

The first factor to consider, in terms of what makes renewable resource enterprises succeed, may be the ability to blend tradition and innovation (Table 3). This does seem to make commercial enterprises stronger; country food stores do this by offering jobs ranging from traditional hunting to meat processing and vacuum-packing, and store operation. This may also contribute to the success of smaller-scale outfitters and fishermen, who combine traditional approaches to resource harvesting or travel, with some new elements of customer service. Alternatively, projects which were very traditional in nature, such as a simple native camp for tourist visits, or collection of driftwood for firewood, seemed to have a lower success rate. At the other end of the scale, very modern enterprises, such as some experiments in the fur and by-products sector, have tended to be very technology-oriented, removing the operators from their traditional skills; they have been less successful.

> **TABLE 2.** NWT Community Categories
>
> **Level One: Developed market** communities have the most potential for displacing major southern supply centres. They have developed business and transportation sectors. Traditional native economic activities are still pursued by many people, though participation in the wage economy is more common. This includes Yellowknife, Fort Smith, Hay River and Inuvik.
>
> **Level Two: Emerging market** communities have significant potential to expand their roles as regional supply centres and to expand the local range of goods and services. They may have a key industry or commercial development, though traditional harvesting is still pursued. Examples are Coppermine, Iqaluit, Cape Dorset, Tuktoyaktuk, Fort Simpson, and Norman Wells.
>
> **Level Three: Resource** communities have potential for arts and crafts, and other forms of human and natural resource development, but are usually more remote, with intensive involvement in the native economy and few wage-paying jobs. This category includes all other 41 communities.

TABLE 3. Traditional, Modern and Mixed Use of Skills and Resources, Related to Project Continuation[2]

	Traditional skills and resource use patterns	*Mixed skills and resource use patterns*	*Modern skills and resource use patterns*
Number of projects funded	8	29	9
Proportion of projects continuing	50%	79%	67%

Second, it is apparent, particularly in smaller communities where there may be less direct experience of business and management, that enterprises are more successful if they are operated by a community-based group, particularly a development corporation or Hunters and Trappers Association. In the larger communities, private proponents were more numerous in my sample, being involved in 70 to 80% of the projects in those communities. They were most successful in Level Two communities. Seventy-five percent of the sample were continuing to operate at the time of the survey, and had done so for at least several years. In Level One communities, however, which have more developed economies, over a third of projects by private entrepreneurs were feasibility studies only, and of those actually intended to set up enterprises, only 65% of my sample were continuing (Table 4). It seems there is greater commitment to renewable resource projects in Level Two communities, and that they tend to be more successful there. This raises some questions, such as: what factors are at work, to make these enterprises so successful in Level Two communities, and less so in Level One communities? Are they factors that also apply to the situation of Level Three communities? There, private entrepreneurs did not do well, whereas community-based organizations did better, but in addition, many projects in the Level Three sample were large-scale, and technologically innovative. Did potential entrepreneurs in Level Three communities have several strikes against them?

TABLE 4. Ownership and Community Level Related to Continuation Rates

	Private entrepreneur	Hunters and Trappers Association	Development corporations
Level One			
Number of projects	14		
Proportion continuing	67%		
Level Two			
Number of projects	14		
Proportion continuing	75%		
Level Three			
Number of projects	9	7	7
Proportion continuing	29%	86%	71%

TABLE 5. Project Size Related to Continuation

Project scale	Total number of projects	Projects continuing to operate
$1–10K	14	75%
$11–20K	12	75%
$21–30K	15	82%
$31–90K	13	75%
$111 ≥ $1M	16	69%

The third factor, project size, also has some influence on whether renewable resource-based enterprises flourish. Small and moderate-scale projects enjoyed 75–82% continuation rates, but large projects, ranging from $111,000 to over $1 million did not do as well (Table 5). The moderate and large-scale projects also tended to require subsequent funding — 80% and 67% of the respective samples — whereas only 29% of the small-project group received subsequent funding. A classic example illustrating this, and the previous point about management, is the case of a successful group of women who made sealskin clothing and crafts which were sold around the world. They were put in charge of a new sealskin processing plant project, and eventually gave up the management under the pressures of managing over $1 million. The experiences of private proponents are telling in relation to this question: most private projects were under $30,000, and 79% of those were continuing at the time of the study. There were 14 private proponents with larger projects: nine with projects valued from $31–90,000 achieved 57% continuation, while of the five with projects valued from $111,000 to over $1 million, only 20% were continuing.

TABLE 6. Product Type and Location of Markets Related to Continuation Rates

Type of product	Number of projects sampled	Proportion continuing
Commodities	44	66%
— for northern markets	27	72%
— for southern markets	17	55%
Tourism, sport hunting and fishing	23	83%

Finally, the location of markets makes a difference to project viability. As we saw with the commercial fishing projects, those dependent on markets in Montreal or Chicago are very vulnerable to high transportation costs, fluctuating prices, and competition from more cheaply-produced farmed fish. Equally, country food products must currently meet federal inspection standards if they are exported from the NWT. Furs, leathers and by-products may find a readier market in the North than in some parts of the South. Indeed, my sample of these three "commodities" sectors showed that most were oriented to local and regional markets, and import replacement (including production of country food, fish and leathers, furs or craft supplies), and they have a much greater tendency to continue than those which are aimed at export markets (Table 6). Ironically, most of the commodity-producing projects surveyed in Level Three communities were aimed at exports rather than import replacement, which may also have contributed to lower success rates among Level Three communities' projects in the sample. Furthermore, 34% of the projects funded in these sectors were feasibility studies, test fisheries and pilot projects, reflecting perhaps a tentativeness about government or proponent commitment to them.

The tourism, sport hunting and fishing sector is different; it caters largely — though not exclusively — to southern visitors. The 23 projects sampled in this sector showed a high continuation rate. Obviously, catering to southern markets, with the unique tourism opportunities of northern Canada, is a relatively successful way of contributing to northern community economies, though it must be noted that these sectors have had a great deal of government support in product development and marketing. Critics also comment that communities must be wary of changes in tourism fashion, which will take tourists to new, more exotic places and away from the North. On the other hand, it takes only a relatively few tourists to make a difference to a community economy. For example, Pond Inlet sees perhaps 250 tourists a year, but ten years ago, the community gained relatively little income from visitors who came. Today, new special interest tours and other products and services, for example, are increasing the revenues from tourism to about $250,000 (Myers and Forrest, in prep.).

It is important to note that incomes from renewable resource-based enterprises may not be high; and especially in large, capital-intensive ventures, high associated costs may consume most of the income. Workers' earnings from these projects may range from several hundred dollars per fishing season for small-scale fishers (Yonge 1988, 1989; Mayo, 1991), to $5,000 for hunters involved in commercial game harvests (Whittles, pers. comm.), and more for those employed in country food outlets on a regular basis. On an individual front, there is considerable evidence that commercial earnings may be used to supplement domestic "earnings," and that there are other "psychic income" benefits to people as well (Usher and Weihs 1989; Wenzel 1989; Kruse 1991; Condon et al. 1995). Furthermore, evidence from a community fishery in the Central Arctic illustrates that people are more concerned with sharing income throughout the community (Yonge 1989) — that is, there seems to be a concern with sufficiency of income rather than accumulation of wealth. Thus, income from these ventures may not make anyone rich, but it can help to augment peoples' cash and non-cash revenues, making them more self-reliant, and supporting other activities.

As well, renewable resource-based ventures may tend to be seasonal in nature. This may add to the normal Arctic seasonal rush of on-the-land activity in spring and summer, and could cause some conflict in balancing personal and commercial endeavours, if they have to be mutually exclusive. In some situations, however, domestic and commercial wildlife harvesting may be carried out simultaneously (Condon et al. 1995); as well, some commercial fisheries are also carried out in conjunction with domestic harvests. Efforts are being made to extend the tourism season, and ways may be found to extend the seasons for other resources, for instance, by winter fishing, so that commercial enterprise activities may not necessarily conflict with domestic harvesting.

DISCUSSION

Development in the North has historically been southern-driven, with variable benefits for northern residents. In the face of this, the traditional, native renewable-resource based economy has continued to exist, providing not only goods, but reaffirmation of cultural and social values. This, combined with a desire not to lose the young people of the Nunavut communities, whether to the South or to despair, suggests the necessity of creating community-based economic opportunities dependent on resources and skills available and known to the communities. Combined yet again with the increasing need to make Nunavut communities more self-sufficient, these economic options provide the opportunity to generate more of the goods and services that Nunavut residents need, as well as ones which will bring in new dollars from exports or tourist services.

These small-scale, renewable-resource based options will not be enough on their own to support all of Nunavut's residents, or the costs of the Nunavut government, but they could provide a very important complement to the other forms of development that take place in the new territory, and an important economic option for Nunavut residents who may prefer to maintain a land-based livelihood. Such enterprises could help to reaffirm the Inuit culture, identity and tradition (Condon et al. 1995). Finn Lynge, consultant with the Greenland Government, in commenting on the lack of government and economic documentation of production from, and participation in, the traditional harvesting economy, said "our values are tied to small-scale living and it is important for all of us that a significant part of our people keep their ties to land, sea and ice" (Bourgeois 1998).

Pursuing these forms of development would raise some questions that should be explicitly addressed by the new Nunavut government and society. How important are wage employment and cash income versus domestic production to a person's status? Is a person's status to be measured through consumption of material goods, as in the South, or will a lower cash income with productivity on-the-land be equally respectable? Is sufficiency as desirable, or more desirable, than accumulating wealth? What model of development suits the people of Nunavut; the southern industrial/service model or a different one? These will be difficult questions, in the face of strong acculturative forces from the southern economy. But the economic realities of Nunavut might force some reevaluation of the scale of consumption and the nature of "wealth." The fact that a conference on this topic was held in Iqaluit is a hopeful sign that such penetrating concerns are indeed being discussed. These questions are being asked by many in the South as well, as part of defining "sustainable lifestyles" there. As Jyrki Kakonen (1993) has noted, we cannot all use the OECD standard of living as a measure of adequacy; if all regions of the world are to achieve equity, new definitions of development and social welfare must be designed, not necessarily based on continual growth.

John Amagoalik suggested at the Iqaluit conference on the Future of Work (March 3–5, 1997), that Nunavut may develop its own concepts of the role of work in people's lives: "Our people don't want to repeat the rat-race or dog-eat-dog world [...] humans were meant to rise above this sort of thing, and we want this to happen up here" (Nunatsiaq News 1997). Jeremy Rifkin (1995) predicts a work revolution for the industrialized South, where there are insufficient jobs to keep everyone employed full-time, and where people will have to learn to do more with their lives than just work at a job; he suggests that with some vision, this could spark a positive social transformation with more people working for the community, rather than in the market-economy. Nunavut communities could be pointing the way in such a revolution.

To achieve this however, the Nunavut government will need to promote this new model, which would have to include goals of sufficiency rather than excess, and the desirability of traditional land-based lifestyles, as well as the modern office/government work. As part of the global thinking about what "sustainable development" really is, this could be an excellent example to the rest of the world, if Nunavut residents can live within the sustainable limits of their environment, balance economic development and environmental considerations, and recognize social and cultural values as much as economic ones.

The purpose of this paper has been to explore some alternatives to traditional Western forms of economic development, that are more aligned with Inuit culture, skills and resources. In exploring the successes of such enterprises in Nunavut, it is apparent that certain characteristics can contribute to their success or failure. Further analysis of such enterprises could lead to the development of more successful or appropriate models for diversifying the economies of Nunavut communities. As Inuit culture traditionally blended society, environment/resources and economy, Nunavut's new economic model could equally ensure a blend of social, cultural and environmental/resource values.

RECOMMENDATIONS FOR NUNAVUT DEVELOPMENT

The Nunavut government has the opportunity to show, in concrete terms, what sustainable development can mean in northern indigenous communities. As communities in Nunavut grow, and continue to require cash and employment opportunities, enterprise development is possible which fully embodies the values, skills and resources of Nunavut. Based on the experiences of entrepreneurs outlined above, what should the Nunavut government do to promote sustainable economic development in the new territory? I recommend the following measures:

1. Predicate economic development planning in Nunavut on models which are more appropriate to the Inuit lifestyle, resources and values. Develop acceptance of land-based enterprises as desirable, modern, sustainable options for young and old alike; acknowledge the validity of part-time or seasonal work that complements domestic production in the traditional mixed household economy of the North.
2. Find ways to support small businesses, because of their proven potential for generating employment and income. This may mean making loans available that respect seasonality in enterprises and therefore in repayments, for instance. One alternative, as Pretes and Robinson (1989) suggest, is to use trust funds that are based on non-renewable resource development on claims lands, to support such alternative forms of development.
3. Tailor management and ownership options to the needs and preferences of the communities in which they are located. Make training in entrepreneurship and management available, both for individuals and for community-based groups. Earlier government custom was to "get businesses running then leave them to it;" this did not work well; new entrepreneurs need "after-care."
4. Recognize that an important complement to tourism and export-oriented enterprises are products that serve northern markets. Assistance in marketing and transportation will likely be necessary to promote these at first, at least for new enterprises.
5. Ensure that these renewable resource-based enterprises work within the capacities of the resources themselves, not only to abide by Inuit concepts of stewardship, but to make these enterprises less vulnerable to the boom-and-bust nature of non-renewable resource development, and in order to be able to prove to the rest of the world that these are sustainable uses. Malouf (1986), in his examination of the sealing issue, reported that the majority of the public would not object to killing of animals for food and clothing if they did not suffer needlessly, and if conservation were not an issue.

NOTES

1. As the study was focused on enterprises that created employment and income in the NWT communities, it did not include in this total some projects that were funded by these programs, such as preparation of brochures of attendance at trade fairs. Feasibility studies were included, however, in order to assess the proportion of funding used for them.
2. Continuation rate has been calculated to reflect the number of action-oriented projects continuing to operate at the time of the study; it corrects for feasibility studies, test fisheries and pilot projects which were not necessarily intended to create on-going enterprises.

REFERENCES

AMES, RANDY, DON AXFORD, PETER USHER, ED WEICK, GEORGe WENZEL and CLAIRE GIGANTES. 1988. *Keeping on the land: A study of the feasibility of a comprehensive wildlife harvest support programme in the Northwest Territories*, Ottawa, Canadian Arctic Resources Committee.

BONE, ROBERT M. 1992. *The geography of the Canadian North: Issues and challenges*, Toronto, Oxford University Press.

BOURGEOIS, ANNETTE. 1998. Who records the value of country food?, *Nunatsiaq News Headline News*, http://www.nunatsiaq.com/nunavut/nvt80731_10.html.

BRODY, HUGH. 1987. *Living Arctic: Hunters of the Canadian North*, London, Faber and Faber.

BUREAU OF STATISTICS. 1994a. *1994 Labour Force Survey, Report No.1: Overall results and community detail*, Yellowknife, Government of the Northwest Territories.

———. 1994b. *1994 Labour Force Survey, Community labour force profiles*, Yellowknife, Government of the Northwest Territories.

CONDON, RICHARD G., PETER COLLINGS and GEORGE WENZEL. 1995. The best part of life: Subsistence hunting, ethnicity, and economic adaptation among young adult Inuit males, *Arctic*, 48(1): 31–46.

HAAGEN, BIRTE. 1982. The coal mine at Qullissat in Greenland, *Études/Inuit/Studies*, 6(1): 75–97.

HOBART, CHARLES. 1982. Inuit employment at the Nanisivik mine on Baffin Island, *Études/Inuit/Studies*, 6(1): 53–74.

KAKONEN, JYRKI. 1993. Growth-oriented economy, development and sustainable development, in J. Kakonen (ed.), *Politics and sustainable growth in the Arctic*, Aldershot, England, Dartmouth Publishing Company.

KLEINFELD, JUDITH, JACK KRUSE and R. TRAVIS. 1983. Inupiat participation in the wage economy: Effects of culturally adapted jobs, *Arctic Anthropology*, 20(1): 1–21.

KRUSE, JACK. 1991. Alaska Inupiat subsistence and wage employment patterns: Understanding individual choice, *Human Organization*, 50(4): 317–326.

MALOUF, A. 1986. *Seals and sealing in Canada: Report of the Royal Commission*, Ottawa, Supply and Services Canada.

MAYO, JANE. 1991. *Report on Great Slave Lake Commercial Fishery Surveys*, Yellowknife, Department of Economic Development and Tourism, GNWT.

MYERS, HEATHER. 1994. *An evaluation of renewable resource development experience in the Northwest Territories, Canada*, unpublished doctoral thesis, Cambridge, England, Cambridge University.

MYERS, HEATHER and SCOTT FOREST. in prep. While Nero fiddles; a decade in the economy of Pond Inlet.

NUNATSIAQ NEWS. 1997. Quick Time movie of John Amagoalik's closing comments, http://natsiq.nunanet.com/~nunat/pages/work.html#2.

NUNAVUT IMPLEMENTATION COMMISSION. 1995. *Footprints in new snow*, Iqaluit, Nunavut Implementation Commission.

PRETES, MICHAEL and MICHAEL ROBINSON. 1989. Beyond boom-and-bust: A strategy for sustainable development in the North, *Polar Record*, 25(153): 115–120.

RIFKIN, JEREMY. 1995. *The end of work: The decline of the global labor force and the dawn of the post-market era*, New York, G.P. Putnam's Sons.

ROBINSON, MICHAEL, MARK DICKERSON and MICHAEL PRETES. 1991. Sustainable development in small northern communities: A micro perspective, in *Old pathways and new directions: Towards a sustainable future. Proceedings from the AINA 1st annual Kluane Lake Conference, Kluane Lake Field Station, September 1989*, Calgary, Arctic Institute of North America.

USHER, PETER J. and FRED H. WEIHS. 1989. *Towards a strategy for supporting the domestic economy of the NWT*, Yellowknife, Legislative Assembly of the NWT.

WENZEL, GEORGE. 1989. Sealing at Clyde River, NWT: A discussion of Inuit economy, *Études/Inuit/Studies*, 13(1): 3–22.

———. 1991. *Animal rights, human rights: Ecology, Economy and ideology in the Canadian Arctic*, Toronto, University of Toronto Press.

WHITTLES, MARTIN. 1994. Personal communication, Scott Polar Research Institute, Cambridge, England.

WWW.SSIMICRO.COM. 1998. graemeda/framework/wildlife/html/body_conclusions.html.

YONGE, LINDA. 1988. *An economic analysis of the 1987 Whale Cove commercial char fishery*, Yellowknife, Department of Economic Development and Tourism, GNWT.

———. 1989. *An economic analysis of the Eskimo Point and Maguse River commercial char fishery, summer 1988*, Yellowknife, Department of Economic Development and Tourism, GNWT.

(d) Institutionalized Adaptation: Aboriginal Involvement in Land and Resource Management[†]

David C. Natcher

INTRODUCTION

The community of Whitefish Lake is located on the west and north shores of Utikuma Lake in north-central Alberta, Canada (Indian Reserves 155, 155A, 155B). The 1,400 members of the Whitefish Lake First Nation (WFLFN) represent the western extreme of the Strongwoods Cree division. Located north of the Saskatchewan River, the WFLFN inhabit a predominately boreal forest environment with transition zones south to the prairies and west to the Rocky Mountain foothills. The forest cover is made up principally of aspen, balsam poplar, jackpine, white and black spruce dispersed among a diversity of wetlands, peatlands, lakes, and streams.

Owing to the ecological characteristics of the boreal environment Whitefish Lake Band members have become well accustomed to conditions of resource uncertainty. Because resources in the boreal forest tend to be localized in specific areas rather than scattered and distributed evenly, Whitefish Lake residents can be characterized as people constantly coping with problems of resource availability. Because of this, competition over valued resources, whether with neighboring First Nations or settler populations, has long been a consideration of the subsistence harvester. However, unlike the competition of the past that occurred generally along shared borders or territorial edges, the pressure that is now being placed upon the Whitefish Lake territory is occurring not on the periphery but rather in the heart of the Whitefish Lake territory.

Over the last four decades, the traditionally used territory of the WFLFN has been targeted for the extraction of both renewable and non-renewable natural resources to the extent of limiting all other forest uses, including the traditional land use patterns of Whitefish Lake residents. As a result of industrial and regulatory impacts, the WFLFN has found itself nested within a landscape of competing and dominating interests that have failed to recognize the cultural significance of the land in the formation of the Whitefish Lake identity. Owing to the interplay of interests that have come to exist within the same geographical landscapes, and because access to lands and resources remains fundamental to Cree culture, Whitefish Lake has recognized the need to establish an interdependent relationship with competing interests or risk continued marginalization or possible displacement. Accomplished through the Whitefish Lake Cooperative Management Agreement, the reordering of existing social relationships has provided an institutional space to articulate local land use concerns, has facilitated local involvement in the land man-

---

[†] From *The Canadian Journal of Native Studies*, 20(2) (2000): 2563–82. Reproduced with permission of the publisher.

agement process, and has established mechanisms of self-empowerment through which the acquisition of knowledge, skills, and economic self-sufficiency can provide a wider range of options for Whitefish Lake to call upon when dealing with competing interests. Viewed in this context, the Whitefish Lake Cooperative Management Agreement represents a coping mechanism or a way of dealing with people and resources to attain goals and overcome immediate and future obstacles. Whether regarded as a process of adjustment or a means of compromise, institutional change ultimately rests on a behavioral adjustment among individuals and/or groups in the course of realizing goals, goals that in this analysis include achieving a measure of influence over traditionally used lands and resources.

Central to this analysis is the concept of the ecological niche. The ecological niche has been a widely and inconsistently used concept in anthropological research. Odum (1959), followed by Geertz (1963), has compared the niche to the profession or a way of life of the organism while noting that the habitat is equivalent to its address. Coe and Flannery (1964) define the niche, or microenvironment, as a culturally and physically delimited segment of the gross habitat that contains a resource or set of resources used by a human population, such as an estuary, grove, or cultivated field. Similar to Coe and Flannery's microenvironment, Barth (1969) defines the niche as a position in the environment as if it were a segment in the human habitat. However, Barth's departure from Coe and Flannery is in his emphasis on human relations that function within that delimited environment. According to Barth (1969: 19) where two or more ethnic groups are in contact, their adaptations may include the following characteristics: (1) the groups may occupy distinct niches in the natural environment and be in minimal competition for resources; (2) they may monopolize separate territories, in which case they are in competition for resources and their articulation will involve politics along the borders; (3) they may provide important goods and services for each other (i.e., occupy reciprocal and therefore different niches but in close interdependence); and, (4) the two groups are in at least partial competition within the same niche. It is Barth's contention that this type of relationship will result ultimately in the displacement of the subordinate group, or an accommodation involving an increasing complementary or interdependent relationship will develop. Thus for the purpose of this analysis the ecological niche is best framed as "the place of a group in the total environment, and its relation to resources and competitors" (Barth, 1956: 1079).

The environment with which we are concerned consists of two basic niches for adaptation. The first is the niche of the Whitefish Lake community, which consists of the living conditions that promote a particular way of life (i.e., hunting, fishing, trapping, and gathering). The second niche consists of the natural resources (i.e., timber, minerals, oil/gas) that are exploited by the industrial society. Using Barth's concept of the niche I am distinguishing the differential use of resources by each group within the same geographical area. The adaptive strategy of one group must, therefore, consider not only the characteristics of the physical environment but also the strategies employed by neighboring competitors (Bennett, 1969). Although these groups are not competing directly for the same ecological niche, the exploitation of one niche by the dominant group (state/industry) will to a large extent affect the other, resulting in a direct alteration of that particular way of life (Svensson, 1983).

This distinction is similar to Grambling and Freudenburg's (1996: 362) example of how large-scale strip mining operations in Wyoming utilize a given niche in a very different way than ranchers who live in the same region, or for that matter naturalists who would prefer to see the same area devoted to hiking or as a wildlife refuge. Thus differing forms of resource use will vary to the extent in which a given niche can be used by others, whether at the same time or subsequently (Grambling and Freudenburg, 1996: 362).

It is important to note that the competing interests that function within this delineated environment also constitute two distinct forms of economy that are based on diverging forms of sustainability. The industrial society, whose interests emphasize profit maximization and economic gain, tend to be guided by the normative values of the group; that is, economic growth is essential. For the Cree of Whitefish Lake, interest in the land base is not solely motivated by their need for a collective means of subsistence, but is also intimately linked to the landscape as it has come to define their collective and individual identities. Within the traditionally used territory of the WFLFN now exists a number of competing interests that have influenced the land and resource use of Whitefish Lake residents. As a result, each of these interests [has] individually and collectively influenced the adaptive strategies of the WFLFN.

RESOURCE COMPETITION

Although it had generally been believed that the western Cree represented a late 18th and early 19th Century westward migration from the eastern regions of Lake Winnipeg, research (Ives, 1993) has shown that the WFLFN, as well as the other Strongwoods Cree First Nation, had long been present in the area, perhaps since 900 A.D.

Throughout the 19th Century the WFLFN maintained a seasonal mobility pattern. Depending on resource availability, Band members distributed themselves accordingly, whether in response to long term resource changes or temporary resource fluctuations. Seasonal residency patterns consisted of summer months living in tents along the northwest shore of Utikuma Lake where their horses could graze and women and children could fish and snare small game. The men, using the summer camp as a base, would pursue moose and deer along the lake shore and nearby wetland areas, enabling them to return to camp each night. This was also a time of socialization and a time to reinforce social bonds. Nearing the end of summer and early fall, Band members would begin preparing for winter by drying moose meat and fish and storing berriers for the months ahead. With preparations complete, Band members would break into family units and disperse throughout their winter trapping territories.

In 1820, seasonal residency was altered somewhat owing to the establishment of a Hudson's Bay Company post on the northwestern shore of Utikuma Lake. Although some families chose to be oriented near the post, the overall mobility of Bank members remained to a large extent unaffected. However, nearing the end of the 1800s changes in Whitefish Lake's mobility began to occur as growing numbers of European settlers, and ultimately treaty negotiators, entered the Whitefish Lake territory.

For nearly a decade before the signing of Treaty Eight (1899) the Government of Canada debated the merits of coming to terms with the Indians from the Lesser Slave Lake and upper Peace River area (Leonard, 1995: 16). However, after recognizing that the area housed sufficient natural wealth (mineral and agricultural potential) a treaty arrangement was believed to be advisable. Word of the proposed treaty arrangement was, however, met with considerable apprehension and resistance by First Nation leaders. Whitefish Lake in particular refused to enter into treaty negotiations with the Government of Canada and was considered generally "hostile" to the entire treaty process.[1] One of the primary concerns of Whitefish Lake, as well as other First Nation groups in the area, was the enactment and enforcement of fish and game regulations by government officials and the disruption that would result to their traditional ways of life. In addition, the establishment of Reserves was seen as a major threat to their continued seasonal mobility, a mobility pattern that was integral to the Whitefish Lake culture. Concerns regarding the centration and sedentary policies of the Crown were also expressed by one Indian Affairs official, J.A. McKenna, who confided:

> ... as the country is not one that will be settled extensively for agricultural purposes, it is questionable whether it would be good policy to even suggest grouping them in the future. The reserve system is inconsistent with the life of a hunter....[2]

Despite their expressed concerns, Whitefish Lake entered into treaty in the summer of 1901, with the guarantee that:

> ... there is no intention to make you live on them [Reserves] if you do not want to, but, in years to come you may change your minds.[3]

With the further assurance that:

> ... your forest and river life will not be changed by the treaty, and you will have your annuities, as well, as long as the sun shines and the earth remains.[4]

Despite the promises made by government negotiators, their assurances were promptly superseded by a system of paternalistic Reserve administration that extinguished any claim to territorial rights. Because the Reserve system was seen as an interim measure advanced by the federal government for the purpose of assimilation (e.g., Friesen, 1987; Elias, 1991; Miller, 1991), the right to resources off-Reserve was never considered essential to the economic development of the Whitefish Lake community. Consequently, Whitefish Lake had been given no authority on the basis of Aboriginal title[5] nor on the basis of customary use to regulate access to resources within their traditional territory. As a result, the lands that have fallen outside Reserve boundaries, lands which — from a community perspective — represent their traditionally used and occupied territory, are now recognized legally as unoccupied provincial Crown lands. Considered, by government, to lack "productive" uses these lands are made largely available to development initiatives deemed to be in the public's best interest (Hrenchuk, 1993).

Lacking regulatory control over off-Reserve lands and resources, coupled with the growing global demand for energy and natural resources, Whitefish Lake first began to encounter resource developers in the mid-1950s. Arriving in "large trucks", oil workers began clearing exploratory seismic lines on the south and northeastern shores of Utikuma Lake. Owing to the difficulty of travel, as well as the expense associated with the development of this still remote area, only a few wells had been established north of Utikuma Lake. However, by the 1960s, seismic activity and road access had begun to reach some of the most remote areas of the Whitefish Lake territory.

With the completion of an all-weather road that extended north from the community of Slave Lake (now Rt. 88), a network of industrial access roads soon spread throughout the Whitefish Lake territory. Since this time, the industrialization of Whitefish Lake's traditionally used territory has intensified to the point of limiting all other forest uses. Within this region now exist approximately 875 petroleum wells, 127 petroleum depots, numerous hazardous waste sites, and a supporting infrastructure of primary and secondary access roads, pipelines, electrical powerlines and seismic exploration corridors. In addition to oil and gas development, the Whitefish Lake territory has come under increased pressure from the timber industry. As of 1997 the annual allowable cut for the S-9 Forest Management Unit (FMU) is 160,000 m^3 of conifer and deciduous timber (Tolko Ltd., 1997). To compound the effects of this industrialization, "No Trespassing" signs have been [posted] warning local residents of these now private industrialized areas.

As noted above a residual effect of the industrialization of the Whitefish Lake territory has been the development of an extensive infrastructure of primary and secondary access roads, right-of-way corridors, and seismic lines that have effectively opened up and made accessible even the most remote areas of the Whitefish Lake territory. As a result of this increased accessibility Whitefish Lake residents have experienced growing competition from non-Aboriginal hunters over declining numbers of moose and other game species.

With the growth of the regional population, non-Aboriginal sportsmen are being attracted from the nearby communities of Slave Lake and High Prairie, as well as the provincial centers of Edmonton, Red Deer and Calgary. Further, non-Aboriginal outfitters are hosting a growing number of US, European, and Asian [sportsmen] who have further "saturated the backyard" of the WFLFN with additional hunting pressure (Northern Moose Management Program Progress Report, 1998 [NMMPPR]). While harvest figures for guides and outfitters can be tabulated, it has proven difficult to ascertain accurate figures for the total harvest of game species owing to the limitations common to survey methodologies. Because of this, total harvest figures can only be estimated. However, since 1993 the Natural Resource Division of Alberta Environmental Protection has initiated the Northern Moose Management Program (NMMP) in response to the declining moose population in northern Alberta. Funded through the Fish and Wildlife Trust Fund, the NMMP is developing and enacting measures in an effort to reverse the declining moose population that ranges throughout the Whitefish Lake territory. To date, however, the moose population in the Whitefish Lake territory remains in serious decline. According to Band members this decline is believed to be a result of several interrelated factors which include increased hunting pressure from recreational hunters, growing access to remote areas facilitated by road development, and an overall decline of productive moose habitat resulting from industrial development.

Placing an additional limitation on Whitefish Lake's land use has been the establishment of the Gift Lake Métis Settlement in the western region of the Whitefish Lake territory. As it applies to land use conflicts, Métis Settlements rep-

TABLE 1. Sport Harvest Data (Heckbert, 1999)

WMU[1] 544, 542, 520	1997	1996	1995	1994	Total
Moose	322	209	306	280	1117
Black Bear	X	16	51	35	102
Mule Deer	17	0	28	15	60
White-tailed Deer	85	48	123	141	397

[1] The traditional territory of the WFLFN is provincially managed as three distinct Wildlife Management Units (WMU 544, 542, 520).

resent somewhat of an anomaly. That us, only in Alberta have the Métis succeeded in establishing their own communal land base. Through the Métis Betterment Act of 1938/40 more than 500,000 hectares (1.25 million acres) of land have been provided along with hunting and fishing rights, socio-economic benefits, and health programs for Alberta Métis (Notzke, 1994:186).

While serving as a major advancement for the Métis, the establishment of Metis Settlements has had significant impact on the contemporary land use patterns of neighboring First Nations and particularly on the land use patterns of the WFLFN. Adjacent to Utikuma Lake, the Gift Lake Métis Settlement is bounded by Peavine Métis Settlement to the west and the Whitefish Lake Reserve (R. 155) to the east. Comprising a 83,916 hectare (207,273 acres) land base, Gift Lake represents the second largest Métis Settlement in Alberta (McCully and Seaton, 1982: 16).

Although the signing of Treaty Eight has assured Whitefish Lake of the continued right to hunt, trap, and fish for food in all seasons of the year on all unoccupied Crown lands, Métis settlement lands have been classified as private lands administered by the province, thereby withdrawing them from First Nation access. Thus the establishment of the Gift Lake Settlement subsequently removed 839 km^2 (324 mi^2) of land and resources from the use of Whitefish Lake residents despite its representing a significant portion of their traditionally used and occupied territory.

COOPERATIVE MANAGEMENT

Recognizing the limitations of the provincial land-tenure system as well as the perceived strain being placed on local lands and resources resulting from that system, the WFLFN long pursued a greater role in the institutional management of their traditional lands. Despite their efforts, gaining any measure of influence over off-Reserve lands and resource had been met with considerable resistance and little success. However, in 1985 opportunity finally presented itself. At this time it was recognized by Whitefish Lake that when their Reserves were established (1908) the Crown had failed to administer a land base to which the Whitefish Lake Band had

FIGURE 1

Whitefish Lake First Nation
I.R. 155, 155A, 155B

Cooperative Management Area

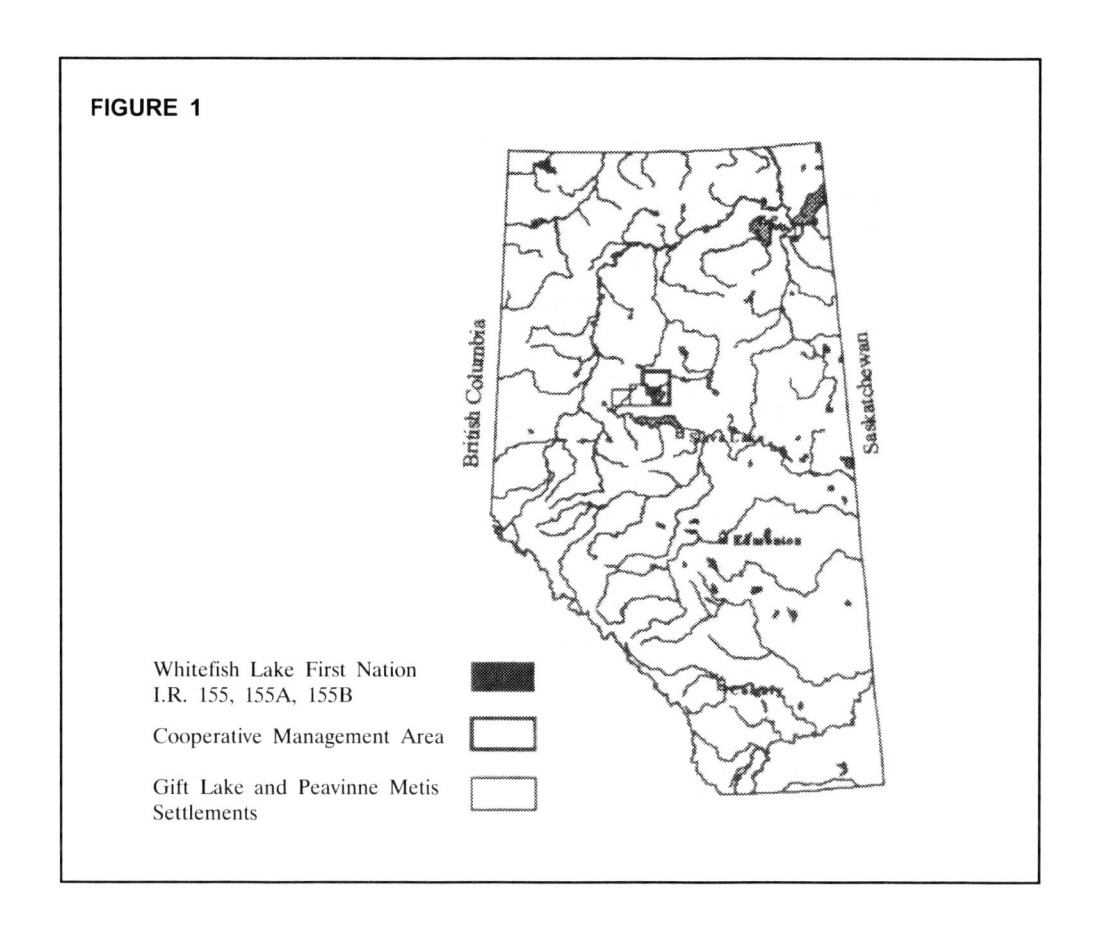

Gift Lake and Peavinne Metis Settlements

legally been entitled. Thus, in 1985 the WFLFN submitted a Treaty Land Entitlement Claim to the Government of Canada. In April of 1986, the Treaty Land Entitlement Claim was validated by the Crown, resulting in the ratification of a Memorandum of Intent in November of 1988.

In addition to providing a supplementary land base and financial settlement, Whitefish Lake was successful in negotiating a clause within the Memorandum that indicated that the province of Alberta and the WFLFN would enter into discussions regarding cooperative approaches to land, wildlife, and fisheries management in the area surrounding the Whitefish Lake Reserve (2,700 sq.km.) (see Figure 1). Through these negotiations, the WFLFN was successful in establishing the only First Nation — Province of Alberta Cooperative Management Agreement to date, as recognized under the terms of a treaty land entitlement claim. Signed in 1994, this agreement is in the form of a Memorandum of Understanding (MOU) between Alberta Environmental Protection, Alberta Aboriginal Affairs, and the WFLFN.

The vehicle used to fulfil the objectives of the MOU is the Implementation Plan for the Cooperative Management Agreement. Developed jointly by the WFLFN and the province of Alberta, this plan represents the framework for discussion between the WFLFN and the province leading towards the cooperative management of lands and resources. Following four years of negotiations and political maneuvering, terms of reference and objectives for the Whitefish Lake Cooperative Management Agreement were finalized and implementation began in January of 1998.

Administering the implementation and operation of the Agreement is the Cooperative Management Implementation Committee. This committee is comprised of three representatives from the WFLFN and three senior regional representatives from the Department of Environmental Protection, as well as designated support staff and other government and non-government representatives. The Implementation Committee is responsible for establishing work plans, working procedures and operating guidelines as well as for establishing and overseeing specific working groups that may be created to address specific management issues. In general, the Committee mandate calls for cooperative approaches to land and resource management through the identification of key resource management issues, establishing an equitable process to address those issues, and for recommending processes leading towards resolution — including policy interpretation and changes in policy that may be required to achieve agreed upon objectives. The Committee is also responsible for the long-range management planning of fish, wildlife, and timber resources and to cooperatively develop future forest management plans. Additionally, because education, training and economic development opportunities are seen by both Whitefish Lake and the province as being central to the cooperative management process, specific measures have been incorporated into the Implementation Plan to enhance these capacity-building opportunities. These initiatives include (western) resource management training for interested Whitefish Lake residents, wildlands fire suppression training, commercial fishing opportunities, silvi-culture and agro-forestry opportunities, eco-tourism, outfitting and guiding, as well as cooperatively seeking out and securing business contracts and joint-ventures (i.e., road gravelling and pipeline maintenance) with industry.

Throughout the development of the Implementation Plan a number of concerns had been expressed by Whitefish Lake residents regarding the perceived health and sustainability of the local environment. These concerns have formed the basis of a preliminary list of discussion items to be addressed by the Implementation Committee and local Working Groups. Arising directly from Committee review specific management objectives have been implemented in order to address community concerns [including] the reclamation of abandoned industrial sites, environmental health research, and traditional/contemporary land use research.

RECLAMATION OF INDUSTRIAL ACTIVITY

Over the past three decades, industrial land disturbance activities such as exploration, pipeline construction, road access, seismic work and sand and gravel extraction have resulted in ecologically unbalanced and aesthetically unappealing areas in the Whitefish Lake territory. Under the 1973 Land Surface Conservation and Reclamation Act,[7] these areas are to be returned to a condition which will allow for "productive" use. However, owing to provincial regulatory limitations (i.e., limited funds and man-power to enforce provincial regulations) these abandoned industrial areas are often left unreclaimed, leaving the landscape scarred by past industrial activities.

Through the cooperative management agreement, Whitefish Lake is establishing a process that facilitates local involvement in the reclamation of these industrial areas. By working directly with the Canadian Forest Service, Alberta Lands and Forests and industry, Whitefish Lake plans to ensure that disturbed areas located within their traditional territory are reclaimed in a manner that incorporates the interests of the WFLFN, be it wildlife habitat recovery, watershed benefits or recreational opportunities.

As no two disturbance areas are the same, government, industry and the WFLFN will work cooperatively on a site-by-site basis to determine the most appropriate reclamation approach. This direct involvement also allows Whitefish Lake to be involved in the actual reclaiming process, thereby providing an economic benefit to local contractors while facilitating a transfer of skills that can be applied to other reclamation projects outside the Whitefish Lake territory.

ENVIRONMENTAL HEALTH RESEARCH

There is a growing concern among the Whitefish Lake residents regarding the impact of industrial development on the health of local wildlife and community residents (e.g., industrial residues, roadside/right-of-way herbicide spraying). In response, environmental health research is being conducted in cooperation with the Canadian Circumpolar Institute at the University of Alberta to identify specific areas of concern, including the perceived contamination of country foods, the identification of specific contaminants and the resulting effects on environmental health (human/non-human), and the documentation of local perceptions regarding the functioning ecosystem in relation to temporal and spatial change. Through the cooperative management process a vehicle for dialogue has been established that enables the concerns of community residents to be expressed in a forum that has the means and authority to enact change in contested industrial practices.

LAND USE RESEARCH

It has been recognized by both the WFLFN and the provincial government that in order to make informed land management decisions a thorough understanding of community land and resource use patterns and needs is required. Therefore, through the cooperative management process, the WFLFN has undertaken land use research that documents the cultural landscape values of Whitefish Lake residents and has integrated those values with the economic interests of resource developers operating in the area; thus the identification of both market and non-market values has been initiated. The ultimate purpose of this research is not to restrict future land and resource use *per se*, nor is it a form of cultural triage, but rather it is to be used as a guide for sound land use initiatives that serve to preserve and protect the cultural values of the WFLFN while providing an information base necessary for making informed land management decisions.

In cooperation with Alberta Community Development (Cultural Facilities and Historic Resources Division), Alberta Lands and Forests and the Canadian Circumpolar Institute the cultural values of the WFLFN, which include grave sites, sacred sites, historic sites and archaeological sites are being recorded and placed under

Protective Notations through the Historical Resources Act, thereby ensuring the preservation and protection of these areas from future development.[8] To date a total of 40 individual burial sites have been documented and registered that were previously at risk from unknowing development. In most cases these sites are places that individuals or families had once occupied. While some of the graves have visible markings, such as headstones, wooden crosses, or fenced areas, many of these areas are marked only in the memories of Whitefish Lake Elders, making the documentation and protection of these sites even more important.

Local knowledge regarding fish and wildlife habitat is also being used to safeguard specific locales. By working with the Alberta Department of Fish and Wildlife, areas such as medicinal plant locations, berry locations, mineral licks, waterfowl nesting and staging areas, and other critical wildlife areas have been recorded and are being placed under Protective or Consultative Notations, again serving to safeguard these areas from future development. When development plans are slated for these specific areas Whitefish Lake representatives, industry representatives and government personnel review the plans, make recommendations and then decide how best to proceed in a cooperative manner.

An additional objective of Whitefish Lake has been the recording of community held place-names, or toponyms of the local landscape. Seen as being integral to sound management, Whitefish Lake has recognized the importance of establishing common terms of reference for physical features of the landscape. Although the recording of named places, together with their spatial and epistemological correlates, have long been the subject of anthropological inquiry, the recording and use of local place-names has received no regard from government/industry land managers operating within the traditional territory of the Whitefish Lake Cree. In addition, the provincial maps generally used by industry and government planners refer to landscape [features] by names that have no relevance to local residents and are sometimes represented by only a number and a legal description of its location. However, owing to the significance of "place" to the WFLFN, the establishment of common toponyms is an attempt to illustrate the relationship local residents have with the surrounding landscape.

The above research initiatives are being technically supported through the development of an automated land management system that will enable Whitefish Lake to incorporate industrial land management data with their own traditional land and resource use information. Through on-going land use research, the WFLFN is developing the capacity to convert local land use knowledge into a GIS computer based system (ArcView) which can visually display, edit and analyze geographically referenced material. This system is enabling the WFLFN to overlay industrial land management plans with local land and resource use information in order to collectively identify and then protect landscape values prior to the occurrence of any industrial activity.

DISCUSSION

The ecological approach chosen in this research emphasizes adaptive behavior that evolves in response to uncertainty and increased competition over the use of, and access to, resources. Ostrom (1990), and others (e.g., Berkes and Folke, 1994;

Hanna *et al.*, 1996; Holling *et al.*, 1998), have referred to this adaptive behavior as a society's cultural capital, which refers to factors that provide human societies with the means to adapt to the natural environment as well as to actively modify it. Consistent with the definition employed by Honigman (1983: 150), adaptive behavior is a process whereby an individual or group acts to seize opportunities and resources available in both the social and physical environments. It is the problem solving mechanisms in human behavior that facilitate a dynamic approach to environmental interaction. The term adaptive capital has also been used to describe this capacity, but as Berkes and Folke (1994) have noted, the use of adaptive capital often fails to describe adequately a group's potential to not only adapt to, but also actively modify its socio-natural setting.

It is important to note that the process of adaptation possesses a certain level of contradiction in relation to collective and individual behavior. That is, what may be adaptive for the WFLFN may be maladaptive for competing interests (i.e., government, industry); and conversely, what may be adaptive for competing interests may prove maladaptive to the WFLFN and/or the environment [they occupy]. Further, an adaptive capacity does not guarantee success. Rather, adaptation represents a behavioral stage that can be evaluated as being ultimately successful or unsuccessful in both the long and short term. If cooperative management is perceived by Whitefish Lake as being unsuccessful a new process may be initiated bringing alternative strategies into play (Honigman, 1983). If, however, cooperative management is perceived as a successful strategy a period of stability may occur. This "success" may then promote the adoption of similar strategies (institutions) among other First Nations who perceive it to be to their own advantage.

Ostrom (1990) has shown that in highly competitive environments, such as the one presented here, groups who fail to incorporate strategies that may enhance their net standing will ultimately lose out to those who are successful in adopting better rules, strategies, and institutions. Thus individuals caught in social dilemmas are far more likely to innovate and try to change the structure of existing institutions in order to improve outcomes, thus far more accepting of strategies promoting change (Ostrom, 1998). North (1990: 81) has noted similarly that a group that permits the maximum generation of adaptive strategies will most likely be able to solve problems through time by providing incentives that encourage the development of decentralized decision-making institutions that explore alternative ways of problem solving.

It has been suggested (e.g., Caulfield, 1997), however, that co-management arrangements that fail to establish a broad framework for political and economic rights risk the creation of incipient forms of social differentiation within Aboriginal communities. It has further been warned that the adoption of co-management institutions may actually hasten the acculturation of Aboriginal peoples through a process of institutional cooptation (e.g., Stevenson, 1997). While it is true that involvement in cooperative management arrangements may further challenge Aboriginal communities already coping with socioeconomic change, concerns regarding the cultural viability of Aboriginal communities involved in institutional management seem to presuppose a static perception of Aboriginal culture. That is, Aboriginal peoples have been adapting to socio-economic change for centuries. Rather than being locked into a static cultural continuum, Aboriginal peoples, as they exist today, have exhibited a cultural dynamism that has enabled them to maintain a distinct cultural identity while coping (to be sure, some more successfully than others) with continuous cultural, economic and environmental changes. It must be remembered that culture is adaptive; adaptive, in that it forms the basis of survival by allowing individuals and communities to cope [with], as well as influence, socio-environmental change. Therefore it is important to recognize that Aboriginal involvement in institutional resource management is a further demonstration of the cultural [flexibility] that has long enabled Aboriginal peoples to adapt to external pressures and competing demands for lands and resources.

Thus Whitefish Lake's involvement in the cooperative resource management process is testimony to the cultural flexibility that has enabled them to maintain their cultural integrity while incorporating the most strategic cultural components from competing populations. This adaptive efficiency has therefore made possible the maintenance of traditional values while integrating new knowledge and strategies (i.e., institutions) that together, have enhanced ecological resilience and their own cultural survival. Thus by borrowing from multiple cultural traditions, Whitefish Lake has developed a richer cultural capital and a wider range of adaptive options to call upon when dealing with competing interests (Begossi, 1998: 148).

CONCLUSION

While still in its infancy the success of the Whitefish Lake Cooperative Management Agreement can be attributed to several factors. First, Whitefish Lake entered into the cooperative management process recognizing that owing to the prevailing political constraints that continue to govern their relationship with off-Reserve lands and resources (i.e., Treaty arrangements), gaining exclusive regulatory authority over their traditionally used territory was not a realistic objective. Recognizing this current political reality, Whitefish Lake has maintained well-defined objectives that, above all, promote greater institutional involvement in resource management decisions. Their initial and primary objective has not been the exclusion of competing interests but rather in establishing a process in which issues can be mutually resolved and recommendations can be made regarding land use planning that takes into account the concerns and aspirations of Whitefish Lake residents. Second, because Whitefish Lake has been to a large extent excluded from education, training, and economic opportunities, developing skills and gaining access to capacity-building opportunities is seen as fundamental in assuring a more equitable role in the cooperative management process in the future. Because of this, Whitefish Lake has maintained a long term vision of institutional development that recognizes that success will depend largely on their own self-empowerment. In this way, issues that most directly affect Whitefish Lake residents can be decided and acted upon locally thereby contributing to their own self-defined development.

Thus by demonstrating a cognitive capacity to visualize change, the WFLFN has adapted to its evolving socio-natural environment through the conception and formation of a new institution that promotes efficiency, equity and desired outcomes for the Whitefish Lake community. The Whitefish Lake Cooperative Management Agreement therefore represents a strategy promoting social reform which has provided an alternative basis in which future decisions are made regarding the allocation, distribution and conservation of resources, thereby establishing an institutional framework that has the potential to redefine the social relationships that have evolved within this shared geographical landscape.

While the Whitefish Lake Agreement is proving to have a direct impact on the way in which Whitefish Lake's traditionally used lands and resources are being managed, the implementation of this Agreement may prove ultimately to have an even greater effect on the way in which Alberta's lands and resources are to be managed in the future. That is, because there [remain] twelve treaty land entitlement claims yet to be settled with Alberta First Nations, the implementation of the Whitefish Lake Agreement will no doubt influence the settlement of these claims by becoming a familiar, and tested construct, in which other First Nations can follow. Thus by adopting similar strategies based upon informed [decisions], as well as the experiences gained by Whitefish Lake and other First Nations who are involved in similar situations, Aboriginal communities are recognizing the strategic value in establishing interdependent relationships with government and industry as a means of enacting fundamental change in the institutions most responsible for the management of their traditionally used land and resources. Thus by seeking out, and entering into cooperative management arrangements, Aboriginal communities are effectively influencing the behavioral patterns of government and industry so as to allow for institutional change to occur. This in turn has allowed for the integration of local value systems with new knowledge, skills and capacity-building opportunities that together, can enhance ecological resilience as well as their own cultural sustainability; thereby enabling Aboriginal communities to not only cope with socio-environmental change, but to initiate change as well.

NOTES

1. PAA 281/149, Holmes to Bishop Young, 3 June 1899.
2. NAC RG 10 Vol. 3484 file 75236–1, McKenna to Superintendent General of Indian Affairs, 17 April 1899.
3. Speech made by Commissioner Ross (in Leonard, 1995: 24).
4. Speech read by Father Lacombe (in Leonard, 1995: 24).
5. The Supreme Court of Canada's decision in Delgamuukw (December 11, 1997) provided the first comprehensive definition of Aboriginal title. The court affirmed that Aboriginal title is first, a right of exclusive use and occupation of that land that allows the Aboriginal group to utilize that land for a variety of reasons not limited to traditional activities; second, the right to choose to what purposes the land can be put; and third, that lands held pursuant to Aboriginal title have an inescapable economic component.
6. The traditional territory of the WFLFN is provincially managed as three distinct Wildlife Management Units (WMU 544, 542, 520).
7. The provincial Land Surface Conservation and Reclamation Act was enacted in 1973. The act is now being revised and will be integrated into the Alberta Environmental Protection and Enhancement Act.
8. Protective Notations are legal instruments used by the provincial government to protect and/or buffer geographical sites of paleontological, archaeological, prehistoric, historic, natural, scientific, or aesthetic significance.

REFERENCES

BARTH, FREDRIK. 1969. *Ethnic Groups and Boundaries: The Social Organization of Cultural Differences*. Boston: Little, Brown and Company

———. 1956. Ecological Relations Among Ethnic Groups in Swat, North Pakistan. *American Anthropologist* 58: 1079–1089.
BEGOSSI, ALPINA. 1998. Resilience and Neo-Traditional Populations: The Caicaras (Atlantic Forest) and Caboclos (Amazon, Brazil). In Fikret Berkes and Carl Folke (Editors): *Linking Social and Ecological Systems: Management Practices and Social Mechanisms for Building Resilience*. Cambridge: Cambridge University Press.
BENNETT, JOHN W. 1969. *Northern Plainsmen: Adaptive Strategy and Agrarian Life*. Chicago, Illinois: Aldine Publishing Company.
BERKES, FIKRET and CARL FOLKE. 1994. Investing in Cultural Capital for Sustainable Use of Natural Resources. In AnnMari Jansson, Monica Hammer, Carl Folke and Robert Constanza (Editors): *Investing In Natural Capital: The Ecological Economics Approach to Sustainability*. International Society for Ecological Economics. Washington D.C., Island Press.
CAULFIELD, R.A. 1997. *Greenlanders, Whales and Whaling: Sustainability and Self Determination*. University of New England Press.
COE, M. and K. FLANNERY. 1964. Microenvironments and Meso-American Prehistory. *Science* 143: 650–654.
ELIAS, P. 1991. *Development of Aboriginal People's Communities*. North York, Ontario: Captus Press.
FRIESEN, G. 1987. *The Canadian Prairies: A History*. Toronto, Ontario: University of Toronto Press.
GEERTZ, CLIFFORD. 1963. *Agricultural Involution: The Process of Ecological Change in Indonesia*. Berkeley: University of California.
GRAMLING, ROBERT and WILLIAM R. FREUDENBURG. 1996. Environmental Sociology: Toward a Paradigm for the 21st Century. *Sociological Spectrum* 16: 347–370.
HANNA, SUSAN S., CARL FOLKE and KARL-GORAN MALER. 1996. *Rights to Nature: Ecological, Economic, Cultural, and Political Principles of Institutions for the Environment*. Beijer International Institute of Ecological Economics, The Royal Swedish Academy of Science, Stockholm Sweden, Island Press.
HECKBERT, MARK. 1999. Outfitter-Guide Allocation and Harvest Data: Wildlife Management Units 544, 542, 520. High Prairie, Alberta: Alberta Environmental Protection, Natural Resource Division.
HOLLING, C.S., FIKRET BERKES and CARL FOLKE. 1998. Science, Sustainability and Resource Management, pp. 342–362 in Fikret Berkes and Carl Folke (Editors): *Linking Social and Ecological Systems: Management Practices and Social Mechanisms for Building Resilience*. Cambridge: Cambridge University Press.
HONIGMAN, JOHN. 1983. Adaptations in Canadian Circumpolar Towns, pp. 149–162 in L. Muller-Wille, P. Pelto, Li. Muller-Wille, and R. Damell (Editors): *Consequences of Economic Change in Circumpolar Regions*. Edmonton, Alberta: Boreal Institute for Northern Studies.
HRENCHUK, CARL. 1993. Native Land Use and Common Property: Whose Common?, pp. 69–86 in Julian T. Inglis (Editor): *Traditional Ecological Knowledge: Concepts and Cases*. Ottawa, Ontario: International Program on Traditional Ecological Knowledge and International Development Research Center.
IVES, JOHN W. 1993. Ten Thousand Years Before The Fur Trade in Northeast Alberta, pp. 5–31 in P.A. McCormack and R.G. Ironside (Editors): *The Uncovered Past: Roots of Northern Alberta Societies. Circumpolar Research Series No. 3*. Edmonton, Alberta: Canadian Circumpolar Institute, University of Alberta.
LEONARD, DAVID W. 1995. *Delayed Frontier: The Peace River Country to 1909*. Calgary, Alberta: Detselig Enterprises Ltd.
McCULLY, AL and HUGH SEATON. 1982. *Gift Lake Metis Settlement Land Use Planning Inventory*. Municipal Planning Section, Planning Branch Alberta Municipal Affairs.
MILLER, JAMES. 1991. *The Skyscrapers Hide the Heavens: a History of Indian-White Relations in Canada*. Toronto, Ontario: University of Toronto Press.
NORTH, DOUGLASS C. 1990. *Institutions, Institutional Change and Economic Performance*. Cambridge: Cambridge University Press.
NOTZKE, CLAUDIA. 1994. *Aboriginal Peoples and Natural Resources in Canada*. York: Captus University Publications.
ODUM, E. 1959. *Fundamentals of Ecology*. 2nd Edition. Philadelphia: Saunders.
OSTROM, ELINOR. 1998. A Behavioral Approach to the Rational Choice Theory of Collective Action. Presidential Address, American Political Science Association. *American Political Science Review* 92(1): 1–21.

―――. 1990. *Governing the Commons: The Evolution of Institutions for Collective Action*. Cambridge: Cambridge University Press.
STEVENSON, MARC. 1997. Inuit and Co-Management: Principles, Practices and Challenges for the Millennium. Paper presented at the NAMMCO International Conference, "Sealing the Future", St. John's, Newfoundland, 25–27 November.
SVENSSON, TOM G. 1983. The Effects of Economic Changes on the Ecology, Culture and Politics of Reindeer Samis in Sweden, pp. 215–234 in L. Muller-Wille, P. Pelto, Li. Muller-Wille, and R. Darnell (Editors): *Consequences of Economic Change in Circumpolar Regions*. Edmonton, Alberta: Boreal Institute For Northern Studies, University of Alberta.
TOLKO INDUSTRIES LTD. 1997. *Tolko Preliminary Forest Management Plan*. High Prairie, Alberta: Tolko Industries Ltd.

(e) Inuit Perceptions of Contaminants and Environmental Knowledge in Salluit, Nunavik[†]

Sylvie Poirier and Lorraine Brooke

INTRODUCTION

In 1993, we were asked to participate in a multidisciplinary research project to inquire into the multifaceted aspects of food chain contaminants in Canada's Eastern Arctic and their potential negative effects on human health. The project was provided funding by the Tri-Council of Canada, as an Eco-research program. Within the nine sub-projects of the program *Avativut/Ilusivut* (Our Environment/Our Health), the objectives of our specific research were two-fold. First, it aimed at achieving a more comprehensive understanding of Inuit perceptions and interpretations of contamination and contaminants issues on the basis of their own language, system of knowledge, values, experiences and practices on the land. We wished to draw a qualitative evaluation of how and to what extent these perceptions might (or might not) affect their long-lasting relationship with the land and their hunting, fishing, and gathering activities.

Our second objective was to contribute, within the Eco-Research program, to the development of a "trans-cultural discourse" (Milton, ed. 1993) on the issue of contaminants in Nunavik. When dealing with issues and concepts concerning contaminants, the facts and figures of "hard science" come face to face with the cultural, social and economic realities of Inuit life. Thus, in order to contribute to the development of a cross-cultural dialogue and collaboration on the issue of contaminants in Nunavik, we must seek ways to bridge the gap between the Inuit knowledge system, and that of western science[. Both] knowledge systems are value-laden[;] both are authoritative in their own cultural context[;] both are con-

―――
[†] From *Arctic Anthropology*, Vol. 37, No. 2, pp. 78–91. © 2000. Reproduced by permission of the University of Wisconsin Press.

structed in terms of their own cultural objectivity according to different ontological and epistemological principles. These two systems draw on different substantive and methodological grounds (Inglis, ed. 1993; Agrawal 1995). The point, we want to stress, is not to set western science in opposition to indigenous knowledge or to emphasize competition in their respective areas of competence, an attitude qualified as unfruitful (Agrawal 1995), but to better understand and develop ways that one can complement the other as far as local and regional issues are concerned.

It is worth pointing out that while many research efforts have explored indigenous ecological knowledge and its relationship with development and environmental issues, since the 1980s and in various northern regions, at the time of our research, very few had actually approached the issue of contaminants as [interpreted] within the system of knowledge and practices of these modern [hunters] and gatherers.[1] Many of the questions, difficulties and issues raised, however, by the studies on Traditional Ecological Knowledge (TEK) and the eventual integration with western science, with a view toward improving environmental management and local empowerment, are no doubt relevant to the issues of contaminants. Among these, social researchers have stressed the difficulties inherent in identifying and defining the scope and range of TEK (Usher 2000, Wenzel 1999), while most of them have also warned against the dangers of compartmentalization, distillation and translation inherent in any studies on TEK (Nadasdy 1999, Brooke 1993), or the risks of dispossession and appropriation of TEK. As Cruikshank [has] outlined, there is also the risk that indigenous knowledge may "be presented as an object for science rather than as a system of knowledge that could inform science" (Cruikshank 1998:50). Or, as pointed out by Mary Simon (1994) at a seminar on the topic: "Indigenous knowledge not only has value for the cultures within which it has evolved, but it can also contribute to an improved understanding of the Arctic and to seeking solutions to environmental and development problems. Indigenous peoples and their organizations are clearly prepared to work with the western scientific community and give guidance and direction.... They will not, however, accept that indigenous knowledge continue to be treated as a research topic or as an adjunct to projects initiated by non-indigenous researchers." All the current emphasis on Traditional Ecological Knowledge, though needed, reflects nevertheless a definite modernist concern with epistemology, or with knowing rather than with being, neglecting the local ontological principles that inform any system of knowledge. From the Inuit point of view, and according to Nadasdy, "traditional knowledge is not so much knowledge, as it is a way of life" (1994:4). Though, in this paper, we don't address these questions specifically, they did present themselves to us, in one way or another, through our research.

THE COMMUNITY OF SALLUIT

Lying north of the 55th parallel, Salluit is one of the 16 communities that make up what is known as Nunavik in northern Quebec (see Fig. 1). Salluit is located on the southern shore of Sugluk Bay on the coast of Hudson Strait. Its population is approximately 1000. The community is situated in a very resource-rich region and continues to have a diverse and active subsistence economy. The mainland provides an abundance of big and small game, as well as freshwater and anadromous fish.

FIGURE 1. Map of Nunavik

Map by Strata360, Montreal

Recent expansion of the George River/Leaf River caribou herds and the resulting change in migration behaviors have resulted in caribou being accessible to the community during winter months. Marine mammal hunting, however, continues to be the preferred activity. Ringed seals are plentiful in the coastal waters. Beluga whales migrate in spring and fall and are eagerly awaited by hunters. Walrus can be found on the large offshore islands.

Salluit was selected on the basis of its long history with a variety of contamination issues and even crises. As early as the mid-1970s, in the course of a National Health and Welfare testing program, Inuit in the community were found to have very high levels of methyl-mercury in their blood and hair. Health advisories were issued against eating certain parts of marine mammals. This was done without evidence as to the origin of the contamination, and without a community strategy or community information program. By 1979–1980, mercury levels had dropped dramatically. The source of the incident was eventually traced to an unusually high consumption of lake trout (a species high in the food chain and therefore a source of mercury contamination) in the winter of 1977. Ice conditions were very bad that year, and hunting patterns shifted from seal hunting to freshwater fish. People were however, left frightened and confused by the events.

During the same era, the community became more aware of the potential dangers associated with the large, open-pit asbestos mine operated by Asbestos Corporation at Asbestos Hill and Deception Bay, 65 km to the east of Salluit. Begun in the late 1960s in the absence of any environmental standards or means to enforce the measures that did exist, asbestos was mined and refined at Asbestos Hill and transported by truck to Deception Bay where it was stored and then loaded on large ocean-going freighters by using a piece of equipment called a blower. The area was literally covered with measurable amounts of asbestos fiber. No information was made available at the time concerning direct dangers to human health. After the signing of the James Bay and Northern Quebec Agreement in 1975, many requests were made to government agencies to research and advise the community on potential impacts of abestos on fish and marine mammals in particular. Little was done and the mine closed. More recently, the negotiations have taken place leading to an impact and benefit agreement with the communities of Salluit and Kangirsujuaq, regarding a nickel mine at Raglan Lake operated by Falconbridge. These discussions specifically identified community concerns regarding pollution and contamination. Mitigation measures were identified and a monitoring program proposed. Only time and experience will permit an evaluation of whether these measures are effective or sufficient.

DATA COLLECTING

Fieldwork in Salluit took place in August 1995. With Lucy Grey, a young Inuk, who acted as research-assistant and translator, we conducted 15 open-ended interviews, involving 29 people, men and women, of different age groups and professional cohorts on the issue of contaminants in relation to hunting and fishing activities. Seventy percent of the informants were senior male hunters. We prepared for each interview by identifying broad categories of information or areas of interest the individual or group might best contribute to, but were careful not to arbitrarily limit the range of conversation. All the interviews were conducted in Inuktituut by Lucy Grey, with one or the two of us also present. The interviews were taped and translated into English by a professional translator in Salluit.

One of the benefits of the open-ended (or semi-directed) interviews, considered as the key method of data collection (Usher 2000:189), is that they allow for a fair amount of flexibility and adaptability for the researcher and the informant. The informant can express his/her point of view, relate to personal experiences, narrate stories or anecdotes; all elements that might contain relevant information for the researcher. While the researcher proposes the leading thread, the interviews take more the form of a dialogue rather than a formal question and answer session. All the people interviewed were more than willing to express and communicate their views on, and understandings of, contaminants and contaminant issues.

As the work progressed, it was evident that letting the people speak for themselves was the most productive and meaningful way to proceed. The work, therefore, and the resulting reports relied primarily on the transcripts of the interviews. Every attempt was made to respect the words of the people in the organization of the responses, categorization and elaboration of conclusions or recommendations — an approach we have carried over to this discussion. Consistent with accepted practice in northern work respecting confidentiality, the quotes are not attributed.

INUIT AS MODERN HUNTER-GATHERERS

Before inquiring into Inuit understandings of contaminants in relation to their environmental knowledge and hunting practices, it is essential to consider a number of specific elements of their social and cultural reality. In today's context, Inuit can be viewed as modern hunter-gatherers (Bird-David, 1992), meaning that while they have, in many respects, maintained their specific way of relating to the land, they have also diversified their methods of subsistence via the adoption of *Qallunaat* (non-Inuit) technologies and a cash income economy. In this context of transformation, the Inuit are nonetheless still guided by a web of local values, representations, and practices that continue to inform their understanding of contaminants and contaminant issues on the land. We shall briefly consider three dimensions of Inuit sociocultural reality which are relevant to our topic.

Inuit Ontology: The Man-Animal Relationship

In Inuit ontology, the environment is seen as a complex system of interacting agencies (and variables) and they appreciate well that interference with one part of the system has implications for the other part (Freeman 1993:155). As hunters, they view and experience their relationship with the environment and the animal world in a particularly intimate, communicative, and reciprocal manner. Human beings, animals, and the environment are all perceived as sharing partners; their modes of becoming are intrinsically linked. It corresponds to what Ingold presents as an ontology of engagement (Ingold 1996) with and within a sentient landscape. In the Inuit world, animals are sentient beings endowed with personhood and thus intentions and awareness (Fienup-Riordan 1999).

An additional theme which has emerged from current research on modern hunter-gatherers, irrespective of the ecosystem, is their deep trust in the environment (Bird-David 1990), despite all the risks and uncertainty that might be the daily lot of hunters who are engaged in harvesting resources. In Salluit, this dimension of trust and confidence towards the environment, and in their own ecological and environmental knowledge, came out quite clearly during the interviews (see below). Thus, Inuit cultural ontology and specific ways of relating to the animal world and engaging with the environment, taken with this dimension of trust and the acute ecological knowledge they have developed as hunters, all combine to shape and influence their perceptions of contamination issues. Interestingly, Inuit seem much more concerned about potential dangers to animals and subsequent impacts on hunting and eating behaviors than about direct dangers to human health.

The Socio-cultural Importance of Country Food

"For Inuit, eating *niqituinnaq* and being Inuk are inseparable" (Usher et al., 1995:117).

> If we are to keep eating country food, hunting has to continue. If I became unable to go out, and no one else had the abilities required, animals will be only that, animals. [They] will no longer be available for food.

Another aspect worth considering when dealing with the perceptions of contaminants in Inuit communities is certainly the socio-cultural importance of country food. Even though their patterns of consumption have gone through major changes in the last decades, amounting to higher intakes of southern food (these might vary according to communities and age groups), the Inuit (and social scientists) continue to stress the importance of country food within the individual and collective conception of health and well-being (Usher et al., 1995:118–132; Therrien 1987a, b). The close relationship between the person and his/her eating habits is indeed an embodied value in Inuit experiences, collective expressions and sense of identity. This cultural reality is best expressed in the words of an elder of Salluit who said: "Animals are our body." Speaking of traditional times, another Inuk expressed the same idea in the following manner: "...as the animals seem to be part of us then." These statements highlight the symbolic implication of country food for Inuit wellbeing and identity, both in individual and collective terms but also the social and cultural values attached to hunting, fishing, and gathering. The importance of country food for Inuit and the clear distinction they make between it and *Qallunaat* food are local realities that also shape and influence their perceptions of scientific discourses on contaminants and "poisoned food."

Reciprocity as Social Practice: Sharing as an Embodied Value

Anthropological studies on hunters and gatherers often stress the importance of sharing within the social fabric and the local systems of values and practices. In the context of contemporary living, this strong ethic of sharing (Bird-David 1990:195) or this ecology of sharing has hardly been affected; the continuation of norms of reciprocity among settled hunter-gatherers is well known and has been well-documented in numerous studies (Myers 1988:269). Inuit societies are no exception to this rule, as was made clear during fieldwork in Salluit. The concept of sharing can be taken a step further by saying that Inuit, like other hunter-gatherers, engage in a sharing relationship with their environment and the animal world.

For an Inuk, sharing is not a duty; sharing is not performed for prestige or out of generosity either. It is even more than a responsibility toward others, it is an embodied value and practice. The sharing of country food, to cite only this example, as it bears most directly on the topic of this paper, is still part of the social fabric. As such, it is vital to the management and the continuation of local interpersonal relationships within contemporary Inuit communities. During fieldwork, it became evident that country food, either dried, frozen, or fresh, was being extensively shared between members of the extended family and beyond. Sharing is an ongoing practice and a way of relating to others that is not so easily quantified (in relation here to statistical studies).

The sharing of knowledge is also highly valued in these societies of oral traditions (Usher et al., 1995:144) and where hunting skills and environmental knowledge are learned, not in a didactic manner, but through observation and practice. In today's context, even though the traditional means of such knowledge transmission have been disrupted in many ways, the bulk of each hunter's environmental knowledge is still very important. As regards the contamination issue, the Inuit expect to share with the researchers their respective knowledge. They expect also that a cross-cultural dialogue will be established, one based on reciprocity and where the two systems of knowledge, values, and practices on the land would be considered on equal footing. Finally, there was an expectation of being informed once the information gathering process was concluded, understanding that certain types of information can only come from laboratory and other analyses, as a basis for jointly developing strategies to minimize or eliminate exposure.

INUIT PERCEPTIONS OF CONTAMINATION AND CONTAMINANTS

As a general rule, Sallumiut are not unduly concerned by the issue of contaminants, which does not mean, on the other hand, that they are totally oblivious or ignorant of the issue. Like the average person in the South, they have a certain media-derived understanding of, and concern for, airborne and waterborne pollutants such as nuclear wastes. One of the differences from Southerners though, is that as hunters their concern is equally directed towards the animals, the land, and humans as elements of an interconnected whole. We first explore here the contamination issue, from the Inuit point of view in a broad sense; that is, as anything that might be perceived by Inuit as having a negative impact on their land and more crucially, on their relationship with it. Secondly, we focus on their perceptions of contaminants and on their growing understanding of the effects of contaminants within the whole food chain.

With respect to local [systems] of values and practices, one of the main concerns, at least for the Elders and senior hunters we interviewed, is the changes they have noticed in the quality of the relationships between humans and animals. In Inuit ontology, the lives of human beings and animals are intrinsically linked; whatever might affect one will affect the other. In that light, generally speaking, the Inuit correlate the changes that have occurred in their own way of life with changes in animal behavior. When asked if they had noticed any change in animal behavior in the last decades, most informants referred to how the sounds and smells of *Qallunaat* technologies and by-products have scared the fish and sea mammals away from the bay adjacent to the community. Most of the Elders we interviewed voiced this view, not so much out of feelings of nostalgia as from a concern that a breach in the quality of the relationships binding hunters and animals might prove detrimental to future generations. The following statements by two Elders provide illustration of this correlation:

>...the animals around here were practically our neighbors.... This is a thing of the past. All the game have been forced elsewhere by the arrival of Qallunaat goods. Perhaps our descendants will simply starve.... However, it is fair to say that we ourselves have contributed in good measure to this, with Qallunaat ammunition [having] been made easily available.... We adopted a much easier way and wound up nearly working ourselves into a period of hard times, or so it seems to me, at any rate.
>
> I tend to think that with the increase in motor boats and other noise-including machines, it is just that the wildlife has been avoiding the area. Noise from outboard motors [is] the same, in effect, as directions to avoid a certain area. The noise [serves] as warning to animals. There are animals around. Mind you there are cycles that cause animals to be abundant for a while and then decline in availability, but generally, the only thing to my mind that has affected wildlife in terms of immediate availability are the [noises] generated today by human activity.

It must be emphasized at this point that while most informants do in fact mention a decrease in the presence of wildlife in the bay adjacent to Salluit, they did not think the same applied in the case of the surrounding countryside, where animals were as abundant as ever, notwithstanding natural cycles. Broadly speaking, contamination is here correlated with changes in their own way of life and is understood as a lessening in the quality and the extent of the close relationships between humans and animals. These changes have in turn affected the traditional dimensions of sustainability, recyclability, and renewal.

Sallumiut have demonstrated a high degree of awareness and concern for the harmful effects of contaminants on lands surrounding the community. For example, it has become common knowledge that, because of inadequate sewage and garbage disposal facilities, country food — be this plants, animals, fish or mussels — are not to be harvested around the community. The caribou that can be observed ambling just outside the community limits are not hunted because they eat from the local dump. The following statements by two senior hunters are illustrative.

> There is the run-off from the sewage disposal site that we consider has ill-effects on things like mussels, clams and sculpins. We don't harvest much of that from around there. Caribou also. We don't kill the caribou that are feeding around there much. This is due to the sewage disposal site on the mountain top there, which runs off down into the bay. If that community service system were not there, we would still harvest from all around the immediate area of the community.
>
> I am wary of collecting mussels from the areas of tidal flat that the sewage effluent goes by. Our solid waste and waste water disposals are located in the mountain, and the sewage is [disposed] in such a way that it runs downhill into the sea water in our bay here. I don't gather mussels from there, but I still do so in neighboring areas.

Another concern expressed by people of all ages, involves the garbage left around summer cabins or in the countryside by hunting groups. People are concerned that such waste might eventually have a particularly harmful effect on the spawning grounds of fish at the heads of inlets. Generally speaking, however, community members are quite aware that they alone are responsible for leaving garbage in the countryside, in contrast with contaminants like mercury and PCB's, over which they have no control.

We will deal now with the issue of contaminants as such, and local understandings of the origins, causes, and pathways. While we recognize that there are differences among community members as to the degree of concern for, and understanding of, contaminants, it is still possible to draw some general outline. As a general rule, Sallumiut perceptions of contaminants have evolved over recent decades, and the initial fears and misunderstandings of the 1970s during the mercury crisis have given way today to more informed attitudes and views. In this process, Sallumiut have learned as much through their own experiences and observations on the land, particularly at Deception Bay on the site of the old Asbestos mine, as through the scientific information they have been presented with over the years. But, when asked to recall their past experience, informants agreed that mercury contamination was perceived at that time as something deadly.

> When a person was told he or she was "contaminated," at first we thought that person was doomed and would maybe even die in short order due to the literal meaning of the word used for contaminant which means "destructive agent". This is because of maybe a lack of understanding of what was meant — a person [who] had ingested "destructive agents" with their food did not necessarily become destroyed after all. It dawned upon us later that these "destroyers" were only destructive to humans at certain levels and that having a tolerable amount, while not desirable, was also possible.
>
> I did have hair samples taken. People who had high levels of mercury in their hair roots were sent away for treatment. Those of us with perceptible but lower levels were not sent away.... Back then, I felt that if this were the case that many people were going to die because of the seriousness which seemed attached to the issue. Those individuals [who] were found to have high levels of mercury obviously thought they were going to die soon, and worried greatly about it.
>
> I even discarded a beluga, a fine healthy, young adult male at his best, because I thought it had mercury in him. He had this noticeable but tiny hole in his skin. I'd heard somewhere that there were people who injected mercury into beluga and was afraid that this one had been thus contaminated. I just left a perfectly fine animal there after I killed it.

The last statement provides clear illustration of the initial degree of misunderstanding present at one time among members of the community as to the origin of the mercury. These views have since been supplanted by better informed opinions. Today, this man harvests and eats beluga meat. Like most other people in Salluit, he has regained trust in his knowledge and ability to detect an animal that is unfit for consumption (see below) after having momentarily doubted it at one time.

The word most commonly used in Inuktituut for "contaminant" is *sukunaktuit*, which means literally "destructive agents." Though the word itself is not quite adequate, it seems by now to have made its way into the local language and knowledge. The question was put to some informants if they had a better word to suggest. The following statement by a senior hunter summarizes a widespread feeling:

> It is difficult to come with a single word. However, the word by itself has too severe a meaning. We can't use *piusirsugnnainartuq*, because people again would understand that to mean to be crippled somehow, and we can't just say that it affects one's normal physical characteristics. I don't really know. The word has been derived from animal research, I know that. But the word itself is confusing: an animal ingests a substance which it isn't meant to have, and then is eaten by an Inuk in turn. Since the animal had "destructive agents" in it, those are passed on to the Inuk. This is the correlation that gave rise to that meaning. However, the person does not die, or become crippled somehow, or otherwise become different, so the word itself does seem inappropriate, but again it is difficult to think of a more suitable name for it.

While the majority of the people we met considered that they lacked effective information on the issue of contaminants, most had a general understanding of the pathways and negative effects of contaminants on the whole food chain, and, as mentioned earlier, their primary concern goes first to the animals as food rather than to human health. Such understanding and primary concern are made evident in the following statement.

> From past observation in Deception [Bay], which is to say from what I have seen in the summer by travelling on a Honda (ATV), I would not wish to see another area so treated. Old chemicals, oils and fuel tanks along the length of that road are leaking their contents into the environment. I've always been against doing harm to wildlife habitats; animals unknowingly sample many things which are potentially harmful, and I'm sure there's been some impacts on some species. I don't wish to see this happen again. Also, whatever chemicals or petroleum products are put in the environment will eventually makes [their] way through the watershed and end up in lakes which have fish in them. These fish in turn travel to the sea and are eaten by other wildlife. The whole food chain can be affected in this way.

Previous and current mining activities and explorations in the area are directly correlated with contamination and contaminants — much more so than air and waterborne pollutants identified with the Southern activities. While Sallumiut have expressed a clear dissatisfaction in the lack of informative and preventive measures in the case of the asbestos mine in the 1970s, they usually agree that the situation has improved with the nickel mine at Raglan Lake operated by Falconbridge. Having signed an impact and benefit agreement with the company and being informed of its activities, they feel they have gained a certain control that was non-existent in previous decades. This does not mean though that Sallumiut are not concerned by eventual damages made to their territory. From their own observations at Deception Bay, they are aware that on a long-term basis the by-products of the mining activities could cause major damages to the reproductive cycle, mainly those of the fish population. The president of the local hunters association expressed his point of view in the following manner:

> To my way of thinking, I would say there should not be any mining activity there, first of all. However, since there has been an agreement reached with us for that project to proceed, and since in all probability it would proceed without our consent anyway, we cannot prevent it from going ahead. I know firsthand that mining companies use very dangerous substances in their work. Substances which could cause contaminants like mercury to be introduced. Miners traditionally are very callous in their treatment of the environment and are prone to dumping substances which we ourselves would not dump in certain places. Chemicals can access lakes and main river systems very easily, even if they are not released directly into the main water bodies; all the minor streams and inclines form the collective watershed which feed the main rivers and lakes. For this reason, I want to see an environmental monitor to ensure the fish in particular are not poisoned.[2]

Over the years and owing to their own observations, Sallumiut have come to a negative appreciation of the culture of the miners, qualifying their general attitude towards the land as callous, in contrast with their own values and practices. Interestingly, abandoned fuel drums have become a symbol for the Inuit of what they fear most about development, namely [an] unknown presence in their territory, lack of information and control and the potential of minor or massive destruction. There are many examples of Inuit linking the presence of abandoned fuel drums with a negative environmental or ecological [phenomenon]. Time and time again, Deception Bay and the asbestos mine came up in the interviews as a concrete example of the relationships between industrial activity or pollution, and diseased or deformed fish. The Deception Bay experience is interesting for our purpose because in the total absence of any information about the mine and its potential impacts, the Inuit developed their own ways of dealing with, and avoiding species (particularly fish) which they felt may have been contaminated by tailings of asbestos dust.

TRUST IN LOCAL KNOWLEDGE

As has been stressed already, the Inuit draw a clear qualitative distinction between country food acquired through hunting, fishing and gathering and *Qallunaat* food coming from the South and bought at the store. At the qualitative and quantitative levels, the distinction remains a culturally sensitive matter. Surely, any visitor to an Inuit community will quickly attest to the fact that they, and mostly the younger generation, consume indeed a fair amount of store-bought food. But the point we want to stress is that, as a general rule, country food as well as hunting and fishing activities are still highly valued as individual and collective vectors of health, well-being, and identity. For the adults and the Elders, such qualitative dimension attached to country food is best expressed in terms of health and identity.

> In the winter we feel that wild meat is better to keep warm and for the body to feel good. We even bring frozen meant with us to eat while we are out, because it is better for maintaining warmth and vitality out on the land. It is different in this way from Qallunaat food, like chicken and other fry pan type foods because when we eat this instead we get cold more easily and become hungry again rather quickly. These are not considered as staples like wild meat is, since our bodies are not used to them.
>
> I am an Inuk and my way is to eat this. I cannot do without it, because it is intrinsic to who I am. Even if I am told that it is unsafe to eat, I think I could not refrain from doing so.

Younger people, more prone to eating *Qallunaat* food and having developed a taste for it, still questioned its degree of contamination and raised the point that they have no way of controlling the processing and handling of such food.

> I think wild meat is less hazardous to eat then some Qallunaat food. We've heard of processed meats having caused illnesses, even recently. Somehow during the handling stages of the meat preparation process, harmful elements may be introduced. We've heard of the so-called hamburger disease which causes meningitis in the South. Although our food can cause illness if not prepared properly, I feel this risk is much smaller than with Qallunaat food. Even after going through all the quality control mechanisms, this food can still spoil in transit, by thawing out and re-freezing repeatedly en route to their destination. I think this is much more likely to cause harm than the usual Inuit methods of food handling.
>
> I think our traditional food is better than Qallunaat food because as our Elders prepare it, it is free of anything that may be harmful to eat, whereas Qallunaat food may have foreign substances in it.
>
> We don't really worry about it much. Our Elders won't give us food that isn't good to have, and therefore we don't worry. We rely on our Elders to discern the quality of the food they are going to prepare.

The young people seem to have arrived at a compromise integrating media-derived and health authorities discourses and information gained from the Elders. We are aware though that if the questions were put to them in terms of preferred taste, we might have received different answers. However, the last statement takes us to the point we wish now to address, one which is fundamental to the development of a cross-cultural discourse on the issue of contaminants, namely local ecological knowledge.

Inuit Elders and the senior hunters have a profound understanding and highly developed knowledge and capacity for detecting unfit country food in addition to an awareness of abnormalities and sicknesses occurring among animals. As they are confident in their own knowledge, they feel quite skeptical toward any warnings that have been issued from the South stating that their food might be poisoned or unfit for consumption. As for the younger people, they recognize that they lack some of the knowledge the Elders have, but they nevertheless feel confident that hunters would not give them food that was tainted in any way.

> Certainly, we will continue to eat these things as long as they aren't obviously abnormal in some way. [...] When it becomes quite obvious that a certain tissue is not the way it should be, then we don't eat it. It's that simple...Inuit are very capable of determining what is good and what is not. There are very knowledgeable people out there. Some people can even tell whether the igunak (putrefied delicacies) before them is good, or has spoiled and become poisonous. This is from experience...I am confident with my ability in this way and would most certainly eat what I deem to be safe.
>
> When an animal is unfit for consumption, the hunters will know it from examination and we do not keep bad meat here. It is obvious when an animal is unwell. When it is thin in appearance during the fat season, for instance.
>
> ...when a tissue is obviously hazardous to eat, or when fat for example isn't right, we regard these as being potentially harmful and don't eat them, as a matter of normal practice.

In order to produce a diagnostic, hunters rely on a whole range of perceptible signs, such as the behavior of the animal, the color and texture of its organs, its fur, or fatty tissues. It is often during the evisceration and butchering process that the hunter or his wife notices that the animal is unfit for consumption. When in doubt or unsure of the quality of the meat, the hunters may discuss the case between themselves. Parasites, for example, which were mentioned on a regular basis, were presented as part of a natural process that can nevertheless cause humans to be very sick. A young hunter expressed the following caution:

> Some [animal] species have parasites in them. When the older people talk about this or provide instruction, attention should be paid. For example, we are advised to remove the head of the caribou we kill at certain times, to prevent the parasites in its throat from moving further into the animal as its body temperature cools.

Throughout the interview process, we were able to collect an entire series of signs from the senior hunter informants. These are presented in Table 1. Their sense of deep trust in local knowledge doesn't mean however, that they are oblivious to the possibility of error. Once in a while, as in other places, some serious cases of food poisoning do occur.

LOCAL RESISTANCE TO SCIENTIFIC DISCOURSES ON CONTAMINANTS

This is our own distinct type of diet and it has always been uncertain as to how we'll respond to orders not to have it.

Being confident in their own knowledge, Sallumiut feel uneasy and suspicious whenever biologists tell them an animal (or meat) that looks perfectly good to the naked eye might actually be contaminated and possibly detrimental to human health. Our informants pointed out that even if a sick animal — caribou, sea mam-

TABLE 1. Signs of Game Unfit for Consumption		
Caribou	External signs	• caribou injured after a battle • hides that look old • loss of hair during the time animal should not be shedding • behavioral signs suspect
	Internal signs	• excess fluid in the joints • abdominal areas seem bluish in color • parasites (not necessarily a sign all meat should be discarded)
Fish	External and Internal signs	• thin, sluggish or weak • discolored spots on liver
Sea Mammals	External and Internal signs	• yellow fat • white patches or spots on liver • hard texture of liver (a normal liver is soft enough to dissect with one's fingers) • red spots on mattaq • kidneys, mushy or shrunken in appearance

mal, fish, or other — is occasionally encountered, this does not mean that the entire species is endangered.

> Wildlife have always had their own peculiar traits, and like humans, there is the occasional sickly animal that is encountered. This is how it seems to me as a lifelong hunter. Some animals, like people, will become sick and it is my opinion that a whole species is never suspect.
> ...we've always been able to tell the harmful from the benign. There were people who knew about this before I did. There have always been animals which were not healthy, and we discern this on a case-by-case basis.
> Fish are found to be abnormal only rarely, seal liver or seal parts and beluga, marine mammals in general too are found to have abnormal characteristics only once in a long while.

In the previous statements, these hunters reiterate trust in their own ability to detect a sick animal, one that might be unfit for consumption. These statements also show that Inuit are not terribly concerned about the general health of wildlife, simply because they have not observed any increase in the number of animal illnesses and abnormalities, other than those which naturally occur. Finally, it is our view that these statements can be understood as a local response to a perceived tendency among members of the scientific community to reach occasionally hasty conclusions, fearing that a whole species may be endangered when in fact only a few specimens are involved. These statements provide a good example with which to compare Inuit and western ways of relating to the environment. As mentioned above, the Inuit perceive their relationship with animals in a particularly intimate, communicative, and reciprocal manner. Accordingly, as hunters, they consider every animal as a sentient being or other-than-human person, with its own characteristics, awareness and motivations, and not simply as a representative of another wildlife species that needs to be monitored or managed.[3]

During the 1970s, when the Inuit of Salluit were first advised to refrain from eating presumably contaminated country food, these warnings produced the effect of a bombshell among this community of hunters. Everyone was worried or concerned to some degree, but not everybody did as they were advised. In fact, it appears that very few heeded the warnings. Some seasons later, those families who had refrained from going out into the land began once more to visit their hunting territories. One informant and his family never stopped eating sea mammals, and began looking upon these warnings suspiciously, seeing them as a strategy by the government to denigrate the Inuit way of life. Then as now, this particular view did not, however, appear to be widely held in Salluit.

Most people interviewed expressed concerns about the fish population at Deception Bay, the site of the Asbestos mine. They had encountered a fair amount of abnormal or sick specimens, but not enough to cause them to avoid the area. In Salluit, there are no traditional hunting or fishing grounds avoided by people out of concerns for contaminants. The only country food that some Sallumiut refrained from eating because they were told they were contaminated are the liver and kidneys of caribou. As caribou have never been a staple of Sallumiut, these restrictions do not represent a great hardship. The following statements are illustrative of a widespread attitude:

> I hunt wherever I wish without concern. It is only when I harvest an animal that has an ailment of some kind that I am wary of the individual's quality. I don't feel there are any areas where I should not harvest animal wildlife.
>
> I've never altered my diet. I know that there are others like me who have never stopped having food which [has] been declared unsafe. We also know that bit of conventional wisdom that goes to say that as long as we moderate our daily intake of different food groups, then we should be and are fine.

Distrust does not account entirely for the Inuit's skepticism in taking what researchers tell them about potentially contaminated food at face value. As seen above, Inuit confidence in their own knowledge and methods for identifying unfit animals or animal parts is another reason. This entrenched pride as hunters is at the core of their cultural resistance. It is also a reflection of a strong sense of identity. What is more, over the years, the Inuit have come to a certain understanding of the "limitations" of scientific knowledge about contaminants. The interviews made clear that in the warnings the Inuit received in the 1970s, they sensed (as now) a serious lack of consistent information and a lack of follow-up information, subsequent to the testing and the issuance of advisories.

Local resistance to scientific discourses on contaminants also partly stems from, and is based on, the fact that Inuit hunters have not noticed any permanent and significant changes in animal behavior, nor any increase in diseases or abnormalities that would signify the wildlife has been substantially affected or endangered in some way. The following statement by a woman who worked also as health official is illustrative of local understanding of man-animal relationships as regards contaminants:

> We do not inflict injustices on the animals and trust that they in turn are good for us, we who do not wrong them in some way. Simultaneously, we would like to take heed to these warnings but since we don't create any circumstances ourselves which would render wildlife unfit to eat, we simply continue as before.

TOWARDS CO-OPERATION AND LOCAL CONTROL

There should be a better dialogue between the researchers involved and the community on wildlife studies. Only in this way, by cooperating with each other, will satisfactory information be acquired by everyone

Many Inuit commented on the need for much broader co-operation between local hunters and scientific researchers in dealing with the issue of contaminants in country food. They do not want to see the mistakes of the past repeated, when researchers issued warnings, often on the basis of inadequate and inconclusive science, without consulting them, without considering their knowledge, and without discussing this issue with them. On the whole issue of communication, crucial in establishing a cross-cultural discourse, most of the people interviewed deplored a serious lack in consistent information and follow up after testing was done or advisories issued.

> We've been told not to eat the liver and stomach of caribou, for example, but I don't know what the specific reasons are. No doubt there are others who have heard more. I was also advised some time ago not to eat seal liver, but have not heard lately if there's been any other development on that.

Inuit expressed the desire for a partnership between hunters and scientists in order to deal with the issue of contaminants in wild food. This partnership should be developed through the entire process — research, testing, analysis, generating information, and communications. In the following statement, a hunter expresses his views on such collaboration:

> This is why I, as a hunter, although I don't go out every single day, suggested that I for one could work in conjunction with a researcher. I have the firsthand knowledge required to differentiate between abnormal and normal specimens and this could [complement] the tools which the researchers would have in turn, to achieve the best possible results using both sides.... If, however, I and a biologist were together and I was to state my opinion of a harvested animal's liver being unfit, I wonder if the biologist would concur. In other words, would this biologist also be of the mind that it was contaminated? I ask this because as an Inuk, although I am not a scientist, I can tell when whatever is in front of me is not good to eat from examination.

Other experiences of the authors, working with Inuit and other indigenous peoples, make us confident in stating that local involvement and control is important not only for developing and conducting appropriate research, but for engaging local people and their institutions in problem solving and decision making. This approach to involvement is now, to a degree, required under most modern-day northern land claims agreements. There is also an evolving, positive trend within the southern scientific community to want to work directly with local people to construct research programs that respond to and meet the needs of northern peoples.

Relevant to this discussion, is the work of the Kuujjuaq Research Center under Makivik Corporation — an Inuit owned corporation created through the 1975 James Bay and Northern Quebec Agreement, representing the Inuit of Nunavik. Begun in the late 1970's, this research center has grown into a facility equipped professionally and technically to conduct a wide variety of work with contaminants. The center works directly with communities to design research programs, involves local Inuit at all stages of the work and places great emphasis on communicating results, responding to requests for testing and information, and collaborating with local health officials.

CONCLUSION

The results of the work indicate clearly that the possible presence of contaminants is not modifying how Inuit hunt, prepare and eat their food. This does not mean they are not concerned, but rather that they feel confident that their own means for distinguishing what is edible from what is not still serves them well. When advisories are issued or concerns communicated, there is sometimes a short-term modification. The eating habits of pregnant [women] are a possible exception, particularly those who are under regular medical supervision. An examination of this group would require a much more focused research effort.

The often poor, confusing, and sometimes alarmist information circulating about contaminants and contamination still has an impact. People may not modify their behavior, or if they do, it does not last. But that does not mean they are not sometimes uneasy and worried. While it is acknowledged that the situation has evolved since the 1970s, there is still great room for improvement.

It was clear to us that Inuit seek to be involved in all aspects of research. They also insist on better communication and timely dissemination of information. Currently some skepticism exists about the degree to which Inuit knowledge and values are actually taken into account. While the discourse has changed over the past 20 years, Inuit feel that the scientific community remains in control of the information and research agenda.

For the Inuit, as for the scientific community, the initial fears and misunderstandings of the 1970s in connection with contaminated country food have given way to better informed attitudes and views. The knowledge and views of both groups have evolved, and both have more to gain today from a complementary approach. No doubt, researchers and other public health agents have learned from the initial mistakes made in [the] 1970s during the mercury scare. Irresponsible scientific investigations, which issue premature reports of potential dangers and neglect to follow up with actual findings, have a considerable negative on these communities. In fact, researchers have come to realize that the negative social impact of such methods is as damaging to local communities as the effects of the contaminants themselves. Generally speaking, as a result, today's research protocols on contaminants are much more sensitive to Inuit cultural values and practices. Furthermore, and in the context of indigenous claims to self-determination, definite efforts have been made at establishing collaborative working relationships with Inuit representatives.

Within the scientific community over the last decade or so, there has been a major shift in the discourse on the intake of country food and its impact on human health. During the 1970s, the Inuit were told to refrain from eating some of their country food because it was said to be poisoned, whereas today they are being told that the benefits of country food in terms of its nutritive value outweigh (or surpass) the potential negative effects of contaminants (Grondin, Proulx, Bruneau and Dewailly 1994). To be sure, these changes in the discourse concerning contaminants reflect greater sensitivity to Inuit values and practices, but the discourse nevertheless carries its share of paradoxical messages. We could add also that, whether the Inuit are told to refrain from eating country food, or to eat it as long as it has not actually been proven detrimental to human health, uneven relations of power and authority are interfering with their life choices.

In the best of all scenarios, the development of a cross-cultural discourse between Inuit and the Western Scientific [Community] should mean that the two knowledge systems are [working] on equal footing; but for many reasons, things are not so simple. In addition to the structure of differences, questions of power and authority necessarily come into play, with the biomedical sciences either "claim[ing] their privileged knowledge about hidden dangers" (Scott 1997:24) or continually raising questions about the "potential" danger of contaminants [to] human health. Owing to their past experience, the Inuit have developed a form of cultural resistance to scientific discourses on contaminants (O'Neil, Elias and Yassi 1997); likewise, as a general rule, biomedical scientists remain resistant to an explicit and collaborative recognition of indigenous knowledge (Silitoe 1998). Despite the positive changes in research codes of ethics, it seems that Inuit voices and hunting knowledge continue, within the issue of contaminants, to be considered as knowledge of secondary importance, as being in no way as reliable or as tangible as biomedical knowledge.

While efforts are certainly being made to broaden the dialogue among Inuit and various members of the biomedical community, during the course of our work we noted a mutual skepticism. Perhaps owing to its position of authority and the assumed rigors of science, the biomedical community can appear to Inuit as lacking the openness necessary to any genuine collaborative working relationship. Inuit knowledge and their approaches to problem-solving can appear to the biomedical community as lacking in precision and foundation. Inuit and bio-medical researchers share in the experience of cultural resistance, each resisting the influence of the other's system of knowledge, each skeptical about the validity and value of the other system of knowledge. The two groups share a skepticism concerning unfamiliar ways of knowing. These factors contribute to the difficulties in the development of a cross-cultural dialogue on contaminants, making the achievement of this goal a complex and continuous challenge.

A young Inuk archeologist from Nunavik, who sadly died in 1981, had much to say on this subject. He was considered a spokesperson on behalf of Nunavik Inuit in their dealings with southern scientists and many refer to his ideas today. In an unpublished manuscript Daniel Weetaluktuk (1980) [...] had the following observations to share:

> What it boils down to is "defensive research" and "positive research." Defensive research is when southern needs and methods are resisting the Inuit desires and needs. This becomes positive research when Inuit are given a fair consideration in developing their own research and when there is an understanding of the Inuit need. A new method of research design aimed at encouraging, including and supporting Inuit chances to get into the scientific community without totally giving up their own ways and ideas must come about. This of course does not mean deterioration of the research quality, as southern parties are often worried

about. It would give the northern perception of southern people a much wider scope and fuller understanding, at least for those who have enough of a broad mind to grasp it.

NOTES

1. The report by Usher et al. (1995) has certainly proved a valuable contribution to understanding the issue of contaminations within Aboriginal communities in Canada, and aided us significantly in developing our methodological framework. See also O'Neil et al. (1997), and Scott (1997). In addition, much of the work of the 5-year Northern Contaminants Program; Phase II, begun in 1998, has focused on communicating research results to northern communities. As partners, the Federal and Territorial governments and northern Aboriginal [organizations] have designed a program where the emphasis has shifted from assessing levels and confirming sources, to human health research, developing effective community dialogue, increasing community participation, and working towards international agreements to control the release of contaminants (Indian and Northern Affairs Canada, 1999). It is very interesting to note how many of the issues raised in our research have shown themselves to be common across northern Canada.
2. The Raglan Agreement did set in place an environmental monitoring program and trained local monitors.
3. In her analysis of Yup'ik Eskimo knowledge on geese, Fienup-Riordan has also stressed "...this fundamental conflict between the non-Native view of geese as manageable wildlife and the Yup'ik view of geese as persons possessing awareness and acting intentionally ..." (1999:15). See also Nadasdy (1999:7–8).

REFERENCES

AGRAWAL, ARUN. 1995. Indigenous and Scientific Knowledge: Some Critical Comments. *Indigenous Knowledge and Development Monitor.* Vol. 3(3):3–5.
BIRD-DAVID, NURIT. 1992. Beyond the Hunting and Gathering Mode of Subsistence: Culture-Sensitive Observations on the Nayaka and Other Modern Hunter-Gatherers. *Man* 27:19–44.
———. 1990. The Giving Environment: Another Perspective on the Economic System of Gatherer-Hunters. *Current Anthropology* 31:189–96.
BROOKE, LORRAINE. 1993. *The Participation of Indigenous Peoples and the Application of their Environmental and Ecological Knowledge in the Arctic Environmental Protection Strategy*, Inuit Circumpolar Conference, Ottawa.
CRUIKSHANK, JULIE. 1998. *The Social Life of Stories: Narrative and Knowledge in the Yukon Territory.* University of British Columbia Press, Vancouver.
FIENUP-RIORDAN, ANN. 1999. Yaqulget Quaillun Pilartat (What the Birds Do): Yup'ik Eskimo Understanding of Geese and Those Who Study Them. *Arctic* 52(1):1–22.
FREEMAN, MILTON. 1993. Traditional Land Users as a Legitimate Source of Environmental Expertise. In: *Traditional Ecological Knowledg., Wisdom for Sustainable Development*, edited by Nancy M. Williams and Graham Baines, pp. 153–161. Centre for Resource and Environmental Studies, Australian National University, Canberra.
GRONDIN, JACQUES, JEAN-FRANÇOIS PROULX, SUZANNE BRUNEAU and ERIC DEWAILLY. 1994. Santé publique et environment au Nunavik. *Études/Inuit/Studies* 18(1–2):225–251.
INDIAN AND NORTHERN AFFAIRS CANADA. 1999. Summary of the Northern Contaminants Program: Projects for 1999–2000, Ottawa.
INGLIS, JULIAN (ed.). 1993. *Traditional Ecological Knowledge: Concepts and Cases*. International Program on Traditional Ecological Knowledge and International Development Research Center, Ottawa.
INGOLD, TIM. 1996. Hunting and Gathering as Ways of Perceiving the Environment. In: *Redefining Nature. Ecology, Cultural and Domestication*, edited by Roy Ellen and Katsuyoshi Fukui, pp. 117–156. Berg, Oxford.
MILTON, KAY (ed.). 1993. *Environmentalism: The View from Anthropology*. Routledge, London and New York.
MYERS, FRED R. 1988. Critical Trends in the Study of Hunter-Gatherers. *Annual Review of Anthropology* 17:261–82.
NADASDY, PAUL. 1999. The Politics of TEK: Power and the "Integration" of Knowledge. *Arctic Anthropology* 36(1–2):1–18.

O'NEIL, JOHN, BRENDA ELIAS, and ANNALEE YASSI. 1997. Poisoned Food: Cultural Resistance to the Contaminant Discourse in Nunavik. *Arctic Anthropology* 34(1):29–40.

SCOTT, RICHARD. 1997. *Becoming a Mercury Dealer: Moral Implications and the Construction of Objective Knowledge for the James Bay Cree*.:AGREE, Discussion Papers Series (3). McGill University.

SILITOE, PAUL. 1998. The Development of Indigenous Knowledge. A New Applied Anthropology. *Current Anthropology* 39(2):223–235.

SIMON, MARY. 1994. *Indigenous Knowledge, Sustainable Development and Sustainable Utilization: the Need to Move from Rhetoric to Practice*. Paper presented at the Arctic Environmental Protection Strategy Seminar on Integration of Indigenous Peoples Knowledge, Reykjavik.

THERRIEN, MICHELE. 1987a. *Le corps inuit*. Société linguistique et anthropologique de France, Presses Universitaires de Bordeaux.

———. 1987b. La parole partagée, l'homme et l'animal arctiques. *Cahiers de littérature orale* 22:105–130.

USHER, PETER. 2000. Traditional Ecological Knowledge in Environmental Assessment and Management. *Arctic* 53(2):183–193.

USHER, PETER, MAUREEN BAIKIE, MARIANNE DEMMER, DOUGLAS NAKASHIMA, MARC G. STEVENSON and MARK STILES. 1995. *Communicating about Contaminants in Country Food: The Experience in Aboriginal Communities*. Inuit Tapirisat of Canada, Ottawa.

WEETALUKTUK, DANIEL. 1980. *Inuit and Science: Understanding the Problem*. MS. reproduced with the permission of the author's family in Brooke (1993).

WENZEL, GEORGE. 1999. Traditional Ecological Knowledge and Inuit: Reflections on TEK Research and Ethics. *Arctic* 52(2):113–124.

CHAPTER 4

Forestry

(a) First Nations Economic Development:
    The Meadow Lake Tribal Council[†]

Robert B. Anderson and Robert M. Bone

INTRODUCTION

The people of the First Nations in Canada are expanding their economic development activities. Through the creation of business ventures competing at the regional, national and international scales, they are struggling to find a place in the new global economy that will allow them to achieve their broader objectives, which include: (i) greater control of activities on their traditional lands, (ii) self-determination, and (iii) an end to dependence through economic self-sufficiency. Two key elements of their strategy are: (i) capacity building through education, institution building and the acquisition of land and resources, and (ii) the formation of business alliances between First Nations and non-First Nation companies. At the same time, and at least in part in response to the success of these two elements of First Nations' strategy, a growing number of corporations are adopting business alliances with Aboriginal people as a part of their strategy for long-term corporate survival.[1] The Meadow Lake Tribal Council's (MLTC) activities provide an excellent case study of this First Nations' approach to economic development in action.

[†] First appeared in *Journal of Aboriginal Economic Development* 1(1) (1999): 13–34. Reproduced with permission of CANDO.

FIRST NATIONS ECONOMIC DEVELOPMENT

The First Nations of Canada are understandably unhappy with their current socioeconomic circumstances. In the words of George Erasmus, past National Chief of the Assembly of First Nations (AFN) and Co-Chair of the Royal Commission on Aboriginal Peoples: "Our people have been relegated to the lowest rung on the ladder of Canadian society; suffer the worst conditions of life, the lowest incomes, the poorest education, and health; and can envision only the most depressing futures for our children" (Erasmus 1989, 1). According to the Federation of Saskatchewan Indian Nations (FSIN), "only one of every three First Nations citizens in Saskatchewan is employed and over 60% of the province's First Nations people are classified as living in poverty — roughly four times the average found in non-Aboriginal communities" (Peters 1996, 8).

Erasmus says that the people of the First Nations in Canada believe that this situation can be turned around. According to Erasmus, this turn around will require a return to the principles of the treaties between the First Nations and Europeans.

> All across North America today First Nations share a common perception of what was then agreed: we would allow Europeans to stay among us and use a certain amount of our land, while in our own lands we would continue to exercise our own laws and maintain our own institutions and systems of government. We all believe that that vision is still very possible today, that as First Nations we should have our own governments with jurisdiction over our own lands and people. (Erasmus 1989, 1 & 2)

The people of the First Nations do not expect that exercising political jurisdiction over their traditional lands will automatically result in an improvement in their socioeconomic circumstances. Instead, they acknowledge that economic development is required to break away from financial dependence and lay the ground-work for self-government. Confirming this, Chapter 5 Volume 2 of the report of the Royal Commission on Aboriginal People (entitled Economic Development) begins with the sentence: "Self-government without a significant economic base would be an exercise in illusion and futility" (RCAP 1997 Volume 2, Chapter 5, 1). In a similar vein, Ovide Mercredi, current Grand Chief of the Assembly of First Nations (AFN), states that, "If we gain [political] power for the community but we don't get the economy, we have power that cannot exercise itself" (Mercredi 1994, 7). He goes on to say that "without an economic base the culture is either dying or dead. So what we have to do is restore an economic base ... everything else will fall in place in terms of self-esteem, in terms of community spirit and in terms of improving the standard of living in our community" (Mercredi 1994, 7).

The approach to economic development that has emerged among the First Nations as a result of these circumstances, objectives and beliefs is briefly described in the following section.

First Nations' Approach to Economic Development

Overall, individual First Nations exhibit a predominately collective approach to economic development that is closely tied to each First Nation's traditional lands, its identity as a Nation and its desire to be self-governing. The First Nations development approach is intended to serve three purposes: the improvement of socioeconomic circumstances, the attainment of economic self-sufficiency in support of self-government, and the preservation and strengthening of traditional culture, values and languages.[2] This view is confirmed by the Report of the Royal Commission of Aboriginal Peoples, which says that, for Aboriginal people, economic development is about:

> much more than individuals striving to maximize incomes and prestige, as many economists and sociologists are inclined to describe it. It is about maintaining and developing culture and identity; supporting self-governing institutions; and sustaining traditional ways of making a living. It is about giving people choice in their lives and maintaining appropriate forms of relationship with their own and with other societies (RCAP 1997 Volume 2, Chapter 5, 5).

It is this strong collective concern with a 'national' focus and the emphasis on culture, values and languages that distinguish the First Nations' approach to economic development from the approach of other Canadian communities of a similar size and in similar locations.

The First Nations believe that they can achieve their development objectives through participation in the global capitalist economy. They expect profitable businesses competing successfully in this economy to: (i) provide them with greater control over economic activities on their lands, (ii) create employment, and (iii) generate the wealth necessary to support self-government and improve socioeconomic conditions. Importantly, in spite of their national status, individual First Nations exhibit many characteristics associated with the local/regional scale (population, size and location of land base, etc.), as opposed to those commonly expected at the national scale. Acknowledging this, First Nations realize that to succeed in the global economic environment, they must form business alliances with other people and groups (First Nation and non-First Nation). Finally, the First Nations recognize that for their economic development approach to be successful they must build capacity through: (i) education, training and institution-building, and (ii) the realization of treaty and Aboriginal rights to land, resources and self-government.

This First Nations' economic development approach is an excellent example of what Sayre Shatz (1987) calls the 'assertively pragmatic approach' to participation in the global capitalist economy. He suggests that this approach is becoming the strategy of choice among developing people around the world as they reject both the 'acceptance' and 'rejection' approaches born of the modernization/neo-liberal and dependence perspectives, respectively.[3] The essence of the pragmatic approach of the First Nations is captured in the following statement from the Tahltan people of British Columbia.

> We wish to make it very clear that the Tahltan People and the Tahltan Tribal Council are not inherently opposed to any specific type of business or resource development within our country. However, we do feel strongly that any development within our tribal territory must adhere to some basic principles.
>
> Before a resource development project can commence within Tahltan territory, it will be necessary for the developer and the Tahltan Tribal Council to enter into a project participation agreement that encompasses the following elements and basic principles:
>
> 1. assurance that the development will not pose a threat of irreparable environmental damage;
> 2. assurance that the development will not jeopardize, prejudice or otherwise compromise the outstanding Tahltan Aboriginal rights claim;
> 3. assurance that the project will provide more positive than negative social impacts on the Tahltan people;

4. provision for the widest possible opportunity for education and direct employment-related training for Tahltan people in connection with the project;
5. provision of the widest possible employment opportunities for the Tahltan people with respect to all phases of the development;
6. provision for substantial equity participation by Tahltans in the total project;
7. provision for the widest possible development of Tahltan business opportunities over which the developer may have control or influence;
8. provision for the developer to assist the Tahltans to accomplish the objectives stated above by providing financial and managerial assistance and advice where deemed necessary. (Notzke 1994, 215)

THE ECONOMIC DEVELOPMENT ACTIVITIES OF THE FIRST NATIONS OF THE MEADOW LAKE TRIBAL COUNCIL

The economic development activities of the nine First Nations of the Meadow Lake Tribal Council provide an excellent example of the First Nations' approach to development 'in action'. This case study that follows explores these activities, paying particular attention to the role of mutually beneficial alliances (MBAs) among First Nations and between First Nation and non-First Nation partners. In exploring the role of MBAs, the following factors are considered:

1. The location of First Nations, the nature of resources owned or controlled by the First Nations and the importance of these resources to the success of the joint venture.
2. The significance of a particular project for the overall objectives of the non-First Nations business.
3. The approach of the non-First Nation business to long-run organizational survival and social responsibility.
4. The community development goals and business development strategies and structures of First Nations.
5. The degree to which the expected and actual outcomes of a MBA (and the methods used to attain those outcomes) are consistent with community goals and strategies and are considered acceptable by the community.

The case study begins with a description of the study area — its geographic location, its communities, and its people and their demographic and socioeconomic characteristics. Next, attention shifts to the MLTC and its efforts to improve the socioeconomic circumstances of the people of its member First Nations. Finally, considerable attention is devoted to the MLTC's economic development activities in the forestry sector and the preparation of the Tribal Council's 20-year development plan.

Study Area

The study area is defined by the boundaries of the Meadow Lake Tribal Council (see Figure 1). The First Nations of the MLTC are located in the Churchill River Basin.[4] The southern part of the MLTC territory is drained by the Beaver River and its tributaries (in particular, the Waterhen and Meadow Rivers), into Lac Ile-a-La-Crosse. The northern section is drained by a number of rivers into La

FIGURE 1. The Meadow Lake Tribal Council District

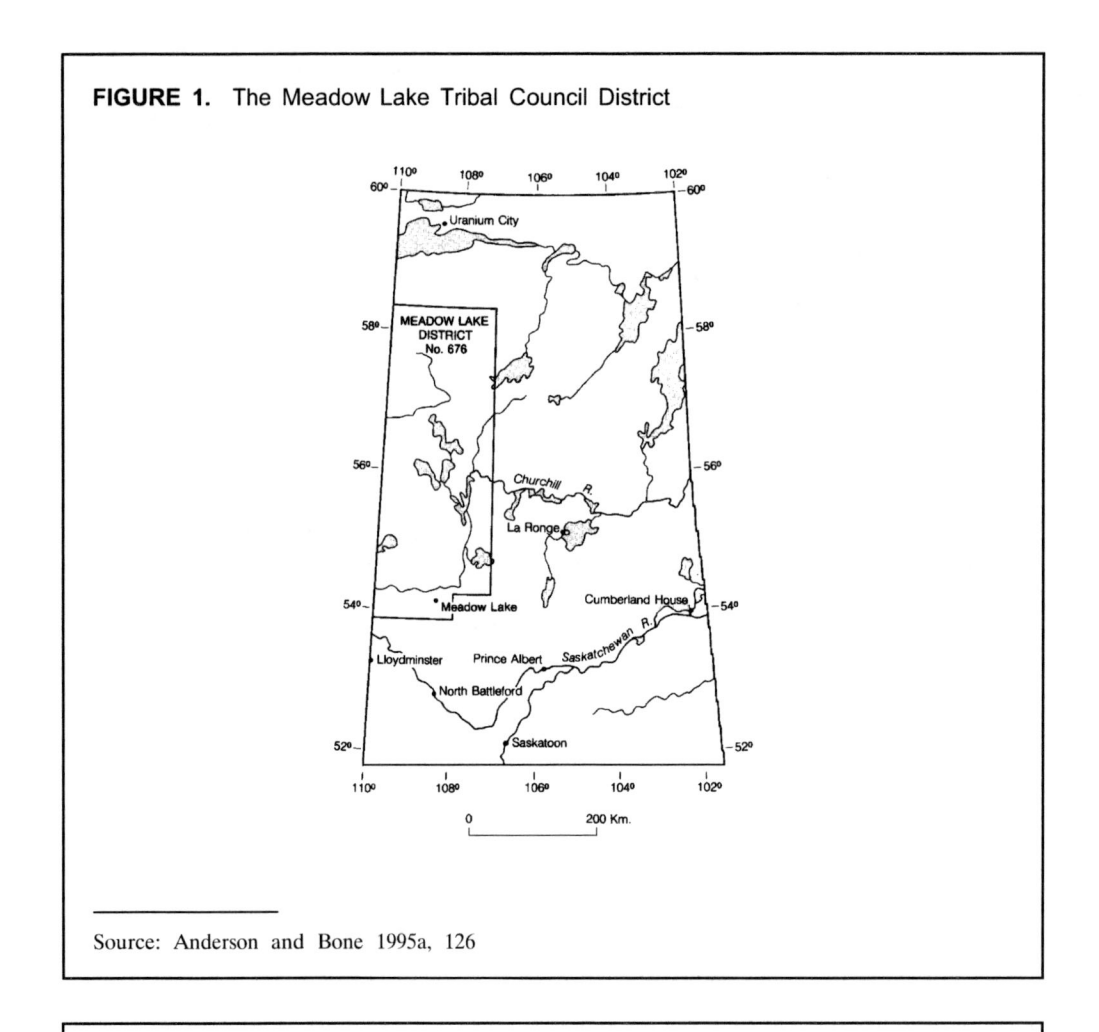

Source: Anderson and Bone 1995a, 126

TABLE 1. MLTC First Nations

Cree First Nations	Dene First Nations
Canoe Lake	Birch Narrows
Flying Dust	Buffalo River
Island Lake	Clearwater River
Makwa Sahgaiehcan	English River
Waterhen Lake	

Loche, Turnor, Peter Pond and Churchill Lakes, which in turn drain into Lac Ile-a-La-Crosse and the Churchill River proper.

There are nine First Nations in MLTC, four Dene and five Cree (see Table 1). At the end of 1993, according to the MLTC, the total population of these First Nations was about eight thousand, "with 3,907 living on their own reserve, 466 liv-

TABLE 2. Non-First Nation Communities

South Urban (Town, Villages and Hamlets)	Rural Municipalities
Meadow Lake	Meadow Lake #588
Gregg Lake	Loon Lake #561
Makwa	Beaver River # 622
Loon Lake	
Goodsoil	
Pierceland	

North — Villages and Hamlets

Green Lake	Patuanak
Cole Bay	Buffalo Narrows
Jans Bay	St. Georges Hill
Beauval	Michel Village
Pinehouse	La Loche
Ile a La Crosse	Turnor Lake

ing on another reserve, and 3275 living off reserve" (MLTC 1995b, iii). According to the 1986 census, the reported on-reserve population of the nine was 4,972, up from 4,334 in the 1981 census.

Within the geographic boundaries of the MLTC there are a number of non-First Nation communities and three rural municipalities (see Table 2). According to the 1986 census, this non-First Nation population totalled 16,637 (9,923 in the South and 6,714 in the north). Most of the non-First Nation population in the north are Metis. The demographic and socioeconomic conditions of the people living in the MLTC region are described in greater detail in the next section.

The Demographic and Socioeconomic Conditions

Data about the socioeconomic conditions of the people living within the study area at the start of the study period were drawn from the 1986 Census. The communities within census divisions of the study area have been divided into four categories. The first category is 'southern urban', and the second is 'southern rural municipalities'. The third category is 'northern villages and hamlets'. The fourth category is 'First Nations', consisting of two sub-categories: (i) 'southern First Nations' and (ii) 'northern First Nations'. Values for various socioeconomic variables for each census division within each category were combined and, when necessary, a weighted average calculated (e.g., household income) to arrive at the value for each variable for each of the community categories. The values for each variable for each category were then converted to proportions to permit comparisons among the categories of communities.

Two demographic characteristics are particularly worthy of note (Table 3). First, the data indicate that the people of the rural municipalities and of the town,

TABLE 3. Population in 1981 and 1986

	Non-Aboriginal			Aboriginal			Study Area	Province
	Rural Municipalities	Town, Villages & Hamlets — South	Total Non-Aboriginal	Villages & Hamlets — North	First Nations	Total Aboriginal		
Population:								
Population — 1986	4,676	5,247	9,923	6,714	4,972	11,686	21,609	1,009,613
Population — 1981	4,694	5,029	9,723	5,522	4,334	9,856	19,579	968,313
Percent growth	-0.38%	4.33%	0.06%	21.59%	14.72%	18.57%	10.37%	4.27%
% Aboriginal Origin	7.00%	22.00%	15.00%	93.00%	99.00%	96.00%	59.00%	

Source: 1986 Census of Canada

TABLE 4. Labour Force Participation and Unemployment Rates, 1986

	Rural Municipalities	Town, Villages & Hamlets — South	Non-Aboriginal	Villages & Hamlets — North	First Nations	Aboriginal	Study Area	Province
Population 15 years and older	3,405	3,825	7,230	4,145	2,810	6,955	14,185	751,090
In the labour force	2,495	2,270	4,765	2,140	1,070	3,210	7,975	501,750
Employed	2,300	2,055	4,355	1,440	720	2,160	6,515	461,515
Unemployed	195	220	415	695	350	1,045	1,460	40,225
Participation rate	73%	59%	66%	52%	38%	46%	56%	67%
Unemployment rate	8%	10%	9%	32%	33%	33%	18%	8%
Per cent of population 15 years and older employed	68%	53%	60%	35%	26%	31%	46%	61%

Source: 1986 Census of Canada

villages and hamlets in the southern part of the study area were predominately non-Aboriginal (93% and 78%, respectively) while the people of the First Nations and the northern villages and hamlets were overwhelmingly Aboriginal (99% and 96%, respectively). Members of the Meadow Lake First Nations (MLFNs) living on reserve accounted for almost 25% of the population of the study area. Aboriginal people (First Nations and Metis) made up 60% of the region's population.

The second item of note from Table 3 is the rate of population growth from 1981 to 1986. The rate for the region as a whole was 10.4%, well above the provincial average of 4.3%. Significantly, there was a great difference between rates of population growth of the First Nation and non-Aboriginal communities. From 1981 to 1986, the First Nation on reserve population increased by 14.7% (more than three times the provincial rate), while the non-Aboriginal population in the area grew by only 2.1% (half the provincial rate).

The difference in the growth rates between First Nation and non-Aboriginal groups was reflected in the age distributions of their populations (Figure 2). In 1986, 44% of the people of the region's First Nations were under 15 years old. In contrast, only 27% of the people of the non-Aboriginal groups were under 15. The figure for the province as a whole was 25%. A similar difference existed at the older end of the age distribution. For both the province and the non-Aboriginal people of the study area, 20% of the population was older than 54. In contrast, only 7% of the population of the First Nations was over that age. The youthfulness of the First Nations population and the high growth rate have obvious and significant implications. The most important of these are the looming growth in the potential labour force and resulting increase in the already very high levels of unemployment.

In 1986, there was a clear difference in participation and employment patterns between the people of the MLFNs and the non-Aboriginal people of the region (Table 4). Only 38% of the people of the First Nations participated in the labour force whereas 66% of non-Aboriginal people and 52% of the residents of northern villages and hamlets did. The difference in employment patterns between First Nation and non-Aboriginal people in the study area extended beyond participation rates to the unemployment rates. According to the 1986 census, 33% of the people in the First Nation workforce were unemployed (32% — northern villages and hamlets). This compared very unfavourably with the 9% unemployment rate for non-Aboriginal people.

Taken together, the participation rate and unemployment rate for each group tell a graphic tale. In 1986, 60% of all the potential non-Aboriginal labour force (age ≥ 15) of the study area were employed. The percentages for the two Aboriginal categories were markedly lower — 35% for northern villages and hamlets, and only 26% for First Nations. This highly unsatisfactory situation has the potential to deteriorate sharply given the high rate of population growth and the related large and growing pool of First Nation young people who will be entering the labour force in next few years. The implications are obvious. There is a desperate need to create employment opportunities for the people of the MLFNs, as there is for the other Aboriginal people of the region.

The sources of 1986 household income (Figure 3) are consistent with the low participation and high unemployment rates described and the resulting reliance by

FIGURE 2. Age Distribution, 1986

Source: 1986 Census of Canada

FIGURE 3. Source of Income, 1986

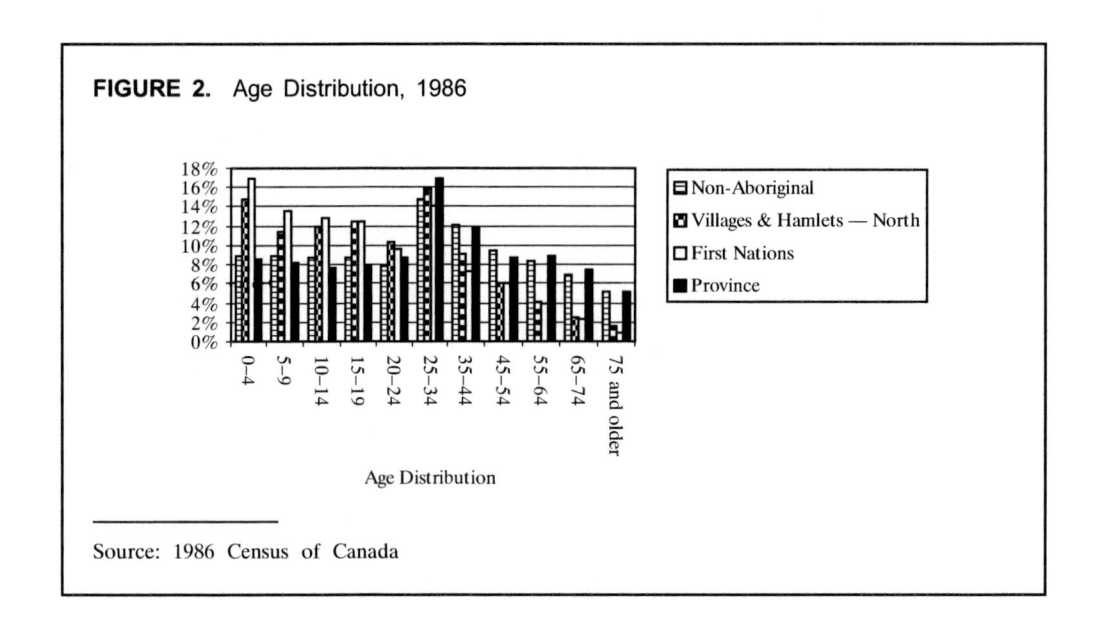

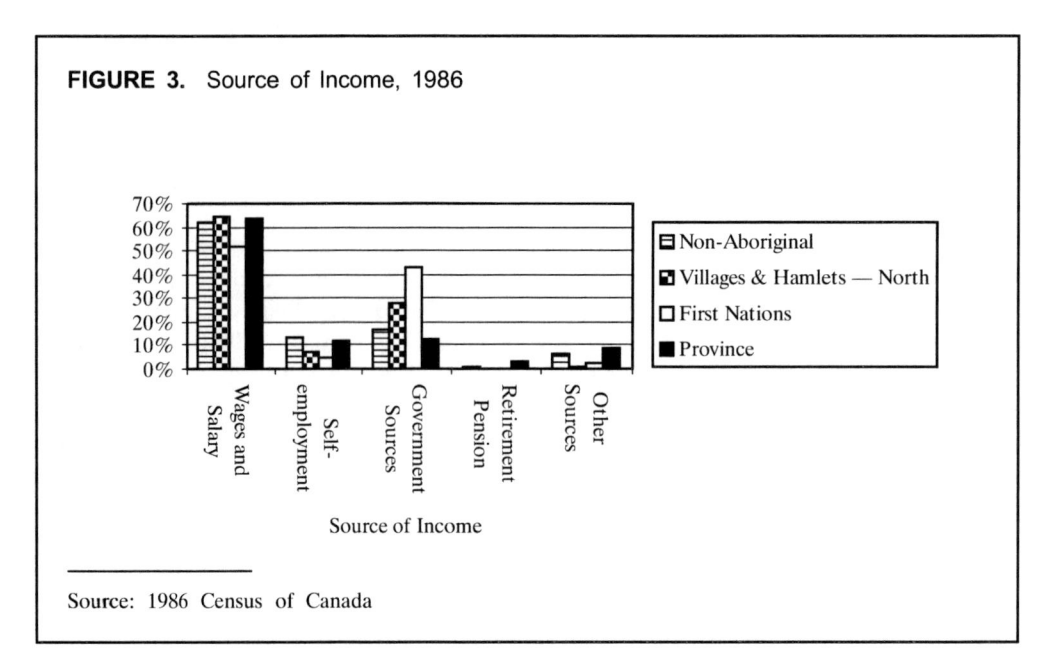

Source: 1986 Census of Canada

many First Nation people on various forms of government transfer payments (social assistance, unemployment insurance, training allowances and the like). Just over 50% of the people of the First Nations reported employment as their primary source of income. In contrast, the figures reported by non-Aboriginal people, the people of the northern villages and hamlets, and the province as a whole were

FIGURE 4. Household Income, 1986

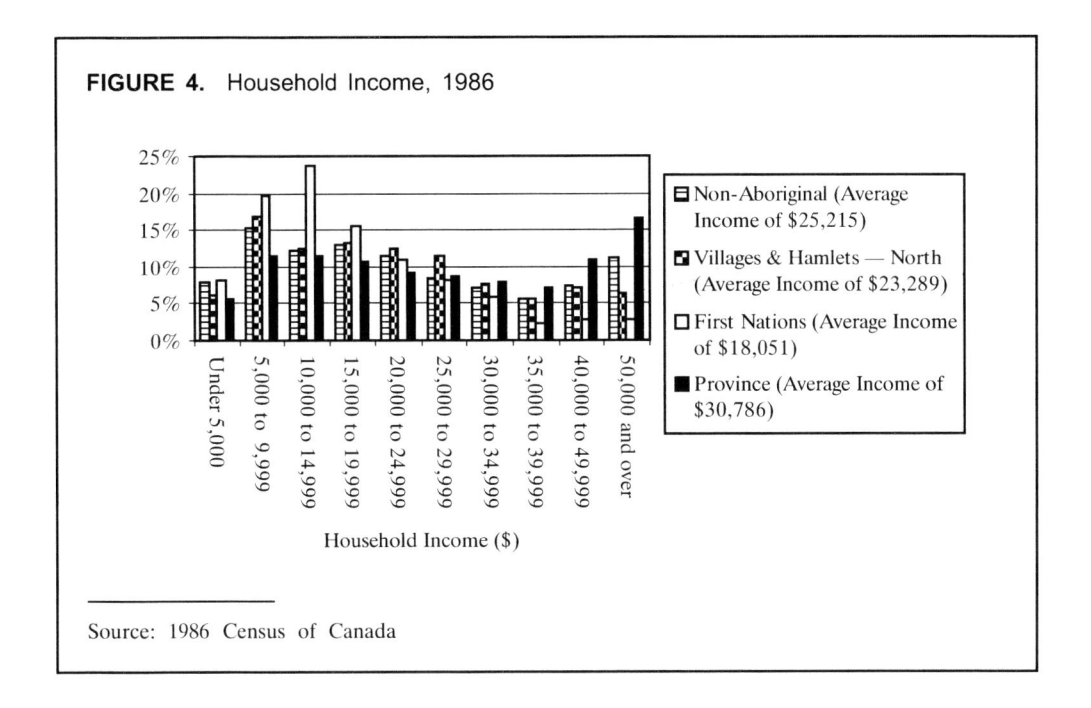

[Bar chart showing household income distribution across four groups: Non-Aboriginal (Average Income of $25,215), Villages & Hamlets — North (Average Income of $23,289), First Nations (Average Income of $18,051), and Province (Average Income of $30,786). X-axis: Household Income ($) with categories Under 5,000; 5,000 to 9,999; 10,000 to 14,999; 15,000 to 19,999; 20,000 to 24,999; 25,000 to 29,999; 30,000 to 34,999; 35,000 to 39,999; 40,000 to 49,999; 50,000 and over. Y-axis: 0% to 25%.]

Source: 1986 Census of Canada

62%, 64% and 64%, respectively. As one would expect, this pattern reversed with respect to income from government sources as a primary source, with First Nations reporting the highest level at 43%, non-Aboriginal people at 17%, northern villages and hamlets at 28%, and the province at 13%. There were also clear but smaller differences among the groups in the other income source categories. For example, self-employment income stood at 5% for First Nations, in contrast to rates at more than twice that level for non-Aboriginal people and the province as a whole (13% and 12%, respectively).

Household income (Figure 4) and household size (Figure 5) offer additional insight into the relative economic circumstances of the groups in the study area. In 1986, fully 52% of the people of the First Nations lived in households with an annual income less than $15,000. In contrast, only 36% of the residents of northern villages, 35% of non-Aboriginals in the study area, and 29% for the province as a whole reported household incomes below $15,000. A similar pattern of inequality existed at the upper end of household income. Only 8% of the people of the First Nations reported household income in excess of $35,000, compared to 10% for northern villages and hamlets, 25% for non-Aboriginal communities and 35% for the province.

While the lack of employment opportunities in First Nations and northern communities was the major cause of the low participation and high unemployment rates of both Aboriginal groups, relative education levels were a contributing factor (see Figure 6). Fifty-three percent of First Nations members 15 and older had an education less than grade nine. The figure for the residents of the northern villages and hamlets was 47%. These levels compare unfavourably with the levels of the

FIGURE 5. Household Size, 1986

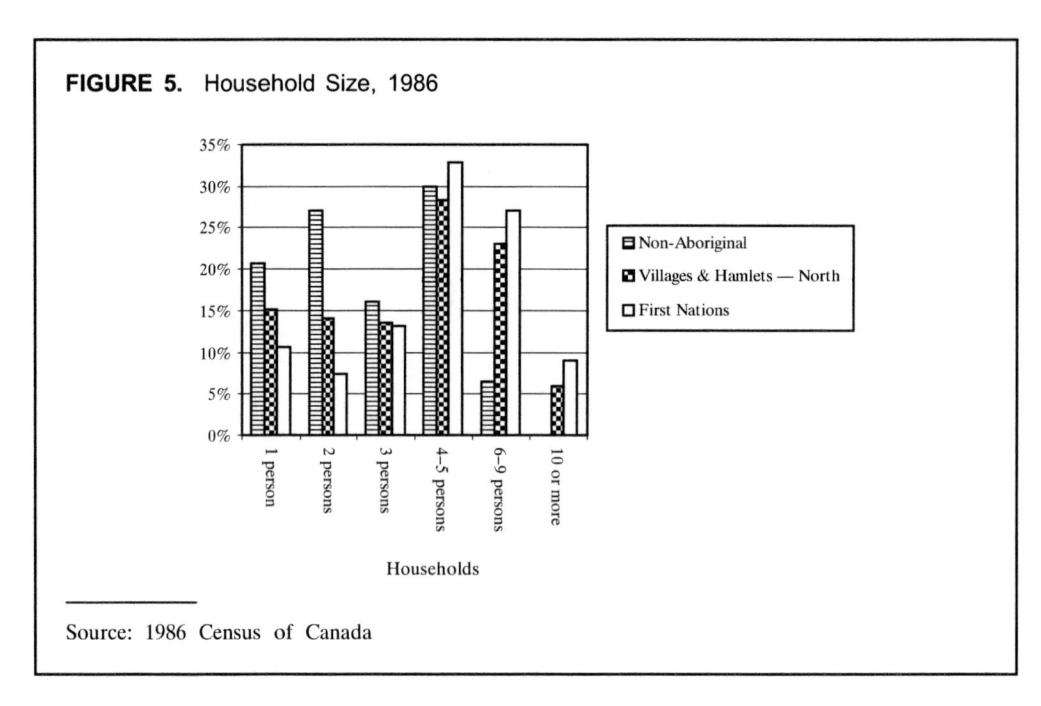

Source: 1986 Census of Canada

FIGURE 6. Education Level, 1986

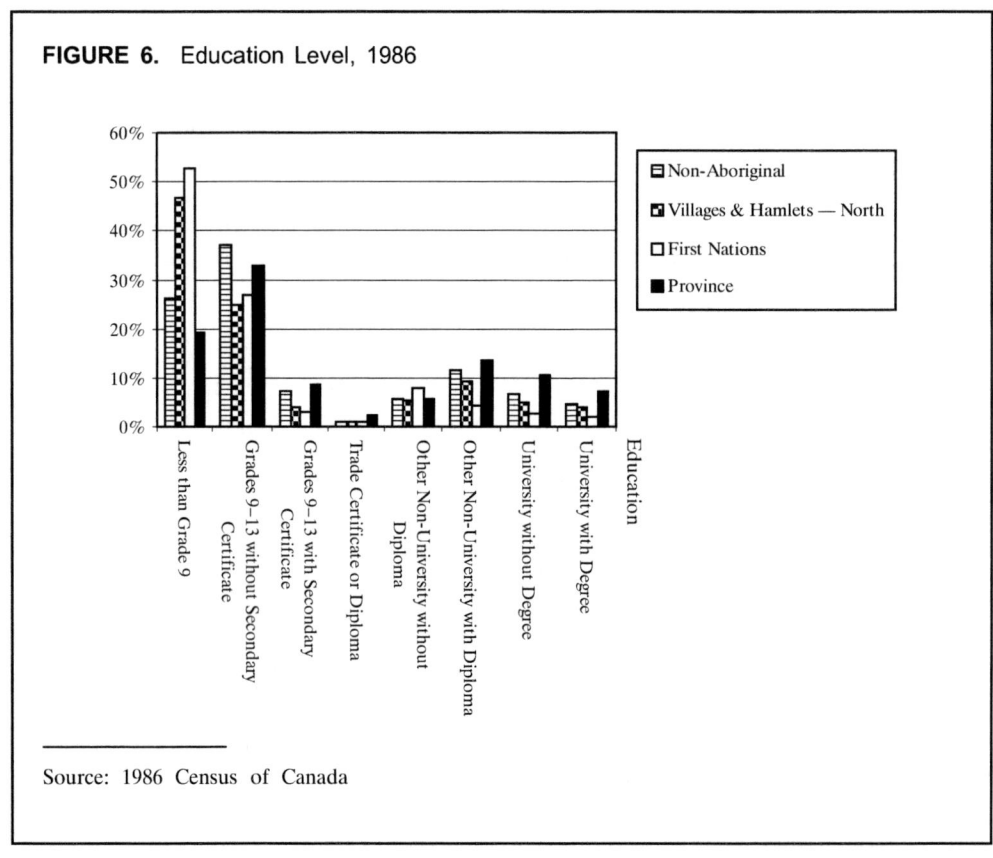

Source: 1986 Census of Canada

non-Aboriginal people of the study area and the people of the province as a whole, which were 26% and 19%, respectively. Equally significant is the disparity between the proportion of people with an education level of grade 12 or higher — First Nations 21%, northern villages and hamlets 28%, non-Aboriginals in the study area 37% and the province 48%.

As is evident from the preceding figures, the socioeconomic circumstances of the people of the First Nations of the MLTC were far from satisfactory in 1986. Further, it is obvious, given the age distribution and population growth rate, that these circumstances were bound to worsen unless significant economic development occurred creating employment opportunities in large numbers. It is also evident that education levels would have had to improve if the people of the First Nations (existing participants and new entrants to the labour force) were to have the capacity to take advantage of any employment and business opportunities created. The efforts of the Meadow Lake Tribal Council, described in the following sections, were directed to these ends.

The Meadow Lake Tribal Council

According to its 1992–93 annual report, "the Meadow Lake Tribal Council is the political, service and corporate organization of the nine Meadow Lake First Nations" (MLTC 1993, 4). In 1986, the Tribal Council was formed as the result of the reorganization and expansion of the Meadow Lake District Chiefs Joint Venture that had been formed in 1981. The responsibilities of the Tribal Council and the authority necessary to carry out those responsibilities are delegated to it by the people of its member First Nations.

> The Tribal Council is governed by the nine First Nation Chiefs who are elected by the eligible membership of each First Nation. The Chiefs set policy and direction for the Tribal Council, bringing forward the issues and concerns from their First Nation members (MLTC 1995b, iii).

Since its inception in 1986, economic development for its member Nations has been one of the primary objectives of the Tribal Council. According to its 1990–91 Annual Report, the MLTC had been operating a business development program for the previous six years. The objective of the program was to "stimulate economic growth for First Nations and to encourage an entrepreneurial spirit among our people" (MLTC 1991, 26). According to that same annual report, 106 business projects were undertaken during the six years of the program ending in 1991. Of this total, 65% were reported to be still operating at the time of the preparation of the 1990–91 report. Norsask Forest Products Ltd. and MLTC Logging and Reforestation Ltd. were among the projects begun during this period.

Results 1986–1991

A comparison of 1991 census values with the 1986 values for selected socioeconomic measures provides an indication of the impact of the MLTC's development efforts during this five year period (Tables 5 and 6). This is not to say that the MLTC's business development activities were the sole cause for any improvement in employment and income. However, it is reasonable to assume that the 66 or so

TABLE 5. Unemployment and Participation, 1986 to 1991

	1986			1991			Change		
	First Nation	North Villages Hamlets	Non-Aboriginal	First Nation	North Villages Hamlets	Non-Aboriginal	First Nation	North Villages Hamlets	Non-Aboriginal
Population 15 years and older	2,810	4,145	7,230	3,080	4,230	7,250	270	85	50
In the labour force	1,070	2,140	4,765	1,205	2,015	5,185	135	-125	420
Employed	720	1,440	4,355	855	1,415	4,790	135	-25	435
Unemployed	350	695	415	350	575	400	0	-120	-15
Participation rate	38%	52%	66%	39.1%	48%	72%	1.1%	-3%	6%
Unemployment rate	33%	32%	9%	29%	29%	8%	-4%	-3%	-1%
Per cent of population 15 years and older employed	26%	35%	60%	27.8%	33%	66%	1.8%	-2%	6%

Source: 1986 and 1991 Censuses of Canada

businesses started by the MLTC between 1986 and 1991 created jobs and income that otherwise would not have been created.

There was a modest improvement in the employment, participation and unemployment rates of the people of the MLFNs between 1986 and 1991 (Table 5). The potential labour force grew by 270 over the five years while the workforce grew by half that number (135). This resulted in a 1.1 percentage point increase in the 1991 participation rate over that of 1986. Coincidentally, the number of people employed in 1991 also increased by 135 over 1986 levels. It seems likely that much of this increase was a result of the 66 or so new businesses created as a result of the MLTC's business development program. As a result of this increase in employment, between 1986 and 1991 the unemployment rate fell by 4 percentage points, and the proportion of the potential labour force employed increased by almost 2 percentage points over the period. It is noteworthy that in all aspects of employment reported in Table 5, the improvement in performance of the First Nations over the period exceeded that of the other Aboriginal group — northern villages and hamlets. However, in spite of this improvement, in 1991 the performance of the First Nations fell far short of that for the non-Aboriginal category.

There was also a change in household income distribution over the same period (Table 6). The number of First Nation households reporting an income of less than $30,000 in 1991 declined by 9% from the number in 1986, while the number with income above that level increased by a similar amount. During the same period, there was a 6% decline in the number of northern village and hamlet households reporting income less than $30,000 and a decline of 20% in the number of non-Aboriginal households. As with the employment data, the performance of First Nations households was superior to that of households in the northern villages and hamlets category but fell short of that of non-Aboriginal households.

In an effort to gain further insight into the change in income amount and composition, Table 7 compares average employment income and numbers between 1986 and 1991. The average full time employment income in 1991 differed by slightly less than $3,000 between the First Nations and non-Aboriginal categories (up from a difference of $1,200 in 1986). This difference was substantially lower than the $10,000 difference in 1991 household income between the two categories. This can be attributed to at least two factors: (i) the lower participation rate and resulting greater reliance on non-employment (generally lower) income sources by First Nations households, and (ii) the larger number of two income households among non-Aboriginal people.

The differences between the changes in employment numbers between 1986 and 1991 for the two Aboriginal categories are striking in two ways. First, the average full-time employment income among First Nations increased by 16%, almost double the 9% rate of increase among the people of the northern villages and hamlets. Second, full-time employment among the people of the First Nations increased by 23% while full-time employment among those from the northern villages and hamlets fell by 20% over the five years. This raises the question: why was the relative employment and income performance of the First Nations over the period 1986–1991 superior to that of northern villages and hamlets?

Between 1986 and 1991, the two Aboriginal groups differed in their approach to economic development. The MLFNs through the MLTC had a much more

TABLE 6. Household Income, 1986 to 1991

	1986			1991			% Change		
	First Nation (%)	North Villages Hamlets	Non-Aboriginal (%)	First Nation (%)	North Villages Hamlets	Non-Aboriginal (%)	First Nation	North Villages Hamlets	Non-Aboriginal
less than $10,000	28	23	23	24	17	6	-4	-6	-17
10,000–14,999	24	13	12	20	18	13	-4	5	1
15,000–19,999	16	13	13	16	13	10	0	0	-3
20,000–29,999	19	24	19	18	19	20	-1	-5	1
30,000–39,999	8	14	13	11	13	16	3	-1	3
40,000–49,999	3	7	8	6	8	13	3	1	5
50,000 and over	3	6	11	6	13	21	3	7	10

Source: 1986 and 1991 Censuses of Canada

TABLE 7. Change in Average Employment Income and Numbers, 1986–1991

	1986			1991			% Change		
	First Nation	Northern Villages Hamlets	Non-Aboriginal	First Nation	Northern Villages Hamlets	Non-Aboriginal	First Nation	Northern Villages Hamlets	Non-Aboriginal
Males — full year, full time	160	560	1,410	160	380	1,570	0	-32	11
Average employment income	$20,185	$24,624	$21,111	$23,296	$27,441	$27,932	15	11	32
Males — part year or part time	475	1,000	1,355	480	680	1,305	1	-32	-4
Average employment income	$6,320	$8,628	$11,043	$7,436	$9,275	$17,847	18	7	62
Females — full year, full time	100	295	525	160	305	900	60	3	71
Average employment income	$17,160	$18,781	$18,337	$20,656	$21,920	$19,406	20	17	6
Females — part year or part time	215	570	1200	245	425	1,270	14	-25	6
Average employment income	$6,267	$7,296	$7,270	$6,317	$8,220	$9,511	1	13	31
All — full year, full time	260	855	1,935	320	685	2,470	23	-20	28
Average employment income	$19,022	$22,608	$20,358	$21,976	$24,983	$24,826	16	11	22
All — part year or part time	690	1,570	2,555	725	1,105	2,575	5	-30	1
Average employment income	$6,304	$8,144	$9,271	$7,316	$8,869	$13,735	16	9	48

Source: 1986 and 1991 Censuses of Canada

collective and planned approach to the process, and that approach seems to have borne fruit. The leaders among the people of the northern hamlets and villages appear to have agreed with this conclusion. In the early 1990s, through an association of northern municipalities, they began to develop a common economic development strategy. In March of 1990, the 14 members of the Northwest Saskatchewan Municipalities Association formed Keewatin Dahze Developers Inc. "as their formal body to address economic development initiatives" (K. D. Developers 1993, viii). One of the projects undertaken by K. D. Developers was the creation of Northwest Logging and Reforestation. The objective was to create "a commercially viable woodland contracting operation" (K. D. Developers 1993, viii) providing the people of the member communities with an "opportunity to participate at an unprecedented level in the forest industry in Saskatchewan's northwest" (K. D. Developers 1993, x).

Building on the modest success achieved between 1986 and 1991 and in response to the larger unmet challenge of parity with non-Aboriginal people, the economic development mission, objectives and strategies of the MLTC have evolved and matured. By 1993, a clear vision for the future was in place and, the role to be played by economic and business development in the realization of that vision identified. According to its 1993–94 annual report:

> [The] MLTC's vision is to support its member individuals, families and communities in achieving health and a state of well-being. This state of well-being means achieving health and a balance in the spiritual, physical, mental and emotional aspects of life. The MLFNs wish to achieve increased self-reliance in all aspects of life as part of this approach and philosophy (MLTC 1994, 4).

In pursuit of this self-reliance:

> the Chiefs of the MLTC have jointly mandated a twenty year plan of economic development strategy aimed at achieving parity with the province in terms of employment rate and income level. In short, we are striving to create and maintain 3,240 good-paying jobs in the next 20 years (MLTC 1994, 20).

The basic strategy adopted to achieve this objective was to "develop and establish 'anchor' businesses around which smaller enterprises can flourish bringing long lasting economic activities and benefits" (MLTC 1994, 20). The MLTC had decided, as far back as 1988 with the purchase of 50% of the Meadow Lake Sawmill, that forestry offered a particularly good opportunity for the creation of such an anchor business.

Since 1991, the MLFNs have greatly expanded their forestry activities. They have also prepared a comprehensive 20-year development plan indicating how they expect to achieve their objective of 'socioeconomic parity' with the non-Aboriginal people of the province. The forestry activities of the MLTC and the 20-year plan and the process used to develop it are interrelated. The experience in forestry development and, in particular, the crisis that occurred in 1992/93 (described in the following section) pointed out the need and provided the impetus for the preparation of the 20-year plan. The MLTC's forestry activities and the development of its 20-year plan are the subjects of the next two sections of this chapter.

MLTC Forestry Developments

The MLTC's involvement in the forestry industry began in 1988 when the Chiefs of MLTC First Nations negotiated the purchase of 50% of the Meadow Lake Sawmill from the provincial government. At the time of this sale, the mill had been losing money for a number of years and was virtually shut down (Price Waterhouse 1994b). The remaining 50% interest in the saw mill was purchased by Techfor Services Ltd., a company wholly owned by the mill employees. The company was renamed Norsask Forest Products Ltd. (Norsask). Norsask's most valuable asset was (and still is) the Forest Management License Agreement (FMLA) it holds from the Province of Saskatchewan. This FMLA gives Norsask the harvesting rights (for both softwood and hardwood) and reforestation responsibilities for 3.3 million hectares of Crown Land in the Meadow Lake District (see Figure 7). While its mill only used softwood, the FMLA required that Norsask develop the capacity to use the hardwood (poplar) in the licence area within four years or the rights to the poplar stock would be lost (Star Phoenix 1993, A2). In addition, the FMLA required that residents of the licence area be given priority for employment and that a co-management process be established involving "complete consultation between the sawmill [Norsask] and northern communities over issues including harvesting, hauling, reforestation, road construction, as well as trapping and fishing" (Price Waterhouse 1994a, 5).

Norsask's rights and responsibilities under the FMLA were central to the MLTC's forestry-based development strategy. They set the stage for the formation of a network of business alliances and joint ventures among the First Nations of the MLTC, between them (through Norsask) and a non-First Nation corporate partner — Millar Western Ltd., and among the non-First Nation residents of the communities in the FMLA area. The key alliance in the network was the joint venture between Norsask Forest Products Ltd. and Millar Western Ltd.

At the time that MLTC was searching for a way to exploit the business and employment opportunities presented by the FMLA, Millar Western Ltd., a privately-owned Alberta corporation, wanted to build a 'zero pollution' pulp mill that used poplar instead of softwood as a raw material. The company saw this mill as the cornerstone of its strategic plan for the future. Throughout its market area (particularly in the United States), increasingly rigorous environmental regulations were rendering older paper plants using the chlorine-based bleaching process economically obsolete. For Millar Western, the cost of refitting an old plant to meet new standards compared to the cost of a new chlorine-free plant favoured the latter. However, forest resources suitable to supply a new plant were not available in Alberta. All had already been licensed to other pulp producers. Therefore, the company's owners had to look elsewhere for an assured supply of poplar. They found such a supply just over the provincial border in Saskatchewan in the hands of the MLTC. The potential for a mutually beneficial alliance in these circumstances was obvious to the leaders of both parties.

Millar Western required access to an assured supply of poplar at a globally competitive price. They had the expertise and capital necessary to develop the pulp mill. Consistent with subcontracting/strategic alliances as elements of flexible production, the company was quite prepared to subcontract the harvesting and reforestation activities to outside organizations while it focused on its core activity, the

FIGURE 7. Norsask's FMLA

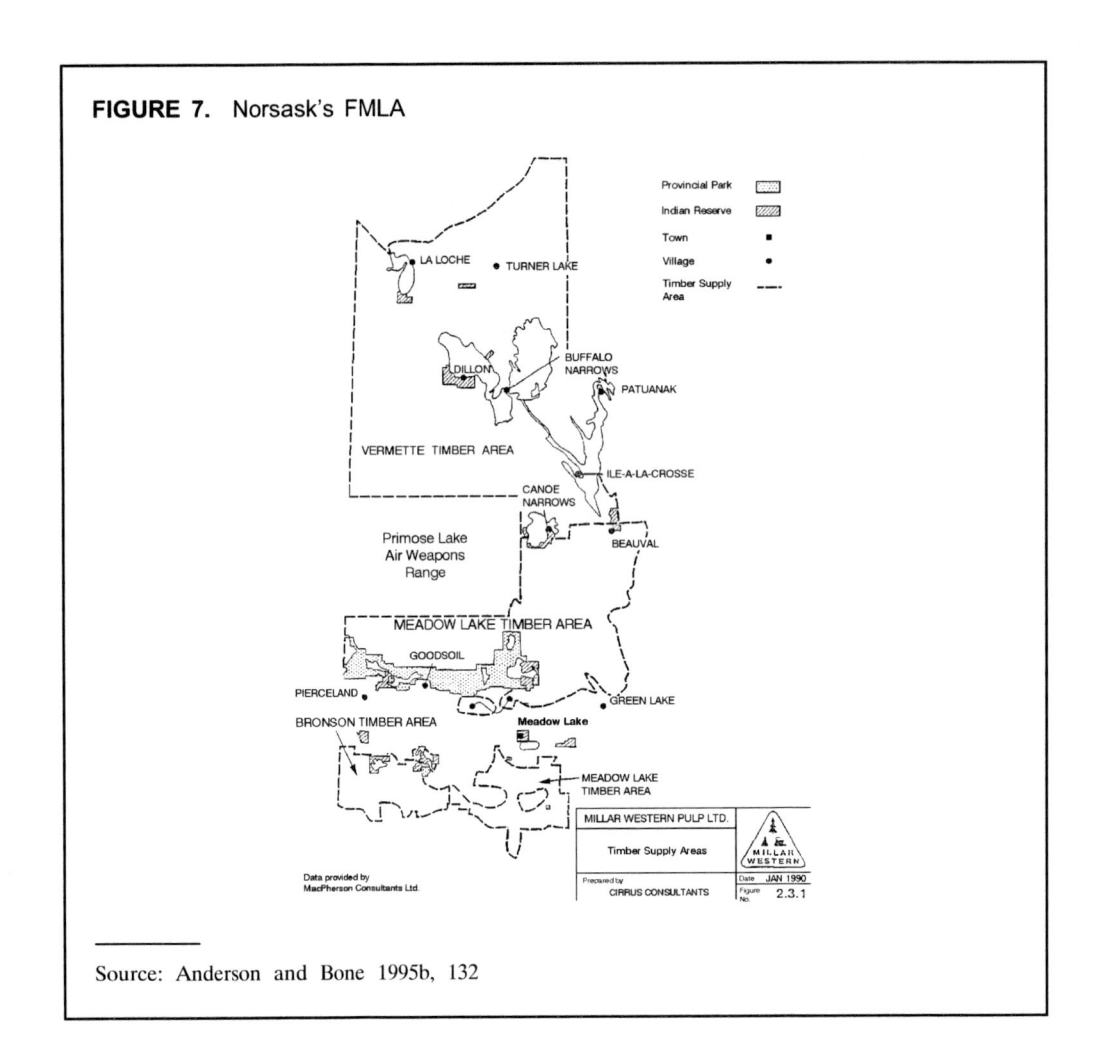

Source: Anderson and Bone 1995b, 132

production and sale of pulp. Millar Western was willing to accept conditions that served the needs and objectives of the MLTC, so long as it received competitively priced feed stock. On their part, the MLTC controlled access to a suitable (to Millar Western) supply of poplar. They needed a use for this hardwood to satisfy the requirements of the FMLA and to realize its inherent employment and business development potential. However, they lacked the capital and expertise to develop this capacity. The leaders of the two groups negotiated an agreement with terms and conditions intended to satisfy the objectives of both. Figure 8 illustrates the structure that emerged from these negotiations.

Millar Western, along with the Crown Investment Corporation of the Province of Saskatchewan, established a company called Millar Western Pulp Ltd. to build and operate the pulp mill at Meadow Lake. Millar Western owns a controlling interest (51%) in Millar Western Pulp. Millar Western Pulp acquired a 20% interest in Norsask Forest Products (10% from each of the two original owners, Techfor

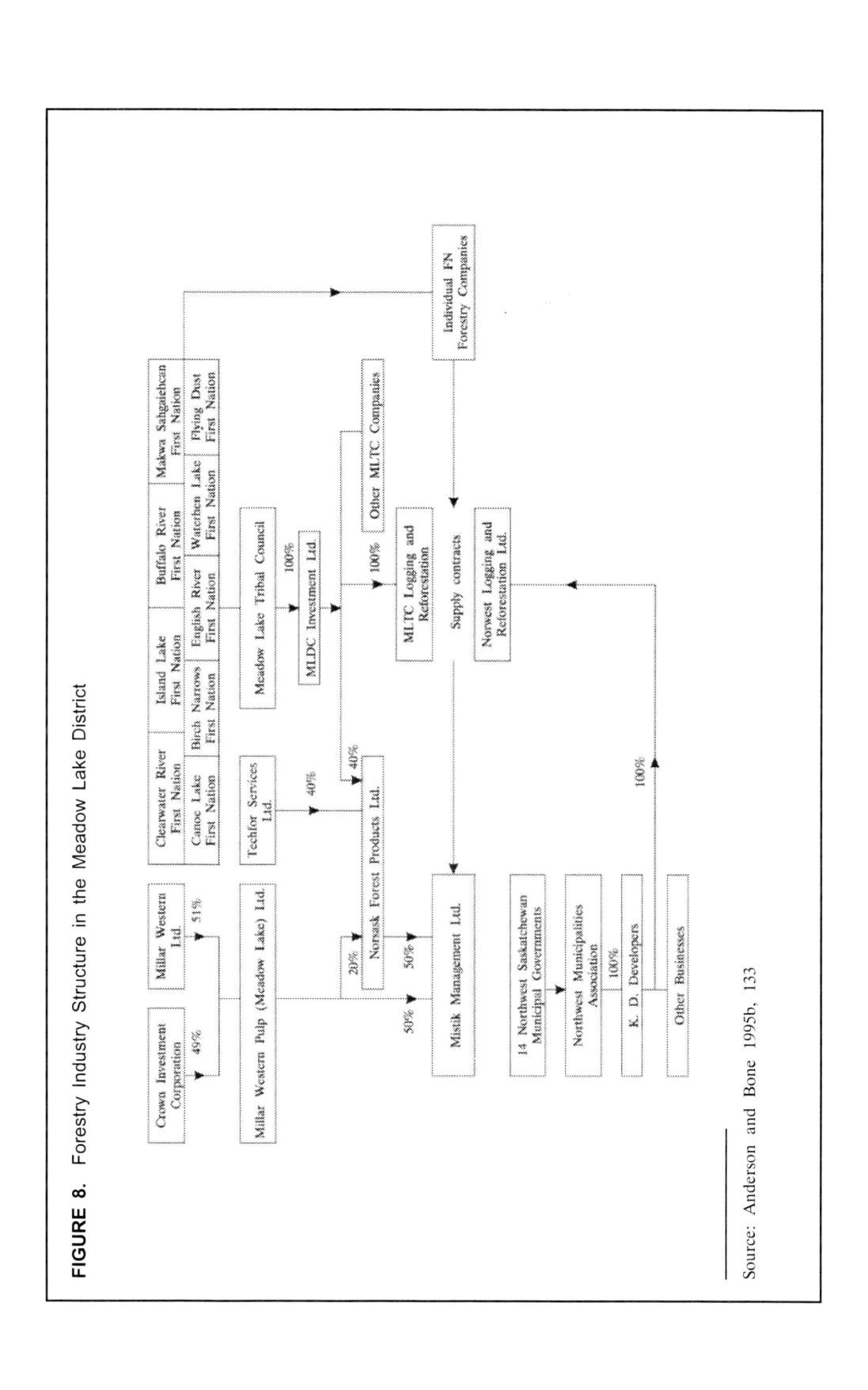

FIGURE 8. Forestry Industry Structure in the Meadow Lake District

Source: Anderson and Bone 1995b, 133

and Norsask). This left the MLTC with a 40% interest in Norsask. Norsask Forest Products and Millar Western Pulp then established a joint venture company called Mistik Management Ltd. (Mistik means wood in Cree), with each parent holding a 50% interest. Mistik was assigned the responsibility to manage all forest operations under the terms and conditions of the FMLA. Mistik was not expected to do the actual work but, rather, to contract to have it done through operating companies. It was through these operating companies that most benefits (employment, business creation and profits) were expected to reach the people of the MLFNs.

In June 1990, the MLTC created its own operating company, MLTC Logging and Reforestation Ltd., to realize the benefits from forest operations for the citizens of its member First Nations. Under contract with Mistik, the company provides logs to both mills and undertakes other activities, such as road building, log hauling and reforestation. Some individual First Nations, as well as some First Nations individuals, also created operating companies. As well, non-First Nations people (mostly Metis and non-status Indians) living in the 14 northern villages and hamlets of the area also saw participation in forestry as a key to employment and economic development. Through an association of their municipal governments, they created an operating company called Norwest Logging and Reforestation Ltd.

> The company [Norwest Logging and Reforestation Ltd.] signed a contract with Mistik "for the provision of logging services starting in 1991/92 (year 1). The contract includes a schedule of annual wood volume allocations which increase from an initial volume of 50,000 m^3 to a maximum of 250,000 m^3 in year four and thereafter (K. D. Developers 1993, x).

Individuals from these communities also formed companies to participate in forestry activities.

To build the capacity of their people to participate in forestry industry as employees and business persons, the Tribal Council developed and offered two post secondary education programs. One was a diploma program in Integrated Resource Management developed offered in partnership with the Saskatchewan Indian Institute of Technology. The other was a three year university Diploma in Business Administration program in partnership with the Saskatchewan Indian Federated College.

By 1994, the Millar Western Pulp Ltd. mill was fully operational. The total harvest in the FMLA area that year was 1,000,000 m^3, up from the 300,000 m^3 harvested in 1990. Of the 48 contractors involved in meeting this demand in 1994, MLTC Logging and Reforestation was by far the largest. The company harvested 300,000 m^3 in 1994, up from the 50,000 m^3 harvested in 1992. This increase in logging and related activities had a significant impact on First Nation employment. MLTC Logging and Reforestation's output in 1994 provided employment for 140 people and placed the company among the top 10% of logging companies in Canada. Norsask Forest Products by the same date was ranked in the top 6% of Canadian saw mills, employing 103 people (Price Waterhouse, 1994a). In addition to these 243 direct jobs, according to same Price Waterhouse report, these First Nations companies created an additional 730 indirect jobs in the region (most of them since 1993). Employment is expected to remain stable at this level in the future.

Almost all of the 243 direct jobs created by Norsask Forest Products and MLTC Logging and Reforestation are held by members of the First Nations of the

MLTC, as are at least 50%, or 365 (a very conservative estimate), of the indirect jobs. The sawmill and supporting forest operations were virtually shut down in 1986, so these are "new jobs" created since the 1986 census. Given that only 730 members of the MLTC First Nations reported themselves employed in the 1986 census, the creation of these 600 or more good-paying, permanent jobs for people from the MLFN is a considerable accomplishment. At the same time, these results emphasize the scale of the challenge facing the people of the MLFNs as they struggle to achieve their 20-year objective of employment parity with the province — 600 jobs created, 2,640 permanent, good-paying jobs to go.

In addition to the jobs created and other spin-off benefits to the region, "during the last three years, the companies [Norsask and MLTC Logging and Reforestation], in aggregate, have paid $10.7 million in corporate taxes and withheld income taxes on wages" (Price Waterhouse 1994b, 8). The MLTC is justifiably proud of these taxes paid, arguing that they represent an excellent return to the Government of Canada on the $1.3 million in grants that the MLTC received to purchase and modernize Norsask. According to the leaders of the MLTC, these results provide evidence of the benefits to all people in Canada — First Nation and non-First Nation — of a policy of support for First Nations business development by the federal and provincial governments. This is an example of the outcome that is anticipated by The Royal Commission on Aboriginal People. The thrust of the commission's conclusions is that additional money — up to $2 billion more per year for the next 20 years — invested now in capacity building and economic development by Aboriginal people will be returned manifold in the future through (i) reduced government expenditures to deal with the otherwise exploding unemployment and other social costs, and (ii) increased tax revenues.

"Bottom-up" Reaction

While the people of the MLFNs were satisfied with the increase in employment and business activity generated through forestry, many were unhappy with certain operating decisions and actions taken by Mistik Management and MLTC Logging and Reforestation. This is particularly true for certain members of the Canoe Lake First Nation. Much of the logging was occurring on Canoe Lake traditional lands. Concerns centred on two issues. The first was the effect that clear cut logging with mechanical harvesters was having on their land and their ability to continue traditional practices. Second, and beyond the specific issue of clear cutting, the people of Canoe Lake felt that they lacked an effective method of influencing the operating decisions taken by Mistik Management and MLTC Logging and Reforestation, and that they were not receiving a fair share of the benefits from forestry activities in their area.

By May 13, 1992, dissatisfaction had become so intense that protesters, led by Elders from the Canoe Lake First Nation, established a blockade on Highway 903, 65 kilometres north of Meadow Lake that halted the operations of MLTC Logging and Reforestation in the area (Windspeaker 1992a, 12). The protesters formed an organization called 'The Protectors of Mother Earth'. Allan Morin, head of the organization, in describing its members' demands, said that:

> The Elders object to clear cutting and the use of mechanical harvesters. They want control over their own resources, compensation for their people, [and] financial and technical compensation for local people who want to start their own forestry related businesses (Windspeaker 1993b, r2).

It is important to note that the protesters from Canoe Lake were not demanding an end to forestry activities in their area. Rather, they sought to change the terms of their participation in the activity in order to increase the benefits to, and decrease the negative impacts on, their community and its people.

Speaking about the blockade on behalf of the MLTC, Vice-Chief Oniell Gladdue "blamed the dispute on a lack of communication. He said many of the concerns will be resolved once the communities get more information" (Windspeaker 1992b, 12). He was speaking about the plans being put in place to incorporate community involvement in the decision-making process. A process had just begun (to be completed by the end of the winter of 1992/93) to establish the community co-management boards required under the terms of the FMLA. Barry Peel, president of Mistik Management, said that these co-management boards would give the people of the communities in the region "a say on issues such as where and how logging should take place, including the size and shape of cuts, location of roads, harvesting methods, reforestation and operating plans" (Star Phoenix 1992b, E1). Peel credited the Canoe Lake blockade with speeding up the introduction of the co-management process.

In late August 1992, while these co-management boards were being introduced, a meeting was held between the Protectors of Mother Earth, Norsask Forest Products, Mistik Management, and the MLTC. At this meeting, all agreed that the proposed co-management boards and process would adequately address the issues underlying the blockade. The Protectors of Mother Earth asked that Norsask and Mistik stop logging in the disputed area until their co-management board and processes were established. The companies refused, citing their responsibilities to the mills and to their employees. The meeting ended without resolving the conflict (Star Phoenix 1992a, A4).

The blockade continued through the winter of 1992/93. Much of this period was marked by legal actions. On December 9, 1992, the provincial government asked the courts to evict the protesters, claiming that they were illegally occupying crown land. The protesters countered by filing a complaint with the Saskatchewan Human Rights Commission. According to Cecilia Iron, a spokesperson for the protesters, the complaint alleged that:

> The government [Saskatchewan] has repeatedly ignored our rights under the treaties, under the Natural Resources Transfer Agreement, and under the constitution. An agreement [the FMLA] between the government and a local forestry company [Norsask Forest Products] completely ignores Aboriginal rights and licenses to trap, hunt fish for food and harvest wild rice (Windspeaker 1992c, 2).

The Court of Queens Bench ruled on May 12, 1993 that the protesters must remove their blockade within fifteen days unless an appeal was launched. The Elders refused to leave the blockade site, and negotiations with Norsask Forest Products resumed (Windspeaker 1993a, 3). On October 12, 1993, a tentative agreement was reached between the protesters and Norsask Forest Products. According to Ray Cariou, chairman of Norsask, the people of the Canoe Lake First Nation, through a co-management board, would have the right to participate in decisions about such things as logging methods, the location of roads, and the accommodation of traplines and other traditional land uses (Windspeaker 1993c, r2).

It is significant that Millar Western remained one step removed from this dispute throughout. The company was neither the target of the protesters nor a negotiator of the settlement. It was able to concentrate on its core activities and leave local and regional issues in the hands of its partners, an outcome entirely consistent with flexible competition and the company's expectations when it entered into its alliance with the MLTC. Instead, the dispute and its resolution involved the people of the region through their own bodies — corporate (Norsask Forest Products), governmental (MLTC), and 'grass-roots' (the Protectors of Mother Earth). The issues were identified and a solution found by the people directly affected — a local/regional mode of social regulation in action.[5]

Will this bottom-up mode of social regulation be successful over the long run? To be judged so, it must simultaneously satisfy the requirements of the mills as they compete in the global economy; the development objectives of the MLTC; the needs and objectives (traditional and modern) of the people of the First Nations and non-First Nations communities of the region; and the requirements of the FMLA. While there are bound to be disagreements among the involved parties in the future and occasional economic difficulties, based on the successful resolution of the Canoe Lake conflict and recent financial and job creation results, prospects for continuing success of this bottom-up mode of social regulation seem promising.

The unfolding of events in forestry, particularly the Canoe Lake protest and its resolution, had significant impacts beyond that sector. The experience resulted in a maturing and refining of the MLTC's economic development mission, objectives, strategies and processes — particularly those relating to consultation, participation and traditional values. This impact is evident in the content of the MLTC's 20-year development plan, "From Vision to Reality", and the process used to prepare it between April 1993 and October 1995.

MLTC 20-Year Plan

In 1993, the MLTC began the process that culminated in the completion of the MLTC 20-year development plan, "From Vision to Reality" in October of 1995. Preparation of the plan over this period involved extensive consultation with Elders and members of the MLFNs. Key aspects of this consultative process included: a meeting the representatives from the nine MLFN in April 1993; a meeting of Elders in January 1994; a survey of the members of the MLFN during 1994; and, in April of 1995, a three-day economic development symposium for members of the MLFN.

According to the 20-year plan:

> The Meadow Lake First Nations' (MLFN) vision of the future is one of "healthy individuals, families and communities." This state of well being reflects balance and harmony in the spiritual, physical, emotional and mental aspects of life. Our vision includes self-sufficiency, self-reliance, and self-government. We will have control over our own lives and over decisions that impact our quality of life. We will have hope for the future and for the future of our children (MLTC 1995b, i).

This vision had its birth in April 1993, when members of the MLFN met for three days to discuss "all areas of community and family life and relationships with the environment and each other" (MLTC 1995b, I-6).

The next key step in the development of the 20-year plan occurred in January of 1994 when the Elders of the MLFN met to discuss traditional culture and values.

> The Elders were specifically asked about the important values that contributed to healthy individuals, families, and communities in the past. The event was critical to developing the values regarding future economic development planning within the MLTC District (MLTC 1995b, I-7).

Self-sufficiency and self-reliance, sharing, community decision-making, respect for the environment, and the preservation of traditional lifestyles and culture emerged as key values. The Elders particularly stressed that the key to attaining the vision of "healthy individuals, families and communities" was the replacement of the current destructive dependence on welfare with self-reliance. Typical of the Elders' views, one said:

> In the future, hunting, trapping, fishing and gathering will not provide the self-sufficiency that is required. Young people will not live the same as the Elders live. The people cannot go back to the old days. We cannot turn back. We need to look ahead and know where to go next (MLTC 1995b, II-15).

In looking to the future, the Elders concluded that employment opportunities created through economic development were necessary to "allow people to regain self-reliance and self-sufficiency, and increase individual and community pride" (MLTC 1995b, II-3).

As the next step in preparing the plan, over 500 people from the nine First Nations were interviewed. Among other things, respondents were asked to rate the relative importance of maintaining a number of traditional values as part of the economic development process. Those surveyed overwhelmingly rated the maintenance of the following as very important: obtaining advice on economic development from Elders; getting the approval of MLFN peoples for economic development projects; protecting the environment; sharing the benefits of economic development; developing on reserve or community employment; and achieving First Nation self-sufficiency and self-reliance.

Those surveyed were also asked the question: "Can traditional lifestyles co-exist with modern enterprises or businesses?" Seventy-five percent of the respondents answered "yes" to this question. Typical comments from those answering "yes" included:

- The two types of lifestyle already do, and it's working.
- We have to work with Native and non-Native lifestyles.
- Strong family relationships are needed.
- Mixing the two types of lifestyles requires honesty, cooperation and communication.
- It's up to us to make it work (MLTC 1995b, 9).

The concerns expressed by those who felt the two couldn't and/or shouldn't be mixed included:

- Modern lifestyles overpower traditional lifestyles.
- Our culture is being lost.

- People can't live both ways.
- The two lifestyles conflict (MLTC 1995b, 9).

Respondents were also asked to identify the obstacles to achieving economic development goals, and the roles and responsibilities of individuals, families, First Nations, the Tribal Council, the federal and provincial government, and the private sector in overcoming these obstacles. Those surveyed identified the following as the primary barriers to development:

- accessible education/job training
- alcohol-free and drug free society
- equality and fairness in job distribution
- availability of permanent jobs
- community members working together supportively
- self-sufficiency and self-reliance versus welfare
- funding and financial programs for small business (MLTC 1995b, 15).

The key roles and responsibilities identified for individuals in overcoming these barriers included: having positive attitudes and motivation, striving for self-sufficiency, obtaining education and training, and starting small businesses. Those identified for the family included the ones for individuals, as well as: providing healthy family lifestyles, providing support (moral, emotional, financial), and preserving language, culture and traditions.

The roles and responsibilities of each First Nation in overcoming these barriers were felt to include:

1. providing effective and responsible leadership, with a particular focus on ensuring community-based long-term economic development intended to provide members with a good standard of living.
2. providing and encouraging education, training and wellness programs.
3. encouraging self-reliance through business planning and marketing assistance, offering workshops and training programs, providing information on funding and providing loans for small business.
4. direct involvement in economic development through business development initiatives as individual Nations and in partnerships with others.
5. protecting the environment.

Expectations relating to the role and responsibilities of the Tribal Council included those listed for individual First Nations. In addition, the Tribal Council was expected to undertake larger development initiatives, often in joint ventures with outside partners, and to provide support to the First Nations and their members as they pursue their own initiatives.

The federal and provincial governments' roles and responsibilities were felt to include: funding for education, assistance to start large businesses, providing grants and loans to businesses, providing marketing and other advice and support, and developing long-term economic development strategies. The expectations of the private sector included: providing financing (banks and credit unions), serving as mentors, providing business planning assistance, providing employment, and participating in joint ventures.

The initial meeting with representatives of the First Nations, the consultation with Elders, and the survey of community members resulted in the formation of a widely held vision and a general consensus as to the objective of economic development — "the achievement of employment and income parity with the Province of Saskatchewan" (MLTC 1995b, ix). Further, it was clearly established that this was to be done in a manner consistent with important traditional values, particularly those of self-reliance and self-sufficiency, protection of the environment, sharing of economic benefits, community decision-making and respect for the wisdom of the Elders.

In April of 1995, a three-day economic development symposium was held to provide members of the MLFN with information about progress on the plan to date and to receive additional input. Approximately 150 members of the nine MLFNs participated in workshops that identified current economic development activities, opportunities for future economic development, and barriers to economic development for the MLTC in general and, most important, from the perspective of each member First Nation.

Consistent with survey respondents' views as to responsibilities, those at the seminar endorsed the strategy that called for the MLTC to establish the larger anchor business and for individual First Nations and their members to create small and medium-sized businesses associated with these anchors. Participants reconfirmed the importance of the key traditional values, including consultation with Elders, local decision-making, sharing of economic benefits and care of the environment. They also stressed the importance of continued human and financial capacity building for the creation of viable businesses and the development of a workforce capable of taking advantage of the employment opportunities such businesses will create.

Following the economic development symposium, the final 20-year development plan was drafted. Building on the strategy of anchor businesses, the plan identifies four key sectors as the main pillars of the economic development strategy. They are tourism, mining, forestry and traditional activities, including hunting, fishing, trapping, and agriculture/gathering. The plan goes on to evaluate each of these sectors in detail (at the Tribal Council and First Nation levels), focusing on opportunities and the barriers to realizing them. The plan establishes short-, medium- and long-term business and job creation objectives for the four key sectors as well as for those sectors identified as secondary (retail/service, construction/trades, oil and gas, environmental, management, professional/scientific, and public administration).

"From Visions to Reality" forms the foundation for the business development plans of the MLFNs as they strive to realize their vision over the next twenty years. English River First Nation's purchase of Tron Power provides an example of a First Nation building on this foundation.

In January 1997, the English River First Nation announced the purchase of Tron Power, a construction and janitorial company servicing northern mines and businesses. The company is also involved in Cameco's gold mine in Kyrgyzstan. In addition to its northern international operations, Tron has industrial maintenance contracts in Saskatoon. This added to the company's appeal, in that the investment will also provide employment opportunities for English River citizens who choose to live in that city rather than 'on Reserve'.

According to English River's press release, the First Nation and Tron Power had been involved in successful joint ventures since 1995. Before that they were partners in an employment equity plan intended to increase Aboriginal employment at the mines in northern Saskatchewan. In summarizing these circumstances, Chief Archie Campbell said:

> Many English River citizens already work for Tron Power, and our joint venture has given First Nations people the opportunity to become supervisors, journeymen welders, electricians, carpenters and pipe fitters. The purchase of the company will include First Nations employment in skilled areas, including management (English River First Nation 1997, 3).

According to Frank Lai, Economic Development Director for English River, financing the purchase was made possible by the First Nation's treaty land entitlement settlement.[6] Frank also commented (as does the press release) on the fact that the recently announced federal government's "Procurement Strategy for Aboriginal Businesses" figured prominently in the decision to purchase the company. According to the press release:

> Tron will be an instrument for targeting other construction and janitorial projects under the "Set Aside Program" of the Federal Procurement Strategy announced last year by Minister Irwin (English River First Nation 1997, 4).

CONCLUDING COMMENTS

The forestry development activities of the Meadow Lake Tribal Council provide an excellent example of the role that can be played by business alliances in First Nations economic development. The forestry activities of the MLTC consist of a number of joint ventures and alliances. First, the MLTC itself is an alliance of nine First Nations. In fact, when formed in 1981 it was called the Meadow Lake District Chiefs Joint Venture. The foundation of the forestry activities and the holder of the critical asset (the FMLA) Norsask Forest Products was formed as a joint venture between the MLTC and Techfor. The impetus for growth in the forestry industry came from two interdependent alliances. One was between Millar Western and Crown Investments to build the pulp mill. The other was the joint venture between Norsask and Millar-Western to create Mistik Management to manage the forest resource under the terms of the FMLA. Finally, the benefits to the people of the region (particularly employment) have been delivered through arrangements (although not joint ventures) between Mistik Management and various operating companies, including MLTC Logging and Reforestation (a joint venture of the MLFN) and Norwest Logging and Reforestation (a joint venture of the 14 northern villages and hamlets). Results to date indicate that this system of alliances has been successful from the perspective of Millar Western and the MLTC and its people. What does this successful system of alliances say about the five factors identified at the beginning of Section 3?

Clearly, the FMLA, controlled by the MLTC, is the key to the entire web of alliances. It made it possible for the MLTC to attract willing partners and establish arrangements meeting their (MLTC) objectives (Factor 1). The establishment of a zero-polluting hardwood pulp plant was central to Millar Western's long-term strategy. To successfully implement this strategy, it was essential that the company acquire a source of poplar. The MLTC controlled one of a very few sufficiently large uncommitted supplies of this resource (Factor 2). Consistent with flexible competition, Millar Western was prepared to enter into a beneficial long-term alliance with a key supplier that met the needs of both (Factor 3). The development goals and strategies of the MLTC required that they establish large anchor businesses in key sectors — particularly forestry. Joint ventures were considered the best vehicle for establishing these ventures (Factor 4). The financial and employment outcomes of the forestry development process were consistent with expectations, and the project was successful by those criteria. The methods adopted to achieve this success were not considered acceptable by some (the Canoe Lake protest). However, within the web of alliances a means (co-management boards and, more generally, the 20-year plan process and content) was found to address the problem in a manner consistent with community goals and standards (Factor 5).

Beyond validating the five factors, the MLTC forestry activities (and other business activities) and the process and content of the 20-year plan are consistent with the characteristics of First Nations economic development described in Section 2. The approach has been national and collective, with many of the businesses owned by the Tribal Council or by individual First Nations. The activities take place on traditional lands. The purpose is to attain economic self-sufficiency in support of self-government and improve the socioeconomic conditions. The process adopted involves participation in the global economy through the creation of profitable businesses, often in partnership with outside companies. Business ownership has provided the Indian people greater control over the activities on their land. Culture and traditional values are incorporated into the structure (ownership by the First Nation(s), not private Indian citizens) and methods of operation (increasing sensitivity to traditional land-uses and growing use of consensus-based decision-making processes).

It also clear that the Tribal Council is learning from experience. In an evolutionary way, the process is becoming more consultative, more strongly centred on traditional practices, more nationally oriented (from the perspective of the First Nations), and more strongly focused on business development and successful competition in the global economy.

NOTES

1. See Anderson 1997 for an in-depth discussion of the evolving relationship between First Nations and non-First Nations business corporations.
2. These conclusions flow from research conducted and results reported previously. See Anderson and Bone 1995a&b, Anderson 1995 and Anderson 1997.
3. See Anderson and Bone 1995a and Anderson 1995 for a discussion of the 'contingency perspective on economic development' that is emerging among Aboriginal peoples in Canada and developing peoples around the world.
4. The far north of the MLTC District is drained by the Clearwater River, part of the Athabaska system; however, none of the reserves of the nine MLTC Nations are located that far north, nor are any currently economically viable timber blocks.
5. See Anderson and Bone 1995a and Anderson 1995 for a discussion of modes of social regulation in the context of a "contingency perspective on First Nations' economic development."
6. Treaty rights flow from agreements between the British Crown and, later, the Canadian government and various Aboriginal groups that were negotiated throughout the entire period of British colonization of what is now Canada. Commonly, individual First Nations either did not receive all the land they were entitled to under the terms of their particular treaty, or they later lost a portion of the land reserved for them. Across the county, various Aboriginal groups are laying

claim to the land they consider theirs by right of treaty. For example, 28 First Nations in the province of Saskatchewan (English River among them) recently signed an agreement giving them $527,000,000 in compensation for land that they should have received under treaty but did not. In addition, treaty making between the Government of Canada and Aboriginal people in areas not yet covered by treaty continues today. Modern treaties have already been negotiated in the Northwest Territories (e.g., the Inuvialuit and Nunavut Agreements) and in the province of British Columbia (e.g., the Nis'ga Agreement). To provide a sense of the size of these settlements, it is estimated the final cost of all the treaties under negotiation in the province of British Columbia will exceed $10,000,000,000.

REFERENCES

ANDERSON, ROBERT B. (1997). "First Nations Economic Development: The Role of Corporate Aboriginal Partnerships", *World Development*. 25(9): 1483–503
———. (1995). "The Business Economy of the First Nations in Saskatchewan: A Contingency Perspective", *The Canadian Journal of Native Studies* 15(2): 309–346.
ANDERSON, ROBERT B., and ROBERT M. BONE. (1995a). "First Nations Economic Development: A Contingency Perspective", *The Canadian Geographer* 39(2): 120–130.
———. (1995b). "Aboriginal People and Forestry in the Churchill River Basin: The Case of the Meadow Lake Tribal Council" in *The Proceedings of the Churchill River Conference*, pp. 128–37. Saskatoon: University of Saskatchewan.
CANDO. (1995a). "Community Economic Development Organizations", *Mawiomi Journal* 2(2): 10–14.
———. (1995b). "Indigenous International Trade", *Mawiomi Journal* 2(2): 15–18.
———. (1995c). "Partners for Progress". Winnipeg: CANDO.
———. (1995d). "Education: A Foundation for Economic and Community Development". Winnipeg: CANDO.
ENGLISH RIVER FIRST NATION. (1997). "Tron Power Purchase". English River: Press Release.
ERASMUS, GEORGE. (1989). "Twenty Years of Disappointed Hopes", in B. Richardson (ed.), *Drum Beat: Anger and Renewal in Indian Country*, pp. 1–15. Toronto: Summerhill Press.
FSIN. (1993). "Annual Report". Saskatoon: The Federation of Saskatchewan Indian Nations.
K. D. DEVELOPERS. (1993). "Executive Summary". Meadow Lake: Keewatin Dahze Developers.
LAFOND, L. (1985). "Self Government in Perspective". in Sinclair (ed.) *Native Self-Reliance Through Resource Development*, pp. .Vancouver: Hemlock Printers Ltd.
MERCREDI, OVIDE. (1994). "A Conversation With National Chief Ovide Mercredi", *Mawioni Journal* Winter(2): 4–9.
MLTC. (1995a). "Meadow Lake Tribal Council Annual Report, 1994–1995", Meadow Lake: Meadow Lake: Meadow Lake Tribal Council.
———. (1995b). "Meadow Lake First Nations 20 Year Plan: From Vision to Reality". Meadow Lake: Meadow Lake Tribal Council.
———. (1994). "Meadow Lake Tribal Council Annual Report, 1993–1994". Meadow Lake: Meadow Lake Tribal Council.
———. (1993). "Meadow Lake Tribal Council Annual Report, 1992–1993". Meadow Lake: Meadow Lake Tribal Council.
———. (1992). "Meadow Lake Tribal Council Annual Report, 1991–1992". Meadow Lake: Meadow Lake Tribal Council.
———. (1991). "Meadow Lake Tribal Council Annual Report, 1990–1991, 1989–1990". Meadow Lake: Meadow Lake Tribal Council.
NAFT. (1996). "The Promise of the Future: Achieving Economic Self-Sufficiency Through Access to Capital". Ottawa: National Aboriginal Financing Task Force.
NOTZKE, CLAUDIA. (1994). "Aboriginal Peoples and Natural Resources in Canada". North York: Captus Press.
PADC. (1993). "Prince Albert Development Corporation: Company Profile". Prince Albert Grand Council.
PETERS, CELESTE. (1996). "FSIN Deals a Winning Hand", *Aboriginal Times* 4(December): 6–9.
PRICE WATERHOUSE. (1994a). "MLTC Logging and Reforestation, Inc. and Norsask Forest Products, Inc.: Performance Evaluation Relative to Industry". Saskatoon: Price Waterhouse.
———. (1994b). "MLTC Logging and Reforestation, Inc. and Norsask Forest Products, An Evaluation of Various Financial Results". Saskatoon: Price Waterhouse.
RCAP. (1997). "Report of the Royal Commission on Aboriginal People", Canada: Royal Commission on Aboriginal People.

SHATZ, SAYRE. (1987a) "Socializing Adaptation: A Perspective on World Capitalism", in D.G. Becker and R. Sklar (eds.), *Postimperialism: International Capitalism and Development in the Late Twentieth Century*, pp. 161–177. Boulder Colorado: Lynne Rienner Publishers, Inc.
———. (1987b). "Assertive Pragmatism and the Multinational Enterprise", in D.G. Becker and R. Sklar (eds.) *Postimperialism: International Capitalism and Development in the Late Twentieth Century*, pp. 93–105. Boulder Colorado: Lynne Rienner Publishers, Inc.
Star Phoenix. (1995). "30,000 New Jobs Targeted by FSIN", *Star Phoenix* Jan 7: a3.
———. (1993). "Protectors of Mother Earth Plan to Continue Blockade", *Star Phoenix* May 17: a2.
———. (1992a). "Talks on Forestry Issue, Blockade Make Little Progress", *Star Phoenix* August 29: A4.
———. (1992b). "Natives to Co-manage Future Forests", *Star Phoenix* September 25: E1.
Windspeaker. (1993a). "Blockade to Celebrate Birthday", *Windspeaker* 11(3): 26.
———. (1993b). "Saskatchewan Protesters Defy Court-ordered Eviction", *Windspeaker* 11(6): 7.
———. (1993c). "Meadow Lake Protesters Reach Agreement with Norsask", *Windspeaker* 11(10): 7.
———. (1992a). "Protesters Want Logging Control", *Windspeaker* 10(5): 8.
———. (1992b). "Protesters Continue Blockade", *Windspeaker* 10(8): 20.
———. (1992c). "Logging Protesters Continue to do Battle", *Windspeaker* 10(19): 21.

(b) First Nations in Forestry[†]

First Nations Forestry Program

SECHELT INDIAN BAND

In the quest to provide band members with employment and opportunities, the Sechelt Indian Band of British Columbia has actively pursued a diversified resource management strategy which promotes growth as well as sustainable development.

Since 1992 Sechelt Indian Band Forestry (SIBFOR) has had a constructive working relationship with International Forest Products in forestry projects on the Sechelt Band's land along the Sunshine Coast. The Sechelt Band has directly benefitted from the partnership with Interfor through employment, training, and the development of forestry related expertise. More importantly they have gained greater responsibility in resource management decisions.

The Band's involvement with forestry has grown since initial silviculture and creek-clearing work, to encompass contract work with Interfor in such vital environmental monitoring activities as stream classification, water quality, and fish stock levels.

In addition to increased involvement in forest management, the Sechelt Nation also actively manages regional fisheries resources by operating a salmon hatchery. For over 15 years, as part of a co-management initiative with the Department of Fisheries and Oceans, the Sechelt fishery technicians have put back into their resources by restocking local streams with Coho, Chinook, Pink, and Chum salmon raised at the McLean Bay hatchery.

[†] From <www.fnfp.gc.ca>. Reproduced with the permission of the Minister of Public Works and Government Services, 2002 and Courtesy of Natural Resources Canada, Canadian Forest Service.

Not only have the Sechelt Band members become active partners in resource management, they are now taking their path of development into their own hands. The acquisition of skills gained through these projects has prepared the way for coordinating an overall forestry business strategy to create growth and viable enterprises for the Band.

The Sechelt Indian Band has recently embarked upon a consultation project aimed at identifying business opportunities and planning sustainable forest-based economic development. The initiative is designed to bolster the Band's long-term forest resource management position. Elements of the strategy include developing a timber sale application, ensuring continued access to tenure for band enterprises, and the potential completion of a value-added facility on Band property. The Band's initial investment in the project was backed up by a $25,000 grant from the First [Nations] Forestry Program.

The Sechelt Band's application was among the 43 projects supported in this dynamic forest economic development program jointly funded by the Canadian Forest Service/Natural Resources Canada and the Department of Indian Affairs and Northern Development. According to Nello Cataldo, British Columbia Collaborative Forestry Program Manager at the Pacific Forestry Centre, the program is receiving an increasing number of proposals from bands across the province for creating opportunities to participate in forest-based businesses.

The Sechelt Band is one of many British Columbia First Nations exploring opportunities to expand the scope of their investment in forestry. A value-added facility would [complement] their current projects and provide vital training opportunities. With this approach the [Band is] looking to make the transition from the seasonal employment created by silviculture work to value-added manufacturing and partnerships which will allow a more diversified forest business strategy.

In making decisions and implementing key resource development projects, the Sechelt Indian Band have been able to take advantage of opportunities in key sectors of the economy which will guarantee the participation of band members. Adding to their knowledge and expertise in forest resource management ensures their future. "We all have respect for the land and its resources," says Sechelt Chief Garry Feschuk.

Guided by a well-balanced equilibrium aimed at protecting the environment, managing resources, and incorporating traditional values as guardians of the land, the Sechelt are well along the path of self-sufficiency and sustainability.

BABINE FOREST PRODUCTS

Babine Forest Products Ltd. is the longest-standing joint venture of its kind in Canada. Located on the Burns Lake Reserve in the Prince George Forest District, the company's 20-year-old sawmill is one of the largest in British Columbia. The sawmill produces over 225 million board feet of dimension lumber annually. About 95 percent of the lumber produced by Babine is sold in the United States and the remaining 5 percent is sold in Japan.

Babine Forest Products' sawmill employs 268 workers. Approximately 34 percent of the mill's employees are Native. This high ratio roughly matches the percentage of Natives as a proportion of the surrounding region.

Weldwood of Canada owns 58 percent of Babine Forest Products, West Fraser Timber Co. owns 32 percent and the Burns Lake Native Development Corporation (BLNDC) owns 10 percent.

The BLNDC is made up of five First Nations bands: Broman Lake, Burns Lake, Cheslatta, Lake Babine and Nee-Tahi-Buhn. The BLNDC is not only involved with managing the Native interest in Babine however. Another one of the corporation's other major functions is providing financial advice as well as economic support to Native groups or individuals who are attempting to establish their own businesses.

The [Burns] Lake Native Development Corporation receives no government funding and pays no dividends to individual bands. The revenue for the corporation comes from the BLNDC's interest in Babine Forest Products as well as its other investments.

"We now have financial resources and environmental controls," BLNDC former chairman Wilf Adam said. "Before 1974 there was damage to trap lines, berry picking sites and archaeological grounds. Now that we're in the boardroom, this no longer happens."

Babine is showing its commitment to the environment in other ways as well. The company is a member of the Forest Data Exchange Pilot Project. This project was created with the intent of creating protocols to allow forestry information to pass smoothly from the private forestry industry to the government and vice versa.

Babine Forest Products is also the principal client in a research project mounted by the Lake Babine Band, the University of Northern British Columbia, the Forest Resources and Practices Team and the Ministry of Forests to determine how changes in landscape disturbance practices have influenced the forest use and cultural practices of the Lake Babine Band. The project hopes to examine through retrospective studies the landscape processes which have played the greatest role in shaping land use practices of the Lake Babine First Nation. One of the project's major objectives is to consider how current silviculture practices can be adapted to provide continued support for cultural practices and traditional harvesting among the members of the Lake Babine Band. The information gathered by this study will be presented via seminars and workshops to foresters, logging contractors, wildlife biologists and the forest-enjoying public.

DEZTI WOODS LIMITED

Although the Stoney Creek, Nadleh Whut'en and Stellaten First Nations are within 100 kilometres of each other, this is the first time they have ventured into business together. "Neduchun" means "our wood" in Carrier, the three Nations' common language. It is also the name of the joint venture company formed by the three Nations, Neduchun Forest Products, Ltd.

Neduchun's story began as the vision of the Stoney Creek Elders Society. They were seeking an employment and economic development project for their youth in the competitive Prince George Timber Supply Area (TSA). The company has just realised its plan to build a value-added mill in Vanderhoof, 100 kilometres east of Prince George, the geographical centre of British Columbia. Neduchun owns

51% of the mill, called Dezti Woods, Ltd., and the other 49% of the ownership is split between Vanderhoof Speciality Wood Products and Slocan Forest Products, Neduchun's joint venture partners.

The name "Dezti" means something of value in Carrier, and was the word closest in meaning to the term "value-added". "We're in the laminated post business," says Barry Vickers, a member of Dezti's board of directors. "We buy many different types of wood from various primary sawmill businesses and turn it into posts and other products for the Japanese construction industry." The plant also makes finger-jointed studs.

Management, Life Skills and Pre-Employment Training are some of biggest rewards of this joint venture. A management trainee was chosen from each of the three Nations. Crystal Casimel, now working in finance for Dezti Wood, was the Stellaten trainee. Her previous experience was in the Band office, and she says she had a hard time making the transition from fund-type accounting to a for-profit system, but she's quickly making the transition.

Casimel says that Dezti is cutting ties, in a manner of speaking, with its partners. It needed financial backing from Slocan, who entered the arrangement for the 8-year fibre agreement. Vanderhoof Speciality Wood Products (VSWP) brought experience in the value-added industry in terms of marketing and management. However, in accordance with Dezti's mandate to provide sustainable economic development in the First Nations communities, Dezti is moving out of VSWP's office and into their own facility.

The economic power of the three Nations involved has improved substantially because of the employment spin-offs from the mill. "We have 100% Native employment from the three Bands," says Paul Heit, a director on the Dezti board. Casimel adds, "We have equal representation from the three Bands. When you hear that someone is a Dezti worker, your first question is: 'Which Band are they from?'"

The company is using employee incentive policies, such as a recognition program, which adds $1/hour to the wages of staff with perfect attendance for an entire pay-period. Crews are rewarded with pizza or breakfast, depending on their shift, when production records are broken. These strategies seem to be working, too. Keith Spencer, Dezti's original manager, told Casimel that he was impressed with the dedication his crews have shown, and their good attitude toward attendance.

"We may be the first North American plant to get JAS certification for posts," says Vickers. This certification allows the company to place a JAS sticker on all its lumber going to the Japanese market, which will indicate a product manufactured to strict quality specifications. "You earn this right by proving the ability to test the product's quality throughout production. It's very stringent." For a company with less than a year's experience producing posts, this certification is a mark of success.

Forest Renewal B.C. allotted the joint venture $213,000, much of which was used for training costs. No other outside funding was required to get the project off the ground.

"What impresses me is that three partners who have different perspectives can get together and work out their problems," says Paul Heit, director on the Dezti board. "As long as the partners continue to think and respond in a flexible manner for the common good of the business, owners and employees, we will continue to grow as a company as we have done successfully to this point."

CREE NORTH LOG HOMES

With a shortage of housing and a wealth of jack pine and spruce trees on their territory, Chapleau Cree First Nation decided to start building log homes. They called their business Cree North Log Homes.

By the spring of 1998, there were six log houses on the reserve and two more were being sold off-reserve, according to Chapleau Cree First Nation CEO Michael Cachagee. "We are open for business and ready to build homes and provide training in other communities," says Cachagee. "The design has been within our community for a few hundred years. We revitalized it, and maximized the use of trees by using both vertical and horizontal logs."

The homes have a very rustic look, as all the logs are hand-peeled. Cree North has developed a few different floor plans. Their First Nation training program runs about one year.

Prior to the project, reserve housing was not affordable. A fair-sized new home would normally run between $75,000 to $100,000 to build, says Cachagee. The two lumber companies located outside of Chapleau were cutting boards and shipping them out, so there was a strong possibility of starting a value-added industry nearby. Now the community builds its own log homes, and offers training to assist other First Nations to establish their own milling and home-building operations.

It all began in the spring of 1995 with funding from the Canadian Forest Service (CFS), explains Cachagee. A forest management plan was adopted. On-reserve GIS (computer mapping) forestry consultant company, Cree Tech, mapped and inventoried the area. The four square-mile territory included a wealth of poplar, jack pine, birch and other conifers such as balsam. By the fall of 1995, after working with a forester, they identified the areas where they should cut. In the winter of 1996, preliminary roads were built and cutting began soon after.

Later in 1996, the first Cree North log home was built on-reserve, with logs cut by a local mill. The next summer, four more homes went up, with vertical logs being cut by Mike and Mike's Logging — a reserve business. Mike and Mike's is a team of a guy named Mike and his horse of the same name. Then eight trainees from both the Anishanabe and Chapleau Cree First Nations worked to do the milling, grooving and building of the homes. They used their own mill machines, designed with the assistance of the First [Nations] Forestry Program. Only three of the eight workers had previous experience in the industry. Logs used for the horizontal-style log homes were cut by a local mill.

"The Band is not in competition with private enterprise," notes Cachagee. "But this has given us a business on which to focus. The Band will take inventory and remain active in this venture. And with other First Nations, we can help them implement their own initiative, and get it up and running."

LAKE SUPERIOR FIRST NATIONS DEVELOPMENT TRUST

A non-profit organization working to encourage more Aboriginal people to tackle a career in forestry is making a difference in Thunder Bay, Ontario.

Lake Superior First Nations Development Trust eventually plans to establish a stand-alone Aboriginal Forestry Management School. But for now, with some funding from the First [Nations] Forestry Program, they are publishing a catalogue listing available courses Ontario Aboriginal forestry workers might take for career skill development while they look for or continue to work.

Beginning in September 1998, two or three forestry-related courses not offered by other educational institutions are set to be offered by Lake Superior First Nations Development Trust. One course will teach industrial policy and procedures, looking at forest companies in Ontario and how they are structured and operated. For example, if a company is publicly traded, they must release certain information. Some private companies also provide background information. Another course will offer GIS (Computer Mapping) training for forestry and other applications. A third course will look at business proposal writing.

According to Continuing Education Research Co-ordinator, Brian Walmark, the Lake Superior First Nations Development Trust courses will take the form of seminars and workshops in their Thunder Bay classroom, through distance education or by correspondence. Students will be able to take some courses, or eventually, take all of them and earn a certificate.

Walmark says the catalogue and training have been created to encourage more Aboriginal young people to stay in school and to consider a career in forestry. "Industry people and forestry academics were beginning to realize few Aboriginals were taking advantage of forestry jobs," he says. "Most of them were becoming labourers or cutting trees. There were only a handful of Aboriginal foresters. We needed a pro-active approach."

Also, fewer and fewer forestry grads in Ontario seemed to be getting jobs. So, Walmark did an employment survey to pinpoint the problem. The survey allowed industry to identify the skills graduates should have, but did not. Technically, it found students required more computer training GIS skills, tree marking and scaling, and silviculture training (e.g. planting seedlings). They also required better negotiating skills and a better grasp of government policy and procedure and corporate policy. Smaller companies surveyed [said,] graduates needed more entrepreneurial skills. They found that while graduates had good technical skills. they needed to know how to market their skills. They also needed to be able to write business proposals and have a better understanding of business and administration.

So, Lake Superior First Nations Development Trust decided to offer some courses to fill the gaps, and to better equip forestry grads for the job market.

PINE CREEK FIRST NATION LOGGING INC.

When the Pine Creek First Nation, located on Lake Winnipegosis, Manitoba, went into the logging business in February 1997, things began to happen.

Pine Creek First Nation Logging Inc. has really made a difference for the First Nation community, according to Ernie Urbanowski, general manager. Urbanowski and his family have lived on the outskirts of the reserve for a number of years, working in partnership with the First Nation people on a number of collaborative projects.

"It has taken eight families off social assistance and put them in the workforce. It also earns the First Nation some income, from timber sales," explains Urbanowski.

Some First Nation people from the area had always worked in this industry, says Urbanowski, but they were always working for someone else. "These people were never able to fly on their own. Now they have the [opportunity] to hold their heads high."

The project was originally initiated in April 1995. Start-up cost, to purchase new equipment, was $899,000. The First Nation provided $100,000 of its own funds, $240,000 came from Aboriginal Business Canada and the rest was borrowed at a low nterest rate. The company landed a contract with Louisiana Pacific — which buys their poplar wood to make wafer board, a product used in house construction.

"Once we got started, everything fell into place," says Urbanowski.

To get things rolling, some up-to-date Timberjack equipment was purchased before the operation opened for business. Equipment included: a $485,000-850 feller buncher, to knock out trees and two 460 grapple skidders. Also, $42,000 was provided by the **First Nation Forestry Program** to provide training for First Nation staff. Training started in June 1997. In addition to equipment operation, it also focused on safety and efficiency.

While the first year, which ends March 31, has been a somewhat challenging one, when things get started again in the fall Urbanowski is sure the venture will generate much more work and income. Their current work season runs from September to March. He is very positive about the future.

In addition to the logging business, Pine Creek also began a [complementary] sawmill operation, in collaboration with the Waterhen First Nation in May, 1997. Between the sawmill and the logging, 20 people from both communities are now employed. At the mill, four men saw logs into timbers to be shipped to furniture companies in Winnipeg such as Pa D'or Manufacturing and Bay Ridge Lumber as well as Aspen Forest Industries in Roblin, Manitoba.

The sawmill pretty much operates at cost, with income covering workers' salaries while the logging operation brings in about $40,000 to $50,000 every two weeks.

Currently, Pine Creek First Nation Logging subcontracts its slashing, where trees are cut to an eight-foot length, and the shipping of its product, by semi. In the future, they plan to buy a new slasher and employ two more people. One community member has also purchased a truck, and tackles some delivery jobs.

Pine Creek First Nation Logging is now pursuing a contract with Tolko, Manitoba (formerly Repap Manitoba). They could be working summer cuts by the spring of 1998.

Harvey Payne, a consultant to the Pine Creek band on natural resource matters, says overall the project looks good and is definitely on the right track.

"Forestry is a tough and competitive business," says Payne, "but Pine Creek is doing well."

ECOLINK FORESTRY SERVICES

"For a company that started with only 15 people, we've really grown," says Bill Chelsea, president of Ecolink Forestry Services. Ecolink started operations in June of 1990, with only 15 employees and an annual revenue of $150,000. By 1994, the company was employing more than 3 times the workers and had revenues totaling more than $1 million. Just last year, this successful joint venture generated over $3 million in revenue and employed more than 80 workers.

Ecolink is a joint venture between Williams Lake-based Lignum Woods Ltd. and the Alkali Lake Band, with Lignum providing management and marketing expertise and the band providing manpower and resources for the company. Employees of Ecolink don't just come from the Alkali Lake Band however. "Of the 80 people working last year, about 4 were non-natives and the rest were hired from eight different bands from the surrounding area[,"] says Chelsea. Approximately 80 per cent of the company's work is silviculture (falling and burning beetle-infested trees, brush clearing, seed collection and juvenile spacing) while the other 20 per cent is logging. While the partnership between Lignum and the Alkali Lake Band has been very successful, there are limitations. "The work is real employment, but it is seasonal," says Chelsea, "When a project is over, new contracts must be won in order to continue operations."

During the winter months, the work force reduces to about 20 people who continue silviculture operations, but the rest of the Ecolink staff are not idle. "We are always trying to update our skills.", says Chelsea. From December to March, employees undergo training in supervisory skills, accounting, tree-falling, small engine repair and timber cruising. The intent behind the training is for Ecolink employees to learn new career-focused skills that will make them better forestry workers, and Ecolink a better forestry company. "Right now, we want to educate more heavy-duty machine operators because we are using more heavy-duty machinery as operations increase. Ecolink is a great way to create skilled employment and with the right training, we could work anywhere in the forestry industry", says Chelsea.

Creating training and skilled employment was only one of many reasons that the Alkali Lake Band became involved with Ecolink. As the name suggests, Ecolink is a company that is helping to protect and rejuvenate the environment. The company has also created many opportunities for First Nations that would not have existed otherwise. Besides employing many community members of the surrounding First Nations, Ecolink also subcontracts work to other bands — contracts that Ecolink can win because of its size and organization.

Lignum Woods Manager Brian LaPointe believes Ecolink is a positive force. "We're building good relationships," he says, "From my perspective, I think we no longer see the First Nations community as something apart. We are part of their lives and they are part of ours."

(c) Aboriginal Forestry in Canada[†]

Michael J. McDonald

INTRODUCTION

Before embarking upon a detailed analysis of how forestry is impacted by aboriginal law matters, it should be noted that by virtue of section 35 of the *Constitution Act, 1982* (the "Constitution"), aboriginal rights (including title) and treaty rights are now constitutionally protected. Section 35 reads as follows:

> 35.(1) The existing aboriginal and treaty rights of the aboriginal peoples of Canada are hereby recognized and affirmed.
>   (2) In this Act, the "aboriginal peoples of Canada" includes the Indian, Inuit and Metis people of Canada.
>   (3) For greater certainty, in subsection (1) "treaty rights" includes rights that now exist by way of land claim agreements or may be so acquired.
>   (4) Notwithstanding any other provision of this Act, the aboriginal and treaty rights referred to in subsection (1) are guaranteed equally to male and female persons.

The importance of the protection provided by the Constitution to aboriginal peoples is that their unique status in Canada in finally recognized. As a result of such constitutional recognition, aboriginal peoples are given more permanency to their existence and sustenance in Canada.

Although aboriginal peoples view their rights in a much broader context, there is a judicially recognized right for at least the following:

(a) fishing for food, ceremonial and social purposes;
(b) hunting over Crown lands and over some unoccupied private lands;
(c) aboriginal title, which encompasses the right to exclusive use and occupation of land for a variety of purposes that need not be aspects of practices, customs and traditions integral to a distinctive aboriginal culture; and
(d) a right to sell or barter roe on kelp.

So far these are the rights which the courts have recognized as being aboriginal rights within the meaning of section 35 of the Constitution. The existence of an aboriginal right protected by section 35 must be determined in accordance with certain tests established in the jurisprudence and discussed further below. However, the fact that a particular First Nation is unable to prove its aboriginal rights in accordance with such tests does not mean that those rights have been extinguished.

OVERVIEW OF ABORIGINAL RIGHTS AND TITLE IMPACTING FORESTRY

The Supreme Court of Canada's decision in *Delgamuukw v. British Columbia*[1] has been heralded as "probably the single most important judicial pronouncement in

---

[†] Paper prepared for the Aboriginal Law Conference 1998 (Vancouver: The Native Investment & Trade Association, 1998). Appendices omitted. Reproduced with permission of the publisher.

the long and somewhat convoluted history of aboriginal rights in Canadian courts."[2] For the first time in Canadian judicial history, the Supreme Court of Canada specifically addressed the issue of unextinguished aboriginal title to land and articulated the specific nature and content of such title. The landmark decision in *Delgamuukw* represents the culmination of a series of cases involving aboriginal rights decided by the Supreme Court of Canada over the past two years.

At the outset it should be noted that by virtue of the changes of Canada's Constitution in 1982, the aboriginal and treaty rights then existing were constitutionally entrenched. In practical terms, this constitutional status means that aboriginal rights cannot be significantly affected by federal or provincial laws without clear justification, which must be established by the federal or provincial government. Aboriginal title is one type of aboriginal right entitled to such constitutional protection. The significance of the recognition of aboriginal title in the *Delgamuukw* decision is that aboriginal title is a right in and to the land itself, thereby making it a part of property law.

A detailed analysis of aboriginal rights and aboriginal title is not intended to be covered in this paper. Rather a review of *process* rights arising out of these [rights] will be reviewed as it is the greatest source of conflict with forestry matters.

The *Sparrow*, Supreme Court of Canada first laid out process rights in this context by a test for justification of infringement. First, infringement of the aboriginal right must be in furtherance of a legislative objective that is compelling and substantial. According to the Court in *Delgamuukw*, a compelling and substantial objective is one which is directed at either one of the purposes underlying the recognition and affirmation of aboriginal rights by section 35(1). These purposes are the recognition of the prior occupation of Canada by aboriginal peoples and the reconciliation of this prior occupation with the assertion of sovereignty by the Crown.

By way of example, the Chief Justice of Canada in *Delgamuukw* identified the following as possible valid legislative objectives:

(a) the development of agricultural, forestry, mining, and hydroelectric power;
(b) the general economic development of a province;
(c) the protection of the environment or endangered species;
(d) the building of infrastructure; and
(e) the settlement of foreign populations to support those aims.

The second requirement of the justification test is that the infringement must be consistent with the special fiduciary relationship between the Crown and aboriginal peoples. In applying this stage of the justification test to the infringement of aboriginal title, the Supreme Court in *Delgamuukw* held that the operation of the fiduciary duty, both in terms of the standard of scrutiny and the form of that duty, will depend on the nature of aboriginal title. In this regard, the Chief Justice noted the relevance of three [particular] aspects of aboriginal title:

(a) aboriginal title encompasses the right to exclusive use and occupation of the land;
(b) aboriginal title encompasses the right to choose to what uses the land can be put; and

(c) lands held pursuant to aboriginal title have an inescapable economic component.

First, aboriginal title encompasses the right to the exclusive use and occupation of the land. Accordingly, the Court in *Delgamuukw* held that in order to satisfy its fiduciary obligation towards aboriginal peoples, the Crown will be required to demonstrate that both the process by which it allocated the land's resources and the actual allocation of those resources reflect the prior interest of the aboriginal title holder. This aspect of the Crown's fiduciary duty may require, for example, the participation of aboriginal peoples in the development of resources on aboriginal title lands, or the reduction of economic barriers, such as licensing fees, to aboriginal uses of the lands.

Second, the fact that aboriginal title encompasses the right to choose to what uses the land can be put imposes a duty upon the Crown to consult the aboriginal group holding title prior to dealing with the land. The Supreme Court described the degree and scope of the consultation required as follows:

> The nature and scope of the duty of consultation will vary with the circumstances. In occasional cases, when the breach is less serious or relatively minor, it will be no more than a duty to discuss important decisions that will be taken with respect to lands held pursuant to aboriginal title. Of course, even in these rare cases when the minimum acceptable standard is consultation, this consultation must be in good faith, and with the intention of substantially addressing the concerns of the aboriginal peoples whose lands are at issue. In most cases, it will be significantly deeper than mere consultation. Some cases may even require the full consent of an aboriginal nation, particularly when provinces enact hunting and fishing regulations in relation to aboriginal lands.[3]

Third, as aboriginal title has an inescapable economic component due to the modern uses to which aboriginal title lands can be put, the Court in *Delgamuukw* held that fair compensation will ordinarily be required whenever aboriginal title is infringed. The amount of compensation payable will vary with the nature of the particular aboriginal title affected and with the nature and severity of the infringement and the extent to which aboriginal interests were accommodated. In most cases, the measurement of the economic component of aboriginal title and the compensation required will lead to many difficult questions of law and economics.

Conclusion

By its decisions in cases such as *Van der Peet* and *Delgamuukw*, the Supreme Court of Canada has made it clear that both aboriginal rights (including aboriginal title) and Crown sovereignty exist in Canada. The current challenge facing all Canadians is the reconciliation of the pre-existence of aboriginal societies with the sovereignty of the Crown in order to ensure the co-existence of the different cultures each represents.

The recognition of aboriginal title by the Supreme Court of Canada in the *Delgamuukw* decision creates a new dimension of government in Canada. As a result of the constitutional entrenchment of aboriginal title, the combined will of Parliament and the Provincial Legislatures will not be sufficient to implement a program desired by both levels of government, where aboriginal title is unjustifiably infringed. Real consultation, if not the consent of the aboriginal group affected, will be required. In many cases, compensation for the infringement will also be necessary. Where the *Delgamuukw* principles (including proper justification of any infringement) are not followed, governmental actions may be reviewed by the courts upon application by the affected aboriginal group.

TREATY RIGHTS

While there is some uncertainty regarding the measure to which treaty rights, such as hunting, trapping and fishing, may be regulated or affected by the Crown, it is clear that those rights set out in the treaties have constitutional protection by virtue of section 35 of the Constitution. (*Simon v. R.*, [1985] 2 S.C.R. 387; *R. v. Sioui*, [1993] C.N.L.R. 127 (S.C.C.).) Despite such equal protection, the majority of the Supreme Court of Canada case law deals with the application of the constitutional safeguard in the context of aboriginal rights. However, the recent case of *R. v. Badger*, [1996] 4 W.W.R. 457, provides guidance in identifying the principles to be applied in approaching treaty interpretation.

In *Badger*, the Supreme Court of Canada recognized that previous case law, and in particular *R. v. Sparrow*, [1990] 1 S.C.R. 1075, was concerned with only aboriginal rights, and not treaty rights. The Court therefore concluded that the criteria set out in *Sparrow* would apply equally to the infringement of treaty rights due to the fact that section 35 of the Constitution applies to treaty rights as well as aboriginal rights.

NATURE OF INDIAN TREATIES IN CANADIAN LAW

For decades, Canadian courts have struggled with the legal characterization to be given to aboriginal treaties. The key argument has been whether such treaties should be regarded as legal contracts capable of international recognition.

In respect of the nature of aboriginal treaties and treaty rights, the majority of the Supreme Court of Canada, per Cory J., made the following remarks in *Badger*:

> There is no doubt that aboriginal and treaty differ in both origin and structure. Aboriginal rights flow from the customs and traditions of the native peoples. To paraphrase the words of Judson J. in *Calder, supra*, at p. 328, they embody the right of native people to continue living as their forefathers lived. Treaty rights, on the other hand, are those contained in official agreements between the Crown and the native peoples. Treaties are analogous to contracts, albeit of a very solemn and special, public nature. They create enforceable obligations based on the mutual consent of the parties. If follows that the scope of treaty rights will be determined by their wording, which must be interpreted in accordance with the principles enunciated by this Court.

In 1985, the decision of the Supreme Court of Canada in *Simon* clarified the issue of the nature of aboriginal treaties and held that such treaties were neither contracts, nor treaties as understood within the international law context. The Court maintained that "while it may be helpful in some instances to analogize the principles of international treaty law to Indian treaties, these principles are not determinative. An Indian treaty is unique; it is an agreement *sui generis* which is neither created nor terminated according to the rules of international law." Based on this characterization of aboriginal treaties, the *Simon* decision created a starting point from which all future analysis of aboriginal treaties would originate.

In 1990, in the case of *Sioui*, the Supreme Court of Canada attempted again to accurately depict the nature of aboriginal treaties and treaty rights. The Court followed the reasoning in *Simon* and stated that "the courts should show flexibility in determining the legal nature of a document recording a transaction with the Aboriginal peoples" and that aboriginal treaties should be liberally construed, with any uncertainties being resolved in favour of the aboriginal peoples. The Court acknowledged that the task of analyzing aboriginal treaties in contemporary Canadian law is not an easy one. However, it noted that once a treaty is indeed found to exist, that treaty must be given "a just, broad and liberal construction." Lamer C.J. cited the following passage from the 1899 United States Supreme Court decision in *Jones v. Meehan*, 175 U.S. 1 (1899), in support of the proposition of liberal construction:

> I must always ... be borne in mind that the negotiations for the treaty are conducted, on the part of the United States, an enlightened and powerful nation, by representative skilled in diplomacy, masters of a written language, understanding the modes and forms of creating the various technical estates known to their law, and assisted by an [interpreter] employed by themselves; that the treaty is drawn up by them and in their own language; that the Aboriginal peoples, on the other hand, are a weak and dependent people, who have no written language and are wholly unfamiliar with all forms of legal expression, and whose only knowledge of the terms in which the treaty is framed is that imparted to them by the [interpreter] employed by the United States; and that the treaty must therefore be construed, not according to the technical meaning of its words to learned lawyers, but in the [sense] in which they would naturally be understood by the Aboriginal peoples.

In *Sioui*, the Supreme Court of Canada set out a number of factors to be taken into consideration in respect of the interpretation of aboriginal treaties. These factors include the following:

(a) continuous exercise of a right in the past and at present;
(b) the reasons why the Crown made a commitment;
(c) the situation prevailing at the time the document was signed;
(d) evidence of relations of mutual respect and esteem between the negotiators; and
(e) the subsequent conduct of the parties.

The Court also noted in *Sioui* that the historical context, which is used to demonstrate the existence of a treaty, may equally assist in interpreting the extent of the rights contained in it. In this regard, the Court quoted the following passage from *Taylor and Williams* (1981), 62 C.C.C. (2d) 227, per McKinnon A.C.J.:

> Cases on Indian or aboriginal rights can never be determined in a vacuum. It is of importance to consider the history and oral tradition of the tribes concerned, and the surrounding circumstances at the time of the treaty, relied on by both parties, in determining the treaty's effect. Although it is not possible to remedy all of what we now perceive as past wrongs in view of the passage of time, nevertheless it is essential and in keeping with established and accepted principles that the courts not create, by a remote, isolated current view of past events, new grievances.

It should be noted that certain decisions have concluded that the *Sioui* case allows signatories of more recent treaties to benefit from special rules of interpretation even where their level of sophistication does not so require it. For example, the Supreme Court of Canada made the following comments in respect of undue special treatment of interpretation in the case of *R. v. Howard*, [1994] 2 S.C.R. 299 at 306:

> The 1923 Treaty does not raise the same concerns as treaties signed in the more distant past or in more remote territories where [one] can legitimately question the understanding of the Indian parties. The 1923 Treaty concerned lands in close proximity to the urbanized Ontario of the day. The Hiawatha signatories were businessmen, a civil servant and all were [literated]. In short, they were active participants in the economy and society of their province. The terms of the Treaty and specifically the basket clause are entirely clear and would have been understood by the seven signatories.

Based on such concerns of special treatment, it now appears that any analysis or interpretation of aboriginal treaties and/or treaty rights must occur within the context of the test for justification of infringement as advanced in the case of *R. v. Sparrow*, [1990] 1 S.C.R. 1075. Even though the *Sparrow* decision involved aboriginal rights and not treaty rights, the Supreme Court of Canada nevertheless confirmed that the fiduciary duty of the Crown to justify infringement extends beyond the [surrender] of reserves and beyond land rights, as evidenced by the following statement:

> The *sui generis* nature of Indian title, and the historic powers and responsibility assumed by the Crown constituted the source of such fiduciary obligation. In our opinion, *Guerin*, together with *R. v. Taylor and Williams* (1981), 34 O.R. (2d) 360, ground a general principle for s. 35(1). That is, the Government has the responsibility to act in a fiduciary capacity with respect to aboriginal peoples. The relationship between the Government and the aboriginals is trust-like, rather than adversarial, and contemporary recognition and affirmation of aboriginal rights must be defined in light of this historic relationship.

In the decision of the Northwest Territories Territorial Court in *R. v. Noel*, [1995] N.W.T.J. 92, the Court discussed the appropriate manner for the interpretation of aboriginal treaties and treaty rights. The Court followed the reasoning in *Simon* and *Sioui* and held that when interpreting treaties, they should be liberally construed and doubtful expressions resolved in favour of the aboriginal peoples. It went on to note that the Crown owes a fiduciary obligation to the aboriginal peoples which stems from the nature of aboriginal title (*sui generis*) and the history of powers and responsibilities assumed by the Crown.

THE CURRENT STATE OF THE LAW — *R. v. BADGER*

The most recent decision of the Supreme Court of Canada to consider the nature of aboriginal treaties and treaty rights is *Badger*. In *Badger*, the Court affirmed that the criteria set out in *Sparrow* in respect of section 35 of the Constitution apply equally to the infringement of treaty rights as to aboriginal rights. Notwithstanding such similar treatment, however, the Court recognized that aboriginal and treaty rights differ in both origin and structure. Aboriginal rights, on the hand, flow from the customs and traditions of aboriginal peoples, whereas treaty rights, on the other hand, are those rights contained within official agreements negotiated between the Crown and aboriginal peoples. As a result, treaties are very much like contracts, albeit of a much more special and public nature, and, therefore, the scope of treaty rights will inevitably be determined by their wording.

Despite such differences though, the Court in *Badger* found that aboriginal rights and treaty rights posses significant similarities. First, both aboriginal and treaty rights possess in common a unique, *sui generis* nature. In each situation, the Crown is engaged through its relationship with aboriginal peoples. Second, given that treaty rights are the result of mutual agreement, they, like aboriginal rights, may be unilaterally abridged. Accordingly, like aboriginal rights, infringements of treaty rights must be justified.

In respect of *prima facie* infringement of treaty rights, the Court, per Lamer C.J., made the following remarks at paragraph 82:

> In my view, it is equally if not more important to justify *prima facie* infringements of treaty rights. The rights granted to Aboriginal peoples by treaties usually form an integral part of the consideration for the surrender of their lands. For example, it is clear that the maintenance of as much of their hunting rights as possible was of paramount concern to the Aboriginal peoples who signed Treaty No. 8. This was, in effect, an aboriginal right recognized in a somewhat limited form by the treaty and later modified by the NRTA. To the Aboriginal peoples, it was an essential element of this solemn agreement.

In *Badger*, the Court set out some of the applicable principles of interpretation of aboriginal treaties. These principles are summarized as follows:

(a) A treaty represents an exchange of solemn promises between the Crown and the various "Indian nations". It is an agreement whose nature is sacred. (*Sioui; Simon*)

(b) The honor of the Crown is always at stake in its dealing with "Indian people". Interpretation of treaties and statutory provisions which have an impact upon treaty or aboriginal rights must be approached in a manner which maintains the integrity of the Crown. It is always assumed that the Crown intends to fulfill its promises. No appearance of "sharp dealing" will be sanctioned. (*Sparrow; Taylor and Williams*)

(c) Any ambiguities or doubtful expressions in the wording of the treaty or documents must be resolved in favour of the aboriginal peoples. A corollary to this principle is that any limitation which restricts the rights of aboriginal peoples under treaties must be narrowly construed. (*Sioui; Simon*)

(d) The onus of proving that a treaty or aboriginal right has been extinguished lies upon the Crown. There must be "strict proof of the fact of extinguishment" and evidence of a clear and plain intention on the [part] of the government to extinguish treaty rights. (*Sioui; Simon*)

The Court in *Badger* went on to say that when considering a treaty, courts must take into account that treaties and statutes relating to aboriginal peoples should be liberally construed and any uncertainties, ambiguities or doubtful expressions should be resolved in favour of the aboriginal peoples. In addition, courts must consider the context in which the treaties were negotiated, conducted and committed to in writing. The treaties, as written documents, recorded an agreement that had already been reached orally and often they did not [...] record the full extent of the oral agreement. As a result, it is well settled that the words in the treaty must not be interpreted in their strict technical sense nor subjected to rigid modern rules of construction. Rather, they must be interpreted in the sense that they would naturally have been understood by the aboriginal peoples at the time of the signing. This applies, as well, to those words in a treaty which impose a limitation on the right which has been granted.

In *R. v. Horseman*, Wilson J. in dissent stated that Indian treaties were the product of negotiation between very different cultures and the language used in them probably does not reflect, and should not be expected to reflect, with total accuracy each party's understanding of their effect at the time they were entered into. This is why the Court must be especially sensitive to the broader historical context in which such treaties were negotiated. They must be prepared to look at the historical context in order to ensure that they reach a proper understanding of the meaning that particular treaties held for their signatories at the time. Furthermore, Indian treaties must be given the effect the signatories obviously intended them to have at the time they were entered into even if they do not comply with today's formal requirements.

While a treaty (as reviewed in *Horseman* and *Badger*) was obviously intended to enable the government of Canada to pass regulations with respect to hunting, fishing and trapping, it becomes clear when one places the treaty in its historical context that the government of Canada committed itself to regulate hunting in a manner that would respect the lifestyle of the Aboriginal peoples and the way in which they had traditionally pursued their livelihood. Because any regulations concerning hunting and fishing were to be "in the interest" of the aboriginal peoples, and because the Aboriginal peoples were promised that they would be as free to hunt, fish and trap "after the treaty as they would be if they never entered into it", such regulations had to be designed to preserve an environment in which the Aboriginal peoples could continue to hunt, fish and trap as they had always done. The whole emphasis of Treaty 8 was on the preservation of the Aboriginal peoples' traditional way of life. But this surely did not mean that the Aboriginal peoples were to be forever consigned to a diet of meat and fish and were to have no opportunity to share in the advances of modern civilization over the next 100 years.

According to Alan Pratt in his Discussion Paper for the Royal Commission on Aboriginal Peoples entitled "The Numbered Treaties and Extinguishment: A Legal Analysis", Mr. Pratt states that the law of Canada has strained to acknowledge the unique character of aboriginal treaties. While Canadian jurisprudence has acknowledged the unique nature of the relationship between the aboriginal peoples and the Crown and the unique nature of aboriginal title, the unique nature of aboriginal treaties and treaty rights has not been completed recognized by Canadian courts. Where treaty rights are discussed in court cases, it is usually done in a very narrow context, without any regard to whether or not the treaty right has been extinguished or, in the alternative, whether the infringement of the treaty right in question can be justified.

According to Mr. Pratt, aboriginal treaties may be deemed to possess the following characteristics:

> they are *sui generis* agreements, neither mere contracts nor Treaties in international law;
>
> they were entered into between one party (the Crown) who owed fiduciary duties to the other (the Treaty Nations);
>
> the honour of the Crown is always involved in their fulfillment;
>
> ambiguous terms are always to be resolved in favour of the Indian parties;

they are to be given a broad and liberal interpretation in light of the understanding of the Indian parties at the time of the Treaty (except for certain more recent Treaties);

while they can be modified by a competent Constitutional enactment, but only to the extent that the enactment evinces a clear intention to effect such a modification;

existing Treaty rights have been recognized and affirmed by section 35(1) of the *Constitution Act, 1982*, and are subject to the analysis set out in the *Sparrow* case.

In the recent case of *R. v. Paul*, [1988] 1 C.N.L. 209, the New Brunswick Court of Queen's Bench Trial Division dealt with the issue of whether the cutting of trees on Crown land licensed to a third party by an aboriginal person was unlawful. The Court held that the respondent was not acting unlawfully because the respondent possessed a broad treaty right (Dummer's Treaty) relating to trade and had a right to harvest and sell the land. In determining the treaty rights of the respondent, the Court made the following remarks:

> The written terms of a treaty can be misleading and must be interpreted in light of the historical and legal milieu of the time and in light of the words that were spoken when the Dummer's Treaty was signed. Indians in New Brunswick can harvest any and all trees they wish on Crown lands as an appurtenance of their land rights under Dummer's Treaty. The Royal Proclamation of 1763 did not alter the nature of the Indian title agreed to at Dummer's Treaty. Indians of New Brunswick possess land rights that are treaty rights. These rights are not personal rights but rather full rights of beneficial ownership and possession. This is in keeping with the Supreme Court of Canada's direction that treaties are *sui generis*.... The Crown has jurisdiction and dominion over all land. The New Brunswick legislature and the federal Parliament can enact laws that affect Indian treaty rights in New Brunswick. The *Crown Lands and Forests Act* did not meet the guidelines set by the Supreme Court of Canada in Sparrow, and therefore the *Crown Lands and Forests Act* is not applicable to the Indians of New Brunswick.

IMPACT OF *DELGAMUUKW* ON TREATIES

The Supreme Court of Canada's decision in *Delgamuukw v. British Columbia*[4] is an obvious legal landmark and has provoked an enormous amount of commentary, most of it focussed on the monumental impact the case will have on the Province of British Columbia. In *Delgamuukw*, the Supreme Court for the first time recognized and defined the concept of aboriginal title. Obviously the Court's recognition of aboriginal title is of great significance to British Columbia in particular because unlike other provinces where treaties were negotiated with local First Nations many decades ago, very few treaties exist in British Columbia. As a result of B.C.'s distinct history, many commentators are currently speculating on how assertions of aboriginal title and aboriginal land claims in the wake of *Delgamuukw* will affect, on one level, the treaty negotiation process in B.C., and on a broader level, the whole of the B.C. economy.

However, this focus on the impact of *Delgamuukw* in B.C. should not overshadow the fact that the decision requires all governments throughout Canada to recognize and respect aboriginal title, aboriginal laws and aboriginal oral histories. For the rest of Canada outside of B.C., the Supreme Court's recognition of aboriginal title as an aboriginal right constitutionally protected by section 35(1) of the Constitution raises another key legal question: does aboriginal title still exist in those parts of Canada already covered by treaty?

The Supreme Court of Canada in *Delgamuukw* did not address the issue of extinguishment of aboriginal title in the face of a treaty. It has always been widely assumed by non-aboriginals that the treaties entered into by First Nations in different provinces across Canada extinguished aboriginal title to those treaty lands. However, there are two aspects of the *Delgamuukw* decision that give new impetus to the re-examination and renovation of existing treaties. The first aspect relates to the Supreme Court of Canada's treatment of aboriginal oral histories. The second aspect relates to the Court's discussion of aboriginal legal systems and how aboriginal title originated in part from pre-existing systems of aboriginal law. These two aspects and the implications they raise for existing treaties will be discussed in more detail below.

If the existence of a treaty does not necessarily extinguish aboriginal title to the lands covered by the treaty, this development has the potential of reopening the whole issue of aboriginal title over reserve lands and treaty areas from coast to coast. What the *Delgamuukw* decision does is open the door to a renewal and implementation of existing treaties in light of the Supreme Court's recognition of aboriginal title. Where the argument is made that treaty rights have not extinguished aboriginal title, treaty First Nations will now be able to argue that they have the right to exploit both the resources on reserve and treaty lands, as well as the resources below the surface such as oil, gas and minerals. The Supreme Court in *Delgamuukw* expressly recognized that aboriginal title to land includes subsurface rights.

There is no doubt that the *Delgamuukw* decision will have a significant impact on existing treaties both from an evidentiary perspective in terms of the use of oral histories and from a substantive perspective in terms of the existence of aboriginal title. The effects of this impact remain to be seen. However, if the principles in *Delgamuukw* are successfully used to rebut the current presumption that the treaties did extinguish aboriginal title with the consent of the aboriginal nations, then aboriginal title and the concomitant rights to the land's resources will be back on the bargaining table for treaty First Nations.

INFRINGEMENT OF ABORIGINAL AND TREATY RIGHTS

In *Sparrow*, Dickson C.J. and La Forest J. advanced a two-tier test for determining whether government infringement of aboriginal rights can be justified. According to the *Sparrow* test of justification, the government must demonstrate that:

(a)   it was acting pursuant to a valid legislative objective; and
(b)   its actions are consistent with its fiduciary duty to aboriginal peoples.

In respect of the second part of the test, the Court noted that there are further questions which need to be addressed. These questions include:

> ... whether there has been as little infringement as possible in order to effect the desired result; whether, in a situation of expropriation, fair compensation is available; and, whether the aboriginal group in question has been consulted with respect to the conservation measures being implemented....

As was noted with respect to the question of infringement, the framework for analyzing aboriginal rights laid down in *Sparrow* depends to a considerable extent on the "legal and factual context" of each appeal. Accordingly, the Supreme Court of Canada in *R. v. Gladstone*, [1996] 2 S.C.R. 723, adapted the *Sparrow* test in order to apply it to the circumstances of that appeal. The two points of variation noted by the Court which warranted adaptation of the *Sparrow* test were:

(a) the aboriginal rights recognized and affirmed in each case differed significantly (that is, *Sparrow* involved social and ceremonial rights and *Gladstone* involved commercial rights); and

(b) the articulation of the Crown's fiduciary duty in terms of priority require refinement in order to take into account the varying circumstances which arise when the aboriginal right in question has no internal limitations (for instance, in *Sparrow*, the right in question was internally limited as it was a right to fish for food, ceremonial and social purposes; whereas in *Gladstone*, the right to sell fish commercially was only limited by supply and demand and therefore did not require the strict application of the *Sparrow* test which would have amounted to an unintended result, that is an exclusive right of the aboriginal peoples to exploit the fishery on a commercial basis).

In *Delgamuukw*, the Court stated that "the general principles governing justification laid down in *Sparrow*, and embellished by *Gladstone*, also operate with respect to infringements of Aboriginal title." Accordingly, at paragraph 161, the Court stated that the test of justification for the infringement of aboriginal title must satisfy two parts: first, the infringement of the aboriginal right must be in furtherance of a legislative objective that is compelling and substantial; and, second, the infringement must be consistent with the special fiduciary relationship between the Crown and aboriginal peoples.

In *Badger*, the Court found that the criteria set out in *Sparrow* would apply equally to the infringement of treaty rights based on the fact that section 35 of the Constitution applies to both aboriginal and treaty rights. Based on the acceptance of such equal treatment, it follows that, even though the Court in *Delgamuukw* considered the "justification of aboriginal rights and title" and did not concern itself directly with the issue of treaty rights, the infringement of treaty rights will be susceptible to the same test for justification as set forth by the Supreme Court of Canada in *Delgamuukw*.

PART ONE: FURTHERANCE OF A LEGISLATIVE OBJECTIVE

In *Delgamuukw*, the Court noted that the compelling and substantial legislative objectives for which an infringement may be justified are those which are directed at either one of the purposes underlying the recognition and affirmation of aboriginal rights by section 35(1) of the Constitution. In identifying such purposes, Lamer C.J. referred to his decision in *Gladstone* in which he described such purposes as:

(a) the recognition of the prior occupation of North America by aboriginal peoples; or

(b) the reconciliation of aboriginal prior occupation with the assertion of sovereignty of the Crown.

The Court noted that, in the wake of *Gladstone*, the range of legislative objectives that can justify the infringement of aboriginal title is fairly broad. Furthermore, it noted that the majority of such objectives can be traced to the latter purpose of reconciliation, which entails the recognition that "distinctive aboriginal societies exist within, and are a part of, a broad social, political and economic community". The Court listed the following objectives as those which are consistent with the purpose of reconciliation and that, in principle, are capable of justifying infringement of aboriginal title: the development of agriculture, forestry, mining, and hydroelectric power; the general economic development of the interior of British Columbia; protection of the environment or endangered species; and, the building of infrastructure and the settlement of foreign populations to support those aims.

The latter purpose is generally the most relevant for purposes of justification for the following reasons, as set out at paragraph 73 of the *Gladstone* decision:

> Because ... distinctive aboriginal societies exist within, and are part of, a broader social, political and economic community, over which the Crown is sovereign, there are circumstances in which, in order to pursue objectives of compelling and substantial importance to that community as a whole (taking into account the fact that aboriginal societies are part of that community), some limitation of those rights will be justifiable. Aboriginal rights are a necessary part of the reconciliation of aboriginal societies with the broader political community of which they are part; limits placed on those rights are, where the objectives furthered by those limits are of sufficient importance to the broader community as a whole, equally a necessary part of that reconciliation.

Ultimately, however, it remains a question of fact to be determined on a case-by-case basis whether a particular government act or measure can be explained by reference to an objective consistent with this purpose.

PART TWO: WHETHER INFRINGEMENT IS CONSISTENT WITH THE CROWN'S FIDUCIARY DUTY

As mentioned in the foregoing, the second part of the test involves an assessment of whether the infringement is consistent with the special fiduciary relationship between the Crown and aboriginal peoples. The manner in which the fiduciary duty will be articulated in each case will depend on the nature of the aboriginal title infringed. However, in *Delgamuukw*, the Court commented that there are three aspects of aboriginal title relevant to a determination of the manner in which the fiduciary duty operates in the second stage of the test of justification. These factors are:

(a) the exclusive nature of aboriginal title;
(b) aboriginal title encompasses within it a right to a choose [to] what ends a piece of land can be put; and
(c) lands held pursuant to aboriginal title have an inescapable economic component.

The first factor is relevant to the degree of scrutiny applied to the infringing measure or action. The degree of scrutiny is a function of the nature of the aboriginal right at issue. The exclusive nature of aboriginal title will require the government to demonstrate that both the *process* by which the resource(s) in question are allocated (i.e., consultation, notice, inclusion of aboriginal concerns and interests from a broad perspective, etc.) and the *actual* allocation percentage of the resource(s) in question are justified and reflect the prior interests of the holders of the aboriginal title. In this regard, the following statement of Lamer C.J. is worth noting:

> By analogy with *Gladstone*, this might entail, for example, that governments accommodate the participation of aboriginal peoples in the development of resources in British Columbia, that conferral of fee simples for agriculture, and of leases and licenses for forestry and mining reflect the prior occupation of aboriginal title lands, that economic barriers to aboriginal uses of their lands (e.g., licensing fees) be somewhat reduced. This list is illustrative and not exhaustive.

The second factor influences the nature and scope of the duty of consultation imposed on the Crown. For the most part, the nature and scope of the duty of consultation will vary with the circumstances. As stated by the Court in *Delgamuukw*, there will be the occasional circumstance in which the breach is so minor that the Crown's fiduciary duty will require it to do no more than discuss with the aboriginal peoples involved the important decisions that will be taken with respect to the lands held pursuant to aboriginal title. However, the Court noted that even in such rare circumstances when the minimum acceptable standard is consultation, this consultation must be carried out in good faith, and with the intention of substantially addressing the issues and concerns of the aboriginal groups whose lands are at issue. In most cases, therefore, it appears that the Court's duty will carry with it a requirement to do more than mere consultation.

The third factor brings that the issue of compensation to the forefront in matters of justification. According to the Court, "aboriginal title has an inescapable economic element, particularly when one takes into account the modern uses to which lands held pursuant to aboriginal title can be put." The Court went on to say that in fact "compensation for breaches for fiduciary duty are a well-established part of the landscape of aboriginal rights." Accordingly, fair compensation will inevitably flow from an infringement of aboriginal title. The amount of compensation payable, however, will depend on the nature of the particular aboriginal title affected and the severity of the infringement.

In respect of the issue of fair compensation, La Forest, speaking for the minority of the Court, made the following comments in *Delgamuukw*:

> Indeed, the treatment of "aboriginal title" as a compensable right can be traced back [to] the Royal Proclamation, 1763. ... Clearly, the Proclamation contemplated that aboriginal peoples would be compensated for the surrender of their lands.... It must be emphasized, nonetheless, that fair compensation in the present context is not equated with the price of a fee simple. Rather, compensation must be viewed in terms of the right and in keeping with the honour of the Crown. Thus, generally speaking, compensation may be greater where the expropriation relates to a village area as opposed to a remotely visited area. I add that account must be taken of the interdependence of traditional uses to which the land was put.

TEST OF JUSTIFICATION WITH RESPECT TO TREATY RIGHTS

In *R. v. Badger*, [1996] 4 W.W.R. 457, the Supreme Court of Canada confirmed that the test for justification as advanced in *Sparrow* with respect to aboriginal rights applies equally to treaty rights. While the *Badger* decision benefits First Nations by requiring the government to consult and justify infringements of treaty rights, the decision is not entirely beneficial to Treaty No. 9 members. The application of the justification test as enunciated in *Sparrow* to treaty rights means that the government can justify infringement of treaty rights. The importation of the justification test into treaty rights will necessarily make treaty rights more vulnerable to attack. Prior to the *Badger* decision, treaty rights were viewed as far less malleable than aboriginal rights. As advanced by the Supreme Court of Canada in the cases of *R. v. Simon*, [1985] 2 S.C.R. 387 and *R. v. Sioui*, [1993] C.N.L.R. 127, prior to the *Badger* decision, the principles for interpretation of aboriginal treaties involve flexibility in determining the legal nature of the document and liberal construction with any ambiguities or uncertainties being resolved in favour of the aboriginal peoples. Such principles suggested that significant protection would be afforded to treaty rights over and above the constitutional protection embodied within section 35(1) of the Constitution.

In *R. v. Corbiere*, [1996] O.J. No. 3121, the Ontario Court of Justice followed the decision of the Supreme Court of Canada in *Badger* and held that following the passage of section 35(1) of the Constitution and the decision in *Sparrow*, the distinction between aboriginal and treaty rights in relation to infringement by either provincial or federal laws has lost much of its importance. It went on to cite the comment of Cory C.J. in *Badger* that "a statute or regulation which constitutes *prima facie* infringement must be justified."

Although the decision of the Supreme Court of Canada in *R. v. Delgamuukw*, [1997] S.C.J. No. 108, has elevated the scope and degree of consultation required by the Crown with aboriginal groups whose lands are affected by legislative measures, it is uncertain whether the decision in *Badger* will be revisited by the Court for purposes of restoring the protection previously granted to treaty rights or will be interpreted in a way so as to provide the inalienability of treaty rights which existed prior to *Badger*. In the writers' view, the test will be higher since there has already been a significant degree of "reconciliation" of prior occupation with the assertion of the crown sovereignty embodied in the treaty itself.

Given that the test for justification as laid out in *Sparrow* and *Delgamuukw* involved aboriginal rights and title, respectively, and did not involve treaty rights, it is not surprising that the foregoing must be revised in order to take into account the differences between aboriginal rights and treaty rights. As mentioned by Lamer C.J. in *Delgamuukw* and *Gladstone*, the purposes underlying the recognition and affirmation of aboriginal rights by section 35(1) of the Constitution include:

(a) the recognition of the prior occupation of North America by aboriginal peoples; and
(b) the reconciliation of aboriginal prior occupation with the assertion of sovereignty of the Crown.

With respect to aboriginal rights, most of the legislative objectives for which justification becomes an issue can be traced to the later purpose of reconciliation. Due to the fact that aboriginal societies exist within a much broader social, political and economic community, over which the Crown is sovereign, it is not unlikely that circumstances will arise in which, in order to pursue objectives of a compelling and substantive nature to that community as a whole, some limitations to the aboriginal rights in question will be justifiable. However, since the very nature of aboriginal treaties embodies a reconciliation of aboriginal prior occupation with the assertion of sovereignty, it appears that legislative objectives which may be justified within the context of aboriginal rights will not be so justified within the context of treaty rights. Treaty rights therefore appear to be more susceptible to a test of justification which traces legislative objectives to the purpose of recognition and, therefore, such legislative objectives may be prone to a higher degree of scrutiny in terms of justification.

In *R. v. Noel*, [1995] N.W.T.J. No. 92, the Northwest Territorial Court had to determine whether the accused, treaty member was lawfully charged with discharging a firearm in a restricted zone and discharging a firearm without regard for safety pursuant to section 2 of the Regulations made under the *Area Management Act* of the Northwest Territories. The Court held that there was indeed an existing aboriginal right to hunt in the area in question based on both history and Treaty No. 8. Accordingly, the effect of the zoning regulations constituted a *prima facie* interference with protected aboriginal rights under section 35(1) of the Constitution. Furthermore, the Court held that there was no evidence to suggest that the people whose rights were affected were adequately consulted prior to implementing the regulations. In determining whether the infringement of the treaty right to hunt was in furtherance of a valid legislative objective, the Court made the following comments at paragraph 33:

> The objective is not to undermine legislative ability and responsibility, but to guarantee that such regulation treats aboriginal peoples in a manner that ensures their rights are taken seriously. The constitutional recognition and affirmation of aboriginal rights may give rise to conflicts with the interests of others, but the constitutional aboriginal right must receive priority to ensure the protection of the rights is taken seriously.

In the recent decision of the Saskatchewan Provincial Court in *R. v. Couillonneur*, [1997] 1 C.N.L.R. 130, the Court determined whether an [accused treaty] member was lawfully charged with fishing with a gill net having a smaller mesh size than that allowed by Saskatchewan *Fishery Regulations* made pursuant to the *Fisheries Act*, R.S.C. 1985, c. F-14. In deciding whether the *prima facie* infringement by the Saskatchewan government of the accused's treaty right to fish was justified in the context of this case, the Court reviewed the decisions of *Sparrow* and *Badger*. From a reading of these cases, the Court concluded that in determining whether a treaty right is justified, the Court must consider a sequence of questions. These questions are as follows:

(a) Is there a valid legislative objective to the regulation?
(b) Does the regulation honour the special trust relationship between aboriginal peoples and the government?
(c) Does the law infringe the treaty right as minimally as possible?

(d) Were the aboriginal people who are affected by the regulation consulted by the government prior to the enactment?

Based on the foregoing, it appears that while aboriginal rights and treaty rights may be subject to similar infringement, the test for justification to such infringement may be slightly higher for treaty rights where there has in fact been prior reconciliation.

CONSULTATION — A COMMON LAW AND CONSTITUTIONAL DUTY

The duty to consult aboriginal peoples in respect of issues that affect their aboriginal title and treaty rights to land arises both at common law and by constitutional enactment. As enshrined in section 35 of the Constitution, the Crown always bears a common law duty to consult with aboriginal peoples where aboriginal and treaty rights issues arise. The common law duty of the Crown to consult with aboriginal peoples where aboriginal and treaty rights issues arise stems from its special fiduciary relationship with aboriginal peoples on which the honour of the Crown rests: *R. v. Guerin*, [1984] 2 S.C.R. 335; *Sparrow*. In respect of certain resources, such as forestry for example, the Crown may also bear a statutory duty to consult aboriginal peoples whose lands are at issue (*TransCanada Pipelines Ltd. v. Beardmore* (Township), [1997] O.J. No. 5316).

In *Noel*, the Northwest Territories Territorial Court, in its analysis of whether the infringement by the Crown of the [accused treaty] member's aboriginal right to hunt was justifiable, considered whether the aboriginal people in question were properly consulted in respect of the proposed legislative measure. The Court held that the letter from the Deputy Minister of Municipal and Community Affairs of the Northwest Territories advising what the government was proposing in respect of no-shooting zones and the one meeting that followed the letter which explained the proposed regulation and at which the government was made aware of the objections of the aboriginal peoples to be affected, did not amount to meaningful consultation. In respect of the failure to adequately consult the aboriginal group whose treaty right to hunt was affected, the Court made the following statement at paragraph 35:

> The priority that must be given to the constitutionally protected aboriginal right in question does not seem to have been recognized on the part of the government. Consultation must require the government to carry out meaningful and reasonable discussions with the representatives of aboriginal people involved. The fact that the time frame for action was short does not justify the government to push forward with the proposed regulation without proper consultation. Otherwise, the recognition and affirmation of the aboriginal rights in section 35(1) of the *Constitution Act, 1982* would become another hollow promise to aboriginal people. Since the judgment in *R. v. Sparrow* in 1990, no process has been established to appropriately deal with the requirement of consultations. Such a process would set a standard to be met as to what is required for proper consultation and would provide for the necessary sensitivity to and respect for the rights of aboriginal peoples. Again, I am not satisfied that the onus on the government to show justification has been met on the consultation issue.
>
> ... This does not mean that the government cannot implement regulations which infringe upon aboriginal rights, however, the proper steps and standards set out above must be met. I do not intend to infer that aboriginal people's rights cannot be infringed for a

valid objective after the necessary steps have been taken and the standards met that ensures sensitivity to and respect for the rights of aboriginal people. As well, aboriginal people must recognize that their protected rights can be infringed as Canadian society develops and the interest of everyone is considered. In the circumstances of this case, if the government had shown the infringement was as little as necessary to reach the desired result and proper consultation had occurred, then the regulation may well be proper and enforceable.

It appears that the concern raised in *Noel* over the lack of a standard for proper consultation as mentioned in the above passage has been met by the Supreme Court of Canada in *Delgamuukw*. In fact, the Supreme Court of Canada's decision in *Delgamuukw* represents a significant departure from the conventional approach to Crown consultation with aboriginal peoples. As a result of *Delgamuukw*, the Crown is now required to consult at a minimum, and in many cases the approval and consent of aboriginal groups will be required. Pre-*Delgamuukw* precedents therefore no longer provide us with the appropriate standard for consultation and, thus, should no longer be used in this context. *Delgamuukw* reinforces the notion that consultation is a key component to justifying infringement. The level of consultation that is now required by virtue of *Delgamuukw* includes the following three elements:

(a) consultation is a minimum acceptable standard, only in rare circumstances;
(b) consultation must be in good faith; and
(c) consultation must be done with the intention of substantially addressing the concerns of aboriginal peoples whose lands are at issue.

In the recent case of *Cheslatta Carrier Nation v. British Columbia (Environment Assessment Act, Project Assessment Director)*, [1998] B.C.J. No. 178 (Vancouver Registry No. A954336), the British Columbia Supreme Court, per Williams C.J.S.C., was faced with the issue of determining whether the Crown had met its duty, at common law and by statute, to consult with the First Nations petitioners in respect of decisions made by the Respondent Ministers regarding a mining project pursuant to the *Environment Assessment Act*, S.B.C. 1994 (now R.S.B.C. 1996, c. 119). The First Nations petitioners challenged the approval process of the mining project in question on the basis that the Respondent Ministers had not adequately consulted with the First Nations in respect of the impacts of the mining project on wildlife and the consequent potential adverse effect on First Nations' aboriginal [title]. Williams C.J.S.C. followed the decision of the Supreme Court of Canada in *Delgamuukw* and held that the Respondent Ministers had both a common law duty and a statutory duty to consult with the First Nations petitioners. In determining whether or not a duty to consult has been discharged, Williams C.J.S.C. noted that it "will depend on the facts and circumstances of each particular case." Moreover, he stated that it is equally clear that consultation means "meaningful" consultation.

With respect to the issue of "meaningful" consultation, Williams C.J.S.C. made reference to the case of *R. v. Sampson* (1995), 16 B.C.L.R. (3d) 226 at 251 (C.A.), in which the British Columbia Court of Appeal stated:

> In our respectful view the requirement of consultation, as set out in Sparrow, is not fulfilled by the DFO merely waiting for a Band to raise the question of its Indian food fish requirements discussing those requirements, and attempting to fulfill those requirements.

> Consultation embraces more than the foregoing. It [includes] being informed of the [conservation] measures being implemented.

Williams C.J.S.C. also made reference to the decision of the Yukon Territories Trial Court in *R. v. Noel*, [1995] 4 C.N.L.R. 78 (Y.T.T.C), where the following comments were made in respect of the issue of "meaningful" consultation:

> A further issue is with regard to whether the Aboriginal people in question had been consulted with respect to the measure to be implemented.... The one meeting that followed was to explain the proposed regulation and the government was made aware of the objections of the representatives of the aboriginal people to be affected. Other alternatives were suggested which the government representatives either ignored or did not consider seriously. In my view this does not amount to *meaningful* consultation or a deliberation of people on a project.... *Consultation must require the government to carry out meaningful and reasonable discussions with the representatives of Aboriginal people involved*. The fact that the time frame for action was short does not justify the government to push forward with the proposed regulation without proper consultation. Otherwise, the recognition and affirmation of Aboriginal rights in s.35(1) of the *Constitution Act, 1982* would become another hollow promise to Aboriginal people. [emphasis added]

Williams C.J.S.C. referred to the decision of the British Columbia Court of Appeal in *R. v. Jack* (1995), 16 B.C.L.R. (3d) 201 at 222–223, in which the duty of the Crown to pursue "meaningful" consultation was also discussed, as set out in the following:

> We consider that there was a duty on the DFO to ensure that the Indian Band was provided with full information on the conservation measures and their effect on the Indians and other user groups. The DFO had a duty to fully inform itself of the fishing practices of the aboriginal group and their views of the conservation measures.

Finally, Williams C.J.S.C. cited the decision of the British Columbia Supreme Court in *Halfway River First Nation v. British Columbia (Ministry of Forests)*, [1997] B.C.J. No. 1494, Vancouver No. A963993, in which the Court held that the British Columbia Ministry of Forests had a duty to consult with the Halfway River First Nation Prior to approving a forest company's cutting permit application. The Court held that the Ministry's duty to consult arose both as a requirement of procedural fairness and out of the fiduciary relationship of the Crown to aboriginal peoples. Accordingly, due to the failure of the Ministry to make all reasonable efforts to consult with the Halfway River First Nation prior to approving the cutting permit, the Court quashed the approval decision to issue a forestry permit and expressed its hope that no further decision would be made without including the Halfway River First Nation. In determining whether the Crown, on behalf of the Ministry of Forests, had discharged its fiduciary obligation to consult with the First Nations affected by the approval of the forestry permit in question in this case, the Court, per Dorgan J., made the following remarks:

> Based on the *Jack*, *Noel* and *Delgamuukw* cases, the *Crown has an obligation to undertake reasonable consultation with a First Nation which may be affected by its decision*. In order for the Crown to consult reasonably, it must fully inform itself of the practices and of the views of the Nation affected. In so doing, it must ensure that the group affected is provided with full information with respect to the proposed legislation or decision and its potential impact on aboriginal rights. [emphasis added]

In *Cheslatta*, Williams C.J.S.C. concluded that the Crown's duty to consult aboriginal peoples is met where there is "adequate" and "meaningful" consultation. Given that the Respondent Ministers had failed to adequately consult the First Nations Petitioners in respect of the wildlife issue in question, the Respondents were in breach of their duty to consult. Furthermore, it was held that the First Nations affected by the proposed project were entitled to data sufficient to make a reasonable assessment of the project's impact on their people, their territories, and the exercise of their rights in those territories. In discussing the extent to which the consultation process must provide First Nations with information necessary to determine the full impact of a proposed project on their aboriginal title, Williams C.J.S.C. reckoned that the demands of the First Nations must not be unreasonable. Moreover, he stated that the affected First Nations groups must not complain if they refuse to be consulted in an effective forum created in good faith for such consultation.

The end result in *Cheslatta* was that the Respondent Ministers were ordered to produce the various mapping information that was necessary for a review of the proposed project by the First Nations affected by it. In addition, the Respondent Ministers were ordered to establish a new committee through which a "meaningful" consultation process in reference to the wildlife issues could be completed in a timely and effective manner. Such a result was inevitable given the recent decision of the Supreme Court of Canada in *Delgamuukw* in which consultation was deemed to be a minimum acceptable standard only in rare cases and one that must be performed in good faith and with the intention of substantially addressing the concerns of aboriginal peoples whose lands are at issue.

In *TransCanada Pipelines Ltd. v. Beardmore* (Township), the Ontario Court of Justice was faced with three applications for judicial review brought by NAN, Long Lac 58 First Nation, the Nishnawbe-Aski Nation and the Ginoogaming First Nation ("GFN"). The aboriginal parties in this case asserted constitutional protection of their treaty and aboriginal rights in respect of proposed by-laws to annex previously unincorporated or unorganized territory into the municipality of Greenstone. The aboriginal parties argued that such annexation would affect their rights and title to the land. Moreover, they argued that pursuant to section 25.3(4) of the *Municipal Act* (Ontario), the provincial Crown had a statutory duty to consult with "such other bodies and persons as the Commission considers appropriate." The Court held that the provincial Crown was under a statutory obligation to conduct reasonable investigations and research about the long-standing land claims of the aboriginal peoples on the impacted area and the treaty rights of the affected parties. After such reasonable investigations, the Court held that the Crown was then under a further obligation to properly, adequately and meaningfully consult with the aboriginal peoples affected by the proposed by-laws. The Court concluded that basis for the duty to consult with the aboriginal groups stemmed from the fact that these groups had *bona fide*, unresolved land claims and were the people that would have been most impacted by the annexation. While the Court did not embark upon a section 35(1) analysis, its decision is noteworthy because of the extent to which the Court elevated the obligation on the Crown to conduct meaningful consultation with "other bodies and persons", particularly where such bodies constitute aboriginal groups with genuine aboriginal and treaty rights in affected areas.

JUSTIFICATION OF INFRINGEMENT BY REGULATORY BODIES

While it is clear that the Crown holds both a fiduciary duty and a constitutionally enshrined common law duty to consult with aboriginal peoples whose lands are affected by legislative measures, it is uncertain the extent to which regulatory bodies will be affected by the heightened duty to consult as provided for in the recent decision of the Supreme Court of Canada in *Delgamuukw*.

Whether a regulatory tribunal will be held to the same fiduciary duty to consult aboriginal peoples as the Crown appears to be a function of the duty performed by the regulatory body. If a regulatory tribunal is quasi-judicial and capable of being viewed as an independent decision-making body operating at arm's length from government, it is likely that the tribunal will not be held to the same fiduciary duty to consult aboriginal peoples. In the case of *Quebec (Attorney General) v. Canada (National Energy Board)* (1994), 112 D.L.R. (4th) 129, the Supreme Court of Canada held the National Energy Board (the "NEB") to be an independent decision-making body operating at arm's length from government. The NEB, therefore, was not [to] be held to the same requirements as the Crown. Accordingly, where a quasi-judicial tribunal is operating at arm's length from government, it would be contrary to the [...] separations of power to hold the tribunal to the same fiduciary duty as the Crown.

If a regulatory tribunal performs administrative or investigative functions, as opposed to adjudicative functions, it is likely that the tribunal will be held to the same fiduciary duty to consult aboriginal peoples as the Crown. In the case of *Halfway River First Nation v. British Columbia (Ministry of Forests)* [1997], 4 C.N.L.R. 45, the British Columbia Supreme Court found the District Manager of the Ministry of Forests, a representative of the Crown, responsible for meeting the Crown's fiduciary duty to consult with the aboriginal peoples involved. The function of the District Manager is purely an administrative [one] in that it acts as a decision-maker on behalf of the Crown with respect to the granting of cutting permits. In no way can the District Manager be regarded as an independent decision-making tribunal operating at arm's length with the Crown. Accordingly, where a regulatory body performs administrative or investigative [functions] and cannot be seen as operating independently of the Crown, the tribunal will be held to [the] same fiduciary duty to consult aboriginal peoples as the Crown.

One issue that arises out of the extension of the Crown's fiduciary duty to consult aboriginal peoples to administrative and investigative regulatory bodies is whether such bodies are responsible for ensuring that the Crown's obligations have been fulfilled before the tribunal may proceed with the legislative measures in question. At this point in time, it appears that unless the governing legislation of the regulatory tribunal provides for the jurisdiction to consider and/or review the duty to consult imposed on the Crown, the regulatory tribunal will have no authority to ensure that the Crown meet its fiduciary obligations to the aboriginal peoples. (Wallace, Brian: *Delgamuukw* and Regulatory Bodies: The Effect of the Doctrine of Aboriginal Title Upon Regulatory Administrative Practice "A First Look", 1998.)

THE ONTARIO FORESTRY CONTEXT

The above principles laid down by Courts should apply in the forestry context. The main difference is two-fold. First, while government actions in the fisheries context often involve conservation objectives, government action in the forestry context is predominantly development/exploitation oriented. That is to say, while conservation measures are generally preservative, logging measures are obviously destructive. Second, problems (re: "excepting ... lands ... for ... lumbering") referred to in many of the treaties rights may make it more difficult to determine the application of *Sparrow* and now *Badger*. The court in *Halfway River* did not consider this a significant problem however.

The destructive nature of logging could be significant with respect to the justification stage in the *Sparrow* decision. As outlined in the above, once a prima facie infringement of aboriginal or treaty rights is established, the government must seek to justify such infringement by first establishing a valid legislative objective. Conservation is recognized by the Supreme Court of Canada in *Sparrow* as a valid legislative objective. Courts have not considered whether the economic benefits of logging related activities will fulfill the requirement of a valid legislative objective. What is certain from *Sparrow* is that mere "public interest" is so vague as to be unhelpful and therefore not a valid justification for infringement. However, *Gladstone* opened the door to public interests of significance as possible reasons for limiting aboriginal, and perhaps treaty rights. This is clarified by *Delgamuukw* which identified the following "valid legislative objectives":

(a) the development of agricultural, forestry, mining, and hydroelectric power;
(b) the general economic development of a province;
(c) the protection of the environment or endangered species;
(d) the building of infrastructure; and
(e) the settlement of foreign populations to support these aims.

A requirement for sustainability of the forestry resource would likely be a minimum requirement in forestry legislation particularly since it has significant correlation to the maintained exercise of hunting, fishing and trapping rights. This requires a thorough review of "sustainability" from the aboriginal perspective as a matter of fact and under the new *Crown Forest Sustainability Act* which, pursuant to s. 6, provides that this Act "does not abrogate, derogate from or add to any aboriginal or treaty right that is recognized and affirmed by section 35 of the *Constitution Act, 1982*". This review would relate to AAC levels for a particular area and **the legal importance of treaty rights** in conflict with forestry activities. (This should be the focus as opposed to trapping as a mere recreation, hobby, business or other pursuit.) In addition, in circumstances where forestry activity permits or results in a loss of hunting habitat for wildlife or loss or damage of some other aboriginal right which is integral to an Aboriginal Group's culture and identity, no logging or forestry service roads could, on their face, appear justifiable.

The Supreme Court of Canada, in *Gladstone*, maintained the *notion* of the *priority of the right* in applying the *Sparrow* test. In the case of treaty rights in conflict with forestry, the notion of the priority of the treaty rights [for] a trapping economy should be maintained in attempting to reconcile forest industry objectives with treaty rights. Treaties with "solemn promises" should not [...] be affected by the various winds of compelling public interests.

In addition, this opens the door to First Nations scrutinizing the government process by which it allocates the forestry resource given the priority of the treaty rights. This should create a procedural requirement for the Ontario Ministry of Natural Resources (the "MNR"). The MNR also has a substantive requirement to allocate forest resources in such a way as to reflect the prior interest of the First Nations in their traditional land based economies. This may not be an exclusive right to the resource but must give priority to the aboriginal (or treaty) right. This requires the MNR not to take the least impairment action available to it, but rather to take into account the priority and significance of the treaty right. Some specific questions for the MNR in this analysis are as follows:

1. Have all those inquiries relating to consultation and compensation set in *Sparrow* and *Delgamuukw* been made?
2. Has the MNR accommodated the exercise of the treaty rights land based economies?
3. Does the regulatory scheme reflect the priority of the holders of treaty rights?

If this new test is applied to treaty rights and on a case by case basis, "full information" and consultation will be key ingredients to the analysis.

Consultation is not just a question of the interpretation and application of the forest legislation, and the new Forest Management Planning Manual, but should apply to all legislation and regulation pertaining to or affecting any watershed area within the traditional territory and land use area of the First Nations. This would, for example, include consultation prior to issuing or renewing permits or licenses under water licensing or environmental legislation, Crown land leases, etc. Any matter that combines government discretion in these area should include aboriginal and treaty rights as a factor in the decision making process. If not, then this decision might be subject to judicial review or even delayed upon injunctive relief until proper consultation can be assured.

It is the opinion of the writer that with the inception of the Crown *Forest Substainability Act*, and the recent class environmental assessment containing "Condition 77", there is a new context for operating timber harvesting arrangements in Ontario. Together with the new body of law regarding the potential infringement on the aboriginal and treaty rights by forest management practices, the Province of Ontario should be required to be actively involved in a broad analysis of all existing legislation and regulation impacting on aboriginal or treaty rights from a watershed context and establishing a thorough and holistic policy regarding the impacts on aboriginal and treaty rights. This should not, in the writer's opinion, be done on a piecemeal and case-by-case basis, particularly where the aboriginal peoples affected have not been provided with sufficient notice or resources to respond on the consultation issues or to analyze their specific rights over their territories. Unfortunately, neither the current Native Consultation Guidelines nor Condition 77 of the Class Environmental Assessment address the Crown's obligation in a proper and equitable manner and as such, the honour of the Crown, in the context of the sustained and high level of harvesting is subject to disrepute.

THE BRITISH COLUMBIA MINISTRY OF FORESTS POLICY

The Province of British Columbia's Ministry of Forests recently developed a policy on the protection of aboriginal rights. The policy outlines the Ministry's process of identifying aboriginal rights, determining whether these rights have been or may be infringed, and accommodating these rights with forest management activity. The policy provides for consultation with First Nations to obtain their participation in operational planning and approval of forest development plans.

The policy applies to Ministry of Forests operational planning and approval processes. The application of this policy may be superseded by a Treaty or by court decisions concerning aboriginal rights. It is the stated policy of the Ministry of Forests to prevent or justify the infringement of rights by proposed forest management activities while maintaining a timely approval process.

On June 25, 1993, the British Columbia Court of Appeal ruled that aboriginal rights were not extinguished. Section 35 of the *Constitution Act* (1982), protects these rights. The effect of this protection is that aboriginal rights must not be unjustifiably infringed upon by the resource development activities of the Crown, or its licensees. As a result, all resource management decisions must now be examined to determine whether they will infringe on aboriginal rights.

All initial forest management activities which directly affect the land (i.e., road building, allocations of Crown timber, bridge building, etc.) will be referred to First Nations. Where aboriginal rights have been assessed, follow-up management activities (i.e., such as brushing and weeding, spacing, pruning, etc.) need not be referred on a site-specific basis, however it is expected that 5 year silviculture plans would be discussed with First Nations.

The policy recognizes that [the First Nations'] view of aboriginal rights often [differs] from that of the provincial government, and that many First Nations view aboriginal rights as rights which have existed since time immemorial that will continue irrespective of court decisions. The policy explains that the First Nations' view of aboriginal rights may include the land itself, as well as the use, ownership, jurisdiction, and sovereignty over their traditional territory.

The policy cites *R. v. Gladstone* for the principal that an aboriginal group may now be able to establish an aboriginal right to harvest and trade in a resource on a commercial basis, if it can show that they traded in that resource, on a scale best characterized as commercial, as an integral part of their distinctive culture prior to European contact.

The text of the policy is attached hereto as Appendix "A". [Not included in this reproduction.]

A sample response letter to government is attached hereto as Appendix "B". [Not included in this reproduction.]

THE IDEAL CONSULTATION PROCESS

In view of the above authorities, any meaningful consultation should involve the following stages:

1. At the first stage, the government (through any ministry) would identify a decision or action which would have some [effect] on Crown Lands or upon private lands relating to aboriginal or treaty rights. Upon identification, the affected First Nation would be notified and be given full information as to the nature and extent of the proposed activity over those lands.
2. The First Nation would respond to the government stating that they are very concerned about this pending activity or decision and require sufficient time and financial resources (both technical and financial) to review the pending decision/activity. A budget could be drawn up and the necessary resources would be provided to the First Nation.
3. The First Nation would analyze all the technical information and then determine the area of traditional lands potentially affected.
4. Over *this* area of traditional lands, the First Nation would carry out and compile an aboriginal or treaty rights inventory. First, they would seek legal advice over the scope of "rights" now recognized by the Courts. Second, they would train and employ community members to assist in compiling the "inventory" (interviewing elders and chiefs, gathering written data, carrying out archeological surveys and assessments, etc.). These would all be funded by the Crown since the First Nation would be replying to the Crown's legal obligation to consult.
5. The First Nation would then carry out analysis of the impact of the proposed activity on those aboriginal or treaty rights. Where this requires financial or technical assistance, the Crown would assist.
6. The First Nation and the Crown would enter into discussions to determine the possibilities to mitigate (or justify) any impact by altering activities, by entering into an interim [measure] or co-management agreement or by a business arrangement with the proponent business involved. In this stage, the Crown would endeavour to seek the consent of the First Nation ensuring the honour of [the] Crown in its dealing with the First Nations.
7. Where infringement of aboriginal or treaty rights is present, and it is unavoidable and accommodation cannot be agreed upon, the Crown would seek to justify the proposed decision/activity.

A major problem faced by Aboriginal Peoples or First Nations is the lack of readily available information and resources to enter into a meaningful negotiation and consultation process. Usually the government would specify a time limit for consultation. The question is who has the burden to obtain to provide the necessary information and spend the resources to analyze the relevant information. The *Jack* decision could be seen as putting such onus on the government as it requires the Ministry to "fully inform itself" of the practice and views of Aboriginal Peoples.

AGREEMENT TO CONSULT

Because of the uncertainties surrounding the consultation issue, it may be advisable for the First Nation to negotiate an agreement with the Department of Indian Affairs regarding the extent of the consultation. A further advantage of an agreement is that it clarifies obligations as to consultation and allows the First Nation to raise concerns other than relating to aboriginal and treaty rights, as illustrated by the following decision.

In *Wilps Gutginuxs v. British Columbia (District Manager)*, the Wilps Gutginuxs, a house of the Gitxsan people, reached a tripartheid agreement with the MOF and the logging company. It provided for a process of consultation of 10 days. The Ministry agreed to engage a terrain specialist, an archaeologist and a forest ecosystem specialist. The agreement allowed the Band to raise all of its concerns, which is not limited to those relating to aboriginal rights. At the conclusion of the 10 day period, the action by Wilps Gutginux to set aside the cutting permit issued was before the Court. The Court found that the District Manager failed to consider concerns raised by the Wilps Gutginux that [were] not related to aboriginal rights. The Court found this to be contrary to the agreement and order further consultation to be conducted. After further consultation, the District Manager modified the terms of the Cutting Permit to create a wider wildlife corridor and to provide greater stream protection.

The plaintiffs' action to set aside the Cutting Permit was unsuccessful because the Court found full and fair consideration was given to the aboriginal rights. This latter part of the decision [seems] to be incorrect as the fact of consultation itself should be sufficient to save the government action from being attacked for violating s.35(1). Consultation is only one of the factors in determining whether a prima facie infringement may be justified.

This decision does show, however, how Aboriginal Groups may use an agreement to consult to their advantage. It also shows that such agreement will be enforced in courts.

STUMPAGE REDUCTION TO FIRST NATIONS

Given the recent *Delgamuukw* decision of the Supreme Court of Canada, it is clear that most timber harvesting will infringe aboriginal title. The question becomes whether the infringement is justifiable. The onus is upon the Crown to justify the infringement.

In order for an infringement to be justified, the Crown must satisfy two tests. First, the infringement must accord with a "valid legislative objective". In *Delgamuukw*, the Supreme Court of Canada cited that "forestry" and "the general economic development of the interior of British Columbia" could constitute a valid legislative objective. In the particular situation, we would assume that the Crown would not have difficulty in satisfying this test.

The second test involves the general fiduciary obligation the Crown owes to aboriginal people. The manner in which the fiduciary duty operates is really a function of the nature of the particular aboriginal title. The three main aspects of aboriginal title relevant here are as follows:

(a)   aboriginal title is *exclusive* as to use and occupation of land;
(b)   aboriginal title encompasses the *right to choose the use* for that land; and
(c)   aboriginal title has an inescapable, economic component.

The economic value of aboriginal title includes the value of the land and also the resources upon that land in the shape of forestry and timber resources.

This, of course, would include current forest licence holders in traditional aboriginal lands.

The exclusive nature of aboriginal title will require the Ministry of Forests to demonstrate that both the *process* by which the timber and forestry resources are allocated (i.e. consultation, notice, inclusion of aboriginal concerns and interests from a broad perspective) and the *actual allocation* percentage of the resource are justified. In this regard, Chief Justice Lamer stated:

> By analogy with *Gladstone*, this might entail, for example, that governments accommodate the participation of aboriginal peoples in the development of resources in British Columbia, that conferral of fee simples for agriculture, and of **leases and licenses for forestry** and mining reflect the prior occupation of aboriginal title lands, that economic barriers to aboriginal uses of their lands (eg.: licensing fees) be somewhat reduced. This list is illustrative and not exhaustive. [**emphasis added**]

This statement has two key components. First, the Court is strongly suggesting to the Province of B.C. that when the Ministry of Forest awards forest licenses, the participation of First Nations are accommodated. Such accommodation could be carried out by forcing current licensees to conduct business with aboriginal peoples in a manner which provides aboriginal peoples economic development opportunities and otherwise secures their participation in the development of forestry resources.

Second, as Lamer, C.J. suggests, this accommodation will result in the *"conferral of licenses for forestry"*. Where a timber supply area within the traditional territory of an aboriginal group is already close to or at maximum annual allowable cut levels, this may result in the reduction of AAC levels to accommodate First Nations [licences] or requirements of existing licence holders to conduct business of one sort or another with aboriginal groups. Where there is the possibility for new timber tenures to be made available to aboriginal groups, new licences might well be provided to aboriginal businesses, even by way of direct award. The other alternative is that new licencees be awarded on the basis that [licencees] create a joint venture relationship with aboriginal groups or that they have already made other prior business arrangements with aboriginal groups. Perhaps it is too great an assumption that the Province of British Columbia will assume the full measure of [a] First Nation's aboriginal title and change its timber tenure allocation in the above manner. This creates great doubt about the likely breaches of forestry statutes and administrative law that might result from conferral of licenses to First Nations and reduction in stumpage to those First Nation licensees.

CRITICAL ABORIGINAL FORESTRY ISSUES

There still remain a great many questions for the First Nations, Government and Forestry Companies to determine in this context. Some of the critical issues affecting aboriginal and treaty rights are as follows:

1. What constitutes meaningful consultation as per the *Delgamuukw, Sparrow* and *Badger* decisions in the forest industry in Northern Ontario? What time, money, expertise and other resources are necessary to comply with any fiduciary duty of the Crown relating to resource development over traditional territories? In view of Treaty 9 provisions, is the Crown's continued manage-

ment of the forests justification for infringement of constitutionally protected treaty and aboriginal rights?
2. What strategies are available to First Nations wishing to ensure appropriate consultation? Are there any lobbying, administrative or legal remedies available to slow the process of development down until First Nations concerns are addressed? For example, where there exists discretion on the part of government to demand from licensees various hearings, reports, studies or assessments relating to treaty or aboriginal rights, does a First Nation demand for such analysis prior to a decision trigger a positive exercise of that discretion?
3. Are there business solutions to these problems? Is it possible to be involved in business in the forest sector and still address integrity issues over traditional territories?
4. Recent court decisions have considered consultation and the involvement of First Nations in the public review process as a factor in injunctive relief decisions where conflicts have arisen between government and [the] forest industry on one side and First Nations on the other. There seems to be a burden (or onus) placed upon First Nations to specify the specific aboriginal or treaty rights affected by various resource developments. Is a "traditional use or native values mapping study" sufficient for this purpose?

While these are not land claims per se, there [appear] to be small but consistent battles over traditional territories going on every day as government, industry and First Nations struggle with the interpretation and application of *Delgamuukw, Badger* and *Sparrow* in the forestry context. Current policy and legislation does not appear to be doing the job. This requires First Nations to keep up to date on all forest development in their territories, maintain a high level of consultation, be fully aware of their specific aboriginal and treaty rights so far recognized by the courts, and seek business and political solutions while treaty land entitlement and self government negotiations continue.

NOTES

1. *Delgamuukw v. British Columbia* (1997), 153 D.L.R. (4th) 193.
2. Brian Slattery, "The Definition and Proof of Aboriginal Title," a paper presented at the conference. *The Supreme Court of Canada Decision in Delgamuukw*, Feb. 12–13, 1998, at p. 1.
3. *Ibid.*, at p. 265.
4. *Delgamuukw v. British Columbia* (1997), 153 D.L.R. (4th) 193.

CHAPTER 5

Hunting/Trapping/Country Food

(a) First Nations Claim Equal Rights to Manage National Parks[†]

Dennis White Bird

At the outset of my presentation, I wish to make it clear that the Assembly of First Nations does not find serious fault with the general aims and objectives of Bill C-27. For our part, the protection and conservation of environmental integrity of lands, water, plants and wildlife is an exceptionally worthy purpose and it is appropriate and commendable for the Government of Canada to be taking these particular steps that we are now considering.

Bill C-27 seeks to ensure that ecological integrity is paramount in the federal parks agenda and as part of the necessary measures for carrying out this important task, it will include increased penalties for wildlife poaching and illegal trafficking in protected wildlife, rare plants and fossils. In our view, these are all well intentioned, deserving and non-contentious objectives.

This is not to suggest, however, that we have no concerns whatsoever to bring forward. We have a number of issues with regard to the consultation process behind the Bill and as to how the First Nations might fit into [a] new Canadian national parks regime.

[†] From *Canadian Speeches*, 14(4) (September/October 2000): 24–27. Notes omitted. Reproduced with permission of the author.

Firstly, one issue that the Assembly of First Nations wishes to bring to your attention has to do more with the role of the First Nations in how the pertinent decision-making to attain these objectives are made and how these measures shall be eventually carried out. As you are all aware, the First Nations hold certain rights with respect to much of the lands under consideration within the discussion of Bill C-27. We also have certain expectations of the Government of Canada as to the future of national parks management and the role of the First Nations in the management process that we want to bring to your attention today.

In terms of the policy development and decision-making process, we seek to ensure that First Nations will be appropriately consulted and allowed to participate. Our concerns as to the role of First Nations are focused upon the need for accommodation of our legal, moral and constitutional rights and the relevance of the proposed legislative framework for the establishment and implementation of meaningful shared management arrangements between the Government of Canada and the First Nations.

While I do not wish to dwell in the past, there is a purpose in calling attention to the fact that it was not too many years ago, in 1969, that the Government of Canada was in a position to propose that the First Nations should have no claim to Aboriginal rights. At that same time, Canada was seriously considering whether or not the ancient treaties that it signed with our nations were indeed still compelling and deserving of honour within a modern context. Here, of course, I am referring to that highly charged social, legal and political debate that surrounded the 1969 "White Paper" which was put forth as a solution to the problems circumscribing the "Indian problem."

We, the First Nations of Canada, saw that proposed solution as a distinct and exorbitant threat to our existence as nations and as peoples. It represented a dire threat to our culture, our rights and our heritage. It also represented a call for an increased awareness in relation to the need for better understanding and disclosing the true history of Canada's formative years and a call for extra vigilance about matters such as our Aboriginal rights, our treaties and our cultural and political identities.

Fortunately, in 1973, with the prudent assistance of the Supreme Court of Canada in Calder[1], we were able to put those concerns and conceptual misgivings to rest. Yet, we are still nonetheless left with an enduring and stubborn legacy from those foreboding days and the outdated and misinformed philosophies that fostered them.

In Calder, the majority decision held that the Nisga'a possessed Aboriginal rights to their traditional territories and that these rights had survived European settlement. This decision was later followed by Guerin v. The Queen[2] wherein the Supreme Court found that Aboriginal rights that have not been extinguished are recognized by the common law and are enforceable by the courts. It was also held that the effect of federal jurisdiction over Indian lands subject to an existing Aboriginal title gave rise to a fiduciary duty on the Crown.

In Sparrow,[3] the Supreme Court of Canada held that section 35 of the Constitution Act, 1982 recognized and affirmed the "existing" Aboriginal fights for a member of the Musqueam Indian Band to carry out salmon fishing in the Fraser River "where his ancestors had fished from time immemorial." The Court also found that this constitutional recognition and affirmation provided sufficient protection for carrying out those activities despite federal legislation which would have otherwise proscribed those fights and activities.

Section 35(1) of the Constitution Act, 1982 relates directly to the rights of the Aboriginal peoples of Canada. It states that "The existing Aboriginal and treaty rights of the Aboriginal peoples of Canada are hereby recognized and affirmed."

The Sparrow decision also set a standard for justification that any legislation that impaired an Aboriginal right would have to meet in order to be valid as against the Aboriginal right. Aboriginal and treaty rights may be regulated by federal law only if those laws can be shown to be meet the applicable criteria under the Sparrow Test.

In the past, it had been held that Aboriginal and Treaty rights have been vulnerable to unilateral regulation and extinguishment by the federal government. This vulnerability to [unilateral] extinguishment has now been nullified as these rights are now entrenched in s. 35 of the Constitution Act, 1982.

Of course, the regulation of Aboriginal and Treaty rights is still possible but subject to the test set out in Sparrow. Recently, in Badger[4] and again in Marshall[5], the Supreme Court of Canada has affirmed that s. 35 Aboriginal and Treaty rights are indeed subject to federal regulatory measures. However, such regulation must be shown by the Crown to be justified as per the Sparrow test on the basis of conservation or for some other grounds of compelling public importance. Of course, Sparrow also stands for the principle that the Crown must carry out meaningful consultations with the First Nations in the carrying out of activities and the development of policies that will impact upon our rights and gain our consent to such developments.

In the 1998 [Sundown][6] decision, the Supreme Court was asked to address issues related to the application of Province of Saskatchewan's Parks Act[7] and Parks Regulations[8] and the Natural Resource Transfer Agreement[9] in relation to the incidental hunting and fishing rights of a Treaty 6 Indian. In this decision, which involves consideration of provincial legislation in an analysis that closely parallels the other "federal" cases I just mentioned, the Indian respondent had cut trees in a provincial park in order to build a temporary hunting cabin. He asserted that this activity was a part of his entitlement under treaty and that it was a necessary aspect of his exercise of hunting and fishing rights. He was charged with contravening the provisions of the provincial legislation by building a dwelling on park land without permission.

He was subsequently convicted, then he successfully appealed that conviction and the Supreme Court held, on further appeal, that his building activity was "reasonably incidental" to the exercise of his treaty rights:

Treaty rights, like Aboriginal rights, must not be interpreted as if they were common law property rights. Any interest in the hunting cabin is a collective right that is derived from the treaty and the traditional expeditionary method of hunting; it belongs to the band as a whole ...[10] While this case involved a consideration of the Natural Resource Transfer Agreement and constitutional principles and the relevance of Treaty 6, it actually turned on the application of the Sparrow test to provincial legislation. The Supreme Court dismissed the provincial appeal and this case is especially helpful to this discussion because it illustrates for us the unique character of First Nation treaty rights and how they interact with legislation that purports to limit or prohibit the exercise of those sui generis rights.

We take note that, in certain situations, the national parks regime will need to be able to address Aboriginal and treaty rights that are clustered. By this I mean to refer to those places within national parks where there are Aboriginal or treaty rights associated with sacred sites or burial grounds. These situations will call for imaginative and flexible arrangements for the purposes of accommodating the exercise of collective First Nations' rights and to provide for appropriate protection of the sites themselves.

One such site that comes to mind is the burial ground that was uncovered several years ago within the bounds of Fort Temiscamingue National Historic Site. This is a matter of great concern to the Timiskaming First Nation. However, due to the impediments presented by the current Comprehensive Claims Policy, the federal [Minister of Indian Affairs and Northern Development] cannot recognize the existing Aboriginal title or rights within the historic site. For that matter, the minister of heritage is also restricted in her ability to address the issues presented by this situation due to the limitations of the current legislative mandate. We need to seriously consider these matters further and my colleague, Mr. David Nahwegahbow, will have more to say about that later on in today's schedule of presentations.

In closing my presentation, I wish to say a few things about our inherent rights and jurisdiction. It is our belief that the inherent rights and jurisdiction of the First Nations [come] from the Great Spirit. [They are] neither granted nor subject to the approval of any other nation. As First Nations we have the sovereign right to jurisdiction rule within our traditional territories. Our lands are a sacred gift. These lands have been provided to us for the continued use, benefit and enjoyment of our people, and it is our ultimate obligation to the Great Spirit to care for and protect it.

Several years ago Canada responded to the recommendations of the Report of the Royal Commission on Aboriginal Peoples. The main focus of that policy response entitled "Gathering Strength" was to renew the relationship with the Aboriginal people of Canada. The new [approach] to our issues builds upon the principles of mutual respect, recognition, responsibility and sharing. It has four key objectives: renewing the partnerships, strengthening Aboriginal governance, developing a new fiscal relationship, and supporting strong Aboriginal communities, people and economies. We look to this commitment for mutual guidance and assistance in the recommendations we make for this process today.

For us, Aboriginal title and rights means that we, as First Nations Indian people, hold legal rights of property to our lands and resources and we have the right to maintain our sacred connection to our lands by governing our territories through our own forms of traditional governance systems.

We have responsibilities towards these lands and to the plants and wildlife that inhabit the land and provide for us. These responsibilities include our role as stewards and protectors of the land and all that live within our territories in order [to] achieve a balance and harmony with nature. This is the essence of our traditional relationship with the land and all of our spiritual wisdom points to this principle as a cornerstone of our identity and existence as Aboriginal people and as nations. We have the right to exercise our jurisdiction within our traditional territories so as to maintain our sacred connection to our lands through prudent management and conservation of the resources for the economic survival and well being of our communities.

In the new regime for the management of national parks, the First Nations must have a clear role and accommodation as a full partner with Canada in relation to:

- Food-gathering through hunting, fishing, trapping, and harvesting for the well-being of our First Nations;
- Conservation, management and environmental protection of the our traditional territories and all renewable and non-renewable resources within it;
- Economic rights including access to resources and commercial activities;
- Spiritual rights to practice our religion, spiritual customs, traditions and culture including protection of our sacred lands within our care;
- Accommodation of traditional activities and pursuits;
- Co-operative management, training and employment opportunities;
- Enhanced interpretation of First Nations history and culture.
- List of Recommendations:
  1) It is recommended that all necessary steps be taken during the legislative and policy development of the new Canada National Parks Act and any related regulatory framework to ensure that all affected First Nations are provided with the opportunity for meaningful consultation.
  2) It is further recommended that the legislation to be drafted for establishment of this new national parks regime provide the Minister of Canadian Heritage with a sufficient mandate and authority to develop and implement, in partnership with First Nations, the wide range of arrangements necessary to accommodate their rights and to protect their interests within Canada's National Parks.
  3) It is also recommended that arrangements be made to ensure that First Nations are consulted and have a role in the development of any legislative measures, including regulations, that involve or may impact upon their rights and interests in the proposed new national parks regime being considered under Bill C-27.

(b) The Harvest of Beluga Whales in Canada's Western Arctic: Hunter-based Monitoring of the Size and Composition of the Catch[†]

Lois A. Harwood, Pamela Norton, Billy Day, and Patricia A. Hall

INTRODUCTION

The belugas (Deiphinapterus leucas) that occur in the Beaufort Sea during summer migrate to spend the winter in the Bering Sea. Each spring, they travel along the north coast of Alaska to their summer range in the Mackenzie River estuary, Beaufort Sea, and Amundsen Gulf (Fraker, 1979; Richard et al., 2001). They share the Bering Sea wintering areas with at least three other stocks of belugas: those that summer in Bristol Bay, Norton Sound, and the eastern Chukchi Sea (Brennin et [al.], 1997; O'Corry-Crowe and Lowry, 1997; O'Corry-Crowe et al., 1997). Together these four stocks, as well as stocks that summer in Russian waters, make up the Bering Sea beluga population (Burns and Seaman, 1985).

The hunting of belugas by Inuit, for use as human and dog food, has a long history. For 500 or more years, the aboriginal people of the Western Arctic have successfully hunted the beluga whale in the Mackenzie River estuary (McGhee, 1988). Limited information is available on the size of the beluga harvest during the pre-contact (prior to 1888) and commercial whaling (1888–1907) periods (Bockstoce, 1986), or from the end of the commercial bowhead whaling era up until the 1950s. Available data suggest that harvests in those times were likely higher than at present (Nuligak, 1966; Smith and Taylor, 1977; McGhee, 1988; Strong, 1989; Friesen and Arnold, 1995; Billy Day, unpubl. data).

Each summer, contemporary hunters and their families from Inuvik, Aklavik, and Tuktoyaktuk, Northwest Territories (Fig. 1) travel to traditional whaling camps along the eastern Beaufort Sea coast (Fig. 2). The hunt has always been conducted mainly during the month of July. It lasts for four to six weeks, while the belugas are aggregated in three main areas of the Mackenzie River estuary: Kugmallit Bay, Beluga Bay, and Shallow Bay (Fraker et al., 1979; Norton and Harwood, 1986).

The Inuvialuit of Holman and Paulatuk, Northwest Territories (Fig. 1) also have a history of hunting the beluga. Hunting takes place when the whales travel close to shore near these communities, after they have left the Mackenzie River estuary, usually in late July and August (Norton and Harwood, 1985). Results from recent satellite telemetry studies have shown that belugas taken by hunters from Paulatuk are likely from the same stock as those taken in the Mackenzie River estuary, but are taken later in the season, once the whales have moved to offshore feeding areas (Richard et al., 2001).

[†] From *Arctic*, 55(1) (March 2002): 10–20. Permission to reproduce has been granted from the Arctic Institute of North America.

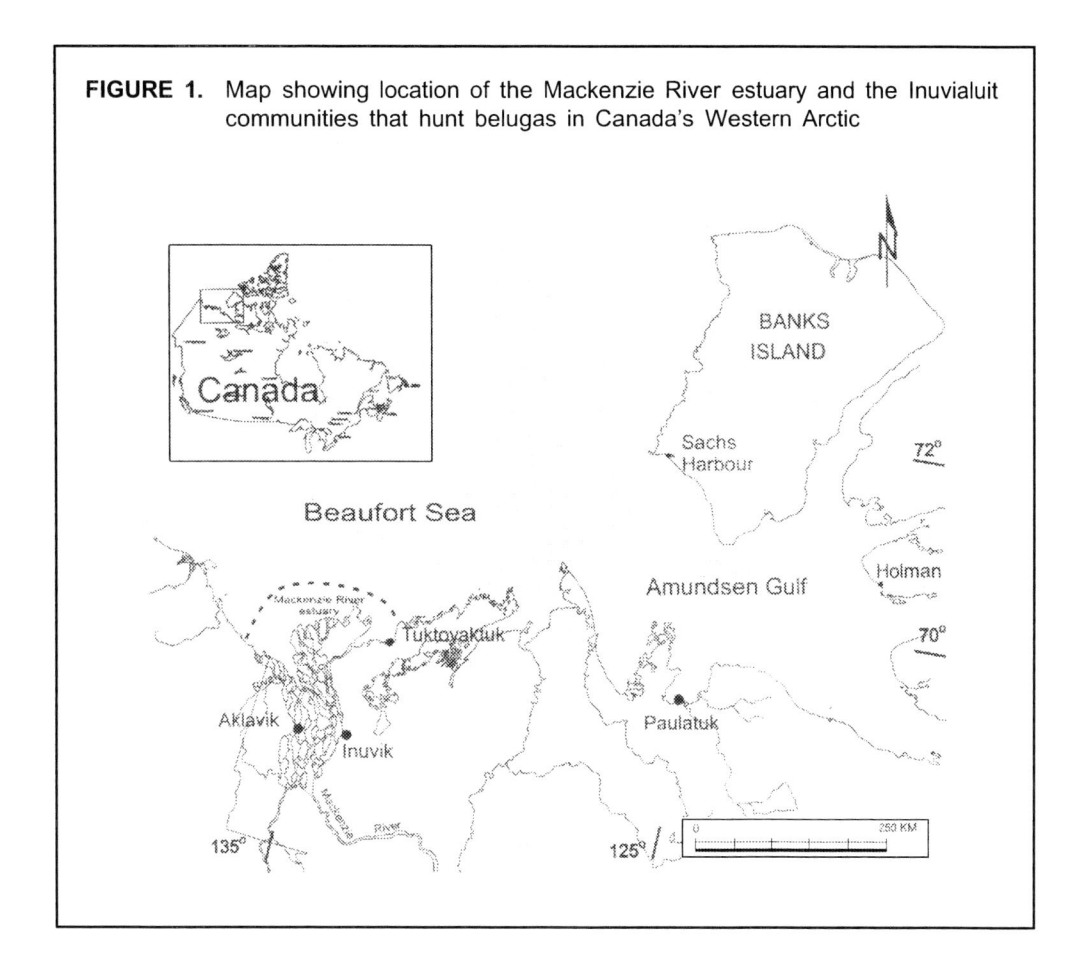

FIGURE 1. Map showing location of the Mackenzie River estuary and the Inuvialuit communities that hunt belugas in Canada's Western Arctic

During their spring and fall migrations, the belugas of the Beaufort Sea stock are also hunted by Inuit of Alaskan villages (i.e., Little Diomede, Kivalina, Point Hope, Barrow, Wainwright, and Kaktovik; Lowry et al., 1988). Residents of the Chukotskiy Peninsula, Russia, probably also take whales from this stock. Harvests in Russian waters since 1990 have been low, probably not exceeding 20–30 animals per year (Melnikov et al., 1998; Belikov, 1999). The origin of the small number of belugas being taken in Russia at the present time is not entirely known and may include more than one stock.

The first written records about harvesting of belugas from the Beaufort Sea stock in Canada are found in Royal Canadian Mounted Police (RCMP) and territorial game officer reports from 1954, which reported that 210 belugas had been landed (Smith and Taylor, 1977). Smith and Taylor (1977) report that the harvest averaged 120 per year between 1960 and 1963, while Strong (1989) reports an average harvest of 146 per year between 1960 and 1966.

A formal harvest-monitoring program was conducted from 1973 to 1975 by the Fisheries and Marine Service of the Government of Canada (Hunt, 1979). Monitor-

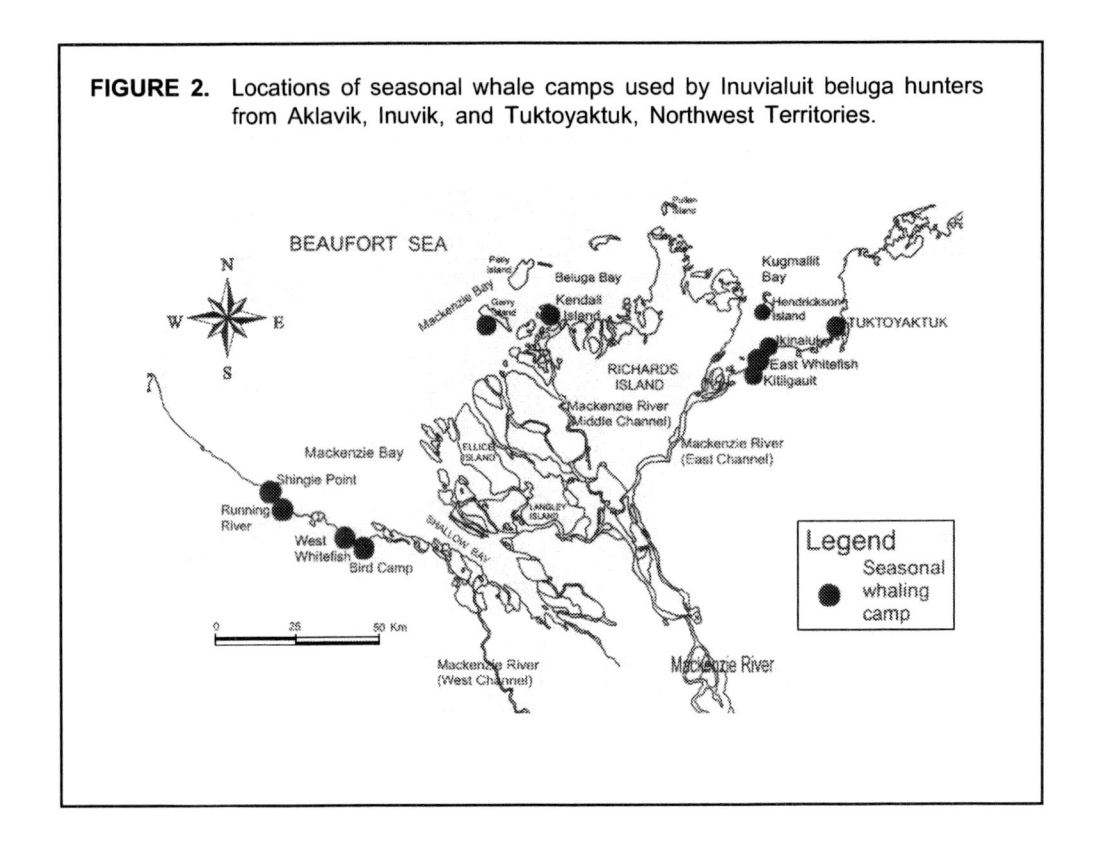

FIGURE 2. Locations of seasonal whale camps used by Inuvialuit beluga hunters from Aklavik, Inuvik, and Tuktoyaktuk, Northwest Territories.

ing was continued from 1977 through 1982 by an oil and gas industry-sponsored program (Fraker, 1977, 1978; Fraker and Fraker, 1979, 1981; Norton Fraker, 1983) and from 1981 through 1986 by a program led by Fisheries and Oceans Canada (DFO) (Strong, 1990; Weaver, 1991). Finally, the Fisheries Joint Management Committee (FJMC) has conducted programs annually from 1987 to the present.

In all years, data were collected from hunters at the seasonal whaling camps on the size and timing of the harvest and the number of whales struck, landed, and lost. From 1980 onward, the landed whales were measured and sexed, and biological samples were taken. This information was collected to document the magnitude and trend of the harvest and to obtain data necessary to assess stock status and the impact of the harvest on that stock. This series of programs has produced the longest and largest database on harvested beluga whales in Canada.

The main objective of the beluga harvest-monitoring programs was to detect changes in the harvest and the beluga stock over time through measurement of certain parameters. In this paper, we collate and summarize the available data on the number of whales struck, landed, and lost from the Beaufort Sea stock during the last four decades. We also provide a summary of the biological data collected from the monitoring programs for the 20 yr period between 1980 and 1999.

METHODS

Sampling Landed Whales

Before 1980, appropriate biological data were collected on an opportunistic basis, when an independent contractor and a local hunter were present in a whaling camp. During these visits, which usually took place every 5–7 days, the hunters were interviewed as to how many whales had been struck since the previous visit. The contractors would also sample any whales that happened to be landed during the course of the camp visit (Fraker, 1977, 1978; Fraker and Fraker, 1979, 1981; Fraker et al., 1979; Norton Fraker, 1983).

In 1980, sampling was intensified, with as many as six local hunters hired each season. Within the Mackenzie Delta, one hunter was assigned to each of the six core whaling areas: 1) Shingle Point/Running River, 2) West Whitefish/Bird Camp, 3) Kendall Island/Garry Island, 4) Hendrickson Island, 5) Tuktoyaktuk, and 6) East Whitefish. These hunters, termed "beluga monitors," collected hunt-related and biological data at their own and neighbouring (usually extended family) whaling camps throughout the whaling season. The monitors received pre-season training from a biologist, either individually or as a group. Often the same hunter held the beluga monitor position in a given camp year after year. Billy Day worked at the same site for all but one year between 1977 and 1999.

After each hunt, the monitor interviewed each hunt captain to obtain information on how many whales were struck, landed, and lost. The benefit of this approach is that the monitor personally observes and counts each landed whale. The monitor also sees and records the names of the different hunters on the hunt, which thus rules out the potential for double counting of a landed whale by more than one hunter on the same hunt. The monitors also collect samples, determine the sex of the landed whales, and measure the standard length of as many whales as possible, according to a standard protocol (American Society of Mammalogists, 1961). Other measurements include fluke and flipper widths (E. McLean, FJMC, unpubl. data, 1988–2000).

Lower mandibles were collected, labelled, and air-dried in the field and were later separated into left and right dentaries. These were trimmed by cutting transversely through the bone, posterior to the tooth row. Teeth were prepared following methods described by Wainwright and Walker (1988). Dentaries were boiled gently to facilitate extraction of two mandibular teeth, usually the second and fifth, for age estimation. These were embedded in clear casting resin and longitudinally thin-sectioned at ~0.3 mm intervals, using a diamond wafering blade. Finished thin sections were stored in 70% ethanol.

Thin sections were examined wet, using a dissecting microscope and reflected light. A single "reader" made the age estimates using counts of dentinal growth layer groups (GLGs) to estimate minimum age. A growth layer group consists of two adjacent growth layers, one light and one dark (Perrin and Myrick, 1980). For each tooth, the mean of three individual counts became the final GLG estimate. Chronological age, based on the assumption that belugas deposit two GLGs annually (Goren et al., 1987), was rounded upward to the next integer. However, recent studies have challenged this assumption (Hohn and Lockyer, 1999), so we have also provided the number of GLGs beside each age estimate.

Analysis

A database of all whales sampled from 1974 to 1999 was prepared from the original data sheets and published reports. These data are now archived as Lotus 123 files at the FJMC office in Inuvik.

The number of whales struck and the number landed were tabulated from the literature for the 1960s and 1970s (Smith and Taylor, 1977; Strong, 1989) and from the database for subsequent years. Spearman's correlation (Sokal and Rohlf, 1995) was used to determine whether the number of whales landed per year was related to the size of the human population in a given community. Human population data, provided by Statistics Canada, represent all ages and ethnic groups. Data from the 1981, 1986, 1991, and 1996 national censuses (Statistics Canada, 1994, 1998) were examined. In addition, we obtained from the Inuvialuit Regional Corporation (IRC) data for 1988 through 1996 on the number of beneficiaries aged 18 years and older, by community, living in the Inuvialuit Settlement Region (M. Tingmiak, IRC, unpubl. data, 1998).

The annual harvest-related removal of belugas from the Beaufort Sea stock was set as the number of whales struck in a given year. No independent data are available with which to assess the completeness of the reporting of struck and lost whales. Like the landed whale data, however, the struck data were collected immediately after the hunt by the monitor, himself a peer and a beluga hunter.

Recorded annual removal of belugas from the Beaufort Sea stock was calculated by summing Inuvialuit strikes and the reported number of whales struck from this same stock in Alaska.

Biological Measurements

The proportion of the catch from the Mackenzie River estuary that was measured each year for standard length, sex, age, and colour was tabulated from the database. In 1977–79, the proportion of the landed whales that was sampled was low (e.g., on average, only 24% were measured for standard length, and sex was determined for only 36%). From 1980 onward, monitors were tasked with sampling as many of the landed whales in their monitoring area as possible. We have limited our analyses of basic biological parameters to the years 1980–99, when sample size was large (588 females, 1428 males) and more complete (90.8% for standard length, 92.5% for sex, 86.2% for colour).

A Kolmogorov-Smirnov 2-sample test (Kiefer, 1959) was used to compare the length frequency distribution of males and females from the Mackenzie River estuary harvest. A one-way analysis of variance (SAS, 1996) was then used to test for differences in the mean length of harvested belugas between years, separately for males and females. The Duncan Multiple Range test (Zar, 1974) was used to rank and compare the mean annual standard lengths of belugas, separately for each sex, using SAS (1996).

Estimated ages of 368 belugas were available for the years 1988–1994. Median ages were determined separately for each sex. Age-frequency histograms were prepared for each sex and compared using a Kolmogorov-Smirnov 2-sample test (Kiefer, 1959).

Gompertz growth curves for standard length (cm) were fitted to the data using a non-linear regression available in SAS (1996), according to Stewart (1994) and the equation [1]:

$$L_s = A(e^{(e-k \cdot \text{age} + k \cdot t_o)}) \quad [1]$$

where A is the asymptote (cm), k and t_o are fitted constants, e is the base of the natural logarithm (approximately 2.7183), age is the estimated age of the whale (yr) and L_2 is the standard length (in cm) that is predicted from the equation. Annual differences in the asymptotic length of male belugas were examined by comparing predicted values and the associated 95% confidence intervals.

For the other years in the database, teeth were not collected or estimated ages are not yet available. For this reason, the monitors' colour category assignments of white (includes white with yellow, or moulting, skin), white with gray, gray, and dark gray were used to estimate the relative age of landed whales. The mean standard lengths of whales (by sex) in each colour category were compared using an analysis of variance and the Duncan Multiple Range test (Zar, 1974) to reveal specific differences between categories. The proportions of harvested whales in each colour category were tallied, and the relative age of whales in those category assignments were estimated from age and colour data available for 335 whales sampled between 1988 and 1992.

RESULTS

The Landed Harvest

Inuvialuit hunters travel from the communities of Inuvik, Aklavik, and Tuktoyaktuk to whaling camps along the Beaufort Sea coast. The seasonal camps are located on the shores of Kugmallit Bay, Beluga Bay, Mackenzie Bay, and Shallow Bay within the Mackenzie River estuary, and along the northern Yukon coast as far west as King Point (Fig. 2). Beluga hunting has also been conducted approximately 350 km east of Tuktoyaktuk, at Paulatuk, Northwest Territories, by residents of that community. The annual landed harvest from both the Mackenzie estuary and Paulatuk areas averaged 131.8 (SD 26.5, n = 1337) from 1970 to 1979, 124.0 (SD 23.3, n = 1240) from 1980 to 1989, and 111.0 (SD 19.0, n = 1110) from 1990 to 1999 (Table 1). Most (91.8%) of the belugas were landed in the Mackenzie River estuary by hunters from Aklavik (17.0%), Inuvik (34.7%), and Tuktoyaktuk (40.1%) areas. The remaining were landed near Holman and Paulatuk. Residents of Holman reported one beluga landed in 1973, seven in 1975, and two in 1978 ([Strong], 1989). Hunters at Paulatuk landed four belugas in 1966, three in 1985, and one in 1987 (Strong, 1989), and they report a "regular" annual harvest since 1989 (a total of 91 whales landed between 1990 and 1999; mean = 9.1 whales/yr).

The average number of belugas harvested has declined over the last three decades, while the number of Inuvialuit beneficiaries has increased. Between 1988 and 1996, the number of beneficiaries aged 18 years and older living in the Inuvialuit Settlement Region increased by 14% (M. Tingmiak, IRC, unpubl. data, 1998).

Statistics Canada reports an overall increase in the aboriginal population of 26.4% for Inuvik, Tuktoyaktuk, Aklavik, and Paulatuk between 1981 and 1996.

TABLE 1. Number of beluga whales struck, landed, and lost in the Mackenzie River estuary and Paulatuk hunting areas, 1970–99 (data from Strong, 1989; Weaver, 1991; FJMC, unpubl. data).

Year	Struck	Landed	Lost	Percent Lost
1970	nr (1)	115	nr	nr
1971	nr	79	nr	nr
1972	nr	113	nr	nr
1973	nr	178	nr	nr
1974	nr	128	nr	nr
1975	nr	149	nr	nr
1976	nr	154	nr	nr
1977	172	148	24	14.0
1978	157	129	28	17.8
1979	nr	144	nr	nr
Mean	164.5	133.7	26.0	15.9
SD		26.0		
1980	85	85	nr	nr
1981	155	155	nr	nr
1982	146	126	20	13.7
1983	102	86	16	15.7
1984	156	141	15	9.6
1985	148	120	28	18.9
1986	199	150	49	24.6
1987	174	144	30	17.2
1988	139	116	23	16.5
1989	156	117	39	25.0
Mean	146.0	124.0	27.5	17.7
SD		23.3		
1990	106	87	19	17.9
1991	144	116	28	19.4
1992	130	121	9	6.9
1993	120	110	10	8.3
1994	149	141	8	5.4
1995	143	129	14	9.8
1996	139	120	19	13.7
1997	123	114	9	7.3
1998	93	86	7	7.5
1999	102	86	16	15.7
Mean	124.9	111.0	13.9	11.2
SD	19.5	19.0		

(1) nr = no record.

There were no positive correlations between the size of the human population and the size of the beluga harvest for the 1981, 1986, 1991, and 1996 census data (Inuvik: /r/ = 0.62, p = 0.3789; Tuktoyaktuk: /r/ = 0.46, p = 0.5403; Aklavik: /r/ = 0.74, p = 0.2611). The same was true for comparisons between the number of Inuvialuit beneficiaries and the size of the beluga harvest (Inuvik: /r/ = 0.12, p = 0.7523; Tuktoyaktuk: /r/ = 0.08, p = 0.8428; Aklavik: /r/ = 0.23, p = 0.5517).

Total Removal

The average number of belugas struck but lost, expressed as a percentage of the total number struck, was lower in the 1990s (mean = 11.2%), than in the 1970s (estimated mean = 15.9%) or the 1980s (mean = 17.7%; Table 1). The past and present efficiency of this hunt, and the factors that affect it, are relevant here for the calculation of the total number of belugas removed from the stock by the harvest. Including strikes by all Inuvialuit hunters, the number of belugas struck averaged 124.9 per year (SD 19.5, n = 1249) during the period from 1990 to 1999 (Table 1).

Inupiat, living along the northern coast of Alaska, struck an estimated 64 belugas per year (range 42–117) during the period from 1995 through 2000, from this same stock (Suydam and Frost, 2001). Struck and loss rates are just becoming available for this harvest, as programs are in place to address this data gap (Adams et al., 1993).

Combining what is known about Alaskan harvests from this stock with data on removals by the Inuvialuit indicates a total removal of approximately 189 belugas per year (not including any that may be taken in Russian waters).

The latest aerial surveys, conducted in 1992, gave an index of abundance of 19 629 belugas in the southeast Beaufort Sea and western Amundsen Gulf (95% confidence interval = 15 134–24 125; Harwood et al., 1996). It is now known that the total area occupied by Beaufort Sea belugas during summer was not covered, and that a considerable but as yet undetermined number of whales remained underwater during aerial counts. Thus, the index is undoubtedly lower than the actual stock size, which remains unknown. The present removal of an average of 189 belugas per year is less than 1% of even this most minimal index of stock size. If a hypothetical take in Russia of an additional 25 belugas was included in the calculation, the removal rate would still only be 1.1%.

Composition of the Mackenzie River Estuary Beluga Harvest

Sex was determined for 92.5% (2016/2192) of the belugas that were landed between 1980 and 1999 (Table 2), with males outnumbering females in the harvest 2.3:1 (mean = 29.3% females per year, range = 15.3–48.3%). The proportion of males and females in the harvest each year was calculated and plotted as a frequency histogram. The sex ratio remained consistent in the 20 consecutive years examined here (Fig. 3). In the 1980s, the average number of females landed per year was 34.7, while in the 1990s, the average was 24.1 per year.

The ages of 368 belugas harvested between 1988 and 1994 were available for 80 females and 286 males, representing 48.5% of the total landings (n = 758) dur-

TABLE 2. Proportion of beluga whales landed that were measured, aged, sexed, and assessed for colour in the Mackenzie River estuary beluga monitoring programs during 1977–99(1)

Year of Harvest	Total Landed	Number Measured	% Measured	Number Aged	% Aged	Number Sexed	% Sexed
1977	98	15	15.3	–	–	21	21.4
1978	114	24	21.1	–	–	44	38.6
1979	121	42	34.7	–	–	59	48.8
1980	82	77	93.9	–	–	77	93.9
1981	146	107	73.3	–	–	116	79.5
1982	107	96	89.7	–	–	98	91.6
1983	86	74	86.0	–	–	83	96.5
1984	141	99	70.2	–	–	111	78.7
1985	118	101	85.6	–	–	102	86.4
1986	131	109	83.2	–	–	121	92.4
1987	134	94	70.1	–	–	122	91.0
1988	114	94	82.5	62	54.4	111	97.4
1989	114	78	68.4	51	44.7	101	88.6
1990	87	63	72.4	53	60.9	78	89.7
1991	100	75	75.0	60	60.0	99	99.0
1992	103	89	86.4	73	70.9	103	100.0
1993	107	96	89.7	26	24.3	99	92.5
1994	133	117	88.0	43	32.3	128	96.2
1995	118	108	91.5	–	–	114	96.6
1996	95	90	94.7	–	–	93	97.9
1997	107	104	97.2	–	–	102	95.3
1998	84	67	79.8	–	–	82	97.6
1999	85	77	90.6	–	–	76	89.4

Year of Harvest	No. With Colour Recorded	% Colour Recorded
1977	2	2.0
1978	3	2.6
1979	0	0.0
1980	75	91.5
1981	62	42.5
1982	99	92.5
1983	81	94.2
1984	112	79.4
1985	106	89.8
1986	118	90.1
1987	119	–88.8
1988	95	83.3
1989	107	93.9
1990	75	86.2
1991	90	90.0
1992	94	91.3
1993	83	77.6
1994	127	95.5
1995	109	92.4
1996	86	90.5
1997	97	90.7
1998	74	88.1
1999	64	75.3

(1) Does not include Paulatuk harvests.

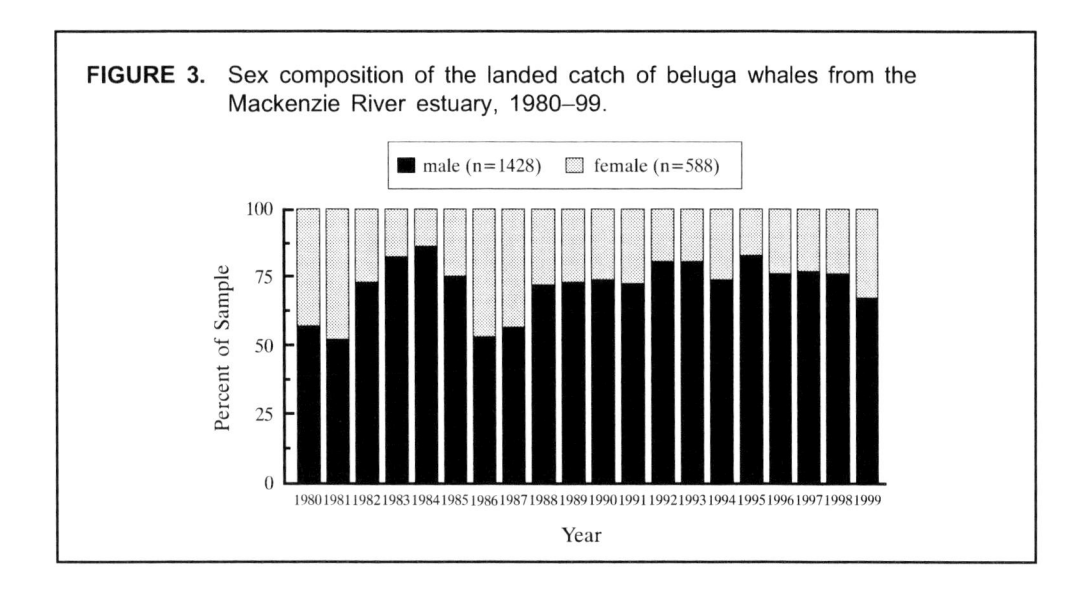

FIGURE 3. Sex composition of the landed catch of beluga whales from the Mackenzie River estuary, 1980–99.

ing that period. The age-frequency histogram (Fig. 4) shows a wide range of ages in the sampled harvest, with 92.9% (351/368) being 10 or more years old (20 GLG). Females sampled from 1988 to 1994, for which age estimates are available, ranged from 0 to 49 yr (0–98 GLG), with a median of 23.5 yr (47 GLG). Males ranged from 3 to 57 yr (6–114 GLG), with a median of 24 yr (48 GLG). The age-frequency distributions of males and females were not statistically different (Kiefer, 1959; Kolmogorov-Smirnov test, $[KS.sub.a] = 1.233$, $n = 366$, $p > KSa = 0.1003$).

Colour was recorded for 1873/2192 or 86.2% of the belugas landed in the Mackenzie River estuary between 1980 and 1999 (Table 2). The proportion of the catch in each colour category was tallied. For both males and females, the mean standard lengths of the "white" and "white with gray" belugas were not different from each other, but they were different from that of the more variable but generally smaller "gray" category (females, $F = 39.92$, $df = 2,449$, $p > F < 0.001$; males, $F = 116.22$, $df = 2,1190$, $p > F < 0.0001$). Focusing on a seven-year subset of data for which age, colour, and standard length data were all available (1988–94), the mean ages corresponding to each colour category were 27.1 yr for "white" (SD 10.8, $n = 274$); 20.4 yr for "white with gray" (SD 8.0, $n = 25$); and 17.3 yr for "gray" (SD = 9.8, $n = 35$). The age of our one "dark gray" beluga was estimated at 3 yr (6 GLGs). The data reflect the fact that during the 20 years of monitoring in which colour category assignments were made, the hunters [actively] selected for older whales. Most (88.7%, or 1662/1873) were in the white/white-with-gray category). The data from 1988–94 indicate that the average age of belugas in this white/white-with-gray category was 24.5 yr (49 GLG) for females ($n = 55$) and 27.0 yr (54 GLG) for males ($n = 243$).

A length-frequency histogram was prepared for male and female belugas landed in the Mackenzie River estuary during 1980–99 (Fig. 5). Standard length was determined for 82.5% (1809/2192) of the landed whales. The length-frequency

FIGURE 4. Age-frequency distribution of male and female belugas landed in the Mackenzie River estuary, 1988–94.

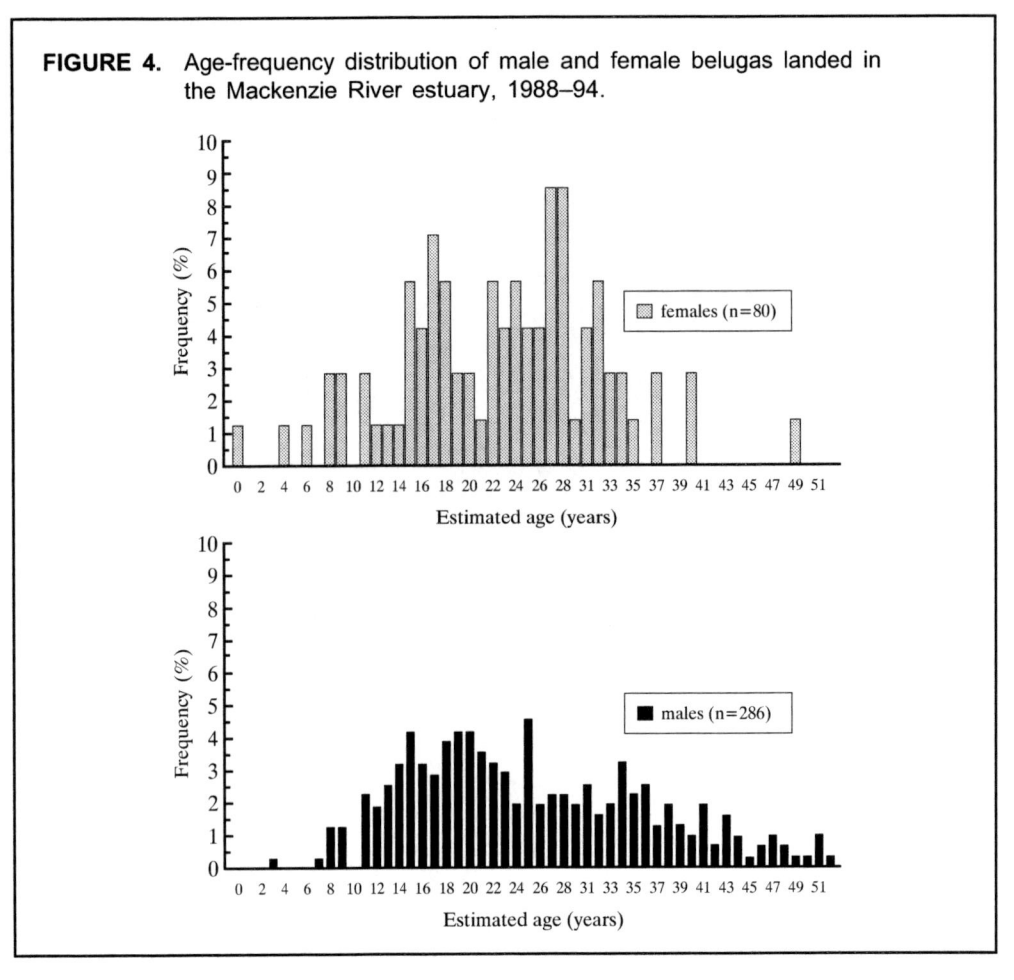

FIGURE 5. Length-frequency distribution of male and female belugas landed in the Mackenzie River estuary, 1980–99.

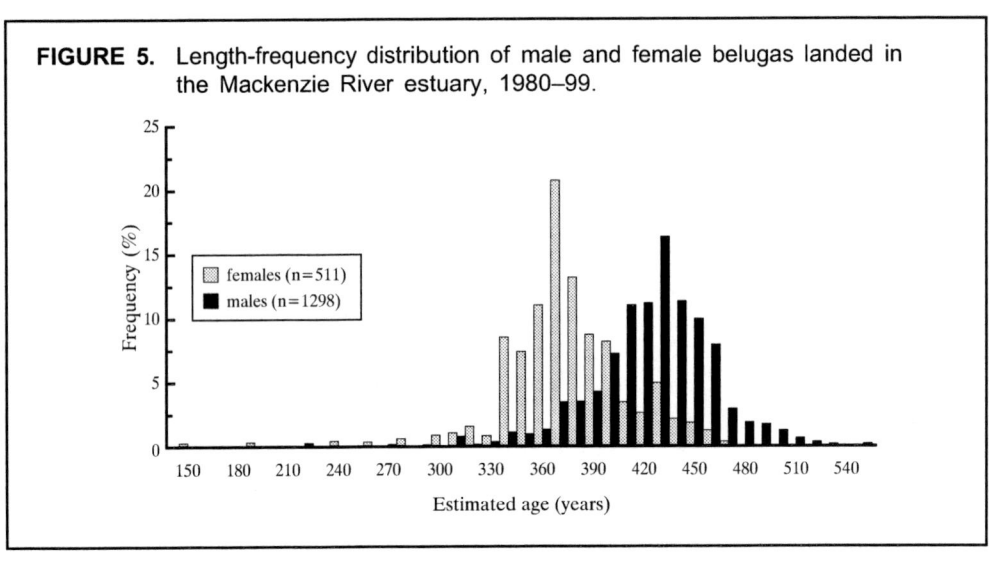

TABLE 3. Asymptotic lengths of male belugas harvested from the Mackenzie River estuary, 1988–94.

Year	Asymptotic length (cm)	SD	df	95% confidence interval lower	upper
1988	450.6	12.5	42	425.2	475.9
1989	446.9	13.8	37	418.9	474.8
1990	437.2	5.6	39	425.9	448.5
1991	433.1	3.4	47	426.2	440.0
1992	429.0	6.8	63	415.4	442.6
1993	443.2	14.7	20	412.3	474.1
1994	422.2	17.2	35	387.3	457.2
Years Pooled	432.6	2.6	289	427.5	437.6

distribution shows the modal 10 cm size class for females (370–380 cm) to be 60cm less than the modal size class for males (430–440 cm). The length-frequency distributions for males and females were significantly different from each other ([KS.sub.a] 11.62, p > [KS.sub.a] < 0.0001, n = 1809).

Asymptotic lengths, predicted by the Gompertz curves (Stewart, 1994) for our 1988–94 sample of aged belugas, were 432.0 cm (SD 2.47, n = 3282; 95% CI = 427.1–436.8 cm) for males and 386.2 cm (SD 4.39, n = 379; 95% CI = 377.4–394.9 cm) for females. Between-year differences in the asymptotic lengths were not apparent for males (Table 3). Sample size was not sufficient to make this comparison for females.

The mean standard length of all males taken in the Mackenzie River estuary varied among years (F = 2.69, df = 19, 1297; p > F = 0.0001). The mean standard length of all females taken in the same area also varied among years (F = 1.86, df = 19, 510, p > F = 0.0148). There were no trends toward increasing or decreasing size for either sex over the 20 years for which data are available (Fig 6).

Composition of the Paulatuk Harvest

Hunters from Paulatuk, located 350 km northeast of the Mackenzie River estuary, landed 95 belugas between 1989 and 1999. The annual take during this time averaged 9.5 belugas per year and ranged from 0 (1990) to 25 (1996). The sex ratio of belugas landed by Paulatuk hunters (3.7 males: 1 female) showed the same strong bias toward males as was the case for the Mackenzie River estuary harvest.

The average age of belugas taken by Paulatuk hunters between 1991 and 1993 was 15.1 years (30.2 GLG) for females (n = 8, range = 7–32 yr) and 15.1 years (30.2 GLG) for males (n = 7, range = 12–20 yr). In contrast, males taken from the Mackenzie River estuary averaged 26.9 yr, while females averaged 24.6 yr, for the same period. These differences were statistically significant (for males, F =

FIGURE 6. Mean standard length of male and female belugas landed in the Mackenzie River estuary, 1980–99.

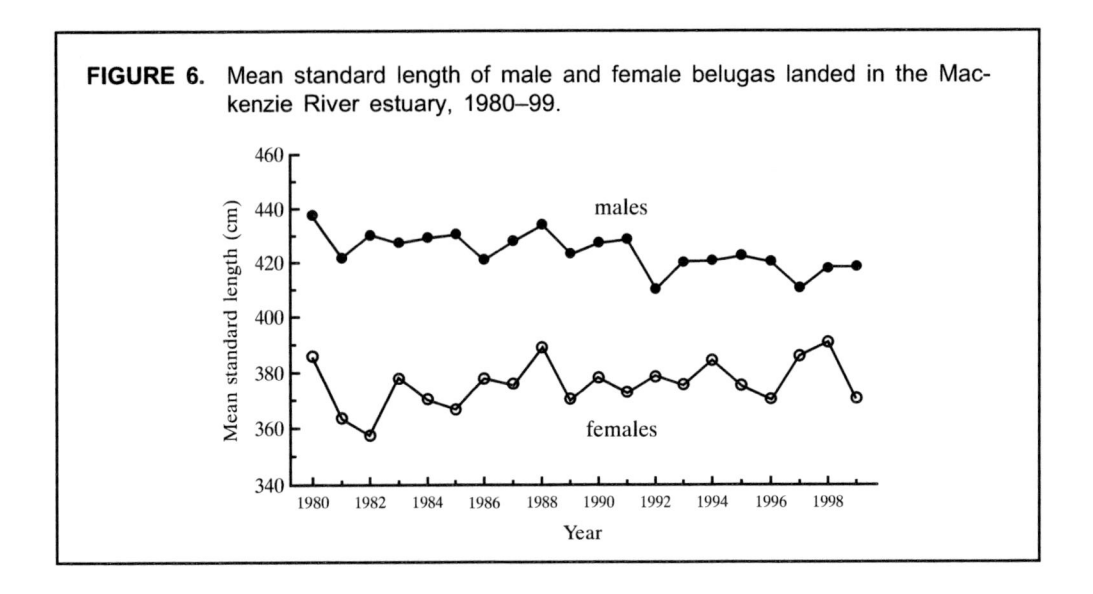

14.72, df = 239, 6, p > F = 0.0025, [T.sub.unequal] = 8.80, df = 12.2, p > t < 0.001; for females, F = 1.18, df = 63, 7, p > F = 0.8981; [T.sub.equal] = 3.01, df = 70, p > t = 0.0037). Despite this difference in average age at these hunting locations, hunting effort in both locations was directed toward males.

Further work on the size and age structure of the Paulatuk harvest is warranted, as data were available for only three of eleven years of recent hunting. Although belugas taken by Paulatuk hunters were on average younger than those taken in the Mackenzie River estuary, the size of the whales taken in these two areas was similar. The mean standard lengths of the pooled white/white with gray belugas, by sex, from Paulatuk harvests (males, 429.7 cm, n = 49; females, 383.3, n = 10) were not different from those of belugas taken in the Mackenzie River estuary during the corresponding period (1989–99; males = 425.5 cm, n = 607, females, 385.0, n = 153; comparing males, F = 1.17, df = 606, 48, p > F = 0.5168; [T.sub.equal] = 1.00, df = 654, p > T = 0.3192; comparing females, F = 1.67, df = 9, 152, p > F = 0.2020, [T.sub.equal] 0.16, p > T = 0.8463).

DISCUSSION

The Inuvialuit and their ancestors of the Western Arctic have a long history of hunting belugas. The size of the present-day harvest, averaging 111.0 belugas per year over the last decade, appears to be smaller than that of past harvests. Present-day harvests are lower than the estimated takes before commercial whaling (Nuligak, 1966) and those for the several decades since then for which harvest data exist (1960s, 1970s, and 1980s). In the late 1800s, the annual take of whales may have been upwards of 300 whales per summer (Nuligak, 1966). Nuligak recalls a communal drive hunt that took place in Kugmallit Bay when he was a small boy, which landed 150 belugas in a single day.

Between 1981 and 1996, the human population increased by more than 26%, yet there was not a corresponding increase in the average catch of belugas landed by the Inuvialuit. Billy Day considers this to be the result of recent trends toward a reduction in the consumption of traditional food, in particular for items requiring special equipment and knowledge to hunt and process, such as the beluga.

Although there has been an overall downward trend in the mean harvest level, annual harvests varied among years, fluctuating by as much as a factor of two between the extreme low and high harvest years in a given decade. The reasons for these variations have not been quantified, but likely include a variety of factors. For example, changes in local subsistence needs (i.e., during periods of increased wage employment in the oil and gas industry in the late 1970s and early 1980s) or in the requirement for beluga products for trade, barter, and sale to other Inuvialuit communities (i.e., when such opportunities increased after the signing of the Inuvialuit Final Agreement in 1984) would have influenced the level of the harvest in any given year. As well, environmental factors such as wind, weather, and ice conditions are known to affect the local distribution and availability of whales in a given whaling season. During 1985, for example, whales did not come into Kugmallit Bay until late in the season because of the late breakup of the ice (Norton and Harwood, 1986).

Fabijan et al. (1995) compared the beluga harvest data from the Inuvialuit Harvest Study (IHS, interview of all Inuvialuit hunters in the Inuvialuit Settlement Region monthly, using the hunter-recall interview as the method of data collection) and the number of landed beluga whales reported by the beluga monitors. Although the data collection methods were not the same, this is the only available independent data set with which to compare harvest totals. Between 1988 and 1992, the IHS reported a combined total of 494 belugas landed by hunters from Tuktoyaktuk, Aklavik, Inuvik, and Paulatuk (Fabijan et al., 1995). The FJMC program recorded 557 belugas for the same period (Table 1), 12.7% higher than the IHS data. This prompted a matching of individual records for landed whales recorded by each study (Fabijan et al., 1995). This comparison revealed that the beluga monitors' records were more complete, because hunters and hunts were not missed by the "on-the-beach" method used by the monitors, as opposed to the [IHS] method of hunter recall interviews in the month following hunting.

Data from the monitoring programs indicate that hunters direct their effort toward adult males. This practice has the benefit of conserving adult females. The majority of whales (92.9%) taken in this harvest were older than 10 yr (20 GLG), and thus had contributed offspring to the stock before they were removed through the harvest. In other areas of the Canadian Arctic, belugas tend to be harvested at a younger age. For example, the mean ages of belugas sampled from the hunt in Nunavut Territory were 8.3 yr (n = 52) for females and 11.5 yr (n = 70) for males at Arviat; 8.5 yr (n = 7) for females and 7.0 yr (n = 25) for males at Pangnirtung, and 5.6 yr (n = 12) for females and 5.2 yr (n = 18) for males at Grise Fiord (Stewart, 1994).

Hunters from Paulatuk also direct their harvests to adult male belugas; however, these appeared to be younger than the adult males taken in the Mackenzie. This is consistent with information gained from satellite tagging efforts, which have shown that the largest males are the most likely to travel to distant summer feeding areas (e.g., Viscount Melville Sound). It is the smaller males and the females that tend to spend the summer in Amundsen Gulf, where they are accessible to Paulatuk hunters (Richard et al., 2001), and thus appear in the Paulatuk harvests.

The Eastern Beaufort Sea beluga stock is harvested at a rate well below the 2.0–3.85% annual rate of increase expected for beluga stocks reported by Kingsley (1996, 1998) and Cosens et al. (1998). The proportion removed is not known in relation to the actual size of the stock. Actual stock size is much larger than the index of abundance (19 629 belugas, Harwood et al., 1996). It is expected that the population size is above the maximum net productivity level and that the present level of harvest is sustainable (Innes, 1996; Cosens et al., 1998; Hill and DeMaster, 1999; DFO, 2000).

The number of whales lost due to orphaning of calves by removal of adult females (in Alaskan and Canadian waters), is still to be determined. To illustrate how this aspect could contribute to the total removal, a hypothetical example is instructive. If orphaned calves are included at a rate of one calf lost [for] every three adult females landed (L. Harwood, unpubl. data), then the estimate of total removal would increase by a further 9 whales in the Inuvialuit Settlement Region and a further 11 in Alaska. This assumes a sex ratio of 1:1 in the Alaskan harvest. Adding these whales to the removal estimate of 189 described above yields a removal of 209 belugas, still well below the expected rate of increase of a beluga stock.

Results from the hunter-based sampling programs reported here indicate that the harvest of southeastern Beaufort Sea belugas is sustainable. The low rate of removal, the continued availability of large and old individuals after centuries of harvest, and the apparent lack of change in the size and age structure of the catch in recent years all suggest that the present harvest is not causing a decline in stock size.

Hunter-based sampling through the FJMC beluga monitoring program is ongoing. It would be fruitful in the future if the monitors were trained to perform a basic on-site examination of female reproductive tracts. This information, together with the results of ovarian analyses, would be used to determine the reproductive status and history of individual females. Data on other reproductive parameters, including age of maturation, age at first birth, and age-specific calving interval, which at the present time are not documented for this stock, would also be obtained (Harwood and Smith, in press; DFO, 2000).

The hunter-based nature of this program has provided a mechanism for the Inuvialuit to be active partners in the collection of biological data used to assess the well-being of the beluga stock on which they depend. The Inuvialuit have been partners in other beluga research projects, including capture and handling for satellite telemetry studies (Richard et al., 2001) and the conduct of aerial surveys to examine the distribution and size of the stock (Harwood et al., 1996). These projects have elevated awareness and ownership of Beaufort Sea beluga management issues and initiatives at the levels of the hunter, the user, and the community.

NOTES

1. Fisheries and Oceans Canada, Box 1871, Inuvik, Northwest Territories X0E 0T0, Canada; harwoodl@dfo-mpo.gc.ca

2. Riptide Consulting Services Ltd., 2717 Rock Bay Avenue, Victoria, British Columbia V8T 4R8, Canada
3. Fisheries Joint Management Committee, Box 2120, Inuvik, Northwest Territories X0E 0T0, Canada; fjmc@jointsec.nt.ca
4. Fisheries and Oceans Canada, 501 University Crescent, Winnipeg, Manitoba R3T 2N6, Canada; hallp@dfo-mpo.gc.ca

REFERENCES

ADAMS, M., FROST, K.J., and HARWOOD, L.A. 1993. Alaska and Inuvialuit Beluga Whale Committee (AIBWC) — An initiative in "at home management." Arctic 46(2):134–137.
AMERICAN SOCIETY OF MAMMALOGISTS. 1961. Standardized methods for measuring and recording data on the smaller cetaceans. Journal of Mammalogy 42(4):471–476.
BELIKOV, S. 1999. The status of the white whale population (Delphinapterus leucas) inhabiting the Russian Arctic. International Whaling Commission SC/51/SM21. 19 p.
BOCKSTOCE, J.R. 1986. Whales, ice and men: The history of whaling in the Western Arctic. Seattle: University of Washington Press. 400 p.
BRENNIN, R., MURRAY, B.W., FRIESEN, M.K., MAIERS, D., CLAYTON, J.W., and WHITE, B.N. 1997. Population genetic structure of beluga whales (Delphinapterus leucas): Mitochondrial DNA sequence variation within and among North American populations. Canadian Journal of Zoology 75:795–802.
BURNS, J.J., and SEAMAN, G.A. 1985. Investigations of belukha whales in coastal waters of western and northern Alaska. II. Biology and ecology. Final Report submitted to NOAA, Outer Continental Shelf Environmental Assessment Program, Alaska Department of Fish and Game, 1300 College Road, Fairbanks, Alaska 99701, U.S.A. 129 p.
COSENS, S.E., de MARCH, B.G.E., INNES, S., MATHIAS, J., and SHORTT, T.A. 1998. Report of the Arctic Fisheries Scientific Advisory Committee for 1993/94, 1994/95 and 1995/96. Canadian Manuscript Report of Fisheries and Aquatic Sciences No. 2473. Winnipeg: Western Region, DFO.
DFO (DEPARTMENT OF FISHERIES AND OCEANS CANADA). 2000. Eastern Beaufort Sea beluga. DFO Science Stock Status Report E5-38 (2000). Available at www.dfompo.gc.ca/csas.
FABIJAN, M., SNOW, N., NAGY, J., and FERGUSON, M. 1995. Evaluation of the Inuvialuit Harvest Study data for the years 1988–1992. Unpubl. Report available from the Joint Secretariat, Box 2120, Inuvik, Northwest Territories X0E 0T0, Canada. 133 p.
FRAKER, M.A. 1977. The 1977 whale monitoring program, Mackenzie Estuary, N.W.T. Report by F.F. Slaney and Company, Limited, Vancouver, British Columbia. Available at Fisheries and Oceans Canada, Box 1871, Inuvik, Northwest Territories X0E 0T0, Canada. 53 p.
———. 1978. The 1978 whale monitoring program, Mackenzie Estuary, N.W.T. Report by F.F. Slaney and Company, Limited, Vancouver, BC. Available at Fisheries and Oceans Canada, Box 1871, Inuvik, Northwest Territories X0E 0T0, Canada. 28 p.
———. 1979. Spring migration of bowhead (Balaena mysticetus) and white whales (Delphinapterus leucas) in the Beaufort Sea. Fisheries and Marine Service Technical Report 859. Winnipeg: Dept. of Fisheries and Environment. 36 p.
FRAKER, M.A., and FRAKER, P.N. 1979. The 1979 whale monitoring program, Mackenzie Estuary. Report by LGL Ltd., Sidney, BC. Available at Fisheries and Oceans Canada, Box 1871, Inuvik, Northwest Territories X0E 0T0, Canada. 51 p.
FRAKER, M.A., GORDON, C.D., McDONALD, J.W., FORD, J.K.B., and CAMBERS, G. 1979. White whale (Delphinapterus leucas) distribution and abundance and the relationship to physical and chemical characteristics of the Mackenzie Estuary. Fisheries and Marine Service Technical Report 863. Winnipeg: Dept. of Fisheries and Environment. 56 p.
FRAKER, P.N., and FRAKER, M.A. 1981. The 1980 whale monitoring program, Mackenzie Estuary. Report by LGL Ltd., Sidney, BC. Available at Fisheries and Oceans Canada, Box 1871, Inuvik, Northwest Territories X0E 0T0, Canada. 98 p.
FRIESEN, T.M., and ARNOLD, C.D. 1995. Zooarchaeology of a focal resource: Dietary importance of beluga whales to pre-contact Mackenzie Inuit. Arctic 48(1):22–30.
GOREN, A.D., BRODIE, P.F., SPOTTE, S., RAY, G.C., KAUFMAN, H.W., GWINNETT, A.J., SCIUBBA, J.J., and BUCK, J.D. 1987. Growth layer groups (GLGs) in the teeth of an adult belukha whale (Delphinapterus leucas) of known age: Evidence for two annual layers. Marine Mammal Science 3:14–21.

HARWOOD, L.A., and SMITH, T.G. In press. Whales of the Inuvialuit Settlement Region in Canada's Western Arctic: An overview and outlook. Arctic.

HARWOOD, L.A., INNES, S., NORTON, P., and KINGSLEY, M.C.S. 1996. Distribution and abundance of beluga whales in the Mackenzie Estuary, south-east Beaufort Sea, and west Amundsen Gulf during late July 1992. Canadian Journal of Fisheries and Aquatic Sciences 53:2262–2273.

HILL, P.S., and DeMASTER, D.P. 1999. Alaska marine mammal stock assessments 1999. U.S. Department of Commerce, NOAA-TM-NMFS-AFSC-110. 166 p. Available from the National Marine Mammal Laboratory, Alaska Fisheries Science Center, 7600 Sand Point Way NE, Seattle, Washington 98115, U.S.A.

HOHN, A.A., and LOCKYER, C. 1999. Growth layer patterns in teeth from two known-history beluga whales: Reconsideration of deposition rates. International Whaling Commission Scientific Committee Report No. SC/51/SM14.

HUNT, W.J. 1979. Domestic whaling in the Mackenzie Estuary, Northwest Territories. Canadian Fisheries and Marine Service Technical Report 769. Winnipeg: Dept. of Fisheries and Environment. 14 p.

INNES, S. 1996. Report of the National Peer Review Committee, Winnipeg, Manitoba, February 7–8, 1996. Appendix 3. Eastern Beaufort Sea beluga (1996 update) for AFSAC. Available at Fisheries and Oceans Canada, 501 University Crescent, Winnipeg, Manitoba R3T 2N6, Canada. 15–20.

KIEFER, J. 1959. K-sample analogues of the Kolmogorov-Smirnov and Cramer-von Mises tests. Annals of Mathematical Statistics 30:420–447.

KINGSLEY, M.C.S. 1996. Population index estimate for the belugas of the St. Lawrence in 1995. Canadian Technical Report of Fisheries and Aquatic Sciences 2117. Winnipeg: Western Region, DFO. 38 p.

———. 1998. Population index estimates for the St. Lawrence belugas, 1973–1995. Marine Mammal Science 14:503–530.

LOWRY, L.F., BURNS, J.J., and FROST, K.J. 1988. Recent harvests of belukha whales in western and northern Alaska and their potential impact on provisional management stocks. International Whaling Commission Scientific Committee Report No. SC\40\SM4.

MELNIKOV, V.V., ZELENSKY, M.A., and AINANA, L.I. 1998. Distribution and migrations of the belukha (Delphinapterus leucas) in the Chukchi Sea and northern Bering Sea. International Whaling Commission Scientific Committee Report No. SC/50/SM4. l2p.

McGHEE, R. 1988. Beluga hunters: An archaeological reconstruction of the history and culture of the Mackenzie Delta Kittegaryumiut. Newfoundland Social and Economic Series No. 13. St. John's: Institute of Social and Economic Research, Memorial University of Newfoundland. 124 p.

NORTON FRAKER, P. 1983. The 1982 white whale monitoring program, Mackenzie Estuary. Prepared by LGL Ltd., Sidney, B.C., for Esso Resources, Dome Petroleum, and Gulf Canada, Calgary, Alberta. Available at Fisheries and Oceans Canada, Box 1871, Inuvik, Northwest Territories X0E 0T0, Canada. 53 p.

NORTON, P., and HARWOOD, L.A. 1985. White whale use of the southeastern Beaufort Sea, July– September 1984. Canadian Technical Report of Fisheries and Aquatic Sciences 1401. Winnipeg: Western Region, DFO. 46 p.

———. 1986. Distribution, abundance and behaviour of white whales in the Mackenzie Estuary. Environmental Studies Revolving Funds Report 036. Ottawa: ESRF. 73 p.

NULIGAK. 1966. I, Nuligak. The autobiography of a Canadian Eskimo. Toronto: Simon and Schuster of Canada. 191 p.

PERRIN, W.F., and MYRICK, A.C., Jr., eds. 1980. Report of the Workshop. Age determination of toothed whales and sirenians. Report of the International Whaling Commission, Special Issue 3:2.

O'CORRY-CROWE, G.M., and LOWRY, L.L. 1997. Genetic ecology and management concerns for the beluga whale (Delphinapterus leucas). In: Dizon, A.E., Chivers, S.J., and Perrin, W.F., eds. Molecular genetics of marine mammals. Society for Marine Mammalogy, Special Publication No. 3. 249–274.

O'CORRY-CROWE, G.M., SUYDAM, R.S., ROSENBERG, A., FROST, K.J., and DIZON, A.E. 1997. Physiology, population structure and dispersal patterns of the beluga whale, Delphinapterus leucas, in the Western Nearctic revealed by mitochondrial DNA. Molecular Ecology 6:955–970.

RICHARD, P.R., MARTIN, A.R., and ORR, J.R. 2001. Summer and autumn movements of belugas of the eastern Beaufort Sea stock. Arctic 54(3):223–236.

SAS (STATISTICAL ANALYSIS SYSTEM). 1996. SAS Users guide: Statistics Version 6. Cary, North Carolina: SAS Institute Inc.

SMITH, T.G., and TAYLOR, D. 1977. Notes on marine mammal, fox and polar bear harvests in the Northwest Territories 1940 to 1972. Fisheries and Marine Service Technical Report 694. Winnipeg: Dept. of Fisheries and Environment. 37 p.
SOKAL, R.R., and ROHLF, F.J. 1995. Biometry. 3rd ed. San Francisco: W.H. Freeman and Company.
STATISTICS CANADA. 1994. Canada's Aboriginal population by census subdivision and census metropolitan areas. Edmonton: Advisory Services, Statistics Canada.
———. 1998. Ad-hoc retrieval for census of population for 1981, 1986, and 1996 censuses. Edmonton: Advisory Services, Statistics Canada.
STEWART, R.E.A. 1994. Size-at-age relationships as discriminators of white whale (Delphinapterus leucas) stocks in the eastern Canadian Arctic. Bioscience 39:217–225.
STRONG, T. 1989. Reported harvests of narwhal, beluga and walrus in the Northwest Territories, 1948–1987. Canadian Data Report of Fisheries and Aquatic Sciences 734. Winnipeg: Western Region, DFO. 14 p.
———. 1990. The domestic beluga (Delphinapterus leucas) fishery in the Mackenzie River Estuary, Northwest Territories, 1981–1986. Canadian Data Report of Fisheries and Aquatic Sciences 800. Winnipeg: Western Region, DFO. 52 p.
SUYDAM, R., and FROST, K. 2001. Programs, activities, and research of the Alaska Beluga Whale Committee, 2000–2001. Annual Report to National Marine Fisheries Service, NOAA. Barrow, Alaska: Alaska Beluga Whale Committee. 99 p.
WAINWRIGHT, K.L., and WALKER, R.S. 1988. A method of preparing beluga (white whale), Delphinapterus leucas, teeth for aging. Canadian Manuscript Report of Fisheries and Aquatic Sciences 1967. Winnipeg: Central and Arctic Region, DFO. 15 p.
WEAVER, P.A. 1991. The 1987 beluga (Delphinapterus leucas) harvest in the Mackenzie River Estuary, NWT. Canadian Manuscript Report of Fisheries and Aquatic Sciences 2097. Winnipeg: Central and Arctic Region, DFO. 18 p.
ZAR, J.H. 1974. Biostatistical analysis. Englewood Cliffs, New Jersey: Prentice-Hall, Inc.

(c) "A Clear Intention to Effect Such a Modification"[1]: The *NRTA* and Treaty Hunting and Fishing Rights[†]

Robert Irwin

INTRODUCTION: INDIAN HUNTING AND FISHING IN THE PRAIRIE PROVINCES

The issue of Indian hunting and fishing in the Canadian prairie provinces (Alberta, Saskatchewan and Manitoba) is covered in two separate regulatory structures: the Indian treaties and section 12 of the *Natural Resources [Transfer Agreements]*.[2] First, in the course of the treaty negotiations, Indian leaders demanded continued access to fish and game resources in return for their acceptance of the treaty. The government's negotiators accepted their demands and, as a result, specific promises were included in the text of Treaties 3 through 8. In Treaties 3, 5 and 6, the promise reads:

[†] This article was previously published in the *Native Studies Review*, 13(2) (2000), pp. 47–84 and is used with permission.

> Her majesty further agrees with Her said Indians, that they, the said Indians, shall have right to pursue their avocations of hunting and fishing throughout the tract surrendered as hereinbefore described, subject to such regulations as may from time to time be made by Her Government of Her Dominion of Canada, and saving and excepting such tracts as may from time to time be required or taken up for settlement, mining, lumbering or other purposes, by Her said Government of the Dominion of Canada, or by any of the subjects thereof duly authorized therefor by the said Dominion.[3]

The clauses in other treaties are similar enough in intent if slightly different in implementation. In Treaties 4, 8 and 10, trapping is itemized as a protected avocation along with hunting and fishing. In Treaty 7, the Blackfoot treaty, only hunting is mentioned. In Treaty 8, "the government of the country" is substituted for "the Government of Her Dominion of [Canada"] as the regulatory authority. The treaty right, as it appears in the written text of the treaty, contains a geographic limitation (the tract surrendered) and is subject to regulations prepared by the federal government.

The *Natural Resources Transfer Agreements* (*NRTA*) corrected a longstanding grievance by Manitoba, Saskatchewan and Alberta concerning their status in Confederation. Following the acquisition of Rupert's Land from the Hudson's Bay Company in 1869, the small province of Manitoba was created, and the North-West Territories evolved slowly from "primitive colonial status under Governor and Council in 1870 to responsible government in 1897 and provincial status in 1905."[4] Unlike other Canadian provinces, however, the three prairie provinces did not control lands and resources. The Manitoba Act (1870), the *Saskatchewan Act*, and the *Alberta Act* (1905) kept the lands and resources under federal government control "for the purposes of the Dominion." Not until 1930, with the passage of the *NRTA* by the Imperial Parliament as a schedule in the *Constitution Act* (1930), did the prairie provinces become "equal" with other provinces in the country. The transfer of control over Crown lands to the provinces meant that the issue of access by Indian peoples had to be discussed. Thus Section 12 of the *NRTA* contains a separate regulatory structure for Indian hunting, fishing and trapping rights.

> In order to secure to the Indians of the Province the continuance of the supply of game and fish for their support and subsistence, Canada agrees that the laws respecting game in force in the Province from time to time shall apply to the Indians within the boundaries thereof, provided, however, that the said Indians shall have the right, which the Province hereby assures to them, of hunting, trapping and fishing game and fish for food at all seasons of the year on all unoccupied Crown lands and on any other lands to which the said Indians may have a right of access.[5]

The *NRTA* provides for provincial regulation of Indian hunting, and provides an expanded geographic area for Indian hunting, fishing, and trapping for food. The provisions of section 12 very quickly became entangled in the issue of treaty rights.

The Canadian courts have been active in interpreting and reconciling these two separate regulatory structures. In the legal opinion of federal government solicitors following the transfer, "section 12 does not import anything new into the relationship between the Indian and the Province but merely restates the Indian's position as already set out in the various treaties."[6] Early court cases provided a similar interpretation. In *R. v. Wesley*, [1932] 2 W.W.R. 337, Justice Lunney of the Alberta Supreme Court noted "the Agreement did not, nor was there any intention that it should, alter the law applicable to Indians." Similarly, in *R. v. Smith*, [1935] 2

W.W.W. 433, Justice Turgeon suggested section 12 should be interpreted "as would establish the intention of the Crown and Legislature to maintain the rights accorded the Indians by Treaty." Historians, however, have been notably negligent in examining the historical context for the making of section 12 of the *NRTA*.

The general textbooks on Indian/White relations in Canada provide a brief introduction to the *NRTA* and its [effect] on Indian hunting, fishing and trapping rights, but provide no interpretive analysis, nor do they cite any sources of information for students.[7] New scholarly accounts of the economic and social structures of the northern areas of the prairie provinces have addressed some of the crises within Aboriginal society, partially induced by the regulatory structure considered here, but do not provide any analysis of the origin of the *NRTA* right and its conflict with the treaty right.[8] In the best study of the transfer of Dominion control of lands to the provinces, Chester Martin provides virtually no information on the government's intent and purpose regarding section 12.[9]

In 1995, historical geographer and Native Studies professor Frank Tough introduced a number of documents he had retrieved on the *NRTA* and called for historians to examine the historical context and the intention and purpose of the framers of section 12.[10] His call for historical investigation seems especially appropriate in light of the Supreme Court's decisions regarding treaty rights. The Supreme Court has identified three important characteristics of treaty rights and the modification of these rights. First, a treaty represents an exchange of solemn promises between the Crown and the various Indian nations. It is an agreement whose nature is sacred. Second, any limitations that restrict the rights of Indians under treaties must be narrowly construed. And third, there must be "strict proof of the fact of extinguishment" and evidence of a clear and plain intention on the part of the government to extinguish treaty rights.[11] In *R. v. Sparrow*, [1990] 1 S.C.R. 1075, the Supreme Court discussed the Crown's fiduciary duty to the Aboriginal peoples of Canada. The *Sparrow* decision placed limits on the power of the Crown to extinguish an aboriginal or treaty right through application of the Sparrow test.[12] The majority noted in *R. v. Badger*, [1996] 1 S.C.R. 771, at 778:

> Any infringement of the rights guaranteed under the Treaty or the *NRTA* must be justified using the *Sparrow* test. This analysis provides a reasonable, flexible and current method of assessing the justifiability of conservation regulations and enactments. It must first be asked if there was a valid legislative objective, and if so, the analysis proceeds to a consideration of the special trust relationship and the responsibility of the government *vis-à-vis* the aboriginal people. Further questions might deal with whether the infringement was as little as was necessary to effect the objective, whether compensation was fair, and whether the aboriginal group was consulted with respect to the conservation measures.

Although the Supreme Court has thus indicated that historical context is important when examining treaty rights, its recent decisions on the *NRTA* and treaty hunting rights have not considered the historical context or the intent and purpose of the framers of section 12 of the *NRTA*.

In three decisions, made as the court enunciated the principles set out above, the Supreme Court concluded that the treaty right to hunt had been merged and consolidated (at first the court used the terms *extinguished* and *replaced*) by the *NRTA*.[13] In *R. v. Horseman*, [1990] 1 S.C.R. 901, the Supreme Court accepted that the treaty contained a right to hunt and fish commercially, but the majority concluded that the right to hunt commercially disappeared following the *NRTA* and, in return, the Crown extended the geographic extent of the right to hunt for food. In this manner, the Supreme Court concluded that the Crown had maintained its integrity and avoided the appearance of "sharp dealing" as noted in *Sparrow*. This logic led the Alberta court of appeal to extend this provision to fishing rights in *R. v. Gladue*, [1996] 1 C.N.L.R. 153. The Supreme Court modified its position in *R. v. Badger*, [1996] 1 S.C.R. 771. In this case, the Supreme Court concluded that the *NRTA* transferred the regulatory authority over the treaty right to the provinces and extinguished the treaty right to hunt commercially, but did not alter the treaty right to hunt for food within the geographic area of the treaty.[14] Although the Supreme Court has considered the historical context for the making of the treaty in these decisions, it has not considered the historical context for the origin of section 12 of the *NRTA*. This paper seeks to provide insights into the negotiations leading to section 12 of the *NRTA* and identify the intent and purpose of the framers.

ARGUMENT: THE INTENT AND PURPOSE OF SECTION 12 OF THE *NRTA*

The Dominion negotiated section 12 of the *NRTA* in the context of regulatory disputes regarding the regulation of Indian rights to hunt, fish and trap. In the period prior to the passage of the *NRTA*, the Dominion government insisted that the treaty right was subject to regulation and that nothing in the treaty was intended to mean that Indian peoples had an unrestricted right to hunt, fish or trap. The records make it clear, however, that the Department of Indian Affairs negotiated with the regulatory authorities for subsistence rights for both treaty and non-treaty Indian peoples during the pre-*NRTA* period. By 1920, the Department of Indian Affairs also recognized that the regulation of hunting and trapping, and the licensing of fishing, was within the provincial sphere of powers in those provinces that controlled their lands, but believed it could use its authority under *BNA Act* sec. 91(24) to secure special provision for Indian peoples. Conflicts with provincial authorities had emerged over this issue not only in the three prairie provinces, but also in Ontario and British Columbia, as provincial authorities sought to include Indian peoples within their regulatory regimes.

With this perspective in mind, three basic objectives of the Department of Indian Affairs can be ascertained during the negotiation of the *NRTA*. First, the department sought to provide for provincial regulation of the Indian peoples' treaty right to hunt and trap, and provincial licensing of Indian fishing rights. Second, it sought to ensure that Indian access to unoccupied Crown lands for hunting and fishing would be continued following the transfer of lands to the provincial sphere. Third, they intended to ensure that the special subsistence privileges for Indian peoples that the department had obtained in the regulatory environment would be maintained. These three objectives remained consistent throughout the negotiations. In negotiations with Alberta leading to the 1926 agreement, the three goals were achieved by a clause providing that Indian access to unoccupied Crown lands to exercise treaty rights to hunt and fish would remain unchanged following the transfer. As the negotiations reached a climax with Manitoba in 1929, however, the third concern of the Department of Indian Affairs became the most important. This concern for the maintenance of subsistence provisions reflects the growing concerns regarding provincial regulation of Indian hunting rights and the need for a provision for Indian peoples in the Treaty 1 and Treaty 2 area where they did not have a treaty right to hunt, fish and trap. Any mention of the treaty right, in this context, would have eliminated the department's ability to protect the subsistence privileges of the Indian peoples in the Treaty 1 and Treaty 2 areas; consequently, mention of the treaty right was removed from section 12 of the *NRTA*. The Dominion government, however, did not intend to merge and consolidate the treaty right with the passage of the *NRTA*. Rather than a limitation on the practice of the treaty right by Indian peoples, the *NRTA* was intended to limit the ability of provinces to regulate Indian hunting, trapping and fishing rights.

THE TREATY RIGHT TO HUNT AND FISH

The hunting and fishing clauses in the treaties did not appear randomly. Continued access to fish and game resources and the maintenance of traditional avocations, including commercial trapping and fishing practices, were an essential aspect of the treaty negotiations. During the negotiations for Treaty 6 at Fort Carlton, the assembled chiefs requested the "liberty to hunt and fish on any place as usual." They were assured by Lieutenant Governor Alexander Morris that "we did not want to take the means of living from you, you have it the same as before, only this, if a man, whether Indian or Half-Breed, had a good field of grain, you would not destroy it with your hunt."[15] Similar promises were heard at most of the treaty negotiations, and in her excellent study of the treaties, historian Jean Friesen notes, "at treaty time the Indians heard nothing that would cause them to question their assumption of Indian open access to resources."[16] The treaties thus contained the specific promise: "Indians shall have the right to pursue their avocations of hunting and fishing throughout the tract surrendered." Indian peoples believed this promise gave them the right to continue pursuing a traditional economy. This right would include commercial and subsistence practices, since both occupied important places in the traditional economic lifestyle.[17]

The Indian hunting and fishing rights set out in the treaties were subject to regulation, nevertheless. Duncan Campbell Scott informed the Indian Affairs minister in 1918:

> We have always held that there is no stipulation in the treaties which would give the Indians exclusive rights to hunting and fishing in the surrendered districts, or which would render them immune from the law, but we have endeavoured to obtain a lenient treatment for them.[18]

Both the Indians and the government, however, understood that regulation meant conservation of the resource for the continued use by Indian peoples. In the period after 1821, for example, the Hudson's Bay Company had made numerous efforts to conserve game resources, and the Indian communities of the prairies were well aware of this issue.[19] Moreover, by the time of the signing of Treaty 6, buffalo and fur-bearing animals had declined in numbers and needed the protection of regulations. Indeed, demands for conservation of the buffalo came from the Indians during the negotiations.[20] Commissioner Morris remarked that he informed the Indians the matter would be considered by the North-West Council. Similarly, several references in the records of Indian Affairs indicate that the government considered regulations designed for conservation purposes to be in the best interests of the Indians. Regulation, consequently, would conserve and protect wildlife for future exploitation. It would not inhibit access as much as improve the commercial exploitation of the resource. Regulation, it was understood, would not interfere in the pursuit of commercial or subsistence hunting and fishing practices but instead ensure their continued viability. This perspective was consistent with the explanations made during the negotiation of the treaties. In explaining the right to continue hunting and fishing in Treaty 8, for example, David Laird noted: "that only such laws as to fishing and hunting as were in the interest of the Indians and were found necessary in order to protect the fish and fur-bearing animals would be made.[21] The sole regulatory authority specified in the treaties, however, was the government of the Dominion, and this soon became an issue of concern.

THE REGULATION OF INDIAN HUNTING AND FISHING

The government's interpretation of constitutional and statutory devices were essential in this regard. Under the *Constitution Act*, section 91(24), governance of Indians and lands reserved for Indians is a federal jurisdiction. This section was the basic head of power under which the treaties and any other government obligation to the Indians could be fulfilled. Perhaps just as important, under section 91(24) the Dominion had responsibility for Indians inside and outside the bounds of treaty. By the time of Confederation, Canada had developed an Indian policy focused on the principles of protection and civilization.[22] The basic tenet of this policy was to teach the Indian how to survive in the modern Western world and encourage them to participate within the Canadian commercial economy. The Dominion implemented this policy through the *Indian Act* and the Department of Indian Affairs. Although Indians clearly fell within Dominion government jurisdiction, Indian hunting rights were not so clearly defined.

Neither hunting nor game are itemized in sections 91 or 92 of the *Constitution Act*. It soon became clear, however, that the power to regulate game fell to the provinces. Regulation of hunting and trapping according to the decision in *R. v. Robertson* [1886] 3 Man R. 613 fell within the bounds of section 92(13) — "matters of a local concern" — and section 92(16) — "civil and property rights" — of the *Constitution Act*. In his decision, Justice Killam at page 616 noted that two issues led to this conclusion:

> One is that the Provincial Legislatures have, from the very inception of the Union, assumed to enact laws of the nature of the game protection clauses in question, while the Dominion Parliament has never attempted to do so, and the right of the Legislatures to do so has never been questioned by the officers of the Crown for the Dominion, either by exercise of the veto power or otherwise; the other is the somewhat analogous subject of "Sea coast and inland fisheries" is [sic] by s.s. 12 of the 91st section of the British North America Act, placed among the subjects upon which the Dominion Parliament has exclusive authority to legislate.

Fisheries were not a local issue because of the migratory nature of fish between sea and river and the relationship between the fishery and the Dominion powers over navigation and shipping. Game, Killam concluded, was not migratory and did not intersect other areas of Dominion government interest, and was thus a local issue. Within a province, he decided, game management was an exclusive domain of the provincial authorities. This concurred with the Dominion decision to grant the power to manage game resources to the North-West Territories Council, a government with far less authority than a province, in 1875.[23]

The regulation of Indian hunting slowly became more, rather than less, confusing. While the provincial governments passed legislation to regulate hunting and trapping, including Indian hunting and trapping, the Department of Indian Affairs continued to consider treaty obligations as an important consideration. The Department of Indian Affairs consequently chose to negotiate with the provinces regarding Indian hunting rights. The department's primary concern was to ensure access to game for subsistence purposes. Early legislation in Manitoba appeared to respond to this issue and also reflected the province's concern regarding the regulation of Indian hunting rights on reserves. Manitoba's first game laws appeared in the *Agricultural Statistics and Health Act* (1883). Section 61 provides that the regulations "shall not apply to Indians within the limits of their reserves with regard to any animals or birds killed at any period of the year for their own use only, and not for the purpose of sale or traffic."[24] Still, the Dominion government sought to ensure that it had the ability to protect Indian peoples from provincial regulations. It acted within the parameters established within the *Indian Act*. An amendment to the *Indian Act* (1890) provided that application of the game laws of Manitoba and North-West Territories to Indian people could occur at the prerogative of the Superintendent General of Indian Affairs.[25] Section 69 remained an important aspect of the *Indian Act* in 1927. It read:

> The Superintendent General may, from time to time, by public notice, declare that, on and after the day therein named the laws respecting game in force in the province of Manitoba, Saskatchewan or Alberta, or the Territories, or respecting such game as is specified in such notice, shall apply to Indians within said province or Territories, as the case may be, or to Indians in such parts thereof as to him seems expedient.[26]

It should be recognized that only the prairie provinces and territories, areas where the federal government controlled the lands and Indian treaties had been negotiated without the concurrent agreement of the provincial authorities, were enumerated in section 69.[27]

Following the Dominion government's disallowance of earlier North-West Territories game ordinances because of the impact these had on Indians, the 1893 game ordinance passed by the North-West Territorial government fell into line with the Dominion's policy. It ordered:

> This Ordinance shall only apply to such Indians as it is specially made applicable to in pursuance and by virtue of the powers vested in the Superintendent General of Indian Affairs of Canada by Section 133 of the *Indian Act*, as enacted by 53 Victoria, Chapter 29, sec. 10.[28]

Following the creation of Alberta, this provision disappeared. The first provincial law in Alberta (1907) made no provision for Indian hunting rights. This led to confusion regarding the actual application of provincial laws regarding hunting and trapping. North-West Territorial game ordinances had been applied to a variety of bands in the territorial districts of Assiniboia, Saskatchewan and Alberta, by announcements made 1 July 1893 and 1 May 1903. When the new provinces of

Alberta and Saskatchewan were created in 1905, the Department of Indian Affairs assumed that the announcements of 1893 and 1903 meant Indians belonging to the enumerated bands were subject to provincial game laws.[29] In *[R. v. Stoney Joe]* (1910 unreported), however, Justice Charles Stuart of the Alberta Supreme Court ruled that only the game law in force at the time of the announcement applied.[30] The Stoney Indians at Morley agency, he decided, were subject to the 1893 game ordinance of the North-West Territories rather than the *Alberta Game Act*. In his reasons, he also noted that in areas where the Dominion had not passed regulations under the section, Indians were subject to provincial game laws of general application. When Alberta requested that the Superintendent General apply provincial game laws to Indians in Alberta, the Deputy Superintendent of Indian Affairs, Frank Pedley, refused. Pedley noted that, under the *Alberta Game Act*, Indian peoples had to pay for licences for subsistence hunting, and this was unacceptable. Alberta eventually agreed to waive the licence fees.[31] The *Alberta Game Act* (1912) provided:

> The Lieutenant Governor in Council may authorize the refund to any treaty Indian of the amount paid by him for any licence under the provisions of this Act upon a certificate being furnished by any Indian agent under his hand that such person is a treaty Indian on the Reserve under his control.[32]

The *Alberta Game Act* also contained a clause providing for unrestricted hunting for food by residents in the north of 55 degrees latitude.[33] Following the passage of this act, the Superintendent General announced in 1914 that the game laws of Alberta would apply to the Stoney Indians at Morley Agency, the most problematic of the hunting bands in Alberta in the eyes of both governments. In the period following this decision the Dominion made no other proclamations for Indian peoples of the prairie provinces.[34]

Despite the ruling in *R. v. Stoney Joe*, the Department of Indian Affairs, as a policy practice, continued to inform Indians that they were subject to provincial regulations, and continued to consider an announcement made under the *Indian Act* of significant importance. This perspective emerged from conflicts in Ontario. Provisions for continued hunting and fishing rights existed in the pre-Confederation Robinson treaties covering the area around the Great Lakes, and problems in Ontario regarding provincial regulation of Indian hunting led the department to seek legal advice from the department of justice. The assistant deputy minister of justice noted in an opinion 5 October 1917:

> It seems to me that it is for your Department [Indian Affairs] to determine, having regard to the terms of the Indian treaties or otherwise, to what extent the Indians should be immune from the Provincial game laws and that then that immunity should be provided by legislation, either of the Province if the Province will yield to the Dominion, otherwise by legislation of the Dominion in the exercise of its paramount power with regard to Indians and lands reserved for Indians.[35]

In a memorandum to the minister in 1919, Duncan Campbell Scott illustrates the confusion in the Department of Indian Affairs:

> There may be some doubt as to whether the game laws of the province [Manitoba] would apply to Indians within that part of the province covered by treaties Nos. 1 and 2 without there formally being applied under Section 66 [later sec. 69] of the *Indian Act*, but there can be no doubt that they would not apply to the other parts of the province in view of

the stipulation in the treaties covering the same, without a formal notice being given under said Section 66 of the *Indian Act*. I think it in the interest of the Indian that the game laws should be made to apply to the whole Province.[36]

Although no announcement was made, the Superintendent General of Indian Affairs, Arthur Meighen, informed the House of Commons in 1920 that Indians outside their reserves had to comply with provincial regulations regarding the preservation of game.[37] Similarly, in a circular letter to Indian agents in 1926, long-serving Department of Indian Affairs Secretary J. D. McLean wrote:

> At the recent conference of the Chief Federal and Provincial Game Officials held at Ottawa, attention was drawn to the fact that many of the Indians do not seem to understand that they are required to respect close seasons for hunting and trapping and other Provincial regulations for the protection of game and fish. Will you please explain to the Indians of your Agency that they must strictly comply with the Game Laws and that failing to do so they render themselves subject to the penalties provided therein.[38]

The Dominion continued to negotiate with the provinces for subsistence rights, nevertheless.[39] The emphasis on subsistence is reflected in the regulatory structure the Dominion developed for the Northwest Territories in this period. While earlier acts regulating game in the Northwest Territories had allowed unlimited hunting by Indians and Inuit,[40] this changed in 1917 and by 1927 the *Northwest Game Act* noted:

> Notwithstanding anything contained in subsections one and three, the game therein mentioned may be lawfully hunted, taken or killed, and the eggs of birds therein mentioned may be lawfully taken, by Indians or Eskimos who are *bona fide* inhabitants of the said territories, and by explorers or surveyors who are engaged in any exploration, survey or other examination of the country, but only when such persons are actually in need of such game or eggs to prevent starvation.[41]

Hunting rights in some areas of Treaty 8 and all of the Treaty 11 area, consequently, had been regulated for conservation purposes excepting hunting the resource for food.

Conditions in the prairie provinces continued to deteriorate in the late 1920s as the increasing number of White settlers, trappers, commercial fishermen and sport hunters threatened game resources. While both the Dominion and the province considered the issue seriously, efforts to solve the problem floundered on the issue of jurisdiction. The Department of Indian Affairs sought to establish exclusive game and trapping preserves for Indian people.[42] The provinces, meanwhile, agreed that such jurisdictions held promise, but sought to restrict Indian hunting and trapping to the preserves. They desired to open other areas of the province to only White hunters and trappers, since the provinces had responsibility for their activities, they voted in provincial elections, and they paid licensing fees to the province for their trap lines. The Department of Indian Affairs, however, expressed significant concerns about this project.

> It is obvious that if the Indians are to confine their trapping activities to the areas set aside for their exclusive use, they will in effect be waiving their treaty right to trap anywhere in the province. It is assumed that any such waiver can only be made by the Indians themselves, and the attitude which they might take towards any such proposition has not been discussed to date with the Indian Department.[43]

The problem eventually led to a collapse of the negotiations. As a result, Indians and White commercial hunters and trappers competed for the game resources and traditional conservation habits disappeared. The discussions of conservation issues [illustrate] a second problem that slowly emerged regarding the regulation of Indian hunting and trapping: Indians were not only hunters and trappers, but also fishermen.

The regulation of the inland fishery in Canada is more complex than the regulation of hunting and trapping.[44] Under the *Constitution Act*, section 91(12), conservation of the inland fishery falls within federal jurisdiction, and the Dominion exercised its authority through the Department of the Marine and Fisheries and the *Fisheries Act*. Section 45 of the *Fisheries Act* (1914) provided for regulation of the inland fishery through order-in-council.[45] Disputes between the Dominion and the province of Ontario in the 1880s and 1890s, however, had resulted in increased provincial participation in the regulation of fisheries. Ontario claimed a proprietary colonial right in many inland lakes and channels under section 109 of the *BNA Act*, and in 1898 the judicial committee of the privy council agreed. The Dominion retained responsibility for catch limits and closed seasons (conservation of the stock), but Ontario, by virtue of its proprietary rights, had the authority to issue licences.[46] Over time, it became Dominion practice to pass provincially drafted regulations for the inland fishery in all provinces except the prairie provinces. In this manner, the Dominion reconciled its power to conserve the fishery with provincial ownership of the fishery.

In subsequent discussions the Dominion and Ontario agreed that provincial regulations, as long as they remained sufficiently general, would apply to Indians.[47] The Dominion government, nevertheless, believed it had the power to protect Indian fishing rights within this arrangement. According to a legal opinion offered by the Department of Justice:

> Such laws passed and not disallowed would be valid and binding even if they operated to deprive Indians of rights assured by treaty. If, however, provisions [are] clearly contrary to treaty it might well be held to be improper and unjustifiable use of the Legislative power.[48]

This perspective continued to influence the Department of Indian Affairs throughout the period under study. Deputy Superintendent General Duncan Campbell Scott informed his minister in 1918 that his department "could not well object to any reasonable legislation being applied to Indians as such legislation would be in their interests as much as in the interests of the white man." The Department, however, did not believe that Indian hunting and fishing privileges secured under treaty were "subject to any legislation that the Legislature of Ontario might see fit to enact."[49] The minister apparently agreed. Arthur Meighen wrote:

> the constitutional power of the Province [Ontario] to regulate fishing and hunting, even as applicable to Indians, is undoubted. The question remaining is, as to how far this Department should, as representing the Indians, endeavour to modify the actual application of Provincial regulations in deference to the Robinson treaties as affecting such Indians.[50]

Meighen also noted that the department could hardly protest regulations designed to conserve the stock since these were in the interests of the Indians themselves.

The fishing disputes in Ontario were important to the decisions on the *NRTA*, since the agreements were intended to set the prairie provinces on an equal footing with the other provinces. Under the terms of the *NRTA*, the prairie provinces gained control of Crown lands and resources and thus obtained a proprietary right in the inland fishery. Section 9 of the *NRTA* gave the provinces ownership of the inland fishery, while the Dominion retained its ability to regulate for the purposes of conservation of the stock under Section 91(12) of the *Constitution Act* and exercised its powers under the *Fisheries Act*. This new regulatory environment appeared consistent with those established in the rest of Canada following the Ontario disputes of the 1890s. It is also important, however, to examine the regulatory regime in place in the prairie provinces prior to the *NRTA*. During this era the Department of Indian Affairs sought special subsistence fishing privileges similar to those on hunting for Indian peoples.

Since the prairie provinces had no proprietary right to the inland fishery prior to 1930, regulation of Indian participation in the fishery of the prairie provinces developed under the control of the Dominion government and the Department of Marine and Fisheries. As early as October 1893, the Department of Indian Affairs identified the necessity of regulating Indian and Metis fishing for commercial purposes while making special provision for subsistence. According to Indian Commissioner Hayter Reed, the department desired that they "might be allowed to fish in the close season to meet their own immediate wants." By November, the Department of Marine and Fisheries had passed regulations "to permit fishing during the prescribed close season, in such cases where the local fishery officer is satisfied that the applicant for licences intends to fish for the supply of local wants, and not for export out of the locality."[51] The newly consolidated regulations, announced in 1894, placed Indian fishermen on equal footing with all other fishermen with the special provision that:

> 16. These regulations shall apply to Indians and half-breeds, as well as to settlers and all other persons; provided always that the Minister of Marine and Fisheries may from time to time set apart for the exclusive use of the Indians, such waters as he may deem necessary, and may grant to Indians or their bands, free licenses to fish during the close-seasons, for themselves or their bands, for the purpose of providing food for themselves, but not for the purpose of sale, barter, or traffic.[52]

The Department of Indian Affairs continued to consider the issue carefully, and the Deputy Superintendent General insisted that the treaty right required *"free"* access to licences, and that it would be preferable to allow Indians to fish during the closed season for subsistence.[53]

This emphasis on protecting Indian subsistence rights continued to be one of the most important issues in designing regulatory structures for the fisheries. Continued declines in the fish stocks led the Dominion to appoint commissions to examine the fisheries in Manitoba, Saskatchewan and Alberta in 1909. The *Dominion Alberta and Saskatchewan Fisheries Commission* conducted public hearings, and met with sport fishermen, local fish and game associations, businessmen and community leaders, Indians, traders and missionaries. The Indians, traders and missionaries all argued that Indians should be able to take and cure fish during the spawning season. First, they noted that the Indians had been promised a continuation of their traditional fishing practices in the treaty; and second, the Indians depended on the large catches during this season, dried and preserved, to feed themselves during the winter trapping season. Still, the commissioners concluded:

to allow the taking of fish in the close season [spawning] is in no wise a solution of the Indian question, and it should be faced in a proper manner by the Indian Department. We cannot uphold this claim of the Indians as being for their own and their children's welfare, not to mention that of the fisheries generally, and therefore recommend a rigid close season be maintained except as elsewhere provided for under the heading "Permit for Indians."[54]

The "Permit for Indians" was defined as:

> Indians and Half-breeds, resident in the two Provinces, should be granted free of charge an annual permit for the use of 60 yards of net, not more than one for each family, the fish to be used solely by the holder of the permit and his family, and no sale of fish is to be allowed. This permit shall allow Indians and Half-breeds to take fish during the close season for their necessary daily consumption, but not for the purpose of curing or hanging.
> If an Indian or Half-breed wishes to fish for sale, he should be placed under the same restrictions as White men.[55]

In their reasons for this decision, the commissioners indicated that their desire to conserve the fish stocks and the jurisdictional questions regarding Indian fishing had influenced their decision. They wrote, "it is the duty of the Fishery Department to conserve the fish that the best results will follow, and to this end a rigid close season is necessary;" and "if the Fishery Department undertakes to practically feed the Indians by allowing them to fish in the close season it is taking upon itself duties which properly belong to the Indian Department." Further, they noted: "If this practice were allowed it would be to the detriment of the Indian himself in a few years. We have found that he has already depleted some lakes."[56] While the treaty right combined Indian Affairs and fishing practices, the Dominion jurisdictional arrangement tended to divide them.

The ensuing regulation of Indian fishing in the prairie provinces shows how the Dominion efforts at conservation intersected with the treaty right to fish and the need for fish for subsistence by Indian peoples. The fisheries department, it is clear, believed that the treaties allowed it to impose regulations for the purpose of conservation. In disputes with the Fisher River band in Manitoba, for example, the Dominion enforced the regulations through the Department of the Marine and Fisheries. These regulations, like those in Ontario, placed Indian people on an equal footing with non-Indian fishermen in the commercial fishery and forced compliance on Indians with regard to net size and the close season. Any Department of Indian Affairs concerns regarding the impact of regulations on the treaty right to fish had to be negotiated with the [Fisheries officials]. The Department of Indian Affairs expressed satisfaction, however, that fisheries laws had not been enforced:

> against the Indians as to prevent their obtaining supplies of fish for their own domestic use....Of course, any Indians engaged in commercial fishing must conform with the laws the same as white people.[57]

This enforcement of the law was clearly discretionary, since the *Fisheries Act* contained no mention of Indian peoples or treaty privileges. The Dominion apparently viewed fishing for subsistence as essential to the community and as posing no threat to conservation measures. It also considered its regulatory position as consistent with the text of the Treaties, which provided for regulation of the Indian avocation fishing.

By the 1920s, therefore, a regulatory environment had emerged on the prairies in which Indians, both treaty and non-treaty, were subject to provincial game laws and federal fisheries regulations. In both of these cases, however, the Department of Indian Affairs had sought concessions for Indian people when hunting or fishing for subsistence. The problem continued to be noted in the *Annual Report of the Department of Indian Affairs* in 1929. The report blamed White commercial hunters and trappers for the shortage of game, and argued special concessions for Indian people were required.[58] Indian agents in the north, meanwhile, frustrated with the attitude of the provincial authorities, suggested some solution had to be worked out during negotiations for the transfer of lands and resources. During this period, they argued, concessions with the province could be won.[59]

THE ALBERTA RESOURCES TRANSFER AGREEMENT OF 1926

The *NRTA*s were intended to correct long-standing grievances from the prairie provinces regarding their status as equal partners in Confederation. The issue of transferring control of Crown lands to the provinces had been discussed as early as 1912 and was one of the key issues promoted by the Progressive Party in the 1920s.[60] Finally, in 1925, the King government entered into serious negotiations with the province of Alberta, the least recalcitrant of the three provinces. The negotiators then asked the Indian Affairs Branch for their input into the process. The Department of Indian Affairs identified the creation of new reserves following future settlement of aboriginal claims, the disposition of unused and surrendered reserve lands and the monies that might accrue from these surrenders, and the necessity for continued Indian access to Crown lands for hunting and fishing as itemized in the treaties as the most pressing concerns. The department also expressed some concern about regulating the Indian hunting and trapping right since game resources fell under provincial jurisdiction.

After discussions with Deputy Superintendent General D. C. Scott, Colonel O. M. Biggar, counsel for Canada in the negotiations, noted the concerns of Indian Affairs regarding game management. In a memorandum of their meeting sent to Scott for his clarification, Biggar remarked that the "Department of Indian Affairs is just as much, or even more concerned to secure the preservation of game than the provincial authorities themselves." He recognized the concerns the department had for hunting Indians in the north, "and it is not without importance that, notwithstanding the game laws, they should be allowed to hunt and fish out of season for their own food." All of these comments came before any mention of the treaties or a treaty right to hunt and fish. Finally Biggar concluded:

> There are provisions about hunting and fishing in all the Alberta treaties (Williams is to send me copies of these). The provisions in certain treaties [give] the Indians a right to hunt and fish on all unoccupied lands subject only to such regulations as the Dominion may make on the subject. The northern territory, however, which is from this point of view the most important, confers the right only subject to such regulations as are now made by law on the subject, and suggest therefore that the Provincial laws might be applicable. Moreover, on the transfer to the Province of the Crown lands, it might at least be argued that the permission the treaties give to enter upon unoccupied lands for the purpose of hunting and fishing came to an end, since these lands were no longer under the control of the authority by which the treaty was made. It would appear, however, that the better opinion would be that, since it was the Crown which made the treaty, and the Province equally with the Dominion was the Crown, the permission to the Indians still stood. It

> would nevertheless be advisable to include in the arrangement with Alberta a provision definitely making the Indian treaty provisions apply. Probably it will not be necessary at this stage to raise the question of whether an Indian properly on unoccupied lands is liable under provincial game laws. It would appear advisable to leave this for subsequent settlement, since the question relates to general legislative administration of Crown lands as such.[61]

This concern for hunting and fishing rights, interestingly, always remained peripheral in debates in the House of Commons.

After reviewing the Indian Affairs material, Colonel Biggar summarized the concerns for the prime minister as: a) a need for land to grant reserves following future surrenders of Aboriginal title; b) protection of former reserve lands and cash accumulated following the disposition of land by bands no longer requiring or agreeing to surrender their reserve; c) guaranteeing Indians right to hunt and fish on unoccupied lands according to treaty; and d) continued relief of Indians from the obligation to comply with provincial fish and game laws. Colonel Biggar argued that the first and second issue were easily covered in a general clause governing reserve lands, and no special provision would be necessary. These two issues form the basis for sections 10 and 11 of the *NRTA* and, once the issue of returning surrendered lands to the domain of the Crown in the right of the province had been solved, caused few disputes during the negotiations.

The third issue was more problematic, he noted. While it might be intimated that the provinces would be bound by the treaties and that the Indians would continue to have access to unoccupied Crown lands for the purpose of hunting and fishing, a special provision would be negotiated. Biggar, noting his discussions with Scott, wrote:

> In the circumstances it would be advisable to include in the agreement a provision that the right of Indians to enter upon all unoccupied Crown lands for the purpose of hunting and fishing should continue, notwithstanding the transfer of lands to the Province, to be the same as if the lands had remained under the administration of the Dominion.[62]

Thus, the issue of Indian hunting and fishing rights was first introduced to the *NRTA* negotiations in terms of continued treaty right of access to Crown lands.

The fourth issue, the relationship between Indian hunters and provincial game laws, was not a problem specific to the prairie provinces. As previously noted, it had also emerged from disputes with Ontario where a similar provision on hunting and fishing rights existed in the pre-Confederation Robinson treaties. Scott believed a clause in the *NRTA* would alleviate future problems over jurisdiction and regulation. It offered an opportunity for Indian Affairs to resolve its conflicts with Alberta over conservation measures as well. Colonel Biggar, however, dismissed the need for inclusion of such a clause. He wrote:

> The fourth point has no relation to lands, but to legislative jurisdiction over Indians as such, and since this is assigned by the British North America Act exclusively to the Dominion. I think that it is unnecessary and would be dangerous to make any reference to the subject in an agreement with the Province of Alberta which must be confirmed by concurrent statutes; the only possible effect of a provision on this point would be to narrow unnecessarily the Dominion's present plenary power.[63]

The Dominion government's position during the negotiations of 1925, consequently, should be regarded as an effort to protect their legislative authority over Indian peoples and to ensure the continuation of the treaty right to pursue the avocation of hunting and fishing on unoccupied Crown lands subject to regulation. Ironically, the fourth point, dismissed by Biggar, would eventually emerge in the *NRTA* and form the central issue of contention in interpreting the agreements.

In the first drafts of the agreement being negotiated with Alberta, the Dominion followed the Indian Affairs Branch recommendations and inserted a clause protecting the right of treaty Indians to hunt and fish on Crown lands. Section 9 of the agreement read:

> To all Indians who may be entitled the benefit of any treaty between the Crown and any band or bands of Indians, whereby such Indians surrendered to the Crown any lands now included within the boundaries of the Province, the Province hereby assures the right to hunt and fish on all unoccupied Crown lands administered by the Province hereunder as fully and freely as such Indians might have been permitted to so hunt and fish if the said lands had continued to be administered by the Government of Canada.[64]

Since the policy of the Department of Indian Affairs had been to make treaty Indians subject to Alberta game laws, this clause was perfectly acceptable to Alberta and remained relatively unchanged throughout the negotiations. The clause called for the continuation of the regulatory environment existing at the time of the transfer of lands to the province. It appeared in the memorandum of agreement reached between Alberta and the Dominion 9 January 1926 and caused no debate in the legislature of the province nor the parliament of the Dominion.

THE 1929 NEGOTIATIONS OF THE *NRTA*

The Alberta deal died in 1926, however, over the protection offered to Roman Catholic school rights in the *Alberta Act*.[65] By the time the Supreme Court assured the Dominion that protecting these school rights was within the Dominion jurisdiction, Manitoba's refusal to accept the terms of the Alberta deal because of the financial terms it contained overshadowed other issues. A royal commission headed by Saskatchewan Justice W. F. A. Turgeon solved the compensation issue with Manitoba in 1928, and subsequently the King government attempted to strike a deal with that province instead of Alberta.[66] The shift to Manitoba had implications for the negotiations from the perspective of Indian Affairs. Most importantly, Treaties 1 and 2 covering southern Manitoba did not contain specific provisions regarding Indian hunting and fishing. As negotiations between Manitoba and the Dominion neared completion in August of 1929, the Department of Justice consulted with Duncan Campbell Scott once again. The two clauses of the Alberta agreement regarding Indian reserves and Indian access to unoccupied Crown lands for hunting and fishing remained unchanged, but Manitoba had requested clarification of the 'privileges of hunting and fishing the Indians within the Province are now entitled to under Dominion laws."[67] Scott's reply to this enquiry transformed the clause in the *Natural Resources Transfer Agreement* and set the tone for subsequent debates over Indian hunting and fishing rights in the prairie provinces.

Scott noted that Manitoba was covered by Treaties 1 through 5. Treaties 1 and 2 contained no provisions regarding hunting and fishing, but Treaties 3, 4 and 5 contained clauses on this issue. These clauses, as previously noted, provided for a continuation of the Indian avocations of hunting and fishing subject to Dominion regulations. Rather than focus on the nature of section 9 and point out that the treaty provided for access to Crown lands not "required or taken up for settlement, mining, lumbering or other purposes," Scott returned to the issue of regulating Indian hunting and fishing rights, which Biggar had dismissed in 1925. He reviewed the jurisdictional arrangement under the terms of the *Indian Act*, and noted no public proclamation by the Superintendent General had been made in the case of Manitoba:

> I am inclined to think that in the absence of Public Notice given under the provision of said Section 69 of the *Indian Act* the Game Laws of the Province could not prevail against the provisions of the Treaties.[68]

He then expressed satisfaction with section 9 of the Alberta agreement and noted it preserved whatever rights the Indians may now enjoy. Scott's position emphasised the paramount authority of the Dominion under section 91(24) and avoided reference to the department's practice of making Indians subject to provincial game laws, Arthur Meighen's attitude while Superintendent General of Indian Affairs, and Justice Stuart's decision in *R. v. Stoney Joe* (supra). It seems deliberately inflammatory, reflected a similar hard-line stance he had taken in 1919, and intimated that Manitoba had no ability to control Indian hunting and fishing within the province without a specific provision, despite departmental practice. Scott appeared to fear that Manitoba desired the complete removal of any mention of Indian hunting and fishing rights in the *NRTA*.

Scott may have been following his Indian agents' advice and using the *NRTA* negotiations to win concessions on Indian hunting and trapping preserves. The provincial authorities had proved unwilling to develop this system and game resources continued to be threatened. With little alternative commercial activity available to northern Indians, the department faced the daunting task of feeding Indians should the game resource fail. Scott returned to the issue of ensuring access to game for subsistence in his letter. He counselled the Acting Deputy Minister of Justice:

> I may say that with the development of the country and the entry of outside hunters and trappers into the northern regions of the Province where the Indians rely almost entirely upon game for their subsistence, their plight is becoming more desperate year by year with the disappearance of game and while, as I stated, I think the Indians in these regions have the full rights granted by treaties it is a question in my mind as to whether it would not be advisable to have it now set forth in this agreement that the Indians in these northern regions shall have the right to take game at all times for their subsistence, and I should like to discuss this matter with you before the agreement is finally completed.[69]

Scott made no mention of fishing. The suggestion that special provision be made for hunting for subsistence is interesting, nonetheless, since Treaty 5 covering the northern regions of Manitoba had clear provisions regarding the continuation of the Indian avocation of hunting and fishing subject to regulation. Similarly, Scott had assured the acting deputy minister that the clause as accepted in 1926 protected these rights. Acting Deputy Minister of Justice Chisholm, despite the opinion of earlier negotiators, agreed to discuss these concerns further with Scott, and the process of changing the clause in the Natural Resources Transfer Agreements had begun. Manitoba's ability to regulate Indians within the game jurisdiction and DIA's desire to incorporate subsistence hunting privileges by Indian communities became the topics of negotiation.

In a draft of the agreement sent to Scott by W. W. Cory, Deputy Minister of the Interior, 7 October 1929, the hunting and fishing clause from the 1926 Alberta agreement remained unchanged, but a note appears following the clause to the effect that Dr. Scott's concern "has not yet been settled." Biggar later forwarded the clauses under discussion to Scott. They clearly attempted to deal with Scott's concern for subsistence hunting in northern regions and solve the regulatory confusion regarding regulation of Indian hunting rights. The clause contained no mention of fish or fishing. Someone at Indian Affairs added the word *fish* after *game* in all areas of the clause, including the words "laws respecting game *and fish* in force in the Province from time to time." By 12 December 1929, a new clause appeared in the draft agreement with Manitoba, making mention only of "laws respecting game in force in the Province" and provoked no response from Indian Affairs or Scott.[70] The new clause incorporated into the Manitoba [sec. 13], Alberta [sec. 12] and Saskatchewan [sec. 12] resource transfer agreements provided:

> In order to secure to the Indians of the Province the continuance of the supply of game and fish for their support and subsistence, Canada agrees that the laws respecting game in force in the Province from time to time shall apply to the Indians within the boundaries thereof, provided, however, that the said Indians shall have the right, which the Province hereby assures to them, of hunting, trapping and fishing game and fish for food at all seasons of the year on all unoccupied Crown lands and on any other lands to which the said Indians may have a right of access[71]

The regulatory aspects of section 12 resembled, in many respects, the practice of regulations negotiated by the Department of Indian Affairs in the years prior to 1930. They reflect the primary importance [of] the third objective of Indian Affairs in the later negotiations.

SECTION 12 AND THE TREATY RIGHT

An "Explanatory Memorandum re: Manitoba Resources Agreement" found in the Indian and Northern Affairs files at the National Archives certainly suggests that the government had no intention of changing the status of the treaties or federal powers to regulate Indian affairs or federal power over Indians in the fishery. It noted:

> Paragraph 13—Section 69 of the *Indian Act* RSC 98, empowers the Superintendent General of Indian Affairs to apply the provincial game laws to the Indians in any of the three Western Provinces, or any part of any of them. What is in effect Canada's agreement by this clause to apply the provincial game laws to the Indians in Manitoba is accordingly compensated for by the provisions of the agreement that the application of these laws shall not deprive the Indians of their right to hunt and fish for food.[72]

The ramifications of section 12 are given even less clarity in the "Explanation to Accompany Bill No. providing for the ratification of the Agreement with Province of Alberta for the Transfer of its Natural Resources," where it reads[,] "The rights of hunting, trapping, and fishing on unoccupied Crown lands are secured to the Indian."[73] Given this explanation of section 12 and Dominion game management regimes established in the Northwest Territories, it is not surprising the section produced no debate in the House of Commons. Surely a clause that had the ramification of changing the treaty rights of Indians and limiting the federal government's constitutional authority to regulate Indian hunting and fishing would produce some debate from one thoughtful member. Indeed, the issue of treaty rights and provincial game laws would be raised by Members of Parliament in subsequent years.[74]

It is possible that the Dominion officials believed that they had protected the Indian treaty right in the *NRTA*. The treaty right was "subject to such regulations as may from time to time be made by Her Majesty Government of Her Dominion of Canada." Delegating this regulatory authority to Manitoba, Alberta and Saskatchewan was not a significantly new perspective. The Dominion had provided for the application of provincial game laws in these provinces under section 69 of the *Indian Act* and had a long-standing policy of making Indians subject to provincial regulation in this field. Remarks by the minister responsible for Indian Affairs follow this logic. Following queries from a Member of Parliament in 1940 regarding the failure of the Dominion to fulfil its treaty obligation regarding the fishing right at Fisher River in Manitoba, the minister, Thomas Crerar, noted that the government saw nothing incompatible between the treaty right to fish and the regulatory environment. Treaty 5 gave the Cree at Fisher River the right to fish subject to regulations. Dominion fishing regulations had therefore been enforced in the region prior to the *NRTA*. Next, Crerar noted that the provisions of the *Indian Act*, sec. 69, provided for the transfer of this regulatory authority to province by public proclamation and this procedure had been followed. The *NRTA*, he continued, confirmed that provincial laws would apply for regulatory purpose. He concluded that a violation of the treaty had therefore not occurred.[75] In other words, Crerar believed section 12 was consistent with the treaty right to pursue the avocation of hunting and fishing.

The intent and purpose of the Dominion government in negotiating Section 12, consequently, could be considered a modification of the treaties to include the provinces in the regulatory authorities under treaty, with an important limitation placed upon the regulatory power of the provinces (but not on the Dominion). The right to hunt and fish for food on unoccupied Crown lands becomes a special privilege granted to all Indian peoples and is separate from the treaty right. Moreover, the new right does not interfere with the treaty right. The disappearance of the word *treaty* from the clause in December 1929 is significant in that all Indians, not simply treaty Indians, were entitled to the right to hunt, trap and fish on unoccupied crown lands for food. Indians subject to treaty still retained the right to pursue the avocation of hunting and fishing on unoccupied Crown lands surrendered by them, subject to regulations.

Government Interpretations of Section 12 after 1930

The statements emerging from Indian Affairs and the Department of the Interior following the *NRTA* demonstrate that the Dominion officials did not believe the *NRTA* had replaced any treaty rights. Scott suggested that an important new right had been granted to Indians. In a circular letter following the transfer he informed the Indian agents:

> This agreement confers a very important privilege upon the Indians which they should avail themselves of with due regard for the purpose for which it is intended. The department

> has received reports of abuses by Indians, such as wanton slaughter, the sale of game to whites, and other [illegal activities]. It is desired that at the Treaty payments during the present year, you will hold a meeting of the Indians of each band and explain to them that while they have the privilege of taking game or fish for food required for their own use, they must not, in any case take game for commercial purposes of any kind, in any way contrary to the law, and that wanton slaughter will not be tolerated.[76]

The opinion of the Department of the Interior, while agreeing that an extraordinary right had been granted, appeared to believe the treaty right continued. Deputy Minister H. H. Rowatt informed the department solicitor, Mr. Daly, in 1933:

> When Premier Anderson was here he spoke to our Minister about the rights of Indians to take game in the Province and our Minister explained that by the Natural Resources Transfer Agreement no new rights were accorded to Indians, that they were merely confirmed in the rights they have had all along; further, that the Province seem to have the remedy for abuses in their own hands because the extraordinary right of the Indian is only to kill for *food* on *unoccupied* lands of the Crown.[77]

Similarly, Rowatt himself had two years earlier acknowledged that the treaty right continued when he requested that the Department of Justice determine if "the Migratory birds treaty over-rides any of the formal Indian treaties which insured the Indians definite hunting rights" in the province of Saskatchewan.[78] He did not ask for a similar review of the *NRTA*.

Other positions taken by Dominion officials indicate that the Dominion never intended to give up its ability to protect Indian hunting and fishing rights in the prairie provinces. In a 1930 letter drafted by Colonel O. M. Biggar, counsel for the Dominion during negotiations, at the request of W. M. Cory, a solicitor with the Department of the Interior, it notes:

> The effect of the agreement with the Province is, of course, in no sense to surrender the right of the regulation now possessed by the Dominion Parliament by which, indeed, any regulatory power of Indians must of necessity remain vested by virtue of the provisions of the British North America Act.[79]

That the Dominion did not believe it had given up authority to legislate on Indian hunting and fishing under section 91(24) following the *NRTA* is apparent in the continued applicability of section 69 of the *Indian Act*. Although section 12 of the *NRTA* would apparently make section 69 of the *Indian Act* redundant, the Dominion did not remove section 69 in its 1936 amendments to the *Indian Act*. This decision suggests they were still unsure of the province's ability to enforce regulations against treaty Indians without the power of the Dominion through the *Indian Act*. When the government did eventually replace sec. 69 in 1952, it broadened the application of provincial authority rather than removing the clause. Section 87 enshrined treaty rights in federal legislation and applied all provincial laws of general application to Indian peoples.

The Department of Indian Affairs, however, accepted a contradictory legal opinion from Deputy Justice Minister W. Stuart Edwards, and communicated it to Saskatchewan Premier J. T. M. Anderson. It noted:

> With regard to the meaning of the term "game" in the proviso of clause 12, the stipulation set out in this clause was embodied in the agreement for the purpose declared in the introductory words, viz., "in order to secure to the Indians of the Province the continuance of the supply of game and fish for their support and subsistence." For the attainment of

> that object, it being no doubt in the interests of the Indians themselves that laws should be enacted and enforced with a view to the preservation of the game and fish, Canada agreed "that the laws respecting game in force in the Province from time to time shall apply to the Indians within the boundaries thereof,['] and thereby undertook not to exercise its paramount legislative power under section 91, head No. 24, of the British North America Act, 1867, so as to override, as to the Indians within the Province, the Provincial Game Laws from time to time in force. But that agreement as to the application of the Provincial Game Laws to the Indians is expressly qualified by the stipulation set out in the proviso whereby "the said Indians shall have the right ... of hunting, trapping and fishing game and fish for food at all seasons of the year on all unoccupied Crown lands."[80]

A second opinion by Edwards follows a similar logic. He argued that all Indians, not simply treaty Indians, were considered in the agreement. He noted the term *Indian* in the *NRTA* had the same meaning as *Indian* in section 91(24) of the BNA Act, and thus implied all Indians had the rights provided in the section.[81] This position follows on his earlier interpretation of section 12 as an agreement not to use the Dominion's paramount authority under section 91(24).

Like the Dominion, Manitoba did not consider its regulatory regime following the 1930 transfer to be a violation of the treaty right. The Manitoba director of game and fisheries, A. G. Cunningham, defended his regulatory authority at Fisher River in 1939, by pointing to the Dominion precedents. He wrote:

> I am informed this [special fishing preserve] or relative matters in respect to special fishing rights allegedly conferred on Indians by the Treaty Agreements have been brought forward recurrently by Indians during the past twenty years. However, the Fishery Administration while a Dominion charge has consistently refused to give any consideration to them and steadfastly maintained that an Indian fishing commercially must submit to the same laws and restrictions as white commercial fishermen. While, as you know, we have made some concessions, it is felt we must in the main adhere to the precedent set by the Dominion.[82]

Manitoba government officials, consequently, did not believe that the treaty right had been extinguished and replaced. They simply argued that the new regulatory environment did not breach the agreement.

CONCLUSIONS

The Supreme Court has concluded that the *NRTA* extinguished the treaty right to hunt commercially. In the most recent case, *R v. Badger*, Justice Cory for the majority noted that the decisions in *Moosehunter* and *Horseman* to the effect that the *NRTA* ended the treaty right to hunt commercially were reasonable and valid. As the Supreme Court decided in *Horseman*:

> The hunting rights reserved to the Indians in 1899 by Treaty No. 8 included hunting for commercial purposes, but these rights were subject to governmental regulation and have been limited to the right to hunt for food only—that is to say, for sustenance for the individual Indian or the Indian's family —by para. 12 of the Transfer Agreement.[83]

The Court in *Badger* also concluded "that the Treaty No. 8 right to hunt has *only* been altered or modified by the *NRTA to the extent that* the *NRTA* evinces a clear intention to effect such a modification."[84] In this regard, the historical evidence clearly indicates that the Dominion intended to transfer the regulatory authority over treaty hunting and trapping rights and the licencing of treaty fishing rights to the provincial governments.

The historical evidence also makes it clear, however, that the Dominion did not seek to limit or extinguish any element of the treaty Indian hunting and fishing rights with the passage of the *NRTA*. What then does the historical evidence suggest the Dominion intended in passing section 12 of the *NRTA*?

First, the Dominion intended to ensure that Indians maintained their treaty right of access to unoccupied Crown lands for the purpose of hunting, trapping and fishing.

Second, the Dominion hoped to conserve game through wise management in the belief that this was important to the Indians because of their treaty right to continue their avocation of hunting and fishing and their reliance upon fish and game for subsistence.

Third, the Dominion recognized that, subsequent to the transfer of lands, the regulatory system for hunting and fishing would resemble that in Ontario where the provincial government set hunting regulations and licensed fishing. The Dominion negotiators therefore sought to ensure to all Indian peoples subsistence privileges on unoccupied Crown lands, consistent with the regulatory structure they had negotiated prior to the *NRTA*, by placing limits on the provincial regulatory authority.

In making its decisions on Indian treaty hunting and fishing rights and the *NRTA*, the Supreme Court has not had the benefit of this historical context. Some members of the Supreme Court have acknowledged the need for historical investigation of the intent and purpose of the negotiators of the *NRTA*. The court divided four to three in *Horseman*, and Justice Wilson for the minority remarked:

> We should not readily assume that the federal government intended to renege on the commitment it had made. Rather we should give it an interpretation, if this is possible on the language, which will implement and be fully consistent with that commitment.
> ...one should be extremely hesitant about accepting the proposition that para. 12 of the Transfer Agreement was also designed to place serious and invidious restrictions on the range of hunting, fishing and trapping related activities that Treaty 8 Indians could continue to engage in.[85]

If the court accepts this historical evidence, then it may address the issue of justification of provincial game regulations that serve to extinguish the treaty right to hunt commercially and provincial fisheries licensing requirements that serve to extinguish the treaty right to fish commercially. These regulations and licensing requirements need to be examined within the parameters of the *Sparrow* test. That the regulation of Indian hunting and trapping under section 12 was intended to "secure to the Indians of the Province the continuance of the supply of game and fish for support and subsistence" seems relevant in any interpretation of these issues. This language reflects the intentions of the treaty negotiators when they discussed regulation with Indian peoples. It adds weight to the historical evidence that suggests the government did not seek to extinguish and replace or merge and consolidate the treaty right with the *NRTA*.

NOTES

1. *R. v. Badger*, [1996] 1 S.C.R. 771, at 805.
2. The *NRTA*s consist of three separate agreements to transfer the land and resources from Dominion to provincial control on the prairie provinces. All were passed by the Dominion Parliament and each province passed its agreement with the Dominion. See *Statutes of Canada*, 20-21 Geo.

V, c. 3, c. 29, and c. 41. The sections, or clauses as they are sometimes called, discussed in this paper are identical in each bill, although they have different numbers in the Manitoba Resources Transfer Agreement. In this paper the sections will be referred to by the numbers given in the Saskatchewan and Alberta agreement. The agreements were confirmed by the Imperial Parliament in the *Constitution Act* (1930), 20-21 Geo. V, c. 26, sec 1, and consequently hold constitutional status.

3. Alexander Morris, *The Treaties of Canada with the Indians of Manitoba and the North-West Territories* (Saskatoon: Fifth House, 1991) contains the text of Treaties 1 through 7. The clause in Treaties 3, 5 and 6 is identical. Some subtle differences exist in Treaties 4 and 7. In Treaties 8 through 11 references to the *Dominion* are replaced by the *Government of the country* and the word *avocation* is replaced by *vocation*. For the text of Treaties 8 and 11, the reader could consult René Fumoleau, *As Long As This Land Shall Last* (Toronto: McClelland and Stewart, 1975).

4. Chester Martin, "The Colonial Policy of the Dominion," *Royal Society of Canada: Proceedings and Transactions*, series 3, vol. 16 (1922), p. 35. See also Chester Martin, *Dominion Lands Policy* (Toronto: Macmillan, 1934, reprinted, 1973); L. H. Thomas, *The Struggle for Responsible Government* (Toronto: University of Toronto Press, 1978); Donald Swainson, "Canada Annexes the West: Colonial Status Confirmed," *Federalism in Canada and Australia: The Early Years*, edited by Bruce Hodgins (Waterloo: Wilfrid Laurier Press, 1978).

5. *Statutes of Canada*, 1929, 20-21 Geo. V., c. 3, sec. 12.

6. Solicitor to H.H. Rowatt (Deputy Minister, Interior), 2 Dec. 1932, RG 22, vol 22, file 91.

7. Donald Purich, *Our Land: Native Rights in Canada* (Toronto: James Lorimer, 1986), 85–87 discusses the *NRTA* only in terms of how the courts have interpreted the *NRTA* right to hunt for food. Olive Dickason, *Canada's First Nations*, 2nd edition (Oxford: Oxford University Press, 1997) makes no mention of the issue. J. R. Miller, *Skyscrapers Hide the Heavens*, rev. ed. (Toronto: University of Toronto Press, 1989), pp. 220–21, provides a single paragraph. A. J. Ray, *I Have Lived Here Since the World Began* (Toronto: Lester, Key Porter Books, 1996), p. 280, states only that "when it [the Dominion] transferred federal control of the natural resources of Manitoba, Saskatchewan, and Alberta to those provinces in 1930, it gave them the power to override the provisions of Treaty 1, 2, and 5 to 8 for the purposes of conservation."

8. Don Wetherell and Irene Kmet, *Alberta's North* (Edmonton: University of Alberta and the Canadian Circumpolar Institute, 2000). Frank Tough, *As Their Natural Resources Fail: Native People and the Economic History of Northern Manitoba, 1870–1930* (Vancouver: University of British Columbia Press, 1996). Anthony Gulig, "Sizing Up the Catch: Native-Newcomer Resource Competition and the Early Years of Saskatchewan's Northern Commercial Fishery," *Saskatchewan History* 47 (1995). Two theses also warrant mentioning here: Anthony Gulig, "In Whose Interest? Government-Indian Relations in Northern Saskatchewan and Wisconsin, 1900–1940" (Ph.D. thesis, University of Saskatchewan, 1997); and Richard Daniel, "Indian Rights and Hinterland Resources: The Case of Northern Alberta" (M.A. thesis, University of Alberta, 1977).

9. Chester Martin, *"Dominion Lands" Policy*, edited with an introduction by L.H. Thomas (Toronto: McClelland and Stewart, 1973), 204–226.

10. Frank Tough, "Introduction to Documents: Indian Hunting Rights, Natural Resources Transfer Agreements and Legal Opinions from the Department of Justice," *Native Studies Review* 10, no. 2 (1995), 121–67.

11. See *Calder v. Attorney-General of British Columbia*, [1973] S.C.R. 313, at p. 404; *Nowegijick v. The Queen*, [1983] 1 S.C.R. 29, at 36; *Simon v. The Queen*, [1985] 2 S.C.R. 387, at 401–2, 406; *R. v. Sioui*, [1990] 1 S.C.R. 1025, at 1035, 1061, and 1063; *R. v. Badger* [1996] 1 S.C.R. 771 at 802.

12. *R. v. Sparrow*, I S.C.R. [19901 1075 at 1123–30. The Sparrow decision was particular to those rights in existence in 1982 and protected under section 35(1) of the *Constitution Act* (1982). Still, the basic parameters of the test seem appropriate to examining any decisions affecting treaty rights prior to 1982 as well.

13. *Frank v. The Queen*, [1978] 1 S.C.R. 95; *Moosehunter v. The Queen*, [1981] 1 S. C.R. 282; and *R. v. Horseman* [1990], 1 S.C.R. 901.

14. For a discussion of the *Badger* case see Catherine Bell, "*R. v. Badger*: One Step Forward and Two Steps Back?" *Constitutional Forum Constitutionnel* 8, no. 2 (1997): 21–26. For an examination of the Crown's fiduciary obligation see Leonard Rotman, "Hunting for Answers in a Strange Kettle of Fish: Unilateralism, Paternalism and Fiduciary Rhetoric in *Badger* and *Van Der Peet*," *Constitutional Forum Constitutionnel* 8, no. 2 (1997): 40–45.

15. Morris, *Treaties*, 215 and 218.

16. Jean Friesen, "Magnificent Gifts: The Treaties of Canada with the Indians of the Northwest 1869–76," *Transactions of the Royal Society of Canada*, Series 5, vol. I (1986), p. 50. See also Friesen, "Grant Me Wherewith to Make My Living," in Kerry Abel and Jean Friesen, *Aboriginal Resource Use in Canada*, (Winnipeg: University of Manitoba Press, 1991), pp. 141–55; and Richard Daniel, "The Spirit and Terms of Treaty Eight," in Richard Price, ed., *The Spirit of the Alberta Indian Treaties* (Edmonton: Pica Pica Press, 1987).
17. The most prolific writer on the subject of Indian economic practice is Arthur J. Ray. For a summary of the evidence he provided in *R. v. Horseman*, [1990] see A.J. Ray, "Commentary on the Economic History of the Treaty 8 Area," *Native Studies Review* 10 no. 2 (1995): 169–95. His two most important books on this subject are *Indians in the Fur Trade* (Toronto: University of Toronto Press, 1974) and The Fur Trade in the Industrial Era (Toronto: University of Toronto Press, 1990). For similar work on Manitoba see Frank Tough, *As Their Resources Fail*, Laura Peers, *The Ojibwa of Western Canada* (Winnipeg: University of Manitoba Press, 1994); and Paul Thistle, *Indian-European Trade Relations* (Winnipeg: University of Manitoba Press, 1987)
18. Memo, Scott to Meighen, 21 Nov. 1918, RG10, vol. 6731, file 420–1.
19. Arthur J. Ray, "Some Conservation Schemes of the Hudson's Bay Company, 1821–50: An Examination of the Problems of Resource Management in the Fur Trade," *Journal of Historical Geography*, 1 (Jan. 1975): 49–68. Lorne Hammond, "Marketing Wildlife: The Hudson's Bay Company and the Pacific Northwest, 1821–9," *Forest and Conservation History* 37 (Jan. 1993): 14–25.
20. Morris, Treaties, 195. See also John Leonard Taylor, "Two Meanings of Treaties 6 and 7," in Richard Price, ed. *The Spirit of the Alberta Indian Treaties* (Edmonton: Pica Pica, 1987): 9–43.
21. "Report of the Commissioners for Treaty Eight," Sessional Papers, 1900, no. 8, xxxvi.
22. L.F.S. Upton, "The Origins of Canadian Indian Policy," *Journal of Canadian Studies* 8, no. 4 (1973), 51–61; John Tobias, "Protection, Civilization, Assimilation: An Outline History of Canadian Indian Policy," *Western Canadian Journal of Anthropology*, (1976) reprinted in R.D. Francis and Howard Palmer, eds., *The Prairie West: Historical Readings*, (Edmonton: Pica Pica Press). John Milloy, "The Early *Indian Acts*: Developmental Strategy and Constitutional Change," in A.S. Lussier and Ian Getty, eds., *As Long As the Sun Shines and the Water Flows*, (Vancouver: University of British Columbia Press, 1983).
23. *Statutes of Canada*, 1875, 38 V., c. 49, sec. 7.
24. *Statutes of Manitoba*, 46-47 V., c. 19, s. 61.
25. *Statutes of Canada*, 1890, 53 V., c. 29, sec. 10
26. *RSC, 1927*, c. 98, s .69.
27. It is hard to understand why the Dominion believed it had to isolate Manitoba and the North-West Territories (later Alberta and Saskatchewan) in section 69. Lands had no impact on game laws and as a result, either all provinces or no provinces needed the assistance of section 69 to enforce game laws against Indians in their domains. If it was the treaty issue problems again emerge. While Ontario played a role in the negotiation of Treaty 9, it did not in Treaty 3 covering the North-West Triangle. Similarly, Treaty 8 extended into the Liard River region of B.C.. Neither B.C. nor Ontario are mentioned in section 69.
28. Territorial Ordinances, 1893, No. 8, sec. 19. This section replaced an earlier provision which noted: "The provisions of this Ordinance, except section 4 [unlawful damage to a bird's nest], shall not apply to Indians in any part of the Territories, with regard to any game actually killed for their own use, and not for purposes of sale or traffic." Territorial Ordinances, 1892, No. 19, sec. 16.
29. RG 10, vol. 6732, file 420-2.
30. Copy of this judgement in RG 10, vol. 6732, file 420-2A.
31. Frank Pedley (Depy Sup't. Indian Affairs) to Duncan Marshall (Alta Min. of Agric.), 7 June 1911; Marshall to Pedley, 29 Sept. 1911; Pedley to Marshall, 5 Oct. 1911, Benjamin Lawton (Game Guardian) to Pedley, 28 Mar. 1912; RG 10, vol 6732, file 420-2A.
32. *Statutes of Alberta*, 1911–12, c. 4, sec. 25(4). Interestingly, this section did not change following the passage of the NRTA. See *Revised Statutes of Alberta* (*RSA*), 1942, c. 70, sec. 64(t).
33. *RSA*, 1942, c. 70, sec. 33.
34. See RG 10, vol. 6732, file 420-2A and 420-2B for numerous pieces of correspondence along these lines. Although no record of an announcement could be found, T.A. Crerar to J.T. Thorson (M.P.), 27 July 1940 suggests that a proclamation (no date specified) regarding Manitoba game laws had been made. RG 10, vol. 6969, file 501/20-2 pt. 1. Duncan Campbell Scott noted that section 69 had not been used with reference to Manitoba. Scott to Deputy Minister of Justice, 4 Sept. 1929, RG 10, vol. 6820, file 492-4-2 pt. 1.

35. Opinion 1447/17,W. Stuart Edwards to Scctt, 5 Oct. 1917. RG 10, vol. 6731, file 420-1. Position quoted in Memorandum to Scott, 6 Feb. 1925. RG 10 vol. 6820, file 492-4-2 pt. 1.
36. Memo Scott to Meighen, 15 Mar. 1919, RG 10, vol. 6731, file 420-1.
37. Canada, *Debates*, 1920, 3379.
38. Circular J.D. McLean to Agents, 26 Apr. 1926, RG 10, vol. 6732, file 420-2B.
39. Statement by Indian Affairs, Dominion and Provincial Game Conference, Jan. 1928, RG 10, vol. 6731, file 420-1-2.
40. *Statutes of Canada*, 1894, 57-58 V., c. 31, sec. 8(a).
41. *RSC*, 1927, c. 141, sec. 4(4). Treaty Indian peoples protested against this restriction as a violation oftheir treaty right to no avail. See Philip Godsell, *Arctic Trader* (New York: A. L. Burt), 193–94 for an account of the protests against these restrictions at Fort Resolution in 1921.
42. This issue was first discussed in 1923. Hoadley to Stewart, 6 Mar. 1923, Scott to Stewart, 13 Nov. 1923, Card to Scott, 22 May 1924 and Scott to Card, 10 June 1924, RG 107 vol. 67327 file 420-2B.
43. Memo to file, 27 Oct. 1926, RG 10, vol. 6732, file 420-2B.
44. For a commentary on the complex jurisdictional arrangement regarding fisheries in Canada see Gerald La Forest, *Natural Resources and Public Property under the Canadian Constitution* (Toronto: University of Toronto Press, 1967), 77–79, 157–60, 165–66, 176–82.
45. *Statutes of Canada*, 1914, 4-5 Geo V., c.8, sec. 45. See *Revised Statutes of Canada (RSC)*, 1927, c. 73, sec. 46.
46. *R. v. Robertson* [1882] 6 S. C. R., 52; and *Attorney General for the Dominion of Canada v. Attorneys General for the Provinces of Ontario Quebec and Nova Scotia* [1898] A. C., 700 in *Decisions of the Judicial Council of the Privy Council relating to The British North America Act*, arranged by Richard Olmsted (Ottawa: Queen's Printer, 1954), 418–435. See Lise C. Hansen, "Treaty Fishing Rights and the Development of Fisheries Legislation in Ontario: A Primer," *Native Studies Review* 7 no. 1 (1991) for a discussion of this issue in Ontario.
47. This followed upon the traditional policy developed by the Department of Marine and Fisheries that regardless of treaty rights, fisheries regulations applied to Indian peoples. See Margaret Beattie Bogue, "To Save Fish: Canada, the United States, the Great Lakes, and the Joint Commission of 1892," *Journal of American History* 79 no. 4 (1993), 1445.
48. This issue was discussed in legal opinion dated 20 July 1897. See "Opinions-Department of Justice" RG 10, vol. 6731, file 420-1.
49. Memorandum, Scott to Meighen, 6 Mar. 1918, RG 10, vol. 6731, file 420-1.
50. Meighen to Scott, 31 Oct. 1918, RG 10, vol. 6731, file 420-1.
51. Hayter Reed to T. Mayne Daly, 28 October 1893, RG 10, vol. 1114; A. E. Forget, Circular letter, 24 Nov. 1893, RG 10, vol. 3581, file 878 pt. A.
52. Order in Council, 8 May 1894, *Canada Gazette*, 26 May 1894.
53. Deputy Superintendent General, "Memorandum for the Information of the Minister re Fishing Privileges Claimed by Indians," 18 Nov. 1895, RG 10, vol. 1117.
54. *Dominion Alberta Saskatchewan Fisheries Commission* (Ottawa, 1912), 31.
55. *Ibid.*, 22.
56. *Ibid.*, 31.
57. J.D. McLean (Assistant Deputy Minister) to T.H. Carter (Agent), 10 April 1915, RG 10, vol. 6969, file 501/20-2 pt. 1.
58. *Annual Report of the Department of Indian Affairs to March 31, 1929*, 7–8.
59. Canada, *Debates*, 1923, 2146. Richard Daniel, "Indian Rights and Hinterland Resources", pp. 167–76.
60. Canada, *Debates*, 1912, 4269. A brief historical summary of the negotiations for each province is found in RG 22, vol. 17, file 70. Readers may also consult Chester Martin, *"Dominion Lands" Policy*, edited with an introduction by L.H. Thomas (Toronto: McClelland and Stewart, 1973), 204–26.
61. Memorandum to Scott, 30 Jan. 1925, RG 10, v. 6820, file 492-4-2 Part 1.
62. Appendix H: Indian Lands in A Memorandum to Prime Minister by Col. Biggar (copy forwarded to D.C. Scott 17 February 1925). RG 10, vol 6820, file 492-4-2 pt. 1.
63. *Ibid*.
64. Draft of Alberta Agreement sent to D.C. Scott, May–June 1925 in RG 10, v. 6820, file 492-4-2 Part 1.
65. Canada, *Debates*, 1926, 557, 3923. Brownlee to King, 7 April 1926, unpublished Sessional Papers, 1926, 1st session, 15th Parliament, paper no. 75a.

66. For correspondence between Manitoba and the King government, see unpublished Sessional Papers, 1926-7, 1st session, 16th Parliament, paper no 172. W.F.A. Turgeon, T.A. Crerar, and Charles Bowman, *Report of the Royal Commission On the Transfer Of Natural Resources Of Manitoba* (Ottawa: King's Printer, 1929).
67. J. Chisholm (Acting Deputy Min. of Justice) to Scott, 22 Aug 1929. RG 10, vol. 6820, file 492-4-2 pt. 1.
68. Scott to Chisholm, 4 Sept. 1929, RG 10 v. 6820, file 492-4-2 Part 1.
69. *Ibid.*
70. Cory to Scott and Draft of Manitoba Resources Transfer Agreement, 7 Oct. 1929; Biggar to Scott and copies of new clauses, 12 December 1929. RG 10, vol. 6820, file 492-4-2 part 1.
71. *Statutes of Canada*, 1929, 20-21 Geo. V., c. 3, sec. 12.
72. RG 22, vol. 3, file 6.
73. *Ibid.*
74. Canada, *Debates*, 1934, 3000–3004.
75. Crerar to Thorson, 27 July 1940, RG10, vol. 6969, file 501/20-2 part 1.
76. Duncan Campbell Scott to Agents, 30 May 1931, copy in RG 10, vol 8860, file 1/18-11-2 pt. 1.
77. Memorandum, H.H. Rowatt to Daly, 23 Jan. 1933, RG 22, vol. 22, file 91.
78. Rowatt to W. Stuart Edwards (Deputy Minister, Justice), 12 Nov. 1931, RG 22, vol. 22, file 91. See Dan Gottesman, "Native Hunting and the Migratory Birds Convention Act: Historical, Political, and Ideological Perspectives," *Journal of Canadian Studies* 18, no. 3 (1983): 67–89, for information on the Migratory Birds Convention and Indian hunting rights.
79. Draft letter to C.F. Newell, K.C. (Edmonton), 3 March 1930, RG 22, vol 17, file 70.
80. W. Stuart Edwards to Scott, 12 Feb. 1931, opinion 198/31; and Minister of the Interior to J.T.M. Anderson, 4 Feb. 1933, RG 22, vol. 22, file 91.
81. See Frank Tough, "Introduction to Documents: Indian Hunting Rights, Natural Resources Transfer Agreements and Legal Opinions from the Department of Justice," *Native Studies Review* 10, no. 2 (1995): 121–67 for a reprint of this legal opinion and several others. See also Kent McNeil, *Indian Hunting, Trapping and Fishing Rights In the Prairie Provinces of Canada* (Saskatoon: Native Law Centre, 1983), pp. 26–9.
82. A.G. Cunningham (Director of Game and Fisheries, Man) to A.G. Hamilton (Inspector of Indian Agencies), 26 July 1939. RG 10, vol 6969, file 501/20-2 part 1.
83. [1990] 1 S.C.R. 901, at 904.
84. [1996] 1 S.C.R. 771, at 805.
85. [1990] 1 S.C.R. 901, at 913 and 922.

(d) Community Perceptions of the Beverly-Qamanirjuaq Caribou Management Board[†]

Anne Kendrick

INTRODUCTION

Caribou co-management arrangements have focused largely on improving communication between government managers and traditional (historically and geographically-rooted) caribou-using communities. Co-management regimes represent *de facto* (informally realized), as well as *de jure* (legally-ensured) sharing of decision-making authority between state bodies and caribou-using communities. This paper will exam-

---

[†] From *The Canadian Journal of Native Studies* 20(1) (2000): 1–33. Reproduced with permission of the publisher.

ine the case of the Beverly-Qamanirjuaq Caribou Management Board (hereafter, "the Board") and the challenges it has tackled perhaps because of, rather than in spite of, its *ad hoc* status.

The Board came into existence as a response to a perceived crisis of declining caribou numbers in the early 1980s. It is not a land claims based co-management arrangement and has no formal status in Canadian law. A distinction is made between claims-based co-management — such as the examples negotiated under the Inuvialuit and Nunavut Final Agreements — and crisis-based co-management, like the Board, by the report of the Royal Commission on Aboriginal Peoples (1996). The report cites the Board as an example of "an *ad hoc*, and possibly temporary, policy response to crisis" (RCAP, 1996:667). However, the Board is often described as one of the most successful and long-standing co-management institutions in northern Canada (Cizek, 1990; Morgan, 1993; Osherenko, 1988; Usher, 1991). In the absence of decision-making authority, the Board has fostered learning and the building of social capital.

Co-management institutions, like the Board, may elucidate the conditions for innovative social learning both by local and state actors and for the building of social capital for cooperation. Social capital is defined here in terms of trust, norms and networks that facilitate coordinated action (Coleman, 1990). Berkes (1997) hypothesizes that trust between actors is one of the critical conditions for successful co-management. This condition of "trust" is explored in terms of learning and the evolution of mechanisms for the transmission of knowledge among all parties to a co-management arrangement. It is the importance of flexible, informal institutions that allow collective learning that is explored in the experience of the Board.

CARIBOU CO-MANAGEMENT

Caribou co-management is a process of cross-cultural learning. Ideally, the knowledge of caribou-hunting communities and government biologists and managers complement each other with the aim of achieving the sustainable use of a culturally and economically important resource. A number of the idealized definitions of co-management are listed [next page]. Co-management may play a part in creating a dialogue between the knowledge of First Nation caribou-hunting communities and government biologists rooted in very different world views. It may also help to synthesize a new resource management science open to participation by resource users rather than as a process for centralized control of local resource management systems.

The ecological knowledge of First Nation communities has been described as an assemblage of empirical, paradigmatic and institutional knowledge (Berkes, 1999). Traditional ecological knowledge (TEK) is a "knowledge-practice-belief complex" where "levels" of knowledge are closely linked and shaped by feedback from one another (Berkes, 1999; Berkes and Folke, 1998). In contrast, formal science, by definition does not include an ethical or belief component (Berkes, 1999:210). However, many academics have challenged the idea that western science is free of a cultural context (Latour, 1998; Longino, 1990; Nadasdy, 1999; Worsley, 1997). The practice of Western science is rooted in a positivist-reductionist paradigm (Pepper, 1984; Evernden, 1985) that perpetuates a human-environment distinction while TEK

(d) Community perceptions of the Beverly-Qamanirjuaq Caribou Management Board

> **Co-management Definitions (modification of Berkes, 1997:6)**
>
> "co-management signifies [a] political claim [by local people] to the right to share management power and responsibility with the state."
>
> McCay and Acheson (1987:32)
>
> "the sharing of power and responsibility between the government and local resource users."
>
> Berkes *et al.* (1991:12)
>
> "the substantial sharing of protected areas management responsibilities and authority among government officials and local people."
>
> West and Brechin (1991:25)
>
> "a blending of these two [first nation and government] systems of management in such a way that the advantages of both are optimized, and the domination of one over the other is avoided."
>
> Royal Commission on Aboriginal Peoples (1996:665–666)

is rooted in a world view that recognizes a "community-of-beings" (Berkes, 1999; Fienup-Riordan, 1990). As explained by a hunter from Baker Lake, Nunavut: "All animals inform each other, all things that have breath in them even if they are from different species" (John Killulark, *Caribou News* 13(1):2).

A quick examination of caribou management institutions across North [America] reveals a great range of community/government power-sharing arrangements for the management of barren-ground caribou (*Rangifer tarandus*) herds. These arrangements stretch from preliminary signs that Alaska will shortly enter into formal co-management of the Western Arctic Caribou Herd, to the well-established co-management of the Porcupine, Beverly and Qamanirjuaq herds. There are no formal efforts for the species-specific co-management of caribou in Quebec and Labrador, although there are failed and/or dormant efforts to establish a co-management institution for the George River caribou herd ranging between Quebec and Labrador (see Figure 1).

Both the Beverly-Qamanirjuaq and Porcupine Caribou Management Boards have undoubtedly helped to clarify and focus discussion between caribou users and outside interests, but the success of the internal dialogue between caribou users and government managers is much more difficult to assess. Feit (1998) has argued that the academic literature on co-management provides very little evidence that meaningful knowledge sharing and decision making between First Nation wildlife using communities and government wildlife managers is occurring. Academics have noted increasing signs of the political empowerment of communities to manage their wildlife resources, but very little work has looked at the success of co-management institutions in facilitating exchanges between Aboriginal wildlife users and government wildlife managers (exceptions include Feit, 1998; Klein *et al.*, 1999; Kofinas,

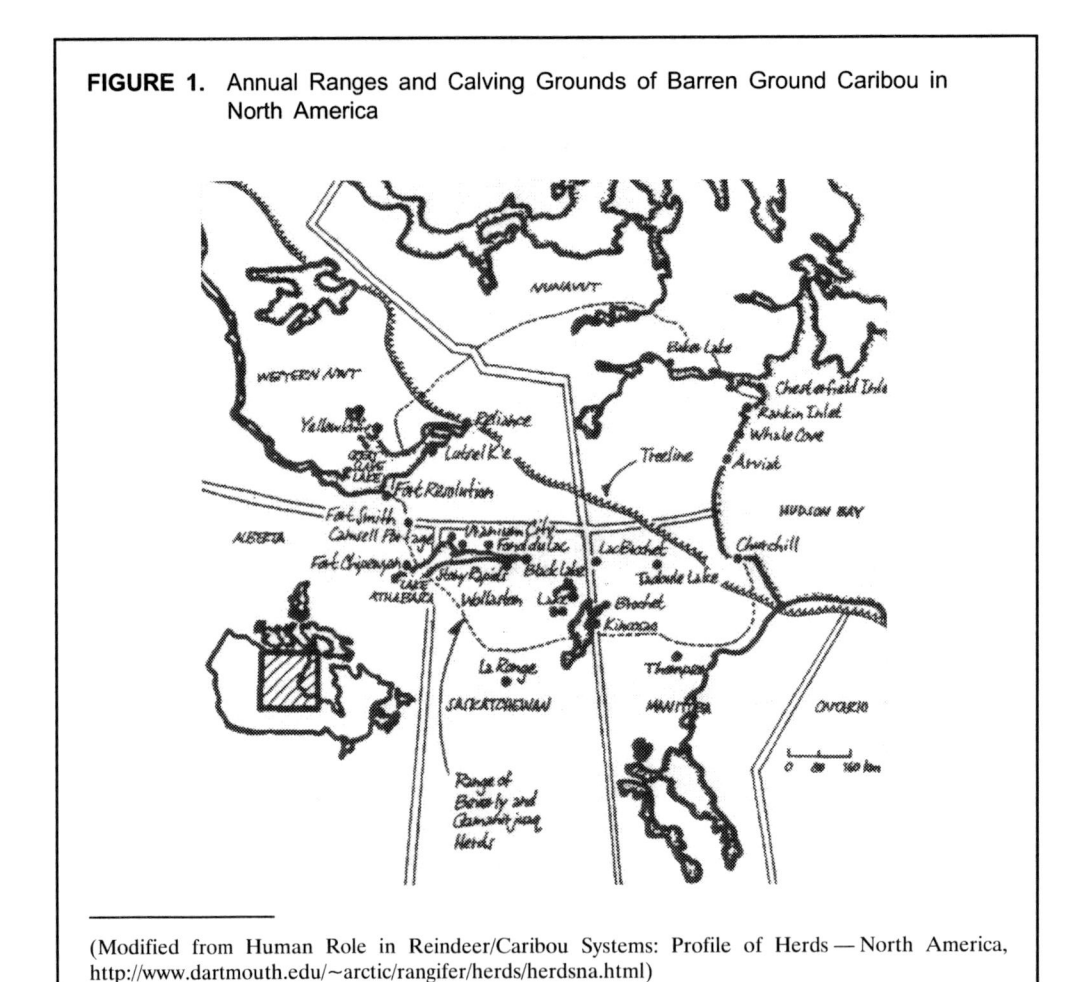

FIGURE 1. Annual Ranges and Calving Grounds of Barren Ground Caribou in North America

(Modified from Human Role in Reindeer/Caribou Systems: Profile of Herds — North America, http://www.dartmouth.edu/~arctic/rangifer/herds/herdsna.html)

1998; Kruse et al., 1998; Singleton, 1998). It is not clear that co-management has led to fundamental or mutually beneficial exchanges between state and Indigenous resource management systems. However, by taking a closer look at one of these co-management systems, insights may be gained about the nature of the dialogue or "conversation" between state and Indigenous resource management systems.

THE BEVERLY-QAMANIRJUAQ CARIBOU MANAGEMENT BOARD

The Board is the first formal caribou co-management institution in Canada. The Board's history illustrates the complexity of the communication involved in attempting to link First Nation and state caribou management systems. The enormity of this task is apparent especially in light of the historical conflict between wildlife biologists and First Nation wildlife users, and the difficulties that come from attempting to match management systems rooted in very different world views.

The Board has served as a "single window" (Usher, 1993) for the consultation of outside interests with caribou users for more than 15 years. However, the success of the internal dialogue occurring behind the Board's "window" is less easily discerned. It appears that the Board's internal discussions in large part represent the construction of an "inner window" between government wildlife managers and First Nation wildlife users. However, the fashioning of this window is a slow and difficult process. The Board has devoted much of its resources to communicating the knowledge of wildlife managers to caribou-using communities. However, the transmission of knowledge from communities back to government wildlife managers has been slow and veiled by a number of conflicts and differences.

HISTORY OF THE BOARD

The Board grew out of a conflict that left little doubt that new forms of communication between communities and government managers was needed. The Board is an advisory body made up of eight First Nation members representing 20 Dene, Métis, Cree and Inuit communities and five members appointed by the provincial, territorial and federal government (Figure 2). The Board provides a setting for the debate and definition of the collective interests of this diversity of communities bound by their cultural and economic dependencies on caribou and therefore, the biological survival of two large caribou herds. The Beverly herd numbers close to 300,000 animals and the Qamanirjuaq, close to 500,000 animals according to 1994 population surveys (*Caribou News*, 15(1):1). The overlapping ranges of these two caribou herds stretch westward from the Hudson Bay coast to Great Slave Lake in the Northwest Territories and from the tundra north of the Arctic Circle south to the spruce lichen woodlands of northern Manitoba and Saskatchewan.

The Board was established in 1982, the first example of a formal co-management board for a game animal in Canada (Usher, 1993). The origins of the Board can be traced to 1978, when government biologists formed a Caribou Working Group in order to develop a management plan to combat what appeared to be a dramatic decline in the numbers of the Qamanirjuaq caribou herd. In the winter of 1979–1980, the neighbouring Beverly herd wintered unusually far south. It is estimated that between 15–20,000 animals were killed in northern Saskatchewan during that winter. Federal and provincial governments as well as First Nation communities received heavy national and international criticism for the winter hunt.

In 1981, Dene and Métis communities on the ranges of the Qamanirjuaq and Beverly caribou herds developed a resolution outlining the formation of a user-only board including both non-treaty and treaty Indians as traditional hunters. Users were concerned that participation in a joint user-government board would erode existing Aboriginal and treaty rights and narrow the extent of eligible user membership. However, a joint user-government Board was created despite the tensions involved in linking the government and First Nation-initiated proposals of the preceding years. Such a marriage was an astounding event at a time of perceived crisis for two large caribou herds, when the miscommunication between government wildlife managers and First Nation communities was high.

FIGURE 2. The Beverly-Qamanirjuaq Caribou Ranges and Traditional Caribou Hunting Communities represented on the Board

(Modified from The Beverly Qamanirjuaq Caribou Management Board website, http://www.arcticcaribou.com/range.html)

In recognition of the fundamental effects of wildlife management decisions on Inuit communities, the government predecessor to the Board (the all-government Caribou Management Working Group) initiated the Kaminuriak (an earlier spelling of Qamanirjuaq) Film/Video Project and *Caribou News*, the Board's newsletter. This video project documented the perspectives of government biologists and Inuit hunters working and living on the range of the Qamanirjuaq caribou herd in the late 1970s. The project spurred discussion between biologists and Inuit hunters who were at odds over the causes and even the existence of a decline in the population numbers of the Qamanirjuaq caribou herd by documenting the viewpoints of all sides of the debate. The Board is convinced that the films facilitated communication and helped to change attitudes. Only two to three years previous to the signing of the Caribou Management Agreement (and the video project) it was not possible to freely discuss topics of caribou management in communities.

GAINING COMMUNITY PERSPECTIVES: STUDY AREA AND METHODOLOGY

The Board was established at a time when the gap in mutual recognition of the ecological knowledge of wildlife managers and caribou-using communities could not be bridged. This discussion continues with an examination of the Board's progress in bridging the communication gap between managers and caribou users by analyzing the activities of the Board between 1982–1993 (including the minutes of the

TABLE 1. Outline of Arviat Interviewees		
Number of Interviewees:	Female	Male
>60 years old	8	4
50–60 years old	5	11
30–50 years old	4	13
<30 years old	1	6

meetings and the Board's newsletter, *Caribou News*). Local perceptions of the Board are illustrated by interviews carried out in the caribou-using communities of Arviat, Nunavut and Tadoule Lake, Manitoba. Arviat is a primarily Inuit community of 1,300 people on the west coast of Hudson Bay. Tadoule Lake is a Dene community of 350 located in spruce lichen woodland on the shores of a lake in northern Manitoba near the Nunavut border. All subsequent discussion of community perceptions of the Board refer to the author's research (Kendrick, 1994) unless otherwise noted.

The author spent parts of the summer of 1993 and winter of 1994 in Arviat and Tadoule Lake and a year beforehand living in the "neighbouring" community of Churchill. Both Arviat and Tadoule Lake are "fly-in" communities that hunt animals from the Qamanirjuaq caribou herd. However, there are a number of prominent differences between the two communities.

Arviat

Arviat is predominantly an Inuit community with a population of over 1,300 people and the southernmost community in the newly emergent Nunavut territory. The town site is a traditional camping area of the *Paallirmiut* Inuit (Caribou Eskimo). A permanent settlement has existed in the area since the 1920s. However, it was not until 1958 that Inuit families in the area settled year-round in Arviat in order to continue to benefit from social assistance programs contingent on Inuit childrens' attendance at Canadian schools. Arviat is today home to people of *Paallirmiut, Harvaqmiut, Hauniqturmiut, Qaimirmiut, Ahialmiut* and *Sallirmiut* backgrounds. While in Arviat the author spoke with 37 men and 14 women about the Board.

Thirty-one of the forty-seven (four were conducted with married couples) interviews were carried out with the help of a translator. The community houses an extensive institutionalized wildlife management infrastructure including local and regional government offices and local and regional hunters and trappers organizations.

Tadoule Lake

The Sayisi-Dene (easternmost Dene) community of Tadoule Lake is represented by a local Band council that is the only formal infrastructure available to act

TABLE 2. Outline of Tadoule Lake Interviewees

Number of Interviewees:	Female	Male
>60 years old	4	6
50–60 years old	0	1
30–50 years old	1	8

as a link between hunters and trappers and anyone from outside the community. While in Tadoule the author spoke with 15 men and 5 women.

Seven of the sixteen (4 were conducted with married couples) interviews were carried out with the help of a translator. Tadoule Lake is still grappling with the legacy of a government relocation of the people from their traditional land use area to Churchill on the Hudson Bay coast in the late 1950s. The community moved back to the Sayisi-Dene's traditional territory in the early 1970s, but not before 117 of the 300 people brought to Churchill in the 1950s had died, half of whom died violently (Bussidor and Bilgen-Reinart, 1997:146–147).

Arviat and Tadoule Lake are shaped by markedly contrasting political realities that make their perceptions of the potential and importance of co-management regimes relatively different. Arviat has a secure base from which to express its plans for land use planning (as a community in Nunavut). However, Tadoule Lake is plagued by uncertainties that outside forces will undermine its ability to negotiate its future on its own terms. Both communities expressed similar ideas about the importance of educating young people about human-wildlife relations. Frustrated efforts to incorporate the knowledge of Elders was also expressed as a common concern in both communities.

Given the depth of the variation among the situations and philosophies of the user communities represented on the Board, Tadoule Lake and Arviat in many ways exemplify the contrasts in the ecological, cultural and political realities of other user communities. The community views expressed in this paper are best represented by the qualitative rather than the quantitative presentation of results. A list of questions was used to guide semi-directed interviews with community members (Table 3).

The questions were designed to bring about discussion of the Board and the issues that people felt most concerned about with respect to their relationships with wildlife officers, biologists and caribou. Interviewees were promised that their comments would be kept confidential so that they felt more comfortable critiquing the Board. For this reason, none of the names of the community members interviewed [is] included in this discussion. It was not possible to compare directly the perspectives drawn out of the conversations in Tadoule Lake versus Arviat. However, generalized conclusions of the parallels and contrasts in the situations in the two different communities can be made.

The Board's prolonged commitment to communication between government wildlife managers and First Nation caribou-using communities has its origins in a

TABLE 3. Questions Used to Structure Semi-Directed Interviews

1. Have you heard of the Caribou Management Board (CMB)?
2. Do you believe that the CMB has done a good job of representing your community's concerns?
3. Have you ever talked with the person in your community who is a member of the CMB to express your thoughts or concerns?
4a. Have you sat in on any of the [CMB's] meetings?
 b. If so, did you participate in any way?
5. Do you read *Caribou News*?
6. What are the issues you feel the CMB or biologists should be most concerned about? — e.g. fire management/border restrictions/wolf control/etc.
7. How important do you think community hunts are to the future of caribou hunting in your community?
8. Can you afford to hunt without the financial support of a community hunt?
9a. Do children get enough opportunities to learn skills out on the land?
 b. Do kids who drop out of school get involved with trapping/hunting/fishing activities?
10. What is the best way to handle/prevent any waste of meat that may occur? — e.g. crippling losses or rotten/freezer-burned meat.
11. What do you think of caribou population estimates?
12. Would you like to see more of the information biologists collect about where caribou are moving through the year?
13. Do you keep in regular contact with neighbouring communities about caribou movements? How? (i.e. by phone, CB radio)
14. Have you ever been involved with a biologist's research?
15. Do you think there is more need for local participation in research?
16. What do you think of the methods biologists use to monitor caribou (i.e. aerial surveys, radio collars)
17. Discussion of *possible future* scenarios:
 a. If caribou were a great distance from town and most hunters were unable to afford the time or the money to hunt, how would you feel about a programme set up to fly hunters out to areas where caribou are located?
 b. If caribou numbers decreased so much that most people could not get as much meat as they needed, how would you react if someone brought reindeer to this area?
18. What kind of information do you feel is important for the community to share with wildlife managers?
19. Do you have any comments you would like to share with people in other caribou-using communities or [with] the CMB?

scenario of low trust levels. However, an analysis of the activities of the Board over its first decade of existence shows that more than 80 percent of the Board's decisions were made by consensus. The topics that have most pervaded management discussions are fire control, the effects of development on caribou habitat, harvest studies and caribou monitoring. Slightly more than 20 percent of the Board meetings centred on the discussion of education and contact between the Board and user communities.

The Board serves an important role as a forum for discussion even though it officially functions only in an advisory capacity. The consistent implementation of the Board's recommendations illustrates that the Board has *de facto* decision-making authority (Swerdfager, 1992). Almost all of the Board's first ten years worth of recommendations have been adopted by the governments involved (Usher, 1993).

The role the Board plays is more apparent as the communities represented by the Board become increasingly politically and legally distinct. The Board has committed a large part of its financial resources to communicating scientific knowledge and perspectives to user communities through its Schools Program and its newsletter, *Caribou News*. However, while the Board has focused its efforts on communication, the incorporation of local perspectives into Board discussions could arguably be stronger. This is undoubtedly due in large part to limited funding and the inability to dedicate more time to strengthening communication between wildlife scientists and communities. But what are the barriers hindering this communication?

RECOGNIZING BARRIERS TO DIALOGUE: THE BEVERLY-QAMANIRJUAQ EXPERIENCE

The hindrances to a balanced and open dialogue may be explained on at least four different fronts. The Board has been slowly working to dissolve or at least acknowledge these obstacles; the curtains that prevent the development of a transparent window between government wildlife managers and caribou-using communities:

1) Historical Conflicts between Caribou Users and Managers,
2) Respect of the Differences in Cross-cultural Ecological Knowledge,
3) Jurisdictional Differences between Communities, and
4) Level of Community Identification with the Board.

The rest of this discussion will expand on these headings, emphasizing the time involved in negotiating these barriers, barriers in essence to trust building, one of Berkes' (1997) preconditions for successful co-management. These barriers are discussed in the light of the local perspectives gained from interviews carried out in Tadoule Lake and Arviat.

HISTORICAL CONFLICTS BETWEEN CARIBOU USERS AND MANAGERS

First Nation caribou-using communities still exhibit a significant level of mistrust of government wildlife management bodies. This is not surprising or unusual (Ames, 1979; Freeman, 1989; Freeman et al., 1992; McCandless, 1985; Swerdfager, 1992). Wildlife management and research has profound implications for communities living nearby or within caribou ranges. Academics have expressed the:

> ...long-standing and largely unaddressed need to critique the current and past use of archaeology and historical anthropological studies by wildlife scientists in order to confront the roots of the historical conflict between wildlife biologists and aboriginal users (Drolet et al., 1987).

The need to address this conflict is as alive today as it was when Drolet and his colleagues addressed it more than ten years ago. Recent findings of a comparative study of the Western Arctic Caribou Herd management system in Alaska and the

Beverly-Qamanirjuaq management system illustrate the persistence of this historically-based conflict (Klein *et al.*, 1999; Kruse *et al.*, 1998). For instance, while 87 percent of the Board's managers feel that the Board has increased traditional caribou users' "sense of control over their lives," only 27 percent of users feel the same way (Kruse *et at.*, 1998:456).

The community of Tadoule Lake illustrates the depth and nature of this conflict. Tadoule still grapples with the legacy of the relocation of the Sayisi-Dene off the land in the late 1950s to the northern Manitoba town of Churchill. The community relocated itself back on the land in the early 1970s. Nevertheless, as mentioned earlier, it is vital to recognize that the Sayisi-Dene were socially and economically devastated by the original relocation (Bussidor and Bilgen-Reinart, 1997; Treeline Productions, 1992). The community of Tadoule Lake is wary of government in general, while the older people the author spoke with feel that wildlife biologists and game wardens helped to justify the government's assimilationist policies in the 1950s by asserting that the Dene were over-hunting caribou in northern Manitoba and should therefore be moved into a settlement. The Sayisi-Dene, who survived on a caribou-based economy before government relocation to Churchill, are still recovering from the legacy of a policy that destroyed their ability to hunt caribou and denied them their self-sufficiency.

Wildlife Management: A "Land-Cropping Art"?

Some Sayisi-Dene Elders expressed their dismay with wildlife management decisions and research methods. One Elder described caribou monitoring methods as an invasion or attack of agricultural peoples' ideas on Dene culture, explaining that in contrast, she would never presume to travel south and tag animals or place limits on the killing of cattle. When explained from this Elder's perspective, wildlife management seems an entirely intrusive and one-sided proposition. Indeed, one of the fathers of modern conservation, Aldo Leopold, wrote that:

> Its [game management's] nature is best understood by comparing it with the other land-cropping arts, and by viewing its present ideas and practices against a background of their own history (1933:3).

The differences in user communities' relationship with caribou and the thinking of government managers and biologists is at times a profound contrast. Co-management structures like the Board are coping day-to-day with the difficulty of linking communities originating from hunting-based societies and wildlife management institutions originating in agriculturally-based societies. There is a profound alienation felt by many First Nation Elders toward wildlife management decision-makers. The continued reverberations in communities' memories of the consequences of early game laws written by southern legislators and geared to suit the needs of sport hunters rather than those who hunted as a way of life should not be forgotten. Leopold's writing epitomizes the biases of early game management:

> Hunting for sport is an improvement over hunting for food in that there has been added to the test of skill an ethical code, which the hunter formulates for himself, and must live up to without the moral support of bystanders (1933:391).

Caribou: A Frontier or Homeland of Thought?

Thomas Berger's (1988) discussion of the paradox of non-Aboriginal concepts of a "wilderness frontier" and Aboriginal concepts of their land use areas as "homelands" has obvious parallels in the growing pains of wildlife management. Poole (1981) describes examples of wildlife research in the Canadian north that failed to consult Aboriginal communities and often disregarded the concerns of these communities. The increased sensitivity of caribou researchers to the knowledge of caribou-using communities is the result of a dialogue between those who see caribou research as an exciting and wide "frontier" of research possibilities and those who see caribou as an animal of profound and long-standing cultural importance, a "homeland" of thought.

Many community members still feel extremely uncomfortable with research methods that require the handling of wild animals. As a result the Board has spent a great deal of time and money consulting with communities specifically about satellite collaring programmes. While the author was conducting interviews in Tadoule Lake in 1993, Band council members asked her not to talk about satellite collaring unless the interviewee mentioned collaring him/herself.

A number of Tadoule Lake Elders did comment on satellite collaring in any case. One Elder recounted a Dene legend that describes a girl who marks a caribou with a cloth ribbon. The girl's action leads to the subsequent deterioration of the relationship of trust between the caribou and Dene people (*Caribou News*, April 1983 2(6):15). Tadoule Lake Elders spoke of the anger the community felt when researchers first began tagging caribou in the 1950s. Caribou were first tagged in northern Manitoba from canoes as they swam across river crossings; crossings considered to be sacred sites. The primary location used to tag caribou was the Duck Lake site from which the Sayisi-Dene were relocated to Churchill in the late 1950s (Miller and Robertson, 1967). This is also the site where photos of caribou carcasses were taken, and distributed by government employees to southern newspapers as evidence of the "slaughter" of caribou by Native peoples in northern Manitoba (Treeline Productions, 1992).

In contrast to depictions of the "wanton slaughter" of caribou (see Kelsall, 1968) anthropologists have extensively documented the historical adherence of Aboriginal communities to behavioural standards of human interactions with animals in both a physical and spiritual context (Brody, 1987; Feit, 1973; Fienup-Riordan, 1990; Tanner, 1973; Ridington, 1988). Although still regarded with trepidation, satellite collaring has been accepted by many Beverly-Qamanirjuaq communities with preconditions because the Board helped to facilitate consultation between wildlife biologists and communities. The Board explained the methods used to collar animals and insists upon the prior consultation of communities before the use of collars in monitoring studies.

The Cost of Doing Research: From a Community Perspective

The examples listed above describe the depth of intrusion many community members (especially Elders) feel that wildlife management actions have made upon their personal lives. Many circumpolar peoples consider the relationship between humans and animals as one of collaborative reciprocity where "the animals [give] themselves to the hunter in response to the hunter's respectful treatment of them as 'persons' in their own right" (Fienup-Riordan, 1990:167). This relationship of reciprocity is very different from Western concepts of the use of natural resources. It is not possible to work toward mutual discussions of resource management without understanding the traditional view of many circumpolar people that animals are non-human persons. Contemporary resource management in the North struggles to acknowledge that traditional hunting and gathering peoples "were more directly affected than others by colonialism and its consequences and an awareness that struggles over allocation of resources today must be waged on non-Indigenous terms and using the discourses and legalities of the more powerful parties" (Hamilton, 1982:242). As a result, the "price" of power-sharing within current caribou co-management regimes is often quite costly to caribou-using communities (see Kofinas, 1998).

RESPECT OF THE DIFFERENCES IN CROSS-CULTURAL ECOLOGICAL KNOWLEDGE

The Board has invested a great deal of resources to communicate the principles of western scientific caribou research to the Board communities. Through Board meetings and the publication of its newsletter *Caribou News*, the Board has attempted to explain the methodologies and rationales behind tagging and collaring programmes, census techniques and statistical uncertainty. The Board has always been anxious to encourage user participation in caribou movement and distribution research in order to validate the information derived from the research of caribou biologists to user communities.

Unfortunately, there are acknowledged problems with this communication. Some of these problems are exacerbated by the Board's limited financial resources. For instance, population surveys are presented primarily in English and in a written format. There are obvious difficulties in affording translation into Dene and Inuktitut syllabics that accommodate the varied dialects present in each language. The jargon of scientific studies is also difficult to translate conceptually into languages that do not recognize human-environment, subject-object and cause-effect relationships in the same way that the English language does. In addition, the challenge involved in representing the results of population surveys in a manner that recognizes the written literacy and numeracy rates of non-scientists cannot be overemphasized. Two surveys in particular required a significant amount of explanation.

The results of the first photo aerial surveys (caribou counts estimated from photographs of the caribou range taken from the air) released in 1984 showed that the earlier visual aerial surveys (counts made by human observers flying overhead) recorded half the number of animals that the photos revealed. Furthermore, in 1989, biologists were at a loss to explain why herd population levels were stable when recruitment levels (the number of calves surviving beyond the first year of life) indicated numbers should be rising. Finally, a 1993 survey of the Beverly herd estimated that the herds' numbers had fallen below the Board's "crisis point" of 150,000. Faced with a situation that indicated a possible dramatic decline in the number of Beverly animals, the Board helped to finance a survey of the herd the following year (surveys are very expensive and not generally carried out within a year of each other) that approximated the herd's size at over three times the number indicated by the previous year's survey (*Caribou News* 15(1):1).

The Board has struggled with community mistrust of the credibility of scientific information given these examples of dramatic differences in population sizes from survey to survey and the large confidence limits of population data. However, the Board has remained consistently open in its acknowledgment of the uncertainties involved in the collection and interpretation of survey data. The research of caribou population dynamics may never equip the Board with the tools to predict a maximum sustained yield or harvest of animals. In fact, the legitimacy of "maximum sustainable yield" harvesting has been challenged within the scientific community for many years (Costanza *et al.*, 1997; Dale, 1989; Gunderson *et al.*, 1995; Maser, 1999). Furthermore, caribou ecology is extremely complex; the variation in the behaviour and movements of caribou populations is high (Klein, 1991; Klein *et al.*, 1999).

However, the Board will continue to struggle with questions of user access to caribou and sustainable use despite the uncertainty involved in interpreting population dynamics. Is it necessary to develop precise population information in order to successfully co-manage caribou (Urquhart, 1996)? The Porcupine Caribou Management Board in the Yukon has successfully challenged this assumption by fostering research incorporating local perspectives that provides answers that will translate into management actions:

> Thus the initial question should not be: "Why is the herd declining?" but, "Are there aspects of the herd's decline that can be mitigated?" If factors such as overharvesting, disturbance and predation can be ruled out through appropriate research, then the causes of the herd's decline become more or less academic since nothing can be done to influence it (Urquhart, 1996:268).

Caribou research is an expensive proposition. Partially in recognition of this reality, the Board recognizes that co-management efforts will be most effective once the knowledge of traditional caribou-using communities and wildlife scientists is synergized. As discussed by Berkes (1999), Johnson (1992) and Mailhot (1993) "each" knowledge system has its limitations and its strengths. One of Tadoule Lake's Elders hopes that in the future the Board will priorize its consultation with communities over the collection of "high tech" information (census data), especially when budget cuts lower the funds available to the Board and government wildlife management agencies. The findings of the comparative study of the Beverly-Qamanirjuaq and Western Arctic caribou management systems echo the same sentiment:

> User-management boards do not appear to be a substitute for a frequent and continued presence of biologists in traditional user communities when it comes to establishing trust in management information and supporting traditional community-based decision making (Kruse *et al.*, 1998:447).

The skepticism found among caribou-using communities when presented with the findings of scientific studies (see Klein *et al.*, 1999; Nadasdy, 1999) is also present among government wildlife managers attempting to understand local ecological knowledge (Ames, 1979; Freeman and Carbyn, 1988; Gunn *et al.*, 1988; Kruse *et al.*, 1998). Dene and Inuit communities may be equally skeptical: Wildlife biologists have misapplied arguments about the sustainability of current Aboriginal harvesting practices with questions about the applicability of Aboriginal knowledge to management efforts in the past (Freeman, 1985:266–269). The differences between western concepts of conservation and historically-based First Nation controls on hunting behaviour are profound (Fienup-Riordan, 1990, 1999; Nelson, 1982). However, this discussion will limit exploration of these differences to an acknowledgement that such contrasts have a large bearing on local versus state perceptions of harvesting practices and wildlife research methodologies and practices (see Klein *et al.*, 1999; Kruse *et al.*, 1998).

Biologists are now recognizing the need for an interdisciplinary approach to the management and conservation of wildlife (Gunn *et al.*, 1988; Knudtson and Suzuki, 1992; Stirling, 1990). Thomas and Schaefer (1991) have acknowledged the significant growth and changes in the attitudes of government and user members toward each other through the Board's development. The social learning inherent in the Board's history and the nature of co-management as a learning process rather than a "quick-fix formula" for cooperation between caribou-using communities and government managers, is evident in the changes seen in the Board over time.

Building Social Capital

Administrative changes, including questions of adequate user representation, as well as the continued minimal linguistic translation available at Board meetings are elements of some of the more obvious gaps in social capital the Board recognizes as problematic. User members have suggested that the reasons communities do not provide more feedback to the Board is because most users do not have the technical experience to communicate with the Board in the language used by managers. Community members the author interviewed emphasized that the Board misses the viewpoints of Elders because user representatives must speak English in order to participate effectively in Board meetings.

The Board holds public meetings in user communities when possible, and usually in conjunction with regular Board meetings held in user communities. It has not been possible, however, for the Board to visit all communities on the caribou ranges given logistical and financial constraints. Twenty-three of the thirty-nine Board meetings held between 1981 and 1993 were held outside of the communities represented by the Board. Half of the communities represented on the Board have never hosted a Board meeting. This means that the concerns of user communities lacking direct representatives on the Board are very difficult to address.

Addressing Caribou User Concerns

The following examples illustrate the time involved in translating user concerns to real policy changes and are discussed below in the context of the social learning gained through the Board's lifetime. User members have always been anxious for the Board's management plan to reflect the issues of utmost concern to users. For instance, user members worried in the early 1980s that the draft management plan did not include the perspectives of users on trapping, logging, fishing and the effects of fire on traditional lifestyles, but only included issues of the protection of caribou winter feeding grounds. Users also felt that the plan's discussion of wolf control did not address the questions of communities; it only addressed the questions of biologists. There was decided pressure on the Board from users not to become yet another bureaucratic institution which glossed over users' primary concerns.

Fire control has been a matter of grave concern to user members in the provinces of the Mackenzie district of the Northwest Territories for many years. User members certainly made it clear that fire suppression is considered one of the primary management issues of communities. Board members agreed that although caribou may survive as a species without a valid program of fire suppression, they would not necessarily survive as a resource. The Board determined to encourage the protection of older forest areas of greater importance as productive caribou feeding grounds.

However, the Board's early attempts to communicate with government ministers about fire control went unheeded. User members worried that if fires continued to burn along the territorial-provincial border, there might be a time when caribou no longer travelled into the provinces. The Board initially encouraged fire managers to consult with user communities in order to place priorities on protecting unburned corridors between burns important as routes for caribou migration and as winter feeding grounds. The Northwest Territories' fire management committee made it clear, however, that it was up to the Board to identify critical areas on the range in need of protection.

Initially, the Board's government members felt that little was known about the effects of fire on caribou movements and the ability of burns to support caribou. However, a user member stated that such a statement was ludicrous given the extent of users' knowledge of the effects of fire. User members successfully argued that it was more important for the Board to identify critical areas for fire suppression than to support further fire research studies.

In 1988, the Board established a Fire Mapping Working Group and by 1991 the group began identifying caribou migration corridors, older forest areas, and "green areas" for user communities. The following year (1992), the Board's Fire Management Committee was established with four user representatives and four government representatives. The Board and the Government of the Northwest Territories were well on their way to incorporating values-at-risk, fire history and critical corridor data into a geographical information system to be used as a management tool. This was an incredible achievement given that before the development of the final Board Fire Management Plan, governments had refused to spend their fire suppression budgets on anything other than areas of merchantable timber.

In recent years the Board has funded an extensive "Important Habitats Project" identifying areas of critical importance to the Beverly and Qamanirjuaq caribou herds. [A series of maps were developed that] illustrate where caribou have travelled at different times of the year over a 30 year period. The project is designed to give the Board the tools it needs to protect critical areas in the face of mining and other industrial developments on the caribou ranges. A traditional knowledge study may eventually include all the Board communities, while the results of traditional mapping already underway in Keewatin communities will be included in the project as soon as the data is available. The Board hopes to use the digital maps to increase its effectiveness in the environmental impact assessment of development activities on the caribou range. By identifying land use activities that could potentially affect caribou and their habitat, the Board plans to develop a classification system for development proposals, and to prepare guidelines for assessing the potential impacts of activities. Such guidelines will be used in conjunction with seasonal range maps and databases.

The time involved to begin to address the concerns of user communities is often lengthy. In the case of fire management it took more than a decade for the concerns of communities to reach the ears of policy-makers and to begin to affect the allocation of fire suppression efforts toward critical caribou habitats. However, the fire management issue is also an example of the contrasting jurisdictional realities of user communities. Communities dependent upon the same resource may face very different political worlds. The next section explores the consequences of these differences and the Board's role in addressing jurisdictional differences.

JURISDICTIONAL DIFFERENCES BETWEEN COMMUNITIES

There are decided regional differences between the political realities of provincial and territorial communities. Provincial economies regard caribou largely as an externality while the Northwest Territories and Nunavut acknowledge the cultural and economic importance of caribou within government policy and legislation. For instance, although the Board's fire management plan received support from the Northwest Territories' government and eventually helped to shape the Northwest Territories' fire suppression activities, Saskatchewan would not provide funding for fire studies in areas where there is no commercial timber and Manitoba does not have a budget for fire suppression in the north of the province.

In addition, imbalances exist in the application of the Board's priority caribou user categories. This inflames questions of accessibility and definitions of commercial use in the provinces versus the territories. The discussion of commercial use has been one of the most controversial issues discussed at Board meetings. The Board established a list of user priorities, allocating domestic use by traditional users the highest priority of use and export use for commercial purposes the lowest priority. The Board risked a fundamental divide between users when it voted after two previous rejections to support a request for a commercial quota for a territorial community while provincial users still had limited access to caribou. The Board supported Manitoba users' long-standing request for access to caribou in the Northwest Territories, but only after the Board supported an Alberta community's request (a community not represented by the Board) for access to caribou in the Northwest Territories. Communities such as Tadoule Lake worry about the effects of commercial quotas on traditional access to caribou meat. For example, will Baffin Islanders end up with indirect access to Qamanirjuaq caribou through a meat processing centre in Rankin Inlet? Should Dene and Inuit communities living near the Beverly caribou range also have access to Qamanirjuaq caribou? Arviat Elders also worry about the implications of the centralization of meat processing out of their home communities.

LEVEL OF COMMUNITY IDENTIFICATION WITH THE BOARD

Interviews in Arviat and Tadoule Lake revealed that less than half of interviewees distinguish the Board from a government management body. Few community members have spoken with their community representatives about the Board or their concerns about caribou research or harvesting practices. However, the Board was described as a "safeguard" despite general mistrust of outside influences on community life. For example, one Arviat Elder described his dislike of the wildlife officers who regulated hunting activity while he was a teenager and his feelings that conditions had improved tremendously with the organization of the Hunters and Trappers' Association and the hiring of Native wildlife officers in recent years.

In contrast, Tadoule Lake is a much smaller provincial community without government wildlife offices, and is much more guarded in its reception of wildlife management activities. Interviewees in Tadoule Lake feel that their thoughts are unlikely to reach expression in policy-making. They do not have a large sense of membership in the Board and its potential to influence government actions. The Board is strongly associated with government and is spoken of in the same context as outside influences such as Manitoba Hydro's plans for future hydro-development of northern rivers. Many individuals clearly continue to consider the Board one of many government and outside interests external to the community.

Many interviewees knew very little about the current activities of the Board or referred to wildlife management agencies as one [homogeneous] force. Community members discussed a range of issues including the importance of community hunts, land skills instruction, the potential for hunting waste and thoughts on caribou monitoring methods. These topics are obviously uppermost in community thinking despite a seeming lack of connection between community members and the Board.

At its 1986 user assembly, the Board was very concerned that most users were uninformed of the Board's goals. Unlike the Board's government members, user members do not have salaries, budgets or programmes to support their representation of the Board to their home communities and the neighbouring communities they represent. In order to address these issues, the Board made adjustments to its organization, establishing an independent user-only meeting to take place in conjunction with each Board meeting and according funds to cover the travel and telephone costs for user members' consultation with communities.

THE BEVERLY-QAMANIRJUAQ CARIBOU MANAGEMENT BOARD IN THE BROADER SCHEME

> The lesson is not that the BQCMB needs to do a better job; rather, the lesson is that the job is bigger than anyone expected (Kruse et al., 1998:456).

The lessons learned from the frame-shifts evident in other co-management systems (Dale, 1989) are also apparent in the Beverly-Qamanirjuaq caribou management system. The complexities of these systems are enormous, from increasing understanding by caribou biologists that caribou ecology is far more variable than anyone imagined 50 years ago, to rising pressures to respond to the impacts of industrial developments on caribou habitat.

The Board had a unique birth in comparison to most other co-management arrangements. Co-management regimes are often categorized as "claims-based" or "crisis-based" (RCAP, 1996). The "crisis" of "crisis-based" wildlife co-management is usually centred on the loss of habitat due to human activities. In the case of the Board, the initial crisis was conceptual; managers worried that caribou numbers were dwindling perhaps due to over-hunting, while many user communities questioned the existence of a decline and certainly questioned the existence of over-harvesting. Without the unity brought about by an identifiable crisis commonly perceived by both users and managers, the Board's growth has been very different from that of the Porcupine Caribou Management Board, a co-management system that has always had a rallying point: the threat of oil and gas development in the herd's calving grounds.

The Board is a unique example of an institution that manages to strengthen the co-management of a resource, without legal definition within a land claims agreement or a clear and undisputed management goal. Is "the sharing of power and responsibility between government and local resource users," (Berkes et al., 1991:12) possible without the legal transfer of political power and responsibility? The Board's creation reflects a recognition that the complexity of human-caribou systems is beyond the capacity of previous management institutions to handle. As phrased by Dale (1989), describing fisheries management, the Board is wrestling with a new kind of social problem, the negotiation of "meta-problems" (complex problems that deal with the whole environment and are impervious to specialized knowledge) "distinguished by such characteristics as difficulty of consensual definition of the problem" (Dale, 1989:50).

The Board's history may illustrate that many of the conditions necessary to strengthen and mature the dialogue between government biologists and user communities are forums that allow innovative collective learning, and that this learning is as vital as the political empowerment of user communities for successful co-management. For instance, the Board's role in changing fire suppression priorities in the Northwest Territories, defending traditional caribou-using communities' access to caribou and in identifying and protecting critical caribou habitat are the result of collective learning in a complicated interjurisdictional context.

In general, co-management systems are seen to function as forums for cross-cultural education and communication (Osherenko, 1988; Usher, 1993). These regimes work to promulgate the social systems that combine socio-economic interests and ecological principles. Co-management systems promise to recognize customary Indigenous infrastructures of resource management and to replace infrastructures of resource management that place restrictive controls on individual common property resource users with "voluntary collective actions" (Feeny et al., 1990:11). However, there is a sea of conflicts and miscommunications to wade through before co-management systems can deliver on such a promise.

The Board has continually addressed fundamental questions about the applicability of Aboriginal and non-Aboriginal value systems to the survival of caribou. The Board attempts to secure a balance of interests to ensure the success of a communal property regime. The Board does serve as a forum for the continual reconciliation of community and government approaches to wildlife management. This lengthy and continuous commitment encompasses profound change; a cross-cultural dialogue that shares and recognizes a variety of knowledge rather than battling to realize the dominance of one body of knowledge over another. The cross-cultural learning involved in this process is often slow. Moreover, it is not clear that "the community" and "the state" equally share the costs of this process, which in many ways is still in a transformative state.

The history of the Beverly-Qamanirjuaq Caribou Management Board illustrates that co-management in practise is the process of securing a balance of interests in a common resource and should not be regarded as the definition of this balance. Co-management is a conceptualization, perhaps comparable with sustainable development, to the extent that it is a process and not a final state, a goal that may never be reached, but that is important to strive toward (Holling et al., 1998:353).

Kofinas (1998), in his analysis of the Porcupine Caribou Management Board, evaluated the transaction costs accumulating to Aboriginal communities participating in the co-management processes. Kofinas' work shows that First Nation communities are taxed by the need to defray the political costs incurred by participation in co-management, in order to benefit from the increased social capital (learning) brought about by co-management participation. Most co-management analyses have implicitly or explicitly assumed that communities represent the lowest cost and most effective fora for communication (Lélé, 1998). However, the concept of "community" is far more "elusive and complex" than previously imagined and even "well-knit" communities (displaying many interdependencies among their members) are complicated by the effects of colonlialistic policies and globalizing economies (Lélé, 1998; Nadasdy, 1999). Kruse et al. (1998) illustrate that caribou management systems (in this case those established for the Western Arctic and Beverly-Qamanirjuaq caribou herds) have not found effective mechanisms to incorporate users' knowledge into decision-making processes. Government managers comment that user observations are often difficult to interpret and that a divergence of user and manager views often stifles efficient management action. Interestingly, however, Kruse and his colleagues do show that the value government managers place in traditional knowledge has shifted significantly in the last two decades. For example one manager stated:

> I've come to realize that there is a very different method of storing this knowledge and of examining what's going on with the caribou that's not related in the numerical sense or in written words (Canadian government manager quoted in Kruse et al., 1998:452).

Increased communication between users and managers may be leading to improved trust and knowledge exchange between government managers and traditional users. The flow of communication between managers and users remains problematic not because of a lack of effort, but perhaps because it is not always effective. This is probably true for the same reasons that most of the lay public is flummoxed by technical scientific language *as well as* the fundamental linguistic and ideological differences between users and government managers (see Fienup-Riordan, 1990; Kofinas, 1998; Roberts, 1996). As expressed by Forester:

> ...public and articulated acknowledgement of conflicting and pressing values does not solve a problem: it works ritualistically to re-build relationships and to prepare the social basis for future practical action (quoted in Meppem and Bourke, 1999:401).

State management knows very little about the manner in which caribou users currently share knowledge, as well as the ways in which users shared knowledge before permanent settlement patterns. It is possible that the hesitancy of communities to accept the methods and techniques of caribou population surveys is also related to the way that such research may undermine local information exchange systems. Caribou management systems displaying increasingly sophisticated monitoring techniques are not necessarily showing increased wisdom about how to limit access or harm to caribou ranges or answering fundamental problems with respect to the access of traditional caribou-using communities to animals that may not move close to permanent settlements for years at a time.

There are important cultural differences about the rules of knowledge and information use. The control of specific knowledge about resources is a form of resource management (operating through restricting access to resources recognized by common property theory (Weinstein, 1996:3). It is not evident that current co-management institutions house mechanisms that recognize this information management. However, global restructuring and government budget cuts may provide opportunities for changes in co-management processes significant for both the state and communities (Feit, 1998). This window for innovative change may provide the conditions for the kind of social learning not possible twenty years ago.

CONCLUSIONS

The Board, an *ad hoc* co-management institution, has served as a forum where social learning has created the conditions to expand beyond a purely *consultative* framework to push *conceptual* boundaries. Beyond the important political questions of equitable and fair procedures for the management of wildlife vital to northern communities, the Board is showing signs that it is a structure which can and will recognize community knowledge as a *process* of thinking about human-environment relations.

This discussion has examined the cross-cultural dialogue between government wildlife managers and Aboriginal wildlife users behind the "single window" the Board provides between outside parties and caribou users. The Board is a forum that is developing the mechanisms to work through significant obstacles to communication. Perhaps it is time to recognize that the "curtains" shading the "window" to two-way communication will involve constant negotiation, not removal. The mechanisms needed to negotiate these hurdles are not just the tools of political empowerment. The Board may yet illustrate that the slow and complex process of linking local and state resource management systems is best achieved in a flexible forum, where the underlying conflicts between biologists and hunters can be salved through learning exchanges such as the Board's fire history mapping project, the negotiation of the "caribou crisis" impasse, and the gradual understanding of the pitfalls and benefits of wildlife research.

Co-option and domination have overwhelmingly marked cross-cultural exchanges in the recent past. Caribou co-management in many ways defines a direct challenge to such historical precedence. No matter what the political and ideological differences between caribou-using communities may be, it is clear that the existence of a forum like the Board has enabled the discussion of diversified interests to grow and the building of trust and social capital. Jurisdictional boundaries may create artificial separations between user groups, but the ecological realities that unite them (shared dependence on caribou) represent a fundamental and shared base that cannot be ignored. An Inuit Elder the author spoke with several years ago, [a] participant in many land claim and wildlife management meetings, emphasized his hope that wildlife management discussions revolve around questions of *how to share* the land *rather than the control* of the land. In essence, his is a profound definition of co-management; the process of learning how to share and protect rather than to control knowledge and resources.

REFERENCES

AMES, R. 1979. *Social, Economic and Legal Problems of Hunting in Northern Labrador*. Labrador Inuit Association.

BERGER, T.R. 1988. *Northern Frontier Northern Homeland: The Report of the Mackenzie Valley Pipeline Inquiry*. Vancouver: Douglas and McIntyre Ltd.

BERKES, F. 1999. *Sacred Ecology — Traditional Ecological Knowledge and Management Systems*. Philadelphia: Taylor and Francis.

———. 1997. New and Not-So-New Directions in the Use of the Commons: Co-management. *The Common Property Resource Digest* 42:5–7.

BERKES, F. and C. FOLKE. 1998. *Linking Social and Ecological Systems: Management Practices and Social Mechanisms for Building Resilience*. Cambridge: Cambridge University Press.

BERKES, F., P. GEORGE and R.J. PRESTON. 1991. Co-Management. *Alternatives* 18(2):12–18.

BUSSIDOR, I. and Ü. BILGEN-REINART. 1997. *Night Spirits — The Story of the Relocation of the Sayisi-Dene*. Winnipeg: The University of Manitoba Press.

BRODY, H. 1987. *Maps and Dreams*. Vancouver: Douglas and McIntyre Ltd.

CIZEK, P. 1990. The Beverly-Kaminuriak Caribou Management Board. A Case Study of Aboriginal Participation in Resource Management. Background Paper #1. Ottawa: Canadian Arctic Resources Committee.

COLEMAN, J.S. 1990. *Foundations of Social Theory*. Cambridge, Mass.: Harvard University Press.

COSTANZA, R., K. CUMBERLAND, H. DALY, R. GOODLAND and R. NORGAARD. 1997. *An Introduction to Ecological Economics*. Boca Raton, Florida: St. Lucie Press.

DALE, N. 1989. Getting to Co-Management: Social Learning in the Redesign of Fisheries Management. *Co-operative Management of Local Fisheries*. Vancouver. University of British Columbia Press.

DROLET, C.A., A. REED, M. BRETON and F. BERKES. 1987. Sharing Wildlife Management Responsibilities With Native Groups: Case Histories in Northern Quebec. *52nd North American Wildlife and Natural Resources Conference*.

EVERNDEN, N. 1985. *The Natural Alien*. Toronto: University of Toronto Press.

FEENY, D., F. BERKES, B.J. MCCAY and J.M. ACHESON. 1990. The Tragedy of the Commons: Twenty-two Years Later. *Human Ecology* 18(1):1–19.

FEIT, H.A. 1998. Reflections on Local Knowledge and Wildlife Resource Management: Differences, Dominance and Decentralization, pp. 123–148 in L.-J Dorais, M. Nagy and L. Müller-Wille (Editors): *Aboriginal Environmental Knowledge in the North*, Université Laval, Québec: GETIC.

———. 1973. The Ethno-Ecology of the Waswanipi Cree; or How Hunters Can Manage Their Resources, pp. 115–125 in B. Cox (Editor): *Cultural Ecology: Readings on the Canadian Indians and Eskimos*. Toronto: McClelland and Stewart.

FIENUP-RIORDAN, A. 1999. *Yaqulget Qaillun Pilartat* (What the Birds Do): Yup'ik Eskimo Understanding of Geese and Those Who Study Them. *Arctic* 52(1):1–22.

———. 1990. *Eskimo Essays: Yup'ik Lives and How We See Them*. New Brunswick, N.J.: Rutgers University Press.

FREEMAN, M.M.R. 1989. Graphs and Gaffs: A Cautionary Tale in the Common Property Resource Debate, pp. 92–109 in F. Berkes (Editor): *Common Property Resources*.

———. 1985. Appeal to Tradition: Different Perspectives on Arctic Wildlife Management, pp. 265–281 in J. Brøsted *et al.* (Editors): *Native Power: The Quest for Autonomy and Nationhood of Indigenous Peoples*. Bergen, Norway: Universitetsforlaget.

FREEMAN, M.M.R. and L.N. CARBYN (Editors) 1988. *Traditional Knowledge and Renewable Resource Management in Northern Regions*. Edmonton, Alberta: IUCN Commission on Ecology and the Boreal Institute for Northern Studies.

FREEMAN, M.M.R., E.E. WEIN and D.E. KEITH. 1992. Recovering Rights: Bowhead Whales and Inuvialuit Subsistence in the Western Canadian Arctic. Edmonton, Alberta: University of Alberta.

GUNN, A., G. ARLOOKTOO and D. KAOMAYOK. 1988. The Contribution of the Ecological Knowledge of Inuit to Wildlife Management in the NWT, pp. 22–30 in M.M.R. Freeman and L.N. Carbyn (Editors): *Traditional Knowledge and Renewable Resource Management in Northern Regions*. Edmonton, Alberta: IUCN Commission on Ecology and the Boreal Institute for Northern Studies.

GUNDERSON, L.H., C.S. HOLLING and S.S. LIGHT (Editors). 1995. *Barriers and Bridges to the Renewal of Ecosystems and Institutions*. New York: Columbia University Press.

HAMILTON, A. 1982. The Unity of Hunting-Gathering Societies: Reflections on Economic Forms and Resource Management, pp. 229–247 in N.M. Williams and E.S. Hunn (Editors): *Resource Managers: North American and Australian Hunter-Gatherers*. Washington, D.C.: American Association for the Advancement of Science.

HOLLING, C.S., F. BERKES and C. FOLKE 1998. Science, Sustainability and Resource Management, pp. 342–362 in F. Berkes and C. Folke (Editors): *Linking Social and Ecological Systems: Management Practices and Social Mechanisms for Building Resilience*. Cambridge: Cambridge University Press.

JOHNSON, M. (Editor) 1992. *Lore: Capturing Traditional Environmental Knowledge*. Ottawa: Dene Cultural Institute, International Development Research Centre.

KELSALL, J.P. 1968. *The Migratory Barren-Ground Caribou of Canada*. Ottawa: Department of Indian and Northern Affairs.

KENDRICK, A. 1994. *Community Perspectives, Caribou User Participation and the Beverly-Qamanirjuaq Caribou Management Board in Northcentral Canada*. Unpublished M.A. Thesis, Montréal: McGill University.

KLEIN, D.R. 1991. Caribou in the Changing North. *Applied Animal Behaviour Science* 29: 279–291.

KLEIN, D.R., L. MOOREHEARD, J. KRUSE, and S.R. BRAUND 1999. Contrasts in Use and Perceptions of Biological Data for Caribou Management. *The Wildlife Society Bulletin* 27(2): 488–498.

KNUDSTON, P. and D. SUZUKI 1992. *Wisdom of the Elders*. Toronto: Stoddart Publishing Company Ltd.

KOFINAS, G.P. 1998. *The Costs of Power Sharing: Community Involvement in Canadian Porcupine Caribou Herd Co-management*. Unpublished Ph.D. Thesis. Vancouver: University of British Columbia.

KRUSE, J., D. KLEIN, S. BRAUD, L. MOOREHEAD, and B. SIMEONE 1998. Co-Management of Natural Resources: A Comparison of Two Caribou Management Systems. *Human Organization* 57(4): 447–458.

LALOUR, B. 1999. *Pandora's Hope: Essays on the Reality of Science Studies*. Cambridge: Harvard University Press.

LÉLÉ, S. 1998. Why, Who, and How of Jointness in Joint Forest Management: Theoretical Considerations and Empirical Insights from the Western Ghats of Kamataka. Paper presented at the International Workshop on Shared Resource Management in South Asia. Feb. 17–19, 1998.

LEOPOLD, A. 1933. *Game Management*. New York: Charles Scribner's Sons.

LONGINO, H.E. 1990. *Science as Social Knowledge — Values and Objectivity in Scientific Inquiry*. Princeton, New Jersey: Princeton University Press.

MAILHOT, J. 1993. *Traditional Ecological Knowledge — The Diversity of Knowledge Systems and Their Study*. Background Paper #4. Great Whale Environmental Assessment.

MASER, C. 1999. *Ecological Diversity in Sustainable Development: The Vital and Forgotten Dimension*. Boca Raton: Lewis Publications.

MCCANDLESS, R.G. 1985. *Yukon Wildlife: a Social History*. Edmonton: University of Alberta Press.

MCCAY, B.J. and J.M. ACHESON (Editors) 1987. *The Question of the Commons — the Culture and Ecology of Communal Resources*. Tucson: University of Arizona Press.

MEPPEM, T. and S. BOURKE 1999. Different Ways of Knowing: A Communicative Turn Toward Sustainability. *Ecological Economies* 30: 389–404.

MILLER, D.R. and J.D. ROBERTSON. 1967. Results of Tagging Caribou at Little Duck Lake, Manitoba. *Journal of Wildlife Management* 31(1): 150–159.

MORGAN, J.P. 1993. *Cooperative Management of Wildlife in Northern Canadian National Parks*. Unpublished Master's Degree Project. Environmental Science, Calgary: University of Calgary.

NADASDY, P. 1999. The Politics of TEK: Power and the "Integration" of Knowledge. *Arctic Anthropology* 36(1–2): 1–18.

NELSON, R.K. 1982. A Conservation Ethic and Environment: The Koyukon of Alaska, pp. 211–228 in N.M. Williams and E.S. Hunn (Editors): *Resource Managers: North American and Australian Hunter-Gatherers*. Washington, D.C.: American Association for the Advancement of Science.

OSHERENKO, G. 1988. Can Comanagement Save Arctic Wildlife? *Environment* 30(6): 6–13, 29–34.
PEPPER, D. 1984. *The Roots of Modern Environmentalism*. London: Routledge.
POOLE, P. 1981. *Conservation and Inuit Hunting: Conflict or Compatibility*. Unpublished Ph.D. Thesis, Montréal, Québec: Department of Geography, McGill University.
RIDINGTON, R. 1988. *Trail to Heaven: Knowledge and Narrative in a Northern Native Community*. Vancouver: Douglas and McIntyre.
ROBERTS, K. 1996. *Circumpolar Aboriginal People and Co-management Practice: Current Issues in Co-management and Environmental Assessment*. Calgary, Alberta: Joint Secretariat, Inuvialuit Renewable Resources Committee.
ROYAL COMMISSION ON ABORIGINAL PEOPLES. 1996. *Restructuring the Relationship*. Volume 2, Part 2, pp. 665–774.
SIMPLETON, S. 1998. *Constructing Cooperation: The Evolution of Institutions of Co-management*. Ann Arbor: The University of Michigan Press.
STIRLING, I. 1990. Guest Editorial: The Future of Wildlife Management in the Northwest Territories. *Arctic* 43(2): iii–iv.
SWERDFAGER, T. 1992. Appendix 8.35 *Cooperative Wildlife Management*. In Alberta *Treaty Indian Hunting and Fishing in Alberta, Background Paper*. Fish and Wildlife Services, Alberta Environmental Protection.
TANNER, A. 1973. The Significance of Hunting Territories Today, pp. 101–113 in B. Cox (Editor): *Cultural Ecology*.
THOMAS, D.C. and J. SCHAEFER. 1991. Wildlife Co-management defined: The Beverly and Kaminuriak Caribou Management Board. *Rangifer*, Special Issue No. 7.
TREELINE PRODUCTIONS. 1992. *Nu Ho Ni Yeh* (Our Story). Tadoule Lake, Manitoba: Sayisi-Dene First Nation. (film/video — 54:23 minutes).
URQUHART, D. 1996. *Caribou Co-Management Needs from Research. Simple Questions — Tricky Answers*. Presented at the Sixth North American Caribou Workshop, Prince George, B.C., March 1–4, 1994, pp. 263–271, in *Rangifer* Special Issue No. 9, 1996.
USHER, P.J. 1993. The Beverly-Kaminuriak Caribou Management Board: An Experience in Co-Management, pp. 111–119 in J.T. Inglis (Editor): *Traditional Ecological Knowledge: Concepts and Cases*. Ottawa: International Development Research Centre.
WEINSTEIN, M. 1996. *Traditional Knowledge, Impact Assessment, and Environmental Planning*. Canadian Environmental Assessment Agency, BHP Diamond Mine Environmental Assessment Panel.
WEST, P.C. and S.R. BRECHIN. 1991. National Parks, Protected Areas, and Resident Peoples: A Comparative Assessment and Integration. *Resident Peoples and National Parks: Social Dilemmas and Strategies in International Conservation*. Tucson: University of Arizona Press.
WILLIAMS, N.M. and E.S. HUNN (Editors) 1982. *Resource Managers: North American and Australian Hunter-Gatherers*. Washington, D.C.: American Association for the Advancement of Science.
WORSLEY, P. 1997. *Knowledges: Culture Counterculture Subculture*. New York: The New Press.

(e) Towards a Model of Co-management of Provincial Parks in Ontario[†]

Roger Spielmann and Marina Unger

INTRODUCTION

This paper is about a new kind of thinking, a new kind of architecture, if you will; an architecture of culture and mind. For First Nations people, this architecture of

---

[†] From *The Canadian Journal of Native Studies*, 20(2): 455–86. Reproduced with permission of the publisher.

culture and mind will have a familiar ring to it, for it is really an ancient architecture and way of thinking deeply entrenched in Aboriginal traditions. There is little written about this new architecture and how it is grounded in these ancient traditions. This paper is intended to introduce the reader to the foundation upon which contemporary environmental planning and design must rest, at least from an Aboriginal perspective.

The purpose of this study is to investigate to what extent First Nations communities participate in the planning and management of parks, and if the current process is successful. This study shows how First Nations' concerns, needs and interests can be reflected in park planning and design practices. Specifically, this study examines the present relationship between Ojibwe First Nations and the Ontario Parks management systems in a contemporary context.

A RATIONALE FOR CO-MANAGEMENT

After many years of forced and rapid social change, First Nations people are now empowering themselves in a more vocal and visually expressive manner. The re-emergence of First Nations cultures is evident in recent land claim settlements, self-government strategies, language revitalization, and political activism. In this light, environmental design/planning professions can be seen as a vehicle to magnify First Nations cultures *visually* in the natural and built environment. This paper has been designed to show how First Nations' approaches to land and the environment in Canada are grounded in a deep understanding of how the land functions, the way its processes work, and how those processes reflect Aboriginal perspectives and spiritual connections.

Few would argue that First Nations cultures around the world have been unjustly treated with regard to their traditional ways of life (Ponting, 1997; Burger, 1990). When European colonization occurred in Canada, pressure for First Nations people to assimilate into an alternative lifestyle was intense. Imposed upon First Nations populations were European views of land use. Many First Nations populations were forced to adopt a new culture and abandon traditions intrinsically tied to sacred lands. Despite these hardships, Native heritages have persisted to the present day. *Understanding and respect* between cultural groups regarding the divisive issues such as land claims and cultural identity has been minimal, therefore more attention is desperately needed.

Those working with First Nations communities, such as anthropologists, linguists, environmental planners, and landscape architects, have a responsibility to recognize the significance of a culture when designing new environments or developing policies to integrate cultural needs within natural systems' limits. Awareness and understanding of the history of an area can lead to a design that is culturally sensitive thus fulfilling the needs of the client and community at large. "Single Group" management of resources is no longer an option, at least from a Native perspective.

A key claim of this study is that First Nations people have been inadequately involved with the land use planning and design issues which have confronted government-run parks in traditional First Nations Territories. This lack of collaboration has contributed to the ongoing tension between First Nations communities and government. Landscape architect Walter Kehm's involvement with the South Moresby/ Haida negotiations in British Columbia and his evaluation of that particular situation [attest] to the great communication and visualization problems which existed between Parks Canada, BC Parks, the timber industry and special interest groups (personal communication, 1996:37). A great sensitizing process was required to enable administrators and policy-makers to understand Aboriginal perceptions and belief systems and to have them incorporated into new policies and plans. A similar scenario is currently being played out in Davis Inlet where we are witnessing at this writing a move to a new location (Sango Bay). In these kinds of situations, crucial questions continue to press: What process of communication exists? What form will the new community take? What cultural-spiritual values will it express? How are people's deep needs and wants recognized and understood?

THE ARGUMENT

From a First Nations perspective, it is no longer acceptable for Canada to operate parks in a monocultural fashion. Land is a spiritual *necessity* in North American First Nations cultures (Ponting, 1997; Burger, 1990). Thus it is imperative for all parties with a vested interest in economic development and environmental planning in traditional First Nations territories to become informed about the values and aspirations of First Nations people if there is to be a true and equitable co-management of resources.

The research we have conducted in Ontario is designed to be of real value in documenting precedents and describing ways to approach planning and design, approaches which could be applied to other situations being played out across Canada. A sense of perspective about how decisions are made in relation to land use, area designations and the provision of infrastructure and facilities is an important contribution that our research makes to the field of environmental planning and co-management in First Nations contexts. Assistance with the interpretation of values is also a critical area of this study and is designed to demonstrate new ways of communicating plans and policies which have greater relevance and sensitivity to local needs and desires. Within the context of this overarching problem, there are four questions that are addressed in this study:

- What means do First Nations people have to participate in the planning and design of a park?
- How do the two parties (park management planners and First Nations cultures) communicate?
- What responsibilities do the two parties have to each other?
- What lessons can be drawn from this comparison?

BACKGROUND INFORMATION

Decades have gone by with minimal changes in the relationship between the federal and provincial governments and First Nations. Ultimately, our natural resources have been considered the priority, and First Nations cultural values a secondary issue. Solutions may be difficult to attain. However, if we can find ways to reduce the frustration and [reverse] these priorities, the process of working toward a common goal will become more achievable.

The differences between Indigenous and European views show a need to redefine public land. European-based people tend to view the world in compartmentalized units, and that the quantity of assets equals worth and wealth (Ponting, 1997; Morse, 1992). Our continued existence as a nation partially depends on the *use* of the environment. Agriculture, timber, shipping and mining are all major international industries in Canada. Bureaucracy has dictated the need to establish laws to control the use and "ownership" of land. European views of the environment have clashed with First Nation views because the two solitudes are so fundamentally different. Aboriginal people have traditionally placed an emphasis on the use of land rather than formal possession. They have unbreakable bonds with the land, commonly referred to in First Nations' traditions as "Mother Earth" and believe if they are without land, they do not have a soul, purpose in life, or identity.[1]

The evolution of trust between First Nations cultures and the government has historically been a struggle. European views of religion, lifestyle and development have been embraced as prevalent societal norms in Canada. Aboriginal people have been forced to accept European values because their experience illustrates that:

> wherever there is a dominant perspective that is so readily accepted and widely influential that it can unconsciously exclude all other perspectives, the process of real communication and understanding is diminished tremendously. Wherever the dominant perspective intentionally ignores or denies the legitimacy and authenticity of other perspectives, the process of communication and understanding is non-existent ... the dominant perspective assumes its perspective to be correct above all others. Because of this, all perspectives are denied or minimized. Indigenous populations have found themselves in the position of the conquered, the subjugated or the annihilated (Clarkson *et al.*, 1992:1).

The challenge of creating trust between the First Nations and the Crown began centuries ago. During the formative years of European colonization, many treaties were drawn up. Treaties were familiar agreements among First Nations as they were used for peace making, aid/relief and education. Europeans also used treaties for many of the same reasons (Ponting, 1997). During the 1850s, Commissioner W.B. Robinson was sent to the northern area of Upper Canada (presently northern Ontario) to negotiate territories with the Ojibwe people. The documents, called the Robinson-Huron and Robinson-Superior treaties, were negotiated by the First Nations and the Crown in order to:

> surrender, cede, grant and convey unto Her Majesty, her heirs and successors forever, all their rights, title and interest to the land, and the right to fish and hunt in the lands they surrendered, until these lands are sold or leased to individuals or companies (OMNR, 1996).

First Nations people agreed to share their traditional lands in return for continued hunting and fishing rights, Reserve lands and annual annuities (Aronson, 1997:24, cited in Smart and Coyle, 1997 [sic]). The treaties, covering lands north of Lake Huron and Lake Superior, set a pattern that other treaties followed. In the Aboriginal perspective, land is believed to be a gift from the Creator. Therefore, when the European settlers wanted to form a treaty, the Native people were not hesitant, as land was meant to be shared, and many First Nations did sign treaties with the federal government.

Representatives of the Crown proposed treaties in order to establish formal relationships with First Nations. The relationship included a degree of trust where both parties (the Crown and the First Nations) agreed to follow certain arrangements. Many First Nations people currently believe they were forced to surrender more than just their traditional territories. Aronson (1997) suggests that:

> historical treaty documents were never drafted by the Aboriginal occupiers of the land, and often the Aboriginal view was that they were not surrendering or giving up all rights to ownership of the land but *that they were sharing the land with the new settlers* (Aronson, 1997:35, in Smart and Coyle, 1997 [sic], emphasis added).

In May, 1990 (*Sioui* vs. *Crown*), Huron Band Indians were legally charged for using an undeveloped section of a provincial park (Quebec, Canada) for camping purposes. They claimed protection with a document signed in 1860 from Quebec provincial law. The court case examined whether or not the provincial regulations were appropriate and whether the document (signed by Gerald Murray, representative of the Crown) could be used. The Huron Band was acquitted as the document was considered a Treaty (Section 88, Indian Act). This court case illustrates the frustration of Native people using land they technically do not own (according to Canadian law) even though all land is Native land in their system of beliefs (Edward, 1994).

THE MINISTRY OF NATURAL RESOURCES AND FIRST NATIONS

The Ontario Ministry of Natural Resources (MNR) manages natural resources with a number of policies and Acts. The regulations are in place to protect, conserve, control development and overuse, and market the unique ecological systems in Ontario. Every provincial park must have a management statement/plan in order to:

> identify the contribution(s) of Park 'X' [made] to the achievement of the four park system objectives (protection, heritage appreciation, recreation, tourism); and to identify management policies aimed at maintaining or enhancing that contribution (Ontario Ministry of Natural Resources, 1992).

To date, the following guidelines are in place to govern the communication, negotiation and partnership with Native people in Ontario:

a) All decisions related to the identification, planning or disposition of provincial park lands, or other lands set aside to protect significant natural or cultural heritage values, will be the subject of public consultation. Aboriginal peoples who identify traditional ties to those lands will be integral to the consultation and decision making processes. In some cases there may be a need for separate consultation or negotiation processes to address Aboriginal interest in park lands. If required, some issues regarding how a park is used may also be the subject of negotiation with Aboriginal people.

b) The Government of Ontario will consider all the available options when seeking to determine the land component, if any, during negotiations involving land claim settlements with First Nations. Options for use that involve lands which are not to be considered for provincial park purposes will be preferred.

c) As described in the Province's Interim Enforcement Policy (1991), aboriginal people hunting or fishing in provincial parks will be subject to all relevant treaties and laws. However, an agreement reached between the Province and a First Nation may modify the application of those treaties and laws (Ontario Ministry of Natural Resources, 1992:23–24).

One key concern in this study is to explore the origins of Ojibwe and European-based perspectives on land and land management, how those perspectives impact on the development and management of provincial parks, and how both might work together to make the Indigenous vision for park management become a reality. The methodology thus relies not only on the existing literature and research relating to the ongoing negotiations between governments and First Nations people, but also on the "living voice" elicited via the ethnographic interview.[2] We interviewed both First Nations people and Ontario MNR officials and employees. Selected interview comments are then interwoven with our analysis and discussion.[3]

CULTURAL EXPRESSION

There are certainly many reasons why the environment has always been, and continues to be, a central theme in the lives of First Nations peoples across Canada. For millennia First Nations in Canada have necessarily been dependent on the land for survival and well-being. While there may be some debate on the origin of the term "Mother Earth," so often invoked in writings about Aboriginal people and used by Aboriginal people themselves, there can be little doubt that there exists a spiritual relationship with the land in virtually every Indigenous tradition around the globe (Campbell, 1996). Ways of maintaining and enhancing this close relationship with the earth were, and are, nurtured and integrated into everyday life. This relationship with "Mother Earth" continues to be a deeply-entrenched theme in the lives of First Nations people in Canada.

This theme can be seen at play in the oral traditions and oral histories of First Nations people today. There continue to be many reminders of this theme embodied in the stories, songs, dances, prayers, ceremonies and sacred teachings of every First Nations tradition in Canada. This theme has profound implications for community decision-making, as well. From our experience working and talking with First Nations people over the years, we have come to understand that, when community decisions are made, the environment is a fundamental consideration. In virtually every decision facing contemporary First Nations communities today, environmental concerns are always an important part of community discussion and consensus decision-making.

First Nations people continue to respect and gather input from their Elders and believe Elders *should* play a significant role in community development. Their wisdom, patience and experiences provide crucial information in the decision-making process. Native people have become very protective of sacred sites and artifacts. As one Elder from the Ojibwe community of Wikwemikong told us:

> Elders, probably our ancestors ... in good faith, they told these people that came into the communities these stories ... and these people went out and dug up artifacts ... and I think that's why these Elders are being quite cautious now, of who they talk to and who they tell this stuff to (personal communication, 1997:30).

In most Anishnaabe (Ojibwe) communities, Elders are viewed as sources of wisdom and knowledge. Traditions, language and ceremonies have been passed on from generation to generation in an oratory fashion. Consultation with Elders is conducted regularly and respectfully because they are able to reflect on previous stories, legends, and experiences and provide visions of growth for the future of their culture (Beck *et al.*, 1992:5). With regard to community development, meetings with Elders are essential because, as one Elder from the community of M'Chigeeng (formerly known as West Bay) told us:

> We have seven generations to look after ... not for today's children, but for tomorrow's and their grandchildren and their great-grandchildren, that's what we are going to head for. We've lived our life, we know how to slug it the rest of the way (personal communication, 1997:30).

Given the degree of respect and influence that Elders have in their surrounding community:

> Anytime an earlier testifies to anything, like my ancestors told me this, their world was taken ... knowledge like a written expert ... so based on that the government has to recognize these Elders as experts (personal communication, 1997:30).

SETTING THE STAGE

Few would argue that cultural knowledge should be respected by Native and non-Native people alike. First Nations cultures pay the consequences when sacred information is abused or taken advantage of. In Ontario, the government has previously minimized and/or completely neglected consultation with Native people with regard to development (personal communication, 1997:23). One Elder we interviewed recalled a story about how the government had plans to install a dam on river in northern Ontario. According to his people's stories, a body was buried somewhere near the proposed dam. The government required an exact burial site in order to *consider* an alternate position. Unfortunately, the body could not be found and the dam was built without knowledge of the scared area. The Elder with whom we spoke about this situation had this to say:

> I think the government has to recognize that a lot of our history has been forgotten and a lot of our history was passed on to us in an oral fashion. We never documented and I think the government has to learn how to trust us and say that there is a body out there somewhere. You have to trust us on that, we can't locate it, but we know it's out there ... and those were stories that were handed down to us (personal communication, 1997:30).

First Nations people are adamant about regaining some future control in government and corporate decision-making. Cultural protection and expression will be possible with an increase of participation in natural resource management. For example, during negotiations between Ontario Parks and Native people, one Native person from the community of Garden River with whom we spoke resolved the following:

> What they are saying (the MNR) is that they have their policies in place in provincial parks, provincial park policy, and we have to adhere by that. Once we start developing we are going to be changing those policies that are culturally appropriate for our community (personal communication, 1997:30).

and,

> When we took part in the negotiations, we made sure that our issues were covered, that our issues were put down there ... so far it seems that they are going to listen to us and abide by what we are trying to do (personal communication, 1997:23).

From the above discussion, three key ingredients for developing an equitable partnership in park planning and design become evident:

- In order for Native people to fully participate in a park plan, the Native voice must be heard and respected;
- First Nations people would prefer to have the government work *with* them by negotiating policies and regulations in the park, e.g. hunting and fishing rights; and,
- If the relationship works, policies in the park *should* reflect the partnership between Ontario Parks and First Nations.

ORIGIN OF PARKS IN CANADA

The relationship between First Nations people and parks is rooted in the origin of parks and treaty rights in Canada. European values entrenched in political systems generally guide the management, planning and design of parks with little or no influence by First Nations people.

The evolution of national parks in Canada began in 1885 at Banff, Alberta. Two employees of the Canadian Pacific Railway (CPR) discovered mineral hot springs and hoped to develop the area for private profit. The federal government refused the claim and created a reserve around the area for public use. Since the inception of national parks, wilderness preservation has not been as influential as economic and social development (McNamee in Dearden *et al.*, 1993:17).

Provincial parks in Ontario were developed for many of the same reasons as national parks: recreation, tourism, protection and heritage appreciation. There were eight provincial parks before 1954 and two hundred and seventy by 1989. The parks are defined as one of six categories: wilderness, access, nature reserve, natural environment, historical and development. The six categories limit what activities can take place in each park (e.g. low impact recreation for day use in nature reserves). The treaties signed between Native people and the government are particularly important in parks. Many Native people use wilderness areas to live, trap, hunt and fish during various times of the year. Native people have had to struggle to keep their treaty rights in place as the general public are not allowed to partake in these activities.

CONTEMPORARY ISSUES

Today, there are feelings of mistrust by First Nations toward the federal and provincial governments. A legacy of three hundred years of broken treaties with First Nations and the federal government has created a very real climate of distrust. However, the relationship is sometimes confusing and often difficult to follow. First Nations have had no choice but to educate themselves about the processes of government. The leading piece of legislation that governs First Nations in Canada is the *Indian Act* (1876). The Act was created by the federal government to strengthen their domination over First Nations people. According to Francis (1995):

> The aim of the Act, as of all Indian legislation, was to assimilate Native people to the Canadian mainstream. Assimilation as a solution to the "Indian problem" was considered preferable to its only perceived alternative: wholesales extermination (Francis, 1995:200).

Despite the number of amendments to the Indian Act, this piece of legislation remains an authoritative voice for government. This voice has historically decided who is Native, where Native people can live, where they are educated, what language they speak and what religion they should practice. For Native people, the concept of building trust with any government is unfathomable at times. The controls that government has instilled on the lives of Native people have also hindered attempts at improving the relationship. As one Elder told us:

> I got the impression that we were seen as government and owning the land, and ... that was a barrier right there. Who we stood for, it was more of an image thing (personal communication, 1997:25).

Negotiation

A conflict since the signing of treaties has been the establishment of provinces. From a European-based perspective, provinces were a wise and economic move. The country's boundaries grew as a result, along with an increase in business and population development and national wealth through natural resource development. A clear struggle occurs when First Nations are approached to negotiate on the issue of natural resources. The provinces, or provincial governments, become additional players in the discussions. As one Native person with whom we spoke stated:

> As soon as you start to recognize the province as a player in all of this, by virtue of doing that, you are giving the province rights and jurisdictional rights where they don't belong (personal communication, 1997:35).

The deficient element of trust in the relationship is evident from the beginning of European colonization. It leaves many First Nations people and Canadians wondering if balanced discussions between the Crown and First Nations can ever occur. Technically, *negotiation* is the process of reaching an agreement where interests are shared and opposed between participants. Once an agreement is made, all parties need to trust and adhere to the approved decisions. According to Fisher and Ury (1991:1):

> Everyone wants to participate in decisions that affect them; fewer and fewer people will accept decisions dictated by someone else.

It is difficult for Native people and the government to ignore previous encounters and cultural differences during negotiations. For example, during a negotiation, one First Nations person with whom we spoke said:

> One of the things that seems to be there from the beginning is when there is that kind of an arrangement or negotiation with the province, the province always wants to assure everybody and to ensure in their negotiations that they still have control and they are never going to surrender that control ... what is presented has the appearance of goodwill, but it always means that something is surrendered, you have to give up something in order to make this kind of arrangement (personal communication, 1997:35).

Consultation

In Ontario, building relationships between MNR and First Nations has been difficult, to say the least. A current problem in northern Ontario is the size of the MNR park planning zone. There are nearly eighty parks and reserves in the zone and the MNR are currently restructuring their staff load. One planning team member believes park superintendents have better opportunities to initialize and maintain contact with groups, however they often have more than one park to manage and are limited with time (personal communication, 1997:25). A parks problem that was discovered from nine MNR employees we interviewed, was that neither the MNR [nor] Native people have a very good understanding of how each other [operates] (personal communication, 1997). Most park superintendents give Native groups the same weight as all other interest groups in park planning.[4] One park superintendent we interviewed stated:

> I would be very surprised if any superintendent did involve, or at least attempt to involve, the First Nation people in the planning process (personal communication, 1997:21).

The conversations we had with MNR employees suggest that very few people have had cross-cultural training in their job placement. In particular, one MNR planner with whom we spoke said:

> No, I have never been told, ... never been encouraged to go to workshops or whatever. It is personal interest and initiative that would drive that. It is more I would say, to choose my words here, the word is contingency ... when you find out something is relevant you learn about it (personal communication, 1997:27).

He maintains that some information about First Nations people does exist within the MNR in published literature and circulated documents, but a limiting factor is definitely time. His exposure to First Nations has been:

> ...some training from First Nations representatives in general. On two occasions: on philosophy of the Aboriginal people and some of their attitudes and where they come from, and some of the things I should be mindful of when dealing with a person or a group of First Nations people. Again that was very general (personal communication, 1997:27).

The MNR does admit to having limited knowledge and understanding about First Nations cultures. For instance, the management planner we interviewed acknowledged the shortcomings of the MNR:

> There are other things that we can't appreciate wholly: sacred use, religious aspects, features that have some sort of meaning in lore that we can read and say "that's good" and we can put it on the map kind of thing, but it does not necessarily mean that we understand fully (personal communication, 1997:27).

To compensate, some staff in the parks unit make a point of looking for unwritten Native traditions and/or legends to aid in the interpretation of Native cultural data in a provincial park (personal communication, 1997:27). The comments from a Native woman from the Ojibwe community of Garden River were in agreement:

> They don't have a big knowledge of who we are, like our culture, where we come from, our traditions, but I think that they are, probably maybe they are being forced to listen and learn, ... so far it has worked out good (personal communication, 1997:23).

The weakness in the process is the number of staff that rely on secondary information (e.g. books, articles) rather than consultation with Native people themselves. One MNR employee illustrated the concern:

> If the process was too fast then we should have slowed it down. We were relying on documented information and perhaps we should have said well there had to be more. Let's stop here, what is the urgency? (personal communication, 1997:27).

A limitation in exposing MNR park employees to the Native culture is the "hands-on" approach to cultural education: there are very few workshops and/or cultural [trainings] held withinn the MNR, [and] thus the education comes on a project-by-project basis. One MNR employee's comments described a park plan situation:

> It involved very few people within MNR. It involved the superintendent, the Native Liaison individual and a Park Planner was brought on specifically to plan the park. It really impacted very few people and the rest of the MNR office was largely unaware (personal communication, 1997:28).

There are many advantages and disadvantages to addressing Native issues on a case-by-case basis. A clear advantage is the opportunity to customize every project to achieve goals and objectives. Comments from one Native woman we interviewed clearly highlight where this advantage has shone through:

> And they have bent over backwards to hear our concerns. Like when we took part in the negotiations, we made sure that our issues were covered, that our issues were put down there, and the same with Thompson [township]. So far, it seems that they are going to listen to us and abide by what we are trying to do, encourage us (personal communication, 1997:23).

This particular woman was very positive and happy with her Band's involvement with the planning of the park. She went on to say:

> You know what I think is really unique is the MNR actually coming to us and willing to sit down with us and negotiate a management plan. Like this would not have happened, probably won't happen anyplace else. I again think it is up to the personnel, or the individuals that they hire. You know, where do they take us? It could have gone in a totally different direction. But I don't know if it is the MNR personnel that works here that are willing to work with us and see our point of view. You know, like I said, some of the Band won't even talk to MNR officials, they kick them [off] the reserve when they see them coming, like you know, stuff like that. And here we have kind of a unique relationship with them, so it doesn't happen all over. And I think we are fortunate that we do have people there, that there are people there working who are willing to listen to us (personal communication, 1997:23).

From a MNR perspective, Parks Ontario is highly policy-driven. The parks system tends to promote natural features before approaching cultural features. A staff member we interviewed found:

> It is not just the Indigenous culture that is sort of overlooked, it is also a lot of our early history as a country that's overlooked. It is just sort by a fluke that a lot of these things get developed (personal communication, 1997:25).

In one particular case, MNR employees held public consultations at Native Band Offices (on Reserve) and township halls. A spokesperson for the MNR said the location helped as:

> The Elders could come and talk and see what we were doing. We recorded all of their comments at that time (personal communication, 1997:22).

Disadvantages range from having little to no consultation with First Nations communities during park planning phases due to insufficient demand from legislation.

MNR RESOURCE MANAGEMENT STRATEGIES

This section describes resource management strategies in the Ontario Parks system. Attempts have been made to link conservation and First Nations cultures in both of the resource management departments. However, evidence shows scarce involvement of First Nations people in the *design* of protected areas.

"Sustainable development", "eco-tourism" and "co-management" are buzz words as we enter the 21st Century. In this particular study, the definition of co-management, specifically addressing First Nations people is as follows:

> The sharing of decision-making power with nontraditional actors in the process of resource management ... those other than either state managers or industry, such as local resource users, environmental groups, or *aboriginal people* ... arrangements ranging from public participation initiatives, to land claim settlements and self-government initiatives (OMNR, 1996, emphasis added).

One of the seven business objectives of the Ontario Parks system is to: "...involve the private sector in program delivery, from service contracts to park contracting to *partnerships*" (OMNR, 1996, emphasis added). There are three examples of which we are aware where this objective has been implemented. The first example is an agreement between Ontario Parks (representing Lake Nipigon Provincial Park) and Sandpoint First Nation. The First Nation band has agreed to cooperate [with] the provincial park in accordance with the terms and conditions set by Ontario Parks. The Band is guided by the park management plan, applicable legislation, policies and procedures and park permits. The Band is also responsible for all staff and maintenance in the park. The benefits to the First Nation Band are employment and (potential) revenue and the benefits to Ontario Parks [are] having a partner operate the park, thus reducing overall costs to the MNR (OMNR, 1996).

A similar example is the relationship between Quetico Provincial Park and the Lac La Croix First Nation. The "Agreement of Co-Existence" evolved from the recognition of the social degradation in the First Nation Band by Quetico Park. The Native community of Lax La Croix have a number of social problems stemming from substance abuse, unemployment, cultural loss and violence. In an effort to lessen these conditions, a partnership with the park was imperative. The Band was involved with the public consultation process which eventually led to an agreement:

> ...to preserve wilderness values and to create social and economic opportunities for the community (OMNR, 1996).

More specifically, the commitment by the band is outlined in part of the message by Chief Leon J. Jourdain (Chief of Lac La Croix First Nation) in the park plan:

> The First Nation has been and will continue to be an active partner in the effective and efficient management of Quetico Park through thoughtful and collaborative efforts in co-

management. The opportunity for the First Nation to act as a partner in this effort is best described by the words of our Elders as "a sacred trust bestowed to the Anishinaabe for the care of the land." The "sacred trust" is what will guide the partners and others in our endeavors to maintain a central focus on the social and economic stability of the community of Lac La Croix (OMNR, 1996).

As described earlier, the definitions of co-management are numerous. Ontario Parks have been chosen by the United Indian Council as the "spiritual caretakers" of the unique petroglyph features in Petroglyphs Provincial Park. Unlike the above examples, only *specific* features in the park are in a co-management arrangement rather than the entire park. The agreement addresses park fees, access to the sacred site, access during the non-operating season and fasting requests by the First Nation. Co-management arrangements could not have been made without resource management guidelines, negotiations, and time. Descriptions of these guidelines and the process of consulting with First Nation groups are found in the paragraphs below.

CO-MANAGEMENT STRATEGIES

Resource managers and planners follow guidelines set by the MNR for the management of cultural and natural resources in provincial parks. The guidelines were established to monitor and continue the effectiveness of park management, standardize development, and formalize approval. Resource management is intended to be flexible within the framework of policies and plans (OMNR, 1992). Defining [terms] of reference is one of the many steps in the management planning process. The procedure requires management objectives and an evaluation of the existing data base. Throughout this phase, the planning team consult and review all information required to formulate a park management plan. The planning team usually consists of specialists related to a number of fields (e.g. landscape architects, environmental planners, and biologists). Unfortunately, this panel of experts do not directly relate to our First Nations issues.

Planning teams also comply with the focus of management of cultural resources dictated by the government of the day. In the previous Ontario government, the Ministry of Natural Resources created Native Liaison positions to foster growth and build bridges with Native people. One MNR staff member we interviewed was pleased to see the government proactively make an effort to better communicate with Native people:

> So, I always felt that somebody has really turned on the light here because MNR is finally going to get into the business of developing the working relationships with the key people on the land here, the Native people (personal communication, 1997:22).

The present provincial government has focused on reducing the Ontario deficit, [and] thus employment cut backs in the provincial government have been dramatic. A retired Native Liaison officer we interviewed revealed his feelings [about] the action taken by the new government:

> There was a brief era there where the MNR actually became, got into, the Native liaison business. We have always liaised with angling and hunting clubs ... but we had this other group of major stakeholders.... They [Native people] don't like to be called that, because they are more than that. But the fact that they are more than that, you'd think we would

have a whole unit dealing with them. We did for awhile, but I don't see it there now, it got pulled out. The funny part of it is that other organizations, like forestry companies, that are planning on dealing a lot with Native people, they do put the time and money into having people who will work and build these relationships and keep the doors open (personal communication, 1997:22).

Occasionally in the MNR, cross-cultural training sessions to educate people and to give them a real awareness of First Nations issues and knowledge are arranged. Attendance is optional and has proved to be beneficial to MNR employees, as one staff person went on to say:

They would take this workshop for two or three days and come out of there with a whole different — sort of overwhelmed. They had a total different appreciation of Native people. I always felt that, you know there was a time when I was uncomfortable going into a reserve and into a band office. After I had some of this cross-cultural training, at these workshops, I got to feel more comfortable in the First Nation office than I did in my own Ministry office (personal communication, 1997:22).

Given this testimony, it is clear that the educational sessions were worthwhile and successful with their intention. As a Native Liaison Officer, he felt that he had developed a good working relationship with Native people. Within the team of Native Liaison officers:

We were very supportive of each other. But when you go back into the district office and worked, you were kind of on your own (personal communication, 1997:22).

Benefits of attending a workshop are evident within the MNR, as one staff member said:

You know, we had various discussions with how to consult with the First Nations. I was more comfortable when we held the public meetings in their community hall (personal communication, 1997:22).

The benefits have also been noticeable, particularly to one First Nation Band:

Like I said, in the past they never consulted with us or took our point of view seriously ... but I think, overall we have a good relationship with MNR. I know some of the First Nations haven't. I know some of them can't stand MNR, or government officials ... I think also it depends on the individual too. I don't know if it has to do with their temperament or their outlook. Do they keep an open mind about everything and stuff like that (personal communication, 1997:23).

As mentioned earlier, cross-cultural training sessions were optional and according to an informant, many of his colleagues remained insensitive to First Nation issues. To date, inviting First Nations to participate in park planning has followed the same procedure as inviting any special interest group. Cultural insensitivity can affect the participation of a First Nation group. As one park superintendent told us:

We didn't know what they wanted. We did not get a reply so we just left it at that then it was up to them whether they would participate or not (personal communication, 1997:21).

From first-hand experience, the retired Native Liaison officer we interviewed believes many MNR employees do not have an understanding of the First Nations culture. He also found his colleagues:

> Work for an organization that has policies and procedures and you have to abide by those I guess. I think there could be a lot more sort of leadership shown by Managers and Directors. I think there needs to be more work done (personal communication, 1997:22).

Mental barriers have to be overcome for true understanding to take place to allow the design process to proceed. Those who work for the MNR tend to be restricted in their capacity as *creative* designers/planners. Limitations have emerged from numerous policies, guidelines and set design standards. In one way, limitations are advantageous as designs become universal and recognizable as "government" amenities. On the other hand, MNR environmental planners *are encouraged* to be creative in their attempt to blend human activities with the environment yet they are confined to MNR regulations. Design limitations and public consultation meetings can go hand in hand.

During our interviews we asked a number of First Nations people how their Native heritage could be represented in a park. We were impressed with their responses, and later wondered if the MNR has ever heard their strong ideas and feelings. The MNR *may not know* how some Native people feel about design as they may never have asked them. Some of the responses that we received include:

- All entrances should be from the east (where the sun comes from)
- Circular designs (buildings, pathways, etc.): the circle represents one continuous journey
- Reading material could be bi- or tri-lingual (e.g. describing the significance of a rock = has a life of its own, spiritual significance)
- Orientation of buildings: circle or six sided design to show that we all go through cycles from life to death
- Significant colours (on/in a building): black, red, yellow, white
- Views of water
- Mark sacred places in a creative way (to protect them and observe them if desired)
- Cleansing or smudging with tobacco upon entrance to the park (personal communication, 1997:36).

Management of natural resources are similar around the globe. The goals and objectives usually follow the same theme (e.g. to protect or preserve natural, cultural and/or historical features in a particular space for public enjoyment).

TOWARDS A SUCCESSFUL CO-MANAGEMENT MODEL: A CASE STUDY

To illustrate what we mean by successful and participatory management planning and design, we present the case of the Mississagi Delta Provincial Nature Reserve (MDPNR), which is located in northern Ontario, Canada. This particular park is unique to the MNR as it is a leading example of "co-management" between Parks Ontario, a First Nation Band and a township. The section entitled "Cultural Resources" contains information solely on the Indigenous influence(s) in the chosen parks.

Mississagi Delta Provincial Nature Reserve (MDPNR)

Native groups who settled on the body of water currently known as the Mississagi River called the water "River Mississaging", "River of Many Mouths" and/or "Big Mouthed River" (OMNR, 1982:25).

Located near the mouth of Mississagi River in northern Ontario is 2,395 hectares of land. The area has been protected by the Ministry of Natural Resources since 1985 as Mississagi Delta Provincial Nature Reserve (MDPNR). MDPNR is seven kilometers west of the town of Blind River and borders the township of Cobden. The park is classified as a Nature Reserve in order to:

> protect distinctive biological, geological and biophysical landscapes; to provide opportunities for unstructured individual exploration, and to foster appreciation of our natural and cultural heritage (OMNR, 1996:2).

Natural Resources

MDPNR protects a number of provincially significant features around the North Channel of Lake Huron. The park includes an island chain called the French Islands along the shore of Mississagi Bay. The islands were formed approximately 10,000 years ago with the movement of melting ice down the south section of the Mississagi River. As a consequence, the landscape of the delta contrasts with the surrounding rocky North Channel shoreline. The shallow water in Mississagi Bay invites wetland formation as the islands offer protection from the wind in the North Channel (OMNR, 1996). The nesting sites located near the French Islands belong to herons, gulls, and cormorants. The flora and fauna of MDPNR include a range of regionally significant species and a rare species called porcupine grass. The North Channel greatly affects the climate in the park as the summers are cool and the winter temperatures are less severe than the surrounding area (OMNR, 1996:4). Topographic features in MDPNR are low and hummocky with elevations reaching 175 to 225 metres. Soils in the park are fairly wet (except in the summer months) and are predominantly Mallard silty loam. The park consists of an upland mixed forest with tree species such as White Pine and Balsam Fir.

Cultural Resources

According to eight archaeological studies completed in the park, evidence from the first occupants in the area [dates] back to 800 AD. The occupants were Native Algonquian speakers (mix of Ojibwe and Cree) and camped mainly in an area known as the Renard Site along the northeast side of Fox Island (OMNR, 1996:25). Their existence depended on hunting (large and small game), fishing and plant resources. During this time, Native people would gather together in the summer months and disperse into smaller groups in the winter. As assortment of artifacts connected to this time period suggest the occupants were skilled at tool making. Another area that indicates occupation is the Falls Site, located in the eastern mainland at Mississagi Chute (OMNR, 1996:26). The river provided an adequate transportation route to Lake Huron and other areas in the interior. There are a number of unexplained circular depressions and rock formations in the park.

A geologist located them in 1975 and compared them to the Pukaskaw Pits in northern Ontario.

The Park Plan

Since the park's inception in 1985, Ontario Parks have directed the park with an Interim Management Statement. A new management plan was initiated with provincial government funding and the Mississauga First Nation Northern Boundary Settlement Agreement in 1994. The land claim had been submitted in the early 1980s and came to a close in 1996. The co-management idea was "kind of a side issue" as Native people were looking for additional parcels of land to *co-manage* (personal communication, 1997:34). The settlement includes a *sharing* of the Blind River by way of the Indian Lands Agreement Act (1986). The Act is a special statute that allows the sharing of jurisdiction (personal communication, 1997:34). One MNR person we interviewed believes the agreement should not be interpreted as *co-management*. In his opinion, co-management means a "partnership", or a relationship that is "50–50" (personal communication, 1997:28). The agreement really describes "cooperation" of the park as the Crown will still have the final say in all decisions. Mississagi Delta is a provincial park and if the agreement really proposed co-management, then the status of the park could no longer remain under the jurisdiction of the Crown. The park would have to be called something else. Therefore, we believe the Ministry of Natural Resources needs to be clear about what "cooperation" and "co-management" means in terms of the future of partnerships with Ontario Parks.

Settlement Agreement

In 1850, the Robinson-Huron Treaty established the Mississauga First Nation Reserve. The size of the Reserve was much larger than what it is today as it included the land between Mississagi River and the Blind (Penowabikong) River, up to the mouth of Lake Duborne. The size of the Reserve changed with the Northern boundary land claim and is proposed to change again with the impending Southern boundary land claim.

The Northern boundary land claim was submitted to the Crown by the Mississauga First Nation on the basis that land for the Native Reserve was improperly surveyed in 1852. The Band "claimed the land which was not included in the survey, and compensation for the loss of use of that land" (Settlement Agreement, 1994). The Agreement was signed by representatives of the Mississauga Band, the Ministry of Indian Affairs and Northern Development, the Ministry Responsible for Native Affairs and the Ministry of Natural Resources on April 27, 1994. In Article 5 of the Agreement, the province of Ontario and the First Nation Band agree to co-manage MDPNR with Thompson Township as an optional participant. In the words of the Agreement, the parties agree to the following:

> (a) a park board, composed of representatives from each of Ontario, Mississagi and, if applicable, the Township of Thompson, to provide advice and recommendations with regard to the planning, management and operations of the Park to the Minister of Natural Resources;

(b) the preparation of a management plan for the Park by the park board, to reflect the commitment of the park board to:
(1) protect the natural values, heritage and integrity of the Park;
(2) protect Mississagi sacred and cultural sites within the Park; and
(3) provide for job opportunities for Mississagi and local residents (Settlement Agreement, 1994:41)

A park board was formulated with two representatives from each of the parties. So far, the park board has met approximately every two months and [is] pleased with this process. In addition to the park board, there was a planning team comprised mainly of MNR staff. The responsibility of the team was to "...provide the park planner with technical expertise" (OMNR, 1996:3) A Park Management Plan has been written and is currently waiting approval from the Minister of Natural Resources.

Consultation

The MNR followed their management planning guidelines and consulted with the public. As mentioned earlier, the process of consulting Native people is comparable to all interest groups. However, in this case some consultation did take place, and one Native person we interviewed found the process to be very rushed:

> the most difficult thing of the whole process was holding the governments back. They were so gung-ho to get ahead with this thing, to get it finalized that we had to constantly keep pulling the reins back and say no, we have to consult with our Elders and get their input into it (personal communication, 1997:30).

The issue of time was later stressed when my informant discussed negotiations in the park plan:

> ...and we have to stick with out agenda, saying, "your agenda is fine, but it can fit into our agenda because this is something new and it is negotiable". But you have to respect our culture and our ways of doing it and if it takes twenty-five years, then I am ready to sit back twenty-five years and deal with it (personal communication, 1997:30).

Public comments were recorded at an open house in January, 1996. The seventeen responses covered the following topics:

camping	fishing (commercial/recreational)	access
permitted uses	mechanized travel	traffic
enforcement	Native issues	protection
trails	funding	tourism
boating	environmental safety	land use permits

More specifically, the responses that discussed Native issues are:

- Native site integrity (involve Native people);
- Properly controlling and enforcing Native hunting
- Have a voluntary ban on Native hunting (or establish and post "Hunting Season") due to effect on visitors watching birds, wildlife, etc. Also, is it necessary [to allow hunting] given the small area of the park?
- Advocate the return of Native artifacts
- Park research projects should have a Native component

- Native enforcement issues should be addressed through Native Conservation Officers
- Concern with land claim's South Boundary and possible influence on park
- Treaty rights and traditional spiritual sites have to be respected
- More hunting and camping allowed for Native people (OMNR, 1996).

Some information that was gathered in the consultations [has] already been addressed by the MNR. For instance, a Native person with whom we spoke said:

> traditionally people have hunted in there [the park] and I think the people, the families that did hunt in that area have the right to continue and practice with what has been handed down to them (personal communication, 1997:30).

As a response, the preliminary management plan states:

> *Treaty rights will continue* e.g. hunting is not allowed in nature reserves, except for Natives permitted through Treaty rights (OMNR, 1996:4).

An issue that can be difficult to deal with is the protection of sacred cultural artifacts and/or sites. One Native person with whom we spoke said many Elders are concerned about the buried sacred belongings (that may be dug up by "souvenir hunters"), the found sacred belongings (that are in museums and universities) and would ultimately like a safe place to have them stored and controlled by Native people (personal communication, 1997:30). Management planning staff find this issue frustrating for two reasons: firstly, once they find out where sacred sites are, the question is how [they can] be protected. Secondly, if management staff do not know where sacred sites are, how can they prevent visitors from stumbling across them or taking them?

An example of where management planners attempted to protect a sacred site is Petroglyphs Provincial Park (Ontario). The petroglyphs are symbols carved on rocks by Ojibwe people. The park has one of the largest collections of petroglyphs in Canada. Management planners initially tried to protect the sacred site with a wire fence around the petroglyphs and a lookout. Later a landscape architect and architect were hired and constructed a more culturally sensitive design around the site (personal communication, 1997:37). Access to the largest sacred site is protected by a gate, [and] a railing and has a flat ["altar"] for those who wish to leave offerings (e.g. tobacco). Visitors can view the petroglyphs from a raised walkway that encircles the carving site. Native people are allowed to walk on the face of the rock provided they remove their shoes or wear moccasins. Other petroglyph sites are not promoted in the park and are restricted only to Native people (OMNR, 1996).[5]

Funding and Development

The issue of funding repeatedly came up in interviews with Native people and MNR staff. For example, many people asked these questions: Will there be any funding? where will funding come from? and when will the park receive funding? Presently, the MNR manages Mississagi Delta as a non-operating park. The parcel of land has minimal development and according to the Nature Reserve classification, preservation is a top priority. The Native people with whom we spoke mentioned the desire to keep the park as pristine wilderness, yet also discussed possible promotion methods of the park (personal communication, 1997). The suggestions ranged from erecting the old Hudson's Bay post and re-developing the site into a contemporary museum or visitor centre, to outdoor education lessons with nearby schools. The services of a landscape architect, for example, could be utilized to fulfill any one of the ideas (e.g. historical restoration). One of the interviewees went into further detail with the following description:

> We want to hopefully educate people more on what we do. We are not going to have big elaborate ceremonies or anything but maybe we can put out booklets and stuff and do a little demonstration of certain things (personal communication, 1997:23).

As mentioned by park board members, promotion of the park would ultimately create job opportunities for Native people and people living in Thompson Township (personal communication, 1997:29). Thompson Township was very keen to get involved with the co-management of Mississagi Delta. The park could be used as a tourism attraction for the town (personal communication, 1997:28). In the words of one Thompson Township resident,

> People in this area need something to give them some hope, right now, because of the mines and because of everything else that was shutting down, there was none. The morale in the whole area was the pits and something like this could give people some pride in the area again and some hope that there are going to be a few jobs created anyway (personal communication, 1997:29).

Current Situation

The management plan for Mississagi Delta is presently waiting approval from the Minister of Natural Resources. From our research, the people we interviewed seemed happy with the arrangement, knowing that certain issues need to be addressed in the future (e.g. the improvement of the relationship between government staff and First Nations, cultural education, and the future of the park). The design of the park was not a major issue with MNR staff nor with the First Nations people with whom we spoke. In their eyes, the park is a large piece of land that needs to be promoted and protected. The agreed-upon principles include: to coordinate the needs and desires of the park board (representatives of the three partners), the greater community, Indigenous community, specific design details (access, future structures), and the park.

CONCLUSIONS AND RECOMMENDATIONS

This study suggests that necessary *effective* communication processes are required in order to ensure equitable participation of First Nations communities in park planning, management and design. To date, the question of understanding different values and the interpretation of place into physical form has been a major problem in resource management. How can we become more sensitized to other points-of-view and make appropriate assessments? Some people believe that weekend cross-cultural exercises are not enough. There *needs* to be constant willingness to learn, teaching and involvement of First Nations cultures by park management systems. This leads to a consideration of what both Native and non-Native people need to bring to problem-solving in order to be relevant, and what processes they can put in place to evolve understandings of place, meaning, and expressive forms. We have come full circle in responding to the questions addressed in this research. In Canada, at least to this date, First Nations people have had few opportunities to be equal partners in developing resource management strategies. There have been efforts made by the MNR to rectify this situation, but there still appears to be a need to better understand First Nations cultures, include First Nations in conservation management, implement culturally appropriate policies, and express First Nations cultures in park management and design. The communication process between First Nations cultures and government systems [depends] on the people involved. In some testimonies by MNR staff, there appeared to be acceptable communication, yet in other interviews the data implied the opposite situation. There were minimal obligations by First Nations people or government staff to one another. Based on the information included in this study, points for discussion are as follows:

1. **The importance of developing and monitoring joint stewardship programs.**

First Nations communities and MNR officials could work together to learn to utilize various technologies, (e.g. Geographic Information Systems (GIS), as a method to monitor wildlife or vegetation health). This system could be used in conjunction with the expertise of First Nations people that use the area for traditional purposes. A written synthesis should be prepared as well as regular updates to the database. GIS is only one system which can be used to gather and interpret data. Cultural inventories using CD ROM and involving local people is a significant area to explore in the parks planning process.

2. **The MNR should work with First Nations communities to find out how *they* wish to express their culture(s) in design and management.**

MNR officials ought to make the effort to find out from First Nations people important elements in the landscape and integrate their findings in site design. Some examples were discovered in our interviews: smudging at the entrance to a park; four sacred colours (architecture or signage); and entrances from the east. Rediscovering Aboriginal language place names (e.g. names and meanings of islands, bilingual signs), would be an important start. The issue of visualization and simulation in a participatory process could be explored in publications, Aboriginal art, logos, paraphernalia (t-shirts), computer images, and Internet sites.

3. **More policies that integrate First Nations' cultural needs and issues should be established.**

An example of the above would be having First Nations Elders work together with MNR planners and policy advisors to alter or create new policies that address cultural issues and/or needs. The end result would be policies that are culturally sensitive and integrated with First Nations values. As mentioned earlier in the MDPNR case study, hunting and year-round traditional camping allowances have been identified as an issue to be resolved with further communication and study (expressed in resource and use management) and written in the management plan.

4. **There should be ongoing research that pertains to First Nations cultures and cultural history relating to the natural environment.**

On many occasions, budget and/or manpower constraints dictate what background information can be collected in resource management. For example, details about trading between First Nations and European settlers were recorded in terms of location, time and traded articles. However, the *treatment* of Native people at the specific locations and with certain parties may not have been documented. A park library may not have that information during the management planning process. The MNR could involve First Nations people in the design of a park by acquiring contemporary information via ethnographic interviews. The information is imperative in order to properly design a space with consideration for First Nations people.

5. **It is important to begin building relationships and developing a formalized and long-term process of communication.**

The MNR could play a part in building relationships with First Nations people by developing a stronger commitment to partnerships with First Nations people; regular cross-cultural training of MNR staff; consultation with First Nations in all park planning decisions; regular assessment of the consultation process; and regular monitoring and up-grading of joint stewardship programs between the MNR and First Nations.

6. **Elders *should* play a significant role in decision-making regarding the planning, use and design of provincial parks in traditional territories.**

The wisdom, patience and experiences of First Nations Elders can provide crucial information in the decision-making process. Native people have been and continue to be very protective of sacred sites and [aware of] the importance of *place*. In most First Nations communities today, Elders continue to be revered as sources of wisdom and knowledge pertaining to the land and the environment. Any decision-making involving park planning and design should, then, include the input of community Elders.

Park planning and resource management can be improved with an emphasis placed on negotiation rather than litigation in conflict resolution situations. This could mean that a broader group of people will have their needs met and hence feel that resources are managed better. There is no doubt that First Nations communities have been inadequately involved with the land-use planning and design issues which have confronted government-run parks in traditional First Nations territories. By looking at successful models of co-management and by making a commitment to co-management partnerships between the MNR and First Nations, First Nations' concerns, values and aspirations can be better reflected in provincial park planning and design practices.

NOTES

1. For Ojibwe people, land is a gift from the Great Mystery. As Ojibwe Elder and historian Basil Johnston writes:

    From beginning to end it nourishes us: it quenches our thirst, it shelters us, and we follow the order of its seasons. It gives us freedom to come and go according to its nature and its extent — great freedom when the extent is large, less freedom when it is small. And when we die we are buried within the land that outlives us all. We belong to the land by birth, by need, and by affection. And no man may presume to own the land (Johnston, 1982:170).

2. When we refer to the "ethnographic interview" as a research methodology, we are referring to a methodology well-entrenched in the western academic tradition, evolving from the discipline of anthropology, and a research method which gives respect and credence to the oral tradition and intuitive analyses of Aboriginal people themselves (Spradley, 1979; Patton, 1987; Kirby and McKenna, 1989). When doing research with First Nations people, qualitative methods have proven to be the most welcome by the people themselves, not to mention the most revealing (Benkovic, 1997; Webster and Nabigon, 1992). The willingness of the researcher to share the results of one's research and to participate in the real lives of the people involved in the research is very much a prerequisite in most Indigenous contexts (Webster and Nabigon, 1992). By encouraging participatory research, common interest and mutual trust [are] able to emerge between the researcher and the ones involved in the research. As a result, the quality of information that is acquired is usually more reliable and beneficial for the people themselves. We found this to be true in our own research, where we were able to not only ask First Nations people questions and "find out things," but to make friends and to participate in their lives.

3. We ended up interviewing seventeen people from First Nations communities represented by the North Shore Tribal Council (NSTC) and the United Chiefs and Councils of Manitoulin (UCCM), including people from the communities of Wikwemikong Unceded First Nation and M'Chigeeng First Nation on Manitoulin Island, and Sagamok and Serpent River along the north shore of Lake Superior. All of the interviews with First Nations people were conducted in English. We also interviewed eight employees of the Ontario Ministry of Natural Resources (OMNR). Anonymity was preserved and university regulations regarding working with human subjects were carefully followed.

4. At the onset of a park management plan, a general mailing goes out to all interest groups to invite their comments in the planning process, including First Nations (MNR Official, personal communication, 1997:27). Given the limitations to relationship building in the MNR, is it possible to improve or develop better communication with Native groups? The answer relates to MNR employee interest and motivation.

5. The Ministry of Natural Resources have demonstrated to Native people and the public that they are able to adequately protect sacred sites. In the case of Mississagi Delta, the park board should be able to suggest methods for the protection of sacred artifacts.

REFERENCES

BECK, P.V., ANNA LEE WALTERS and N. FRANCISCO. 1992. *The Sacred: Ways Knowledge, Sources of Life*. Arizona: Navajo Community Press.
BENKOVIC, ZORICA. 1997. "Break Out Of Your Shell!": An Evaluation of KeyNorth Office Services and Training. Unpublished M.A. thesis. Sudbury, Ontario: Laurentian University.
BURGER, JULIAN. 1990. *First Peoples: A Future for the Indigenous World*. New York: Anchor Books.
CAMPBELL, TRACY. 1996. Co-management of Aboriginal Resources. *Information North* 22(1). (Internet Information: http://www.lib.uconn.edu/Arctic Circle/NatResources/comanagement. html).
CLARKSON, L., V. MORRISSETTE and G. REGALLET. 1992. Barriers to Understanding, pp. 1–2 in *Our Responsibility to the Seventh Generation, Indigenous Peoples and Sustainable Development*. International Institute for Sustainable Development.
FISHER, R. and W. URY. 1991. *Getting to Yes: Negotiating Agreement Without Giving In*. New York: The Penguin Group.
FRANCIS, DANIEL. 1995. *The Imaginary Indian: The Image of the Indian in Canadian Culture*. Vancouver, British Columbia: Arsenal Pulp Press.
JOHNSTON, BASIL. 1982. *Ojibway Ceremonies*. Toronto: McClelland and Stewart Inc.
KIRBY, S. and K. MCKENNA. 1989. *Experience, Research. Social Change: Methods From The Margins*. Toronto: Garamond Press.
MAY, ELIZABETH. 1990. *Paradise Won: The Struggle for South Moresby*. Toronto: McClelland and Stewart Inc.
McNAMEE, KEVIN. 1993. From Wild Places to Endangered Spaces: A History of Canada's National Parks, in Philip Dearden and Rick Rollins (Editors): *Parks and Protected Areas in Canada: Planning and Management*. Toronto: Oxford University Press.

MORSE, BRADFORD W. 1992. Native Land Rights and the Canadian Constitution. *Institute of Canadian Studies Occasional Papers.* Ottawa: Carleton University.
National Parks Act. 1980. No. 66. Wellington, New Zealand.
ONTARIO MINISTRY OF NATURAL RESOURCES. 1996. *Ontario Parks — A New Business Model for Ontario's Provincial Parks, Fact Sheet,* in News Releases and Fact Sheets.
———. 1996. Park Board Meeting: MDPNR. January 25.
———. 1996. Lake Nipigon Park Agreement. Unpublished Report.
———. 1996. Petroglyphs Management Strategy. Unpublished Report.
———. 1996. *Media Scan.* November 25, 26.
———. 1995. Mississagi Delta Provincial Nature Reserve: Background Information.
———. 1995. *Quetico Provincial Park Revised Park Policy.*
———. nd. Mississagi Delta Provincial Nature Reserve Preliminary Park Management Plan.
———. nd. Mississagi Delta Provincial Nature Reserve Management Plan. Queen's Printer for Ontario.
PATTON, J. 1987. How to Use Qualitative Methods in Evaluation. Newbury Park: Sage Publications.
PONTING, RICK (Editor). 1997. *First Nations in Canada: Perspectives on Opportunity, Empowerment, and Self-Determination.* Toronto: McGraw-Hill Ryerson Limited.
PRIDDLE, GEORGE. 1993. The Ontario Park System: Policy and Planning, in Philip Dearden and Rick Rollins (Editors): *Parks and Protected Areas in Canada: Planning and Management.* Toronto: Oxford University Press.
Provincial Parks Act. 1990. *Revised Statutes of Ontario.* Chapter P.34.
Settlement Agreement. 1994. Between The Mississauga Band, Canada and Ontario. April 27.
SPRADLEY, JAMES. 1979. *The Ethnographic Interview.* Toronto: Holt Rinehart and Winston.
WEBSTER, SCHUYLER and HERB NABIGON. 1992. First Nations Empowerment, in Paul Anisef and Paul Axelrod (Editors): *Transitions. Schooling and Employment in Canada.* Toronto: Thompson Educational Publishing.

CHAPTER 6

Water

(a) Water Issues and Treaty Negotiations: Lessons from the Yukon Experience[†]

Andrew R. Thompson and Nancy A. Morgan

I. INTRODUCTION

Water is the lifeblood of all societies. Whether a society's members are engaged in the traditional pursuits of hunting, fishing and gathering or in modern industrial activities, water is key to survival. Water also illustrates our interconnectedness as human beings to one another and to the world which surrounds us. For this reason, water will be one of the most critical issues to be addressed in the treaty negotiation process. As well, because of its migratory characteristics, water is the most difficult to understand and manage of all the natural resources.

The purpose of this paper is to describe how water was dealt with in the Yukon land claims agreements and to consider how the Yukon model may provide us with insights into how water issues may be dealt with in the BC treaty process. We begin by discussing water use and the existing water legislation in Yukon. We then describe the current status of the Yukon land claims agreements. This is followed by a discussion of Chapter 14, the Water Management Chapter, of the Council for Yukon Indians Umbrella Final Agreement ("UFA"). Finally, we consider what lessons the Yukon experience offers to the BC treaty process.

[†] Paper presented at the Aboriginal Law in Canada 1998 Conference, Vancouver, April 20th and April 21st, 1998. Appendix omitted. (Vancouver: The Native Investment & Trade Association, 1998). Reproduced with permission of the publisher.

II. BRIEF HISTORY OF WATER USE IN YUKON

The BC mining industry, including placer mining, has always had close ties with Yukon. This relationship began with mining the gold of the Klondike and continues to this day. The largest user of surface land and water in Yukon continues to be mining (though, as in British Columbia, tourism is catching up). So it is not surprising that mineral industry representatives were the most outspoken of all public interest participants in the negotiations concerning First Nation rights in Yukon to mineral and water resources. Nor is it surprising that interests in British Columbia should look to the Yukon land claims settlements to find a model for British Columbia.

III. EXISTING WATER LEGISLATION IN YUKON

In 1970 the *Northern Inland Waters Act ("NIWA")* was enacted by the federal Parliament to provide a comprehensive waste and water management regime for the Northwest Territories and Yukon, with separate water boards established for each territory to implement the same legislated provisions.

NIWA supplanted common law riparian rights in much the same way that riparian rights had been supplanted in the prairie provinces and BC. This worked in the following fashion: first, the property in flowing water was taken away from riparian owners and vested in the Crown; and second, the Crown then allocated the right to flowing water by a licensing system. In two major respects, the *NIWA* scheme differed from the regimes applying in these other provinces. First, unlike the B.C. case, *NIWA* licences were not perpetual, but were limited to a maximum of 25 years. In practice, the Boards usually issued licences of much shorter duration so that terms and conditions could be brought up to date on a continuing basis. Through these licences, the Boards could impose terms and conditions that would guard riparian-like rights to quantity, quality and rates of flow (QQF). Second, waste discharges would be governed by the same statute and the same licensing board. In effect, through *NIWA*, the common law riparian rights of the downstream user to flow and quality of water would now have to be provided through the terms and conditions of the legislation and the licences issued under it.

In 1993, after significant consultation with industry and other interested parties, the federal government repealed *NIWA* and enacted two separate statutes: the *Yukon Waters Act ("YWA")* and the *Northwest Territories Waters Act*. The new *YWA* was enacted to provide stronger protection for Yukon waters. It was also intended to streamline licensing procedures and to provide greater certainty in water use licensing for development activities. The *YWA* establishes a two-tier licensing procedure to distinguish between minor non-controversial water uses and more significant water uses.

The surprising thing about the enactment of the *YWA* is that it ignores the provisions of the Water Management Chapter of the UFA even though the latter has constitutional paramountcy over any conflicting legislation. Although the UFA had not yet been finalized when the *YWA* was introduced into the House of Commons, the Water Management Chapter had already been initialled and there was good reason to believe that the parties would sign the UFA within months. The *YWA* did not, in fact, come into force until two weeks after the UFA was signed on May 29, 1993. As a result, there are currently two distinct water regimes in Yukon. While the two regimes are in many ways compatible, they directly conflict in several important ways. Some of these conflicts will be considered below in section D of Part V.

IV. CURRENT STATUS OF YUKON LAND CLAIMS AGREEMENTS

On February 14, 1995, the *Yukon First Nations Land Claims Settlement Act* came into force. This federal statute approved, gave effect to and declared valid the four Final Agreements. Two other statutes came into force on that same day: the *Yukon First Nations Self-Government Act* and the *Yukon Surface Rights Board Act*. Under the terms of the UFA, these three statutes had to come into force at the same time.

Of the remaining 10 Yukon First Nations who do not have Final Agreements, six of them are actively negotiating final agreements. When finalized, these agreements will be brought into force by order of the Governor in Council (cabinet) in accordance with the provisions of the *Yukon First Nations Land Claims Settlement Act*. The four Final Agreements are now part of the laws of Canada. They are "super" laws because they qualify as modern treaties that are affirmed pursuant to section 35 of the *Constitution Act, 1982*. This means that their terms and provisions cannot be changed in the future except with the consent of the affected First Nations or, failing their consent, by resorting to the cumbersome process of amending the Constitution. Further, the Yukon Final Agreements, like their forerunner, the Inuvialuit Final Agreement covering the western Arctic, contain a provision that gives paramountcy to the terms and provisions of the Final Agreements in the event there is conflict between these terms and provisions and any law of Canada.

A. First Nations' Concerns

The first task of those instructed to develop a water management regime was to explain riparian rights and the existing water use licensing regime to the members of the CYI caucus (made up of the leaders of each of the 14 Yukon First Nations) so that the concerns of First Nations respecting water preservation and use could be identified. It was plain that their interests focused on how they could be sheltered from the adverse impacts of development projects such as placer mining, road building or mine tailings disposal which threatened both the quality and quantity of water flows in Yukon waterways. In particular, First Nations' anxieties centered on fish, wildlife and their habitats.

First, First Nations wanted protection of water on or flowing through settlement lands (the lands identified as such in a First Nation's Final Agreement). They expected to gain control of this water while on settlement lands, and they wanted protection of this water from the harmful effects of activities located on non-settlement lands upstream from settlement lands.

Second, individual First Nations persons wanted water rights which would continue to support traditional uses of water such as fishing, hunting and trapping, not only on settlement lands but on non-settlement lands as well. This would require assurance that the quality, quantity and rate of flow of water including seasonal flows (QQF) would be given first consideration in Yukon waterways. Individual First Nations persons also expected to have the same rights to obtain water licences on non-settlement lands as do all other residents in Yukon.

Third, First Nations acknowledged that their needs for QQF would often conflict with domestic and industrial uses. Therefore they wanted a water management system that would spell out clearly and fairly how competing demands would be resolved. There would also have to be an effective machinery for settling disputes about avoidance and mitigation measures as well as claims to damages and compensation.

B. Addressing First Nations' Concerns

Once First Nations' concerns were identified and ways of dealing with these concerns were designed, the next step was to draft provisions which would ultimately emerge as Chapter 14 on Water Management in the UFA. This process involved frequent meetings with the CYI caucus and gradually led to consensus as to what positions should be taken by CYI negotiators on various issues. This iterative approach resulted in a draft chapter which could be placed before the federal and territorial governments for negotiation. A guiding principle was to design UFA provisions that would build on the existing legislation (then *NIWA*) so that ultimately there could be integration of the UFA provisions with the existing legislation to achieve a consistent whole.

For example, in the case of water rights of First Nations on settlement land, there had to be reconciled:

(i) the determination of Her Majesty that all water in Yukon would remain the property of Her Majesty;
(ii) the insistence of First Nations that they have the exclusive right to use water on settlement land as if they were the owners; and
(iii) the desire of all parties that all water use (apart from traditional use) should be licensed and subject to upstream/downstream regulation by the Water Board.

These inconsistencies were resolved by UFA provisions that:

(i) acknowledge the property rights of Her Majesty by adopting laws of general application which include section 4 of *YWA* that says "the property in and the right to the use and flow of all waters are vested in Her Majesty in right of Canada" (14.3.0);
(ii) recognize the Yukon First Nations' exclusive right to use water on or flowing through settlement lands, so long as it continues to be on settlement lands (14.5.0);
(iii) give the Yukon First Nations rights to assign the First Nation's exclusive water right in whole or in part (14.5.7) (under the law of property the exclusive right to use water and to transfer this right in whole or in part to another and to have these rights in perpetuity are the equivalent of outright ownership);

(iv) require the Yukon First Nation to obtain a water licence for its water use (apart from traditional use) from the Water Board, but state that the issuance of this licence cannot be refused unless it is proved to the Board that such use will substantially alter the QQF so as to harm downstream users (retaining the licensing authority of the Board with respect to QQF on settlement lands accomplishes two objectives:

it provides for administrative certainty and efficiency and deals with the inherent upstream/downstream characteristics of flowing water).

Further, the difficulties of achieving consistency were reduced early on by agreement that existing water licences and access rights would be respected. This concession by the Yukon First Nations was easier to make because, as noted earlier, Yukon water licences are not perpetual and renewal could be denied by the Board.

Further discussion of the UFA provision is contained in Appendix 1. [Not included in this reproduction.]

C. Inconsistencies Between the UFA and the *Yukon Waters Act*

As we stated above under our discussion of the *YWA* in Part III, there are a number of provisions in the *YWA* which conflict with Chapter 14 of the UFA. Because the terms of First Nation Final Agreements are paramount to all other legislation, any inconsistencies will be resolved in favour of the Final Agreements.

Some key provisions of the *YWA* which conflict with Chapter 14 are the following:

1. Ownership of Waters

As previously stated, section 4 of the *YWA* vests the property in and the **right to the use and flow** of all waters in Her Majesty. The UFA states that a Yukon First Nation has the exclusive right to use water on or flowing through its settlement land (14.5.4) and that a Yukon Indian Person has the right to use water for a traditional use in Yukon (14.5.1). There is an apparent inconsistency between the Crown's vested right to the use of water and the Yukon First Nations' and Indian Persons' rights to use water on Settlement Lands. This inconsistency will persist until the Crown's ownership right is made subject to the rights in the First Nation Final Agreements.

2. Use of Waters

Section 8 of the *YWA* requires that no person use water except in accordance with a licence or as authorized by regulations. Under the UFA, Yukon First Nations can use water without a licence for traditional purposes so long as they do not substantially alter the QQF of the water. Resolving this inconsistency will require regulations recognizing water use for traditional purposes without a licence.

3. Water Board Membership

Section 10 of the *YWA* calls for a minimum of four and a **maximum of nine** members of the Board. The Board must include one nominee from each department "directly concerned with the management of waters" and three nominees of the Yukon Government Leader. Under the UFA there is a requirement that the CYI nominate one-third of the members of the Board (14.4.1). It is possible that four federal departments e.g. Fisheries, Transport, Environment and Indian and Northern Affairs would nominate members. If you added the four federal nominees to the three territorial representatives, it would be impossible for CYI to have one-third representation without going over the limit of nine Board members.

4. Assignment of Licences

Section 19 of the *YWA* requires the Board to authorize assignments of licences if certain conditions are fulfilled. It also states that "except as provided in this section, a licence is not assignable". These provisions are inconsistent with the provision in the UFA which allows Yukon First Nations to assign their rights to use water (14.5.7).

Over the long term, these inconsistencies will have to be resolved by amending the *YWA*. In the short term, however, First Nations and other Yukon residents alike will have to cope with a measure of uncertainty. The uncertainty is limited to some extent because Chapter 14 frequently incorporates "laws of general application".

V. RELEVANCE OF YUKON MODEL TO BRITISH COLUMBIA

As we have said, it is likely that First Nations will look to northern land claims settlements as potential precedents for settlements in British Columbia. In particular, the negotiation of water use provisions should be assisted by an examination of the Water Management Chapter of the UFA. We will highlight only a few situations where Chapter 14 might provide precedents.

But first, a word of caution. Yukon has a unique geography and social history that [encompass] the traditional territories of 14 separate First Nations. A land and water regime suitable for one territory may not be responsive to the needs of First Nations in other parts of Canada. BC has an even greater diversity of geography and culture leading to even greater diversity in needs. Possibly the surprising factor is how much First Nations have in common in the face of such diversity. We have previously identified the concerns expressed by Yukon First Nations — ownership of water adjoining or flowing through settlement lands; protection of traditional uses throughout Yukon; an effective water management system to deal with conflicts that are inherent in a flowing or migratory resource.

We believe that it is likely that these three basic needs would also be identified as the basic needs of BC First Nations. With this understanding, we offer our comments about potential precedents to be derived from the Yukon experience.

A. Structure of Negotiations

The flowing character of water and specifically its upstream/downstream characteristics place restraints on how water can be managed. Such characteristics cannot be effectively addressed on a fragmented basis as would be the case if each First Nation set about to manage water within its traditional territories without regard to the effects that would be imposed on other First Nations' lands. This problem of "spill over" effects applies in the case of other natural resources such as fish or wildlife that have migratory characteristics. In all these situations, the framework for negotiations must be responsive to these migratory characteristics. In Yukon, the 14 First Nations gave primary responsibility for negotiating the UFA to the CYI negotiators. Consequently, throughout most of the negotiations, the Yukon First Nations were able to present a common front at the negotiating table. Individual First Nation autonomy was safeguarded by giving the First Nations political control over the CYI and [by] the right of each First Nation to place its own imprint on the UFA through its First Nation Final Agreement.

In BC there are, of course, more First Nations electing to take part in the treaty negotiation process than the 14 First Nations involved with the Yukon settlements. BC's coastal geography also creates much more complexity in relation to watersheds than in Yukon. These factors suggest a need for First Nations to create a framework for negotiations over water rights in the style of the Yukon process. If a single voice on water issues cannot be agreed for all First Nations in BC, the negotiating process should at least be organized for water management issues on a regional watershed basis. For example, the Fraser River Basin could provide an effective regional basis for negotiating a water management regime with the federal and provincial governments. The B.C. *Water Protection Act*, R.S. Chap. 484, for example, lists the following as regional watersheds: the Frasershed; The Mackenzie Watershed; the Columbia Watershed; the Sheena Watershed; The Nass Watershed; the Stikine Watershed; the Taku Watershed; the Yukon Watershed; the Coastal Watershed.

B. Integration With Existing Water Law

Chapter 14 of the UFA was designed to operate as an "overlay" on the provisions of the existing water legislation, which, at that time, was *NIWA*. So far as possible, this overlay was intended to be consistent with the existing law, but, should there be inconsistency, the overlay would prevail. In the BC context, a water chapter in a treaty could be designed as an overlay on the existing water legislation in BC — the *Water Act*. If this constitutionally protected water chapter were given paramountcy, any inconsistency between the BC First Nation's chapter and the BC *Water Act* would have to be resolved in favour of the water chapter. However difficult it may be, the water use and management components of a BC First Nation's treaty must be recognized by the drafters of a new BC *Water Act* as part of the overall structure that must be taken into account.

C. Effective Enforcement of Water Rights

Experience teaches that property rights are not of much advantage unless there are effective enforcement mechanisms in place. Water rights are a case in point. An example in *NIWA* and now in the *YWA* are the provisions that offer compensation to a person adversely affected by an upstream licensee but only after court remedies have been exhausted sections *YWA* 17(1)(2) and 30(1)). The requirement of court action virtually assures that no remedy will be gained. The reasons are both that court remedies are costly and time-consuming and that they are highly uncertain in outcome. Courts are not used to dealing with the complexities of the water resource or the standards of proof of injury that should be applied.

Chapter 14 of the UFA tries to define more effective remedies. Recognizing that triggering concepts like QQF will require case by case elaboration, Chapter 14 gives an aggrieved person the right to apply directly to the Water Board for a ruling as to the meaning of QQF in a particular case. A Yukon Indian Person who claims a right to compensation for loss or damage to a water right can go directly to the Board for a decision as to entitlement to compensation and how much. The expectation is that the Board over time will build a set of precedents so that water users can enjoy more certainty as to the meaning of their rights. Chapter 14 goes a great distance in detailing what elements can be included in a claim to compensation. As the Board makes decisions defining these elements, a body of precedents will be established for the future.

Court proceedings are not ruled out in the UFA. Where the preferred course of action is resort to the court, Chapter 14 provides that the claimant shall be given the same rights as if the claimant were a riparian owner enjoying riparian rights. This entitlement is particularly helpful where the action is brought against a polluter for failing to have a licence to discharge waste or for breaching the terms of such a licence. A further advantage is conferred on the claimant by a "reverse onus" provision that says if the claimant proves that the defendant was in violation of a waste discharge licence at the point of discharge of the waste, the onus would shift to the defendant to prove that there were no damaging effects downstream.

Probably the most effective enforcement incentive is the power which the Water Board may exert over the water use or waste discharge licence. By a combination of provisions in the *YWA*, as amended by Chapter 14, the Board can amend, suspend or cancel a licence or attach conditions to an assignment of a licence. For example, a person claiming to be adversely affected by a waste discharge in violation of a waste discharge licence can apply for an order requiring the licensee to show cause why the licence should not be suspended pending clean up or other remedial measure. An even more basic power of the Board is its control over any assignment, amendment or renewal of a licence, a power made more significant by the fact that *YWA* licences are not perpetual but have limited durations.

D. Composition of the Water Board

In the tradition of the northern settlement agreements, Chapter 14 provides that one-third of the members of the Yukon Water Board must be CYI nominees. In the northern agreements this method of balancing representation extends to other settlement institutions such as the Yukon Heritage Resources Board and the Fish and Wildlife Management Board. BC settlement agreements will undoubtedly have to make provision for First Nation representation in appropriate situations.

E. Protection of Existing Rights

From the beginning, it was agreed that existing water rights and rights of access to water would be respected. One of the most difficult and protracted negotiations was to reflect this simple principle in the actual text of an agreement. In Yukon, the mining industry in particular is a major user of land and water resources. It became necessary to incorporate in great detail the many circumstances in which claim staking and placer operations require land and water access and use. The fact that these activities were not adequately or clearly provided for in the Yukon mining legislation did not make the task easier. If there is a part of the UFA that will attract litigation to sort out its meaning, it will be land and water access rights.

Basically the approach of the UFA and the *Yukon Surface Rights Board Act* is to define different classes of access and assign them to a category which requires the consent of the affected Yukon First Nation or to a category that does not require such consent, but as to which conditions will be imposed (e.g. that the access is reasonably required and that such access is not also practicable and reasonable across Crown land). Undoubtedly similar difficulties in addressing existing rights will be encountered in British Columbia.

F. Land and Water

In areas like Yukon where the natural resource industries require access to land for exploration and development purposes, there is a need to resolve conflicts with surface owners. In British Columbia and the prairie provinces this need is answered by the enactment of surface rights legislation. This legislation establishes a board to control access so that existing rights to enter and use land are respected but terms and conditions including compensation are imposed to balance the rights of surface owners.

There being no such legislation in Yukon, the UFA required that a surface rights statute be enacted by Parliament at the same time as the enactment of the *Yukon First Nations Land Claims Settlement Act* bringing into effect the first four First Nation Final Agreements. This has been done. An understanding of access rights in Yukon now requires an examination not only of several chapters of the UFA (Chapter 6 — Access; Chapter 7 — Expropriation; Chapter 8 — Surface Rights Board; Chapter 14 — Water Management; Chapter 17 — Forest Resources; Chapter 18 — Non-Renewable Resources), but also the provisions of the new *Yukon Surface Rights Board Act*. The relevance of this experience to BC is that it demonstrates how the treaty-making process can be utilized to require the restructuring of legislation so that it better fits the governance requirements of the First Nations.

These are but a few examples of precedents set by the Yukon Umbrella Final Agreement that may influence BC negotiators. There are many other similar situations.

VI. CONCLUSION

In conclusion, we wish to say that differences in circumstances between Yukon and British Columbia will ultimately dictate the extent to which the treatment of water rights in BC First Nations' treaties will differ in significant ways from the Yukon model.

(b) The Blood Tribe Agricultural Project, Standoff, Alberta[†]

Anna Classen

> We Bloods have had to adapt to white man's ways. BTAP is a way we can overcome obstacles and succeed without losing who we are. We've done it before. The horse and the gun brought us great prosperity. The Indian way of life was improved greatly. Our people lived well.
>
> After the buffalo were wiped out we had to change again. The buffalo was everything to us. It was the heart of all our culture and traditions. When it was gone, the Blackfoot people had to change. Smallpox killed our people and whisky wrecked the lives of many. The Bloods got back on their feet, though. They raised cattle and they went into farming on their own, in their own way. They traded their horses for cattle, they bought a steam engine and plow and broke their land. They farmed their own land in their own way, with no government assistance.
>
> Tractors and big equipment put the Indian farmers out of business. We leased the land to white farmers. We, the landowners, are the best stewards of our land. We care for the land because it is our children's land. It's right for us to manage our own land. The Creator put the land and the water there for us to use. Years ago, we could let nature take care of itself and of us humans who are a part of nature.... Now, there are so many of us, we have to care for the land differently. BTAP is one way we can use the land and the water the Creator has [given] us to sustain ourselves. It's a way to self-sufficiency.
>
> At first BTAP was a dream. We set goals so big no Blood Indian had ever thought of doing them. Now, we've made it a reality. We're proving to the white man and to the world that we can do it. We're proving it to ourselves as well. BTAP is a source of confidence in ourselves. We're achieving our goals, ourselves, in our own way. This project is working, bringing in money and good jobs into the community.
>
> Bringing BTAP from a dream to reality has taken almost 50 years and a lot of work from a lot of very good people.... Doing things our own way is important. Turning back to our own spirituality has helped many of us improve our own lives and those of our communities. In the same way, bringing our own culture and beliefs to irrigation and agribusiness, as we have at BTAP, allows us to succeed on our own terms. BTAP has entered into world trade with its agreement with Sumitomo Corporation of Japan. Our Blood traditions have guided us in the development of this international relationship with its promise of prosperity for many of our people.
>
> We Bloods can use this project as a springboard for agribusiness and other enterprises. BTAP proves we can be successful. We just have to build from here. We have to thank many people, from Chief Jim Shot Both Sides and his council, through Chief Roy Fox and his council who negotiated with the politicians, to Francis First Charger and his staff who turned that dream into a reality.
>
> Chief Standing Alone
BTAP Annual Report, 1997/98

HISTORY

When the Bloods signed their first treaty (Treaty 7) in 1877, they didn't think they would ever need to give up their nomadic, bison hunting lifestyle to settle on reserve.[11] It wasn't long, however, before the buffalo were nearly extinct, and land

---

[†] First appeared in "CANDO Aboriginal Economic Development Recognition Awards", *Journal of Aboriginal Economic Development*, 1(2) (2000): 23–27. Reproduced with permission of the author and CANDO.

came to have a greater importance. In 1881 Chief Red Crow renegotiated with the federal government to settle on the land between the Belly and St. Mary's Rivers, all the way to the Rocky Mountains, and a new treaty was signed on July 2nd, 1883.[12] In 1889, Chief Red Crow planted crops of oats, wheat and turnips. He was one of the first Blood Indians to use horses to plow his fields, and paved the way for the Bloods' agricultural future. Over the next several years, the Bloods continued to develop their agricultural skills, learning to adjust to their new way of life.

Fifty years ago, the Federal Government asked the Blood Tribe to surrender 5,800 acres of land to accommodate construction of the St. Mary's dam and reservoir in the southeast portion of the reserve, and another 1,677 acres to allow for the construction of the distribution canal from the Belly River. Chief Shot Both Sides agreed to both requests, but demanded access to water to irrigate 25,000 acres of Blood lands in exchange. The "Big Lease" was established in 1957 for lease on behalf of Blood Tribe members.

> "Chief Shot Both Sides started the whole thing to provide employment for our children and our future people. This whole project is for our children. We're working for the next generation so they can fit into the world."[13]

In 1978, the Blood Tribe presented a brief to Alberta Environment's Oldman River Basin water management study. They outlined the reserve's social and economic depression, and highlighted the potential benefits of their involvement in future agricultural and irrigation development. The Council's final report urged the federal and provincial governments to support on-reserve irrigation development.

AN AGREEMENT IS SIGNED

The Blood Tribe first met with Provincial cabinet ministers in February of 1980 to discuss irrigation development on the reserve and formed a Tripartite Committee of federal, provincial, and Blood Tribe officials. In 1981 through 1983, the Blood Tribe, Agriculture Canada, and Alberta Agriculture conducted a multi-disciplinary study to assess the feasibility of irrigating the "Big Lease", the northeastern portion of the Blood Reserve.[14] The completed report (1983) found that the project was feasible in all areas, but it was not until 1986 that further discussions took place between the three parties.

From the beginning, Band membership played an important role in the development of the project. A November 1988 referendum asked whether they would allow the Government of Canada to transfer the lands originally surrendered in the 1950s to the Province of Alberta. Although a seemingly innocuous question, it was clear in all the informational literature that this was a referendum on the Blood Indian irrigation project. An agreement could be signed only if the land was transferred to the province. Band members said yes.

The Blood Tribe Irrigation Project Agreement was signed February 24, 1989 by:

- Government of Canada
- Province of Alberta
- Band Council of the Blood Band

- Blood Tribe Agricultural Project Inc.

   Funding agencies and Tripartite Committee members included:
   - Blood Tribe
   - Government of Canada through the Department of Indian and Northern Affairs, Agriculture Canada, and the Native Economic Development Program
   - Province of Alberta through Alberta Agriculture and Alberta Environment

Two subcommittees of the Tripartite Committee were formed to ensure the success of the project. The Implementation Advisory Committee (IAC) was formed to facilitate project implementation, and has an advisory role in project construction and financial management. The Environmental Advisory Committee (EAC) focuses on environmental mitigation, monitoring, and enhancement measures as outlined in the recommendations of the Environmental Impact Assessment Report.

Finally, the Blood Tribe incorporated the Blood Tribe Agricultural Project to oversee construction, operate the Irrigation Project once completed, and ensure that Blood Tribe members benefitted from the project in a variety of ways. With an estimated total cost of $64.5 million over the next ten years, the irrigation project would prove to be an enormous undertaking.

THE BLOOD TRIBE IRRIGATION PROJECT

On June 9, 1994 the water was turned on and flowed through the newly built canals, drop structures, reservoirs, and pipelines, the pivots spraying some 2300 acres for the first time.

Over the last ten years, BTAP has been responsible for administering and implementing the irrigation project, has coordinated the installation of 98 pivots and is now responsible for irrigating 19,000 acres of the Big Lease. Although the construction schedule was in large part dictated by the weather's cooperation (or lack thereof), the Blood Tribe Irrigation Project has largely been on schedule and on budget.

The Blood Tribe Agricultural Project (BTAP)[15] leases land from the band, and then turns around and re-leases most of it as fully serviced irrigated land to off-reserve farmers. The irrigated land is leased at about $100–$150 per acre, which may seem high at first blush, but is an all inclusive rate.

BTAP staff run the entire irrigation system, set and fix the pivots, and ensure that the right amount of water is delivered at the right time. The system is monitored and operated by a state-of-the-art network of computers

BTAP also strove to ensure that the project was implemented in a way that did not compromise the environmental integrity of the Big Lease. Following the recommendations of the Environmental Advisory Committee, BTAP ensured that:

- water for on-farm irrigation flowed underground
- all pipes used in construction were plastic
- canals were designed to reduce seepage
- erosion control was addressed

- soils were tested for salinity, water erosion and waterlogged conditions
- farming practices that reduced the loss of topsoil were encouraged

BTAP has met its targeted 1999 construction completion date and is the biggest single-owner irrigation project in Canada, with 98 pivots and 19,000 irrigated acres.

TRAINING, TRAINING, TRAINING

In December of 1989, Chief Roy Fox stated that his primary concern was to ensure that as many Blood Tribe members as possible were put to work on the project. The Blood Tribe negotiated a clause in the irrigation agreement that made it mandatory for outside contractors to hire as many Reserve tradesmen and labourers as was feasible. BTAP also decided to select contractors through invitations to tender; they would then be able to select from a number of contractors who were willing to make a commitment to hire a 75% reserve work force.

And BTAP was successful in this endeavour. More than $5 million in payroll has gone out to Blood residents through wages and construction contracts. But BTAP did not hire unqualified people to do the work. A comprehensive human resources plan was developed in 1992 that outlined the number of positions required over the next ten years, and the skills needed to fill those positions. BTAP then started gearing up.

Francis First Charger (past BTAP General Manager) spent a great deal of time and effort recruiting the right people and then investing in the training needed to make that person a part of the team. BTAP employees were often recruited one to two years before they would be asked to fill the position, and would be trained in the interim. BTAP set up personalized training programs through Red Crow College, Lindsay Manufacturing, Nebraska Central Community College, University of Lethbridge, Lethbridge Community College, Cremona hay plant, and many other educational and industry partners.

Agriculture Canada through the First Nations Resource Council supported an international exchange where BTAP personnel travelled to the Ak-Chin Indian Community, Maricopa, and the Gila River Farms in Arizona to learn about other on-reserve irrigation projects. Employees spent six months in Arizona working with flood irrigation projects that have been running since 1968.

> "I have a lot of responsibility, if a pivot breaks down, we have to be able to get it running again. Everybody just pitches in to keep ahead of farmers and get the job done" (BTAP employee, 1997/98 Annual Report).

BTAP has also started investing in future generations by sponsoring and organizing a yearly summer camp for Aboriginal youth that focuses on alcohol and drug abuse prevention, and offers various camping and cultural activities. About 50 youth aged 11 through 14 have participated each year.

TIMOTHY HAY PROCESSING PLANT

In October 1996, eleven BTAP delegates travelled to Japan on a trade mission sponsored by Aboriginal Business Canada, Ipex, and New-Way Irrigation in Lethbridge. BTAP representatives met with the head office of Sumitomo Corporation[16] to discuss partnership possibilities. BTAP had the opportunity to promote its development, and became the first supplier to see the entire end-use process.

Because of Japan's large and dense population, there is not much room to farm large agricultural crops. There are many dairy farms in operation, though, and timothy hay is in high demand for cattle and race horses. Valued at $90–$190 per tonne in Canada, timothy hay is worth $330 (US) in Yokohama, Japan, and Japanese farmers pay a price of around $450 per tonne. The Sumitomo Corporation needed hay that could meet the Japanese Government's stringent import regulations,[17] and that could be compressed into bales 40 percent of normal size. BTAP felt they could deliver.

As a result of this trade mission, the Blood Tribe, Transfeeder Inc. of Olds Albers, and the Sumitomo Corporation of Japan signed a forage processing and export agreement on October 27, 1997. Blood Tribe Forage Processing (BTFP) started running on June 1st 1998, and within two weeks had filled two separate orders to Japan, the first of which was ahead of schedule by two days. Operations at the plant are currently on schedule, with three shifts running per day, and an employment roster of more than 40 people. The BTFP export agreement will eventually process and ship up to 30,000 tonnes of timothy hay per year.

INTERNATIONAL PARTNERSHIPS

In addition to the partnership with Sumitomo Corporation of Japan, BTAP has shown off its irrigation model to people representing more than thirty countries including, among others: USA, China, Sudan, India, Uruguay, Egypt, St. Lucia, Zimbabwe, Pakistan, Taiwan, Australia, France, Israel, Mexico, Hungary, and Spain.

Lee Mapplebeck of the Bank of Nova Scotia in Lethbridge said that the irrigation project has become the model for all First Nations on how to plan, implement, and operate a commercial venture on reserve. BTAP has also become a model for the development and operation of large irrigation projects around the world.

> "BTAP has opened a lot of doors, not just in agriculture, but in telecommunications, business application and international investments for our people. It is a source of pride for all of us" Narcisse Blood, Tribal Councillor.

PRIDE

One could point to a number of factors that have contributed to BTAP's success — hard work, good partnerships, government support through training programs and funding. But I think more than anything, BTAP has been successful because of the pride that BTAP staff and the Blood Tribe have taken in their work on the irrigation project.

Regular newsletters starting in 1989 have provided comprehensive updates to Band members on BTAP staffing, progress, and financial status. Photos of countless smiling Band members working on various stages and components of the project are proudly displayed. Blood elder Pete Standing Alone and Susumo Ono[18] stand hand in hand at Mr. Ono's induction into the Kainai Honourary Chieftainship. And Chief Roy Fox, on the Grand Opening of the irrigation project, remarked, "Watching the water flow down the canals and spray onto the fields was an experience I will never forget. Even today, as I view the continued construction, I am proud to be a Blood Indian."[19]

NOTES

1. Owned and operated by the Cape Mudge Band on Quadra Island.
2. Discovery Harbour's high-end shop of Aboriginal West Coast art.
3. "The project marks the first time in British Columbia that a real estate company and a native group ... have created a joint venture to develop and own a shopping centre on aboriginal land, said Mr. Richter" *The Globe and Mail*, "A mall with a native touch" by Ann Gibson, Wednesday, June 3, 1995.
4. Part of the Band lands under water was filled in to accommodate the development.
5. Igors Sigalias, Senior Vice-President, Westcoast Group of Companies.
6. Architectural drawing.
7. Northern Pipleline took 75% of the profits because it owned all of the equipment. This was later to prove to be a major factor in the Cowichan Tribe's decision to invest in their own equipment and set up their own pipeline company.
8. W. Edwards Deming started the total quality movement. These come from his 14 Points for Management. More information on total quality managment can be found by looking for W. Edwards Deming's writings, contacting the International Organization for Standardization (ISO) at <www.iso.ch>, or the Standards Council of Canada, phone: (613) 328-3222, fax: (613) 995-4564, E-mail: info@scc.ca, Web site: <www.scc.ca>.
9. Al. Solheim, *The Unlimited Potential of Limited Partnerships*, CANDO, 1999, p. 12.
10. An Alberta based Aboriginal financial company.
11. Hugh Dempsey, "Beginning of the Blood Reserve" *Official Opening, Blood Tribe Agricultural Project, June 9, 1994, Souvenir Program*, p. 28.
12. Although the Bloods believed that the 1883 treaty simply confirmed Chief Red Crow's understanding, they did not get all the land between the rivers to the mountains. This was a source of a bitter dispute with the government for many years, and many still believe today that the Bloods received far less than they were entitled to.
13. BTAP employee 1997–98 Annual Report.
14. The partners studied ten components: mapping, land classification, agricultural potential, engineering, groundwater and salinization, economics, environmental and social impacts, implementation, and conclusions and recommendations.
15. The incorporated arm that administers the irrigation project.
16. Japan's largest bank and trading company.
17. Japan wants to ensure that no disease or parasite enters their country, so if a bale has a single head of quack grass, mold, or soil on it, the entire shipment will be sent back.
18. Manager of Sumitomo Feeds and Fertilizer Division.
19. Chief Roy Fox, 1994, on irrigation Grand Opening — BTAP newsletter Winter 1994.

CHAPTER 7

Fishery

(a) Lobster Wars[†]

Parker Barss Donham

If you followed the national news last fall, you know the Supreme Court of Canada, citing ancient treaties, gave Mi'kmaqs the right to hunt and fish whenever and wherever they want, without regard to seasons or other conservation rules. You know hundreds of Natives rushed to embrace the freshly bestowed rights, descending on the lobster grounds in a massive new commercial fishery. You know white fishermen, barred by federal regulation from taking lobster out of season, watched helplessly as Mi'kmaqs threatened to wipe out the resource that had sustained their families for generations. You know their frustration and fear eventually sparked violent confrontations between the traditional license holders and the native [interlopers]. You know the confrontations ended only after the Mi'kmaqs backed off and the Supreme Court of Canada clarified its ruling, belatedly giving Ottawa the right to regulate the Native lobster fishery.

If you are like most well-informed Canadians, you know all these things — and you are dead wrong.

Media Aids White Hysteria

To understand the fractious aftermath of the Supreme Court's September 17 decision acquitting Donald Marshall Jr. of fishing eels out of season, you should begin by forgetting everything you "know" about the ensuing crisis. The court did

---

[†] From *Canadian Dimension*, 34(1) (1999): 26–28. Copyright © 2000 by Parker Donham <parker@donham.ca>. Reproduced by permission. All rights reserved.

not declare open season for Mi'kmaq fishermen. It did not put Native hunters and fishermen beyond reach of federal regulation. Hundreds of Mi'kmaqs did not suddenly start catching lobster. The modest Native fishery that followed did not, by the wildest stretch of the imagination, threaten lobster stocks or the livelihood of any white fishermen. The Supreme Court's supplementary ruling in late November did not so much clarify its earlier decision as reiterate the limited and balanced decision it had already rendered.

The white community's hysterical overreaction to the Marshall ruling, and the violent confrontations that followed, looked at first like a simple case of racism. Bigotry certainly played a central and disheartening role. But bad and incomplete reporting — the media's paralyzing inability or unwillingness to provide necessary context, combined with a ritual focus on confrontation — played at least as big a part in fostering and sustaining the ersatz crisis.

On an August morning six and a half years ago, a shy, middle-aged Mi'kmaq pushed his outboard-powered skiff into Pomquet Harbour on Nova Scotia's northern coast for a day of eel fishing. Without a license and out of season, Donald Marshall Jr. caught 463 pounds of eels, which he sold for $787.10. He was arrested and charged, events that doubly secured his place as one of the most pivotal figures in Nova Scotia history, a man whose impact on future generations ranks with the province's most illustrious premiers and generals.

It was Marshall's second conviction. In 1971, he was falsely imprisoned for murder. The discovery of this grotesque miscarriage, after 11 years of wrongful incarceration, led to a royal commission that forced reform upon Nova Scotia's justice system and began the tortuous process of extracting the province from its pervasive culture of corruption. His act of civil disobedience in 1993, fishing eels out of season and without a license, led the Supreme Court of Canada to affirm Canada's obligation to honour a series of 240-year-old treaties in a spirit that could forever alter relations between whites and Natives.

"Nothing less [than acquitting Marshall] would uphold the honour and integrity of the Crown in its dealings with the Mi'kmaq people to secure their peace and friendship, as best the content of those treaty promises can now be ascertained," wrote Mr. Justice Ian Binnie for the court's 5-2 majority.

What the Treaties Left Out

Critics of the Marshall decision like to describe the treaties at issue as ancient. They are of the same vintage as the Treaty of Paris, which transferred Acadia, Quebec and much of the rest of North America from France to Britain, an outcome whose validity most of the same critics endorse. Signing treaties with the Mi'kmaq was the lynchpin of Gov. Charles Lawrence's strategy for pacifying a militarily formidable ally of the French, following the Acadian expulsion.

Lawrence's treaties do not, as the few critics who have bothered to read them point out, explicitly confer upon Mi'kmaqs any right to trade the fruits of their hunting and gathering. Rather, they impose an obligation on Mi'kmaqs to trade only at truck houses established by the British.

The treaties were negotiated orally by the British and the Mi'kmaq, but written down only by the British. The Mi'kmaq had no written language, aside from wampum belts, which no one alive today can decipher. The obvious danger is that the written words might not correspond to what was agreed upon. In the case of the treaties covered by the Marshall decision, the British kept meticulous notes on negotiations as they progressed. These notes leave no doubt that some of the terms agreed to orally were omitted from the written version of the treaty. The court concluded it would be "unconscionable" to limit the scope of the treaty to its written version, when one party was illiterate, and we know the transcription did not include all the agreed-upon-items.

What the Ruling Really Says

While affirming the Mi'kmaqs' treaty-enshrined right to trade the fruits of their hunting and gathering for what the treaties called "necessaries," the court rejected any suggestion that this entailed an unlimited commercial harvest. It interpreted "necessaries" to mean more than subsistence but less than a "right to trade generally for economic gain." It means "sustenance," or "a modest livelihood."

The court said federal regulations could be used to contain the right within those limits, and further still in the name of some overarching social concern like conservation. But such regulation could only be imposed after consultation with the Mi'kmaqs both as to their content and the means of arriving at them.

In short, it was a nuanced, balanced decision affirming a right to harvest whose limits, though significant, could only be precisely defined through negotiations. In keeping with earlier decisions on Aboriginal and treaty rights, those negotiations would have to be conducted in a manner consistent with "the honour of the Crown." Binnie cited the words of the 1996 decision in R. v. Badger:

> [T]he honour of the Crown is always at stake in its dealings with Indian people.... It is always assumed that the Crown intends to fulfill its promises. No appearance of 'sharp dealing' will be sanctioned.

Reactions Unjustified

In the days following the decision, reporters naturally turned to fishing communities for reaction — particularly to communities where natives were already exercising their right to catch lobster. When hotheads in two of those communities — Yarmouth, NS, and Burnt Church, NB — angrily denounced the presence of Natives in their traditional fishing grounds, the media focus narrowed further.

What followed was a barrage of shrill diatribes on the fancied implications of a decision few of the combatants had actually read. Most of this commentary was wildly out of sync with the Marshall decision, and much of it was frankly racist. One Yarmouth fisherman told CBC Radio that Nova Scotia should handle the Mi'kmaq the way Newfoundland had handled the Beothuk — "extinct em." All this was dutifully reported, along with the far more restrained responses of Mi'kmaq leaders and fishermen, who didn't make nearly as good copy.

John Risley, the multimillionaire lobster baron whose company, Clearwater Seafoods, holds a virtual monopoly on offshore lobster licenses, went through the witless exercise of guessing that a moderate livelihood might mean $30,000, multiplying this figure by 12,000 (a number equivalent to every status Mi'kmaq man, woman and child in Atlantic Canada), and concluding that a third of a billion dollars could be diverted from the lobster industry to Mi'kmaqs.

Nightly television images of the escalating conflict left the impression a small armada of Mi'kmaq vessels had invaded traditional white fishing villages. In fact, small numbers of Mi'kmaqs had been fishing lobster for years, ever since the 1990 Sparrow decision authorized a limited food fishery, and under a federal program that bought commercial licenses from retiring fishermen and turned them over to Native bands.

White Over-Fishing

A month into the controversy, the Mi'kmaq fishing effort remained minuscule by comparison with the white lobster fishery. In the Scotia Fundy region, which runs from the Maine-New Brunswick border, around the Bay of Fundy and along Nova Scotia's Atlantic coastline to the tip of Cape Breton, fisheries officials estimated there were, at most, 40 Native boats fishing lobster, up from perhaps 35 a year earlier. White fishermen ply the same waters with 2,893 lobster boats.

It didn't matter. By now, white fishermen had been persuaded by their own rhetoric, endlessly fed back to them on the nightly news, that their entire way of life was at stake. Threats of violence escalated to sporadic instances of real violence — a Mi'kmaq boat sunk at Yarmouth, a fish plant trashed and a Native shrine torched at Burnt Church, Native traps hauled and smashed in both locations. At its ugly peak in early November, a mob of thugs surged through the streets of Yarmouth looking for Mi'kmaqs to beat up.

That Yarmouth should be a centre of the protest was ironic. The town sits smack in the middle of Lobster Fishing Area 34, the richest lobster fishery in the world, with landings of $149 million — an average $152,010 per boat — in 1998.

Yarmouth is also a hotbed of illegal fishing — an activity frowned upon in most other parts of Atlantic Canada. Fishermen in LFA 34 can legally set up to 400 traps, 50 per cent more than any other district. Informed observers estimate they set another 25 per cent in illegal traps. It works out to 100,000 illegal traps in the Yarmouth area alone — compared to 5,000 Mi'kmaq traps in all of Nova Scotia.

If the self-appointed vigilantes bleating about the need to conserve stocks from marauding Mi'kmaqs would simply haul their own illegal gear, it would open 20 times the space needed for Mi'kmaq fishing.

Faced with the escalating violence, not a single politician raised his voice to insist that white fishermen respect the rule of law. On the contrary, politicians echoed the demands of white fishermen that the Mi'kmaq back off, and the Supreme Court reopen the case.

This time, the side that played by the rules and waited patiently for the courts to decide the issue was being asked to retreat in the face of ugly, racist bullying. The rallying cry was that everyone would have to fish in the same season by the same rules — the existing white rules. Apparently, only whites could be trusted to devise sound conservationist policies. This must be why we've done so well conserving the Northern Cod.

Quiet Negotiations Under-Reported

Following appeals from Marshall and Grand Chief Ben Sylliboy, most of the Mi'kmaq bands did back off. Encroaching winter weather persuaded the others to stop fishing. Meanwhile, Mi'kmaq bands in various parts of the Maritimes quietly cut deals with local fishermen on protocols for their entry into the lobster fishery. The deals came quickest in areas like Pictou County, NS, where members of the Maritime Fishermen's Union had already been working with would-be Mi'kmaq fishermen, and a relationship of trust and communication had preceded the court ruling. The media mostly ignored these agreements.

The national media, meanwhile, well removed from the story, found it a convenient foil for various ideological hobbyhorses — a judiciary grown too activist, race-based law that made too many concessions to endless Native demands. While columnists at the National Post and the Globe and Mail railed against these perceived abuses, reporters at the same papers continued to misrepresent the decision as having declared an open season for Mi'kmaq fishing, or allowed Mi'kmaqs to hunt and fish out of season.

In rejecting a petition from the West Nova Fishermen's Association to reopen the Marshall case, the Supreme Court reviewed its decision in a 20-page ruling most media characterized as a "clarification" of the earlier judgment. In fact, it was more reiteration than clarification. In 20 pages, the court cites its earlier text no fewer than 54 times.

In focusing upon, and unintentionally fomenting, the white fishing community's hysterical reaction to the Marshall decision, reporters overlooked the ruling's real significance. The decision not only confirms Mi'kmaq access to economic tools that will help extract Native communities from the entrenched poverty that has been their lot, it demands that government fulfill historic obligations to the Mi'kmaq with honour and integrity.

That's a good thing, a promise of hope and reconciliation. We will be counting the Marshall decision's blessings for generations to come — long after the fearmongering, threats of mob violence and repulsive, racist slurs have faded.

(b) Lobster Wars and the Media[†]

Parker Barss Donham

What a turnaround. After suffering a public-relations debacle in the wake of last summer's Marshall decision, the Department of Fisheries and Oceans has exercised almost total control over media coverage of this summer's events at Miramachi and St. Mary's Bays.

[†] From *Canadian Dimension*, 34(5) (1999): 7. Copyright © 2000 by Parker Donham <parker@donham.ca>. Reproduced by permission. All rights reserved.

Day after day, newspapers and broadcasters have allowed Marc-Andre Lentaigne, the department's smooth-talking PR operative, to frame the day's events in highly misleading terms that serve DFO's agenda. No comparable spokesman has emerged on the other side, so the media, especially the national media, has adopted Lentaigne's perspective as its own, elevating his self-serving commentary to the status of objective truth.

Lentaigne constantly stresses the Supreme Court's acknowledgment of DFO's right to regulate the Mi'kmaq fishery, but never mentions the sharp limits the court placed on that regulatory power. The court said DFO can only impose regulations in pursuit of a "pressing and substantial public purpose" like conservation. The regulations can "go no further than is required" to achieve that purpose, and can only be imposed "after appropriate consultation with the aboriginal community." The consultations must be procedurally fair to the Mi'kmaq, and substantively respectful of their right to a limited commercial fishery.

That should have encouraged negotiations similar to those leading to the Native big-game hunt in Nova Scotia, a hunt that takes place in a different season, and according to different rules, than the white hunt. Each Mi'kmaq band could have produced plans for a limited fishery, and DFO could have reviewed the plans' impact on conservation. If not, negotiations could have ensued, with DFO empowered to impose its own rules only if a reasonable agreement could not be reached.

But DFO was terrified of a backlash among white fishermen if Mi'kmaq were allowed to fish on a different schedule than whites. So it attempted an end run around the Marshall decision, offering to provide boats, licenses, gear, training and cash to bands that would adopt existing white rules for the 2000 season.

Most bands took the bribe. Indian Brook and Burnt Church made a principled decision to exercise the rights affirmed in the Marshall decision. They developed careful plans for a limited fishery.

Instead of reviewing those plans, assessing their impact on conservation, and seeking to negotiate changes if necessary, DFO responded with an ultimatum: fish by white rules or limit yourself to a tiny food fishery. (The food fishery, implemented by a 1990 decision of the Supreme Court, limits entire bands to 35 or 40 traps, roughly one-eighth the number a single white fisherman can set.)

Lentaigne and minister Herb Dhaliwal falsely assert that the Marshall decisions merely required the department to provide Mi'kmaqs with "access" to the fishery. They continually cite the 27 bands that signed agreements with DFO, and portray Indian Brook and Burnt Church as renegade bands, deaf and blind to all attempts at reason. They never volunteer that the interim agreements explicitly sidestep the rights affirmed by the Marshall rulings.

Why do so many reporters accept this skewed perspective so unquestioningly? Canadian Press, which prides itself [on] neutrality, refers to "illegal traps." The Globe and Mail calls the disputed fishery "patently illegal" and denounces the Natives' "extreme militancy" and "intransigence." The National Post, which hardly ever likes anything government does, describes DFO's enforcement armada as "cautious but determined" and the Natives as "provocateurs."

Yet the Indian Brook band is so confident of the legality of its position, it has asked the federal court for an injunction to halt DFO's blitzkrieg.

Reporters rarely if ever point out the miniscule quantity of Native traps (less than two-tenths of one per cent of the white total), or the rich history of illegal fishing by white fishermen in some districts, or the Supreme Court's comments on the limits to DFO regulation.

Why is the media so poorly equipped to portray both sides fairly in a conflict that pits bureaucrats against Aboriginals?

I believe race is at the heart of the answer.

Mi'kmaqs are often shy, and loathe to engage in verbal sparring in English, a language utterly different from their native tongue. Although a few Mi'kmaqs have developed impressive media skills — the lawyer Bernd Christmas comes to mind — most bands do not have public-relations operatives on a par with Lentaigne.

White reporters find it easier to chat up familiar white bureaucrats than to enter an unfamiliar Native reserve and immerse themselves in a foreign culture until they understand the position being taken.

Under pressure to produce stories on the latest confrontation, reporters spend less time than they should researching the background to the dispute. Few, I suspect, have read the Marshall decisions.

Too many whites are too ready to believe the worst about Natives. If Lentaigne or Dhaliwal tried to portray a group of Jews or Acadians as truculent, disrespectful of the law, recklessly hostile to conservation, or ready to plunder valuable fish stocks, they wouldn't get to first base.

But let them calmly assert the same thing about Mi'kmaqs, and the media swallows it whole hog.

(c) Lobster Wars: 2001 Edition[†]

Parker Barss Donham

A federal bureaucrat's assertion that Donald Marshall Jr. would be arrested if he went fishing for lobster today shows how little progress Ottawa has made in living up to the landmark Supreme Court decisions that bear Marshall's name.

It wasn't just the words spoken by Paul Sprout, who lugs around the weighty title of associate assistant deputy minister for fisheries management, it was the amalgam of machismo and condescension in his voice.

"You hear a lot of opinions about this," he said. "But I deal in facts."

The facts, according to Sprout, are that even as it affirmed the Mi'kmaq right to fish for a moderate living, the court said "it's a regulated right ... not something you can go out and do anytime, any place in any manner."

Like most DFO statements on Native fishing, this might be called a selection of facts, adding up to less than half a truth.

[†] From *Canadian Dimension*, 35(4) (2001): 5. Copyright © 2001 by Parker Donham <parker@donham.ca>. Reproduced by permission. All rights reserved.

The court did confirm Ottawa's power to regulate Native fishing, but it's a sharply limited power, not one DFO can exercise, to borrow Sprout's phrase, "anytime, any place in any manner."

The Marshall decisions, like previous Supreme Court judgements on Native rights, allow Ottawa to infringe upon Native rights only in pursuit of a pressing and substantial public interest, like conservation. Even then, Ottawa must act in a manner consistent with "the honour of the Crown" and its fiduciary responsibility to Canada's Aboriginal peoples.

In practice, this means Ottawa must deal fairly with Mi'kmaq fishermen, both substantively and procedurally. It must consult them in a bona fide manner. Its regulations must accommodate their right to fish. It must seek the least intrusive way of achieving its overriding policy goals.

In the two and a half years since the Marshall decisions, Ottawa has never consulted [Mi'kmaq] on its proposed regulations. It has simply insisted they follow existing rules for white fishermen, and vowed John Wayne-like reprisals against any injuns ornery enough to defy them.

"We'll be there," DFO tough guy Andre-Marc Lanteigne said last month. "We're ready for anything, our people are trained, we're well-equipped."

The existing rules for white fishermen are not the only route to conservation. Indeed, in most fisheries, DFO rules have failed to conserve stocks. A policy that respected Supreme Court decisions would, at a minimum, require Ottawa to seriously consider alter native [alternative] conservation proposals put forth by various Mi'kmaq bands.

DFO refuses to consider a rights-based fishery, at least in the short term. Instead, it offers to play what Native-rights lawyer Bruce Wildsmith calls, "Let's Make a Deal," throwing money, boats and gear at individual bands in return for their acquiescence to existing white rules.

Why not evaluate the impact of Native fishing proposals on conservation, especially since only a relative handful of boats and traps are involved? Because the hyperventilated reaction of white fishermen to the Marshall ruling makes Ottawa fearful of the political fallout from letting Natives fish when whites can't.

Is this a pressing and substantial public-policy objective, or just political cowardice? Is it respectful of the law, as laid down by the Supreme Court? The Shubenacadie Band has been trying for a year to get a federal court ruling on that question. DFO's Justice Department lawyers have pulled out every legal stop in efforts to keep them from getting one.

The band seeks judicial review of DFO's refusal to consider its plan for fishing in St. Mary's Bay last summer, as well as damages for destruction and seizure of fishing gear, and for assaults on, and false imprisonment of, fishermen.

DFO tried to strike the band's statement of claim. When the court said no, it appealed. It appealed the court's decision to grant intervenor status to the non-status Native Council of Nova Scotia (but not the decision to grant two provinces and two white fishermen's groups the same status).

It has now filed a second motion to strike the Shubenacadie Band's statement of claim, and a motion to keep certain documents out of the appeal court record.

As long as DFO can postpone judicial review, it can continue refusing to implement a rights-based fishery. Natives who object are subject to beatings, boat rammings and seizure of gear and boats, not to mention arrest and prosecution.

Those are the facts Associate Assistant Deputy Sprout and tough guy Lanteigne prefer to overlook. Their omission extends and deepens the centuries-old legacy of betrayal Marshall was intended to redress.

Section 3

Non-Renewable Resources

Section Three contains nine articles on the topic of renewable resources: six of them on petroleum, and three on mining. The purpose of the selected articles is to provide insight into (i) the nature of non-renewable resource development, (ii) the impact of such development on Aboriginal people and (iii) the evolving nature of Aboriginal participation in non-renewable resource development. Before commenting briefly on each article, some general comments are in order.

Non-renewable resources are discovered and exploited where they are found. This "where" is increasingly in remote areas that are the homelands of the world's Indigenous people. Ownership of the resources of these lands is often contested, with Indigenous people claiming rights to the land and resources based on continuous occupancy and use, and nation states claiming ownership by conquest or treaty. To complicate the situation, while often discovered by individuals, non-renewable resources are usually exploited by large multinational corporations. This means that non-renewable resource development brings together Indigenous people, state governments and multinational corporations. Until recently, the history of this coming together has worked to the advantage of the corporations and the nation states, and to the detriment of the Indigenous people involved. As you will find in the articles that follow, this may be changing.

The first three articles — "The Mackenzie Valley Pipeline Inquiry" (Anderson 2002), "Power Shifts in the Canadian North" (Bone 1995) and "New Pipe Dreams" (Bergman 2002) examine the changing relationship among Aboriginal people, governments (the state) and multinational oil and gas companies in northern Canada. In his opening paragraphs, Bone describes the Mackenzie Valley Pipeline Project. As he says, initially it was expected that this project would proceed as others had in the past; after all, it had the support of the government and the multinational corporations and would bring great economic benefits to the country. However, as Bone and Anderson separately discuss, this time Aboriginal interests were considered, and the project did not proceed. The process of consideration — the Berger Inquiry — is described in "The Mackenzie Valley Pipeline Inquiry". As Anderson says, at the end of his inquiry Justice Thomas Berger ordered

> a 10-year moratorium on pipeline construction in the Mackenzie Valley "in order to strengthen native society, the native economy — indeed the whole renewable resource sector — and to enable native claims to be settled" (Berger, 1977). In Berger's view such settlements "must be part of a fundamental re-ordering of the relationship between white and native, in order to entrench their rights to the land and to lay the foundations for native self determination under the Constitution of Canada" (Page, 1986: 119). In reaching this conclusion, Justice Berger ushered in a new era in the relationship between Canada and the Aboriginal people living within its borders.

In his paper, Bone discusses the Inuvialuit Agreement that followed the Berger Inquiry, including the impact of the agreement on non-renewable resource development.

In "New Pipe Dream" Bergman brings us forward in time to the year 2000. As you will read, the Mackenzie Valley pipeline proposal is back. However, this time all three parties — Aboriginal people, multinational corporations and governments — are involved. As Bergman says:

> The biggest change since the 1970s is that the oil and gas industry realizes that aboriginal peoples are an integral part of development ... The territory's current premier [says] *"when we said "No" to the pipeline in the 1970's it wasn't in vain ... Aboriginal peoples are no longer going to be thrown some crumbs and rolled over by industry and government.*

It remains to be seen what will happen, but Aboriginal people now have a strong and respected voice, and the power to stop the project should they choose to do so.

The article "Shell Game" by Stephanie Boyd looks at the issue of Indigenous people and non-renewable resource development in an international context. Here you will read about another conflict between Indigenous people, a national government and a multinational corporation. The Machiguena, Nahua and Kugapakori people faced the same problem in 2000 that the Inuvialuit did in 1974. However, they have not had the benefit a Berger Inquiry. The project has been delayed but only because of a dispute between Shell and the Peruvian government. The government has granted the concession to another company and, according to "Lelis Rivera, Director of the Centre for the Development of Amazon Indigenous Peoples ... local people are prepared for an uphill battle with the new company." Boyd's article raises a pair of interesting questions. To what extent are multinational companies more environmentally and socially responsible now than they were in the past? Will they be more respectful of Indigenous people's rights and interests than they were in the past as a "good business practice", or only if laws and regulations force them to?

The two articles "Metis Concerned About Expansion" and "Sour Gas, Bitter Relations" offer further insight into the relationship between corporations and Aboriginal people in an oil and gas setting outside the far north and in the absence of a comprehensive land claims agreement. As you read the first article, you will see that the Metis of Anzac and Suncor seem to be working towards an understanding that respects the interests and objectives of both. Is this because Suncor must do so because of laws and regulations, or is it because they see working with Metis as a better way of doing business? A similar picture emerges in the second article on the Lubicon and Unocal. The article describes years of failure and distrust. However, it also indicates that a potential for change might be emerging in part because corporations "are restructuring to accommodate and include community concerns ... motivated by the expectation of achieving long-standing agreements ... [and to] reflect recognition of the increasing power and influence of aboriginal groups."

In the final three articles the focus shifts from oil and gas to mining. While all address diamond mining in northern Canada, they offer insight into mining of all types. The first, "The Nasty Game: How Environmental Assessment Is Failing Aboriginal Communities in Canada's North", revisits some of the issues raised by Paul Nadasdy in Section 1 with respect to "incorporating" traditional knowledge into environmental assessment and involving Aboriginals in the process. The article also reinforces material from Section 2 by contrasting non-renewable and renewable resource use, pointing out some of the difficulties in building and sustaining Aboriginal communities on a non-renewable resource base. Wismer concludes that

> it is not clear if mineral development can be a spoke in the mixed economy wheel, which has subsistence at its hub, and the people in the Slave Lake communities know very little more after the BHP review than they did before. The panel did not address this question.

She goes on to say:

> The BHP review has failed the people whose homelands take in the area around Lac de Gras, just as environmental assessment generally is failing Aboriginal peoples all across Canada. Unless and until environmental assessment can begin to pick up where it left off after the Berger Inquiry and start to make a genuine contribution to addressing the complexities of northern development, aboriginal peoples will be forced to pursue other [routes] for asserting their need to act as the legitimate stewards of their territories.

In "Northern Gems", Tom Fennel offers further insight into ongoing Aboriginal concerns about the impact of diamond mining on their lands and way of life.

In the final article, "Nunavut Open for Business", Paul Okalik, Premiere of Nunavut, puts forward a cautiously optimistic argument in favour of mining. He says:

> We are committed to working with our residents, Inuit organizations and the private sector to ensure that we all benefit from mining development in the territory ... [There is a] treasure chest of mineral resources as long as we work together towards sustainable development.

With Premier Okalik's statement we come full circle. It is generally agreed that traditional world views and traditional environmental knowledge will play central roles in a sustainable development paradigm. However, operationalizing the paradigm is the challenge. Progress is being made slowly and fitfully, but it is being made.

CHAPTER 8

Oil and Gas

(a) The Mackenzie Valley Pipeline Inquiry[†]

Robert B. Anderson

In 1974, a consortium of multinational oil companies (called Arctic Gas) made application to the Canadian government to build a pipeline to carry natural gas from the fields in the Mackenzie Delta and Prudhoe Bay in Alaska to markets in southern Canada and the United States.[10] According to Gurston Dacks, the federal government

> favoured and indeed had actively promoted the construction of the Mackenzie Valley pipeline. However, for public-relations reasons and to mollify the New Democratic Party, which at that time held the balance of power in the House of Commons, the cabinet decided that a public inquiry should be held to study the questions surrounding the pipeline.
> (Dacks, 1981: 135)

In March of 1994, Mr. Justice Thomas Berger was appointed to head the inquiry that was established to consider the issues surrounding the pipeline.

As you will see in the material that follows, the government's decision to appoint Justice Berger had a profound influence on the scope and outcome of the inquiry and on the land claims and comprehensive treaty process that has followed. The reasons for this impact are threefold:

1. The respect Aboriginal people had for Justice Berger's honesty and fairness,
2. Justice Berger's experience with and understanding of Aboriginal rights, and
3. Justice Berger's interpretation of the mandate of his inquiry.

[†] From Robert B. Anderson, *Aboriginal Entrepreneurship and Business Development* (North York: Captus Press Inc., 2002), pp. 22–25.

We will consider each of these in turn.

According to Dacks, "Justice Berger was known to be sympathetic to native people" (Dacks, 1981: 136). In fact, he was one of the lawyers who argued the Calder case before the Supreme Court on behalf of the Nisga'a. On the face of it, this would seem to make him an unusual choice for the government given its support for the project. However, this was the very reason he was chosen. According to Robert Page:

> The Trudeau government lacked credibility with native groups as a result of its white paper and its court actions ... the inquiry had to be headed by someone who commanded their respect. ... If native groups participated fully and with some faith in the commissioner, they were more likely to abide by his recommendations in authorizing the pipeline.
> (Page, 1986: 92)

As we will see, Justice Berger lived up to the faith placed in him by Aboriginal people and delivered what has proven to be a wise decision.

Now to the inquiry's terms of reference. They required Justice Berger to inquire into and report on the terms and conditions for granting a pipeline right-of-way under two specific headings:

> 1. The social, environmental, and economic impacts regionally of the construction, operation, and subsequent abandonment of the proposed pipeline;

and

> 2. Any proposals to meet the specific environmental and social concerns.
> (Page, 1983: 93)

From the beginning of the inquiry proponents of the pipeline and those opposing it held differing views about the scope and timing of the inquiry that should flow from these terms of reference.

The proponents of the pipeline felt that Justice Berger was not being asked to determine if the line should be built. In their view, he was only to determine the terms and conditions that would apply to its construction and operation, and he was to do this quickly. Opponents of the pipeline project took a broader view, and so did Justice Berger. He ruled against the proponents on both counts. With regard to timing, he refused to rush the process to suit the commercial interests of the proponents. He ruled that all parties should have a fair opportunity to prepare for the hearings and have an opportunity to be heard. According to Page, on the scope of the hearings he was even more emphatic, saying:

> I take no narrow view of my terms of reference. ...[it will] not [be] confined to the consideration of a pipeline application but related "to the whole future of the North."
> (Page, 1983: 102–103)

Once the inquiry began, it was clear there were contending views on the project and its possible benefits to the people of the region and of Canada as a whole. The proponents espoused the modernization perspective on development. Their views were challenged by Aboriginal groups and others arguing from the neo-Marxist perspective. Justice Berger's conclusions as to the relative merits of these conflicting views are what made the Mackenzie Valley Pipeline Inquiry so important to the Aboriginal capacity-building activities that followed. According to Peter Usher, as a result of Justice Berger's decision "there emerged from those years both a new paradigm of development and social change ... and new processes of directing their course" (Usher, 1993: 99). The new paradigm that emerged in this instance was a part of the broader trend toward alternative/Indigenous approaches to development occurring worldwide.

Arctic Gas and other proponents of the pipeline put the modernization case. They argued that industrialization in northern Canada was "inevitable, desirable, and beneficial — the more the better" (Usher, 1993: 105). They did not deny that the process would have negative impacts on traditional Aboriginal society. In fact, in their view development "required the breakdown and eventual replacements of whatever social forms had existed before" (Usher, 1993: 104). They agreed that the process would be painful for Aboriginal people, but from it would emerge "a higher standard of living, a better quality of life, and greater personal choice ... [while] continued blockage could only lead to deepening dependency" (Usher, 1993: 104–105). A sense of the modernist view can be found in the words of Mayor R. Sykes of Calgary, who described efforts to protect the traditional Aboriginal way of life as:

> misguided attempts to preserve under the meaningless title of culture a primitive life of insecurity and hardship. If they knew a better way of life [the modern way of life], they would hardly wish it [the traditional way of life] on their children.
> (Page, 1986: 113)

In addition to their views on the desirability of industrialization and the inevitability of modernization, proponents of the project held the view that "all Canadians have an equal interest in the North and its resources" (Page, 1986: 114). This view was at odds with the position of Aboriginal people and the recent Calder decision, both of which upheld the principle of Aboriginal title to traditional lands.

The views of the project's proponents were challenged by Aboriginal groups and others. They agreed with the proponents that the pipeline project would introduce "massive development with incalculable and irreversible effects like the settlement of the Prairies" (Usher, 1993: 106). However, unlike the proponents they did not feel that this was a desirable outcome. Instead, they argued from the dependency perspective that:

> this massive assault on the land base of Native northerners threatened their basic economic resources and the way of life that these resources sustained ... when all the riches were taken out from under them by foreign companies, Native land and culture would have been destroyed and people left with nothing.
> (Usher, 1993: 106–107)

This alternative view of the development process was accompanied by a different view about the land in question. Far from believing the lands and resources belonged to all Canadians equally, Aboriginal people felt that these were their traditional lands over which they held "Aboriginal title," and which they had never ceded to the Crown under treaty. This view was consistent with the Calder decision and the newly [established] federal policy on comprehensive land claims.

In 1976, after an exhaustive and exhausting series of hearings, Berger issued the first volume of his report. In it, he recommended a 10-year moratorium on pipeline construction in the Mackenzie Valley "in order to strengthen native society, the native economy — indeed the whole renewable resource sector — and to enable native claims to be settled" (Berger, 1977). In Berger's view such settlements

> must be part of a fundamental re-ordering of the relationship between white and native, in order to entrench their rights to the land and to lay the foundations for native self-determination under the Constitution of Canada.
>
> (Page, 1986: 119)

In reaching this conclusion, Justice Berger ushered in a new era in the relationship between Canada and the Aboriginal people living within its borders. A key characteristic of this new era has been the emergence of business development, based on capacity provided by land claim settlements, as an important aspect of the drive by Aboriginal people for self-reliance, self-government and improved socioeconomic circumstances.

NOTES

10. History repeats itself. On May 29, 2001, Conoco Oil purchased Gulf Canada Resources. According to *The Globe and Mail* (May 30, 2001) the purchase gives
   > Conoco a toe-hold in key underdeveloped Mackenzie Delta gas deposits in the Northwest Territories, at a time when U.S. political leaders are pushing to unlock substantial natural gas reserves in the far north. Archie Dunham, chairman and chief executive officer of Conoco, said the company will push to develop the Mackenzie Delta reserves and the associated Mackenzie Valley pipeline project as quickly as possible.

(b) Power Shifts in the Canadian North: A Case Study of the Inuvialuit Final Agreement[†]

Robert M. Bone

1. NORTHERN WINDS OF CHANGE

Before the 1970s, the frontier perspective held sway in the Canadian North. Resource development, both private and public, took place with little regard for either the environment or local people. Canadian society imagined such projects were "good" for both the region and the country.

With the *Berger Inquiry* into the *Mackenzie Valley Pipeline Project* between 1974 and 1977, this myth, like Humpty Dumpty, was shattered, never to be put together again. But what was the *Mackenzie Valley Pipeline Project*? And why did the failure of this mega-project sponsored by powerful multinational corporations signal the end of the frontier development myth and the beginning of a regional perspective?

[†] From Roland Vogelsang, ed., "Canada in Transition: Results of Environmental and Human Geographical Research (Kanada-Studien im Auftrag des Instituts für Kanada-Studien, Band 22) (Bochum, Germany: Universitätsverlag Dr. N. Brockmeyer, 1996). [Updated by the author for this publication.] Universitätsverlag Dr. N. Brockmeyer, Haarmannsbusch 112, 44797 Bochum. Reproduced with permission of the publisher.

2. THE MACKENZIE VALLEY PIPELINE PROJECT

During the early 1970s, the price of energy rose as a result of the reduction of oil production by the *OPEC* cartel. Natural gas prices also increased, encouraging a consortium of 27 American and Canadian companies to announce plans for the largest private construction project in the world, the *Mackenzie Valley Gas Pipeline Project*. Nearly a meter in diameter, this pipeline was designed to bring massive amounts of natural gas from the Prudhoe Bay oil fields to American markets in the Mid-West. The proposed route would cross into Canada along the Yukon coastal plain to the Mackenzie Delta. At that point, the pipeline would follow a southerly direction along the Mackenzie Valley leading into northern Alberta where it would be connected to the privately owned Canadian natural gas pipeline system.

At first, the magnitude of this development and its role in opening up the Canadian Northwest attracted much positive media attention. Virtually all the initial reports extolled its economic benefits for the Canadian economy. At that time, few suspected that the project would fail to gain approval of the federal government. What happened was a radical shift in power, a remarkable change in attitude within Canadian society, and a major victory for Aboriginal peoples and environmentalists.

Two events in the 1960s combined to cause this power shift. One was the rapid growth of the environmental movement in North America and the other was the emergence of Aboriginal political power. These two forces merged to challenge and eventually defeat the largest private development scheme ever assembled for the North — the *Mackenzie Valley Pipeline Project*. The process of the *Berger Inquiry*, its effect on Canadian society and the ultimate rejection of the development myth marks a watershed event in the Canadian North.

Comprehensive Land Claims settlements are a continuation of that power shift — with power devolving from Ottawa to Aboriginal peoples in the Canadian North. This paper examines that part of that devolution, the impact of the *Inuvialuit Final Agreement* on environmental and wildlife decision-making in the Inuvialuit Settlement Region.

3. COMPREHENSIVE LAND CLAIMS AGREEMENTS

Since the *Berger Inquiry*, power has continued to flow to the North as Aboriginal organizations exert more and more power from the federal government. The key to this devolution was the recognition of Aboriginal Rights by the federal government. One result was comprehensive land claims agreements. These agreements were specifically designed for Aboriginal peoples who had not signed treaties and therefore had not extinguished their Aboriginal Rights, including their claim to lands occupied from time immemorial. In exchange for surrendering Aboriginal Rights, Native groups, such as the Inuvialuit, have obtained title to land, minerals, capital and a dual organizational structure.

The dual organizational structure is an attempt to balance the economic interests and environmental concerns of the Inuvialuit. The *Inuvialuit Regional Council*, on the one hand, manages their lands and capital while, on the other hand, the *Inuvialuit Game Council* (IGC) ensures the long-term well-being of their arctic environment and wildlife.

The *Inuvialuit Final Agreement* represents a fundamental transfer of economic and environment powers to Aboriginal peoples in the North. The first to reach an agreement were the *Inuvialuit* in 1984, the second were the *Gwich'in* in 1993 followed in 1993 by the *Tungavik Federation of Nunavut*.

Within each of these agreements, the cash settlement and the resulting economic ventures are touted by the media as signs of "success". One venture demonstrating the business success of the Inuvialuit is their profitable *Inuvialuit Petroleum Corporation*. This junior oil and gas company has assets close to $80 million, mainly situated in Alberta. Since its establishment in 1985, the *Inuvialuit Petroleum Corporation* has turned a tidy profit each year.

Wildlife management achievements in the field of sustainable harvesting, on the other hand, are often ignored by the media or are not fully appreciated. In fact, the powers gained by the Inuvialuit over the environment and wildlife management may well prove to be more significant to the Inuvialuit in the long run than their business accomplishments. Certainly, the new environmental impact assessment process has fundamentally altered the decision-making system in the Western Arctic. Equally important, it has ensured a future for the Inuvialuit culture and harvesting economy. Authority and responsibility for environmental matters now takes the form of co-managed committees and a co-management process.

4. CO-MANAGEMENT OF THE ENVIRONMENT AND WILDLIFE

After the *Inuvialuit Final Agreement*, a number of co-management bodies and the IGC were created to look after the environment and wildlife in the Inuvialuit Settlement Region. Co-management means that the federal government and the Inuvialuit are both responsible for the environment and wildlife in the Inuvialuit Settlement Region (Figure 1).

Five co-management committees were created. These are:

- Fisheries Joint Management Committee (FJMC)
- Wildlife Management Advisory Council (Northwest Territories) (WMAC-NWT)
- Wildlife Management Advisory Council (North Slope) (WMAC-NS)
- Environmental Impact Screening Committee (EISC)
- Environmental Impact Review Board (EIRB).

Each agency has a permanent secretary who is responsible for the day-to-day affairs of the particular committee. These professional are part of the *Joint Secretariat* located in Inuvik. They comprise the permanent staff of a committee, council or board which are composed of an equal number of members are appointed by the federal and territorial governments and the *Inuvialuit Game Council*. Finance administration is provided as a central service by other staff of the *Joint Secretariat*. Each co-management body has a chairman who is mutually acceptable to both the *Inuvialuit Game Council* and the *Government of Canada*. Each group meets several times a year to review management issues and carry out their functions as per the IFA. During the remainder of the year, the secretary/manager undertakes various research tasks approved by the committee and informs the committee members of

FIGURE 1. Organization Chart for Renewable Resource Management Under the Inuvialuit Final Agreement

```
   Inuvialuit              Joint Management            Government
                             Committees                 Agencies*

                                                      ┌──────────┐
                                                      │  Canada  │
  ┌──────────┐          ┌───────────────────┐         ├──────────┤
  │ Akiavik  │──────────│   Environmental   │─────────│  GNWT    │
  │  HTC     │          │ Impact Screening  │         ├──────────┤
  └──────────┘          │    Committee      │         │  YTG     │
                        └───────────────────┘         └──────────┘

                                                      ┌──────────┐
                                                      │  Canada  │
  ┌──────────┐          ┌───────────────────┐         ├──────────┤
  │ Holman   │──────────│   Environmental   │─────────│  GNWT    │
  │  HTC     │          │ Impact Review Board│        ├──────────┤
  └──────────┘          └───────────────────┘         │  YTG     │
                                                      └──────────┘

  ┌──────────┐
  │ Inuvik   │          ┌───────────────────┐         ┌────────────┐
  │  HTC     │──┐       │    Fisheries Joint│─────────│Canada (DFO)│
  └──────────┘  │  ┌──────────┐  Management │         └────────────┘
                ├──│Inuvialuit│  Committee  │
  ┌──────────┐  │  │  Game    │             │
  │ Paulatuk │──┤  │  Council │             │
  │  HTC     │  │  └──────────┘
  └──────────┘  │

                                                      ┌──────────┐
  ┌──────────┐          ┌───────────────────┐         │   Doe    │
  │ Sachs    │──────────│Wildlife Management│─────────├──────────┤
  │Harbour HTC│         │Advisory Council(NWT)        │  GNWT    │
  └──────────┘          └───────────────────┘         └──────────┘

                                                      ┌──────────┐
  ┌──────────┐          ┌───────────────────┐         │   Doe    │
  │Tuktoyaktuk│─────────│Wildlife Management│─────────├──────────┤
  │  HTC     │          │ Advisory Council  │         │  YTG     │
  └──────────┘          │   (North Slope)   │         └──────────┘
                        └───────────────────┘
        ▲                       ▲                          ▲
        │                       │                          │
        └───────────────┬───────┴──────────────────────────┘
                 ┌──────────────┐
                 │Harvest Study │
                 └──────────────┘
```

* GNWT = Government of the Northwest Territories
YTG = Yukon Territorial Government
DFO = Department of Fisheries & Oceans
DOE = Department of Environment
HTC = Hunters and Trappers Committee

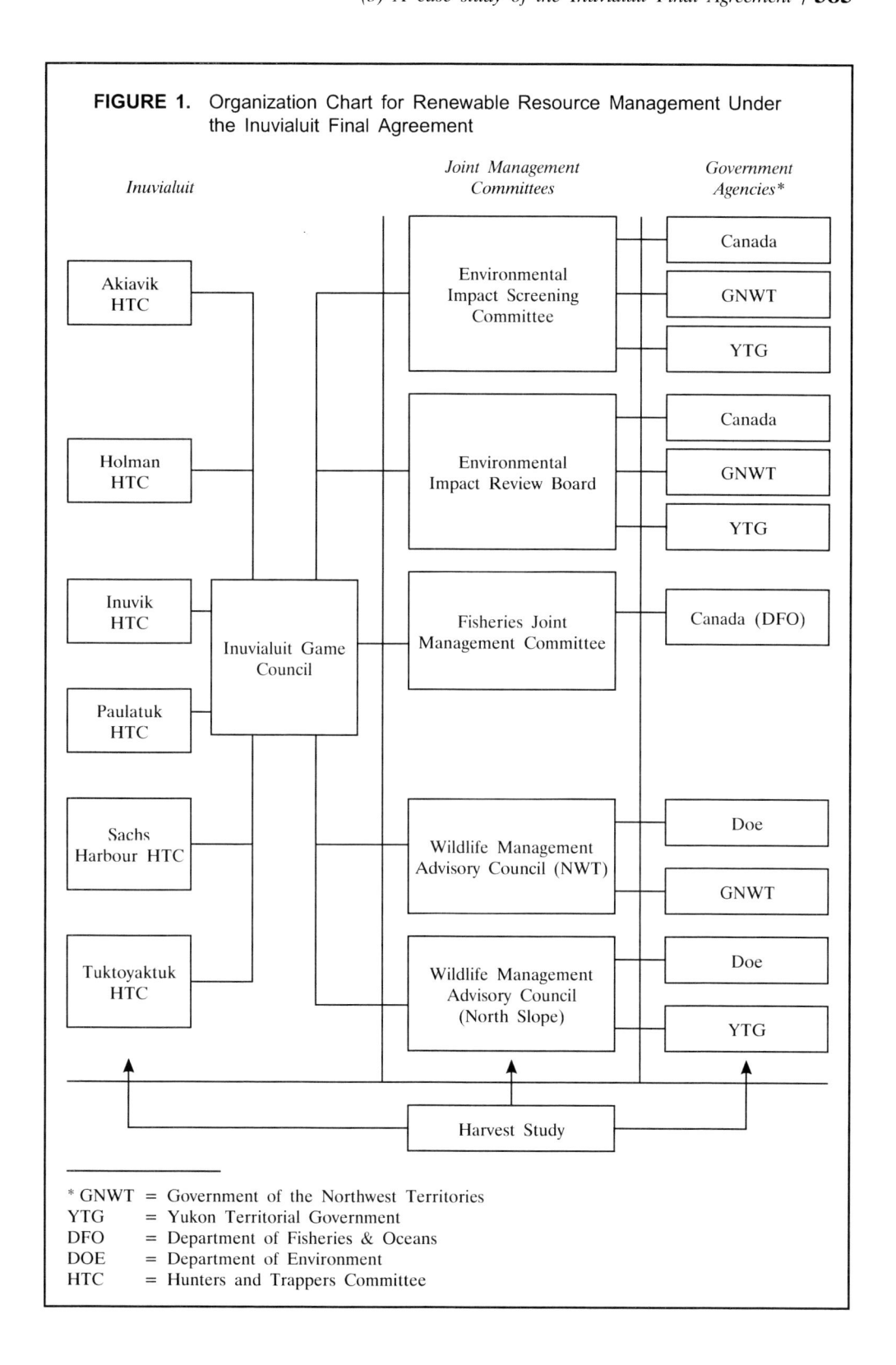

FIGURE 1. Inuvialuit Settlement Region

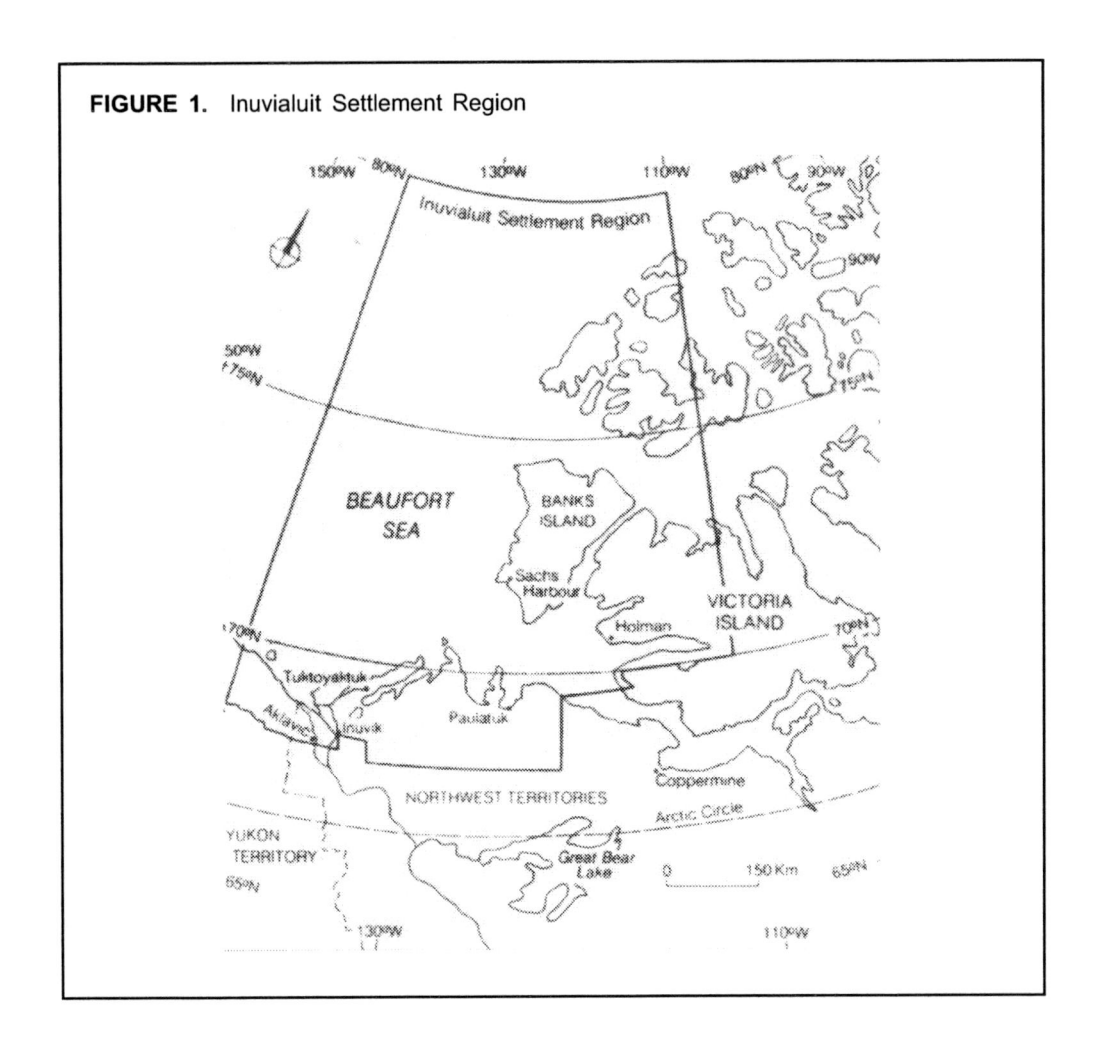

business matters arising from the last meeting and of new issues affecting the environment and wildlife in the Inuvialuit Settlement Region (Figure 2).

5. THE NEW ENVIRONMENTAL IMPACT ASSESSMENT STRUCTURE

By transferring the environmental impact assessment process from Ottawa to Inuvik, the Inuvialuit obtained a measure of control over proposed development projects. This control is exercised through two interrelated co-management bodies, namely the *Environmental Impact Screening Committee* (EISC) and the *Environment Impact Review Board* (EIRB). The EISC assesses all development proposals and refers those that may have a significant impact on the environment or on harvesting to the EIRB (Figure 3). The EIRB conducts a detailed assessment of such proposed projects, holds public meetings, and calls expert witnesses. In

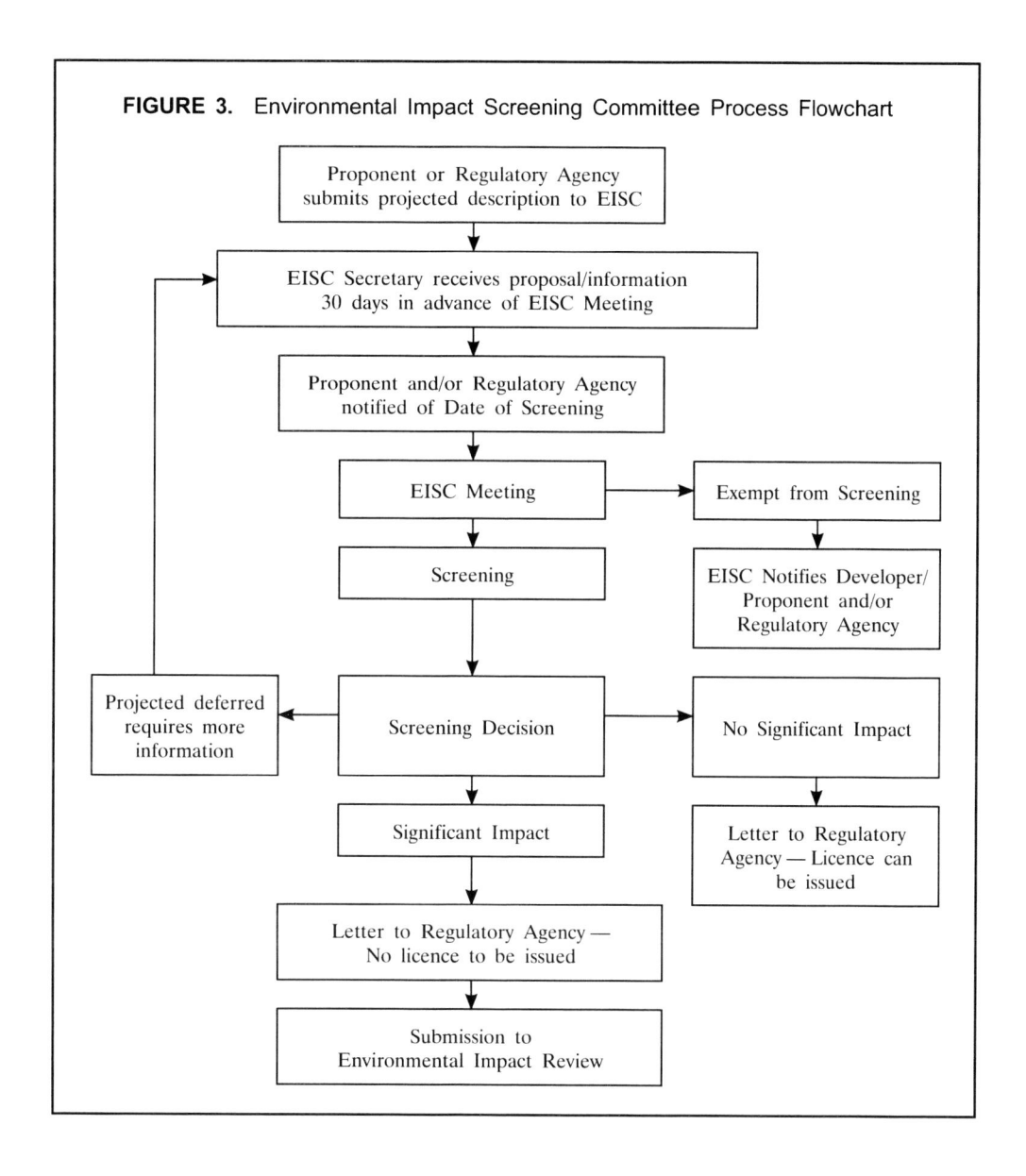

FIGURE 3. Environmental Impact Screening Committee Process Flowchart

```
Proponent or Regulatory Agency
submits projected description to EISC
              │
              ▼
EISC Secretary receives proposal/information
   30 days in advance of EISC Meeting  ◄──────┐
              │                               │
              ▼                               │
Proponent and/or Regulatory Agency            │
   notified of Date of Screening              │
              │                               │
              ▼                               │
        EISC Meeting ─────────►  Exempt from Screening
              │                               │
              ▼                               ▼
          Screening                  EISC Notifies Developer/
              │                      Proponent and/or
              │                      Regulatory Agency
              ▼
  ┌─── Screening Decision ───►  No Significant Impact
  │           │                           │
  ▼           ▼                           ▼
Projected  Significant Impact      Letter to Regulatory
deferred       │                   Agency — Licence can
requires       │                        be issued
more           ▼
information  Letter to Regulatory Agency —
             No licence to be issued
                   │
                   ▼
              Submission to
         Environmental Impact Review
```

the end, the EIRB issues a report which contains its recommendations. These recommendations usually fall into one of three categories: approval, approval with conditions, or rejection. The federal government receives these recommendations and acts on them. Normally, the federal government approves the EIRB recommendations.

All development projects affecting the Inuvialuit Settlement Area must be assessed by the EISC and possibly the EIRB. Development is defined in a broad sense. For example, a recent matter before EISC was the proposal to collect driftwood along the arctic coast and transport it to Inuvik where the driftwood would be processed into lumber and other wood products. Known as *Driftwood Lumber Salvage Proposal*, the developer argued that this business venture would generate jobs and would have minimal effect on the environment. Most opposition came from Delta residents who camp in the area around Shingle Point and who use the land for hunting, fishing and whaling. These residents felt that this project could harm the environment and interfere with their harvesting activities. The proposal was then submitted to the Environmental Impact Review Board.

Until the signing of the *Inuvialuit Final Agreement* (IFA) in 1984, environmental impact assessment in the Western Arctic was conducted by the *Federal Environmental and Review Office* (FEARO). Based in Ottawa, FEARO conducted environmental impact assessments from a national perspective. For that reason, local issues, while discussed at public hearings and duly noted by numerous boards of inquiry, carried little weight in the final deliberations. The primary reason was that the national gain from resource development was judged to be great while the local costs were considered small. In a typical trade-off scenario, proposed projects were approved subject to certain mitigative measures that would reduce the local environmental and social costs to an "acceptable" level.

Evidence of this power shift is revealed in the rejection of one of the two offshore oil drilling proposals to come before the EIRB. Prior to this decision in 1991, hundreds of similar proposals had been approved by Ottawa. The reasons for this rejection illustrate how the Inuvialuit exercise this new power. To understand the Inuvialuit decision-making process, we need to examine the importance of wildlife to the Inuvialuit culture and household economy before reviewing the two drilling programs.

6. INUVIALUIT HUNTING CULTURE

The Inuvialuit hunting culture embodies the harvesting of wildlife from both the land and the sea. The Beaufort Sea is an essential part of that environment. Because the Inuvialuit believe that their future is dependent upon the continued well-being of wildlife, they created two parallel management structures under the *Inuvialuit Final Agreement*. The *Inuvialuit Game Council* is concerned with environment and wildlife while the *Inuvialuit Regional Corporation* is responsible for the management of the lands and monetary compensation resulting from the *Inuvialuit Final Agreement*. The *Inuvialuit Game Council* regionally represents the hunters and trappers residing in the six communities within the I.S.R. Each community has a *Hunters and Trappers Committee*. The *Inuvialuit Game Council* is composed of representatives from these community committees.

Direction for the *Inuvialuit Game Council* therefore comes from local (community level) committees. A prime example is the 1988 request from the *Aklavik Hunters and Trappers Committee* to harvest one bowhead whale. The *Inuvialuit Game Council* endorsed their proposal upon the advice of the *Fisheries Joint Management Committee* and presented it to the *Minister of Fisheries and Oceans*. The request was finally approved in 1991, a licence was issued, and a bowhead whale was taken off Shingle Point in September of that year.

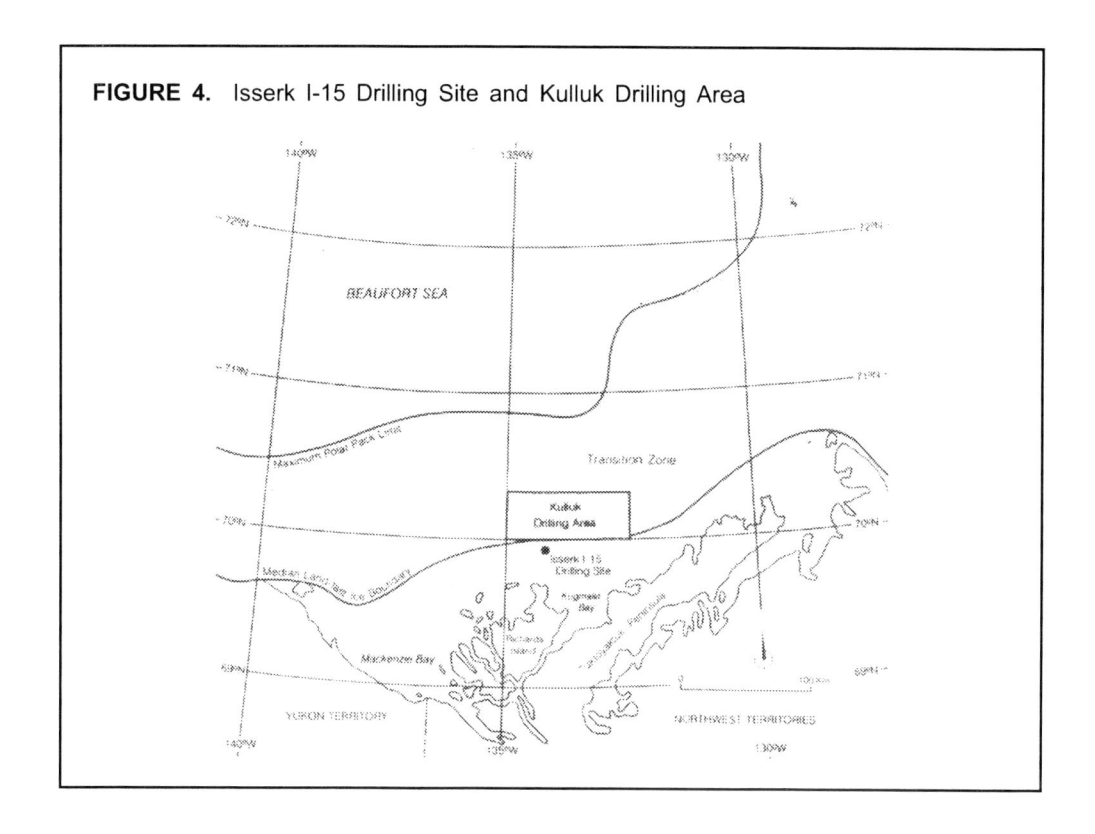

FIGURE 4. Isserk I-15 Drilling Site and Kulluk Drilling Area

7. ESSO'S ISSERK I-15 DRILLING PROGRAM

In 1989, *Esso Resources Canada* and several other companies wished to drill an offshore exploratory well in the Beaufort Sea some 25 km north of Richards Island in some 10 meters of water (Figure 4). The Isserk I-15 well would extend to a depth of 2800 meters. On the basis of seismic data, Esso reported that there was a gas deposit at 1300 meters and a gas/oil deposit at 2200 meters.

Esso submitted its Environmental Impact Statement to the *Environmental Impact Review Board* on September 20th, 1989. The Board was concerned about oil spill possibilities, containment and clean-up measures, and the possible effect of a spill on wildlife. The Board then raised the matter of who would pay for a clean-up and compensate hunters and trappers.

With this in mind, the Board required that Esso produce a 'worst case oil blow-out scenario'. At the public hearings, Esso reported that, while an oil blow-out is extremely unlikely, it could only occur at the 2200 meter horizon where there is a possibility of striking oil. Assuming the Isserk I-15 well is drilled in the summer, the worst case scenario for a blow-out would take place in the late fall when the land-fast ice would prevent access to the well site by ship and a relief drilling rig. In this case, the relief drilling rig would be transported across an ice road to the drill site. This more complicated operation would take 135 days, allowing over

400,000 barrels of oil to escape (ENVIRONMENTAL IMPACT REVIEW BOARD 1989:9).

The *Environmental Impact Review Board* recommended two conditions for approval of the Esso program. One was that drilling in the oil/gas horizon take place after land-fast ice has formed. The presence of ice at the drill site would mean that the oil spill from a blow-out would remain on the ice surface, thus permitting a relatively simple clean-up procedure.

The second requirement was that drilling must be completed with enough time remaining for an oil clean-up before June 15th, 1990. The Board selected June 15th as the date to mark the day that land-ice would no longer support truck traffic on an ice road to the drill site. The last requirement was that Esso sign an agreement to compensate hunters and trappers for damage to wildlife caused by their activities.

Esso agreed to these conditions. Over the next year, the company completed its Isserk I-15 drilling operation without incident.

8. GULF'S KULLUK DRILLING PROGRAM

In the year following Esso's successful drilling program, *Gulf Canada* proposed to drill four oil wells some 40 to 70 km north of Richards Island (Figure 4). The *Kulluk project* would take three years to complete. The well sites would lie in the ice transition zone. This zone lies between the normal extent of the land-fast ice and the polar ice pack. All drilling would take place within 30 km of Gulf's Amauligak oil field. The objective was to add to the already extensive Amauligak oil reserves and thereby hasten its commercial development.

The water depth at the sites of the four wells was around 30 meters. Each well would extend some 3000 to 4500 meters into the ocean floor. Drilling operations for each well would take between 30 to 45 days. Subject to approval by the *Environment Impact Review Board*, the work on the first well would begin in June 1990.

Similar to the Esso hearings, the Board was concerned about oil spill possibilities, containment and clean-up measures, and the possible effect of a spill on wildlife. The Board then raised the matter of who would pay for a clean-up and compensate hunters and trappers.

As before with Esso, the Board required that Gulf produce a 'worst case blow-out scenario' for its Kulluk program. Gulf calculated that it would take 66 days to stop the release of oil from a blow-out at one of the four wells. At a daily release rate of 40,000 barrels, Gulf estimated that 2.6 million barrels of oil would escape into the Beaufort Sea. The scale of the oil spill was astounding for it was ten times the size of the Exxon Valdez spill in Alaska (ENVIRONMENTAL IMPACT REVIEW BOARD 1991:48). Under this worst case scenario, oil would soon reach the shorelines of the arctic coast, causing devastating effects on sea and shore wildlife.

Gulf estimated that the cost of a clean-up was around $400 million (ENVIRONMENTAL IMPACT REVIEW BOARD 1991:48). This figure is considerably lower than the $2 billion cost of cleaning-up the Exxon Valdez spill. Even more revealing was the fact that, unless Gulf was negligent, the maximum liability under federal regulations was only $40 million (ENVIRONMENTAL IMPACT

REVIEW BOARD 1991:48). Under these conditions, the remaining costs would fall to the federal government.

Gulf argued that, given their technology and past experience with exploratory drilling in the Beaufort, such a blow-out was extremely unlikely. Gulf felt that the Board should give more weight to the notion of risk probability than to a worst case scenario. Gulf officials stressed that over the last decade, Gulf had successfully completed over a dozen exploratory oil wells in the Beaufort Sea, including the Amauligak well. They also pointed out that, under the former environment impact assessment process, Gulf's oil drilling programs for the Beaufort Sea were readily approved at the environmental screening level.

The Board rejected the Kulluk drilling project on three grounds. The first factor was the potential damage to the marine environment and wildlife from a major oil spill. The second factor was the difficulty of containing a spill in the ice transition zone. The fear was that the spill would quickly spread to Richards Island and the Tuktoyaktuk Peninsula. Lastly, the Board felt that the issues of liability and the state of preparedness of the company and government for an oil spill clean-up were grossly inadequate. Particularly, the Board faulted the *Canada Oil and Gas Lands Administration*, the federal regulatory agency responsible for frontier exploration and development, for failing to develop adequate oil spill contingency plans.

9. DISCUSSION AND CONCLUSION

The *Inuvialuit Final Agreement* has changed the power structure determining the environmental landscape. In particular, the *Inuvialuit Final Agreement* has provided the Inuvialuit with powerful tools to safeguard their interest in wildlife and the environment. One such tool is the new Environmental Impact Assessment process. With co-management, the Inuvialuit now share the authority and responsibility for assessing development projects with the federal government for the area defined as the *Inuvialuit Settlement Region*. In fact, developments outside the Inuvialuit Settlement Region that affect wildlife within the region are subject to screening and possible review.

The rejection of *Gulf's Kulluk Drilling Program* sent shock waves into the board rooms of Calgary's oil barons and embarrassed the federal government. While the depressed price of oil in the early 1990's caused the oil companies to pull up stakes in the Western Arctic, an added consideration was the rejection of the Kulluk Project and the knowledge that future proposals would be subjected to a "worst case scenario". Major oil companies sold or leased their ice-reinforced drilling rigs and ice breakers to companies operating around Prudhoe Bay and they withdrew all operational units from Tuktoyaktuk and Inuvik. Since the Esso exploratory well in 1990, no drilling has taken place in the Beaufort Sea. The prospects for drilling in the Western Arctic in 1995 are not bright. There are three main reasons. The primary one is that oil prices are still too low to warrant a strong exploratory effort in the Beaufort Sea. Until prices return to $30/barrel, this area will remain unattractive. The second reason is that exploration for oil and gas in the upper Mackenzie Valley and the western provinces is not only less expensive than similar operations in the Beaufort Sea but oil production is more easily transported to major markets in the United States and Canada. The last reason may be the cost associated with the more demanding requirements instituted by the *Canada Inuvialuit Environmental Impact Review Board*. By insisting that the oil companies prove that they have the financial resources to undertake a major oil spill clean-up, the Board increases their costs of operation. For example, if required to post a bond of $500 million for three years at an interest rate of 10%, the additional charge to the company would amount to $150 million.

Recent evidence shows that the oil companies have no 1995 oil exploration plans for the Beaufort Sea which are reflected in recent reports from Calgary. *Shell Canada* and *Chevron Canada* have stated that they have no interest in acquiring exploratory leases in the Beaufort Sea. These statements were a reaction to the announcement in January 1995 by the federal government that more than 616,000 km^2 in the Beaufort Sea and Mackenzie Delta were available for posting. Posting is the first step in acquiring land for petroleum exploration. Oil companies examine the areas posted and advise Ottawa which particular areas, if any, they would like to explore. The next step is for Ottawa to allow companies to bid for the identified lands/seas. Exploration licenses for a set period of time are awarded to the highest bidder.

No doubt the Inuvialuit members of the *Environmental Impact Review Board* were aware that a rejection of Gulf's proposal might trigger a negative reaction by the oil industry to future exploration in the Beaufort Sea. On the other hand, the fear of a Valdez-size oil spill and its effect on the environment and wildlife was simply too much for the Board to ignore. There has been a cost — the loss of jobs and business opportunities in Inuvik and Tuktoyaktuk. But such a cost is a small price to ensure that the cultural base of the Inuvialuit society remains well and strong. In 1991, for instance, the Aklavik hunters harvested their first bowhead whale in over 50 years. For those hunters, the Board's decision was the right one.

REFERENCES

BEAUFORT SEA STEERING COMMITTEE (1991): Issues Arising from the Environmental Impact Review Board: Reviews of the Isserk and Kulluk Drilling Program Applications. Ottawa: DIAND.

BERGER, THOMAS R. (1977): Northern Frontier, Northern Homeland: the Report of the Mackenzie Valley Pipeline Inquiry. 2 Vols. Ottawa: DIAND.

BERKES, FIKRET (1994): "Co-Management: Bridging the Two Solitudes" In: Northern Perspectives 22, 2-3, 18-20.

BONE, ROBERT M. (1992): "The Continuing Importance of Country Food to Northern Natives" In: Focus 41, 4, 7-12.

BONE, ROBERT M. (1994): Inuvialuit Final Agreement, Economic Development and the Environmental Impact Assessment Process. Paper presented at the Western Regional Science Association Annual Meetings in February 1994 at Tucson, Arizona.

CARPENTER, ANDY / HANBIGE, BRUCE M.V. / BINDER, RICHARD M. (1992): Co-Management of Wildlife in the Western Canadian Arctic: An Inuvialuit Perspective. Inuvik: Inuvialuit Game Council.

CAMPBELL, S. (1990): "Kulluk Program Flawed" In: The Inuvik Drum 26, 3, 1-2.

CHERKASOV, A.I. (1994): "Environmental Problems and Native Self-Government: Northern Peoples in the Russian Federation and Canada" In: The Musk-ox 40, 54-58.

ENVIRONMENTAL IMPACT SCREENING COMMITTEE (1994): Operating Guidelines and Procedures. Inuvik: Joint Secretariat.

ENVIRONMENTAL IMPACT REVIEW BOARD (1989): Public Review of the Esso, Chevron et al. Isserk I-15 Drilling Program. Inuvik: Joint Secretariat.

ENVIRONMENTAL IMPACT REVIEW BOARD (1991): Public Review of the Gulf Canada Resources Limited Kulluk Drilling Program 1990–92. Inuvik: Joint Secretariat.
ENVIRONMENTAL IMPACT REVIEW BOARD (1992): Operating Procedures (Second Edition). Inuvik: Joint Secretariat.
FEDERAL ENVIRONMENTAL ASSESSMENT AND REVIEW OFFICE (1984): Beaufort Sea Hydrocarbon Production and Transportation: Final Report of the Environmental Assessment Panel. Report 25. Ottawa: Minister of Supply & Services.
FREEMAN, MILTON M.R. / WEIN, ELEANOR E. / KEITH, DARREN E. (1992): Recovering Rights: Bowhead Whales and Inuvialuit Subsistence in the Western Canadian Arctic. Edmonton: Canadian Circumpolar Institute.
GRIFFITHS, G. (1990): "Environmental Review Under the Inuvialuit Agreement: The Kulluk Drilling Programme in Jeopardy" In: Resources: The Newsletter of the Canadian Institute of Resources Law 31, 1–3.
HLADUN, H. (1990): "Back to Basics, Government, Industry and People from the North are Looking for Ways to Revive Drilling in the Beaufort Sea" In: Arctic Petroleum Review 13, 3, 6–7.
KEEPING, J.M. (1980): The Inuvialuit Final Agreement. Calgary: Canadian Institute of Resources, University of Calgary.
MACLACHLAN, LETHA (1994): "Co-Management of Wildlife in Northern Aboriginal Comprehensive Land-Claim Agreements" In: Northern Perspectives 22, 2–3, 21–27.
MUIR, MAGDALENA A.K. (1992): "Comprehensive Land Claims Agreements and their Implications for Resource Management in the Northwest Territories" In: Musk-Ox 39, 256–259.
MUIR, MAGDALENA A.K. (1994): Comprehensive Land Claims Agreements of the Northwest Territories: Implications for Land and Water Management. Canadian Institute of Resources Law. Calgary: Arctic Institute of North America.
MULLER-WILLE, L. (1987): "Indigenous Peoples, Land-Use Conflicts and Economic Developments in Circumpolar Lands" In: Arctic and Alpine Research 19, 4, 351–356.
PAGE, ROBERT (1987): Northern Development: The Canadian Dilemma. Toronto: McClelland and Stewart.
REED, M.G. (1990): Environmental Assessment and Aboriginal Claims: Implementation of the Inuvialuit Final Agreement. Canadian Environmental Assessment Research Council. Ottawa: CEARC.
SAUNDERS, A. (1991): "Beaufort Blues Again" In: Arctic Circle 1, 5, 15–23.
SPOXTON, MARK (1995): "Oil Companies See Potential in Fort Liard Area" In: News North 49, 37, A-13–14.
USHER, PETER J. / TOUGH, FRANK J. / GALOIS, ROBERT M. (1992): "Reclaiming the Land: Aboriginal Title, Treaty Rights and Land Claims in Canada" In: Applied Geography 12, 109–132.

(c) New Pipe Dreams: In the 1970s, Native Protests Helped Stop the Mackenzie Valley Pipeline. Now, Native Leaders Want to See It Built[†]

Brian Bergman

Along with many other young native activists in the 1970s, Northwest Territories Premier Stephen Kakfwi cut his political teeth fighting against a proposed megaproject to build a northern pipeline through the Mackenzie Valley to the Beaufort Sea. At the time, critics saw the pipeline as a bid by southern-based busi-

---

[†] From *Maclean's* (July 17, 2000): 34–35. Reproduced with permission of the publisher.

ness interests to exploit the vast oil and gas wealth of the North with little regard to the impact on the people who lived there. Fast-forward to the spring and summer of 2000, when Kakfwi can often be found addressing business audiences on the virtues of a project he once denounced. "The construction of a pipeline through the Mackenzie Valley is the key that will unlock the development of our oil and gas," the 49-year-old premier recently told energy executives in Calgary. "We believe the time is right for making this vision a reality."

The bold dream of unleashing the resource riches of the Far North is back — with a vengeance. Record-high natural gas prices and supplies that just can't keep up with the ever-expanding North American demand are turning many industry eyes northward. Technological advances in pipeline construction and drilling have significantly reduced the cost of tapping the resource, both in the Mackenzie Delta and in Alaska's Prudhoe Bay. At the same time, native land claims — the main stumbling block to the pipeline dreams of the 1970s — have, for the most part, been resolved. "It's not so much a matter of if a pipeline will be built, as when," says Roland George, a gas consultant with Calgary-based Purvin & Gertz Inc. "This is going to be the next major frontier for resource development."

At least one proponent, Texas-based Arctic Resources Co. Ltd., is talking about having a preliminary application before Canada's National Energy Board by the end of the year. And even the most conservative industry insiders are predicting that a northern pipeline should be constructed and in operation by 2010. In the meantime, there is a flurry of activity among potential stakeholders in a project that, depending on the route, could cost anywhere from $3 billion to $8 billion. Some key developments:

- In February, four of Canada's largest energy companies — Imperial Oil Resources Ltd., Shell Canada Ltd., Mobil Oil Canada and Gulf Canada Resources Ltd. — launched a joint study into the feasibility of developing and transporting Mackenzie Delta gas. Producers are also intensifying efforts to further "prove up" the extent of delta gas reserves — a critical factor in justifying the costs of building a pipeline.
- Last month, two of Canada's biggest pipeline firms, Westcoast Energy Inc. and TransCanada PipeLines Ltd., confirmed they were jointly studying options for a northern pipeline. One alternative is dusting off the route that Foothills Pipe Lines Ltd. first proposed in the 1970s, to take Alaskan natural gas southward through the Yukon, British Columbia and Alberta to the United States. TransCanada and Westcoast each own a 50-per-cent share of Foothills Pipe Lines.
- At the recent World Petroleum Congress in Calgary, John Browne, chief executive officer of the world's second-largest petroleum producer, BP Amoco PLC, added his voice to the growing consensus that a northern pipeline will likely be built before the end of the decade. Browne said BP Amoco — which has a major stake in Prudhoe Bay and holdings in the Mackenzie Delta — will consider taking an ownership position in any future pipeline.

It was, in fact, just a matter of time before this modern version of the Gold Rush resumed in earnest. The prize is simply too alluring. The National Energy Board estimates there are nine trillion cubic feet of discovered natural gas reserves in the Mackenzie Delta — and at least another 55 trillion yet to be found. In sheer volume, that would amount to more than a third of the known reserves in the more traditional gas fields of Alberta. To the west of the delta, at Prudhoe Bay, there are proven gas reserves of 30 trillion cubic feet and estimated total reserves of more than 100 trillion. Northern Alaska is already a significant oil-producing area, generating over one million barrels per day, which is piped south across Alaska and then put on tanker ships.

The potential resource windfall is what fuelled the original pipeline proposals three decades ago. At that time, Canadian Arctic Gas Pipeline Ltd., a consortium of Canadian and American companies, proposed a route from Prudhoe Bay across the northern Yukon to the Mackenzie Delta, then south to Alberta. Calgary-based Foothills Pipe Lines countered with its plan to bring Prudhoe gas directly south to a route that would parallel the Alaska Highway, and later to add a link to the delta resources along the Yukon's Dempster Highway.

The Canadian Arctic Gas pipeline, in particular, drew the ire of southern environmentalists and northern natives alike. The route traversed the coastal plains of Alaska and the Yukon, traditional calving grounds to the Porcupine caribou herd on which native hunters depended. In 1974, the Trudeau government appointed Thomas Berger, then a B.C. Supreme Court justice, to investigate. Berger took to the task with uncommon enthusiasm. First, he heard in Yellowknife from 300 expert witnesses. Then he travelled to 35 remote communities and listened directly to northerners. The hearings attracted widespread media coverage, giving many residents their first real opportunity to voice their fears, frustrations — and aspirations — to the rest of the country.

In May, 1977, Berger recommended that, for environmental reasons, no pipeline should ever be built along the northern coastal plains. And although Berger concluded that an environmentally sound pipeline could be built through the Mackenzie Valley, he urged a 10-year moratorium on pipeline construction in the region to allow time to settle native land claims. Ottawa endorsed his recommendations.

In a potentially significant footnote, two months after Berger tabled his report the National Energy Board granted regulatory approval to the routing proposed by Foothills — rights-of-way that legally still stand. The company soon abandoned the project in the face of ballooning construction costs and an unexpected gas glut that persisted through much of the 1990s, depressing prices. All that has now dramatically changed: demand is soaring, and the Alberta spot price for gas more than doubled between January and the end of June, from $2.50 per gigajoule (roughly 1,000 cubic feet) to $5.50. That is well above the $4.50 per gigajoule level analysts say is needed to make a northern pipeline viable. Seasonal factors pushed the price back to $4.64 last week, but it is expected to return to a level above $5 later in the year and stay high.

The latest round of pipeline fever began last October when former federal Conservative cabinet minister Harvie Andre unveiled an ambitious $8-billion plan to bring both Prudhoe Bay and delta gas on stream as early as 2005. Andre is a Calgary management consultant and the Canadian chairman of Arctic Resources Co. Ltd., a new consortium launched by a group of Texas financiers. They are proposing a 1,760-km pipeline, from Boundary Lake on the northern B.C.-Alberta border to the Mackenzie Delta, that would connect with a second 520-km line to Prudhoe Bay to be built offshore, in the seabed. Andre argues that the economies of scale realized by harnessing both the Prudhoe and delta reserves would significantly improve the rate of return for producers. He also maintains that, by planting the Prudhoe Bay portion offshore, the environmental risks identified in the 1970s can be sidestepped. "Twenty-five years ago, there weren't a lot of ocean-bottom pipelines," he says. "The technology has changed enormously and today there are thousands of kilometres of them."

Andre has been involved for months in talks with northern aboriginal groups and territorial government officials. So, too, have TransCanada and Westcoast. In addition to the original Foothills line, the pipeline giants are also actively considering the option of a pipeline through the Mackenzie Valley. "There's a lot of meetings going on," reports Nellie Cournoyea, chairwoman of the Inuvialuit Regional Corp., the body that administers the land claim reached by natives in the Beaufort Sea region in 1984. "The major companies are all in this area and we deal with them every day."

Cournoyea, a veteran native leader and former premier of the Northwest Territories, says the biggest change since the 1970s is that the oil and gas industry realizes aboriginal people are an integral part of development, and that they must receive a fair share of resource revenue and have the opportunity to invest directly in pipelines and offshoot businesses. The territory's current premier echoes that view. "When we said 'No' to the pipeline in the 1970s, it wasn't in vain," Kakfwi told Maclean's. "Aboriginal people are no longer going to be thrown some crumbs and rolled over by industry and government."

The exact timing and route for a northern pipeline will largely depend on how quickly producers want to bring the gas to market — and the regulatory hurdles they must overcome. If speed is of the essence, says Calgary-based analyst John Mawdsley, then the nod may go to the $7.6-billion, 2,700-km Foothills line, which follows existing highways and has approved rights-of-way. But if capital costs are the key consideration, then the shorter (1,800-km), cheaper (an estimated $3.6 billion) Mackenzie Valley route may have the edge. Andre's dual pipeline bid to the delta and Prudhoe Bay cannot be ruled out, adds Mawdsley, although the offshore portion would face intense scrutiny from both Canadian and U.S. authorities. Yukon Premier Pat Duncan, for instance, says she would fight an offshore route, as well as any plan for traversing the northern Yukon.

And how does the man who played such a critical role in the last pipeline drama view the sequel? Thomas Berger, who now practises law in Vancouver, is sanguine. "The whole idea behind the inquiry," Berger told Maclean's, "was to protect the environment and ensure that, if there was major development, native people should be players. And they feel ready, I gather, to do that." They do, and the race to the North's riches is back in full throttle.

(d) Shell Game: Transnationals Everywhere Are Attempting to Recast Themselves as Eco-friendly[†]

Stephanie Boyd

They promised this time it would be different. 'Health, safety and environment' was their motto. A 'green' Shell. A friendly Shell. And even after losing a bid to develop the Camisea gas fields in the Peruvian Amazon, Shell claimed the experience gave them a revolutionary guide for environmental regulations and social relations that would 'transform mineral exploration in the new century'.

Not surprisingly, both indigenous communities and environmentalists are uneasy about the legacy of Shell's brave new world in the Camisea concessions of the Lower Urubamba Valley — virgin rainforest just 100 kilometres from the famed Manu National Park. Machiguenga, Nahua and Kugapakori natives still lead a semi-nomadic life in this lush and isolated region of biodiversity. Their leaders are not certain whether a transnational giant like Shell can be trusted, but at the same time they feel they have little choice.

Camisea's estimated 600 million barrels of liquid natural gas are worth billions and communities say working with foreign companies is their only chance to get money for social projects. Peru's central government has ignored native people in the Urubamba Valley for centuries — leaving them without schools, health centres or other services. But environmental groups, like the San-Francisco-based Rainforest Action Network (RAN), want gas companies out of the Amazon. They urge Peru to develop alternative energy resources instead.

RAN claimed victory when Shell Oil and its partner Mobil Corp pulled out of Camisea in 1998 after investing $2.7 billion over two years of exploration. But the real reason the company left was because of a dispute with the Peruvian Government over gas distribution rights and tariffs. Finally last February the contract was awarded to PlusPetrol, an Argentine-led consortium with a bleak environmental record and neither the interest nor the money to invest in social or ecological concerns.

Lelis Rivera, director of the Centre for the Development of Amazon Indigenous Peoples, has worked in the Urubamba Valley with the Machiguenga for 20 years and says local people are prepared for an uphill battle with the new company.

Rivera recalls a Shell executive patting him on the shoulder after the company lost the bid, saying: 'Hey, look, it was worth the trouble fighting all the time because now we have a plan for working with indigenous communities worldwide.'

[†] Reproduced with permission from *New Internationalist*, No. 329 (Nov. 2000): 16–17.

The Urubamba Valley in the Peruvian Amazon

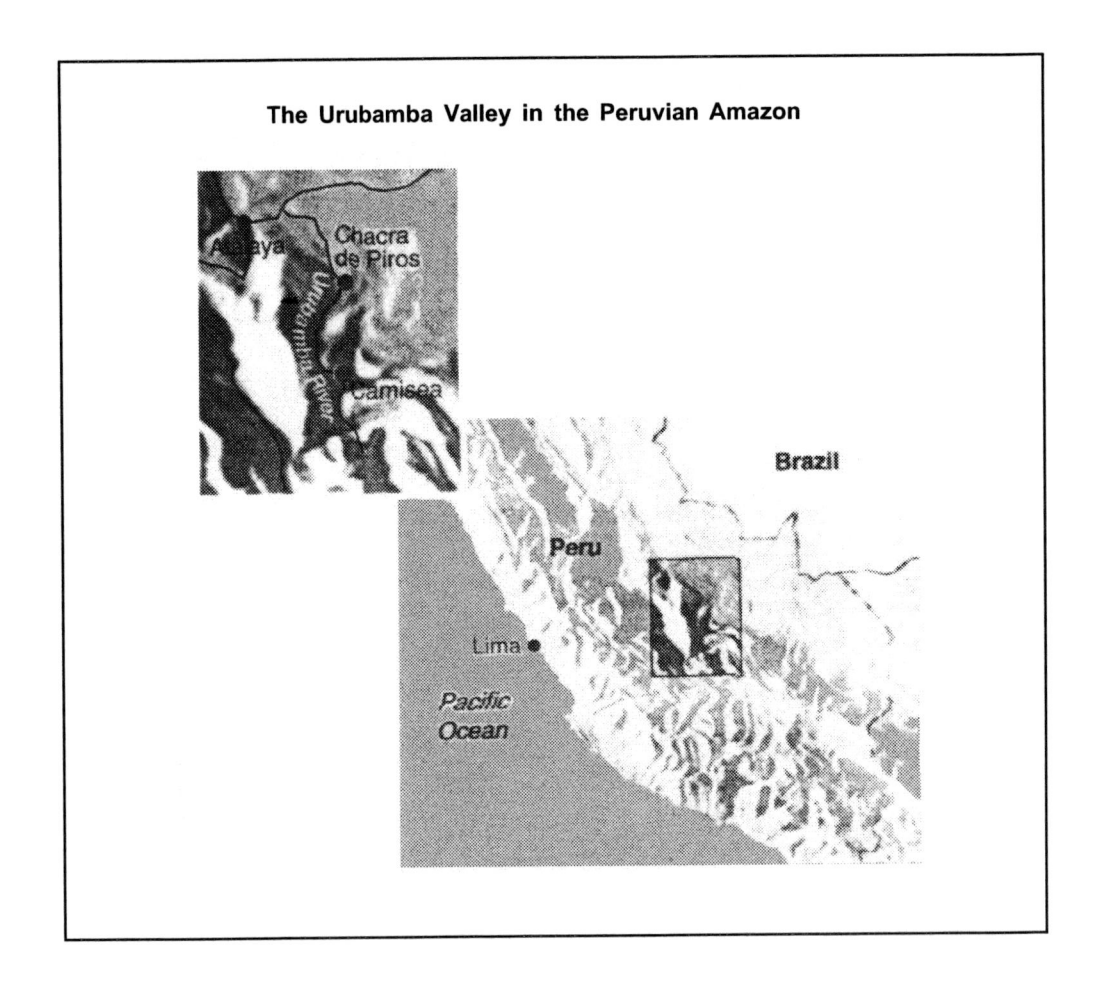

Rivera says Shell first came to the region in the 1980s, with disastrous consequences. Whooping cough and influenza decimated previously uncontacted groups and sexual relations with indigenous women, including many rapes, left sexually transmitted diseases and the ironically named 'baby Shells'. So when Shell returned in 1996 the communities were prepared. By then nearly all the land under exploration had been legally titled to the Machiguenga and they were well versed in their rights under Peruvian and international law.

Still smarting from the public outcry over its alleged human-rights violations in Nigeria, Shell decided to engage in a little image polishing. Bigshots like Washington's Smithsonian Institute were hired, along with a team of Peruvian anthropologists, to handle contact between the company and native people. Shell promised no other company employees would come in contact with locals and agreed not to build major roads, thus preventing an invasion from landhungry peasants eager to turn the forest into farmland or deal in tropical hardwoods. Everything in and out of Shell's camps, from drill rigs to garbage, was supposed to be transported by air or water.

(d) Transnationals everywhere are attempting to recast themselves as eco-friendly / **399**

But the Machiguenga and their advisors were not so easily fooled. They chronicled a series of abuses that first year — including garbage left behind in campsites, abandoned airstrips that were never reforested and dangerous levels of hydrocarbons, cadmium and mercury in local water samples. The study convinced a shame-faced Shell to tighten up monitoring and Rivera says there was marked improvement during the second year.

But there were still unresolved issues. Shell wanted the Government to close a reserve protecting Kugapakori and Nahua peoples and title their land so it could be sold to Camisea. Rivera says this would have been impossible because, in the Nahua and Kugapakori cultures, land is shared among semi-nomadic groups and 'ownership' is not recognized. A sudden introduction to the outside world would also have been devastating.

Shell's belief that everything and everyone is negotiable is wrong, says Rivera: 'There are still places in the world that are not ready to be explored by oil and gas companies.'

Jesus Castro, a young anthropologist who worked as a Shell community-liaison officer, shares many of Rivera's opinions. 'And this was just the exploration phase,' says Castro, pointing out that the construction and operation of natural-gas pipelines have even greater potential for damage. Shell planned to build a massive pipeline snaking through virgin rainforest, ending up in Lima.

'One leak in a pipeline and everything within ten kilometres disappears,' he says. One pipeline explosion in 1989 in Russia, between the towns of Ufa and Asha, blew up two railroad trains and killed 575 people.

The harsh reality facing indigenous groups within the Camisea concession is that although Shell was far from perfect they had a better plan than other companies — including the Argentine consortium now in charge.

Pragmatists applaud Shell's attempts, saying environmentalists need to work with companies in developing greener technology. But in the case of fossil fuels, even 'green' extraction, production and refining can't ameliorate oil's deadly long-term impact on the planet's environment. And although natural gas may be more environmentally 'friendly' than coal or oil, it's still a non-renewable resource.

In a just world the Machiguenga would not have been forced into a position where selling their land — and threatening their way of life — was their only option. And if environmental and social damages were added to the cost (say in some form of tax), projects like Camisea would suddenly seem less profitable and more attention could be focused on developing real green technology.

Wipe away the rhetoric and Shell is still one of the world's top three oil and gas companies and co-owner of such controversial projects as the Bolivia-Brazil natural-gas pipeline which traverses important South American wetlands and forests.

The simple capitalist truism — that corporations exist to make profits — means companies like Shell will invest in the environment and social relations only as long as the game remains profitable. Pragmatists say it doesn't matter as long as the end result is positive. But a false conversion to the faith of sustainable development is as fragile as the Amazon, and likely to be blown away whenever the next consumer fad comes along.

(e) Metis Concerned about Expansion of Suncor's Oil Sands Operations, Called Project Millennium[†]

Marie Burke

The Metis people of Anzac, Alta. have gained intervenor status at the Alberta Energy and Utility Board hearings on Suncor Energy's application to expand their oil sands operations at Fort McMurray, Alta.

The $2.2 billion expansion of Suncor, called Project Millennium, is undergoing regulatory hearings in which the Metis are calling for a commitment to the environment and jobs for their people.

Suncor wants to expand oil sands production to 210,000 barrels of oil by 2002. Suncor must have regulatory board approval before the second phase of Project Millennium can begin.

"This is a big step for a small Metis local," said John Malcolm, president of the Anzac Metis local. Malcolm feels the opportunity to speak to the issues at the hearings will result in a positive situation for the Metis. It's a chance to have a say in how the environment and the people will be affected, he said.

Many of the Aboriginal people in the area still trap for a living, he said. Several trappers told of the decreasing animal populations in the area at the recent Alberta Energy and Utility Board hearing, said Malcolm. He also said the fish coming out of the Athabasca River are no longer edible.

"This place is going to be a desert if we don't address pollution," said Malcolm. He is concerned about increased emissions from the stacks at Suncor settling on the land and water and what the long-term effects will be.

"Suncor has committed to help us with our concerns, but we have been neglected for 30 years," said the Metis president. The massive projects generally just roll through, but this time the Metis will be considered.

The issue of jobs is also something the Metis are concerned about, said Malcolm. Most of the jobs at Suncor where Aboriginal people are employed are not technical, he said. Suncor is promising to increase its number of Aboriginal employees.

"Anzac Metis are not opposed to the project. They do have major socio-economic concerns about their employment situation," said Mark Shaw, director of sustainable development.

In a statement about Project Millennium, the oil production giant has committed to ongoing consultations with the Metis and First Nations people in the region for as long as Suncor is in operation.

"Suncor recognizes industrial development has an impact on traditional hunting and trapping for Aboriginal people," said Brenda Erskine, manager of communications. The on-going consultations with Aboriginal people will address those issues, she said.

[†] From *Windspeaker*, 16(10) (Fall 1999): 39. Website: <www.windspeaker.com>. Reproduced with permission of Aboriginal Multi-Media Society (AMMSA).

The environmental effects initiative of Suncor is looking at the cumulative effects of emissions, said Erskine.

Terms of reference have been completed by the Alberta Environmental Protection's regional sustainable development strategy and Aboriginal people have been identified as one of the stakeholders to ratify the strategy. The strategy will identify how to manage the cumulative [environmental] impact of future oil sand development in the area. Erskine was not sure if the Anzac Metis had ratified the terms of reference.

"Aboriginal business development, as well as employment, is the focus Suncor is taking," said Erskine. "In 1990 there was only $2 million in contracts to Aboriginal people. In 1998 there is now a total of $21.5 million in contracts," she said.

"We have a clear commitment to increasing our Aboriginal workforce. We are sitting at over four per cent of our workforce being Aboriginal," said Erskine. A target of a 12 per cent Aboriginal workforce has been set for Project Millennium in the next three years.

Environment Canada will respond to the Alberta Energy and Utility Board hearings on Suncor's expansion with their own submission on Feb. 2 in Calgary. Suncor is expecting to begin the second phase of Project Millennium in April.

(f) Sour Gas, Bitter Relations[†]

Ginger Gibson, Eric Higgs and Steve E. Hrudey

The Lubicon-Unocal sour gas plant dispute occurred when the Lubicon Cree tribe opposed Unocal Canada's construction of a sour gas plant on their land, fearing that the plant could cause environmental risks. Unocal saw the plant as just another routine development, failing to consider the natives' worldviews.

Poor communication between Unocal and the Lubicon Cree about sour gas risks fostered distrust rather than collaboration

In spite of the rhetoric, communication about risks still often assumes that the experts have all the answers, and the public has none.

For the [Lubicon Cree], a sour gas plant built by Unocal Canada is a regrettable reminder of the accumulating burden of industrial activity in their traditional territory. Since 1979, when the first road reached the community of Little Buffalo in northern Alberta, oil, gas and forestry operations have dramatically altered the Lubicon way of life and economy. The Lubicon have fought for recognition of a

---

[†] From *Alternatives Journal*, 24(2) (1998): 26–31. Reproduced from *Alternatives Journal: Environmental Thought, Policy and Action*. Annual Subscriptions, $25 (plus GST) from Alternatives Journal, Faculty of Environmental Studies, University of Waterloo, Waterloo, Ontario, N2L 3G1. Web site: <www.alternativesjournal.ca>. Reproduced with permission of the authors.

claim to their homeland for more than half a century. The 1988 Grimshaw Accord would have brought a settlement for 95 square miles of territory. But it was not ratified and the [struggle] continues.

Over the years that Unocal Canada has operated in this area, Lubicon political actions have moved from the United Nations, to a boycott of the 1988 Olympics, and a blockade of oil and gas roads. Through such actions the Lubicon have regularly placed themselves in the media spotlight. Yet the siting and construction of a sour gas plant, which pressed the Lubicon into an expensive and ultimately frustrating adjudication through the quasi-judicial Energy and Utilities Board in Alberta (EUB), has received relatively little attention.

Typically in disputes between communities and industry, few walk away from the negotiating table satisfied. This was certainly the case for representatives of Unocal Canada. They viewed the sour gas plant as just another routine development to complement existing infrastructure in a region of rapidly developing oil and gas extraction. It was not easy for them to understand why this particular development had upset the Lubicon sufficiently to force a protracted and adversarial formal process.

Outstanding land claims and the assertion of traditional land-use practices were either outside the reach of their usual procedures or beyond their understanding. During extensive interviews with both groups and also members of the EUB, we learned that perceptions of the dispute varied widely.[1] At bottom, the dispute flared because of different worldviews, but closer to the surface it was a disagreement about the level of risk associated with a sour gas plant.

In the following pages, we examine the risk communication techniques at the heart of the dispute. What the literature in risk communication recommends is not what happened in this case. While the intent of risk communication by a development proponent is usually to engage affected parties as meaningful partners, this was only a remote ideal in the Lubicon-Unocal dispute. After exploring this mismatch between intention and reality, and diagnosing critical problems, we will prescribe some alternative approaches that promise more effective cross-cultural risk communication.

THE SOUR GAS PLANT DISPUTE

Unocal Canada applied in 1994 to the EUB, to process sour gas in the southeast corner of the unresolved Lubicon land claim (see map on [next page]). With the approval of the Lubicon Cree for expansion of existing facilities and construction of feeder lines, the EUB granted Unocal permission to proceed with construction of the sour gas plant. However, the Lubicon were unaware that the plant was intended to process sour gas, as opposed to low sulphur natural gas (i.e., low content of hydrogen sulphide). When they learned of the sour gas, and the attendant toxic risks associated with hydrogen sulphide, they protested the plant approval and called for a full public review.

The public hearing occurred in 1994. The following year, the EUB reaffirmed the approval for Unocal to operate the plant. In communicating with the Lubicon Cree prior to approval, Unocal representatives used a technical language that did not convey critical characteristics of the plant clearly. Unocal officials maintain they

(f) Sour gas, bitter relations / **403**

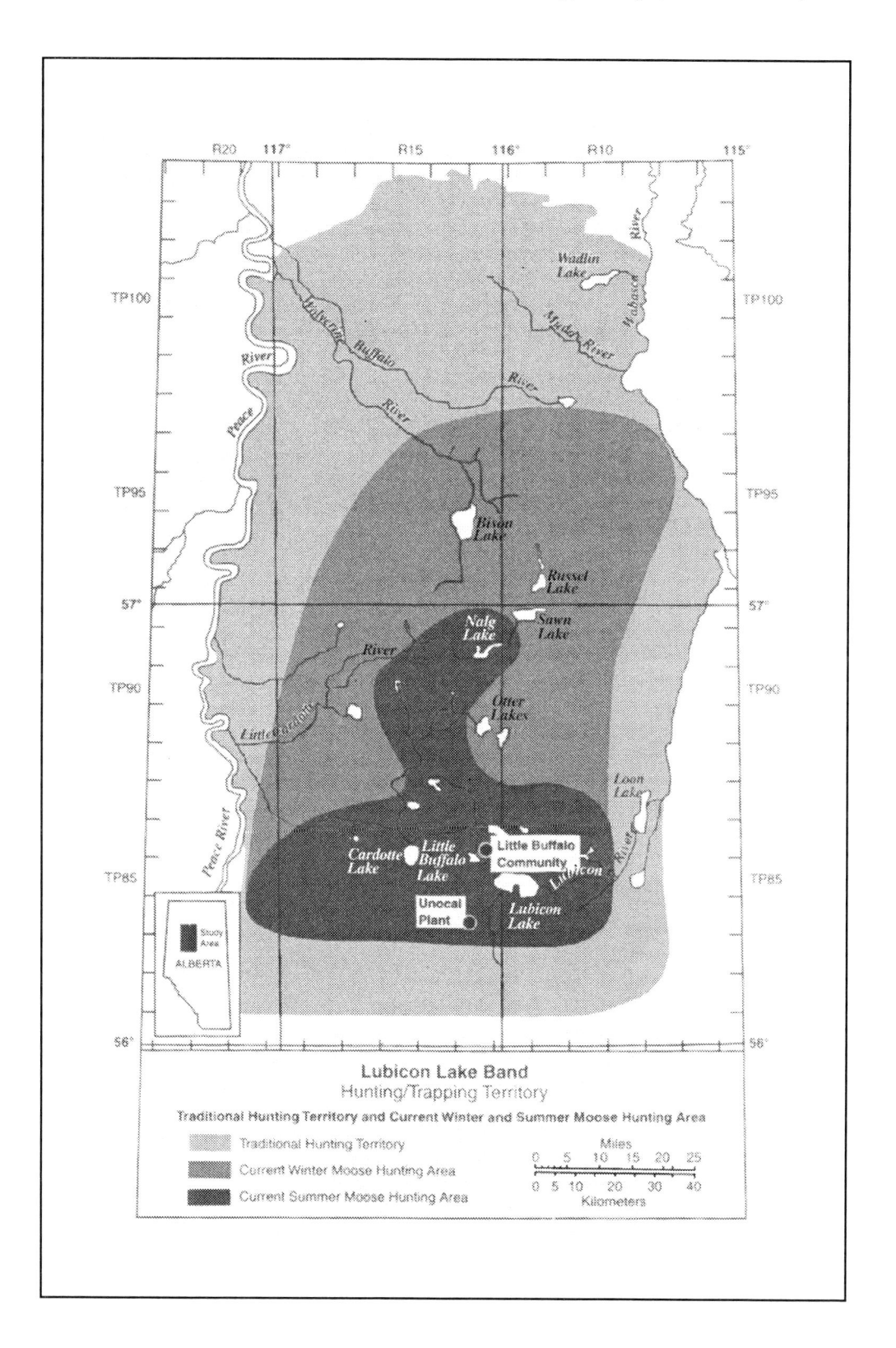

Lubicon Lake Band
Hunting/Trapping Territory
Traditional Hunting Territory and Current Winter and Summer Moose Hunting Area

- Traditional Hunting Territory
- Current Winter Moose Hunting Area
- Current Summer Moose Hunting Area

did not provide all the technical information, because in a previous experience with an aboriginal community they had been asked not to do so. The Lubicon Cree maintain that Unocal deliberately misrepresented the plant to secure Lubicon approval. Unocal denies this charge, and claims their communications were clear. Whatever the case, and the EUB currently has no legal investigative authority for verifying the truth of such claims, a review of this conflict indicates that the risk communication process between Unocal and the Lubicon was a victim of different expectations, approaches, styles and values.

The pervasive and growing industrial presence in Lubicon traditional territory has had a significant effect on the Lubicon Cree. Chief Bernard Ominayak indicates that the community has seen no beneficial return:

> With the billions of dollars that have been extracted by way of natural resources off our traditional territory, there has not been a red cent that has come back to the community other than welfare from the federal government.[2]

Given the countless projects and incursions within the area that they claim, conflict was nearly inevitable once the Unocal sour gas plant was proposed. Past accidents and environmental scares have led to sour gas plant operations becoming a symbol of the threat posed by the oil and gas industry to environment and health in Alberta. In this case, the Lubicon Cree maintain that the plant cannot operate in their traditional territory so close to where they propose to relocate their community when their land claims are successfully negotiated.

Furthermore, even if a single project may have minimal or limited effects, the community evaluates it as part of a cumulative process of development, alongside all other existing and future projects. However, while the Lubicon Cree regarded the sour gas plant against a background of oil and gas expansion in their territory, the EUB currently has no procedure for effectively assessing cumulative effects. And while cumulative effects assessments are now mandated by the Canadian Environmental Assessment Act, implementation remains elusive.

RISK COMMUNICATION IN THEORY

Current theories of risk communication promote two-way dialogue that addresses the concerns of the public who perceive themselves to be at risk, and helps them to interpret assessments of risk.[3] Participatory approaches are advocated because they appear to offer better, less adversarial and less divisive decisions.[4] Through trial and error and many difficult lessons, risk communicators have established guidelines, many of which are "boiler plate" solutions to complex and dynamic situations. For example, the literature calls for: articulating goals; acknowledging the concerns of the public; frequent release of information; recognition that members of the public differ in arenas of involvement, and development of indigenous technical and analytic resources and skills to maximize effective public participation.[5]

Many practitioners of risk communication are aware of a gap between theory and practice. But ways of dealing effectively with this gap are not often articulated. For example, one inconsistency is the theoretical recognition that the public is diverse, while in practice it is treated as a homogeneous group that needs to be educated about the communicators' ideas of "real" risk. Such generalizations about the public, or about aboriginal communities, mask the reality of diversity among and between groups. Differences among groups may relate to beliefs and behaviours in relation to distance and time, worldview, communication style, the value placed on communication, language, discursive style, ethnicity or socio-economic status.[6] But relatively little attention has been directed to accommodating these differences. Ross warns that "it is not sufficient to assume that well-tried Western models ... will work or can be adapted directly for intercultural encounters."[7]

As Ross suggests, genetic assumptions about risk communication cannot be transferred from a process in, say, San Francisco, to northern Alberta. An aboriginal community that has been battling since 1939 in federal and provincial courts, and erecting blockades to secure the integrity of their land, is not likely to perceive industrial development in the same way as middle class urban residents concerned about the health risks of urea-formaldehyde insulation in their homes. Of course, some concerns will be similar. An urban mother and a Lubicon Cree mother share some of the same fears for the health of their children. But key differences will remain.

Recognizing similarities as well as differences is an essential first step, but such attempts must be accompanied by a model for developing long-term relationships between a community and a corporation.[8] Currently, conflicts surrounding development decisions are addressed by an adversarial decision-making system, which often resorts to simple yes or no answers on project development. The EUB has offered suggestions for future relations among parties,[9] but the faith of the Lubicon Cree in the ability of any regulatory body to recognize and protect their interests has been severely undermined by events. Nonadversarial approaches to development decisions may therefore better address the needs and concerns of aboriginal communities and corporations.

As Mulvihill and Jacobs note, in "order for northern development to be sustainable, projects that originate in the South must take into account the different history, periodicity, culture and rhythms of the North." Their work speaks to the importance of context, of the need to be flexible and open-minded in any exchange of information. However, they provide no model for accommodating the critical differences between southern urban proponents and northern residents.

COLLABORATION

Despite an extensive record of mistakes in risk communication, the same ones are still being made. Unocal Canada has relied on incorrect assumptions about the Lubicon. In a public meeting, for example, they brought in an expert medical consultant to address Lubicon health concerns. While these concerns certainly extend to health, the medical expert could not address and understand the environmental, social and political reasons for Lubicon objection to the plant. In fact, no expert brought in by Unocal could have done this, but Unocal nevertheless continues to assume that an expert consoling the public will suffice. Their failure raises at least two questions. Are company employees not learning from the risk communication courses that the company requires those in touch with the public to take? Or are there key ingredients missing in the formulae developed for communicating risks to the public? The answer involves both facets: problems of cultural awareness remain even after sensitivity training (or similar corporate programmes), but there are also inadequacies with the substance of training. based on our analysis of the case, we articulate some of the factors that need to be addressed to succeed in risk communication.

As regulatory agencies are downsized, corporations can no longer rely on the regulator for guidance in the application and development process. Instead, corporate accountability to communities must become more direct. Some corporations in Alberta are restructuring to accommodate and include community concerns (e.g., Syncrude, Suncor, Amoco). They may be motivated by the expectation of achieving long-standing agreements. Alternatively, such actions may reflect recognition of the increasing power and influence of aboriginal groups in Canadian politics.

Some aboriginal groups, however, are understandably cynical about corporate motivations for approaching a community, even as others are more optimistic about working with industry as collaborators, not as adversaries. At least in theory, if a community negotiates directly with corporations, they may guarantee themselves more opportunities (e.g., employment, monitoring the corporation, protected areas) than would be afforded by a strictly adversarial approach.

There are a number of advantages to negotiating a relationship. For both aboriginal groups and corporations, reactive decision making will be avoided (the typical process of decide-announce-defend). If those who are directly affected become involved in more than a merely token fashion, then negotiated agreements may result in more timely and effective decisions. Likewise, agreements will be made and implemented at the local level, rather than being externally imposed. Ultimately, closure might be achieved on some issues, a goal that has eluded Unocal and the Lubicon Cree. One corporate respondent noted the benefits of a collaborative relationship:

> One is that it does make your life easier from a business standpoint. But the other is that there is a higher reason to have a relationship with these people, in that they are a local resource to you. And if you can develop them as a local source of people to employ ... then you have a local thing there. And it is a good thing to do from a business standpoint.

Collaborative arrangements can provide safeguards for the community, especially if the collaboration involves participation in, and control over, aspects of the industrial operation. One community [respondent] stated:

> You just train me and employ me to make sure that whatever it is you're doing on our land is safe and you're following certain standards and we're monitoring you. We're out there from early in the morning fill [till] late at night, making sure that nothing happens with your operation on our land.

And as some industries have learned, ongoing dialogue, though time consuming, can help avert future problems:

> I mean we have maps that show us every trapline, everywhere. Simply because we know it is important. And we still can't assume that because there is no trapline showing, that there isn't one there. And we found that out the hard way. It was a real technical thing — you can go through and look at all the traplines. Well, somebody's trapline wasn't marked there. And it just happened to be the Chief of one of the bands. And we had a huge problem. Kind of a breakdown, because the feeling was that we had lost trust ... Other than just looking at a map that the government gave us — we could have gone out to that community sooner and said, we don't think there is anything out there, but is there?

But there are inherent perils for both aboriginal groups and corporations in collaborative relationships. The generally precarious historical conditions for aboriginal peoples make them especially susceptible. To the people interviewed for this study, the changes to the land since industry came into the area [are], as a community respondent noted, "like night and day. My people were basically self-sufficient. They didn't have no welfare, they didn't know what welfare was". If aboriginal land claims are to be treated seriously, developers must tread carefully and respectfully. There is a serious risk of co-optation of aboriginal communities. By agreeing to negotiate, often privately, it can become more difficult to explain subsequent agreements to community members and the outside world. The spirit of collaboration can mask some invidious and profound differences. In addition, non-adversarial working relationships risk excluding others who are affected by the development (e.g., nearby communities, other corporations, and dissenting voices within a specific community) from participation in the deliberations. A collaborative model also favours long-term benefit over short-term profit, a virtue that may be contrary to a stock value-driven corporate ethos.

There are a number of obstacles to collaborative arrangements. There is often no history of working together, and there may be a legacy of distrust, as arose with the Lubicon Cree and Unocal. Further, there is no traditional or legislative framework to encourage collaborative decision making. Yet a collaborative model holds considerable promise for aligning the practice of risk communication with theory. Establishing an effective relationship requires some key elements: an agreed upon process, resolution of economic benefits, recognition and understanding of underlying political and social issues.

PROCESS

Communities and corporations have identified a few important principles of collaborative relationships. Negotiation of agreements must occur between one community and the corporation. The parties to a negotiation must first lay the framework for discussion; this requires a mutually agreed upon process for negotiation. For example, one company's agreement with a community ensured that no one could take unilateral actions. One corporate employee explained this:

> There is no way that a company should ever be able to ultimately say, well all criticism aside, we're going to drill here. And no way that certain stakeholders should be able to have certain power over decisions either. You have to reach a process, either through a [hearing], or some kind of arbitration/dispute mechanism. Or some huge public process that ultimately resolves it.

Substantial time needs to be invested in achieving common understanding on concepts and intentions. Consistency of representation from both groups ensures that progress can be made on issues, and that a solid relationship is built. Companies are advised to become aware of the community structure, politics and forms of decision making. This point was stressed by one corporate respondent:

> I think that an industry that is really involved in an area, in terms of getting its natural resources from an area, or using the lands in the area for its main access and corridors, is well-advised to get itself thoroughly immersed there ... to be a bit selective about it, because you can't necessarily get that familiar an interest in every place in sight. But I

think that where there is an important physical resource or material tie, that you should get to know the area very thoroughly indeed. And that involves getting to know the administrators and political leaders.

Within the corporation there must be a commitment at the senior level to these issues. Once commitments were made by senior management, some companies drafted policy regarding aboriginal communities, in consultation with the group. Communities can participate in advisory or steering committees of interest to them. Community members emphasized they want to give input into industrial development in their territory. However, this level of involvement can be intimidating for the corporation.

Ultimately, although direction for change may be provided by senior management, real change in attitudes and involvement requires personal dedication from both the community and the corporation.

ECONOMIC FACTORS

For some, participation in environmental decision making is a job; for others, it is a cause, based on deeply-held cultural beliefs. This distinction, at least in community-corporate negotiations, is often tied to different economic means. Participation can often require funding, as was noted by one corporate respondent:

> You have to fund them through the consultation process too. It took me a while to get my head around funding people to come and have meetings with me. But eventually we came around; we truly want them there, providing meaningful input. We are going to have to provide funding to get that.

The need to fund participation is sharpened by the fact that the few salaried first nation members with administrative and technical skill are usually overloaded with responsibilities. Further, first nation participation is valuable in the same way as scientific knowledge; elders and knowledgeable community members have an intricate understanding of the local area, which deserves remuneration. From a strictly pragmatic view, every dollar spent by corporations on consultation will save thousands in corporate and legal costs. Furthermore, some communities will be unable to consult without some financial aid. As one community member noted, "the distance to the hearing made it very difficult for my people, because we are not very rich. We had to travel back and forth. We don't have the funds." Consultation takes time. Implementation of decisions or agreements may require many years. Respondents, however, see this time as worthwhile, as they link this investment of time to fewer misunderstandings and stronger mutually agreeable decisions.

Participants in our study also indicated that establishing trust requires integration of the community into the workforce. Employment equity may be achieved through job training, job shadowing, education or mentoring, co-op programmes and scholarships. Many companies are contracting outside services to local aboriginal contractors. Others have targeted different positions in the corporation such as accounting or engineering, areas that aboriginals may not yet be working in. Employment requires a broad level of support and change. As one corporate respondent noted:

people just naturally gravitate to a place where they see that people like them have had some success. And, they naturally stay away from places in which it is obvious, where nobody looks like them anywhere in sight. And so you have to gradually build up the trust and the confidence that can build up between the company [and] the workforce.

SOCIAL AND POLITICAL FACTORS

Corporations and communities often have different decision-making procedures and social organizations. While corporations tend to be hierarchical, and capable of making decisions quickly, aboriginal groups are generally organized in a more egalitarian manner, and may require more time to reach a consensus decision. This is not always the case — recent exposures of conflict within aboriginal communities between band councils and their memberships indicate that not all representation is direct and accountable. There may also be differing abilities within groups to ratify, endorse or commit to a proposition. Individuals who negotiate with a corporation are generally responsible to an entire group of people. If aboriginal leaders fail continually to report back to their community, or are pushed to make decisions too quickly, they may end up losing the support of their community.

While the political or historical context of a community may seem peripheral to the concerns [of the] corporation, such issues usually need to be understood. For the Lubicon Cree, the historical context played a major part in their distrust of Unocal, and in shaping their view of development. Here, as elsewhere in Canada, even though sovereignty and treaty claims may be issues that no corporation can make decisions on, by discussing these issues, the company comes to understand the position, perspective, and needs of the aboriginal group.

Within corporate circles there is much curiosity about aboriginal culture. Many cross-cultural seminars focus on the obvious differences in behaviour and decision-making structures between corporations and aboriginal groups, or on general aspects of aboriginal culture. While these are important, companies should not just reflect on how aboriginals are different and how to successfully deal with that difference. Cross-cultural training should reflect both on individual biases and the pervasive influence of corporate culture. Recalled one corporate respondent:

> The first thing that I had to learn was incredible patience. Because my training suggests that we are there to get a job done, and the whole value system or business mindset of a company is — if we don't drill there — we call it reduced cycle time — we want to drill there as quickly as possible. We didn't do all that work to wait ten years to find out if there is gas there. We want to build a pipeline and we want to sell it.

To establish a relationship, industry has to be willing to change the way they think and operate on aboriginal territory. While education and understanding will go a long way towards bridging the gap, there remains uneasiness and distrust of current approaches towards cultural or sensitivity training.

CAUTIONS

There may be pitfalls in collaborative processes, such as loss of power, co-optation, or simply issues that need to be public, but are not. Many corporations in Canada are now negotiating private agreements with first nations in the hope of avoiding conflict and the expense of public hearings. But conflict may be necessary sometimes. Regulators must uphold the democratic right of private individuals and advocacy organizations to scrutinize projects that affect community and environmental health. M'Gonigle notes the loss of power that environmentalists in British Columbia have experienced in the CORE/Code/Forest Renewal processes. Environmental groups find themselves with much reduced influence, where "they can be treated as just another interest to be 'managed'."[10] This same loss of power may be a reality for aboriginal groups. And in particular, isolation, both geographically and politically, can affect their ability to meet their own needs, or protect their lands.

FUTURE OF RISK COMMUNICATION

Other aspects that may need to be negotiated include support for education, community development, or aboriginal business development. In the future, an effective risk communication process could provide an opportunity for aboriginal people to advise on where an energy resource development will be located, how it will be developed, and what kind of benefit the community can derive from it. If these issues are negotiated, the foundations can be laid to communicate major development decisions. A framework can be established to negotiate transfer of information and understanding in both directions. With that foundation, the sincere calls for dialogue espoused in the risk communication literature can finally be implemented.

But inevitably, issues of sovereignty aside, the question must be posed: how far should those seeking development go to please a minority? While there is no absolute answer, the question will certainly arise in every community and corporation. The appropriate balance can be found only through deliberation. However, we endorse the proposal of Susskind and Field, that a line be:

> drawn liberally to ensure that almost all parties in a host community perceive themselves as better off. Furthermore, these hard decisions must be made with, not for, the citizens in each community.[11]

An inability to honour this guideline suggests serious flaws in a development proposal. The framework already exists to manage difficult decisions; parties with competing agendas can come together and move from disagreement to consensus. The quasijudicial and judicial processes may become less burdened if collaborative approaches are adopted. However, arbitration processes will remain necessary for many disputes.

The power and economic disparities apparent between aboriginal communities and corporations is still wide in Alberta, and the danger of co-optation is real.

The literature on dispute resolution gives us little reason to believe that the stronger nation is going to exert the patience or consideration to "learn" or "share" without the force of law, the threat of litigation, or the presence of a mutually recognized authority.[12]

However, collaborative processes hold promise for cases involving a community with strong and able leaders who can voice the appropriate community concerns, and a corporation that is willing to begin working in a long-term and participatory fashion.

Collaborative processes can provide a forum for diverse stakeholders to express their interests, needs and concerns in a manner that can be implemented as public policy. They provide an organized structure that integrates environmental, cultural, political and economic elements in negotiated agreements in order to resolve complex development decisions. Such agreements, because they have the support of affected parties, have a better chance of being implemented, and thereby creating meaningful environmental, cultural and economic gains.[13]

NOTES

1. This article is based on Virginia Gibson's MA thesis, Resources, Conflict and Culture: The Sour Gas Plant Dispute Between Unocal Canada and the Lubicon Cree Nation (Edmonton: Department of Anthropology, University of Alberta, 1996). The thesis is available as a research report from the contact author. The research involved public hearing transcript review, interviews, and focus groups with the regulatory board, oil and gas corporations, and select members of the Lubicon Cree Nation and their supporters. To protect the anonymity of sources, individuals quoted in this article are not named, and are only referred to by their corporate or community affiliation.
2. Lubicon Settlement Commission of Review: Final Report (Edmonton: Government of Alberta, 1993), p. 13.
3. Steve Hrudey, Understanding and Managing Environmental Risk (Calgary, Alberta: Proceeding of Canadian Bar Association, National Environmental Law Section, Oct. 20, 1994); and Ann Fisher, "Risk Communication Challenges," Risk Analysis, 11:2 (1991), pp. 173–79.
4. V. Covello, P. Sandman, and P. Slovic, Risk Communication, Risk Statistics, and Risk Comparisons: A Manual for Plant Managers (Washington, DC: Chemical Manufacturer Association, 1988).
5. Fisher, "Perspectives" [note 2]; [Lawrence Susskind] and Patrick Field, Dealing with an Angry Public: The Mutual Gains Approach to Resolving Disputes (New York: The Free Press, 1996); Maria Pavlova, "Superfund and One Community Program," American Journal of Industrial Medicine, 23:10 (1993), pp. 183–89; and Roger Kasperson, "Six Propositions on Public Participation and Their Relevance for Risk Communication," Risk Analysis, 6:3 (1986), pp. 275–81.
6. Peter Usher, et al., Communicating About Contaminants in Country Food: The Experience in Aboriginal Communities (Ottawa: Inuit Tapirisat of Canada, 1995).
7. Helen Ross, "Aboriginal Australians' Cultural Norms for Negotiating Natural Resources," Cultural Survival Quarterly, 19:3 (1995), pp. 33–39.
8. As Peter Mulhivill and Peter Jacobs note, in "order for northern development to be sustainable, projects that originate in the South must take into account the different history, periodicity, culture and rhythms of the North." "Towards New South/North Development Strategies in Canada," Alternatives, 18:2 (1991), p. 38. Their work speaks to the importance of context, of the need to be flexible and open-minded in any exchange of information. However, they provide no model for accommodating the critical differences between southern urban proponents and northern residents.
9. For example, in their decision on the Unocal sour gas plant, the EUC recommended that Unocal "initiate and maintain a meaningful dialogue with the native community that is sensitive to their culture and understanding of technical matters. Unocal has a responsibility as a long-term resident in the area to conduct its affairs with every concern for its neighbours." Energy and Utilities Board, Decision D 95-4: Proceeding Regarding an Approved Sour Gas Plant, Unocal Canada Management Ltd., Slave Field (Lubicon Lake Area) (Calgary: Energy Resources Conservation Board, 1995), p. 27.
10. Michael M'Gonigle, "Behind the Green Curtain," Alternatives, 23:4 (1997), pp. 16–21.
11. Susskind and Field, Dealing [note 4].
12. Laura Nader, "Civilization and Its Negotiations," in Understanding Disputes: The Politics of Argument, Pat Caplan, ed. (Oxford: Berg Publishers, 1995), p. 53.
13. This work was supported by funding for the Eco-Research Chair in Environmental Risk Management provided by the Tri-Council Secretariat representing the Medical Research, the Natural Sciences and Engineering Research and the Social Sciences and Humanities Research Councils of Canada; the Alberta Heritage Foundation for Medical Research; Alberta Environmental Protection; Alberta Health; the City of Edmonton; Syncrude Canada Ltd. and the Alberta Energy and Utilities Board.

CHAPTER 9

Mining

(a) The Nasty Game: How Environmental Assessment Is Failing Aboriginal Communities in Canada's North[†]

Susan Wismer

In the small northern communities surrounding Great Slave Lake, there is much talk of diamonds. The diamonds are located under the ground at Lac de Gras, a few hundred kilometres north. But the area around Lac de Gras is also within the traditional hunting and trapping territories of aboriginal people from the area around Slave Lake and further north. The Dogrib Nation, the Yellowknives Dene First Nation, Metis people and Inuit from Kitikmeot all claim overlapping rights and interests in the area. As well, the diamond area is at the heart of the migration route of the Bathurst caribou herd.

Australia's largest corporation, Broken Hill Proprietary Company Limited (BHP), is proposing to mine the diamonds in an operation that is expected to extract $12 billion worth of diamonds over a 25-year period, resulting in seven billion dollars in profits and $2.5 billion in revenues paid to federal and territorial governments. In the process, it will drain six lakes, use another lake as a tailings dump and become the Northwest Territories' largest single industrial employer.

A beautiful jewel is a delight and a luxury, but not a necessity. A good and happy life can be lived without the gem diamonds lying underneath Lac de Gras.

[†] Reproduced from *Alternatives Journal: Environmental thought, policy and action* 22(4) (1996): 10–17. Annual subscriptions $25.00 (plus GST) from Alternatives Journal, Faculty of Environmental Studies, University of Waterloo, Waterloo, Ontario N3L 3G1. Web site: <www.alternativesjournal.ca>. Reproduced with permission of the author.

For people living in the Slave Lake communities, however, caribou are another matter. The good life cannot be lived without them. People eat them. People use their skins. People understand the world and who they are by living in relationship with them and the land that supports them. The importance of wildlife and of the land which supports it is clear and well-known. Centuries of life on the land have created a rich store of traditional knowledge about its care and well-being.

Unfortunately, traditional knowledge has very few stories to tell about the desirability of diamonds and diamond mining. Although mining is a very old activity in human terms, it has not been a traditional activity during the 9000 known years of aboriginal habitation in Canada's Northwest Territories. Mineral development has been going on in Canada's North for about 100 years. During the course of this century, some aboriginal people have found work that suited them — particularly in exploration and prospecting. The roads and infrastructure that come with mining have been a mixed blessing, because of the people, traffic, pollution and external influences that come with them, but have been of some benefit to small communities close to routes in and out of mine sites. In general, however, most aboriginal experience with mining has been negative.[1]

In a series of recent environmental assessment hearings, many aboriginal participants said that they are not against mineral development — as long as it does not interfere with the environment, the land and the animals. It is very difficult for people in communities to know whether or not the diamond mine can make a positive contribution to their lives. Certainly, they said, the income that may come from jobs, small business development or royalty and taxation arrangements made through yet-to-be negotiated impact and benefit agreements will be welcome. Education and training possibilities also exist, and would be welcomed.

In one presentation after another, however, people said that these things will not be useful to them unless they have a strong say in the pace, scale and timing of resource development, and in how benefits are distributed. For example, the people of Lutsel K'e, a Chipewyan Dene community at the southeast end of Great Slave Lake, told the environmental assessment panel:

> Since time immemorial, the Lutsel K'e First Nation has lived in the Akaitcho Territory, which encompasses the lands where the NWT Diamond mine is to be built. We have survived as a distinct culture and nation by wisely using the Gifts of the Creator on this land: the animals, fish and plants. To this day, we continue to depend on the land for our physical and cultural survival. The Lutsel K'e First Nation will strenuously oppose any development that jeopardizes our culture and livelihood.
>
> Nevertheless, we believe that orderly, planned and environmentally responsible mineral development can be compatible with our traditional culture and economy. Further, we are willing to share the mineral wealth of our land with visitors, provided that they too are willing to share with us through royalties, preferential contracting, adequate training and guaranteed jobs....[2]

WHAT THE COMMUNITIES NEED

Sustainable communities are healthy communities. The foundations of community lie in a clearly defined and strongly interwoven understanding of identity, ethics and place. Identity is about knowing and understanding culture and history. Ethics is about what is important and why — about values. Place is about knowing where home is, geographically and spiritually, and about the sense of shared destiny with others that comes with that knowledge. In order to make a contribution to community health, economic activities should strengthen these foundations. Economic "development" that undermines cultural identity, compromises values, or fails to preserve or enhance environmental quality is neither sustainable nor healthy.

Subsistence activities provide aboriginal people with identity, ethics and a sense of place. These activities include hunting, trapping, fishing, harvesting, the processing of food, the preparation of hides, and the construction and decoration of clothing for ceremonial and [everyday] purposes. They provide a substantial amount of food and clothing for domestic use.[3] This informal economic activity is not counted in standard economic measures, since it is not monetarized, but is distributed on the basis of kinship, social reciprocity or bartering arrangements. Up to 40 percent of food consumed is "country food", acquired through subsistence activities.[4]

Subsistence activities also provide some cash income. They do not very often, however, provide adequate cash income to support family life. Frequently, subsistence activities require financial support from other forms of economic activity. Rifles, ammunition, snow machines, fuel, traps and other equipment all cost money. The apparently marginal economic viability of aboriginal subsistence activity has been seriously misunderstood in the past and, in some quarters, continues to be. The result of this misunderstanding has been pressure on aboriginal people to give up subsistence activities in order to pursue jobs in the waged economy.[5]

Despite their marginal profitability — and indeed their need for subsidies at certain times — subsistence activities are the hub around which other economic activities move in small northern communities. In a perpetually cash-strapped economic situation, they play a critical role in reducing other financial requirements, not only for food and clothing, but also for services. A strong subsistence sector reduces significantly the costs associated with social programmes, health care and remedial education programmes in language, culture and tradition, which become necessary when people are no longer passing traditional knowledge on to one another as part of everyday community and family life.[6]

In addition to their role in avoiding costs, subsistence activities make a key economic contribution by stabilizing the fluctuations associated with the boom and bust nature of northern economic life. They make up in self-reliance and reliability for what they lack in profit margins. Resource developments, business activities and government programmes come and go, based on factors over which small northern communities have very little control. Subsistence activities are community-based and can be pursued in various forms as long as the land and the wildlife are available and in a good state of health.

Sustainability for northern aboriginal communities requires a mixed economy, in which wage and income-based activity is combined with informal, subsistence activity in order to meet family and community needs.[7] In a mixed economy, the most desirable waged jobs are locally based, are flexible or seasonal with respect to allocation of paid working hours, and build upon or complement the skill and knowledge base used in subsistence activities. Small businesses find favour from this point of view, especially if they provide services, equipment or food and fuel requirements to community members; tourism that does not disrupt local human or natural ecologies; and locally based public services in areas such as education and health care. Some jobs in renewable resource sectors such as forestry and fishing

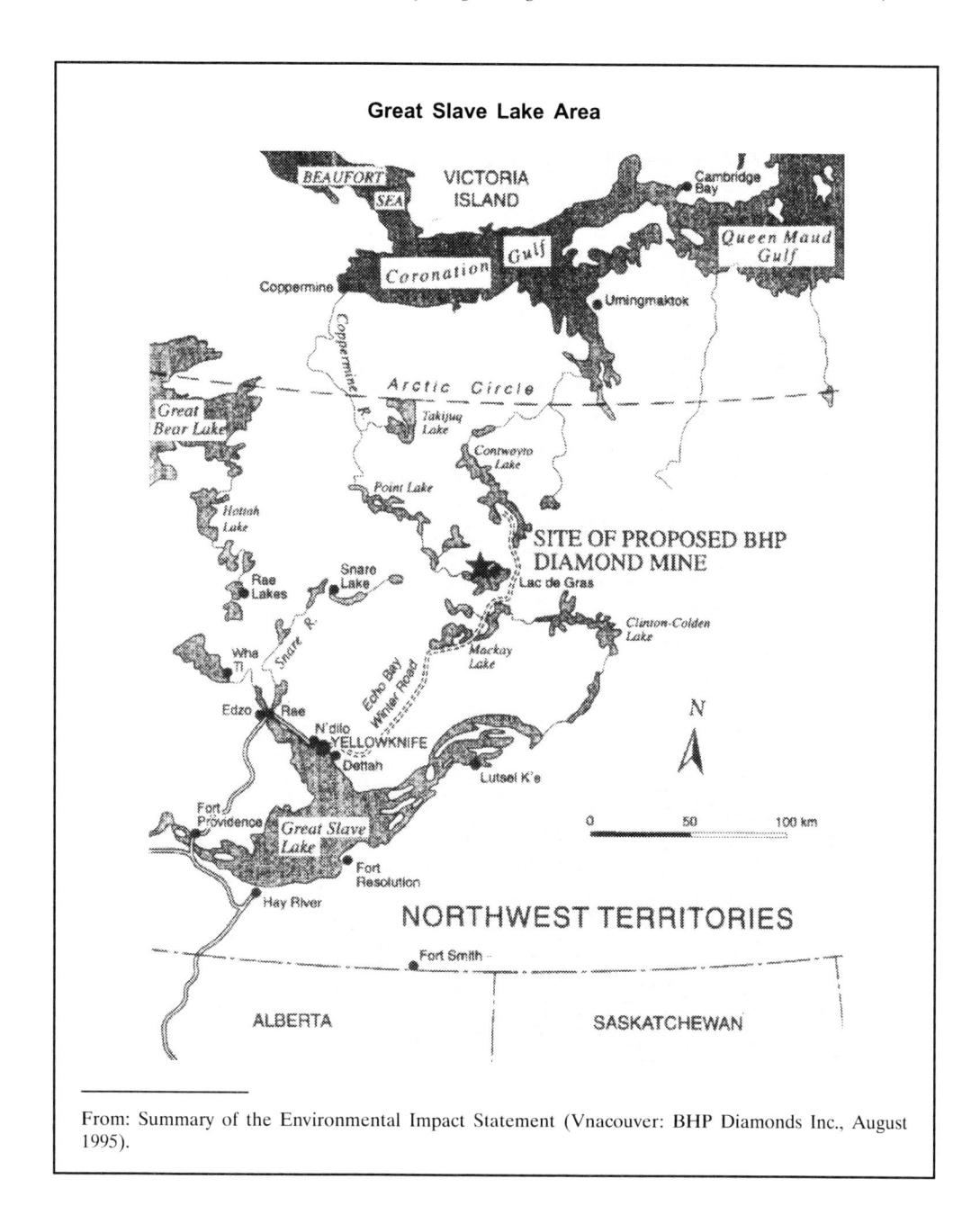

(a) How environmental assessment is failing aboriginal communities in Canada's North / **415**

Great Slave Lake Area

From: Summary of the Environmental Impact Statement (Vnacouver: BHP Diamonds Inc., August 1995).

and in community administration and management also serve the mixed economy. In the non-renewable resource area, exploration work can be compatible with subsistence activities.

Experience with jobs in the mines themselves has been less favourable. The nature of the work, its scheduling into shifts that are often at least two weeks in length, the distance of mine sites from home communities, and the need for a consistent and reliable work-force that does not take time off on a seasonal basis, creates a situation in which the benefits of employment in the mines are often offset by the costs of social and family disruption and loss of opportunities to participate adequately in community life.[8]

Wage-based activity that causes people to lose their capacity to participate in subsistence activities will not be consistent with sustainable development. This does not mean that everyone has to be participating in subsistence activities all the time. But at the community level, the store of traditional knowledge and the capacity of community members — both young and old — to participate, or to learn to participate, in subsistence activities as might be necessary or desired, must not be impaired or diminished as a result of other forms of economic activity.

A similarly negative view is taken of activities that offer wage benefits but threaten to damage the environment upon which subsistence activities rely. This is clear in the submission of the Yellowknives Dene to the environmental assessment panel:

> Our Elders feel that neither government nor mining people really listen to our concerns or want to do anything about them. We have raised many concerns, for instance, about the fuel oil, arsenic and cyanide hauled on winter roads that cross our most spiritually important lands, our current hunting grounds. Our concerns increase as more and more mining companies announce their intention to use the winter road. Yes, companies offer to pay compensation for damaging the waters and the land. But money is no substitute for this land that we love.
>
> We have concerns that our lands will suffer long-term damage, while the economic benefits from the mines will be short term....[9]

ASSESSMENT FAILS TO DELIVER

The BHP diamond mine is the first of several major mineral developments that are proposed or are currently in development in Canada's North. In the business pages of Canada's papers, news about the potential of diamond mining in the Northwest Territories competes for space with speculation about the value of the Voisey's Bay nickel find in Labrador. Behind these multibillion dollar developments others are following, including proposals for up to six new mines in the region where the BHP mine site is located.

When the Department of Indian and Northern Affairs made the referral that resulted in the selection of a federally appointed panel to carry out an environmental assessment review, many people were glad to have the opportunity to examine and comment on the potential impacts of the BHP project before it proceeded. Results of the BHP review are likely to have an impact on decision making for other mineral development projects across the North.

As part of the review, community hearings were held in January and February 1996 in the smaller communities identified as likely to be affected by the mine, as well as in Yellowknife, which was the central venue. Prior to the hearings, people in the affected communities were involved in several months of preparation, which included a requirement to review close to 1000 pages of material in connection with the Environmental Impact Statement (EIS) prepared by BHP.

Preparation was not easy. The EIS became available at a time when many people were out of communities or were very busy. Resources provided were very lim-

> **A Chronology of the BHP Diamond Mining Environmental Assessment**
>
> 1989 — Diamonds are found at Lac de Gras.
>
> 1990 — Broken Hills Proprietary (BHP) of Australia signs a deal to develop North America's first diamond mine.
>
> 1994 — Federal Minister of the Environment, in response to concerns over potential impact of the proposed mine on northern ecosystems and human communities, decides to require a full review of the project, under the old *Environmental Assessment Review Process Guidelines Order*, rather than the soon-to-be-proclaimed *Canadian Envrionmental Assessment Act*.
>
> December 1994 — BHP Diamonds Project Environmental Assessment Panel is appointed
>
> February 1995 — *Canadian Environmental Assessment Act* is proclaimed, but does not apply to BHP hearings. Scoping hearings are held in seven communities to consider what concerns should be addressed by the Panel.
>
> May 1995 — Panel issues *Guidelines for Preparation of the Environmental Impact Statement* (EIS).
>
> July 1995 — BHP submits eight-volume EIS less than two months after the *Guidelines* were issued.
>
> October 1995 — Panel concludes that EIS is sufficient, despite concerns expressed by intervenor groups regarding issues including corporate record, treatment of traditional knowledge, monitoring, mitigation, environmental provisions, community impacts, employment policies. Aboriginal groups state that any decision to go ahead will be a contravention of ongoing land claims and treaty entitlement negotiations which include the mine site.
>
> January 1996 — Hearings take place. Aboriginal communities state in numerous presentations that they are not against mineral development *per se*, as long as they have adequate control over its timing, pace and approach to developments and over distribution of benefits. They state that the federal government is failing to uphold its fiduciary obligations to aboriginal people by proposing to allow the BHP development to go ahead on land that has not been ceded for these uses through land claims or treaty negotiation processes.
>
> February 1996 — Hearings are completed. Formal objections submitted by BHP and by other hearing participants, claiming that the hearing process had been neither fair nor adequately thorough. Panel retires to write its report.
>
> June 1996 — Panel recommends approval. World Wildlife Fund calls for judicial review based on inadequate consideration for protected areas. Other intervenors criticize handling of issues related to land claims, traditional knowledge and cumulative impacts. Federal officials acknowledge that the review was affected by tight timelines, narrow scope and limited funding.
>
> Prepared by Susan Wismer and Brenda Parlee, a master's student in Environment and Resource Studies at the University of Waterloo

ited and did not allow for adequate translation and interpretation of the EIS or for preparation of detailed arguments and positions. Since the full EIS was available in English only and its language was frequently technical, preparatory discussions and workshops were necessary in communities where English is not a first language in order to prepare a response for the hearings even though no resources had been allocated initially for this purpose.[10]

Early in April, after the conclusion of the hearings and prior to the announcement of the panel's June decision, the Canadian Arctic Resources Committee (CARC) organized a workshop that brought together aboriginal people from across Canada's North to discuss together their experiences with mineral development. At the workshop, Innu people from Labrador, preparing for the impending mine development in Voisey's Bay met with people from the Northwest Territories who had just been through the BHP review.

The Innu were exhausted and frustrated after a nine-year struggle through environmental assessment and appeals in an ultimately fruitless effort to eliminate low-level military flights over their hunting grounds. Understandably, they found the prospect of another major development and another major environmental assessment more than a little daunting. What advice, they wondered, did the people who had just been through the BHP review have for them? The question elicited a variety of thoughtful responses regarding the costs and benefits of participating in environmental assessment. Around the table, however, heads nodded everywhere when one participant said, "It's a game. It's a nasty game."

This analysis is a far cry from the vision of environmental assessment on which the federal Environmental Assessment Review Process Guidelines Order and the subsequent Canadian Environmental Assessment Act have been based. Environmental assessment in Canada was created to ensure that environmental concerns were adequately considered in decision making. Twenty years ago, the Berger Inquiry established standards for how that consideration should take place in Canada's North and elsewhere, and they have remained ever since.

Berger established clearly that "environment" includes human social and cultural concerns and cannot be considered adequately without them; that all those affected by the proposal have a right to a fair hearing and to have their concerns included in decision making; and that environmental assessment must be a transparent and accessible process in which traditional knowledge and Western science join forces to produce the best possible information base for decision making. He also made it clear that none of this could be accomplished without adequate time for a thorough review.[11]

Experience with environmental assessment in Canada and elsewhere over the past two decades has confirmed that adequate attention to equity issues is essential. Environmental equity — ensuring that flora, fauna and the land, air and water which support them have representation at the decision-making table — is generally understood as fundamental to the purposes of environmental assessment. Human equity concerns are equally important to effective, fair and efficient environmental assessment, but their role and importance has not historically been recognized. Despite some movement forward, this continues to be the case. The recently proclaimed Canadian Environmental Assessment Act requires assessment of only those human effects that result from impacts on the natural environment, thereby leaving out all direct impacts on human communities. Beyond its substantive devaluation of human community concerns, the act also has serious weaknesses in its procedures and processes with respect to human equity.[12]

Good environmental assessment is not possible without adequate attention to three major dimensions of human equity:

- Political equity ensures that those who will be affected have commensurate influence in decision making. It provides the basis for a concern with adequate community participation and an increasing interest in negotiation and other forms of decision making, creating new possibilities beyond the conflict-based win-lose options inherent in quasi-judicial hearing processes.
- Economic equity ensures that those who create problems bear the costs of solving them and that benefits are fairly distributed. It has generated increasing levels of interest in monitoring, enforcement of mitigation requirements and, in the case of resource development projects, longer term biophysical and socio-economic decommissioning and site reclamation issues.
- Intergenerational equity ensures that the quality of life of future generations is not compromised by decisions made today. It has stimulated interest in cumulative effects. In turn, it has become apparent that traditional knowledge is essential to adequate cumulative effects assessment in the North. Western scientific knowledge is too limited to provide the depth and breadth of data necessary, whereas traditional knowledge provides a reliable source of locally specific intergenerational information.[13]

In the 70s, many people saw the Berger Inquiry as the beginning of an era in which environmental assessment could be used to balance out the inequities inherent in large-scale resource development projects, ensure accountability and inject a suitable tone of precaution into decision making. In the years since then, the importance of community-level participation, negotiation, monitoring, reclamation, cumulative effects and effective consideration of traditional knowledge have been affirmed.[14] Experience with the federal review process suggests, however, the Berger Inquiry may have been the high point of an era, rather than its beginning.

Participants at the CARC workshop came up with a long list of concerns about the process and content of the BHP review. In the opinion of Kevin O'Reilly, a CARC staff member based in Yellowknife, the review was "neither rigorous nor procedurally fair."[15] Communities were not adequately included, in part because the panel was operating with very limited time and financial resources. Among the sections of the EIS most severely criticized were those that deal with monitoring, site reclamation and traditional knowledge.[16]

Experience to date with the BHP review raises serious questions about the state of environmental assessment in Canada. As a regulatory and planning mechanism designed to ensure fair, effective and efficient decision making, it does not seem to be working. At the CARC workshop, the general consensus was that environmental assessment is expensive, time consuming and wearing for all concerned. In the case of BHP, people correctly predicted that the panel's recommendation would be that the mine should go ahead and that its report would not adequately address their concerns and interests.[17] It is tempting to conclude that participation in the exercise of environmental assessment is simply not worthwhile.

ASSESSMENTS COULD SERVE NORTHERN COMMUNITIES

In northern aboriginal communities, the economy is a wheel with many spokes. Families gather together the goods and services they require through a combination of waged and unwaged pursuits, which vary according to individual, season and opportunities. The hub of the wheel, the stable centre, is subsistence activities carried out on the land.

Aboriginal claims to the role of stewards of the northern landscape will not disappear. Aboriginal people will continue to assert that a fair measure of control over land-use planning and development in their traditional territories is essential to successfully carrying out their role. Their unshakeable belief is that the health and sustainability of their communities will always be based on a relationship with their surroundings, which is constructed in large part through subsistence activities. Land claims and treaty entitlement negotiations with the federal government are central to current strategies for securing formal recognition and the right to pursue healthy and sustainable livelihoods.[18]

It is not clear whether mineral development can be a spoke in the mixed economy wheel, which has subsistence at its hub, and people in the Slave Lake communities know very little more after the BHP review than they did before it. The panel did not address this question. Even if it had, the community-directed baseline traditional knowledge studies, which would be necessary to begin to construct an answer, have not taken place.[19] The procedures for community-based monitoring of social, cultural and ecological conditions, which would be necessary for determining if, when and how mining can contribute to community sustainability and for keeping track of cumulative effects, have yet to be developed. Regulatory and legislative mechanisms for ensuring that relevant information is put to good use are also lacking.

The BHP review has failed the people whose homelands take in the area around Lac de Gras, just as environmental assessment generally is failing Aboriginal people all across Canada. Unless and until environmental assessment can begin to pick up where it appears to have left off after the Berger Inquiry and start to make a genuine contribution to addressing the complexities of northern development, [Aboriginal] people will be forced to pursue other routes for asserting their need to act as the legitimate stewards of their territories.

Unfortunately, their choices are limited. Land claims processes are preferred, but are lengthy and expensive to negotiate and subject to interpretation even once in place. Impact and Benefits Agreements negotiated separately between individual communities and corporations are difficult for both parties to enforce outside of a completed land claims agreement. Litigation seems to be most effective as an expensive delaying tactic, buying time, but seldom providing a forum for effective negotiation of agreements. Protest and disruption also buy time and can result in a shift in positions, but are potentially dangerous and destructive for all concerned and, in the aftermath, have serious public relations implications.

Can mining activity make a contribution to the longer-term health and sustainability of communities? This is a question for all Canadians, not just the northern aboriginal peoples who see themselves as stewards of their traditional territories. Aboriginal or not, all Canadians want to live their lives in healthy, sustainable communities. Common sense says that, anywhere in Canada, economic activities should be constructed in ways that move communities toward, rather than away from, health and sustainability.

Environmental assessment can and should be an excellent process for determining whether or not the outcomes of economic development are likely to be positive or negative for communities and for ensuring that environmental and human equity concerns provide the ethical base for decision making about what happens and when. The conditions for creating good environmental assessment have been well-known for over 20 years and are feasible: adequate time for review, careful and thorough information gathering and analysis, which gives full value to traditional knowledge, inclusive and accessible procedures for public participation, and clearly defined strategies for monitoring of impacts and enforcement of recommendations.

Alternative routes to equitable decision making are few and carry with them significant costs and penalties, not just for aboriginal people in the North, but for all Canadians. By allowing environmental assessment to fail, we not only fail to acknowledge the ethics, identity and place of the people and ecosystems of the North, we fail ourselves.

NOTES

1. See Lutsel K'e First Nation, "Lutsel K'e First Nation Submission to the NWT Diamonds Project Federal Environmental Assessment Review Panel" (submitted to the BHP Diamonds Project Panel, February 1996); Natural Resources Canada, Sustainable Development and Minerals and Metals: An Issue Paper (Ottawa: Natural Resources Canada, September 1995); Al Gedicks, The New Resource Wars: Native and Environmental Struggles against Mutli-National Corporations (Boston: South End Press, 1993); Oran Young, Arctic Politics: Conflict and Cooperation in the Circumpolar North (Hanover, New Hampshire: University Press of New England, 1992); David Ross and Peter Usher, From the Roots Up: Economic Development as if Community Mattered (Cronton-on-Hudson, New York: Bootstrap Press, 1986), pp. 141–54; and Michael Asch, "The Dene Economy," Dene Nation: the Colony Within, Mel Watkins, ed. (Toronto: University of Toronto Press, 1977), pp. 47–61.
2. "Lutsel K'e First Nation Submission" [note 1], p.1.
3. BHP/Diamet, NWT Diamonds Project: Summary of Environmental Impact Study (Vancouver: BHP Diamonds Inc., 1995); Young, Arctic Politics [note 1]; Ross and Usher, From the Roots Up [note 1], pp. 78–81.
4. Personal communication, participant (Ottawa: Canadian Arctic Resources Committee Workshop on Aboriginal Communities and Mining in Northern Canada, April, 1996).
5. See Jack Stabler and Eric Howe, "Native Participation in Northern Development: The Impending Crisis in the NWT," Canadian Public Policy XVI:3 (1990), pp. 262–83; and Intergovernmental Working Group on the Mineral Industry, Report on Native Participation in Mining: Phase I (Ottawa: Department of Indian Affairs and Northern Development (DIAND), 1990).
6. Milton Freeman, "Environment, Society and Health: Quality of Life Issues in the Contemporary North," Arctic Medical Research, 47:suppl. 1 (1988), pp. 54–59.
7. See Yellowknives Dene First Nation, "Fact Sheet # 10: Our Position on Development," (submitted to the BHP Diamonds Project Panel, February 1996); Claudia Notzke, Aboriginal People and Natural Resources in Canada (North York: Captus Press, 1994); and Frances Abele, Gathering Strength (Calgary: Arctic Institute, 1989).
8. Personal communication, various participants (Ottawa: CARC Workshop on Aboriginal Communities and Mining in Northern Canada, April 1996).
9. Yellowknives Dene First Nation, "Fact Sheet #10" [note 7].
10. The Government of the Northwest Territories eventually provided funding for the workshops.
11. Justice Thomas Berger, Northern Frontier, Northern Homeland: The Report of the Mackenzie Valley Pipeline Inquiry, Volume 1 (Ottawa: DIAND, 1977).

12. See Robert Gibson, "The New Canadian Environmental Assessment Act: Possible Responses to Its Main Deficiencies," Journal of Environmental Law and Practice, 2:3 (July 1992), pp. 223–55.
13. See Robbie Keith, "Aboriginal Communities and Mining in Northern Canada," Northern Perspectives, 23:3-4 (Fall-Winter 1996), pp. 2–8; and Jackie Wolfe, Indigenous and Western Knowledge and Resource Management (Guelph: University School of Rural Planning and Development, 1992).
14. See, for example, L.G. Smith, Impact Assessment and Sustainable Resource Management (Harlow, Essex: Longman Group, UK Ltd., 1993).
15. Kevin O'Reilly (Ottawa: CARC workshop, April 1996).
16. See Kevin O'Reilly, "A Critique of the Environmental Review of the BHP Diamonds Project," Northern Perspectives, (forthcoming, 1996); and Susan Wismer, "Analysis and Commentary: Sociocultural Concerns and Considerations" (submitted to the BHP Diamonds Project Panel, February 1996).
17. Canadian Environmental Assessment Agency, NWT Diamonds Project (Ottawa: Supply and Services, June 1996); and Doug Saunders, "Diamond-mine scrutiny called shoddy," Globe and Mail. (Toronto: June 18, 1996), p. A8.
18. See Thomas Berger, A Long and Terrible Shadow (Vancouver: Douglas and McIntyre, 1991); and Hon. A.C. Hamilton, A New Partnership (Ottawa: DIAND, 1995).
19. The West Katikmeot Salve Study is a major regional study jointly sponsored by the federal government, GNWT and private partners. Initiated in 1994, it was designed to generate baseline data in the region where BHP will operate. The study has been slow in getting off the ground and, at this writing (April 1996), it is unclear whether or not it will be able to meet its objectives.

(b) Northern Gems: Natives Battle a Proposed $12-billion Diamond Mine[†]

Tom Fennell

It might seem improbable that a lone voice from a tropical nation could block development of a massive diamond mine in Canada's frozen North. But Alex Maun, a soft-spoken businessman from Papua New Guinea, was trying to do just that in Yellowknife last week. The occasion was a federal environmental review hearing on a proposal by Australia's largest corporation, Broken Hill Proprietary Co. Ltd. (BHP), to mine more than $12 billion worth of diamonds at Lac de Gras, 310 km northeast of Yellowknife. Unfortunately for BHP, the proposed mine site is located on the traditional lands of the Dene, and as part of their strategy to wring concessions from the Australians, they invited Maun to explain how waste from a BHP copper mine has poisoned a river in Papua New Guinea. When Maun spoke, natives at the hearing listened intently-even those who support the project because of its potential to create jobs. "We can't drink the water," Maun said. "The river is dead."

BHP officials disputed every allegation Maun made, but their lawyers' attempts to delay Maun's testimony only underscored what is at stake in Yellowknife. The

---

[†] From Maclean's 109(10) (March 4, 1996): 54–55. Reproduced with permission of the publisher.

(b) Northern gems: Natives battle a proposed $112-billion diamond mine

proposed mine contains an estimated 90 million carats, one of the largest and richest diamond finds in history. After factoring in the cost of building the isolated mine and extracting the gems, analysts say it will still generate a profit of more than $7 billion over the mine's 25-year lifespan. Moreover, the federal review will also influence the fate of several other proposed mines in the area, which together contain another $30 billion in diamonds. London-based RTZ Corp., the world's largest mining company, is expected to start building a mine near Lac de Gras in 1999, and other, smaller finds close to both properties are also laden with diamonds. Said John Hainey, an analyst with Eagle & Partners Inc., a Toronto-based research firm: "The diamonds they have found rank right up there in value with the very best in South Africa and Russia."

The sparkling find in the windswept tundra was the product of one man's determined search. For nearly 10 years Kelowna, B.C., geologist Chuck Fipke braved hostile weather and voracious mosquitoes to prove his long-held theory: that diamonds would be found in rock formations near Lac de Gras. Fipke finally discovered his diamonds by accident as he was flying over the area in April, 1990. Just hours before he was set to abandon his search, he spotted an outcropping of soft volcanic rock, known as kimberlite, near the lake. That evening, he chipped away at the rock and revealed its treasure. Hundreds of prospectors soon swarmed over the Barrens. Drill crews worked around the clock, and a lucky few produced core samples that contained the gems. Four months later, Fipke sold 29 percent of his find to BHP. Fipke urged the panel last week to approve the mine. "If we have a delay," he warned, "it could cause BHP to postpone the project."

Before diamonds from the Northwest Territories go on sale in jewelry shops around the world, BHP faces a daunting task. The company must convince the environmental panel in Yellowknife that it can mine the diamonds without causing major damage to the land or wildlife in the area. Native leaders are split on whether the mine can be developed safely, but on one point they agree: all want a share of the treasure as part of a comprehensive land claims agreement. And so the Australians are caught up in a complex political tussle involving the Yellowknives Dene, the Dogrib Dene and the Canadian government. Bill Erasmus, Grand Chief of the Dene nation, from which the Dogrib have withdrawn, told BHP officials at the hearing that they were simply pawns in the land-claims dispute. "I know you want the diamonds, and we are the people that can stop you," Erasmus warned. "We are not here for window dressing."

The panel's finding is due in June, although either side could then ask for a judicial review. A lawyer for BHP has already argued that it was "unfair" to allow Maun to address the hearing because events in New Guinea have no bearing on the company's intentions in Canada. Erasmus countered by reminding panel chairman Letha MacLachlan that Canadian courts recognize the Dene's rights to the land. He promised to take legal action to stop the project from proceeding before the land claim is settled.

That leaves BHP in an awkward position. Project manager Jim Excell told *Maclean's* that while the company does not dispute the Dene's claim, the issue is between aboriginal peoples and the government. BHP, meanwhile, is determined to bring the mine into production on schedule in 1998, creating 650 jobs. "The greatest impact of the Northwest Territories diamonds project is expected to be socio-

BHP'S Diamond Mine

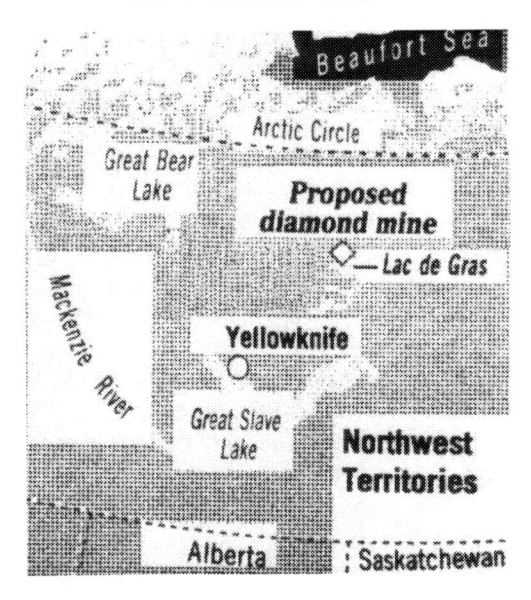

- Discovered: 1990, by Vancouver geologist Chuck Fipke
- Planned start of production: 1998
- Mine lifespan: 25 years
- Estimated vaulue of diamonds: $12 billion

economic," said Karen Azinger, BHP's manager of external affairs. "It is expected to reduce the overall unemployment rate in the Northwest Territories by three percent."

Of the two nations, the Dogrib, who live closest to the mine site, are most supportive of BHP's plan. Dogrib Grand Chief Joe Rabesca has already tried to negotiate a separate agreement with BHP that would create jobs for his people and give them a say in how the mine is developed. But the slow pace of talks prompted Rabesca to withdraw his support for the mine on the first day of public hearings. "I did everything in my power so we could get a benefits agreement," Rabesca told a recent gathering at the Dene village Wha Ti. "I'm open to business, but without this agreement, there is no sense talking."

Erasmus is taking a tougher stand, partially backed by the World Wildlife Fund, the Canadian Arctic Resources Committee and several other environmental groups. Their representatives are pushing the government to involve natives at every stage of the development. The Dene also hired a Toronto-based public relations firm, Crosbie Communications, to distribute an Australian Broadcasting Corp. documentary on the BHP's Papua New Guinea operations. Titled *Broken Hearts and Promises*, it is a compelling portrait of the damage caused by the company's

(b) Northern gems: Natives battle a proposed $112-billion diamond mine / **425**

massive copper mine on the Ok Tedi River. Hundreds of people who live downstream from the site are now suing BHP in Australia for more than a billion dollars. "BHP cannot be trusted," Maun told *Maclean's*. "They have a bad record in Papua New Guinea. They're going to be the same here."

To defend their record, BHP executives in Yellowknife flew in Kipling Uiari, the company's corporate general manager for Papua New Guinea. He said that construction of a tailings dam at the Ok Tedi was halted in early 1984 following two major landslides. Since then, with the government's approval, BHP has continued to dump 88,000 tons of mine tailings a day into the river. BHP has offered downstream landowners $110 million in compensation, and Uiari said he believes most of them are now willing to settle. He also insisted that the river has not been badly damaged by the mine waste. "There's a lot of fish in the river," said Uiari. "The levels of copper are not toxic."

BHP's track record in Canada is far less controversial. In fact, the company has picked up two environmental awards for its Island Copper Mine near Port Hardy on Vancouver Island. And in Yellowknife, BHP has laid out a far-reaching plan that Excell said would protect the land surrounding the Lac de Gras operation. Still, like any giant mining operation it would not be benign. The firm plans to drain five small lakes and then mine the diamonds beneath the lakebeds in open pits. The ore would be crushed and the gems removed, after which the tailings would be contained in a sixth lake. Some independent analysts who have studied BHP's plans say it would be one of the most environmentally safe mines ever built in Canada. Said David James, a mining analyst at Canaccord Capital Corp. in Winnipeg: "I've never seen such well-done environmental and engineering studies."

Critics, however, say BHP's environmental submissions are not sufficiently detailed. Peter McCart, a biologist representing the Northern Environmental Coalition, also told the hearing that the impact on fish in the area could be far worse than the mining company suggests. Complained McCart: "The BHP impact assessment is seriously deficient."

Environmentalists are also concerned about the fate of the area's 350,000-strong caribou herd—still an important source of food for the Dene. The animals migrate over a 100,000-square-mile region, which includes Lac de Gras. Anne Gunn, a biologist with the territorial government, told the panel that BHP has done little scientific work to assess the risk to caribou. Francois Messier, a biologist and consultant to BHP, however, said that while he agrees with the need for studies, he supported the company's conclusions because the mine would cover only a fraction of the caribou's territory.

One of the few organizations in the North which fully supports BHP is the city government of Yellowknife, whose crest features a mine, a shovel and a pick—recalling the community's historic gold-mining past that dates back to 1934. With federal cutbacks now pinching the city, Mayor Dave Lovell predicts "increased prosperity" if the mine project goes ahead. To the mayor's frustration, his dream of a sparkling boom on the Barrens has hit a wall of opposition-and an unassuming man from the sunny Pacific is leading the way.

(c) Nunavut Open for Business: It's a Delicate Balance between Creating a Sustainable Mining Industry Yet Maximizing Our Resources Potential[†]

Paul Okalik

In two short years since the creation of Nunavut in April 1999, our government has begun to make significant changes in the way business is conducted in the territory.

Transforming Nunavut's unrivalled mineral development potential into opportunities for the people of Nunavut and Canada is certainly one of our challenges. During this endeavour, we must also be cognizant of something known as the industry's "social licence," or the need to develop viable projects within a sustainable context.

The mining industry must earn the support of its stakeholders — the communities in which it operates, its employees and aboriginal people whose land may be developed. In order to succeed, the industry must strengthen its partnerships with all those with an interest in mining and its performance.

The government of Nunavut knows that in order for it to succeed in developing mineral resources, we must also embrace these partnerships.

Nunavut encompasses nearly two million square miles, a remarkable one-fifth of the entire country. One need only scan Nunavut's landmass and geology to envision its potential in gold, lead, zinc and diamonds. Moreover, this potential is virtually untapped.

Mining is Nunavut's largest wealth-creating industry and it holds the greatest opportunities for employment and business development in many local communities. One of the most attractive elements to investors is the certainty provided by the signing of the 1993 Nunavut Land Claims Agreement. This agreement provides for a clear and concise development process that includes the Inuit of Nunavut as participants in the development of the territory, socially, politically and economically.

With the establishment of such participation agreements, more of the money from mining will remain in Nunavut and benefit its peoples.

Recently, there has been an increase in the attention being paid to mineral exploration in the territory. We're open for business, and the prospects are positive. But our government is also taking steps to ensure that the lives of Nunavummiut are not negatively impacted through resource development. Many of the decisions that have been made during the past two years reflect a philosophy of sustainability. In fact, responsibility for the mining sector within the territory falls under the Department of Sustainable Development, which is also responsible for the environment.

[†] From *Northern Miner*, 87(30) (Sept. 17/23 2001): 4–5. This is an edited version of a speech given to the Mining Association of Canada at its annual meeting in Halifax, N.S., in June 2001. The author is the premier of Nunavut. Reproduced with permission of the publisher.

The government is committed to fostering an economic milieu that encourages development and prosperity while encompassing respect and protection for our residents, traditions and environment. It's a delicate balance between creating a sustainable mining industry yet maximizing our resources potential.

The mining industry is poised to contribute a solid foundation for a strong and diversified economy. It has been established that the natural capital — in this case, the grade and tonnage of our raw resources — is present in Nunavut.

The ability to mine these resources and the infrastructure needed for that task relate directly to our natural and physical capital. Currently, the national infrastructure program is funded on a per capita basis. That means Nunavut, with a population of about 30,000 and one of the areas of the country in most need of infrastructure development, is allotted a mere 1/16 of 1%, of a nearly $2.5-billion program. We are working with the mining industry, as well as Inuit organizations in Nunavut to identify opportunities for feasible infrastructure development in Nunavut. The Bathurst Port and Road Project, which would support the Hope Bay gold project, the Izok copper-zinc project, and other projects in the Kitikmeot, is one example.

We have also created the Canada-Nunavut Geoscience Office in partnership with Natural Resources Canada and the Department of Indian and Northern Affairs. The office supports the development of basic geoscience infrastructure essential to mineral exploration through topographic mapping projects and public geoscience.

Another pillar of mining and sustainable development relates to society. Mineral exploration and mine development must provide substantive and sustainable benefits to affected people and communities. This is the human, social and organizational investment that will increase in value through direct employment, training and business opportunities.

To this end, we are developing our capacity through a Prospector's Assistance Program. This program includes courses and contributions of up to $5,000 for prospecting, staking claims and collecting rock samples, along with direct technical support in the field. Hunters, who spend countless hours on the land, have taken advantage of this program, resulting in some interesting and potentially significant mineral discoveries.

Currently, there are three operating mines in Nunavut: Polaris and Nanisivik, base-metal mines in the High Arctic, and Lupin, a gold mine in the Kitikmeot region.

Polaris and Nanisivik employ 450 people and generated revenues exceeding $350 million in 2000. The projections for 2001 are $400 million. The Lupin gold mine reopened this year and employs about 350 people.

Toronto-based Tahera has begun developing the Jericho diamond project in western Nunavut. Gold exploration remains a major focus, and Nunavut has three of the largest gold exploration projects in Canada: Miramar and Hope Bay Resources at Hope Bay in the Kitikmeot; Western Mining at Meliadine; and Cumberland Resources at Meadowbank in the Kivalliq, the central region of Nunavut.

Major base-metal projects include the search for nickel and platinum group minerals by Starfield Resources at Ferguson Lake, and Muskox Minerals, south of Kugluktuk. Cominco and Noranda are involved in zinc and copper projects in the

Arctic islands, while Inmet Mining holds the advanced Izok Lake copper-zinc project and is exploring lead-zinc deposits in western Nunavut.

Many new projects are likely to be fly-in/fly-out operations — a practice that speaks to sustaining the mining industry. Fly-in/fly-out operations will allow resident employees to remain in their communities and commute to the mine site. Such operations will eliminate the need to establish, and ultimately abandon, mining settlements. This will also instigate spin-off economies in existing communities.

And when mining operations cease, employees will have the education, skills and experience to seek new mining opportunities elsewhere in the territory.

The mining industry contributed $129.9 million to Nunavut's gross domestic product in 1999 and there is every indication that figure will likely grow in the future.

The government of Nunavut is interested in working with the federal government, the private sector and Inuit organizations in the territory to overcome our challenges.

Under the current system, the majority of royalties accrued from mining development in Nunavut flow to the federal government. The expansion of the mining industry and the ensuing resources royalties would offer the Government of Nunavut the potential to negotiate a method to more directly share in new resource revenue.

Securing this revenue, especially with the renewed interest in resource development, would go a long way towards economic self-determination and allow us to increase our participation in the funding of resource development.

We are committed to working with our residents, Inuit organizations and the private sector to ensure we all benefit from mining development in the territory. Nunavut has the potential to be Canada's treasure chest of mineral resources as long as we work together towards sustainable resource management.